KARL MARX (1818–83) was born into a professional family in Trier in the Rhineland. After studying at the University of Berlin, he became a radical journalist, married the aristocratic Jenny von Westphalen, and converted to communism in Paris in 1844. In 1847 he wrote *The Communist Manifesto* with Friedrich Engels. He took an active part in the 1848 revolution in Germany before settling definitively in London, where the family's poverty was partly responsible for the death of three of his six children. His massive studies of political economy issued in *Capital*, the first volume of which was published in 1867, and on which Marx continued to work until his death.

DAVID McLELLAN is Professor of Political Theory at the University of Kent and author of numerous studies on Marx and Marxism. Among his most recent books are *Simone Weil: Utopian Pessimist* and *Unto Caesar: The Political Relevance of Christianity*. His *Case Law and Political Theory* is forthcoming.

OXFORD WORLD'S CLASSICS

For over 100 years Oxford World's Classics have brought readers closer to the world's great literature. Now with over 700 titles—from the 4,000-year-old myths of Mesopotamia to the twentieth century's greatest novels—the series makes available lesser-known as well as celebrated writing.

The pocket-sized hardbacks of the early years contained introductions by Virginia Woolf, T. S. Eliot, Graham Greene, and other literary figures which enriched the experience of reading. Today the series is recognized for its fine scholarship and reliability in texts that span world literature, drama and poetry, religion, philosophy and politics. Each edition includes perceptive commentary and essential background information to meet the changing needs of readers.

OXFORD WORLD'S CLASSICS

KARL MARX

Capital
An abridged edition

Edited with an Introduction and Notes by
DAVID McLELLAN

OXFORD
UNIVERSITY PRESS

OXFORD

UNIVERSITY PRESS

Great Clarendon Street, Oxford OX2 6DP

Oxford University Press is a department of the University of Oxford.
It furthers the University's objective of excellence in research, scholarship,
and education by publishing worldwide in

Oxford New York

Athens Auckland Bangkok Bogotá Buenos Aires Calcutta
Cape Town Chennai Dar es Salaam Delhi Florence Hong Kong Istanbul
Karachi Kuala Lumpur Madrid Melbourne Mexico City Mumbai
Nairobi Paris São Paulo Singapore Taipei Tokyo Toronto Warsaw

with associated companies in Berlin Ibadan

Oxford is a registered trade mark of Oxford University Press
in the UK and in certain other countries

Published in the United States
by Oxford University Press Inc., New York

British Library Cataloguing in Publication Data

Data available

Library of Congress Cataloging in Publication Data
Marx, Karl, 1818–1883.
[Kapital. English. Selections]
Capital: an abridged edition / Karl Marx ; edited with an
introduction by David McLellan.
p. cm.—(Oxford world's classics)
Includes bibliographical references.
1. Capital.   2. Economics.   I. McLellan, David.
II. Title.   III. Series
HB501.M3625 1995 335.4'1—dc20 94–18783
ISBN 0–19–283872–5

7

Printed in Great Britain by
Clays Ltd, St Ives plc

I wish to record my gratitude to my friend Ellen Sharp for invaluable help in the production of this volume.

CONTENTS

Part V. The Production of Absolute and of Relative Surplus-Value

Part VI. Wages

Part VII. The Accumulation of Capital

INTRODUCTION

FOR a book which has a reputation for length and difficulty, *Capital* is an unlikely best seller. But best seller it is: translated (in its massive entirety) into more than fifty languages, it has proved one of the most widely quoted books of the last hundred years—a world classic indeed.

The title which Marx gave to his great work is neither immediately attractive nor indicative of its richness. It is certainly a book about capital, but not about capital alone nor merely in a dry economic sense. Marx subtitled his book 'Critique of Political Economy', and 'critique' is the operative word here. Marx is concerned to evaluate the importance to the modern world of the rise of capitalism and its concomitant industrial revolution. This is a dramatic story—*the* dramatic story of modern times—and the power and influence of *Capital* can only be understood if it is seen as, in part, a tragic drama of world proportions. Moreover, the themes of this drama are conveyed in and through a meticulous historical scholarship. The result is an unrivalled account of capitalist modernization. Marx is one of the great early modernist writers, a true child of the Enlightenment in the self-confident sweep of his historical perspective who also sees the pathos and contradictions to which the whole modernist project is prone. Like the Mills of God, Marx's account often grinds slowly, but his sharp wit, piercing denunciation and sense of theatre keep on breaking through; and, also like the Mills of God, Marx's accumulation of damning details grinds exceeding small and provides a terrible indictment of the methods by which the vast wealth of his age was acquired. It is this many-layered and many-textured nature of *Capital* that explains its wide and lasting appeal.

Marx's written output was prolific, yet Volume One of *Capital* is the only really substantial work that he ever published. Like most great artistic creations, it is a highly personal work and into it Marx poured the summation of his intense commitment to philosophy, history, politics, and economics. He was 49 years old when *Capital* was published and six years later suffered a stroke which considerably diminished his capacity for creative work. So *Capital* can be seen as the culmination of the thirty years of study which had begun in 1836 when Marx enrolled as a student at the University of Berlin. Here the dominant intellectual force was the great idealist philosopher Hegel who had died only six years earlier. Marx became an ardent disciple, attracted by the way in which Hegel had reintroduced movement into philosophy, pointed to the interconnectedness of all elements in society, and emphasized struggle and contradiction as a force making for progress. Hegel's philosophy was ambivalent: he himself preferred to say that philosophy could only interpret the past and that the owl of Minerva only flew at dusk; but his radical disciples known as the Young Hegelians (with whom Marx associated himself) argued that Hegel's ideas could be turned round to interpret, and shape, the future.

His academic studies crowned with a Ph.D. in philosophy, Marx's powerful personality and quick pen earned him the editorship of the leading liberal newspaper in the Rhineland. In reply to his attacks on its repressive nature the Prussian government banned his newspaper and Marx moved to Paris which was then the centre of early socialist thought. Contact with working-class organizations convinced Marx that productive labour was the key to society and its future—a view which was to be at the heart of *Capital*. However, his support for revolutionary movements to establish a society in which workers could be free to produce for themselves on a communal basis only earned him a further expulsion. He moved to Brussels with Engels, with whom he had established a lifelong friendship, and worked out a theory of history in which successive social groups struggled for control of the forces of production. The wave of revolutions which broke over Europe in 1848 drew Marx back to Germany. He published, with Engels, the *Communist Manifesto* and once again became involved in radical journalism. The collapse of the revolutionary movement and the now familiar expulsion order brought him to England to begin his long sleepless night of exile.

In London, Marx devoted himself to finding out why the revolutionary movement of 1848 had collapsed and when such a movement might be expected to reoccur. He obtained a ticket to the Reading Room of the British Museum and began to read back numbers of the recently published *Economist*. These convinced him that it was the cyclical movements of the economy which had, in its downturn, precipitated revolution and then, in its upturn, frustrated it. Thus since the key to revolution lay in economics, Marx devoted his studies to uncovering what he was to call in *Capital* 'the law of motion of capitalist society'. He had originally signed a contract for a work on economics in Paris as long ago as 1845. But in spite of repeated assertions that he was on the point of finishing, the work made slow progress until the prospect of a crisis in 1857 impelled Marx to compose more than eight hundred pages in less than six months. 'I am working madly through the nights', he wrote to Engels, 'on a synthesis of my economic studies, so that I at least have the main principles clear before the deluge.' This huge manuscript—which became known as the *Grundrisse* (outlines)—contained notes and excursuses for most of the six parts in which Marx intended to publish the results of his studies. However, Marx was only able to write up the small introductory *Critique of Political Economy* before he was enveloped in a time-consuming polemic with Karl Vogt; and in the early 1860s he could only amass more notes for the historical section of the first part (notes subsequently published under the title *Theories of Surplus Value*). This first part then expanded into the three volumes of *Capital*—of which Marx only managed to complete the first, published in 1867, a work to which Marx declared himself to have 'sacrificed health, happiness, and family'. The other two volumes were left in manuscript to be edited by Engels after Marx's death. The other five parts were never even drafted. Volume One of *Capital* thus remains a fragment, albeit a massive one, of Marx's lifelong project.

As Marx says on the first page of *Capital*, 'every beginning is difficult', and the beginning of *Capital* is exceptionally so. There are three reasons for this. First, whereas the rest of the book contains a description of the historical genesis and contemporary reality of capitalism which is at times extremely vivid and readable, the first nine chapters are of a very abstract theoretical nature. Secondly, there is the Hegelian cast of the book. In the 'Afterword' to the second German edition of the book, Marx admitted to 'coquetting with modes of expression peculiar to Hegel'.[1] More substantially, in the same 'Afterword', he explained that he was indeed employing the Hegelian dialectic of which he had discovered the 'rational kernel' inside the 'mystical shell' by 'turning it right side up again'.[2]

The third and most substantial factor which makes the beginning of *Capital* difficult is the fact that the concepts used by Marx are ones quite familiar to economists in the mid-nineteenth century but thereafter abandoned by the orthodox schools of economics. Since the third quarter of the nineteenth century economists in Western Europe and America have tended to look at the capitalist system as given, construct models of it, assuming private property, profit, and a more or less free market, and to discuss the functionings of this model, concentrating particularly on prices. This 'marginalist' school of economics has no

[1] See below, p. 11.
[2] See below, p. 11. Further on this point, see T. Smith, *The Logic of Marx's Capital: Replies to Hegelian Criticisms* (State University of New York Press, Albany, NY, 1990).

concept of value apart from price. To Marx, this procedure seemed superficial for two reasons: first, he considered it superficial in a literal sense, in that it was only a description of phenomena lying on the surface of capitalist society without an analysis of the mode of production that gave rise to these phenomena. Secondly, this approach took the capitalist system for granted whereas Marx wished to analyse 'the birth, life and death of a given social organism and its replacement by another, superior order'.

In order to achieve these two aims, Marx took over the concepts of the 'classical' economists that were still the generally accepted tool of economic analysis, and used them to draw very different conclusions. Ricardo, the most influential of the classical economists, had made a distinction between use value and exchange value. The exchange value of an object was something separate from its price and consisted of the amount of labour embodied in the objects of production, though Ricardo thought that the price in fact tended to approximate to the exchange value. Thus—in contradistinction to later analyses—the value of an object was determined by the circumstances of production rather than those of demand. Marx took over these concepts, but, in his attempt to show that capitalism was not static but a historically relative system of class exploitation, supplemented Ricardo's views by introducing the idea of surplus value. Surplus value was defined as the difference between the value of the products of labour and the cost of producing that labour power, i.e. the labourer's subsistence; for the exchange value of labour power was equal to the amount of labour necessary to reproduce that labour power and this was normally much lower than the exchange value of the products of that labour power.

These first nine chapters of Volume One—the theoretical part—divide easily into three sections. The first section is a rewriting of the *Critique of Political Economy* of 1859 and analyses commodities, in the sense of external objects that satisfy human needs, and their value. Marx established two sorts of value, use value, or the utility of something, and exchange value which is determined by the amount of labour incorporated in the object. Labour is also of a twofold nature according to whether it creates use values or exchange values. Since 'the exchange values of commodities must be capable of being expressed in terms of something common to them all' and the only thing they shared was labour, then labour must be the source of value. This is the only argument that Marx uses to establish the labour theory of value—and it is a very weak one since it is by no means obvious that simply because commodities exchange there *must* be a third entity against which they are measured. In this context it is important to remember that the labour theory of value did not challenge the orthodoxy of the time: it *was* the orthodoxy. In reality, Marx's approach here takes for granted his view, worked out thirty years earlier, of productive labour as the key to human nature and history. But, he continued, since evidently some people worked faster or more skilfully than others, this labour must be a sort of average 'socially necessary' labour time. There followed a difficult section on the form of value and the first chapter ended with a far-reaching account of commodities as exchange values which he described as the 'fetishism of commodities'. The topsy-turvy world thus created, in which money and market exchange came to dominate and replace human relationships (i.e. the most important relationships were between things rather than between people) recalls the account of alienation in the *Paris Manuscripts* and (even more) the *Note on James Mill*. 'In order', said Marx here, 'to find an analogy, we must have recourse to the mist-enveloped regions of the religious world. In that world the productions of the human brain appear as independent beings endowed with life, and entering into relation both with one another and the human race. So it is in the world of commodities with the products of men's hands.'[3] Marx frequently uses religious analogies in *Capital* to express his view of money and profit as the ersatz divinity of the modern world and also, perhaps, to shock people into realizing the contradiction between the values preached by religion and those practised in capitalist society. The section ended with a chapter on exchange and an account of money as the means for the circulation of commodities, the material expression for their values and the universal measure of value.

Marx is very strong on the dehumanizing effects of money, and the second section, a small one on the transformation of money into capital, continues this theme. Before the capitalist era people had sold commodities for money in order to buy more commodities. In the capitalist era, instead of selling to buy, people had bought to sell dearer: they had bought commodities with their money in order, by means of those commodities, to increase their money. Thus the medium had itself become the message: money was the supreme representative of social power in capitalist society and the only social bond in an increasingly divided and fragmented community.

The most important commodity that can be bought in such a society, since it is the only one likely to yield more money, is human labour power which has the characteristic of being able to produce greater value than it has itself. It is here, in the third section, that Marx introduced his key notion of surplus value, the idea that Engels characterized as Marx's principal 'discovery' in economics. It explains the apparent contradiction between the fact that capitalist and wage-labourer exchange equivalents in a 'fair' bargain and the inequality implied by profit. Marx made a distinction between *constant* capital which was 'that part of capital which is represented by the means of production, by the raw material, auxiliary material and instruments of labour, and does not, in the process of production, undergo any quantitative alteration of value' and *variable* capital. Of this Marx said: 'That part of capital, represented by labour power, does, in the process of production, undergo an alteration of value. It both reproduces the equivalent of its own value, and also produces an excess, a surplus value, which may itself vary, may be more or less according to the circumstances.' This variation was the rate of surplus value around which the struggle between workers and capitalists centred. The essential point was that the capitalist got the worker to work longer than was merely sufficient to embody in his product the value of his labour power: if the cost of the labour power of the worker (roughly what it cost to keep him alive) was £4 a day and the worker could embody £4 of value in the product on which he was working in eight hours; then, if he worked ten hours, the last two hours would yield surplus value— in this case £1.

A little further on Marx expanded on the nature of this surplus value as follows:

During the second period of the labour-process, that in which his labour is no longer necessary labour, the workman, it is true, labours, expends labour-power; but his labour being no longer necessary labour, he creates no value for himself. He creates surplus-value which, for the capitalist, has all the charms of a creation out of nothing. This portion of the working-day, I name surplus labour-time, and to the labour expended during that time, I give the name of surplus-labour. It is every bit as important, for a correct understanding of surplus-value, to conceive it as a mere congelation of surplus labour-time, as nothing but materialised surplus-labour, as it is, for a proper comprehension of value, to conceive it as a mere congelation of so many hours of labour, as nothing but materialised labour. The essential difference between the various economic forms of society, between, for instance, a society based on slave-labour, and one based on wage-labour, lies only in the mode in which this surplus-labour is in each case extracted from the actual producer, the labourer.[4]

[4] See below, p. 146.

Thus surplus value could only arise from variable capital, not from constant capital, as labour alone created value. If v is the variable capital, c the constant capital and s the surplus value, then the three vital proportions in Marx's economic theory are: the proportion of c to v—the 'organic composition of capital', the proportion of s to v—the rate of exploitation; and the proportion of s to $c + v$—the rate of profit. Put very simply Marx's reason for thinking that the rate of profit would decrease was that, with the introduction of machinery, labour time would become less and thus yield less surplus value. Of course, machinery would increase productivity and colonial markets would absorb some of the surplus, but these were only palliatives and an eventual crisis was inevitable—themes which Marx takes up at greater length in Volume Three.

Marx now turns to an explanation of the origin of the wage labour implied by the idea of surplus value. These first nine chapters are thus complemented by a masterly historical account of the genesis of capitalism which illustrates better than any other writing Marx's approach and method. Marx particularly made pioneering use of official statistical information that came to be available from the middle of the nineteenth century onwards. A reader who finds the beginning of *Capital* too arid would do well to follow Marx's advice to Mrs Kugelmann[5] and begin by reading the chapters on 'The Working-Day', 'Machinery and Modern Industry', and 'Capitalist Accumulation'. In the chapter on 'The Working-Day', Marx described in detail the 'physical and mental degradation' forced on men, women, and children by working long hours in unhealthy conditions and related the bitter struggle to gain some relief by legal limits on the number of hours worked and the passing of factory acts. Although, Marx concluded, it might seem as though the capitalist and worker exchanged contracts in a free market, the bargain was, in fact, one-sided:

The bargain concluded, it is discovered that he was no 'free agent', that the time for which he is free to sell his labour-power is the time for which he is forced to sell it, that in fact the vampire will not loose its hold on him 'so long as there is a muscle, a nerve, a drop of blood to be exploited'. For 'protection' against 'the serpent of their agonies', the labourers must put their heads together, and, as a class, compel the passing of a law, an all-powerful social barrier that shall prevent the very workers from selling, by voluntary contract with capital, themselves and their families into slavery and death. In place of the pompous catalogue of the 'inalienable rights of man' comes the modest

[5] See K. Marx, F. Engels, *Collected Works* (Lawrence and Wishart, London, 1975–), vol. 42, p. 490.

Magna Charta of a legally limited working-day, which shall make clear 'when the time which the worker sells is ended, and when his own begins'.[6]

Marx continued his indictment of capitalism in the chapter on 'Machinery and Modern Industry', describing the crippling effect of machinery on workers and the environmental effects of capitalist exploitation of agriculture. The existence of wage labour, in the form of people who have to sell their labour power in order to live, is based on the violent separation of the mass of producers from control over the tools and instruments with which they work. The achievement of this transformation—of the worker into a 'hand', a 'factor' of production, a mere 'labour power' is, as Marx says, 'the result of many revolutions, of the extinction of a whole series of older forms of production' and he spends a lot of time detailing this historical process. Summing up his conclusions, however, Marx showed that his view of technological progress under capitalism was not wholly negative:

We have seen how this absolute contradiction between the technical necessities of Modern Industry, and the social character inherent in its capitalistic form, dispels all fixity and security in the situation of the labourer; how it constantly threatens, by taking away the instruments of labour, to snatch from his hands his means of subsistence, and, by suppressing his detail-function, to make him superfluous. We have seen too, how this antagonism vents its rage in the creation of that monstrosity, an industrial reserve army, kept in misery in order to be always at the disposal of capital; in the incessant human sacrifices from among the working-class, in the most reckless squandering of labour-power, and in the devastation caused by a social anarchy which turns every economical progress into a social calamity. This is the negative side. But if, on the one hand, variation of work at present imposes itself after the manner of an over-powering natural law, and with the blindly destructive action of a natural law that meets with resistance at all points, Modern Industry, on the other hand, through its catastrophes imposes the necessity of recognising, as a fundamental law of production, variation of work, consequently fitness of the labourer for varied work, consequently the greatest possible development of his varied aptitudes. It becomes a question of life and death for society to adapt the mode of production to the normal functioning of this law. Modern industry, indeed, compels society, under penalty of death, to replace the detail-worker of today, crippled by life-long repetition of one and the same trivial operation, and thus reduced to the mere fragment of a man, by the fully developed individual, fit for a variety of labours, ready to face any change of production, and to whom the different social functions he performs, are but so many modes of giving free scope to his own natural and acquired powers.[7]

---

[6] See below, pp. 181–2.   [7] See below, p. 292.

Marx considered that such a fully developed individual depended on the overcoming, to some considerable extent, of the division of labour and that this was only possible in a socialist society. Volume One ended with a long section on 'Capitalist Accumulation'—the finest chapter in the book. The capitalist, being prey to 'a Faustian conflict between the passion for accumulation and the desire for enjoyment', was forced to create an 'industrial reserve army' or vast pool of temporarily unemployed workers to serve the fluctuations of the market. This was Marx's long-run prediction:

The greater the social wealth, the functioning capital, the extent and energy of its growth, and, therefore, also the absolute mass of the proletariat, and the productiveness of its labour, the greater is the industrial reserve army. The same causes which develop the expansive power of capital, develop also the labour power at its disposal. The relative mass of the industrial reserve army increases, therefore, with the potential energy of wealth. But the greater this reserve army, the greater is the mass of a consolidated surplus population, whose misery is in inverse ratio to its torment of labour. The more extensive the lazarus-layers of the working class, and the industrial reserve army, the greater is official pauperism. This is the absolute general law of capitalist accumulation.[8]

Marx is thus keen to stress the role of unemployment in depressing wages and thus sustaining capitalist profitability, the polarization of society through the decline of independent producers and those of independent means, the numerical growth of those dependent on a wage or salary contract, and the relative impoverishment of those so dependent. These ideas, though controversial, have not been evidently disproved by subsequent events. Marx synthesized his analysis in a thundering denunciation:

In proportion as capital accumulates, the lot of the labourer, be his payment high or low, must grow worse. The law, finally, that always equilibrates the relative surplus-population, or industrial reserve army, to the extent and energy of accumulation, this law rivets the labourer to capital more firmly than the wedges of Vulcan did Prometheus to the rock. It establishes an accumulation of misery, corresponding with accumulation of capital. Accumulation of wealth at one pole is, therefore, at the same time accumulation of misery, agony of toil, slavery, ignorance, brutality, mental degradation, at the opposite pole, i.e. on the side of the class that produces its own product in the form of capital.[9]

This judgement was supported by a series of detailed studies, moving yet objective, on the condition of the British working classes over

[8] See below, pp. 360–1.   [9] See below, p. 362.

the previous twenty years, the British agricultural proletariat, and the misery of Ireland. Here Marx stresses the restless insecurity of the capitalist system, how the coercive laws of competition and class struggle constantly force the capitalists to control the labourer in the workplace, to force down wages, and to worsen working conditions. But the instability thus produced would bring its own nemesis and Marx rounds off the book with the following famous passage:

Along with the constantly diminishing number of the magnates of capital, who usurp and monopolise all advantages of this process of transformation, grows the mass of misery, oppression, slavery, degradation, exploitation; but with this too grows the revolt of the working class, a class always increasing in numbers, and disciplined, united, organised by the very mechanism of the process of capitalist production itself. The monopoly of capital becomes a fetter upon the mode of production, which has sprung up and flourished along with, and under it. Centralisation of the means of production and socialisation of labour at last reach a point where they become incompatible with their capitalist integument. This integument is burst asunder. The knell of capitalist private property sounds. The expropriators are expropriated.[10]

The subsequent two volumes, being only in draft form, have none of the polished verve of Volume One. There was, however, a long chapter entitled 'Results of the Immediate Process of Production' that Marx seems to have intended to put at the end of Volume One but left out at the last minute. In this chapter Marx discussed how capitalist production reproduced the relationship of capitalist to worker in the total process. There are particularly interesting comments on the alienation involved in the relationship of capitalist to worker and on the tendency of capitalism to 'reduce as much as possible the number of those working for a wage' in the production sphere and increase the number of workers in purely service industries.

Whereas Volume One had dealt with production, Volumes Two and Three investigate what happened outside the factory when the capitalist came to sell his products for cash. In Volume Two Marx traces the circular movement of sale, profit, and the ploughing back of resources for the next cycle of production and the complex factors underlying economic crises. This volume is far less interesting, because of its technical theoretical nature.

The first part of Volume Three appears to be in a more or less final draft, but thereafter the book tails off without any final conclusion. It

[10] See below, pp. 379–80.

begins with a discussion of the conversion of surplus value into profit and thus the relationship between values and prices. Many people on reading Volume One had asked how it came about that, if values were measured by socially necessary labour, they should be so very different from market prices. This is what came to be known as the 'transformation problem'. In particular, given that different industries had different organic compositions of capital, one would expect investment to migrate to the industry with the largest labour costs and thus the highest rate of profit. Eventually the ensuing competition would bring down the rate of profit in this industry and an average rate of profit would be established throughout the economy. But such a change in prices appeared to imply that relative prices did *not* reflect relative labour costs, and the theory of value did not explain the real phenomena of production. The only answer that Marx provided to this problem was to assert that value was 'the centre of gravity around which prices fluctuate and around which their rise and falls tends to an equilibrium' and that, although the prices of individual commodities might differ from their labour values, total values did, in fact, equal total prices. He continued: 'No matter what may be the way in which prices are regulated, the result always is the following: the law of value dominates the movement of prices, since a reduction or increase of the labour-time required for production causes the prices of production to fall or to rise.' But this predominance of the law of value was very approximate: 'The general law of value acts as the prevailing tendency only in a very complicated and approximate manner, as a never ascertainable average of ceaseless fluctuations.' Marx then enunciated in more detail than in Volume One the falling tendency of the rate of profit which forms the centre-piece of the third volume. This law is expressed most succinctly by Marx as follows:

it is the nature of the capitalist mode of production, and a logical necessity of its development, to give expression to the average rate of surplus-value by a falling rate of average profit. Since the mass of the employed living labour is continually on the decline compared to the mass of materialised labour incorporated in productively consumed means of production, it follows that the portion of living labour, which is unpaid and represents surplus-value, must also be continually on the decrease compared to the volume and value of the invested total capital. Seeing that the proportion of the mass of surplus-value to the invested total capital forms the rate of profit, this rate must fall continuously.[11]

[11] See below, pp. 420–1.

Marx then went further into the nature of economic crises which he traced to the basic contradiction between the necessity of a capitalist economy to expand its production without taking into account the level of consumption that alone could make it feasible:

> The *real barrier* of capitalist production is *capital itself*. It is that capital and its self-expansion appear as the starting and the closing point, the motive and the purpose of production; that production is only production for *capital* and not vice versa, the means of production are not mere means for a constant expansion of the living process of the *society* of producers. The limits within which the preservation or self-expansion of the value of capital resting on the expropriation and pauperisation of the great mass of producers can alone move— these limits come continually into conflict with the methods of production employed by capital for its purposes, which drive towards unlimited extension of production as an end in itself, towards unconditional development of the social productivity of labour. This means—unconditional development of the productive forces of society—comes continually into conflict with the limited purpose, the self-expansion of the existing capital.[12]

The conclusion was:

> The last cause of all real crises always remains the poverty and restricted consumption of the masses as compared to the tendency of capitalist production to develop the productive forces in such a way that only the absolute power of consumption of the entire society would be their limit.[13]

Marx then dealt with the factors that could slow down the fall in profits—principally increased exploitation, the cheapening of constant capital, overpopulation, and foreign trade—and attempted to show that they could only be short-term palliatives. There follows a section, entitled 'The Trinity Formula' in which Marx analysed the roles of the trinity of capital, land, and labour in the production process. This section contains the justly famous passage in which Marx calls for a society in which human beings will be able to develop their powers free from the stunting of economic injustice and debilitating greed.[14] Then after two sections on interest-bearing capital and ground rent, the volume ended with the dramatically incomplete section on classes.

From the above sketch it will be obvious that *Capital* can be read in many ways: as economic science, as prophecy, as a tract on the morality of our times, as high drama. Much debate has surrounded the scientific status of Marx's work. Marx certainly saw himself as in some sense a scientist and *Capital* is full of metaphors about removing veils and revealing mysteries on the grounds that 'all science would be superflu-

[12] See below, p. 455.   [13] See below, p. 456.   [14] See below, p. 470.

ous if the outward appearance and the essence of things coincided directly'. Engels, in his speech at Marx's funeral, claimed that 'as Darwin discovered the law of evolution in organic nature, so Marx discovered the law of evolution in human history'.[15] Although it is not true (as has sometimes been claimed) that Marx asked Darwin for permission to dedicate to him Volume Two of *Capital*, he did draw analogies between his own work and biological science. Marx admired Darwin: he followed the same method of moving from simple to complex in his analysis and shared Darwin's teleological view of human progress. And he relished the fact (as he saw it) that Darwin's account of the survival of the fittest in evolutionary biology mirrored the ruthlessly competitive nature of contemporary bourgeois society. Many of the concepts that Marx took over from the classical economists (who had furnished the theoretical underpinning to that society) are now outdated, though a vast literature remains on the precise nature of the labour theory of value and on the mysterious intangibility of how values relate to actual prices. In any case, the power of the labour theory of value has always been less in its technical analysis than in its fundamental moral insight that those who did the work should also get its reward.

Strong though it is on historical analysis, *Capital* (like most works of Victorian modernism) was keen to anticipate the future. Although Marx resolutely refused to write what he dismissively called 'recipes for the cookshops of the future', it is legitimate to ask how far his tenets have been called into question by the twentieth century. First, the revolution of 1917 meant that Marxist orthodoxy was hijacked by the Soviet Union. Although Marx said dismayingly little about the nature of a socialist society, it is clear that Soviet Communism was as far removed as capitalism from his vision of socialism. Further, Marx produced a critique of *capitalist* society and his conceptual framework was not so obviously relevant to Soviet society. But Marx would have been neither surprised nor disappointed by the collapse of Communism. Indeed, the paradox is that, with Russia's now rejoining the historical trajectory marked out in *Capital*, its citizens are likely to find Marx's work now more grimly relevant than they ever did under Soviet rule. Secondly, although Marx foresaw the possibility of revolution in Russia, it was to the capitalist heartlands of the West that he looked for the definitive revolutionary upheaval. The sense of imminent doom that pervades *Capital* became less convincing after the great depression

---

[15] K. Marx, F. Engels, *Selected Works* (Progress Publishers, Moscow, 1962), p. 435.

had been weathered by counter-cyclical Keynesian intervention and the long economic boom following the Second World War. The end of this boom and the return of a more aggressive market capitalism in the 1980s made many turn to *Capital* with renewed interest. Thirdly, the phenomena of imperialism are largely absent from *Capital*. Although Marx emphasized the global nature of capitalism, the main colonial push came after its publication. The concepts of *Capital* need considerable revision to account for the international nature of exploitation in the contemporary world. Fourthly, Marx, like most of his contemporaries, looked to the development of the productive forces to bring about the social changes that he envisaged. He does indeed emphasize the way in which capitalism wastes and ravages natural resources, but he had little sense either of the intrinsic value of the natural world or of the finitude of natural resources that informs contemporary green politics. Lastly, *Capital* is firmly based on a class analysis which tends to ignore other social divisions such as those of gender and race which have achieved considerable prominence in recent social analysis.

During the first few decades after its publication, the main function of *Capital* was to give an apparently scientific vindication to the cause of the nascent working-class movement. That the precise scientific nature of the message was sometimes difficult to decipher mattered little. And, in any case, Marx was more powerful as a prophet in the Old Testament sense than as a social forecaster. But like most interesting scientific endeavours, Marx's work is as shot through with values as any piece of classical drama. Indeed, a large part of the appeal of *Capital* lies in its combination of historical sociology with dramatic narrative. Marx has carefully paced his unfolding of the origin and destiny of capitalist society by interweaving passages of descriptive horror with passages of cool analysis. But it is undoubtedly for the former that *Capital* is most remembered: Marx is fond of quoting Dante and his account often seems to follow Dante's *Inferno* on a guided tour of the circles of hell created by capitalism. On his tour Marx makes use of every rhetorical device. Polyglot and polymath, he employs the rich resources of classical mythology and preaches in a style every bit as forceful as his contemporaries Carlyle, Ruskin, or Kingsley.[16] Although Marx has a sharp eye for hypocrisy, and thus includes comic elements in his drama, it is Greek tragedy which predominates in a story where the characters are subject to an

---

[16] These themes are well explored in S. Prawer, *Karl Marx and World Literature* (Oxford University Press, Oxford, 1976), ch. 12.

inexorable necessity generated by little more than their own self-delusion.

In its economic concepts, its style, its self-confidence, *Capital* is very much a work of its own time. But like any major classic the very manner in which it distils its own age provides insights which continue to be relevant. The world has, of course, changed enormously since Marx wrote. But, for all the blithe contemporary talk of the post-modern, it is the scars inflicted by the all-too-present modern that disfigure our world. Marx can still illuminate with disturbing clarity many of the ills of the late twentieth century.

NOTE ON THE TEXT

THE text of Volume One is taken from the first English edition of 1887, translated by Samuel Moore and Edward Aveling. They used the third German edition published by Engels in 1889 who had revised it in accordance with the French edition of 1872–5 and various instructions found in Marx's manuscripts. The extracts from the *Results of the Immediate Process of Production* have been translated by David McLellan. The material for Volume Three is taken from the anonymous translation published by Progress Publishers in Moscow in 1971 which itself lent heavily on the translation published by Kerr in Chicago in 1909.

Marx's original notes are cued in the text by numerals and are to be found at the end of the text. The editor's explanatory notes are cued by asterisks and are to be found immediately following Marx's notes.

SELECT BIBLIOGRAPHY

Texts of *Capital*

(For further information on the various editions of *Capital*, see A. Uroyeva, *For All Time and All Men* (Progress Publishers, Moscow, 1969).)

Vol. i, ed. F. Engels, trans. S. Moore and E. Aveling (Swan Sonnenschein, London, 1887).

Vol. i, trans. E. Untermann (Kerr, Chicago, 1906).

Vol. i, trans. E. and C. Paul (Dent, London, 1930).

Vol. i, trans. B. Fowkes (Penguin, Harmondsworth, 1976).

Vol. iii, ed. F. Engels, trans. E. Untermann (Kerr, Chicago, 1909).

Vol. iii (Moscow, Progress, 1971).

Vol. iii, trans. B. Fowkes (Penguin, Harmondsworth, 1981).

Commentaries

Althusser, L., and Balibar, E., *Reading Capital* (New Left Books, London, 1968).

Bohm-Bawerk, E. von, *Karl Marx and the Close of his System*, ed. P. Sweezy (Kalley, New York, 1948).

Brewer, A., *A Guide to Marx's Capital* (Cambridge University Press, Cambridge, 1984).

Cleaver, H., *Reading Capital Politically* (University of Texas Press, Austin, 1979).

Cutler, A., *et al.*, *Marx's Capital and Capitalism Today*, 2 vols. (Routledge, London, 1977–8).

Engels, F., *On Capital. Synopsis, Reviews, Letters and Supplementary Material*, trans. L. Mins (Lawrence and Wishart, London, n.d.).

Fine, B., *Marx's Capital* (Macmillan, London, 1975).

Fox, J., and Johnson, W., *Understanding Capital: A Guide to Volume One* (Progress Books, Toronto, 1978).

Harrison, J., *Marxist Economics for Socialists: A Critique of Reformism* (Pluto, London, 1978).

Harvey, D., *The Limits to Capital* (Blackwell, Oxford, 1982).

Howard, M., and King, J., *The Political Economy of Marx* (Longman, London, 1975).

Kemp, T., *Marx's 'Capital' Today* (New Park Publications, London, 1982).

Mandel, E., Introduction to K. Marx, *Capital* (Penguin, Harmondsworth, 1976).

Meek, R., *Studies in the Labour Theory of Value* (Lawrence and Wishart, London, 1973).

Morishima, M., *Marx's Economics: A Dual Theory of Value and Growth* (Cambridge University Press, Cambridge, 1973).

Postone, M., *Time, Labour and Social Domination: A Reinterpretation of Marx's Critical Theory* (Cambridge University Press, Cambridge, 1993).

Pilling, G., *Marx's Capital, Philosophy and Political Economy* (Routledge, London, 1980).

Robinson, J., *An Essay on Marxian Economics* (St Martin's Press, New York, 1942).

Rosdolsky, R., *The Making of Marx's Capital* (Pluto, London, 1977).

Roth, M., and Eldred, M., *Guide to Marx's Capital* (CSE Books, London, 1978).

Rubin, I., *Essays on Marx's Theory of Value* (Black and Red, Detroit, 1972).

Sayer, D., *Marx's Method: Ideology, Science and Critique in Capital* (Harvester, Hassocks, 1979).

Smith, T., *The Logic of Marx's Capital: Replies to Hegelian Criticisms* (State University of New York Press, Albany, NY, 1990).

Steedman, I., *Marx after Sraffa* (New Left Books, London, 1977).

Strachey, J., *The Nature of Capitalist Crisis* (Gollancz, London, 1935).

Sweezy, P., *The Theory of Capitalist Development* (Dobson, London, 1946).

Wolff, R., *Understanding Marx: A Reconstruction and Critique of Capital* (Princeton University Press, Princeton, NJ, 1984).

Zeleney, J., *The Logic of Marx* (Rowman and Littlefield, New York, 1980).

A CHRONOLOGY OF KARL MARX

1818   5 May: Born in Trier, Rhineland, eldest son in a family of eight children, his father a prominent lawyer, his mother of Dutch/Hungarian ancestry, both from Rabbinic families.

1836   Student of philosophy at University of Berlin (until 1841).

1842   Appointed editor of the liberal newspaper *Rheinische Zeitung*.

1843   Marries the aristocratic Jenny von Westphalen and moves to Paris.

1844   Writes *Economic and Philosophical Manuscripts*. In September, meets Engels with whom he begins a lifelong collaboration. Birth of Jenny Marx.

1845   Moves to Brussels. Writes *Theses on Feuerbach* and *The German Ideology*. Birth of Laura Marx.

1846   Birth of Edgar Marx.

1847   Writes *The Communist Manifesto* with Engels.

1848   Year of Revolutions. Appointed editor of *Neue Rheinische Zeitung* in Cologne.

1849   Collapse of revolutionary movement. Arrives in London and settles in Soho in very straitened circumstances. Birth of Guido Marx.

1850   Begins regular study in the British Museum. Death of Guido Marx.

1851   Birth of Franziska Marx.

1852   Writes *The Eighteenth Brumaire of Louis Bonaparte*. Death of Franziska Marx. Numerous articles over the next ten years for the *New York Herald Tribune*.

1855   Birth of Eleanor Marx. Death of Edgar Marx.

1856   After the death of three of his children, Marx moves with his three surviving daughters, Jenny, Laura, and Eleanor, to more salubrious quarters in Kentish Town.

1857–8 Works on a rough draft of *Capital* posthumously published under the title *Grundrisse—Outlines of a Critique of Political Economy*.

1859   Publishes *A Critique of Political Economy*, a summary of the initial ideas of *Capital*.

1862–3 Writes *Theories of Surplus Value* and starts drafts for the three volumes of *Capital*.

1864   Becomes Secretary of the First International.

1867   Publishes Volume One of *Capital* and works intermittently for the rest of his life on drafts of Volumes Two and Three.

1871   Outbreak of Paris Commune. Writes *The Civil War in France*.

1873   Writes Preface to 2nd edition of Volume One of *Capital*.

1875   Writes *Critique of the Gotha Programme*; French edition of Volume One of *Capital*.

1881   Death of Jenny Marx.
1883   14 March: Marx dies and is buried in Highgate Cemetery.
1885   Publication of Volume Two of *Capital*, edited by Engels.
1894   Publication of Volume Three of *Capital*, edited by Engels.

CAPITAL

VOLUME ONE

PREFACE TO
THE FIRST GERMAN EDITION

EVERY beginning is difficult, holds in all sciences. To understand the first chapter, especially the section that contains the analysis of commodities, will, therefore, present the greatest difficulty. That which concerns more especially the analysis of the substance of value and the magnitude of value, I have, as much as it was possible, popularised. The value-form, whose fully developed shape is the money-form, is very elementary and simple. Nevertheless, the human mind has for more than 2,000 years sought in vain to get to the bottom of it, whilst on the other hand, to the successful analysis of much more composite and complex forms, there has been at least an approximation. Why? Because the body, as an organic whole, is more easy of study than are the cells of that body. In the analysis of economic forms, moreover, neither microscopes nor chemical reagents are of use. The force of abstraction must replace both. But in bourgeois society the commodity-form of the product of labour—or the value-form of the commodity—is the economic cell-form. To the superficial observer, the analysis of these forms seems to turn upon minutiæ. It does in fact deal with minutiæ, but they are of the same order as those dealt with in microscopic anatomy.

With the exception of the section on value-form, therefore, this volume cannot stand accused on the score of difficulty. I pre-suppose, of course, a reader who is willing to learn something new and therefore to think for himself.

The physicist either observes physical phenomena where they occur in their most typical form and most free from disturbing influence, or, wherever possible, he makes experiments under conditions that assure the occurrence of the phenomenon in its normality. In this work I have to examine the capitalist mode of production, and the conditions of production and exchange corresponding to that mode. Up to the present time, their classic ground is England. That is the reason why England is used as the chief illustration in the development of my theoretical ideas. If, however, the German reader shrugs his shoulders at the condition of the English industrial and agricultural labourers, or in optimist fashion comforts himself with the thought that in Germany things are not nearly so bad; I must plainly tell him, 'De te fabula narratur!'*

Intrinsically, it is not a question of the higher or lower degree of development of the social antagonisms that result from the natural laws of capitalist production. It is a question of these laws themselves, of these tendencies working with iron necessity towards inevitable results. The country that is more developed industrially only shows, to the less developed, the image of its own future.

But apart from this. Where capitalist production is fully naturalised among the Germans (for instance, in the factories proper) the condition of things is much worse than in England, because the counterpoise of the Factory Acts is wanting. In all other spheres, we, like all the rest of Continental Western Europe, suffer not only from the development of capitalist production, but also from the incompleteness of that development. Alongside of modern evils, a whole series of inherited evils oppress us, arising from the passive survival of antiquated modes of production, with their inevitable train of social and political anachronisms. We suffer not only from the living, but from the dead. *Le mort saisit le vif!**

The social statistics of Germany and the rest of Continental Western Europe are, in comparison with those of England, wretchedly compiled. But they raise the veil just enough to let us catch a glimpse of the Medusa head behind it. We should be appalled at the state of things at home, if, as in England, our governments and parliaments appointed periodically commissions of inquiry into economic conditions; if these commissions were armed with the same plenary powers to get at the truth; if it was possible to find for this purpose men as competent, as free from partisanship and respect of persons as are the English factory-inspectors, her medical reporters on public health, her commissioners of inquiry into the exploitation of women and children, into housing and food. Perseus wore a magic cap that the monsters he hunted down might not see him. We draw the magic cap down over eyes and ears as a make-believe that there are no monsters.

Let us not deceive ourselves on this. As in the 18th century, the American war of independence sounded the tocsin for the European middle-class, so in the 19th century, the American Civil War sounded it for the European working-class. In England the progress of social disintegration is palpable. When it has reached a certain point, it must re-act on the Continent. There it will take a form more brutal or more humane, according to the degree of development of the working-class itself. Apart from higher motives, therefore, their own most important interests dictate to the classes that are for the nonce the ruling ones, the removal of all legally removable hindrances to the free development of the working-class. For this reason, as well as others, I have given so large a space in this volume to the history, the details, and the results of factory legislation. One nation can and should learn from others. And even when a society has got upon the right track for the discovery of the natural laws of its movement—and it is the ultimate aim of this work, to lay bare the economic law of motion of modern society—it can neither clear by bold leaps, nor remove by legal enactments, the obstacles offered by the successive phases of its normal development. But it can shorten and lessen the birth-pangs.

To prevent possible misunderstanding, a word. I paint the capitalist and the landlord in no sense *couleur de rose*. But here individuals are dealt with only in so far as they are the personifications of economic categories, embodiments of particular class-relations and class-interests. My standpoint, from which the evolution of the economic formation of society is viewed as a process of natural history, can less than any other make the individual responsible for relations whose creature he socially remains, however much he may subjectively raise himself above them.

In the domain of Political Economy, free scientific inquiry meets not merely the same enemies as in all other domains. The peculiar nature of the material it deals with, summons as foes into the field of battle the most violent, mean and malignant passions of the human breast, the Furies of private interest. The English Established Church, e.g. will more readily pardon an attack on 38 of its 39 articles than on $\frac{1}{39}$ of its income. Now-a-days atheism itself is *culpa levis*, as compared with criticism of existing property relations. Nevertheless, there is an unmistakable advance. I refer, e.g. to the Blue book published within the last few weeks: 'Correspondence with Her Majesty's Missions Abroad, regarding Industrial Questions and Trades' Unions.' The representatives of the English Crown in foreign countries there declare in so many words that in Germany, in France, to be brief, in all the civilised states of the European Continent, a radical change in the existing relations between capital and labour is as evident and inevitable as in England. At the same time, on the other side of the Atlantic Ocean, Mr Wade, vice-president of the United States, declared in public meetings that, after the abolition of slavery, a radical change of the relations of capital and of property in land is next upon the order of the day. These are signs of the times, not to be hidden by purple mantles or black cassocks. They do not signify that tomorrow a miracle will happen.

They show that, within the ruling-classes themselves, a foreboding is dawning, that the present society is no solid crystal, but an organism capable of change, and is constantly changing.

The second volume of this work will treat of the process of the circulation of capital (Book II), and of the varied forms assumed by capital in the course of its development (Book III), the third and last volume (Book IV), the history of the theory.

Every opinion based on scientific criticism I welcome. As to the prejudices of so-called public opinion, to which I have never made concessions, now as aforetime the maxim of the great Florentine is mine:

'Segui il tuo corso, e lascia dir le genti.'*

AFTERWORD TO
THE SECOND GERMAN EDITION

SINCE 1848 capitalist production has developed rapidly in Germany, and at the present time it is in the full bloom of speculation and swindling. But fate is still unpropitious to our professional economists. At the time when they were able to deal with Political Economy in a straightforward fashion, modern economic conditions did not actually exist in Germany. And as soon as these conditions did come into existence, they did so under circumstances that no longer allowed of their being really and impartially investigated within the bounds of the bourgeois horizon. In so far as Political Economy remains within that horizon, in so far, i.e. as the capitalist régime is looked upon as the absolutely final form of social production, instead of as a passing historical phase of its evolution, Political Economy can remain a science only so long as the class-struggle is latent or manifests itself only in isolated and sporadic phenomena.

Let us take England. Its Political Economy belongs to the period in which the class-struggle was as yet undeveloped. Its last great representative, Ricardo, in the end, consciously makes the antagonism of class-interests, of wages and profits, of profits and rent, the starting-point of his investigations, naïvely taking this antagonism for a social law of Nature. But by this start the science of bourgeois economy had reached the limits beyond which it could not pass. Already in the lifetime of Ricardo, and in opposition to him, it was met by criticism, in the person of Sismondi.

The succeeding period, from 1820 to 1830, was notable in England for scientific activity in the domain of Political Economy. It was the time as well of the vulgarising and extending of Ricardo's theory, as of the contest of that theory with the old school. Splendid tournaments were held. What was done then, is little known to the Continent generally, because the polemic is for the most part scattered through articles in reviews, occasional literature and pamphlets. The unprejudiced character of this polemic—although the theory of Ricardo already serves, in exceptional cases, as a weapon of attack upon bourgeois economy—is explained by the circumstances of the time. On the one hand, modern industry itself was only just emerging from the age of childhood, as is shown by the fact that with the crisis of 1825 it for the first time opens the periodic cycle of its modern life. On the other hand, the class-struggle between capital and labour is forced into the background, politically by the discord between the governments and the feudal aristocracy gathered around the Holy Alliance on the one hand, and the popular masses, led by the bourgeoisie, on the other; economically by the quarrel between industrial capital and aristocratic landed property—a quarrel that in France was concealed by the opposition between small and large landed property, and that in England broke out openly after the Corn Laws. The literature of Political Economy in England at this time calls to mind the stormy forward movement in France after Dr Quesnay's death, but only as a Saint Martin's summer reminds us of spring. With the year 1830 came the decisive crisis.

In France and in England the bourgeoisie had conquered political power. Thenceforth, the class-struggle, practically as well as theoretically, took on more and more outspoken and threatening forms. It sounded the knell of scientific bourgeois economy. It was thenceforth no longer a question, whether this theorem or that was true, but whether it was useful to capital or harmful, expedient or inexpedient, politically dangerous or not. In place of disinterested inquirers, there were hired prize-fighters; in place of genuine scientific research, the bad conscience and the evil intent of apologetic. Still, even the obtrusive pamphlets with which the Anti-Corn Law League, led by the manufacturers Cobden and Bright, deluged the world, have a historic interest, if no scientific one, on account of their polemic against the landed aristocracy. But since then the Free-trade legislation, inaugurated by Sir Robert Peel, has deprived vulgar economy of this its last sting.

The Continental revolution of 1848–9 also had its reaction in England. Men who still claimed some scientific standing and aspired to be something more than mere sophists and sycophants of the ruling-classes, tried to harmonise the Political Economy of capital with the claims, no longer to be ignored, of the proletariat. Hence a shallow syncretism, of which John Stuart Mill is the best representative. It is a declaration of bankruptcy by bourgeois economy, an event on which the great Russian scholar and critic, N. Tschernyschewsky, has thrown the light of a master mind in his 'Outlines of Political Economy according to Mill'.

In Germany, therefore, the capitalist mode of production came to a head, after its antagonistic character had already, in France and England, shown itself in a fierce strife of classes. And meanwhile, moreover, the German proletariat had attained a much more clear class-consciousness than the German bourgeoisie. Thus, at the very moment when a bourgeois science of Political Economy seemed at last possible in Germany, it had in reality again become impossible.

Under these circumstances its professors fell into two groups. The one set, prudent, practical business folk, flocked to the banner of Bastiat, the most superficial and therefore the most adequate representative of the apologetic of vulgar economy; the other, proud of the professorial dignity of their science, followed John Stuart Mill in his attempt to reconcile irreconcilables. Just as in the classical time of bourgeois economy, so also in the time of its decline, the Germans remained mere schoolboys, imitators and followers, petty retailers and hawkers in the service of the great foreign wholesale concern.

The peculiar historical development of German society therefore forbids, in that country, all original work in bourgeois economy; but not the criticism of that economy. So far as such criticism represents a class, it can only represent the class whose vocation in history is the overthrow of the capitalist mode of production and the final abolition of all classes—the proletariat.

That the method employed in 'Das Kapital' has been little understood, is shown by the various conceptions, contradictory one to another, that have been formed of it.

Thus the Paris *Revue Positiviste* reproaches me in that, on the one hand, I treat economics metaphysically, and on the other hand—imagine!—confine myself to the mere critical analysis of actual facts, instead of writing receipts (Comtist ones?) for the cook-shops of the future. The *European Messenger* of St Petersburg in an article dealing exclusively with the method of 'Das Kapital' (May number, 1872, pp. 427–436), finds my method of inquiry severely realistic, but my method of presentation, unfortunately, German-dialectical. It says: 'At first sight, if the judgment is based on the external form of the presentation of the subject, Marx is the most ideal of ideal philosophers, always in the German, i.e. the bad sense of the word. But in point of fact he is infinitely more realistic than all his fore-runners in the work of economic criticism. He can in no sense be called an idealist.' I cannot answer the writer better than by aid of a few extracts from his own criticism, which may interest some of my readers to whom the Russian original is inaccessible.

After a quotation from the preface to my 'Criticism of Political Economy', Berlin, 1859, pp. IV–VII, where I discuss the materialistic basis of my method, the writer goes on:

The one thing which is of moment to Marx, is to find the law of the phenomena with whose investigation he is concerned; and not only is that law of moment to him, which governs these phenomena, in so far as they have a definite form and mutual connexion within a given historical period. Of still greater moment to him is the law of their variation, of their development, i.e. of their transition from one form into another, from one series of connexions into a different one. This law once discovered, he investigates in detail the effects in which it manifests itself in social life. Consequently, Marx only troubles himself about one thing: to show, by rigid scientific investigation, the necessity of successive determinate orders of social conditions, and to establish, as impartially as possible, the facts that serve him for fundamental starting-points. For this it is quite enough, if he proves, at the same time, both the necessity of the present order of things, and the necessity of another order into which the first must inevitably pass over; and this all the same, whether men believe or do not believe it, whether they are conscious or unconscious of it. Marx treats the social movement as a process of natural history, governed by laws not only independent of human will, consciousness and intelligence, but rather, on the contrary, determining that will, consciousness and intelligence. . . . If in the history of civilisation the conscious element plays a part so subordinate, then it is self-evident that a critical inquiry whose subject-matter is civilisation, can, less than anything else, have for its basis any form of, or any result of, consciousness. That is to say, that not the idea, but the material phenomenon alone can serve as its starting-point. Such an inquiry will confine itself to the confrontation and the comparison of a fact, not with ideas, but with another fact. For this inquiry, the one thing of moment is, that both facts be investigated as accurately as possible, and that they actually form, each with respect to the other, different momenta of an evolution; but most important of all is the rigid analysis of the series of successions, of the sequences and concatenations in which the different stages of such an evolution present themselves. But it will be said, the general laws of economic life are one and the same, no matter whether they are applied to the present or the past. This Marx directly denies. According to him, such abstract laws do not exist. On the contrary, in his opinion every historical period has laws of its own. . . . As soon as society has outlived a given period of development, and is passing over from one given stage to another, it begins to be subject also to other laws. In a word, economic life offers us a phenomenon analogous to the history of evolution in other branches of biology. The old economists misunderstood the nature of economic laws when they likened them to the laws of physics and chemistry. A more thorough analysis of phenomena shows that social organisms differ among themselves as fundamentally as plants or animals. Nay, one and the same phenomenon falls under quite different laws in consequence of the different structure of those organisms as a whole, of the variations of their individual organs, of the different conditions in which those organs function, etc. Marx, e.g. denies that the law of population is the same at all times and in all places. He asserts, on the contrary, that every stage of development has its own law of population. . . . With the varying degree of development of productive power, social conditions and the laws governing them vary too. Whilst Marx sets himself the task of following and explaining from this point of view the economic system established by the sway of capital, he is only formulating, in a strictly scientific manner, the aim that every accurate investigation into economic life must have. The scientific value of such an inquiry lies in the disclosing of the special laws that regulate the origin, existence, development, death of a given social organism and its replacement by another and higher one. And it is this value that, in point of fact, Marx's book has.

Whilst the writer pictures what he takes to be actually my method, in this striking and [as far as concerns my own application of it] generous way, what else is he picturing but the dialectic method?

Of course the method of presentation must differ in form from that of inquiry. The latter has to appropriate the material in detail, to analyse its different forms of development, to trace out their inner connexion. Only after this work is done, can the actual movement be adequately described. If this is done successfully, if the life of the subject-matter is ideally reflected as in a mirror, then it may appear as if we had before us a mere a priori construction.

My dialectic method is not only different from the Hegelian, but is its direct opposite. To Hegel, the life-process of the human brain, i.e. the process of thinking, which, under the name of 'the Idea', he even transforms into an independent subject, is the demiurgos of the real world, and the real world is only the external, phenomenal form of 'the Idea'. With me, on the contrary, the ideal is nothing else than the material world reflected by the human mind, and translated into forms of thought.

The mystifying side of Hegelian dialectic I criticised nearly thirty years ago, at a time when it was still the fashion. But just as I was working at the first volume of 'Das Kapital', it was the good pleasure of the peevish, arrogant, mediocre Ἐπίγονοι who now talk large in cultured Germany, to treat Hegel in the same way as the brave Moses Mendelssohn in Lessing's time treated Spinoza, i.e. as a 'dead dog'. I therefore openly avowed myself the pupil of that mighty thinker, and even here and there, in the chapter on the theory of value, coquetted with the modes of expression peculiar to him. The mystification which dialectic suffers in Hegel's hands, by no means prevents him from being the first to present its general form of working in a comprehensive and conscious manner. With him it is standing on its head. It must be turned right side up again, if you would discover the rational kernel within the mystical shell.

In its mystified form, dialectic became the fashion in Germany, because it seemed to transfigure and to glorify the existing state of things. In its rational form it is a scandal and abomination to bourgeoisdom and its doctrinaire professors, because it includes in its comprehension and affirmative recognition of the existing state of things, at the same time also, the recognition of the negation of that state, of its inevitable breaking up; because it regards every historically developed social form as in fluid movement, and therefore takes into account its transient nature not less than its momentary existence; because it lets nothing impose upon it, and is in its essence critical and revolutionary.

The contradictions inherent in the movement of capitalist society impress themselves upon the practical bourgeois most strikingly in the changes of the periodic cycle, through which modern industry runs, and whose crowning point is the universal crisis. That crisis is once again approaching, although as yet but in its preliminary stage; and by the universality of its theatre and the intensity of its action it will drum dialectics even into the heads of the mushroom-upstarts of the new, holy Prusso-German empire.

Karl Marx

London, 24 *January* 1873

PART I
COMMODITIES AND MONEY

CHAPTER 1
COMMODITIES

Section 1. The Two Factors of a Commodity: Use-Value and Value (the Substance of Value and the Magnitude of Value)

The wealth of those societies in which the capitalist mode of production prevails, presents itself as 'an immense accumulation of commodities', its unit being a single commodity. Our investigation must therefore begin with the analysis of a commodity.

A commodity is, in the first place, an object outside us, a thing that by its properties satisfies human wants of some sort or another. The nature of such wants, whether, for instance, they spring from the stomach or from fancy, makes no difference. Neither are we here concerned to know how the object satisfies these wants, whether directly as means of subsistence, or indirectly as means of production.

Every useful thing, as iron, paper, etc., may be looked at from the two points of view of quality and quantity. It is an assemblage of many properties, and may therefore be of use in various ways. To discover the various uses of things is the work of history. So also is the establishment of socially-recognised standards of measure for the quantities of these useful objects. The diversity of these measures has its origin partly in the diverse nature of the objects to be measured, partly in convention.

The utility of a thing makes it a use-value. But this utility is not a thing of air. Being limited by the physical properties of the commodity, it has no existence apart from that commodity. A commodity, such as iron, corn, or a diamond, is therefore, so far as it is a material thing, a use-value, something useful. This property of a commodity is independent of the amount of labour required to appropriate its useful qualities. When treating of use-value, we always assume to be dealing with definite quantities, such as dozens of watches, yards of linen, or tons of iron. The use-values of commodities furnish the material for a special study, that of the commercial knowledge of commodities. Use-values become a reality only by use or consumption: they also constitute the substance of all wealth, whatever may be the social form of that wealth. In the form of society we are about to consider, they are, in addition, the material depositories of exchange-value.

Exchange-value, at first sight, presents itself as a quantitative relation, as the proportion in which values in use of one sort are exchanged for those of another sort, a relation constantly changing with time and place. Hence exchange-value appears to be something accidental and purely relative, and consequently an intrinsic value, i.e. an exchange-value that is inseparably connected with, inherent in commodities, seems a contradiction in terms. Let us consider the matter a little more closely.

A given commodity, e.g. a quarter of wheat is exchanged for x blacking, y silk, or z gold, etc.—in short, for other commodities in the most different proportions. Instead of one exchange-value, the wheat has, therefore, a great many. But since x blacking, y silk, or z gold, etc., each represents the exchange-value of one quarter of wheat, x blacking, y silk, z gold, etc., must, as exchange-values, be replaceable by each other, or equal to each other. Therefore, first: the valid exchange-values of a given commodity express something equal; secondly, exchange-value, generally, is only the mode of expression, the phenomenal form, of something contained in it, yet distinguishable from it.

Let us take two commodities, e.g. corn and iron. The proportions in which they are exchangeable, whatever those proportions may be, can always be represented by an equation in which a given quantity of corn is equated to some quantity of iron: e.g. 1 quarter corn = x cwt. iron. What does this equation tell us? It tells us that in two different things—in 1 quarter of corn and x cwt. of iron, there exists in equal quantities something common to both. The two things must therefore be equal to a third, which in itself is neither the one nor the other. Each of them, so far as it is exchange-value, must therefore be reducible to this third.

A simple geometrical illustration will make this clear. In order to calculate and compare the areas of rectilinear figures, we decompose them into triangles. But the area of the triangle itself is expressed by something totally different from its visible figure, namely, by half the product of the base multiplied by the altitude. In the same way the exchange-values of commodities must be capable of being expressed in terms of something common to them all, of which thing they represent a greater or less quantity.

This common 'something' cannot be either a geometrical, a chemical, or any other natural property of commodities. Such properties claim our attention only in so far as they affect the utility of those commodities, make them use-values. But the exchange of commodities is evidently an act characterised by a total abstraction from use-value. Then one use-value is just as good as another, provided only it be present in sufficient quantity. Or, as old Barbon says, 'one sort of wares are as good as another, if the values be equal. There is no difference or distinction in things of equal value.... An hundred pounds' worth of lead or iron, is of as great value as one hundred pounds' worth of silver or gold.' As use-values, commodities are, above all, of different qual- ities, but as exchange-values they are merely different quantities, and consequently do not contain an atom of use-value.

If then we leave out of consideration the use-value of commodities, they have only one common property left, that of being products of labour. But even the product of labour itself has undergone a change in our hands. If we make abstraction from its use-value, we make abstrac- tion at the same time from the material elements and shapes that make the product a use-value; we see in it no longer a table, a house, yarn, or any other useful thing. Its existence as a material thing is put out of sight. Neither can it any longer be regarded as the product of the labour of the joiner, the mason, the spinner, or of any other definite kind of productive labour. Along with the useful qualities of the prod- ucts themselves, we put out of sight both the useful character of the various kinds of labour embodied in them, and the concrete forms of that labour; there is nothing left but what is common to them all; all are reduced to one and the same sort of labour, human labour in the abstract.

Let us now consider the residue of each of these products; it consists of the same unsubstantial reality in each, a mere congelation of hom- ogeneous human labour, of labour-power expended without regard to the mode of its expenditure. All that these things now tell us is, that human labour-power has been expended in their production, that human labour is embodied in them. When looked at as crystals of this social substance, common to them all, they are—Values.

We have seen that when commodities are exchanged, their ex- change-value manifests itself as something totally independent of their use-value. But if we abstract from their use-value, there remains their Value as defined above. Therefore, the common substance that manifests itself in the exchange-value of commodities, whenever they are exchanged, is their value. The progress of our investigation will show that exchange-value is the only form in which the value of commodities can manifest itself or be expressed. For the present, however, we have to consider the nature of value independently of this, its form.

A use-value, or useful article, therefore, has value only because human labour in the abstract has been embodied or materialised in it. How, then, is the magnitude of this value to be measured? Plainly, by the quantity of the value-creating substance, the labour, contained in the article. The quantity of labour, however, is measured by its duration, and labour-time in its turn finds its standard in weeks, days, and hours.

Some people might think that if the value of a commodity is determined by the quantity of labour spent on it, the more idle and unskilful the labourer, the more valuable would his commodity be, because more time would be required in its production. The labour, however, that forms the substance of value, is homogeneous human labour, expenditure of one uniform labour-power. The total labour-power of society, which is embodied in the sum total of the values of all commodities produced by that society, counts here as one homogeneous mass of human labour-power, composed though it be of innumerable individual units. Each of these units is the same as any other, so far as it has the character of the average labour-power of society, and takes effect as such; that is, so far as it requires for producing a commodity, no more time than is needed on an average, no more than is socially necessary. The labour-time socially necessary is that required to produce an article under the normal conditions of production, and with the average degree of skill and intensity prevalent at the time. The introduction of power-looms into England probably reduced by one-half the labour required to weave a given quantity of yarn into cloth. The hand-loom weavers, as a matter of fact, continued to require the same time as before; but for all that, the product of one hour of their labour represented after the change only half an hour's social labour, and consequently fell to one-half its former value.

We see then that that which determines the magnitude of the value of any article is the amount of labour socially necessary, or the labour-time socially necessary for its production. Each individual commodity, in this connexion, is to be considered as an average sample of its class. Commodities, therefore, in which equal quantities of labour are embodied, or which can be produced in the same time, have the same value. The value of one commodity is to the value of any other, as the labour-time necessary for the production of the one is to that necessary for the production of the other. As values, all commodities are only definite masses of congealed labour-time.

The value of a commodity would therefore remain constant, if the labour-time required for its production also remained constant. But the latter changes with every variation in the productiveness of labour. This productiveness is determined by various circumstances, amongst others, by the average amount of skill of the workmen, the state of science, and the degree of its practical application, the social organisation of production, the extent and capabilities of the means of production, and by physical conditions. For example, the same amount of labour in favourable seasons is embodied in 8 bushels of corn, and in unfavourable, only in four. The same labour extracts from rich mines more metal than from poor mines. Diamonds are of very rare occurrence on the earth's surface, and hence their discovery costs, on an average, a great deal of labour-time. Consequently much labour is represented in a small compass. Jacob doubts whether gold has ever been paid for at its full value. This applies still more to diamonds. According to Eschwege, the total produce of the Brazilian diamond mines for the eighty years, ending in 1823, had not realised the price of one-and-a-half years' average produce of the sugar and coffee plantations of the same country, although the diamonds cost much more labour, and therefore represented more value. With richer mines, the same quantity of labour would embody itself in more diamonds, and their value would fall. If we could succeed at a small expenditure of labour, in converting carbon into diamonds, their value might fall below that of bricks. In general, the greater the productiveness of labour, the less is the labour-time required for the production of an article, the less is the amount of labour crystallised in that article, and the less is its value; and vice versa, the less the productiveness of labour, the greater is the labour-time required for the production of an article, and the greater is its value. The value of a commodity, therefore, varies directly as the quantity, and inversely as the productiveness, of the labour incorporated in it.

A thing can be a use-value, without having value. This is the case whenever its utility to man is not due to labour. Such are air, virgin soil, natural meadows, etc. A thing can be useful, and the product of human labour, without being a commodity. Whoever directly satisfies his wants with the produce of his own labour, creates, indeed, use-values, but not commodities. In order to produce the latter, he must not only produce use-values, but use-values for others, social use-values. Lastly nothing can have value, without being an object of utility. If the thing is useless, so is the labour contained in it; the labour does not count as labour, and therefore creates no value.

Section 2. The Two-Fold Character
of the Labour Embodied in Commodities

At first sight a commodity presented itself to us as a complex of two things—use-value and exchange-value. Later on, we saw also that labour, too, possesses the same two-fold nature; for, so far as it finds expression in value, it does not possess the same characteristics that belong to it as a creator of use-values. I was the first to point out and to examine critically this two-fold nature of the labour contained in commodities. As this point is the pivot on which a clear comprehension of Political Economy turns, we must go more into detail.

Let us take two commodities such as a coat and 10 yards of linen, and let the former be double the value of the latter, so that, if 10 yards of linen = W, the coat = 2W.

The coat is a use-value that satisfies a particular want. Its existence is the result of a special sort of productive activity, the nature of which is determined by its aim, mode of operation, subject, means, and result. The labour, whose utility is thus represented by the value in use of its product, or which manifests itself by making its product a use-value, we call useful labour. In this connexion we consider only its useful effect.

As the coat and the linen are two qualitatively different use-values, so also are the two forms of labour that produce them, tailoring and weaving. Were these two objects not qualitatively different, not produced respectively by labour of different quality, they could not stand to each other in the relation of commodities. Coats are not exchanged for coats, one use-value is not exchanged for another of the same kind.

To all the different varieties of values in use there correspond as many different kinds of useful labour, classified according to the order, genus, species, and variety to which they belong in the social division of labour. This division of labour is a necessary condition for the production of commodities, but it does not follow, conversely, that the production of commodities is a necessary condition for the division of labour. In the primitive Indian community there is social division of labour, without production of commodities. Or, to take an example nearer home, in every factory the labour is divided according to a system, but this division is not brought about by the operatives mutually exchanging their individual products. Only such products can become commodities with regard to each other, as result from different kinds of labour, each kind being carried on independently and for the account of private individuals.

To resume, then: In the use-value of each commodity there is contained useful labour, i.e. productive activity of a definite kind and exercised with a definite aim. Use-values cannot confront each other as commodities, unless the useful labour embodied in them is qualitatively different in each of them. In a community, the produce of which in general takes the form of commodities, i.e. in a community of commodity producers, this qualitative difference between the useful forms of labour that are carried on independently by individual producers, each on their own account, develops into a complex system, a social division of labour.

Anyhow, whether the coat be worn by the tailor or by his customer, in either case it operates as a use-value. Nor is the relation between the coat and the labour that produced it altered by the circumstance that tailoring may have become a special trade, an independent branch of the social division of labour. Wherever the want of clothing forced them to it, the human race made clothes for thousands of years, without a single man becoming a tailor. But coats and linen, like every other element of material wealth that is not the spontaneous produce of Nature, must invariably owe their existence to a special productive activity, exercised with a definite aim, an activity that appropriates particular nature-given materials to particular human wants. So far therefore as labour is a creator of use-value, is useful labour, it is a necessary condition, independent of all forms of society, for the existence of the human race; it is an eternal nature-imposed necessity, without which there can be no material exchanges between man and Nature, and therefore no life.

The use-values, coat, linen, etc., i.e. the bodies of commodities, are combinations of two elements—matter and labour. If we take away the useful labour expended upon them, a material substratum is always left, which is furnished by Nature without the help of man. The latter can work only as Nature does, that is by changing the form of matter. Nay more, in this work of changing the form he is constantly helped by natural forces. We see, then, that labour is not the only source of material wealth, of use-values produced by labour. As William Petty puts it, labour is its father and the earth its mother.

Let us now pass from the commodity considered as a use-value to the value of commodities.

By our assumption, the coat is worth twice as much as the linen. But this is a mere quantitative difference, which for the present does not concern us. We bear in mind, however, that if the value of the coat is double that of 10 yds. of linen, 20 yds. of linen must have the same value as one coat. So far as they are values, the coat and the linen are things of a like substance, objective expressions of essentially identical labour. But tailoring and weaving are, qualitatively, different kinds of labour. There are, however, states of society in which one and the same man does tailoring and weaving alternately, in which case these two forms of labour are mere modifications of the labour of the same individual, and no special and fixed functions of different persons; just as the coat which our tailor makes one day, and the trousers which he makes another day, imply only a variation in the labour of one and the same individual. Moreover, we see at a glance that, in our capitalist society, a given portion of human labour is, in accordance with the varying demand, at one time supplied in the form of tailoring, at another in the form of weaving. This change may possibly not take place without friction, but take place it must.

Productive activity, if we leave out of sight its special form, viz., the useful character of the labour, is nothing but the expenditure of human labour-power. Tailoring and weaving, though qualitatively different productive activities, are each a productive expenditure of human brains, nerves, and muscles, and in this sense are human labour. They are but two different modes of expending human labour-power. Of course, this labour-power, which remains the same under all its modifications, must have attained a certain pitch of development before it can be expended in a multiplicity of modes. But the value of a commodity represents human labour in the abstract, the expenditure of human labour in general. And just as in society, a general or a banker plays a great part, but mere man, on the other hand, a very shabby part, so here with mere human labour. It is the expenditure of simple labour-power, i.e. of the labour-power which, on an average, apart from any special development, exists in the organism of every ordinary individual. Simple average labour, it is true, varies in character in different countries and at different times, but in a particular society it is given. Skilled labour counts only as simple labour intensified, or rather, as multiplied simple labour, a given quantity of skilled being considered equal to a greater quantity of simple labour. Experience shows that this reduction is constantly being made. A commodity may be the product of the most skilled labour, but its value, by equating it to the product of simple unskilled labour, represents a definite quantity of the latter labour alone. The different proportions in which different sorts of labour are reduced to unskilled labour as their standard, are established by a social process that goes on behind the backs of the producers, and, consequently, appear to be fixed by custom. For simplicity's sake we shall henceforth account every kind of labour to be unskilled, simple labour; by this we do no more than save ourselves the trouble of making the reduction.

Just as, therefore, in viewing the coat and linen as values, we abstract from their different use-values, so it is with the labour represented by those values: we disregard the difference between its useful forms, weaving and tailoring. As the use-values, coat and linen, are combinations of special productive activities with cloth and yarn, while the values, coat and linen, are, on the other hand, mere homogeneous congelations of undifferentiated labour, so the labour embodied in these latter values does not count by virtue of its productive relation to cloth and yarn, but only as being expenditure of human labour-power. Tailoring and weaving are necessary factors in the creation of the use-values, coat and linen, precisely because these two kinds of labour are of different qualities; but only in so far as abstraction is made from their special qualities, only in so far as both possess the same quality of being human labour, do tailoring and weaving form the substance of the values of the same articles.

Coats and linen, however, are not merely values, but values of definite magnitude, and according to our assumption, the coat is worth twice as much as the ten yards of linen. Whence this difference in their values? It is owing to the fact that the linen contains only half as much labour as the coat, and consequently, that in the production of the latter, labour-power must have been expended during twice the time necessary for the production of the former.

While, therefore, with reference to use-value, the labour contained in a commodity counts only qualitatively, with reference to value it counts only quantitatively, and must first be reduced to human labour pure and simple. In the former case, it is a question of How and What, in the latter of How much? How long a time? Since the magnitude of the value of a commodity represents only the quantity of labour embodied in it, it follows that all commodities, when taken in certain proportions, must be equal in value.

If the productive power of all the different sorts of useful labour required for the production of a coat remains unchanged, the sum of the values of the coats produced increases with their number. If one coat represents x days' labour, two coats represent 2x days' labour, and so on. But assume that the duration of the labour necessary for the production of a coat becomes doubled or halved. In the first case, one coat is worth as much as two coats were before; in the second case, two coats are only worth as much as one was before, although in both cases one coat renders the same service as before, and the useful labour embodied in it remains of the same quality. But the quantity of labour spent on its production has altered.

An increase in the quantity of use-values is an increase of material wealth. With two coats two men can be clothed, with one coat only one man. Nevertheless, an increased quantity of material wealth may correspond to a simultaneous fall in the magnitude of its value. This antagonistic movement has its origin in the two-fold character of labour. Productive power has reference, of course, only to labour of some useful concrete form, the efficacy of any special productive activity during a given time being dependent on its productiveness. Useful labour becomes, therefore, a more or less abundant source of products, in proportion to the rise or fall of its productiveness. On the other hand, no change in this productiveness affects the labour represented by value. Since productive power is an attribute of the concrete useful forms of labour, of course it can no longer have any bearing on that labour, so soon as we make abstraction from those concrete useful forms. However then productive power may vary, the same labour, exercised during equal periods of time, always yields equal amounts of value. But it will yield, during equal periods of time, different quantities of values in use; more, if the productive power rise, fewer, if it fall. The same change in productive power, which increases the fruitfulness of labour, and, in consequence, the quantity of use-values produced by that labour, will diminish the total value of this increased quantity of use-values, provided such change shorten the total labour-time necessary for their production; and vice versa.

On the one hand all labour is, speaking physiologically, an expenditure of human labour-power, and in its character of identical abstract human labour, it creates and forms the value of commodities. On the other hand, all labour is the expenditure of human labour-power in a special form and with a definite aim, and in this, its character of concrete useful labour, it produces use-values.

Section 3. The Form of Value or Exchange-Value

Commodities come into the world in the shape of use-values, articles, or goods, such as iron, linen, corn, etc. This is their plain, homely, bodily form. They are, however, commodities, only because they are something two-fold, both objects of utility, and, at the same time, depositories of value. They manifest themselves therefore as commodities, or have the form of commodities, only in so far as they have two forms, a physical or natural form, and a value-form.

The reality of the value of commodities differs in this respect from Dame Quickly, that we don't know 'where to have it.'* The value of commodities is the very opposite of the coarse materiality of their substance, not an atom of matter enters into its composition. Turn and examine a single commodity, by itself, as we will, yet in so far as it remains an object of value, it seems impossible to grasp it. If, however, we bear in mind that the value of commodities has a purely social reality, and that they acquire this reality only in so far as they are expressions or embodiments of one identical social substance, viz., human labour, it follows as a matter of course, that value can only manifest itself in the social relation of commodity to commodity. In fact we started from exchange-value, or the exchange relation of commodities, in order to get at the value that lies hidden behind it. We must now return to this form under which value first appeared to us.

Every one knows, if he knows nothing else, that commodities have a value-form common to them all, and presenting a marked contrast with the varied bodily forms of their use-values. I mean their money-form. Here, however, a task is set us, the performance of which has never yet even been attempted by *bourgeois* economy, the task of tracing the genesis of this money-form, of developing the expression of value implied in the value-relation of commodities, from its simplest, almost imperceptible outline, to the dazzling money-form. By doing this we shall, at the same time, solve the riddle presented by money.

The simplest value-relation is evidently that of one commodity to some one other commodity of a different kind. Hence the relation between the values of two commodities supplies us with the simplest expression of the value of a single commodity.

A. Elementary or Accidental Form of Value

x commodity A = y commodity B, or
x commodity A is worth y commodity B.
20 yards of linen = 1 coat, or
20 yards of linen are worth 1 coat.

1. The Two Poles of the Expression of Value. Relative Form and Equivalent Form

The whole mystery of the form of value lies hidden in this elementary form. Its analysis, therefore, is our real difficulty.

Here two different kinds of commodities (in our example the linen and the coat), evidently play two different parts. The linen expresses its value in the coat; the coat serves as the material in which that value is expressed. The former plays an active, the latter a passive, part. The value of the linen is represented as relative value, or appears in relative form. The coat officiates as equivalent, or appears in equivalent form.

The relative form and the equivalent form are two intimately connected, mutually dependent and inseparable elements of the expression of value; but, at the same time, are mutually exclusive, antagonistic extremes—i.e. poles of the same expression. They are allotted respectively to the two different commodities brought into relation by that expression. It is not possible to express the value of linen in linen. 20 yards of linen = 20 yards of linen is no expression of value. On the contrary, such an equation merely says that 20 yards of linen are nothing else than 20 yards of linen, a definite quantity of the use-value linen. The value of the linen can therefore be expressed only relatively—i.e. in some other commodity. The relative form of the value of the linen pre-supposes, therefore, the presence of some other commodity—here the coat—under the form of an equivalent. On the other hand, the commodity that figures as the equivalent cannot at the same time assume the relative form. That second commodity is not the one whose value is expressed. Its function is merely to serve as the material in which the value of the first commodity is expressed.

No doubt, the expression 20 yards of linen = 1 coat, or 20 yards of linen are worth 1 coat, implies the opposite relation. 1 coat = 20 yards of linen, or 1 coat is worth 20 yards of linen. But, in that case, I must reverse the equation, in order to express the value of the coat relatively; and, so soon as I do that, the linen becomes the equivalent instead of the coat. A single commodity cannot, therefore, simultaneously assume, in the same expression of value, both forms. The very polarity of these forms makes them mutually exclusive.

Whether, then, a commodity assumes the relative form, or the opposite equivalent form, depends entirely upon its accidental position in the expression of value—that is, upon whether it is the commodity whose value is being expressed or the commodity in which value is being expressed.

2. The Relative Form of Value

(a) *The Nature and Import of This Form*

In order to discover how the elementary expression of the value of a commodity lies hidden in the value-relation of two commodities, we must, in the first place, consider the latter entirely apart from its quantitative aspect. The usual mode of procedure is generally the reverse, and in the value-relation nothing is seen but the proportion between definite quantities of two different sorts of commodities that are considered equal to each other. It is apt to be forgotten that the magnitudes of different things can be compared quantitatively, only when those magnitudes are expressed in terms of the same unit. It is only as expressions of such a unit that they are of the same denomination, and therefore commensurable.

Whether 20 yards of linen = 1 coat or = 20 coats or = x coats— that is, whether a given quantity of linen is worth few or many coats, every such statement implies that the linen and coats, as magnitudes of value, are expressions of the same unit, things of the same kind. Linen = coat is the basis of the equation.

But the two commodities whose identity of quality is thus assumed, do not play the same part. It is only the value of the linen that is expressed. And how? By its reference to the coat as its equivalent, as something that can be exchanged for it. In this relation the coat is the mode of existence of value, is value embodied, for only as such is it the same as the linen. On the other hand, the linen's own value comes to the front, receives independent expression, for it is only as being value that it is comparable with the coat as a thing of equal value, or exchangeable with the coat.

If we say that, as values, commodities are mere congelations of human labour, we reduce them by our analysis, it is true, to the abstraction, value; but we ascribe to this value no form apart from their bodily form. It is otherwise in the value-relation of one commodity to another. Here, the one stands forth in its character of value by reason of its relation to the other.

By making the coat the equivalent of the linen, we equate the labour embodied in the former to that in the latter. Now, it is true that the tailoring, which makes the coat, is concrete labour of a different sort from the weaving which makes the linen. But the act of equating it to the weaving, reduces the tailoring to that which is really equal in the two kinds of labour, to their common character of human labour. In this roundabout way, then, the fact is expressed, that weaving also, in so far as it weaves value, has nothing to distinguish it from tailoring, and, consequently, is abstract human labour. It is the expression of equivalence between different sorts of commodities that alone brings into relief the specific character of value-creating labour, and this it does by actually reducing the different varieties of labour embodied in the different kinds of commodities to their common quality of human labour in the abstract.

There is, however, something else required beyond the expression of the specific character of the labour of which the value of the linen consists. Human labour-power in motion, or human labour, creates value, but is not itself value. It becomes value only in its congealed state, when embodied in the form of some object. In order to express the value of the linen as a congelation of human labour, that value must be expressed as having objective existence, as being a something materially different from the linen itself, and yet a something common to the linen and all other commodities. The problem is already solved.

When occupying the position of equivalent in the equation of value, the coat ranks qualitatively as the equal of the linen, as something of the same kind, because it is value. In this position it is a thing in which we see nothing but value, or whose palpable bodily form represents value. Yet the coat itself, the body of the commodity, coat, is a mere use-value. A coat as such no more tells us it is value, than does the first piece of linen we take hold of. This shows that when placed in value-relation to the linen, the coat signifies more than when out of that relation, just as many a man strutting about in a gorgeous uniform counts for more than when in mufti.

In the production of the coat, human labour-power, in the shape of tailoring, must have been actually expended. Human labour is therefore accumulated in it. In this aspect the coat is a depository of value, but though worn to a thread, it does not let this fact show through. And as equivalent of the linen in the value equation, it exists under this aspect alone, counts therefore as embodied value, as a body that is value. *A*, for instance, cannot be 'your majesty' to *B*, unless at the same time majesty in B's eyes assumes the bodily form of A, and, what is more, with every new father of the people, changes its features, hair, and many other things besides.

Hence, in the value equation, in which the coat is the equivalent of the linen, the coat officiates as the form of value. The value of the commodity linen is expressed by the bodily form of the commodity coat, the value of one by the use-value of the other. As a use-value, the linen is something palpably different from the coat; as value, it is the same as the coat, and now has the appearance of a coat. Thus the linen acquires a value-form different from its physical form. The fact that it is value, is made manifest by its equality with the coat, just as the sheep's nature of a Christian is shown in his resemblance to the Lamb of God.

We see, then, all that our analysis of the value of commodities has already told us, is told us by the linen itself, so soon as it comes into communication with another commodity, the coat. Only it betrays its thoughts in that language with which alone it is familiar, the language of commodities. In order to tell us that its own value is created by labour in its abstract character of human labour, it says that the coat, in so far as it is worth as much as the linen, and therefore is value, consists of the same labour as the linen. In order to inform us that its sublime reality as value is not the same as its buckram body, it says that value has the appearance of a coat, and consequently that so far as the linen is value, it and the coat are as like as two peas. We may here remark, that the language of commodities has, besides Hebrew, many other more or less correct dialects. The German 'Wertsein', to be worth, for instance, expresses in a less striking manner than the Romance verbs 'valere', 'valer', 'valoir', that the equating of commodity B to commodity A, is commodity A's own mode of expressing its value. Paris vaut bien une messe.*

By means, therefore, of the value-relation expressed in our equation, the bodily form of commodity B becomes the value-form of commodity A, or the body of commodity B acts as a mirror to the value of commodity A. By putting itself in relation with commodity B, as value *in propria persona*, as the matter of which human labour is made up, the commodity A converts the value in use, B, into the substance in which to express its, A's, own value. The value of A, thus expressed in the use-value of B, has taken the form of relative value.

(b) *Quantitative Determination of Relative Value*

Every commodity, whose value it is intended to express, is a useful object of given quantity, as 15 bushels of corn, or 100 lbs. of coffee. And a given quantity of any commodity contains a definite quantity of human labour. The value-form must therefore not only express value generally, but also value in definite quantity. Therefore, in the value-relation of commodity A to commodity B, of the linen to the coat, not only is the latter, as value in general, made the equal in quality of the linen, but a definite quantity of coat (1 coat) is made the equivalent of a definite quantity (20 yards) of linen.

The equation, 20 yards of linen = 1 coat, or 20 yards of linen are worth one coat, implies that the same quantity of value-substance (congealed labour) is embodied in both; that the two commodities have each cost the same amount of labour of the same quantity of labour-time. But the labour-time necessary for the production of 20 yards of linen or 1 coat varies with every change in the productiveness of weaving or tailoring. We have now to consider the influence of such changes on the quantitative aspect of the relative expression of value.

I. Let the value of the linen vary, that of the coat remaining constant. If, say in consequence of the exhaustion of flax-growing soil, the labour-time necessary for the production of the linen be doubled, the value of the linen will also be doubled. Instead of the equation, 20 yards of linen = 1 coat, we should have 20 yards of linen = 2 coats, since 1 coat would now contain only half the labour-time embodied in 20 yards of linen. If, on the other hand, in consequence, say, of improved looms, this labour-time be reduced by one-half, the value of the linen would fall by one-half. Consequently, we should have 20 yards of linen = ½ coat. The relative value of commodity A, i.e. its value expressed in commodity B, rises and falls directly as the value of A, the value of B being supposed constant.

II. Let the value of the linen remain constant, while the value of the coat varies. If, under these circumstances, in consequence, for instance, of a poor crop of wool, the labour-time necessary for the production of a coat becomes doubled, we have instead of 20 yards of linen = 1 coat, 20 yards of linen = ½ coat. If, on the other hand, the value of the coat sinks by one-half, then 20 yards of linen = 2 coats. Hence, if the value of commodity A remain constant, its relative value expressed in commodity B rises and falls inversely as the value of B.

If we compare the different cases in I and II, we see that the same change of magnitude in relative value may arise from totally opposite causes. Thus, the equation, 20 yards of linen = 1 coat, becomes 20 yards of linen = 2 coats, either, because the value of the linen has doubled, or because the value of the coat has fallen by one-half; and it becomes 20 yards of linen = ½ coat, either, because the value of the linen has fallen by one-half, or because the value of the coat has doubled.

III. Let the quantities of labour-time respectively necessary for the production of the linen and the coat vary simultaneously in the same direction and in the same proportion. In this case 20 yards of linen continue equal to 1 coat, however much their values may have altered. Their change of value is seen as soon as they are compared with a third commodity, whose value has remained constant. If the values of all commodities rose or fell simultaneously, and in the same proportion, their relative values would remain unaltered. Their real change of value would appear from the diminished or increased quantity of commodities produced in a given time.

IV. The labour-time respectively necessary for the production of the linen and the coat, and therefore the value of these commodities may simultaneously vary in the same direction, but at unequal rates, or in opposite directions, or in other ways. The effect of all these possible different variations, on the relative value of a commodity, may be deduced from the results of I, II, and III.

Thus real changes in the magnitude of value are neither unequivocally nor exhaustively reflected in their relative expression, that is, in the equation expressing the magnitude of relative value. The relative value of a commodity may vary, although its value remains constant. Its relative value may remain constant, although its value varies; and finally, simultaneous variations in the magnitude of value and in that of its relative expression by no means necessarily correspond in amount.

3. The Equivalent Form of Value

We have seen that commodity A (the linen), by expressing its value in the use-value of a commodity differing in kind (the coat), at the same time impresses upon the latter a specific form of value, namely that of the equivalent. The commodity linen manifests its quality of having a value by the fact that the coat, without having assumed a value-form different from its bodily form, is equated to the linen. The fact that the latter therefore has a value is expressed by saying that the coat is directly exchangeable with it. Therefore, when we say that a commodity is in the equivalent form, we express the fact that it is directly exchangeable with other commodities.

When one commodity, such as a coat, serves as the equivalent of another, such as linen, and coats consequently acquire the characteristic property of being directly exchangeable with linen, we are far from knowing in what proportion the two are exchangeable. The value of the linen being given in magnitude, that proportion depends on the value of the coat. Whether the coat serves as the equivalent and the linen as relative value, or the linen as the equivalent and the coat as relative value, the magnitude of the coat's value is determined, independently of its value-form, by the labour-time necessary for its production. But whenever the coat assumes in the equation of value, the position of equivalent, its value acquires no quantitative expression; on the contrary, the commodity coat now figures only as a definite quantity of some article.

For instance, 40 yards of linen are worth—what? 2 coats. Because the commodity coat here plays the part of equivalent, because the use-value coat, as opposed to the linen, figures as an embodiment of value, therefore a definite number of coats suffices to express the definite quantity of value in the linen. Two coats may therefore express the quantity of value of 40 yards of linen, but they can never express the quantity of their own value. A superficial observation of this fact, namely, that in the equation of value, the equivalent figures exclusively as a simple quantity of some article, of some use-value, has misled Bailey, as also many others, both before and after him, into seeing, in the expression of value, merely a quantitative relation. The truth being, that when a commodity acts as equivalent, no quantitative determination of its value is expressed.

The first peculiarity that strikes us, in considering the form of the equivalent, is this: use-value becomes the form of manifestation, the phenomenal form of its opposite, value.

The bodily form of the commodity becomes its value-form. But, mark well, that this *quid pro quo* exists in the case of any commodity B, only when some other commodity A enters into a value-relation with it, and then only within the limits of this relation. Since no commodity can stand in the relation of equivalent to itself, and thus turn its own bodily shape into the expression of its own value, every commodity is compelled to choose some other commodity for its equivalent, and to accept the use-value, that is to say, the bodily shape of that other commodity as the form of its own value.

One of the measures that we apply to commodities as material substances, as use-values, will serve to illustrate this point. A sugar-loaf being a body, is heavy, and therefore has weight: but we can neither see nor touch this weight. We then take various pieces of iron, whose weight has been determined beforehand. The iron, as iron, is no more the form of manifestation of weight, than is the sugar-loaf. Nevertheless, in order to express the sugar-loaf as so much weight, we put it into a weight-relation with the iron. In this relation, the iron officiates as a body representing nothing but weight. A certain quantity of iron therefore serves as the measure of the weight of the sugar, and represents, in relation to the sugar-loaf, weight embodied, the form of manifestation of weight. This part is played by the iron only within this relation, into which the sugar or any other body, whose weight has to be determined, enters with the iron. Were they not both heavy, they could not enter into this relation, and the one could therefore not serve as the expression of the weight of the other. When we throw both into the scales, we see in reality, that as weight they are both the same, and that, therefore, when taken in proper proportions, they have the same weight. Just as the substance iron, as a measure of weight, represents in relation to the sugar-loaf weight alone, so, in our expression of value, the material object, coat, in relation to the linen, represents value alone.

Here, however, the analogy ceases. The iron, in the expression of the weight of the sugar-loaf, represents a natural property common to both bodies, namely their weight; but the coat, in the expression of value of the linen, represents a non-natural property of both, something purely social, namely, their value.

Since the relative form of value of a commodity—the linen, for example—expresses the value of that commodity, as being something wholly different from its substance and properties, as being, for instance, coat-like, we see that this expression itself indicates that some social relation lies at the bottom of it. With the equivalent form it is just the contrary. The very essence of this form is that the material commodity itself—the coat—just as it is, expresses value, and is endowed with the form of value by Nature itself. Of course this holds good only so long as the value-relation exists, in which the coat stands in the position of equivalent to the linen. Since, however, the properties of a thing are not the result of its relations to other things, but only manifest themselves in such relations, the coat seems to be endowed with its equivalent form, its property of being directly exchangeable, just as much by Nature as it is endowed with the property of being heavy, or the capacity to keep us warm. Hence the enigmatical character of the equivalent form which escapes the notice of the bourgeois political economist, until this form, completely developed, confronts him in the shape of money. He then seeks to explain away the mystical character of gold and silver, by substituting for them less dazzling commodities, and by reciting, with ever renewed satisfaction, the catalogue of all possible commodities which at one time or another have played the part of equivalent. He has not the least suspicion that the most simple expression of value, such as 20 yds. of linen = 1 coat, already propounds the riddle of the equivalent form for our solution.

The body of the commodity that serves as the equivalent, figures as the materialisation of human labour in the abstract, and is at the same time the product of some specifically useful concrete labour. This concrete labour becomes, therefore, the medium for expressing abstract human labour. If on the one hand the coat ranks as nothing but the embodiment of abstract human labour, so, on the other hand, the tailoring which is actually embodied in it, counts as nothing but the form under which that abstract labour is realised. In the expression of value of the linen, the utility of the tailoring consists, not in making clothes, but in making an object, which we at once recognise to be Value, and therefore to be a congelation of labour, but of labour indistinguishable from that realised in the value of the linen. In order to act as such a mirror of value, the labour of tailoring must reflect nothing besides its own abstract quality of being human labour generally.

In tailoring, as well as in weaving, human labour-power is expended. Both, therefore, possess the general property of being human labour, and may, therefore, in certain cases, such as in the production of value, have to be considered under this aspect alone. There is nothing mysterious in this. But in the expression of value there is a complete turn of the tables. For instance, how is the fact to be expressed that weaving creates the value of the linen, not by virtue of being weaving, as such, but by reason of its general property of being human labour? Simply by opposing to weaving that other particular form of concrete labour (in this instance tailoring), which produces the equivalent of the product of weaving. Just as the coat in its bodily form became a direct expression of value, so now does tailoring, a concrete form of labour, appear as the direct and palpable embodiment of human labour generally.

Hence, the second peculiarity of the equivalent form is, that concrete labour becomes the form under which its opposite, abstract human labour, manifests itself.

But because this concrete labour, tailoring in our case, ranks as, and is directly identified with, undifferentiated human labour, it also ranks as identical with any other sort of labour, and therefore with that embodied in the linen. Consequently, although, like all other commodity-producing labour, it is the labour of private individuals, yet, at the same time, it ranks as labour directly social in its character. This is the reason why it results in a product directly exchangeable with other commodities. We have then a third peculiarity of the equivalent form, namely, that the labour of private individuals takes the form of its opposite, labour directly social in its form.

The two latter peculiarities of the equivalent form will become more intelligible if we go back to the great thinker who was the first to analyse so many forms, whether of thought, society, or Nature, and amongst them also the form of value. I mean Aristotle.

In the first place, he clearly enunciates that the money-form of commodities is only the further development of the simple form of value—i.e. of the expression of the value of one commodity in some other commodity taken at random.

There was, however, an important fact which prevented Aristotle from seeing that, to attribute value to commodities, is merely a mode of expressing all labour as equal human labour, and consequently as labour of equal quality. Greek society was founded upon slavery, and had, therefore, for its natural basis, the inequality of men and of their labour-powers. The secret of the expression of value, namely, that all kinds of labour are equal and equivalent, because, and so far as they are human labour in general, cannot be deciphered, until the notion of human equality has already acquired the fixity of a popular prejudice. This, however, is possible only in a society in which the great mass of the produce of labour takes the form of commodities, in which, consequently, the dominant relation between man and man, is that of owners of commodities. The brilliancy of Aristotle's genius is shown by this alone, that he discovered, in the expression of the value of commodities, a relation of equality. The peculiar conditions of the society in which he lived, alone prevented him from discovering what, 'in truth', was at the bottom of this equality.

4. The Elementary Form of Value Considered as a Whole

The elementary form of value of a commodity is contained in the equation, expressing its value-relation to another commodity of a different kind, or in its exchange-relation to the same. The value of commodity A, is qualitatively expressed, by the fact that commodity B is directly exchangeable with it. Its value is quantitatively expressed by the fact, that a definite quantity of B is exchangeable with a definite quantity of A. In other words, the value of a commodity obtains independent and definite expression, by taking the form of exchange-value. When, at the beginning of this chapter, we said, in common parlance, that a commodity is both a use-value and an exchange-value, we were, accurately speaking, wrong. A commodity is a use-value or object of utility, and a value. It manifests itself as this two-fold thing, that it is, as soon as its value assumes an independent form—viz., the form of exchange-value. It never assumes this form when isolated, but only when placed in a value or exchange relation with another commodity of a different kind. When once we know this, such a mode of expression does no harm; it simply serves as an abbreviation.

A close scrutiny of the expression of the value of A in terms of B, contained in the equation expressing the value-relation of A to B, has shown us that, within that relation, the bodily form of A figures only as a use-value, the bodily form of B only as the form or aspect of value. The opposition or contrast existing internally in each commodity between use-value and value, is, therefore, made evident externally by two commodities being placed in such relation to each other, that the commodity whose value it is sought to express, figures directly as a mere use-value, while the commodity in which that value is to be expressed, figures directly as mere exchange-value. Hence the elementary form of value of a commodity is the elementary form in which the contrast contained in that commodity, between use-value and value, becomes apparent.

Every product of labour is, in all states of society, a use-value; but it is only at a definite historical epoch in a society's development that such a product becomes a commodity, viz., at the epoch when the labour spent on the production of a useful article becomes expressed as one of the objective qualities of that article, i.e. as its value. It therefore follows that the elementary value-form is also the primitive form under which a product of labour appears historically as a commodity, and that the gradual transformation of such products into commodities, proceeds *pari passu* with the development of the value-form.

We perceive, at first sight, the deficiencies of the elementary form of value: it is a mere germ, which must undergo a series of metamorphoses before it can ripen into the price-form.

The expression of the value of commodity A in terms of any other commodity B, merely distinguishes the value from the use-value of A, and therefore places A merely in a relation of exchange with a single different commodity, B; but it is still far from expressing A's qualitative equality, and quantitative proportionality, to all commodities. To the elementary relative value-form of a commodity, there corresponds the single equivalent form of one other commodity. Thus, in the relative expression of value of the linen, the coat assumes the form of equivalent, or of being directly exchangeable, only in relation to a single commodity, the linen.

Nevertheless, the elementary form of value passes by an easy transition into a more complete form. It is true that by means of the elementary form, the value of a commodity A, becomes expressed in terms of one, and only one, other commodity. But that one may be a commodity of any kind, coat, iron, corn, or anything else. Therefore, according as A is placed in relation with one or the other, we get for one and the same commodity, different elementary expressions of value. The number of such possible expressions is limited only by the number of the different kinds of commodities distinct from it. The isolated expression of A's value, is therefore convertible into a series, prolonged to any length, of the different elementary expressions of that value.

B. Total or Expanded Form of Value

z Com. A = u Com. B or = v Com. C or = w Com. D or = x Com.
E or = etc.
(20 yards of linen = 1 coat or = 10 lbs. tea or = 40 lbs. coffee or = 1
quarter corn or = 2 ounces gold or = ½ ton iron or = etc.)

1. The Expanded Relative Form of Value

The value of a single commodity, the linen, for example, is now expressed in terms of numberless other elements of the world of commodities. Every other commodity now becomes a mirror of the linen's
value. It is thus, that for the first time, this value shows itself in its true
light as a congelation of undifferentiated human labour. For the labour
that creates it, now stands expressly revealed, as labour that ranks
equally with every other sort of human labour, no matter what its form,
whether tailoring ploughing, mining, etc., and no matter, therefore,
whether it is realised in coats, corn, iron, or gold. The linen, by virtue
of the form of its value, now stands in a social relation, no longer with
only one other kind of commodity, but with the whole world of commodities. As a commodity, it is a citizen of that world. At the same
time, the interminable series of value equations implies, that as regards
the value of a commodity, it is a matter of indifference under what
particular form, or kind, of use-value it appears.

In the first form, 20 yds. of linen = 1 coat, it might, for ought that
otherwise appears, be pure accident, that these two commodities are
exchangeable in definite quantities. In the second form, on the contrary, we perceive at once the background that determines, and is
essentially different from, this accidental appearance. The value of the
linen remains unaltered in magnitude, whether expressed in coats,
coffee, or iron, or in numberless different commodities, the property of
as many different owners. The accidental relation between two individual commodity-owners disappears. It becomes plain, that it is not
the exchange of commodities which regulates the magnitude of their
value; but, on the contrary, that it is the magnitude of their value which
controls their exchange proportions.

2. The Particular Equivalent Form

Each commodity, such as, coat, tea, corn, iron, etc., figures in the
expression of value of the linen, as an equivalent, and, consequently, as
a thing that is value. The bodily form of each of these commodities

figures now as a particular equivalent form, one out of many. In the same way the manifold concrete useful kinds of labour, embodied in these different commodities, rank now as so many different forms of the realisation, or manifestation, of undifferentiated human labour.

3. Defects of the Total or Expanded Form of Value

In the first place, the relative expression of value is incomplete because the series representing it is interminable. The chain of which each equation of value is a link, is liable at any moment to be lengthened by each new kind of commodity that comes into existence and furnishes the material for a fresh expression of value. In the second place, it is a many-coloured mosaic of disparate and independent expressions of value. And lastly, if, as must be the case, the relative value of each commodity in turn, becomes expressed in this expanded form, we get for each of them a relative value-form, different in every case, and consisting of an interminable series of expressions of value. The defects of the expanded relative value-form are reflected in the corresponding equivalent form. Since the bodily form of each single commodity is one particular equivalent form amongst numberless others, we have, on the whole, nothing but fragmentary equivalent forms, each excluding the others. In the same way, also, the special, concrete, useful kind of labour embodied in each particular equivalent, is presented only as a particular kind of labour, and therefore not as an exhaustive representative of human labour generally. The latter, indeed, gains adequate manifestation in the totality of its manifold, particular, concrete forms. But, in that case, its expression in an infinite series is ever incomplete and deficient in unity.

The expanded relative value-form is, however, nothing but the sum of the elementary relative expressions or equations of the first kind, such as

$$20 \text{ yards of linen} = 1 \text{ coat}$$
$$20 \text{ yards of linen} = 10 \text{ lbs. of tea, etc.}$$

Each of these implies the corresponding inverted equation,

$$1 \text{ coat} = 20 \text{ yards of linen}$$
$$10 \text{ lbs. of tea} = 20 \text{ yards of linen, etc.}$$

In fact, when a person exchanges his linen for many other commodities, and thus expresses its value in a series of other commodities, it necessarily follows, that the various owners of the latter exchange them for the linen, and consequently express the value of their various commodities in one and the same third commodity, the linen. If then, we reverse the series, 20 yards of linen = 1 coat or = 10 lbs. of tea, etc., that is to say, if we give expression to the converse relation already implied in the series, we get,

C. *The General Form of Value*

$$
\left.
\begin{array}{l}
1 \text{ coat} \\
10 \text{ lbs. of tea} \\
40 \text{ lbs. of coffee} \\
1 \text{ quarter of corn} \\
2 \text{ ounces of gold} \\
\frac{1}{2} \text{ a ton of iron} \\
x \text{ com. A., etc.}
\end{array}
\right\} = 20 \text{ yards of linen}
$$

1. The Altered Character of the Form of Value

All commodities now express their value (1) in an elementary form, because in a single commodity; (2) with unity, because in one and the same commodity. This form of value is elementary and the same for all, therefore general.

The forms A and B were fit only to express the value of a commodity as something distinct from its use-value or material form.

The first form, A, furnishes such equations as the following:—1 coat = 20 yards of linen, 10 lbs. of tea = ½ a ton of iron. The value of the coat is equated to linen, that of the tea to iron. But to be equated to linen, and again to iron, is to be as different as are linen and iron. This form, it is plain, occurs practically only in the first beginning, when the products of labour are converted into commodities by accidental and occasional exchanges.

The second form, B, distinguishes, in a more adequate manner than the first, the value of a commodity from its use-value; for the value of the coat is there placed in contrast under all possible shapes with the bodily form of the coat; it is equated to linen, to iron, to tea, in short, to everything else, only not to itself, the coat. On the other hand, any general expression of value common to all is directly excluded; for, in the equation of value of each commodity, all other commodities now appear only under the form of equivalents. The expanded form of value comes into actual existence for the first time so soon as a particular product of labour, such as cattle, is no longer exceptionally, but habitually, exchanged for various other commodities.

The third and lastly developed form expresses the values of the whole world of commodities in terms of a single commodity set apart for the purpose, namely, the linen, and thus represents to us their values by means of their equality with linen. The value of every commodity is now, by being equated to linen, not only differentiated from its own use-value, but from all other use-values generally, and is, by that very fact, expressed as that which is common to all commodities. By this form, commodities are, for the first time, effectively brought into relation with one another as values, or made to appear as exchange-values.

The two earlier forms either express the value of each commodity in terms of a single commodity of a different kind, or in a series of many such commodities. In both cases, it is, so to say, the special business of each single commodity to find an expression for its value, and this it does without the help of the others. These others, with respect to the former, play the passive parts of equivalents. The general form of value, C, results from the joint action of the whole world of commodities, and from that alone. A commodity can acquire a general expression of its value only by all other commodities, simultaneously with it, expressing their values in the same equivalent; and every new commodity must follow suit. It thus becomes evident that, since the existence of commodities as values is purely social, this social existence can be expressed by the totality of their social relations alone, and consequently that the form of their value must be a socially recognised form.

All commodities being equated to linen now appear not only as qualitatively equal as values generally, but also as values whose magnitudes are capable of comparison. By expressing the magnitudes of their values in one and the same material, the linen, those magnitudes are also compared with each other. For instance, 10 lbs. of tea = 20 yards of linen, and 40 lbs. of coffee = 20 yards of linen. Therefore, 10 lbs. of tea = 40 lbs. of coffee. In other words, there is contained in 1 lb. of coffee only one-fourth as much substance of value—labour—as is contained in 1 lb. of tea.

The general form of relative value, embracing the whole world of commodities, converts the single commodity that is excluded from the rest, and made to play the part of equivalent—here the linen—into the universal equivalent. The bodily form of the linen is now the form assumed in common by the values of all commodities; it therefore becomes directly exchangeable with all and every of them. The substance linen becomes the visible incarnation, the social chrysalis state of every kind of human labour. Weaving, which is the labour of certain private individuals producing a particular article, linen, acquires in consequence a social character, the character of equality with all other kinds of labour. The innumerable equations of which the general form of value is composed, equate in turn the labour embodied in the linen to that embodied in every other commodity, and they thus convert weaving into the general form of manifestation of undifferentiated human labour. In this manner the labour realised in the values of commodities is presented not only under its negative aspect, under which abstraction is made from every concrete form and useful property of actual work, but its own positive nature is made to reveal itself expressly. The general value-form is the reduction of all kinds of actual labour to their common character of being human labour generally, of being the expenditure of human labour-power.

The general value-form, which represents all products of labour as mere congelations of undifferentiated human labour, shows by its very structure that it is the social resumé of the world of commodities. That form consequently makes it indisputably evident that in the world of commodities the character possessed by all labour of being *human* labour constitutes its specific social character.

2. The Interdependent Development of the Relative Form of Value and of the Equivalent Form

The degree of development of the relative form of value corresponds to that of the equivalent form. But we must bear in mind that the development of the latter is only the expression and result of the development of the former.

The primary or isolated relative form of value of one commodity converts some other commodity into an isolated equivalent. The expanded form of relative value, which is the expression of the value of one commodity in terms of all other commodities, endows those other commodities with the character of particular equivalents differing in kind. And lastly, a particular kind of commodity acquires the character of universal equivalent, because all other commodities make it the material in which they uniformly express their value.

The antagonism between the relative form of value and the equivalent form, the two poles of the value-form, is developed concurrently with that form itself.

The first form, 20 yds. of linen = one coat, already contains this antagonism, without as yet fixing it. According as we read this equation forwards or backwards, the parts played by the linen and the coat are different. In the one case the relative value of the linen is expressed in the coat, in the other case the relative value of the coat is expressed in the linen. In this first form of value, therefore, it is difficult to grasp the polar contrast.

Form B shows that only one single commodity at a time can completely expand its relative value, and that it acquires this expanded form only because, and in so far as, all other commodities are, with respect to it, equivalents. Here we cannot reverse the equation, as we can the equation 20 yds. of linen = 1 coat, without altering its general character, and converting it from the expanded form of value into the general form of value.

Finally, the form C gives to the world of commodities a general social relative form of value, because, and in so far as, thereby all commodities, with the exception of one, are excluded from the equivalent form. A single commodity, the linen, appears therefore to have acquired the character of direct exchangeability with every other commodity because, and in so far as, this character is denied to every other commodity.

The commodity that figures as universal equivalent, is, on the other hand, excluded from the relative value-form. If the linen, or any other commodity serving as universal equivalent, were, at the same time, to share in the relative form of value, it would have to serve as its own equivalent. We should then have 20 yds. of linen = 20 yds. of linen; this tautology expresses neither value, nor magnitude of value. In order to express the relative value of the universal equivalent, we must rather reverse the form C. This equivalent has no relative form of value in common with other commodities, but its value is relatively expressed by a never ending series of other commodities.

Thus, the expanded form of relative value, or form B, now shows itself as the specific form of relative value for the equivalent commodity.

3. Transition from the General Form of Value to the Money-Form

The universal equivalent form is a form of value in general. It can, therefore, be assumed by any commodity. On the other hand, if a commodity be found to have assumed the universal equivalent form (form C), this is only because and in so far as it has been excluded from the rest of all other commodities as their equivalent, and that by their own act. And from the moment that this exclusion becomes finally restricted to one particular commodity, from that moment only, the general form of relative value of the world of commodities obtains real consistence and general social validity.

The particular commodity, with whose bodily form the equivalent form is thus socially identified, now becomes the money–commodity, or serves as money. It becomes the special social function of that commodity, and consequently its social monopoly, to play within the world of commodities the part of the universal equivalent. Amongst the commodities which, in form B, figure as particular equivalents of the linen, and, in form C, express in common their relative values in linen, this foremost place has been attained by one in particular—namely, gold. If, then, in form C we replace the linen by gold, we get,

D. The Money-Form

$$
\left.
\begin{array}{l}
\text{20 yards of linen} = \\
\text{1 coat} = \\
\text{10 lbs. of tea} = \\
\text{40 lbs. of coffee} = \\
\text{1 qr. of corn} = \\
\text{½ a ton of iron} = \\
\text{x commodity A} =
\end{array}
\right\} \quad \text{2 ounces of gold}
$$

In passing from form A to form B, and from the latter to form C, the changes are fundamental. On the other hand, there is no difference between forms C and D, except that, in the latter, gold has assumed the equivalent form in the place of linen. Gold is in form D, what linen was in form C—the universal equivalent. The progress consists in this alone, that the character of direct and universal exchangeability—in other words, that the universal equivalent form—has now, by social custom, become finally identified with the substance, gold.

Gold is now money with reference to all other commodities only because it was previously, with reference to them, a simple commodity. Like all other commodities, it was also capable of serving as an equivalent, either as simple equivalent in isolated exchanges, or as particular equivalent by the side of others. Gradually it began to serve, within varying limits, as universal equivalent. So soon as it monopolises this position in the expression of value for the world of commodities, it becomes the money commodity, and then, and not till then, does form D become distinct from form C, and the general form of value become changed into the money-form.

The elementary expression of the relative value of a single commodity, such as linen, in terms of the commodity, such as gold, that plays the part of money, is the price-form of that commodity. The price-form of the linen is therefore

20 yards of linen = 2 ounces of gold, or, if 2 ounces of gold when coined are £2, 20 yards of linen = £2.

The difficulty in forming a concept of the money-form, consists in clearly comprehending the universal equivalent form, and as a necessary corollary, the general form of value, form C. The latter is deducible from form B, the expanded form of value, the essential component element of which, we saw, is form A, 20 yards of linen = 1 coat or x commodity A = y commodity B. The simple commodity-form is therefore the germ of the money-form.

Section 4. The Fetishism of Commodities and the Secret Thereof

A commodity appears, at first sight, a very trivial thing, and easily understood. Its analysis shows that it is, in reality, a very queer thing, abounding in metaphysical subtleties and theological niceties. So far as it is a value in use, there is nothing mysterious about it, whether we consider it from the point of view that by its properties it is capable of satisfying human wants, or from the point that those properties are the product of human labour. It is as clear as noon-day, that man, by his industry, changes the forms of the materials furnished by Nature, in such a way as to make them useful to him. The form of wood, for instance, is altered, by making a table out of it. Yet, for all that, the table continues to be that common, every-day thing, wood. But, so soon as it steps forth as a commodity, it is changed into something transcendent. It not only stands with its feet on the ground, but, in relation to all other commodities, it stands on its head, and evolves out of its wooden brain grotesque ideas, far more wonderful than 'table-turning' ever was.

The mystical character of commodities does not originate, therefore, in their use-value. Just as little does it proceed from the nature of the determining factors of value. For, in the first place, however varied the useful kinds of labour, or productive activities, may be, it is a physiological fact, that they are functions of the human organism, and that each such function, whatever may be its nature or form, is essentially the expenditure of human brain, nerves, muscles, etc. Secondly, with regard to that which forms the ground-work for the quantitative determination of value, namely, the duration of that expenditure, or the quantity of labour, it is quite clear that there is a palpable difference between its quantity and quality. In all states of society, the labour-time that it costs to produce the means of subsistence, must necessarily be an object of interest to mankind, though not of equal interest in different stages of development. And lastly, from the moment that men in any way work for one another, their labour assumes a social form.

Whence, then, arises the enigmatical character of the product of labour, so soon as it assumes the form of commodities? Clearly from this form itself. The equality of all sorts of human labour is expressed objectively by their products all being equally values; the measure of the expenditure of labour-power by the duration of that expenditure, takes the form of the quantity of value of the products of labour; and finally, the mutual relations of the producers, within which the social character of their labour affirms itself, take the form of a social relation between the products.

A commodity is therefore a mysterious thing, simply because in it the social character of men's labour appears to them as an objective character stamped upon the product of that labour; because the relation of the producers to the sum total of their own labour is presented to them as a social relation, existing not between themselves, but between the products of their labour. This is the reason why the products of labour become commodities, social things whose qualities are at the same time perceptible and imperceptible by the senses. In the same way the light from an object is perceived by us not as the subjective excitation of our optic nerve, but as the objective form of something outside the eye itself. But, in the act of seeing, there is at all events, an actual passage of light from one thing to another, from the external object to the eye. There is a physical relation between physical things. But it is different with commodities. There, the existence of the things *qua* commodities, and the value-relation between the products of labour which stamps them as commodities, have absolutely no connexion with their physical properties and with the material relations arising therefrom. There it is a definite social relation between men, that assumes, in their eyes, the fantastic form of a relation between things. In order, therefore, to find an analogy, we must have recourse to the mist-enveloped regions of the religious world. In that world the productions of the human brain appear as independent beings endowed with life, and entering into relation both with one another and the human race. So it is in the world of commodities with the products of men's hands. This I call the Fetishism which attaches itself to the products of labour, so soon as they are produced as commodities, and which is therefore inseparable from the production of commodities.

This Fetishism of commodities has its origin, as the foregoing analysis has already shown, in the peculiar social character of the labour that produces them.

As a general rule, articles of utility become commodities, only because they are products of the labour of private individuals or groups of individuals who carry on their work independently of each other. The sum total of the labour of all these private individuals forms the aggregate labour of society. Since the producers do not come into social contact with each other until they exchange their products, the specific social character of each producer's labour does not show itself except in the act of exchange. In other words, the labour of the individual asserts itself as a part of the labour of society, only by means of the relation which the act of exchange establishes directly between the products, and indirectly, through them, between the producers. To the latter, therefore, the relations connecting the labour of one individual with that of the rest appear, not as direct social relations between individuals at work, but as what they really are, material relations between persons and social relations between things. It is only by being exchanged that the products of labour acquire, as values, one uniform social status, distinct from their varied forms of existence as objects of utility. This division of a product into a useful thing and a value becomes practically important, only when exchange has acquired such an extension that useful articles are produced for the purpose of being exchanged, and their character as values has therefore to be taken into account, beforehand, during production. From this moment the labour of the individual producer acquires socially a two-fold character. On the one hand, it must, as a definite useful kind of labour, satisfy a definite social want, and thus hold its place as part and parcel of the collective labour of all, as a branch of a social division of labour that has sprung up spontaneously. On the other hand, it can satisfy the manifold wants of the individual producer himself, only in so far as the mutual exchangeability of all kinds of useful private labour is an established social fact, and therefore the private useful labour of each producer ranks on an equality with that of all others. The equalisation of the most different kinds of labour can be the result only of an abstraction from their inequalities, or of reducing them to their common denominator, viz., expenditure of human labour-power or human labour in the abstract.

The two-fold social character of the labour of the individual appears to him, when reflected in his brain, only under those forms which are impressed upon that labour in every-day practice by the exchange of products. In this way, the character that his own labour possesses of being socially useful takes the form of the condition, that the product must be not only useful, but useful for others, and the social character that his particular labour has of being the equal of all other particular kinds of labour, takes the form that all the physically different articles that are the products of labour, have one common quality, viz., that of having value.

Hence, when we bring the products of our labour into relation with each other as values, it is not because we see in these articles the material receptacles of homogeneous human labour. Quite the contrary: whenever, by an exchange, we equate as values our different products, by that very act, we also equate, as human labour, the different kinds of labour expended upon them. We are not aware of this, nevertheless we do it. Value, therefore, does not stalk about with a label describing what it is. It is value, rather, that converts every product into a social hieroglyphic. Later on, we try to decipher the hieroglyphic, to get behind the secret of our own social products; for to stamp an object of utility as a value, is just as much a social product as language. The recent scientific discovery, that the products of labour, so far as they are values, are but material expressions of the human labour spent in their production, marks, indeed, an epoch in the history of the development of the human race, but, by no means, dissipates the mist through which the social character of labour appears to us to be an objective character of the products themselves. The fact, that in the particular form of production with which we are dealing, viz., the production of commodities, the specific social character of private labour carried on independently, consists in the equality of every kind of that labour, by virtue of its being human labour, which character, therefore, assumes in the product the form of value—this fact appears to the producers, notwithstanding the discovery above referred to, to be just as real and final, as the fact, that, after the discovery by science of the component gases of air, the atmosphere itself remained unaltered.

What, first of all, practically concerns producers when they make an exchange, is the question, how much of some other product they get for their own? in what proportions the products are exchangeable? When these proportions have, by custom, attained a certain stability, they appear to result from the nature of the products, so that, for instance, one ton of iron and two ounces of gold appear as naturally to be of equal value as a pound of gold and a pound of iron in spite of their different physical and chemical qualities appear to be of equal weight. The character of having value, when once impressed upon products, obtains fixity only by reason of their acting and re-acting upon each other as quantities of value. These quantities vary continually, independently of the will, foresight and action of the producers. To them, their own social action takes the form of the action of objects, which rule the producers instead of being ruled by them. It requires a fully developed production of commodities before, from accumulated experience alone, the scientific conviction springs up, that all the different kinds of private labour, which are carried on independently of each other, and yet as spontaneously developed branches of the social division of labour, are continually being reduced to the quantitative proportions in which society requires them. And why? Because, in the midst of all the accidental and ever fluctuating exchange-relations between the products, the labour-time socially necessary for their production forcibly asserts itself like an over-riding law of Nature. The law of gravity thus asserts itself when a house falls about our ears. The determination of the magnitude of value by labour-time is therefore a secret, hidden under the apparent fluctuations in the relative values of commodities. Its discovery, while removing all appearance of mere accidentality from the determination of the magnitude of the values of products, yet in no way alters the mode in which that determination takes place.

Man's reflections on the forms of social life, and consequently, also, his scientific analysis of those forms, take a course directly opposite to that of their actual historical development. He begins, post festum,* with the results of the process of development ready to hand before him. The characters that stamp products as commodities, and whose establishment is a necessary preliminary to the circulation of commodities, have already acquired the stability of natural, self-understood forms of social life, before man seeks to decipher, not their historical character, for in his eyes they are immutable, but their meaning. Consequently it was the analysis of the prices of commodities that alone led to the determination of the magnitude of value, and it was the common expression of all commodities in money that alone led to the establishment of their characters as values. It is, however, just this ultimate money-form of the world of commodities that actually conceals, instead of disclosing, the social character of private labour, and the social relations between the individual producers. When I state that coats or boots stand in a relation to linen, because it is the universal incarnation of abstract human labour, the absurdity of the statement is self-evident. Nevertheless, when the producers of coats and boots compare those articles with linen, or, what is the same thing, with gold or silver, as the universal equivalent, they express the relation between their own private labour and the collective labour of society in the same absurd form.

The categories of bourgeois economy consist of such like forms. They are forms of thought expressing with social validity the conditions and relations of a definite, historically determined mode of production, viz., the production of commodities. The whole mystery of commodities, all the magic and necromancy that surrounds the products of labour as long as they take the form of commodities, vanishes therefore, so soon as we come to other forms of production.

Since Robinson Crusoe's experiences are a favourite theme with political economists, let us take a look at him on his island. Moderate though he be, yet some few wants he has to satisfy, and must therefore do a little useful work of various sorts, such as making tools and furniture, taming goats, fishing and hunting. Of his prayers and the like we take no account, since they are a source of pleasure to him, and he looks upon them as so much recreation. In spite of the variety of his work, he knows that his labour, whatever its form, is but the activity of one and the same Robinson, and consequently, that it consists of nothing but different modes of human labour. Necessity itself compels him to apportion his time accurately between his different kinds of work. Whether one kind occupies a greater space in his general activity than another, depends on the difficulties, greater or less as the case may be, to be overcome in attaining the useful effect aimed at. This our friend Robinson soon learns by experience, and having rescued a watch, ledger, and pen and ink from the wreck, commences, like a true-born Briton, to keep a set of books. His stock-book contains a list of the objects of utility that belong to him, of the operations necessary for their production; and lastly, of the labour-time that definite quantities of those objects have, on an average, cost him. All the relations between Robinson and the objects that form this wealth of his own creation, are here so simple and clear as to be intelligible without exertion, even to Mr Sedley Taylor. And yet those relations contain all that is essential to the determination of value.

Let us now transport ourselves from Robinson's island bathed in light to the European middle ages shrouded in darkness. Here, instead of the independent man, we find everyone dependent, serfs and lords, vassals and suzerains, laymen and clergy. Personal dependence here characterises the social relations of production just as much as it does the other spheres of life organised on the basis of that production. But for the very reason that personal dependence forms the ground-work of society, there is no necessity for labour and its products to assume a fantastic form different from their reality. They take the shape, in the transactions of society, of services in kind and payments in kind. Here the particular and natural form of labour, and not, as in a society based on production of commodities, its general abstract form is the immediate social form of labour. Compulsory labour is just as properly measured by time, as commodity-producing labour; but every serf knows that what he expends in the service of his lord, is a definite quantity of his own personal labour-power. The tithe to be rendered to the priest is more matter of fact than his blessing. No matter, then, what we may think of the parts played by the different classes of people themselves in this society, the social relations between individuals in the performance of their labour, appear at all events as their own mutual personal relations, and are not disguised under the shape of social relations between the products of labour.

For an example of labour in common or directly associated labour, we have no occasion to go back to that spontaneously developed form which we find on the threshold of the history of all civilised races. We have one close at hand in the patriarchal industries of a peasant family, that produces corn, cattle, yarn, linen, and clothing for home use. These different articles are, as regards the family, so many products of its labour, but as between themselves, they are not commodities. The different kinds of labour, such as tillage, cattle tending, spinning, weaving and making clothes, which result in the various products, are in themselves, and such as they are, direct social functions, because functions of the family, which, just as much as a society based on the production of commodities, possesses a spontaneously developed system of division of labour. The distribution of the work within the family, and the regulation of the labour-time of the several members, depend as well upon differences of age and sex as upon natural conditions varying with the seasons. The labour-power of each individual, by its very nature, operates in this case merely as a definite portion of the whole labour-power of the family, and therefore, the measure of the expenditure of individual labour-power by its duration, appears here by its very nature as a social character of their labour.

Let us now picture to ourselves, by way of change, a community of free individuals, carrying on their work with the means of production in common, in which the labour-power of all the different individuals is consciously applied as the combined labour-power of the community. All the characteristics of Robinson's labour are here repeated, but with this difference, that they are social, instead of individual. Everything produced by him was exclusively the result of his own personal labour, and therefore simply an object of use for himself. The total product of our community is a social product. One portion serves as fresh means of production and remains social. But another portion is consumed by the members as means of subsistence. A distribution of this portion amongst them is consequently necessary. The mode of this distribution will vary with the productive organisation of the community, and the degree of historical development attained by the producers. We will assume, but merely for the sake of a parallel with the production of commodities, that the share of each individual producer in the means of subsistence is determined by his labour-time. Labour-time would, in that case, play a double part. Its apportionment in accordance with a definite social plan maintains the proper proportion between the different kinds of work to be done and the various wants of the community. On the other hand, it also serves as a measure of the portion of the common labour borne by each individual, and of his share in the part of the total product destined for individual consumption. The social relations of the individual producers, with regard both to their labour and to its products, are in this case perfectly simple and intelligible, and that with regard not only to production but also to distribution.

The religious world is but the reflex of the real world. And for a society based upon the production of commodities, in which the producers in general enter into social relations with one another by treating their products as commodities and values, whereby they reduce their individual private labour to the standard of homogeneous human labour—for such a society, Christianity with its *cultus* of abstract man, more especially in its bourgeois developments, Protestantism, Deism, etc., is the most fitting form of religion. In the ancient Asiatic and other ancient modes of production, we find that the conversion of products into commodities, and therefore the conversion of men into producers of commodities, holds a subordinate place, which, however, increases in importance as the primitive communities approach nearer and nearer to their dissolution. Trading nations, properly so called, exist in the ancient world only in its interstices, like the gods of Epicurus in the Intermundia,* or like Jews in the pores of Polish society. Those ancient social organisms of production are, as compared with bourgeois society, extremely simple and transparent. But they are founded either on

the immature development of man individually, who has not yet severed the umbilical cord that unites him with his fellowmen in a primitive tribal community, or upon direct relations of subjection. They can
arise and exist only when the development of the productive power of
labour has not risen beyond a low stage, and when, therefore, the social
relations within the sphere of material life, between man and man, and
between man and Nature, are correspondingly narrow. This narrow-
ness is reflected in the ancient worship of Nature, and in the other
elements of the popular religions. The religious reflex of the real world
can, in any case, only then finally vanish, when the practical relations of
every-day life offer to man none but perfectly intelligible and reasonable relations with regard to his fellowmen and to Nature.

The life-process of society, which is based on the process of material
production, does not strip off its mystical veil until it is treated as
production by freely associated men, and is consciously regulated by
them in accordance with a settled plan. This, however, demands for
society a certain material ground-work or set of conditions of existence
which in their turn are the spontaneous product of a long and painful
process of development.

Political Economy has indeed analysed, however incompletely, value
and its magnitude, and has discovered what lies beneath these forms.
But it has never once asked the question why labour is represented by
the value of its product and labour-time by the magnitude of that
value.[1] These formulæ, which bear it stamped upon them in unmistakable letters that they belong to a state of society, in which the process
of production has the mastery over man, instead of being controlled by
him, such formulæ appear to the bourgeois intellect to be as much a
self-evident necessity imposed by Nature as productive labour itself.
Hence forms of social production that preceded the bourgeois form,
are treated by the bourgeoisie in much the same way as the Fathers of
the Church treated pre-Christian religions.[2]

CHAPTER 2

EXCHANGE

IT is plain that commodities cannot go to market and make exchanges of their own account. We must, therefore, have recourse to their guardians, who are also their owners. Commodities are things, and therefore without power of resistance against man. If they are wanting in docility he can use force; in other words, he can take possession of them. In order that these objects may enter into relation with each other as commodities, their guardians must place themselves in relation to one another, as persons whose will resides in those objects, and must behave in such a way that each does not appropriate the commodity of the other, and part with his own, except by means of an act done by mutual consent. They must therefore, mutually recognise in each other the rights of private proprietors. This juridical relation, which thus expresses itself in a contract, whether such contract be part of a developed legal system or not, is a relation between two wills, and is but the reflex of the real economic relation between the two. It is this economic relation that determines the subject-matter comprised in each such juridical act. The persons exist for one another merely as representatives of, and, therefore, as owners of, commodities. In the course of our investigation we shall find, in general, that the characters who appear on the economic stage are but the personifications of the economic relations that exist between them.

What chiefly distinguishes a commodity from its owner is the fact, that it looks upon every other commodity as but the form of appearance of its own value. A born leveller and a cynic, it is always ready to exchange not only soul, but body, with any and every other commodity, be the same more repulsive than Maritornes herself.* The owner makes up for this lack in the commodity of a sense of the concrete, by his own five and more senses. His commodity possesses for himself no immediate use-value. Otherwise, he would not bring it to the market. It has use-value for others; but for himself its only direct use-value is that of being a depository of exchange-value, and, consequently, a means of exchange. Therefore, he makes up his mind to part with it for commodities whose value in use is of service to him. All commodities are non-use-values for their owners, and use-values for their non-owners. Consequently, they must all change hands. But this change of hands is what constitutes their exchange, and the latter puts them in relation with each other as values, and realises them as values. Hence commodities must be realised as values before they can be realised as use-values.

On the other hand, they must show that they are use-values before they can be realised as values. For the labour spent upon them counts effectively, only in so far as it is spent in a form that is useful for others. Whether that labour is useful for others, and its product consequently capable of satisfying the wants of others, can be proved only by the act of exchange.

Every owner of a commodity wishes to part with it in exchange only for those commodities whose use-value satisfies some want of his. Looked at in this way, exchange is for him simply a private transaction. On the other hand, he desires to realise the value of his commodity, to convert it into any other suitable commodity of equal value, irrespective of whether his own commodity has or has not any use-value for the owner of the other. From this point of view, exchange is for him a social transaction of a general character. But one and the same set of transactions cannot be simultaneously for all owners of commodities both exclusively private and exclusively social and general.

Let us look at the matter a little closer. To the owner of a commodity, every other commodity is, in regard to his own, a particular equivalent, and consequently his own commodity is the universal equivalent for all the others. But since this applies to every owner, there is, in fact, no commodity acting as universal equivalent, and the relative value of commodities possesses no general form under which they can be equated as values and have the magnitude of their values compared. So far, therefore, they do not confront each other as commodities, but only as products or use-values. In their difficulties our commodity-owners think like Faust: 'Im Anfang war die That.'* They therefore acted and transacted before they thought. Instinctively they conform to the laws imposed by the nature of commodities. They cannot bring their commodities into relation as values, and therefore as commodities, except by comparing them with some one other commodity as the universal equivalent. That we saw from the analysis of a commodity. But a particular commodity cannot become the universal equivalent except by a social act. The social action therefore of all other commodities, sets apart the particular commodity in which they all represent their values. Thereby the bodily form of this commodity becomes the form of the socially recognised universal equivalent. To be the universal equivalent, becomes, by this social process, the specific function of the commodity thus excluded by the rest. Thus it becomes—money.

Money is a crystal formed of necessity in the course of the exchanges, whereby different products of labour are practically equated to one another and thus by practice converted into commodities. The historical progress and extension of exchanges develops the contrast, latent in commodities, between use-value and value. The necessity for giving an external expression to this contrast for the purposes of commercial intercourse, urges on the establishment of an independent form of value, and finds no rest until it is once for all satisfied by the differentiation of commodities into commodities and money. At the same rate, then, as the conversion of products into commodities is being accomplished, so also is the conversion of one special commodity into money.[3]

The direct barter of products attains the elementary form of the relative expression of value in one respect, but not in another. That form is x Commodity A = y Commodity B. The form of direct barter is x use-value A = y use-value B. The articles A and B in this case are not as yet commodities, but become so only by the act of barter. The first step made by an object of utility towards acquiring exchange-value is when it forms a non-use-value for its owner, and that happens when it forms a superfluous portion of some article required for his immediate wants. Objects in themselves are external to man, and consequently alienable by him. In order that this alienation may be reciprocal, it is only necessary for men, by a tacit understanding, to treat each other as private owners of those alienable objects, and by implication as independent individuals. But such a state of reciprocal independence has no existence in a primitive society based on property in common, whether such a society takes the form of a patriarchal family, an ancient Indian community, or a Peruvian Inca State. The exchange of commodities, therefore, first begins on the boundaries of such communities, at their points of contact with other similar communities, or with members of the latter. So soon, however, as products once become commodities in the external relations of a community, they also, by reaction, become so in its internal intercourse. The proportions in which they are exchangeable are at first quite a matter of chance. What makes them exchangeable is the mutual desire of their owners to alienate them. Meantime the need for foreign objects of utility gradually establishes itself. The constant repetition of exchange makes it a normal social act. In the course of time, therefore, some portion at least of the products of labour must be produced with a special view to exchange. From that moment the distinction becomes firmly established between the utility of an object for the purposes of consumption, and its utility for the purposes of exchange. Its use-value becomes distinguished from its exchange-value. On the other hand, the quantitative proportion in which the articles are exchangeable, becomes dependent on their production itself. Custom stamps them as values with definite magnitudes.

In the direct barter of products, each commodity is directly a means of exchange to its owner, and to all other persons an equivalent, but that only in so far as it has use-value for them. At this stage, therefore, the articles exchanged do not acquire a value-form independent of their own use-value, or of the individual needs of the exchangers. The necessity for a value-form grows with the increasing number and variety of the commodities exchanged. The problem and the means of solution arise simultaneously. Commodity-owners never equate their own commodities to those of others, and exchange them on a large scale, without different kinds of commodities belonging to different owners being exchangeable for, and equated as values to, one and the same special article. Such last-mentioned article, by becoming the equivalent of various other commodities, acquires at once, though within narrow limits, the character of a general social equivalent. This character comes and goes with the momentary social acts that called it into life. In turns and transiently it attaches itself first to this and then to that commodity. But with the development of exchange it fixes itself firmly and exclusively to particular sorts of commodities, and becomes crystallised by assuming the money-form. The particular kind of commodity to which it sticks is at first a matter of accident. Nevertheless there are two circumstances whose influence is decisive. The money-form attaches itself either to the most important articles of exchange from outside, and these in fact are primitive and natural forms in which the exchange-value of home products finds expression; or else it attaches itself to the object of utility that forms, like cattle, the chief portion of indigenous alienable wealth. Nomad races are the first to develop the money-form, because all their worldly goods consist of moveable objects and are therefore directly alienable; and because their mode of life, by continually bringing them into contact with foreign communities, solicits the exchange of products. Man has often made man himself, under the form of slaves, serve as the primitive material of money, but has never used land for that purpose. Such an idea could only spring up in a bourgeois society already well developed. It dates from the last third of the 17th century, and the first attempt to put it in practice on a national scale was made a century afterwards, during the French bourgeois revolution.

In proportion as exchange bursts its local bonds, and the value of commodities more and more expands into an embodiment of human labour in the abstract, in the same proportion the character of money attaches itself to commodities that are by Nature fitted to perform the social function of a universal equivalent. Those commodities are the precious metals.

The truth of the proposition that, 'although gold and silver are not by Nature money, money is by Nature gold and silver', is shown by the fitness of the physical properties of these metals for the functions of money. Up to this point, however, we are acquainted only with one function of money, namely, to serve as the form of manifestation of the value of commodities, or as the material in which the magnitudes of their values are socially expressed. An adequate form of manifestation of value, a fit embodiment of abstract, undifferentiated, and therefore equal human labour, that material alone can be whose every sample exhibits the same uniform qualities. On the other hand, since the difference between the magnitudes of value is purely quantitative, the money-commodity must be susceptible of merely quantitative differences, must therefore be divisible at will, and equally capable of being reunited. Gold and silver possess these properties by Nature.

The use-value of the money-commodity becomes two-fold. In addition to its special use-value as a commodity (gold, for instance, serving to stop teeth, to form the raw material of articles of luxury, etc.), it acquires a formal use-value, originating in its specific social function.

Since all commodities are merely particular equivalents of money, the latter being their universal equivalent, they, with regard to the latter as the universal commodity, play the parts of particular commodities.

We have seen that the money-form is but the reflex, thrown upon one single commodity, of the value relations between all the rest. That money is a commodity is therefore a new discovery only for those who, when they analyse it, start from its fully developed shape. The act of exchange gives to the commodity converted into money, not its value, but its specific value-form. By confounding these two distinct things some writers have been led to hold that the value of gold and silver is imaginary. The fact that money can, in certain functions, be replaced by mere symbols of itself, gave rise to that other mistaken notion, that it is itself a mere symbol. Nevertheless under this error lurked a presentiment that the money-form of an object is not an inseparable part of that object, but is simply the form under which certain social relations manifest themselves. In this sense every commodity is a symbol, since, in so far as it is value, it is only the material envelope of the human labour spent upon it. But if it be declared that the social characters assumed by objects, or the material forms assumed by the social qualities of labour under the régime of a definite mode of production, are mere symbols, it is in the same breath also declared that these characteristics are arbitrary fictions sanctioned by the so-called universal consent of mankind. This suited the mode of explanation in favour during the 18th century. Unable to account for the origin of the puzzling forms assumed by social relations between man and man, people sought to denude them of their strange appearance by ascribing to them a conventional origin.

It has already been remarked above that the equivalent form of a commodity does not imply the determination of the magnitude of its value. Therefore, although we may be aware that gold is money, and consequently directly exchangeable for all other commodities, yet that fact by no means tells how much 10 lbs., for instance, of gold is worth. Money, like every other commodity, cannot express the magnitude of its value except relatively in other commodities. This value is determined by the labour-time required for its production, and is expressed by the quantity of any other commodity that costs the same amount of labour-time. Such quantitative determination of its relative value takes place at the source of its production by means of barter. When it steps into circulation as money, its value is already given. In the last decades of the 17th century it had already been shown that money is a commodity, but this step marks only the infancy of the analysis. The difficulty lies, not in comprehending that money is a commodity, but in discovering how, why, and by what means a commodity becomes money.

We have already seen, from the most elementary expression of value, x commodity A = y commodity B, that the object in which the magnitude of the value of another object is represented, appears to have the equivalent form independently of this relation, as a social property given to it by Nature. We followed up this false appearance to its final establishment, which is complete so soon as the universal equivalent form becomes identified with the bodily form of a particular commodity, and thus crystallised into the money-form. What appears to happen is, not that gold becomes money, in consequence of all other commodities expressing their values in it, but, on the contrary, that all other commodities universally express their values in gold, because it is money. The intermediate steps of the process vanish in the result and leave no trace behind. Commodities find their own value already completely represented, without any initiative on their part, in another commodity existing in company with them. These objects, gold and silver, just as they come out of the bowels of the earth, are forthwith the direct incarnation of all human labour. Hence the magic of money. In the form of society now under consideration, the behaviour of men in the social process of production is purely atomic. Hence their relations to each other in production assume a material character independent of their control and conscious individual action. These facts manifest themselves at first by products as a general rule taking the form of commodities. We have seen how the progressive development of a society of commodity-producers stamps one privileged commodity with the character of money. Hence the riddle presented by money is but the riddle presented by commodities; only it now strikes us in its most glaring form.

CHAPTER 3

MONEY, OR THE CIRCULATION OF COMMODITIES

Section 1. The Measure of Values

Throughout this work, I assume, for the sake of simplicity, gold as the money-commodity.

The first chief function of money is to supply commodities with the material for the expression of their values, or to represent their values as magnitudes of the same denomination, qualitatively equal, and quantitatively comparable. It thus serves as a *universal measure of value*. And only by virtue of this function does gold, the equivalent commodity *par excellence*, become money.

It is not money that renders commodities commensurable. Just the contrary. It is because all commodities, as values, are realised human labour, and therefore commensurable, that their values can be measured by one and the same special commodity, and the latter be converted into the common measure of their values, i.e. into money. Money as a measure of value, is the phenomenal form that must of necessity be assumed by that measure of value which is immanent in commodities, labour-time.[4]

The expression of the value of a commodity in gold—x commodity A = y money-commodity—is its money-form or price. A single equation, such as 1 ton of iron = 2 ounces of gold, now suffices to express the value of the iron in a socially valid manner. There is no longer any need for this equation to figure as a link in the chain of equations that express the values of all other commodities, because the equivalent commodity, gold, now has the character of money. The general form of relative value has resumed its original shape of simple or isolated relative value. On the other hand, the expanded expression of relative value, the endless seriles of equations, has now become the form peculiar to the relative value of the money-commodity. The series itself, too, is now given, and has social recognition in the prices of actual commodities. We have only to read the quotations of a price-list backwards, to find the magnitude of the value of money expressed in all sorts of commodities. But money itself has no price. In order to put it on an equal footing with all other commodities in this respect, we should be obliged to equate it to itself as its own equivalent.

The price or money-form of commodities is, like their form of value generally, a form quite distinct from their palpable bodily form; it is, therefore, a purely ideal or mental form. Although invisible, the value of iron, linen and corn has actual existence in these very articles: it is ideally made perceptible by their equality with gold, a relation that, so to say, exists only in their own heads. Their owner must, therefore, lend them his tongue, or hang a ticket on them, before their prices can be communicated to the outside world. Since the expression of the value of commodities in gold is a merely ideal act, we may use for this purpose imaginary or ideal money. Every trader knows, that he is far from having turned his goods into money, when he has expressed their value in a price or in imaginary money, and that it does not require the least bit of real gold, to estimate in that metal millions of pounds' worth of goods. When, therefore, money serves as a measure of value, it is employed only as imaginary or ideal money. This circumstance has given rise to the wildest theories. But, although the money that performs the functions of a measure of value is only ideal money, price depends entirely upon the actual substance that is money. The value, or in other words, the quantity of human labour contained in a ton of iron, is expressed in imagination by such a quantity of the money-commodity as contains the same amount of labour as the iron. According, therefore, as the measure of value is gold, silver, or copper, the value of the ton of iron will be expressed by very different prices, or will be represented by very different quantities of those metals respectively.

If, therefore, two different commodities, such as gold and silver, are simultaneously measures of value, all commodities have two prices— one a gold-price, the other a silver-price. These exist quietly side by side, so long as the ratio of the value of silver to that of gold remains unchanged, say, at 15:1. Every change in their ratio disturbs the ratio which exists between the gold-prices and the silver-prices of commodities, and thus proves, by facts, that a double standard of value is inconsistent with the functions of a standard.

Commodities with definite prices present themselves under the form: a commodity A = x gold; b commodity B = z gold; c commodity C = y gold, etc., where a, b, c, represent definite quantities of the commodities A, B, C and x, z, y, definite quantities of gold. The values of these commodities are, therefore, changed in imagination into so many different quantities of gold. Hence, in spite of the confusing variety of the commodities themselves, their values become magnitudes of the same denomination, gold-magnitudes. They are now capable of being compared with each other and measured, and the want becomes technically felt of comparing them with some fixed quantity of gold as a unit measure. This unit, by subsequent division into aliquot parts, becomes itself the standard or scale. Before they become money, gold, silver, and copper already possess such standard measures in their standards of weight, so that, for example, a pound weight, while serving as the unit, is, on the one hand, divisible into ounces, and, on the other, may be combined to make up hundred-weights. It is owing to this that, in all metallic currencies, the names given to the standards of money or of price were originally taken from the pre-existing names of the standards of weight.

As *measure of value*, and as *standard of price*, money has two entirely distinct functions to perform. It is the measure of value inasmuch as it is the socially recognised incarnation of human labour; it is the standard of price inasmuch as it is a fixed weight of metal. As the measure of value it serves to convert the values of all the manifold commodities into prices, into imaginary quantities of gold; as the standard of price it measures those quantities of gold. The measure of values measures commodities considered as values; the standard of price measures, on the contrary, quantities of gold by a unit quantity of gold, not the value of one quantity of gold by the weight of another. In order to make gold a standard of price, a certain weight must be fixed upon as the unit. In this case, as in all cases of measuring quantities of the same denomination, the establishment of an unvarying unit of measure is all-important. Hence, the less the unit is subject to variation, so much the better does the standard of price fulfil its office. But only in so far as it is itself a product of labour, and, therefore, potentially variable in value, can gold serve as a measure of value.

It is, in the first place, quite clear that a change in the value of gold does not, in any way, affect its function as a standard of price. No matter how this value varies, the proportions between the values of different quantities of the metal remain constant. However great the fall in its value, 12 ounces of gold still have 12 times the value of 1 ounce; and in prices, the only thing considered is the relation between different quantities of gold. Since, on the other hand, no rise or fall in the value of an ounce of gold can alter its weight, no alteration can take place in the weight of its aliquot parts. Thus gold always renders the same service as an invariable standard of price, however much its value may vary.

In the second place, a change in the value of gold does not interfere with its functions as a measure of value. The change affects all commodities simultaneously, and, therefore, *caeteris paribus*, leaves their relative values *inter se*, unaltered, although those values are now expressed in higher or lower gold-prices.

Just as when we estimate the value of any commodity by a definite quantity of the use-value of some other commodity, so in estimating the value of the former in gold, we assume nothing more than that the production of a given quantity of gold costs, at the given period, a given amount of labour. As regards the fluctuations of prices generally, they are subject to the laws of elementary relative value investigated in a former chapter.

A general rise in the prices of commodities can result only, either from a rise in their values—the value of money remaining constant—or from a fall in the value of money, the values of commodities remaining constant. On the other hand, a general fall in prices can result only, either from a fall in the values of commodities—the value of money remaining constant—or from a rise in the value of money, the values of commodities remaining constant. It therefore by no means follows, that a rise in the value of money necessarily implies a proportional fall in the prices of commodities; or that a fall in the value of money implies a proportional rise in prices. Such change of price holds good only in the case of commodities whose value remains constant. With those, for example, whose value rises, simultaneously with, and proportionally to, that of money, there is no alteration in price. And if their value rise either slower or faster than that of money, the fall or rise in their prices will be determined by the difference between the change in their value and that of money; and so on.

Let us now go back to the consideration of the price-form.

By degrees there arises a discrepancy between the current money-names of the various weights of the precious metal figuring as money, and the actual weights which those names originally represented.

These historical causes convert the separation of the money-name from the weight-name into an established habit with the community. Since the standard of money is on the one hand purely conventional, and must on the other hand find general acceptance, it is in the end regulated by law. A given weight of one of the precious metals, an ounce of gold, for instance, becomes officially divided into aliquot parts, with legally bestowed names, such as pound, dollar, etc. These aliquot parts, which thenceforth serve as units of money, are then subdivided into other aliquot parts with legal names, such as shilling, penny, etc. But, both before and after these divisions are made, a definite weight of metal is the standard of metallic

money. The sole alteration consists in the subdivision and denomination.

The prices, or quantities of gold, into which the values of commodities are ideally changed, are therefore now expressed in the names
of coins, or in the legally valid names of the subdivisions of the gold
standard. Hence, instead of saying: A quarter of wheat is worth an
ounce of gold; we say, it is worth £3 17s. 10½d. In this way commodities
express by their prices how much they are worth, and money serves as
money of account whenever it is a question of fixing the value of an
article in its money-form.

The name of a thing is something distinct from the qualities of that
thing. I know nothing of a man, by knowing that his name is Jacob. In
the same way with regard to money, every trace of a value-relation
disappears in the names pound, dollar, franc, ducat, etc. The confusion
caused by attributing a hidden meaning to these cabalistic signs is all
the greater, because these money-names express both the values of
commodities, and, at the same time, aliquot parts of the weight of the
metal that is the standard of money. On the other hand, it is absolutely
necessary that value, in order that it may be distinguished from the
varied bodily forms of commodities, should assume this material and
unmeaning, but, at the same time, purely social form.

Price is the money-name of the labour realised in a commodity.
Hence the expression of the equivalence of a commodity with the sum
of money constituting its price, is a tautology, just as in general the
expression of the relative value of a commodity is a statement of the
equivalence of two commodities. But although price, being the exponent of the magnitude of a commodity's value, is the exponent of its
exchange-ratio with money, it does not follow that the exponent of this
exchange-ratio is necessarily the exponent of the magnitude of the
commodity's value. Suppose two equal quantities of socially necessary
labour to be respectively represented by 1 quarter of wheat and £2
(nearly ½ oz. of gold), £2 is the expression in money of the magnitude
of the value of the quarter of wheat, or is its price. If now circumstances
allow of this price being raised to £3, or compel it to be reduced to £1,
then although £1 and £3 may be too small or too great properly to
express the magnitude of the wheat's value, nevertheless they are its
prices, for they are, in the first place, the form under which its value
appears, i.e. money; and in the second place, the exponents of its
exchange-ratio with money. If the conditions of production, in other
words, if the productive power of labour remain constant, the same
amount of social labour-time must, both before and after the change in

price, be expended in the reproduction of a quarter of wheat. This circumstance depends, neither on the will of the wheat producer, nor on that of the owners of other commodities.

Magnitude of value expresses a relation of social production, it expresses the connexion that necessarily exists between a certain article and the portion of the total labour-time of society required to produce it. As soon as magnitude of value is converted into price, the above necessary relation takes the shape of a more or less accidental exchange-ratio between a single commodity and another, the money-commodity. But this exchange-ratio may express either the real magnitude of that commodity's value, or the quantity of gold deviating from that value, for which, according to circumstances, it may be parted with. The possibility, therefore, of quantitative incongruity between price and magnitude of value, or the deviation of the former from the latter, is inherent in the price-form itself. This is no defect, but, on the contrary, admirably adapts the price-form to a mode of production whose inherent laws impose themselves only as the mean of apparently lawless irregularities that compensate one another.

The price-form, however, is not only compatible with the possibility of a quantitative incongruity between magnitude of value and price, i.e. between the former and its expression in money, but it may also conceal a qualitative inconsistency, so much so, that, although money is nothing but the value-form of commodities, price ceases altogether to express value. Objects that in themselves are no commodities, such as conscience, honour, etc., are capable of being offered for sale by their holders, and of thus acquiring, through their price, the form of commodities. Hence an object may have a price without having value. The price in that case is imaginary, like certain quantities in mathematics. On the other hand, the imaginary price-form may sometimes conceal either a direct or indirect real value-relation; for instance, the price of uncultivated land, which is without value, because no human labour has been incorporated in it.

Price, like relative value in general, expresses the value of a commodity (e.g. a ton of iron), by stating that a given quantity of the equivalent (e.g. an ounce of gold), is directly exchangeable for iron. But it by no means states the converse, that iron is directly exchangeable for gold. In order, therefore, that a commodity may in practice act effectively as exchange-value, it must quit its bodily shape, must transform itself from mere imaginary into real gold, although to the commodity such transubstantiation may be more difficult than to the Hegelian 'concept', the transition from 'necessity' to 'freedom', or to a lobster the casting of his shell, or to Saint Jerome the putting off of the old Adam.[5] Though a commodity may, side by side with its actual form (iron, for instance), take in our imagination the form of gold, yet it cannot at one and the same time actually be both iron and gold. To fix its price, it suffices to equate it to gold in imagination. But to enable it to render to its owner the service of a universal equivalent, it must be actually replaced by gold. If the owner of the iron were to go to the owner of some other commodity offered for exchange, and were to refer him to the price of the iron as proof that it was already money, he would get the same answer as St Peter gave in heaven to Dante, when the latter recited the creed—

> 'Assai bene è trascorsa
> D'esta moneta già la lega e'l peso,
> Ma dimmi se tu l'hai nella tua borsa.'*

A price therefore implies both that a commodity is exchangeable for money, and also that it must be so exchanged. On the other hand, gold serves as an ideal measure of value, only because it has already, in the process of exchange, established itself as the money-commodity. Under the ideal measure of values there lurks the hard cash.

Section 2. The Medium of Circulation

(a) *The Metamorphosis of Commodities*

We saw in a former chapter that the exchange of commodities implies contradictory and mutually exclusive conditions. The differentiation of commodities into commodities and money does not sweep away these inconsistencies, but develops a *modus vivendi*, a form in which they can exist side by side. This is generally the way in which real contradictions are reconciled. For instance, it is a contradiction to depict one body as constantly falling towards another, and as, at the same time, constantly flying away from it. The ellipse is a form of motion which, while allowing this contradiction to go on, at the same time reconciles it.

In so far as exchange is a process, by which commodities are transferred from hands in which they are non-use-values, to hands in which they become use-values, it is a social circulation of matter. The product of one form of useful labour replaces that of another. When once a commodity has found a resting-place, where it can serve as a use-value, it falls out of the sphere of exchange into that of consumption. But the former sphere alone interests us at present. We have, therefore, now to consider exchange from a formal point of view; to investigate the change of form or metamorphosis of commodities which effectuates the social circulation of matter.

The comprehension of this change of form is, as a rule, very imperfect. The cause of this imperfection is, apart from indistinct notions of value itself, that every change of form in a commodity results from the exchange of two commodities, an ordinary one and the money-commodity. If we keep in view the material fact alone that a commodity has been exchanged for gold, we overlook the very thing that we ought to observe—namely, what has happened to the form of the commodity. We overlook the facts that gold, when a mere commodity, is not money, and that when other commodities express their prices in gold, this gold is but the money-form of those commodities themselves.

Commodities, first of all, enter into the process of exchange just as they are. The process then differentiates them into commodities and money, and thus produces an external opposition corresponding to the internal opposition inherent in them, as being at once use-values and values. Commodities as use-values now stand opposed to money as exchange-value. On the other hand, both opposing sides are commodities, unities of use-value and value. But this unity of differences manifests itself at two opposite poles, and at each pole in an opposite way. Being poles they are as necessarily opposite as they are connected. On the one side of the equation we have an ordinary commodity, which is in reality a use-value. Its value is expressed only ideally in its price, by which it is equated to its opponent, the gold, as to the real embodiment of its value. On the other hand, the gold, in its metallic reality, ranks as the embodiment of value, as money. Gold, as gold, is exchange-value itself. As to its use-value, that has only an ideal existence, represented by the series of expressions of relative value in which it stands face to face with all other commodities, the sum of whose uses makes up the sum of the various uses of gold. These antagonistic forms of commodities are the real forms in which the process of their exchange moves and takes place.

Let us now accompany the owner of some commodity—say, our old friend the weaver of linen—to the scene of action, the market. His 20 yards of linen has a definite price, £2. He exchanges it for the £2, and then, like a man of the good old stamp that he is, he parts with the £2 for a family Bible of the same price. The linen, which in his eyes is a mere commodity, a depository of value, he alienates in exchange for gold, which is the linen's value-form, and this form he again parts with for another commodity, the Bible, which is destined to enter his house as an object of utility and of edification to its inmates. The exchange becomes an accomplished fact by two metamorphoses of opposite yet supplementary character—the conversion of the commodity into money, and the re-conversion of the money into a commodity. The two phases of this metamorphosis are both of them distinct transactions of the weaver—selling, or the exchange of the commodity for money; buying, or the exchange of the money for a commodity; and, the unity of the two acts, selling in order to buy.

The result of the whole transaction, as regards the weaver, is this, that instead of being in possession of the linen, he now has the Bible; instead of his original commodity, he now possesses another of the same value but of different utility. In like manner he procures his other means of subsistence and means of production. From his point of view, the whole process effectuates nothing more than the exchange of the product of his labour for the product of some one else's, nothing more than an exchange of products.

The exchange of commodities is therefore accompanied by the following changes in their form.

Commodity—Money—Commodity.

C—M—C.

The result of the whole process is, so far as concerns the objects themselves, C—C, the exchange of one commodity for another, the circulation of materialised social labour. When this result is attained, the process is at an end.

C—M. First Metamorphosis, or Sale

The leap taken by value from the body of the commodity, into the body of the gold, is, as I have elsewhere called it, the salto mortale* of the commodity. If it falls short, then, although the commodity itself is not harmed, its owner decidedly is. The social division of labour causes his labour to be as one-sided as his wants are many-sided. This is precisely the reason why the product of his labour serves him solely as exchange-value. But it cannot acquire the properties of a socially recognised universal equivalent, except by being converted into money. That money, however, is in some one else's pocket. In order to entice the money out of that pocket, our friend's commodity must, above all things, be a use-value to the owner of the money. For this, it is necessary that the labour expended upon it, be of a kind that is socially useful, of a kind that constitutes a branch of the social division of labour. But division of labour is a system of production which has grown up spontaneously and continues to grow behind the backs of the producers. The commodity to be exchanged may possibly be the product of some new kind of labour, that pretends to satisfy newly arisen requirements, or even to give rise itself to new requirements. A particular operation, though yesterday, perhaps, forming one out of the many operations conducted by one producer in creating a given commodity, may today separate itself from this connexion, may establish itself as an independent branch of labour and send its incomplete product to market as an independent commodity. The circumstances may or may not be ripe for such a separation. Today the product satisfies a social want. Tomorrow the article may, either altogether or partially, be superseded by some other appropriate product. Moreover, although our weaver's labour may be a recognised branch of the social division of labour, yet that fact is by no means sufficient to guarantee the utility of his 20 yards of linen. If the community's want of linen, and such a want has a limit like every other want, should already be saturated by the products of rival weavers, our friend's product is superfluous, redundant, and consequently useless. Although people do not look a gift-horse in the mouth, our friend does not frequent the market for the purpose of making presents. But suppose his product turn out a real use-value, and thereby attracts money? The question arises, how much will it attract? No doubt the answer is already anticipated in the price of the article, in the exponent of the magnitude of its value. We leave out of consideration here any accidental miscalculation of value by our friend, a mistake that is soon rectified in the market. We suppose him to have spent on his product only that amount of labour-time that is on an average socially necessary. The price then, is merely the money-name of the quantity of social labour realised in his commodity. But without the leave, and behind the back, of our weaver, the old-fashioned mode of weaving undergoes a change. The labour-time that yesterday was without doubt socially necessary to the production of a yard of linen, ceases to be so today, a fact which the owner of the money is only too eager to prove from the prices quoted by our friend's competitors. Unluckily for him, weavers are not few and far between. Lastly, suppose that every piece of linen in the market contains no more labour-time than is socially necessary. In spite of this, all these pieces taken as a whole, may have had superfluous labour-time spent upon them. If the market cannot stomach the whole quantity at the normal price of 2 shillings a yard, this proves that too great a portion of the total labour of the community has been expended in the form of weaving. The effect is the same as if each individual weaver had expended more labour-time upon his particular product than is socially necessary. Here we may say, with the German proverb: caught together, hung together. All the linen in the market counts but as one article of commerce, of which each piece is only an aliquot part. And as a matter of fact, the value also of each single yard is but the materialised form of the same definite and socially fixed quantity of homogeneous human labour.

We see then, commodities are in love with money, but 'the course of true love never did run smooth'. The quantitative division of labour is brought about in exactly the same spontaneous and accidental manner as its qualitative division. The owners of commodities therefore find out, that the same division of labour that turns them into independent private producers, also frees the social process of production and the relations of the individual producers to each other within that process, from all dependence on the will of those producers, and that the seeming mutual independence of the individuals is supplemented by a system of general and mutual dependence through or by means of the products.

The division of labour converts the product of labour into a commodity, and thereby makes necessary its further conversion into money. At the same time it also makes the accomplishment of this transubstantiation quite accidental. Here, however, we are only concerned with the phenomenon in its integrity, and we therefore assume its progress to be normal. Moreover, if the conversion take place at all, that is, if the commodity be not absolutely unsaleable, its metamorphosis does take place although the price realised may be abnormally above or below the value.

The seller has his commodity replaced by gold, the buyer has his gold replaced by a commodity. The fact which here stares us in the face is, that a commodity and gold, 20 yards of linen and £2, have changed hands and places, in other words, that they have been exchanged. But for what is the commodity exchanged? For the shape assumed by its own value, for the universal equivalent. And for what is the gold exchanged? For a particular form of its own use-value. Why does gold take the form of money face to face with the linen? Because the linen's price of £2, its denomination in money, has already equated the linen to gold in its character of money. A commodity strips off its original commodity-form on being alienated, i.e. on the instant its use-value actually attracts the gold, that before existed only ideally in its price. The realisation of a commodity's price, or of its ideal value-form, is therefore at the same time the realisation of the ideal use-value of money; the conversion of a commodity into money, is the simultaneous conversion of money into a commodity. The apparently single process is in reality a double one. From the pole of the commodity-owner it is a sale, from the opposite pole of the money-owner, it is a purchase. In other words, a sale is a purchase, C—M is also M—C.

Up to this point we have considered men in only one economic capacity, that of owners of commodities, a capacity in which they appropriate the produce of the labour of others, by alienating that of their own labour. Hence, for one commodity-owner to meet with another who has money, it is necessary, either, that the product of the labour of the latter person, the buyer, should be in itself money, should be gold, the material of which money consists, or that his product should already have changed its skin and have stripped off its original form of a useful object. In order that it may play the part of money, gold must of course enter the market at some point or other. This point is to be found at the source of production of the metal, at which place gold is bartered, as the immediate product of labour, for some other product of equal value. From that moment it always represents the realised price of some commodity. Apart from its exchange for other commodities at the source of its production, gold, in whose-so-ever hands it may be, is the transformed shape of some commodity alienated by its owner; it is the product of a sale or of the first metamorphosis C—M. Gold, as we saw, became ideal money, or a measure of values, in consequence of all commodities measuring their values by it, and thus contrasting it ideally with their natural shape as useful objects, and making it the shape of their value. It became real money, by the general alienation of commodities, by actually changing places with their natural forms as useful objects, and thus becoming in reality the embodiment of their values. When they assume this money-shape, commodities strip off every trace of their natural use-value, and of the particular kind of labour to which they owe their creation, in order to transform themselves into the uniform, socially recognised incarnation of homogeneous human labour. We cannot tell from the mere look of a piece of money, for what particular commodity it has been exchanged. Under their money-form all commodities look alike. Hence, money may be dirt, although dirt is not money. We will assume that the two gold pieces, in consideration of which our weaver has parted with his linen, are the metamorphosed shape of a quarter of wheat. The sale of the linen, C—M, is at the same time its purchase, M—C. But the sale is the first act of a process that ends with a transaction of an opposite nature, namely, the purchase of a Bible; the purchase of the linen, on the other hand, ends a movement that began with a transaction of an opposite nature, namely, with the sale of the wheat. C—M (linen—money), which is the first phase of C—M—C (linen—money—Bible), is also M—C (money—linen), the last phase of another movement C—M—C (wheat—money—linen). The first metamorphosis of one commodity, its transformation from a commodity into money, is therefore also invariably the second metamorphosis of some other commodity, the retransformation of the latter from money into a commodity.

M—C, or Purchase. The Second and Concluding Metamorphosis of a Commodity

Because money is the metamorphosed shape of all other commodities, the result of their general alienation, for this reason it is alienable itself without restriction or condition. It reads all prices backwards, and thus, so to say, depicts itself in the bodies of all other commodities, which offer to it the material for the realisation of its own use-value. At the same time the prices, wooing glances cast at money by commodities, define the limits of its convertibility, by pointing to its quantity. Since every commodity, on becoming money, disappears as a commodity, it is impossible to tell from the money itself, how it got into the hands of its possessor, or what article has been changed into it. Non olet,*from whatever source it may come. Representing on the one hand a sold commodity, it represents on the other a commodity to be bought.

M—C, a purchase, is, at the same time, C—M, a sale; the concluding metamorphosis of one commodity is the first metamorphosis of another. With regard to our weaver, the life of his commodity ends with the Bible, into which he has reconverted his £2. But suppose the seller of the Bible turns the £2 set free by the weaver into brandy M—C, the concluding phase of C—M—C (linen, money, Bible), is also C—M, the first phase of C—M—C (Bible, money, brandy). The producer of a particular commodity has that one article alone to offer; this he sells very often in large quantities, but his many and various wants compel him to split up the price realised, the sum of money set free, into numerous purchases. Hence a sale leads to many purchases of various articles. The concluding metamorphosis of a commodity thus constitutes an aggregation of first metamorphoses of various other commodities.

If we now consider the completed metamorphosis of a commodity, as a whole, it appears in the first place, that it is made up of two opposite and complementary movements, C—M and M—C. These two antithetical transmutations of a commodity are brought about by two antithetical social acts on the part of the owner, and these acts in their turn stamp the character of the economic parts played by him. As the person who makes a sale, he is a seller; as the person who makes a purchase, he is a buyer. But just as, upon every such transmutation of a commodity, its two forms, commodity-form and money-form, exist simultaneously but at opposite poles, so every seller has a buyer opposed to him, and every buyer a seller. While one particular commodity is going through its two transmutations in succession, from a commodity into money and from money into another commodity, the owner of the commodity changes in succession his part from that of seller to that of buyer. These characters of seller and buyer are therefore not permanent, but attach themselves in turns to the various persons engaged in the circulation of commodities.

The complete metamorphosis of a commodity, in its simplest form, implies four extremes, and three dramatis personæ. First, a commodity comes face to face with money; the latter is the form taken by the value of the former, and exists in all its hard reality, in the pocket of the buyer. A commodity-owner is thus brought into contact with a possessor of money. So soon, now, as the commodity has been changed into money, the money becomes its transient equivalent-form, the use-value of which equivalent-form is to be found in the bodies of other commodities. Money, the final term of the first transmutation, is at the same time the starting-point for the second. The person who is a seller in the first transaction thus becomes a buyer in the second, in which a third commodity-owner appears on the scene as a seller.

The two phases, each inverse to the other, that make up the metamorphosis of a commodity constitute together a circular movement, a circuit: commodity-form, stripping off of this form, and return to the commodity-form. No doubt, the commodity appears here under two different aspects. At the starting-point it is not a use-value to its owner; at the finishing point it is. So, too, the money appears in the first phase as a solid crystal of value, a crystal into which the commodity eagerly solidifies, and in the second, dissolves into the mere transient equivalent-form destined to be replaced by a use-value.

The two metamorphoses constituting the circuit are at the same time two inverse partial metamorphoses of two other commodities. One and the same commodity, the linen, opens the series of its own metamorphoses, and completes the metamorphosis of another (the wheat). In the first phase or sale, the linen plays these two parts in its own person. But, then, changed into gold, it completes its own second and final metamorphosis, and helps at the same time to accomplish the first metamorphosis of a third commodity. Hence the circuit made by one commodity in the course of its metamorphoses is inextricably mixed up with the circuits of other commodities. The total of all the different circuits constitutes *the circulation of commodities*.

The circulation of commodities differs from the direct exchange of products (barter), not only in form, but in substance. Only consider the course of events. The weaver has, as a matter of fact, exchanged his linen for a Bible, his own commodity for that of some one else. But this is true only so far as he himself is concerned. The seller of the Bible, who prefers something to warm his inside, no more thought of exchanging his Bible for linen than our weaver knew that wheat had been exchanged for his linen. B's commodity replaces that of A, but A and B do not mutually exchange those commodities. It may, of course, happen that A and B make simultaneous purchases, the one from the other; but such exceptional transactions are by no means the necessary result of the general conditions of the circulation of commodities. We see here, on the one hand, how the exchange of commodities breaks through all local and personal bounds inseparable from direct barter, and develops the circulation of the products of social labour; and on the other hand, how it develops a whole network of social relations spontaneous in their growth and entirely beyond the control of the actors. It is only because the farmer has sold his wheat that the weaver is enabled to sell his linen, only because the weaver has sold his linen that our Hotspur is enabled to sell his Bible, and only because the latter has sold the water of everlasting life that the distiller is enabled to sell his *eau-de-vie*, and so on.

The process of circulation, therefore, does not, like direct barter of products, become extinguished upon the use-values changing places and hands. The money does not vanish on dropping out of the circuit of the metamorphosis of a given commodity. It is constantly being precipitated into new places in the arena of circulation vacated by other commodities. In the complete metamorphosis of the linen, for example, linen—money—Bible, the linen first falls out of circulation, and money steps into its place. Then the Bible falls out of circulation, and again money takes its place. When one commodity replaces another, the money-commodity always sticks to the hands of some third person. Circulation sweats money from every pore.

Nothing can be more childish than the dogma, that because every sale is a purchase, and every purchase a sale, therefore the circulation

of commodities necessarily implies an equilibrium of sales and purchases. If this means that the number of actual sales is equal to the
number of purchases, it is mere tautology. But its real purport is to
prove that every seller brings his buyer to market with him. Nothing
of the kind. The sale and the purchase constitute one identical act,
an exchange between a commodity-owner and an owner of money,
between two persons as opposed to each other as the two poles of a
magnet. They form two distinct acts, of polar and opposite characters,
when performed by one single person. Hence the identity of sale and
purchase implies that the commodity is useless, if, on being thrown
into the alchemistical retort of circulation, it does not come out again
in the shape of money; if, in other words, it cannot be sold by its owner,
and therefore be bought by the owner of the money. That identity
further implies that the exchange, if it do take place, constitutes a
period of rest, an interval, long or short, in the life of the commodity.
Since the first metamorphosis of a commodity is at once a sale and a
purchase, it is also an independent process in itself. The purchaser has
the commodity, the seller has the money, i.e. a commodity ready to go
into circulation at any time. No one can sell unless some one else
purchases. But no one is forthwith bound to purchase, because he has
just sold. Circulation bursts through all restrictions as to time, place,
and individuals, imposed by direct barter, and this it effects by splitting
up, into the antithesis of a sale and a purchase, the direct identity that
in barter does exist between the alienation of one's own and the acquisition of some other man's product. To say that these two independent
and antithetical acts have an intrinsic unity, are essentially one, is the
same as to say that this intrinsic oneness expresses itself in an external
antithesis. If the interval in time between the two complementary
phases of the complete metamorphosis of a commodity become too
great, if the split between the sale and the purchase become too pronounced, the intimate connexion between them, their oneness, asserts
itself by producing—a crisis. The antithesis, use-value and value; the
contradictions that private labour is bound to manifest itself as direct
social labour, that a particularised concrete kind of labour has to pass
for abstract human labour; the contradiction between the personification of objects and the representation of persons by things; all these
antitheses and contradictions, which are immanent in commodities,
assert themselves, and develop their modes of motion, in the antithetical phases of the metamorphosis of a commodity. These modes therefore imply the possibility, and no more than the possibility, of crises.
The conversion of this mere possibility into a reality is the result of a

long series of relations, that, from our present standpoint of simple circulation, have as yet no existence.

(b) *The Currency of Money*

The change of form, C—M—C, by which the circulation of the material products of labour is brought about, requires that a given value in the shape of a commodity shall begin the process, and shall, also in the shape of a commodity, end it. The movement of the commodity is therefore a circuit. On the other hand, the form of this movement precludes a circuit from being made by the money. The result is not the return of the money, but its continued removal further and further away from its starting-point. So long as the seller sticks fast to his money, which is the transformed shape of his commodity, that commodity is still in the first phase of its metamorphosis, and has completed only half its course. But so soon as he completes the process, so soon as he supplements his sale by a purchase, the money again leaves the hands of its possessor. It is true that if the weaver, after buying the Bible, sell more linen, money comes back into his hands. But this return is not owing to the circulation of the first 20 yards of linen; that circulation resulted in the money getting into the hands of the seller of the Bible. The return of money into the hands of the weaver is brought about only by the renewal or repetition of the process of circulation with a fresh commodity, which renewed process ends with the same result as its predecessor did. Hence the movement directly imparted to money by the circulation of commodities takes the form of a constant motion away from its starting-point, of a course from the hands of one commodity-owner into those of another. This course constitutes its currency (cours de la monnaie).

The currency of money is the constant and monotonous repetition of the same process. The commodity is always in the hands of the seller; the money, as a means of purchase, always in the hands of the buyer. And money serves as a means of purchase by realising the price of the commodity. This realisation transfers the commodity from the seller to the buyer and removes the money from the hands of the buyer into those of the seller, where it again goes through the same process with another commodity. That this one-sided character of the money's motion arises out of the two-sided character of the commodity's motion, is a circumstance that is veiled over. The very nature of the circulation of commodities begets the opposite appearance. The first metamorphosis of a commodity is visibly, not only the money's movement, but also that of the commodity itself; in the second metamorphosis, on the contrary, the movement appears to us as the movement of the money alone. In the first phase of its circulation the commodity changes place with the money. Thereupon the commodity, under its aspect of a useful object, falls out of circulation into consumption. In its stead we have its value-shape—the money. It then goes through the second phase of its circulation, not under its own natural shape, but under the shape of money. The continuity of the movement is therefore kept up by the money alone, and the same movement that as regards the commodity consists of two processes of an antithetical character, is, when considered as the movement of the money, always one and the same process, a continued change of places with ever fresh commodities. Hence the result brought about by the circulation of commodities, namely, the replacing of one commodity by another, takes the appearance of having been effected not by means of the change of form of the commodities, but rather by the money acting as a medium of circulation, by an action that circulates commodities, to all appearance motionless in themselves, and transfers them from hands in which they are non-use-values, to hands in which they are use-values; and that in a direction constantly opposed to the direction of the money. The latter is continually withdrawing commodities from circulation and stepping into their places, and in this way continually moving further and further from its starting-point. Hence although the movement of the money is merely the expression of the circulation of commodities, yet the contrary appears to be the actual fact, and the circulation of commodities seems to be the result of the movement of the money.

Again, money functions as a means of circulation only because in it the values of commodities have independent reality. Hence its movement, as the medium of circulation, is, in fact, merely the movement of commodities while changing their forms. This fact must therefore make itself plainly visible in the currency of money. Thus the linen, for instance, first of all changes its commodity-form into its money-form. The second term of its first metamorphosis, C—M, the money-form, then becomes the first term of its final metamorphosis, M—C, its reconversion into the Bible. But each of these two changes of form is accomplished by an exchange between commodity and money, by their *reciprocal displacement*. The same pieces of coin come into the seller's hand *as the alienated form of the commodity* and leave it as *the absolutely alienable form of the commodity*. They are displaced twice. The first metamorphosis of the linen puts these coins into the weaver's pocket, the second draws them out of it. The two inverse changes undergone by the same commodity are reflected in the displacement, twice repeated, but in opposite directions, of the same pieces of coin.

If, on the contrary, only one phase of the metamorphosis is gone through, if there are only sales or only purchases, then a given piece of money changes its place only once. Its second change of place always expresses the second metamorphosis of the commodity, its re-conversion from money. The frequent repetition of the displacement of the same coins reflects not only the series of metamorphoses that a single commodity has gone through, but also the intertwining of the innumerable metamorphoses in the world of commodities in general. It is a matter of course, that all this is applicable to the simple circulation of commodities alone, the only form that we are now considering.

Every commodity, when it first steps into circulation, and undergoes its first change of form, does so only to fall out of circulation again and to be replaced by other commodities. Money, on the contrary, as the medium of circulation, keeps continually within the sphere of circulation, and moves about in it. The question therefore arises, how much money this sphere constantly absorbs?

In a given country there take place every day at the same time, but in different localities, numerous one-sided metamorphoses of commodities, or, in other words, numerous sales and numerous purchases. The commodities are equated beforehand in imagination, by their prices, to definite quantities of money. And since, in the form of circulation now under consideration, money and commodities always come bodily face to face, one at the positive pole of purchase, the other at the negative pole of sale, it is clear that the amount of the means of circulation required, is determined beforehand by the sum of the prices of all these commodities. As a matter of fact, the money in reality represents the quantity or sum of gold ideally expressed beforehand by the sum of the prices of the commodities. The equality of these two sums is therefore self-evident. We know, however, that, the values of commodities remaining constant, their prices vary with the value of gold (the material of money), rising in proportion as it falls, and falling in proportion as it rises. Now if, in consequence of such a rise or fall in the value of gold, the sum of the prices of commodities fall or rise, the quantity of money in currency must fall or rise to the same extent. The change in the quantity of the circulating medium is, in this case, it is true, caused by the money itself, yet not in virtue of its function as a medium of circulation, but of its function as a measure of value. First, the price of the commodities varies inversely as the value of the money, and then the quantity of the medium of circulation varies directly as the price of the commodities. Exactly the same thing would happen if, for instance, instead of the value of gold falling, gold were replaced by silver as the measure of value, or if, instead of the value of silver rising, gold were to thrust silver out from being the measure of value. In the one case, more silver would be current than gold was before; in the other case, less gold would be current than silver was before. In each case the value of the material of money, i.e. the value of the commodity that serves as the measure of value, would have undergone a change, and therefore so, too, would the prices of commodities which express their values in money, and so, too, would the quantity of money current whose function it is to realise those prices. We have already seen, that the sphere of circulation has an opening through which gold (or the material of money generally) enters into it as a commodity with a given value. Hence, when money enters on its functions as a measure of value, when it expresses prices, its value is already determined. If now its value fall, this fact is first evidenced by a change in the prices of those commodities that are directly bartered for the precious metals at the sources of their production. The greater part of all other commodities, especially in the imperfectly developed stages of civil society, will continue for a long time to be estimated by the former antiquated and illusory value of the measure of value. Nevertheless, one commodity infects another through their common value-relation, so that their prices, expressed in gold or in silver, gradually settle down into the proportions determined by their comparative values, until finally the values of all commodities are estimated in terms of the value of the metal that constitutes money. This process is accompanied by the continued increase in the quantity of the precious metals, an increase caused by their streaming in to replace the articles directly bartered for them at their sources of production. In proportion therefore as commodities in general acquire their true prices, in proportion as their values become estimated according to the fallen value of the precious metal, in the same proportion the quantity of that metal necessary for realising those new prices is provided beforehand. A one-sided observation of the results that followed upon the discovery of fresh supplies of gold and silver, led some economists in the 17th, and particularly in the 18th century, to the false conclusion, that the prices of commodities had gone up in consequence of the increased quantity of gold and silver serving as means of circulation. Henceforth we shall consider the value of gold to be given, as, in fact, it is momentarily whenever we estimate the price of a commodity.

On this supposition then, the quantity of the medium of circulation is determined by the sum of the prices that have to be realised. If now we further suppose the price of each commodity to be given, the sum of the prices clearly depends on the mass of commodities in circulation. It requires but little racking of brains to comprehend that if one quarter of wheat costs £2, 100 quarters will cost £200, 200 quarters £400, and so on, that consequently the quantity of money that changes place with the wheat, when sold, must increase with the quantity of that wheat.

If the mass of commodities remain constant, the quantity of circulating money varies with the fluctuations in the prices of those commodities. It increases and diminishes because the sum of the prices increases or diminishes in consequence of the change of price. To produce this effect, it is by no means requisite that the prices of all commodities should rise or fall simultaneously. A rise or a fall in the prices of a number of leading articles, is sufficient in the one case to increase, in the other to diminish, the sum of the prices of all commodities, and, therefore, to put more or less money in circulation. Whether the change in the price correspond to an actual change of value in the commodities, or whether it be the result of mere fluctuations in market-prices, the effect on the quantity of the medium of circulation remains the same.

Suppose the following articles to be sold or partially metamorphosed simultaneously in different localities: say, one quarter of wheat, 20 yards of linen, one Bible, and 4 gallons of brandy. If the price of each article be £2, and the sum of the prices to be realised be consequently £8, it follows that £8 in money must go into circulation. If, on the other hand, these same articles are links in the following chain of metamorphoses: 1 quarter of wheat—£2—20 yards of linen—£2—1 Bible—£2—4 gallons of brandy—£2, a chain that is already well known to us, in that case the £2 cause the different commodities to circulate one after the other, and after realising their prices successively, and therefore the sum of those prices, £8, they come to rest at last in the pocket of the distiller. The £2 thus make four moves. This repeated change of place of the same pieces of money corresponds to the double change in form of the commodities, to their motion in opposite directions through two stages of circulation, and to the interlacing of the metamorphoses of different commodities. These antithetic and complementary phases, of which the process of metamorphosis consists, are gone through, not simultaneously, but successively. Time is therefore required for the completion of the series. Hence the velocity of the currency of money is measured by the number of moves made by a given piece of money in a given time. Suppose the circulation of the 4 articles takes a day. The sum of the prices to be realised in the day is £8, the number of moves of the two pieces of money is four, and the quantity of money circulating is £2. Hence, for a given interval of time during the process of circulation, we have the following relation: the quantity of money functioning as the circulating medium is equal to the sum of the prices of the commodities divided by the number of moves made by coins of the same denomination. This law holds generally.

The total circulation of commodities in a given country during a given period is made up on the one hand of numerous isolated and simultaneous partial metamorphoses, sales which are at the same time purchases, in which each coin changes its place only once, or makes only one move; on the other hand, of numerous distinct series of metamorphoses partly running side by side, and partly coalescing with each other, in each of which series each coin makes a number of moves, the number being greater or less according to circumstances. The total number of moves made by all the circulating coins of one denomination being given, we can arrive at the average number of moves made by a single coin of that denomination, or at the average velocity of the currency of money. The quantity of money thrown into the circulation at the beginning of each day is of course determined by the sum of the prices of all the commodities circulating simultaneously side by side. But once in circulation, coins are, so to say, made responsible for one another. If the one increase its velocity, the other either retards its own, or altogether falls out of circulation; for the circulation can absorb only such a quantity of gold as when multiplied by the mean number of moves made by one single coin or element, is equal to the sum of the prices to be realised. Hence if the number of moves made by the separate pieces increase, the total number of those pieces in circulation diminishes. If the number of the moves diminish, the total number of pieces increases. Since the quantity of money capable of being absorbed by the circulation is given for a given mean velocity of currency, all that is necessary in order to abstract a given number of sovereigns from the circulation is to throw the same number of one-pound notes into it, a trick well known to all bankers.

Just as the currency of money, generally considered, is but a reflex of the circulation of commodities, or of the antithetical metamorphoses they undergo, so, too, the velocity of that currency reflects the rapidity with which commodities change their forms, the continued interlacing of one series of metamorphoses with another, the hurried social interchange of matter, the rapid disappearance of commodities from the sphere of circulation, and the equally rapid substitution of fresh ones in their places. Hence, in the velocity of the currency we have the fluent unity of the antithetical and complementary phases, the unity of the conversion of the useful aspect of commodities into their value-aspect, and their re-conversion from the latter aspect to the former, or the unity of the two processes of sale and purchase. On the other hand, the retardation of the currency reflects the separation of these two processes into isolated antithetical phases, reflects the stagnation in the change of form, and therefore, in the social interchange of matter. The circulation itself, of course, gives no clue to the origin of this stagnation; it merely puts in evidence the phenomenon itself. The general public, who, simultaneously with the retardation of the currency, see money appear and disappear less frequently at the periphery of circulation, naturally attribute this retardation to a quantitative deficiency in the circulating medium.

The total quantity of money functioning during a given period as the circulating medium, is determined, on the one hand, by the sum of the prices of the circulating commodities, and on the other hand, by the rapidity with which the antithetical phases of the metamorphoses follow one another. On this rapidity depends what proportion of the sum of the prices can, on the average, be realised by each single coin. But the sum of the prices of the circulating commodities depends on the quantity, as well as on the prices, of the commodities. These three factors, however, state of prices, quantity of circulating commodities, and velocity of money-currency, are all variable. Hence, the sum of the prices to be realised, and consequently the quantity of the circulating medium depending on that sum, will vary with the numerous variations of these three factors in combination. Of these variations we shall consider those alone that have been the most important in the history of prices.

The law, that the quantity of the circulating medium is determined by the sum of the prices of the commodities circulating, and the average velocity of currency may also be stated as follows: given the sum of the values of commodities, and the average rapidity of their metamorphoses, the quantity of precious metal current as money depends on the value of that precious metal. The erroneous opinion that it is, on the contrary, prices that are determined by the quantity of the circulating medium, and that the latter depends on the quantity of the precious metals in a country; this opinion was based by those who first held it, on the absurd hypothesis that commodities are without a price, and money without a value, when they first enter into circulation, and that, once in the circulation, an aliquot part of the medley of commodities is exchanged for an aliquot part of the heap of precious metals.

(c) *Coin and Symbols of Value*

That money takes the shape of coin, springs from its function as the circulating medium. The weight of gold represented in imagination by the prices or money-names of commodities, must confront those commodities, within the circulation, in the shape of coins or pieces of gold of a given denomination. Coining, like the establishment of a standard of prices, is the business of the State. The different national uniforms worn at home by gold and silver as coins, and doffed again in the market of the world, indicate the separation between the internal or national spheres of the circulation of commodities, and their universal sphere.

The only difference, therefore, between coin and bullion, is one of shape, and gold can at any time pass from one form to the other. But no sooner does coin leave the mint, than it immediately finds itself on the high-road to the melting pot. During their currency, coins wear away, some more, others less. Name and substance, nominal weight and real weight, begin their process of separation. Coins of the same denomination become different in value, because they are different in weight. The weight of gold fixed upon as the standard of prices, deviates from the weight that serves as the circulating medium, and the latter thereby ceases any longer to be a real equivalent of the commodities whose prices it realises. The history of coinage during the middle ages and down into the 18th century, records the ever renewed confusion arising from this cause. The natural tendency of circulation to convert coins into a mere semblance of what they profess to be, into a symbol of the weight of metal they are officially supposed to contain, is recognised by modern legislation, which fixes the loss of weight sufficient to demonetise a gold coin, or to make it no longer legal tender.

The fact that the currency of coins itself effects a separation between their nominal and their real weight, creating a distinction between them as mere pieces of metal on the one hand, and as coins with a definite function on the other—this fact implies the latent possibility of replacing metallic coins by tokens of some other material, by symbols serving the same purposes as coins. The practical difficulties in the way of coining extremely minute quantities of gold or silver, and the circumstance that at first the less precious metal is used as a measure of value instead of the more precious, copper instead of silver, silver instead of gold, and that the less precious circulates as money until dethroned by the more precious—all these facts explain the parts historically played by silver and copper tokens as substitutes for gold coins. Silver and copper tokens take the place of gold in those regions of the circulation where coins pass from hand to hand most rapidly, and are subject to the maximum amount of wear and tear. This occurs where sales and purchases on a very small scale are continually happening. In order to prevent these satellites from establishing themselves permanently in the place of gold, positive enactments determine the extent to which they must be compulsorily received as payment instead of gold. The particular tracks pursued by the different species of coin in currency, run naturally into each other. The tokens keep company with gold, to pay fractional parts of the smallest gold coin; gold is, on the one hand, constantly pouring into retail circulation, and on the other hand is as constantly being thrown out again by being changed into tokens.

The weight of metal in the silver and copper tokens is arbitrarily fixed by law. When in currency, they wear away even more rapidly than gold coins. Hence their functions are totally independent of their weight, and consequently of all value. The function of gold as coin becomes completely independent of the metallic value of that gold. Therefore things that are relatively without value, such as paper notes, can serve as coins in its place. This purely symbolic character is to a certain extent masked in metal tokens. In paper money it stands out plainly. In fact, ce n'est que le premier pas qui coûte.*

We allude here only to inconvertible paper money issued by the State and having compulsory circulation. It has its immediate origin in the metallic currency. Money based upon credit implies on the other hand conditions, which, from our standpoint of the simple circulation of commodities, are as yet totally unknown to us. But we may affirm this much, that just as true paper money takes its rise in the function of money as the circulating medium, so money based upon credit takes root spontaneously in the function of money as the means of payment.

The State puts in circulation bits of paper on which their various denominations, say £1, £5, etc., are printed. In so far as they actually take the place of gold to the same amount, their movement is subject to the laws that regulate the currency of money itself. A law peculiar to the circulation of paper money can spring up only from the proportion in which that paper money represents gold. Such a law exists; stated simply, it is as follows: the issue of paper money must not exceed in amount the gold (or silver as the case may be) which would actually circulate if not replaced by symbols. Now the quantity of gold which the circulation can absorb, constantly fluctuates about a given level. Still, the mass of the circulating medium in a given country never sinks below a certain minimum easily ascertained by actual experience. The fact that this minimum mass continually undergoes changes in its constituent parts, or that the pieces of gold of which it consists are being constantly replaced by fresh ones, causes of course no change either in its amount or in the continuity of its circulation. It can therefore be replaced by paper symbols. If, on the other hand, all the conduits of circulation were today filled with paper money to the full extent of their capacity for absorbing money, they might to-morrow be overflowing in consequence of a fluctuation in the circulation of commodities. There would no longer be any standard. If the paper money exceed its proper limit, which is the amount in gold coins of the like denomination that can actually be current, it would, apart from the danger of falling into general disrepute, represent only that quantity of gold, which, in accordance with the laws of the circulation of commodities, is required, and is alone capable of being represented by paper. If the quantity of paper money issued be double what it ought to be, then, as a matter of fact, £1 would be the money-name not of ¼ of an ounce, but of ⅛ of an ounce of gold. The effect would be the same as if an alteration had taken place in the function of gold as a standard of prices. Those values that were previously expressed by the price of £1 would now be expressed by the price of £2.

Paper money is a token representing gold or money. The relation between it and the values of commodities is this, that the latter are ideally expressed in the same quantities of gold that are symbolically represented by the paper. Only in so far as paper money represents gold, which like all other commodities has value, is it a symbol of value.

Finally, some one may ask why gold is capable of being replaced by tokens that have no value? But, as we have already seen, it is capable of being so replaced only in so far as it functions exclusively as coin, or as the circulating medium, and as nothing else. Now, money has other functions besides this one, and the isolated function of serving as the mere circulating medium is not necessarily the only one attached to gold coin, although this is the case with those abraded coins that continue to circulate. Each piece of money is a mere coin, or means of circulation, only so long as it actually circulates. But this is just the case with that minimum mass of gold, which is capable of being replaced by paper money. That mass remains constantly within the sphere of circulation, continually functions as a circulating medium, and exists exclusively for that purpose. Its movement therefore represents nothing but the continued alternation of the inverse phases of the metamorphosis C—M—C, phases in which commodities confront their value-forms, only to disappear again immediately. The independent existence of the exchange-value of a commodity is here a transient apparition, by means of which the commodity is immediately replaced by another commodity. Hence, in this process which continually makes money pass from hand to hand, the mere symbolical existence of money suffices. Its functional existence absorbs, so to say, its material existence. Being a transient and objective reflex of the prices of commodities, it serves only as a symbol of itself, and is therefore capable of being replaced by a token. One thing is, however, requisite; this token must have an objective social validity of its own, and this the paper symbol acquires by its forced currency. This compulsory action of the State can take effect only within that inner sphere of circulation which is co-terminous with the territories of the community, but it is also only within that sphere that money completely responds to its function of being the circulating medium, or becomes coin.

Section 3. Money

The commodity that functions as a measure of value, and, either in its own person or by a representative, as the medium of circulation, is money. Gold (or silver) is therefore money. It functions as money, on the one hand, when it has to be present in its own golden person. It is then the money-commodity, neither merely ideal, as in its function of a measure of value, nor capable of being represented, as in its function of circulating medium. On the other hand, it also functions as money, when by virtue of its function, whether that function be performed in person or by representative, it congeals into the sole form of value, the only adequate form of existence of exchange-value, in opposition to use-value, represented by all other commodities.

(a) *Hoarding*

With the very earliest development of the circulation of commodities, there is also developed the necessity, and the passionate desire, to hold fast the product of the first metamorphosis. This product is the transformed shape of the commodity, or its gold-chrysalis. Commodities are thus sold not for the purpose of buying others, but in order to replace their commodity-form by their money-form. From being the mere means of effecting the circulation of commodities, this change of form becomes the end and aim. The changed form of the commodity is thus prevented from functioning as its unconditionally alienable form, or as its merely transient money-form. The money becomes petrified into a hoard, and the seller becomes a hoarder of money.

As the production of commodities further develops, every producer of commodities is compelled to make sure of the nexus rerum or the social pledge. His wants are constantly making themselves felt, and necessitate the continual purchase of other people's commodities, while the production and sale of his own goods require time, and depend upon circumstances. In order then to be able to buy without selling, he must have sold previously without buying. This operation, conducted on a general scale, appears to imply a contradiction. But the precious metals at the sources of their production are directly exchanged for other commodities. And here we have sales (by the owners of commodities) without purchases (by the owners of gold or silver). And subsequent sales, by other producers, unfollowed by purchases, merely bring about the distribution of the newly produced precious metals among all the owners of commodities. In this way, all along the line of exchange, hoards of gold and silver of varied extent are accumulated. With the possibility of holding and storing up exchange-value in the shape of a particular commodity, arises also the greed for gold. Along with the extension of circulation, increases the power of money, that absolutely social form of wealth ever ready for use. 'Gold is a wonderful thing! Whoever possesses it is lord of all he wants. By means of gold one can even get souls into Paradise.' (Columbus in his letter from Jamaica, 1503.) Since gold does not disclose what has been transformed into it, everything, commodity or not, is convertible into gold. Everything becomes saleable and buyable. The circulation becomes the great social retort into which everything is thrown, to come out again as a gold–crystal. Not even are the bones of saints, and still less are more delicate res sacrosanctæ, extra commercium hominum able to withstand this alchemy. Just as every qualitative difference between commodities is extinguished in money, so money, on its side, like the radical leveller that it is, does away with all distinctions. But money itself is a commodity, an external object, capable of becoming the private property of any individual. Thus social power becomes the private power of private persons. The ancients therefore denounced money as subversive of the economic and moral order of things. Modern society, which, soon after its birth, pulled Plutus by the hair of his head from the bowels of the earth, greets gold as its Holy Grail, as the glittering incarnation of the very principle of its own life.

A commodity, in its capacity of a use-value, satisfies a particular want, and is a particular element of material wealth. But the value of a commodity measures the degree of its attraction for all other elements of material wealth, and therefore measures the social wealth of its owner. To a barbarian owner of commodities, and even to a West-European peasant, value is the same as value-form, and therefore to him the increase in his hoard of gold and silver is an increase in value. It is true that the value of money varies, at one time in consequence of a variation in its own value, at another, in consequence of a change in the values of commodities. But this, on the one hand, does not prevent 200 ounces of gold from still containing more value than 100 ounces, nor, on the other hand, does it hinder the actual metallic form of this article from continuing to be the universal equivalent form of all other commodities, and the immediate social incarnation of all human labour. The desire after hoarding is in its very nature unsatiable. In its qualitative aspect, or formally considered, money has no bounds to its efficacy, i.e. it is the universal representative of material wealth, because it is directly convertible into any other commodity. But, at the same time, every actual sum of money is limited in amount, and, therefore, as a means of purchasing, has only a limited efficacy. This antagonism between the quantitative limits of money and its qualitative boundlessness, continually acts as a spur to the hoarder in his Sisyphus-like labour of accumulating. It is with him as it is with a conqueror who sees in every new country annexed, only a new boundary.

In order that gold may be held as money, and made to form a hoard, it must be prevented from circulating, or from transforming itself into a means of enjoyment. The hoarder, therefore, makes a sacrifice of the lusts of the flesh to his gold fetish. He acts in earnest up to the Gospel of abstention. On the other hand, he can withdraw from circulation no more than what he has thrown into it in the shape of commodities. The more he produces, the more he is able to sell. Hard work, saving, and avarice, are, therefore, his three cardinal virtues, and to sell much and buy little the sum of his political economy.

By the side of the gross form of a hoard, we find also its æsthetic form in the possession of gold and silver articles. This grows with the wealth of civil society. 'Soyons riches ou paraissons riches'* (Diderot). In this way there is created, on the one hand, a constantly extending market for gold and silver, unconnected with their functions as money, and, on the other hand, a latent source of supply, to which recourse is had principally in times of crisis and social disturbance.

Hoarding serves various purposes in the economy of the metallic circulation. Its first function arises out of the conditions to which the currency of gold and silver coins is subject. We have seen how, along with the continual fluctuations in the extent and rapidity of the circulation of commodities and in their prices, the quantity of money current unceasingly ebbs and flows. This mass must, therefore, be capable of expansion and contraction. At one time money must be attracted in order to act as circulating coin, at another, circulating coin must be repelled in order to act again as more or less stagnant money. In order that the mass of money, actually current, may constantly saturate the absorbing power of the circulation, it is necessary that the quantity of gold and silver in a country be greater than the quantity required to function as coin. This condition is fulfilled by money taking the form of hoards. These reserves serve as conduits for the supply or withdrawal of money to or from the circulation, which in this way never overflows its banks.

(b) *Means of Payment*

In the simple form of the circulation of commodities hitherto considered, we found a given value always presented to us in a double shape, as a commodity at one pole, as money at the opposite pole. The owners of commodities came therefore into contact as the respective representatives of what were already equivalents. But with the development of circulation, conditions arise under which the alienation of commodities becomes separated, by an interval of time, from the realisation of their prices. It will be sufficient to indicate the most simple of these conditions. One sort of article requires a longer, another a shorter time for its production. Again, the production of different commodities depends on different seasons of the year. One sort of commodity may be born on its own market place, another has to make a long journey to market. Commodity-owner No. 1, may therefore be ready to sell, before No. 2 is ready to buy. When the same transactions are continually repeated between the same persons, the conditions of sale are regulated in accordance with the conditions of production. On the other hand, the use of a given commodity, of a house, for instance, is sold (in common parlance, let) for a definite period. Here, it is only at the end of the term that the buyer has actually received the use-value of the commodity. He therefore buys it before he pays for it. The vendor sells an existing commodity, the purchaser buys as the mere representative of money, or rather of future money. The vendor becomes a creditor, the purchaser becomes a debtor. Since the metamorphosis of commodities, or the development of their value-form, appears here under a new aspect, money also acquires a fresh function; it becomes the means of payment.

The character of creditor, or of debtor, results here from the simple circulation. The change in the form of that circulation stamps buyer and seller with this new die. At first, therefore, these new parts are just as transient and alternating as those of seller and buyer, and are in turns played by the same actors. But the opposition is not nearly so pleasant, and is far more capable of crystallisation. The same characters can, however, be assumed independently of the circulation of commodities. The class-struggles of the ancient world took the form chiefly of a contest between debtors and creditors, which in Rome ended in the ruin of the plebeian debtors. They were displaced by slaves. In the middle ages the contest ended with the ruin of the feudal debtors, who lost their political power together with the economic basis on which it was established. Nevertheless, the money relation of debtor and creditor that existed at these two periods reflected only the deeper-lying antagonism between the general economic conditions of existence of the classes in question.

Let us return to the circulation of commodities. The appearance of the two equivalents, commodities and money, at the two poles of the process of sale, has ceased to be simultaneous. The money functions now, first as a measure of value in the determination of the price of the commodity sold; the price fixed by the contract measures the obligation of the debtor, or the sum of money that he has to pay at a fixed date. Secondly, it serves as an ideal means of purchase. Although existing only in the promise of the buyer to pay, it causes the commodity to change hands. It is not before the day fixed for payment that the means of payment actually steps into circulation, leaves the hand of the buyer for that of the seller. The circulating medium was transformed into a hoard, because the process stopped short after the first phase, because the converted shape of the commodity, viz., the money, was withdrawn from circulation. The means of payment enters the circulation, but only after the commodity has left it. The money is no longer the means that brings about the process. It only brings it to a close, by stepping in as the absolute form of existence of exchange-value, or as the universal commodity. The seller turned his commodity into money, in order thereby to satisfy some want; the hoarder did the same in order to keep his commodity in its money-shape, and the debtor in order to be able to pay; if he do not pay, his goods will be sold by the sheriff. The value-form of commodities, money, is therefore now the end and aim of a sale, and that owing to a social necessity springing out of the process of circulation itself.

The buyer converts money back into commodities before he has turned commodities into money: in other words, he achieves the second metamorphosis of commodities before the first. The seller's commodity circulates, and realises its price, but only in the shape of a legal claim upon money. It is converted into a use-value before it has been converted into money. The completion of its first metamorphosis follows only at a later period.

The function of money as the means of payment implies a contradiction without a terminus medius. In so far as the payments balance one another, money functions only ideally as money of account, as a measure of value. In so far as actual payments have to be made, money does not serve as a circulating medium, as a mere transient agent in the interchange of products, but as the individual incarnation of social labour, as the independent form of existence of exchange-value, as the universal commodity. This contradiction comes to a head in those phases of industrial and commercial crises which are known as monetary crises. Such a crisis occurs only where the ever-lengthening chain of payments, and an artificial system of settling them, has been fully developed. Whenever there is a general and extensive disturbance of this mechanism, no matter what its cause, money becomes suddenly and immediately transformed, from its merely ideal shape of money of account, into hard cash. Profane commodities can no longer replace it. The use-value of commodities becomes valueless, and their value vanishes in the presence of its own independent form. On the eve of the crisis, the bourgeois, with the self-sufficiency that springs from intoxicating prosperity, declares money to be a vain imagination. Commodities alone are money. But now the cry is everywhere: money alone is a commodity! As the hart pants after fresh water, so pants his soul after money, the only wealth. In a crisis, the antithesis between commodities and their value-form, money, becomes heightened into an absolute contradiction. Hence, in such events, the form under which money appears is of no importance. The money famine continues, whether payments have to be made in gold or in credit money such as bank-notes.

If we now consider the sum total of the money current during a given period, we shall find that, given the rapidity of currency of the circulating medium and of the means of payment, it is equal to the sum of the prices to be realised, plus the sum of the payments falling due, minus the payments that balance each other, minus finally the number of circuits in which the same piece of coin serves in turn as means of circulation and of payment. Hence, even when prices, rapidity of currency, and the extent of the economy in payments, are given, the quantity of money current and the mass of commodities circulating during a given period, such as a day, no longer correspond. Money that represents commodities long withdrawn from circulation, continues to be current. Commodities circulate, whose equivalent in money will not appear on the scene till some future day. Moreover, the debts contracted each day, and the payments falling due on the same day, are quite incommensurable quantities.

Credit-money springs directly out of the function of money as a means of payment. Certificates of the debts owing for the purchased commodities circulate for the purpose of transferring those debts to others. On the other hand, to the same extent as the system of credit is extended, so is the function of money as a means of payment. In that character it takes various forms peculiar to itself under which it makes itself at home in the sphere of great commercial transactions. Gold and silver coin, on the other hand, are mostly relegated to the sphere of retail trade.

When the production of commodities has sufficiently extended itself, money begins to serve as the means of payment beyond the sphere of the circulation of commodities. It becomes the commodity that is the universal subject-matter of all contracts. Rents, taxes, and such like payments are transformed from payments in kind into money payments. To what extent this transformation depends upon the general conditions of production, is shown, to take one example, by the fact that the Roman Empire twice failed in its attempt to levy all contributions in money. The unspeakable misery of the French agricultural population under Louis XIV, a misery so eloquently denounced by Boisguillebert, Marshal Vauban, and others, was due not only to the weight of the taxes, but also to the conversion of taxes in kind into money taxes. In Asia, on the other hand, the fact that state taxes are chiefly composed of rents payable in kind, depends on conditions of production that are reproduced with the regularity of natural phenomena. And this mode of payment tends in its turn to maintain the ancient form of production. It is one of the secrets of the conservation of the Ottoman Empire. If the foreign trade, forced upon Japan by Europeans, should lead to the substitution of money rents for rents in kind, it will be all up with the exemplary agriculture of that country. The narrow economic conditions under which that agriculture is carried on, will be swept away.

In every country, certain days of the year become by habit recognised settling days for various large and recurrent payments. These dates depend, apart from other revolutions in the wheel of reproduction, on conditions closely connected with the seasons. They also regulate the dates for payments that have no direct connexion with the circulation of commodities such as taxes, rents, and so on. The quantity of money requisite to make the payments, falling due on those dates all over the country, causes periodical, though merely superficial, perturbations in the economy of the medium of payment.

From the law of the rapidity of currency of the means of payment, it follows that the quantity of the means of payment required for all periodical payments, whatever their source, is in inverse proportion to the length of their periods.

The development of money into a medium of payment makes it necessary to accumulate money against the dates fixed for the payment of the sums owing. While hoarding, as a distinct mode of acquiring riches, vanishes with the progress of civil society, the formation of reserves of the means of payment grows with that progress.

(c) *Universal Money*

When money leaves the home sphere of circulation, it strips off the local garbs which it there assumes, of a standard of prices, of coin, of tokens, and of a symbol of value, and returns to its original form of bullion. In the trade between the markets of the world, the value of commodities is expressed so as to be universally recognised. Hence their independent value-form also, in these cases, confronts them under the shape of universal money. It is only in the markets of the world that money acquires to the full extent the character of the commodity whose bodily form is also the immediate social incarnation of human labour in the abstract. Its real mode of existence in this sphere adequately corresponds to its ideal concept.

Within the sphere of home circulation, there can be but one commodity which, by serving as a measure of value, becomes money. In the markets of the world a double measure of value holds sway, gold and silver.

Money of the world serves as the universal medium of payment, as the universal means of purchasing, and as the universally recognised embodiment of all wealth. Its function as a means of payment in the settling of international balances is its chief one. Hence the watchword of the mercantilists, balance of trade. Gold and silver serve as international means of purchasing chiefly and necessarily in those periods when the customary equilibrium in the interchange of products between different nations is suddenly disturbed. And lastly, it serves as the universally recognised embodiment of social wealth, whenever the question is not of buying or paying, but of transferring wealth from one country to another, and whenever this transference in the form of commodities is rendered impossible, either by special conjunctures in the markets, or by the purpose itself that is intended.

Just as every country needs a reserve of money for its home circulation, so, too, it requires one for external circulation in the markets of the world. The functions of hoards, therefore, arise in part out of the function of money, as the medium of the home circulation and home payments, and in part out of its function of money of the world. For this latter function, the genuine money-commodity, actual gold and silver, is necessary. On that account, Sir James Steuart, in order to distinguish them from their purely local substitutes, calls gold and silver 'money of the world'.

The current of the stream of gold and silver is a double one. On the one hand, it spreads itself from its sources over all the markets of the world, in order to become absorbed, to various extents, into the different national spheres of circulation, to fill the conduits of currency, to replace abraded gold and silver coins, to supply the material of articles of luxury, and to petrify into hoards. This first current is started by the countries that exchange their labour, realised in commodities, for the labour embodied in the precious metals by gold and silver-producing countries. On the other hand, there is a continual flowing backwards and forwards of gold and silver between the different national spheres of circulation, a current whose motion depends on the ceaseless fluctuations in the course of exchange.

Countries in which the bourgeois form of production is developed to a certain extent, limit the hoards concentrated in the strong rooms of the banks to the minimum required for the proper performance of their peculiar functions. Whenever these hoards are strikingly above their average level, it is, with some exceptions, an indication of stagnation in the circulation of commodities, of an interruption in the even flow of their metamorphoses.

PART II

THE TRANSFORMATION OF MONEY INTO CAPITAL

CHAPTER 4

THE GENERAL FORMULA FOR CAPITAL

THE circulation of commodities is the starting-point of capital. The production of commodities, their circulation, and that more developed form of their circulation called commerce, these form the historical ground-work from which it rises. The modern history of capital dates from the creation in the 16th century of a world-embracing commerce and a world-embracing market.

If we abstract from the material substance of the circulation of commodities, that is, from the exchange of the various use-values, and consider only the economic forms produced by this process of circulation, we find its final result to be money: this final product of the circulation of commodities is the first form in which capital appears.

As a matter of history, capital, as opposed to landed property, invariably takes the form at first of money; it appears as moneyed wealth, as the capital of the merchant and of the usurer. But we have no need to refer to the origin of capital in order to discover that the first form of appearance of capital is money. We can see it daily under our very eyes. All new capital, to commence with, comes on the stage, that is, on the market, whether of commodities, labour, or money, even in our days, in the shape of money that by a definite process has to be transformed into capital.

The first distinction we notice between money that is money only, and money that is capital, is nothing more than a difference in their form of circulation.

The simplest form of the circulation of commodities is C—M—C, the transformation of commodities into money, and the change of the money back again into commodities; or selling in order to buy. But alongside of this form we find another specifically different form: M—C—M, the transformation of money into commodities, and the change of commodities back again into money; or buying in order to sell.

Money that circulates in the latter manner is thereby transformed into, becomes capital, and is already potentially capital.

Now let us examine the circuit M—C—M a little closer. It consists, like the other, of two antithetical phases. In the first phase, M—C, or the purchase, the money is changed into a commodity. In the second phase, C—M, or the sale, the commodity is changed back again into money. The combination of these two phases constitutes the single movement whereby money is exchanged for a commodity, and the same commodity is again exchanged for money; whereby a commodity is bought in order to be sold, or, neglecting the distinction in form between buying and selling, whereby a commodity is bought with money, and then money is bought with a commodity. The result, in which the phases of the process vanish, is the exchange of money for money, M—M. If I purchase 2,000 lbs. of cotton for £100, and resell the 2,000 lbs. of cotton for £110, I have, in fact, exchanged £100 for £110, money for money.

Now it is evident that the circuit M—C—M would be absurd and without meaning if the intention were to exchange by this means two equal sums of money, £100 for £100. The miser's plan would be far simpler and surer; he sticks to his £100 instead of exposing it to the dangers of circulation. And yet, whether the merchant who has paid £100 for his cotton sells it for £110, or lets it go for £100, or even £50, his money has, at all events, gone through a characteristic and original movement, quite different in kind from that which it goes through in the hands of the peasant who sells corn, and with the money thus set free buys clothes. We have therefore to examine first the distinguishing characteristics of the forms of the circuits M—C—M and C—M—C, and in doing this the real difference that underlies the mere difference of form will reveal itself.

Let us see, in the first place, what the two forms have in common.

Both circuits are resolvable into the same two antithetical phases, C—M, a sale, and M—C, a purchase. In each of these phases the same material elements—a commodity, and money, and the same economic dramatis personæ, a buyer and a seller—confront one another. Each circuit is the unity of the same two antithetical phases, and in each case this unity is brought about by the intervention of three contracting parties, of whom one only sells, another only buys, while the third both buys and sells.

What, however, first and foremost distinguishes the circuit C—M—C from the circuit M—C—M, is the inverted order of succession of the two phases. The simple circulation of commodities begins with a sale and ends with a purchase, while the circulation of money as capital begins with a purchase and ends with a sale. In the one case both the starting-point and the goal are commodities, in the other they are money. In the first form the movement is brought about by the intervention of money, in the second by that of a commodity.

In the circulation C—M—C, the money is in the end converted into a commodity, that serves as a use-value; it is spent once for all. In the inverted form, M—C—M, on the contrary, the buyer lays out money in order that, as a seller, he may recover money. By the purchase of his commodity he throws money into circulation, in order to withdraw it again by the sale of the same commodity. He lets the money go, but only with the sly intention of getting it back again. The money, therefore, is not spent, it is merely advanced.

In the circuit C—M—C, the same piece of money changes its place twice. The seller gets it from the buyer and pays it away to another seller. The complete circulation, which begins with the receipt, concludes with the payment, of money for commodities. It is the very contrary in the circuit M—C—M. Here it is not the piece of money that changes its place twice, but the commodity. The buyer takes it from the hands of the seller and passes it into the hands of another buyer. Just as in the simple circulation of commodities the double change of place of the same piece of money effects its passage from one hand into another, so here the double change of place of the same commodity brings about the reflux of the money to its point of departure.

Such reflux is not dependent on the commodity being sold for more than was paid for it. This circumstance influences only the amount of the money that comes back. The reflux itself takes place, so soon as the purchased commodity is resold, in other words, so soon as the circuit M—C—M is completed. We have here, therefore, a palpable difference between the circulation of money as capital, and its circulation as mere money.

The circuit C—M—C comes completely to an end, so soon as the money brought in by the sale of one commodity is abstracted again by the purchase of another.

If, nevertheless, there follows a reflux of money to its starting-point, this can only happen through a renewal or repetition of the operation. If I sell a quarter of corn for £3, and with this £3 buy clothes, the money, so far as I am concerned, is spent and done with. It belongs to the clothes merchant. If I now sell a second quarter of corn, money indeed flows back to me, not however as a sequel to the first transaction, but in consequence of its repetition. The money again leaves me, so soon as I complete this second transaction by a fresh purchase. Therefore, in the circuit C—M—C, the expenditure of money has nothing to do with its reflux. On the other hand, in M—C—M, the reflux of the money is conditioned by the very mode of its expenditure. Without this reflux, the operation fails, or the process is interrupted and incomplete, owing to the absence of its complementary and final phase, the sale.

The circuit C—M—C starts with one commodity, and finishes with another, which falls out of circulation and into consumption. Consumption, the satisfaction of wants, in one word, use-value, is its end and aim. The circuit M—C—M, on the contrary, commences with money and ends with money. Its leading motive, and the goal that attracts it, is therefore mere exchange-value.

In the simple circulation of commodities, the two extremes of the circuit have the same economic form. They are both commodities, and commodities of equal value. But they are also use-values differing in their qualities, as, for example, corn and clothes. The exchange of products, of the different materials in which the labour of society is embodied, forms here the basis of the movement. It is otherwise in the circulation M—C—M, which at first sight appears purposeless, because tautological. Both extremes have the same economic form. They are both money, and therefore are not qualitatively different use-values; for money is but the converted form of commodities, in which their particular use-values vanish. To exchange £100 for cotton, and then this same cotton again for £100, is merely a roundabout way of exchanging money for money, the same for the same, and appears to be an operation just as purposeless as it is absurd. One sum of money is distinguishable from another only by its amount. The character and tendency of the process M—C—M, is therefore not due to any qualitative difference between its extremes, both being money, but solely to their quantitative difference. More money is withdrawn from circulation at the finish than was thrown into it at the start. The cotton that was bought for £100 is perhaps resold for £100 + £10 or £110. The exact form of this process is therefore M—C—M′, where M′ = M + ΔM = the original sum advanced, plus an increment. This increment or excess over the original value I call 'surplus-value'. The value originally advanced, therefore, not only remains intact while in circulation, but adds to itself a surplus-value or expands itself. It is this movement that converts it into capital.

Of course, it is also possible, that in C—M—C, the two extremes C—C, say corn and clothes, may represent different quantities of value. The farmer may sell his corn above its value, or may buy the clothes at less than their value. He may, on the other hand, 'be done' by the clothes merchant. Yet, in the form of circulation now under consideration, such differences in value are purely accidental. The fact that the corn and the clothes are equivalents, does not deprive the process of all meaning, as it does in M—C—M. The equivalence of their values is rather a necessary condition to its normal course.

The repetition or renewal of the act of selling in order to buy, is kept within bounds by the very object it aims at, namely, consumption or the satisfaction of definite wants, an aim that lies altogether outside the sphere of circulation. But when we buy in order to sell, we, on the contrary, begin and end with the same thing, money, exchange-value; and thereby the movement becomes interminable. No doubt, M becomes M + ΔM, £100 become £110. But when viewed in their qualitative aspect alone, £110 are the same as £100, namely money; and considered quantitatively, £110 is, like £100, a sum of definite and limited value. If now, the £110 be spent as money, they cease to play their part. They are no longer capital. Withdrawn from circulation, they become petrified into a hoard, and though they remained in that state till doomsday, not a single farthing would accrue to them. If, then, the expansion of value is once aimed at, there is just the same inducement to augment the value of the £110 as that of the £100; for both are but limited expressions for exchange-value, and therefore both have the same vocation to approach, by quantitative increase, as near as possible to absolute wealth. Momentarily, indeed, the value originally advanced, the £100 is distinguishable from the surplus-value of £10 that is annexed to it during circulation; but the distinction vanishes immediately. At the end of the process, we do not receive with one hand the original £100, and with the other, the surplus-value of £10. We simply get a value of £110, which is in exactly the same condition and fitness for commencing the expanding process, as the original £100 was. Money ends the movement only to begin it again. Therefore, the final result of every separate circuit, in which a purchase and consequent sale are completed, forms of itself the starting-point of a new circuit. The simple circulation of commodities—selling in order to buy—is a means of carrying out a purpose unconnected with circulation, namely, the appropriation of use-values, the satisfaction of wants. The circulation of money as capital is, on the contrary, an end in itself, for the expansion of value takes place only within this constantly renewed movement. The circulation of capital has therefore no limits.

As the conscious representative of this movement, the possessor of money becomes a capitalist. His person, or rather his pocket, is the point from which the money starts and to which it returns. The expansion of value, which is the objective basis or main-spring of the circulation M—C—M, becomes his subjective aim, and it is only in so far as the appropriation of ever more and more wealth in the abstract becomes the sole motive of his operations, that he functions as a capitalist, that is, as capital personified and endowed with conscious-ness and a will. Use-values must therefore never be looked upon as the real aim of the capitalist; neither must the profit on any single trans-action. The restless never-ending process of profit-making alone is what he aims at. This boundless greed after riches, this passionate chase after exchange-value, is common to the capitalist and the miser; but while the miser is merely a capitalist gone mad, the capitalist is a rational miser. The never-ending augmentation of exchange-value, which the miser strives after, by seeking to save his money from circu-lation, is attained by the more acute capitalist, by constantly throwing it afresh into circulation.

The independent form, i.e. the money-form, which the value of commodities assumes in the case of simple circulation, serves only one purpose, namely, their exchange, and vanishes in the final result of the movement. On the other hand, in the circulation M—C—M, both the money and the commodity represent only different modes of existence of value itself, the money its general mode, and the commodity its particular, or, so to say, disguised mode. It is constantly changing from one form to the other without thereby becoming lost, and thus assumes an automatically active character. If now we take in turn each of the two different forms which self-expanding value successively assumes in the course of its life, we then arrive at these two propositions: Capital is money: Capital is commodities. In truth, however, value is here the active factor in a process, in which, while constantly assuming the form in turn of money and commodities, it at the same time changes in magnitude, differentiates itself by throwing off surplus-value from itself; the original value, in other words, expands spontaneously. For the movement, in the course of which it adds surplus-value, is its own movement, its expansion, therefore, is automatic expansion. Because it is value, it has acquired the occult quality of being able to add value to itself. If brings forth living offspring, or, at the least, lays golden eggs.

Value, therefore, being the active factor in such a process, and assuming at one time the form of money, at another that of commodities, but through all these changes preserving itself and expanding, it requires some independent form, by means of which its identity may at any time be established. And this form it possesses only in the shape of money. It is under the form of money that value begins and ends, and begins again, every act of its own spontaneous generation. It began by being £100, it is now £110, and so on. But the money itself is only one of the two forms of value. Unless it takes the form of some commodity, it does not become capital. There is here no antagonism, as in the case of hoarding, between the money and commodities. The capitalist knows that all commodities, however scurvy they may look, or however badly they may smell, are in faith and in truth money, inwardly circumcised Jews, and what is more, a wonderful means whereby out of money to make more money.

In simple circulation, C—M—C, the value of commodities attained at the most a form independent of their use-values, i.e. the form of money; but that same value now in the circulation M—C—M, or the circulation of capital, suddenly presents itself as an independent substance, endowed with a motion of its own, passing through a life-process of its own, in which money and commodities are mere forms which it assumes and casts off in turn. Nay, more: instead of simply representing the relations of commodities, it enters now, so to say, into private relations with itself. It differentiates itself as original value from itself as surplus-value; as the father differentiates himself from himself qua the son, yet both are one and of one age: for only by the surplus-value of £10 does the £100 originally advanced become capital, and so soon as this takes place, so soon as the son, and by the son, the father, is begotten, so soon does their difference vanish, and they again become one, £110.

Value therefore now becomes value in process, money in process, and, as such, capital. It comes out of circulation, enters into it again, preserves and multiplies itself within its circuit, comes back out of it with expanded bulk, and begins the same round ever afresh. M—M′, money which begets money, such is the description of Capital from the mouths of its first interpreters, the Mercantilists.

Buying in order to sell, or, more accurately, buying in order to sell dearer, M—C—M, appears certainly to be a form peculiar to one kind of capital alone, namely, merchants' capital. But industrial capital too is money, that is changed into commodities, and by the sale of these commodities, is re-converted into more money. The events that take place outside the sphere of circulation, in the interval between the buying and selling, do not affect the form of this movement. Lastly, in the case of interest-bearing capital, the circulation M—C—M′ appears abridged. We have its result without the intermediate stage, in the form M—M′, 'en style lapidaire' so to say, money that is worth more money, value that is greater than itself.

M—C—M′ is therefore in reality the general formula of capital as it appears prima facie within the sphere of circulation.

CHAPTER 5

CONTRADICTIONS IN THE GENERAL FORMULA OF CAPITAL

THE form which circulation takes when money becomes capital, is opposed to all the laws we have hitherto investigated bearing on the nature of commodities, value and money, and even of circulation itself. What distinguishes this form from that of the simple circulation of commodities, is the inverted order of succession of the two antithetical processes, sale and purchase. How can this purely formal distinction between these processes change their character as it were by magic?

But that is not all. This inversion has no existence for two out of the three persons who transact business together. As capitalist, I buy commodities from A and sell them again to B, but as a simple owner of commodities, I sell them to B and then purchase fresh ones from A. A and B see no difference between the two sets of transactions. They are merely buyers or sellers. And I on each occasion meet them as a mere owner of either money or commodities, as a buyer or a seller, and, what is more, in both sets of transactions, I am opposed to A only as a buyer and to B only as a seller, to the one only as money, to the other only as commodities, and to neither of them as capital or a capitalist, or as representative of anything that is more than money or commodities, or that can produce any effect beyond what money and commodities can. For me the purchase from A and the sale to B are part of a series. But the connexion between the two acts exists for me alone. A does not trouble himself about my transaction with B, nor does B about my business with A. And if I offered to explain to them the meritorious nature of my action in inverting the order of succession, they would probably point out to me that I was mistaken as to that order of succession, and that the whole transaction, instead of beginning with a purchase and ending with a sale, began, on the contrary, with a sale and was concluded with a purchase. In truth, my first act, the purchase, was from the standpoint of A, a sale, and my second act, the sale, was from the standpoint of B, a purchase. Not content with that, A and B would declare that the whole series was superfluous and nothing but Hokus Pokus; that for the future A would buy direct from B, and B sell direct to A. Thus the whole transaction would be reduced to a single act forming an isolated, non-complemented phase in the ordinary circulation of commodities, a mere sale from A's point of view, and from B's, a mere purchase. The inversion, therefore, of the order of succession, does not take us outside the sphere of the simple circulation of commodities, and we must rather look, whether there is in this simple circulation anything permitting an expansion of the value that enters into circulation, and, consequently, a creation of surplus-value.

Let us take the process of circulation in a form under which it presents itself as a simple and direct exchange of commodities. This is always the case when two owners of commodities buy from each other, and on the settling day the amounts mutually owing are equal and cancel each other. The money in this case is money of account and serves to express the value of the commodities by their prices, but is not, itself, in the shape of hard cash, confronted with them. So far as regards use-values, it is clear that both parties may gain some advantage. Both part with goods that, as use-values, are of no service to them, and receive others that they can make use of. And there may also be a further gain. A, who sells wine and buys corn, possibly produces more wine, with given labour-time, than farmer B could, and B on the other hand, more corn than wine-grower A could. A, therefore, may get, for the same exchange-value, more corn, and B more wine, than each would respectively get without any exchange by producing his own corn and wine. With reference, therefore, to use-value, there is good ground for saying that 'exchange is a transaction by which both sides gain'. It is otherwise with exchange-value. The value of a commodity is expressed in its price before it goes into circulation, and is therefore a precedent condition of circulation, not its result.

Abstractedly considered, that is, apart from circumstances not immediately flowing from the laws of the simple circulation of commodities, there is in an exchange nothing (if we except the replacing of one use-value by another) but a metamorphosis, a mere change in the form of the commodity. The same exchange-value, i.e. the same quantity of incorporated social labour, remains throughout in the hands of the owner of the commodity, first in the shape of his own commodity, then in the form of the money for which he exchanged it, and lastly, in the shape of the commodity he buys with that money. This change of form does not imply a change in the magnitude of the value. But the change, which the value of the commodity undergoes in this process, is limited to a change in its money-form. This form exists first as the price of the commodity offered for sale, then as an actual sum of money, which, however, was already expressed in the price, and lastly, as the price of an equivalent commodity. This change of form no more implies, taken alone, a change in the quantity of value, than does the change of a £5 note into sovereigns, half sovereigns and shillings. So far therefore as the circulation of commodities effects a change in the form alone of their values, and is free from disturbing influences, it must be the exchange of equivalents. Little as Vulgar-Economy knows about the nature of value, yet whenever it wishes to consider the phenomena of circulation in their purity, it assumes that supply and demand are equal, which amounts to this, that their effect is nil. If therefore, as regards the use-values exchanged, both buyer and seller may possibly gain something, this is not the case as regards the exchange-values. Here we must rather say, 'Where equality exists there can be no gain.' It is true, commodities may be sold at prices deviating from their values, but these deviations are to be considered as infractions of the laws of the exchange of commodities, which in its normal state is an exchange of equivalents, consequently, no method for increasing value.

Hence, we see that behind all attempts to represent the circulation of commodities as a source of surplus-value, there lurks a *quid pro quo*, a mixing up of use-value and exchange-value.

If commodities, or commodities and money, of equal exchange-value, and consequently equivalents, are exchanged, it is plain that no one abstracts more value from, than he throws into, circulation. There is no creation of surplus-value. And, in its normal form, the circulation of commodities demands the exchange of equivalents. But in actual practice, the process does not retain its normal form. Let us, therefore, assume an exchange of non-equivalents.

In any case the market for commodities is only frequented by owners of commodities, and the power which these persons exercise over each other, is no other than the power of their commodities. The material variety of these commodities is the material incentive to the act of exchange, and makes buyers and sellers mutually dependent, because none of them possesses the object of his own wants, and each holds in his hand the object of another's wants. Besides these material differences of their use-values, there is only one other difference between commodities, namely, that between their bodily form and the form into which they are converted by sale, the difference between commodities and money. And consequently the owners of commodities are distinguishable only as sellers, those who own commodities, and buyers, those who own money.

Suppose then, that by some inexplicable privilege, the seller is enabled to sell his commodities above their value, what is worth 100 for 110, in which case the price is nominally raised 10%. The seller therefore pockets a surplus-value of 10. But after he has sold he becomes a buyer. A third owner of commodities comes to him now as seller, who in this capacity also enjoys the privilege of selling his commodities 10% too dear. Our friend gained 10 as a seller only to lose it again as a buyer. The net result is, that all owners of commodities sell their goods to one another at 10% above their value, which comes precisely to the same as if they sold them at their true value. Such a general and nominal rise of prices has the same effect as if the values had been expressed in weight of silver instead of in weight of gold. The nominal prices of commodities would rise, but the real relation between their values would remain unchanged.

Let us make the opposite assumption, that the buyer has the privilege of purchasing commodities under their value. In this case it is no longer necessary to bear in mind that he in his turn will become a seller. He was so before he became buyer; he had already lost 10% in selling before he gained 10% as buyer. Everything is just as it was.

The creation of surplus-value, and therefore the conversion of money into capital, can consequently be explained neither on the assumption that commodities are sold above their value, nor that they are bought below their value.

In relation to circulation, producers and consumers meet only as buyers and sellers. To assert that the surplus-value acquired by the producer has its origin in the fact that consumers pay for commodities more than their value, is only to say in other words: The owner of commodities possesses, as a seller, the privilege of selling too dear. The seller has himself produced the commodities or represents their producer, but the buyer has to no less extent produced the commodities represented by his money, or represents their producer. The distinction between them is, that one buys and the other sells. The fact that the owner of the commodities, under the designation of producer, sells them over their value, and under the designation of consumer, pays too much for them, does not carry us a single step further.

To be consistent therefore, the upholders of the delusion that surplus-value has its origin in a nominal rise of prices or in the privilege which the seller has of selling too dear, must assume the existence of a class that only buys and does not sell, i.e. only consumes and does not produce. The existence of such a class is inexplicable from the standpoint we have so far reached, viz., that of simple circulation. But let us anticipate. The money with which such a class is constantly making purchases, must constantly flow into their pockets, without any exchange, gratis, by might or right, from the pockets of the commodity-owners themselves. To sell commodities above their value to such a class, is only to crib back again a part of the money previously given to it. The towns of Asia Minor thus paid a yearly money tribute to ancient Rome. With this money Rome purchased from them commodities, and purchased them too dear. The provincials cheated the Romans, and thus got back from their conquerors, in the course of trade, a portion of the tribute. Yet, for all that, the conquered were the really cheated. Their goods were still paid for with their own money. That is not the way to get rich or to create surplus-value.

Let us therefore keep within the bounds of exchange where sellers are also buyers, and buyers, sellers. Our difficulty may perhaps have arisen from treating the actors as personifications instead of as individuals.

A may be clever enough to get the advantage of B or C without their being able to retaliate. A sells wine worth £40 to B, and obtains from him in exchange corn to the value of £50. A has converted his £40 into £50, has made more money out of less, and has converted his commodities into capital. Let us examine this a little more closely. Before the exchange we had £40 worth of wine in the hands of A, and £50 worth of corn in those of B, a total value of £90. After the exchange we have still the same total value of £90. The value in circulation has not increased by one iota, it is only distributed differently between A and B. What is a loss of value to B is surplus-value to A; what is 'minus' to one is 'plus' to the other. The same change would have taken place, if A, without the formality of an exchange, had directly stolen the £10 from B. The sum of the values in circulation can clearly not be augmented by any change in their distribution, any more than the quantity of the precious metals in a country by a Jew selling a Queen Anne's farthing for a guinea. The capitalist class, as a whole, in any country, cannot over-reach themselves.

Turn and twist then as we may, the fact remains unaltered. If equivalents are exchanged, no surplus-value results, and if non-equivalents are exchanged, still no surplus-value. Circulation, or the exchange of commodities, begets no value.

The reason is now therefore plain why, in analysing the standard form of capital, the form under which it determines the economic organisation of modern society, we entirely left out of consideration its most popular, and, so to say, antediluvian forms, merchants' capital and money-lenders' capital.

The circuit M—C—M, buying in order to sell dearer, is seen most clearly in genuine merchants' capital. But the movement takes place entirely within the sphere of circulation. Since, however, it is impossible, by circulation alone, to account for the conversion of money into capital, for the formation of surplus-value, it would appear, that merchants' capital is an impossibility, so long as equivalents are exchanged; that, therefore, it can only have its origin in the two-fold advantage gained, over both the selling and the buying producers, by the merchant who parasitically shoves himself in between them. It is in this sense that Franklin says, 'war is robbery, commerce is generally cheating'. If the transformation of merchants' money into capital is to be explained otherwise than by the producers being simply cheated, a long series of intermediate steps would be necessary, which, at present, when the simple circulation of commodities forms our only assumption, are entirely wanting.

What we have said with reference to merchants' capital, applies still more to money-lenders' capital. In merchants' capital, the two extremes, the money that is thrown upon the market, and the augmented money that is withdrawn from the market, are at least connected by a purchase and a sale, in other words by the movement of the circulation. In money-lenders' capital the form M—C—M is reduced to the two extremes without a mean, M—M, money exchanged for more money, a form that is incompatible with the nature of money, and therefore remains inexplicable from the standpoint of the circulation of commodities. Hence Aristotle:

Since chrematistic is a double science, one part belonging to commerce, the other to economic, the latter being necessary and praiseworthy, the former based on circulation and with justice disapproved (for it is not based on Nature, but on mutual cheating), therefore the usurer is most rightly hated, because money itself is the source of his gain, and is not used for the purposes for which it was invented. For it originated for the exchange of commodities, but interest makes out of money, more money. Hence its name (τόχος interest and offspring). For the begotten are like those who beget them. But interest is money of money, so that of all modes of making a living, this is the most contrary to Nature.

In the course of our investigation, we shall find that both merchants' capital and interest-bearing capital are derivative forms, and at the same time it will become clear, why these two forms appear in the course of history before the modern standard form of capital.

We have shown that surplus-value cannot be created by circulation, and, therefore, that in its formation, something must take place in the background, which is not apparent in the circulation itself. But can surplus-value possibly originate anywhere else than in circulation, which is the sum total of all the mutual relations of commodity-owners, as far as they are determined by their commodities? Apart from circulation, the commodity-owner is in relation only with his own commodity. So far as regards value, that relation is limited to this, that the commodity contains a quantity of his own labour, that quantity being measured by a definite social standard. This quantity is expressed by the value of the commodity, and since the value is reckoned in money of account, this quantity is also expressed by the price, which we will suppose to be £10. But his labour is not represented both by the value of the commodity, and by a surplus over that value, not by a price of 10 that is also a price of 11, not by a value that is greater than itself. The commodity owner can, by his labour, create value, but not self-expanding value. He can increase the value of his commodity, by adding fresh labour, and therefore more value to the value in hand, by making, for instance, leather into boots. The same material has now more value, because it contains a greater quantity of labour. The boots have therefore more value than the leather, but the value of the leather remains what it was; it has not expanded itself, has not, during the making of the boots, annexed surplus-value. It is therefore impossible that outside the sphere of circulation, a producer of commodities can, without coming into contact with other commodity-owners, expand value, and consequently convert money or commodities into capital.

It is therefore impossible for capital to be produced by circulation, and it is equally impossible for it to originate apart from circulation. It must have its origin both in circulation and yet not in circulation.

We have, therefore, got a double result.

The conversion of money into capital has to be explained on the basis of the laws that regulate the exchange of commodities, in such a way that the starting-point is the exchange of equivalents. Our friend, Moneybags, who as yet is only an embryo capitalist, must buy his commodities at their value, must sell them at their value, and yet at the end of the process must withdraw more value from circulation than he threw into it at starting. His development into a full-grown capitalist must take place, both within the sphere of circulation and without it. These are the conditions of the problem. Hic Rhodus, hic salta!*

CHAPTER 6

THE BUYING AND SELLING OF LABOUR-POWER

THE change of value that occurs in the case of money intended to be converted into capital, cannot take place in the money itself, since in its function of means of purchase and of payment, it does no more than realise the price of the commodity it buys or pays for; and, as hard cash, it is value petrified, never varying. Just as little can it originate in the second act of circulation, the re-sale of the commodity, which does no more than transform the article from its bodily form back again into its money-form. The change must, therefore, take place in the commodity bought by the first act, M—C, but not in its value, for equivalents are exchanged, and the commodity is paid for at its full value. We are, therefore, forced to the conclusion that the change originates in the use-value, as such, of the commodity, i.e. in its consumption. In order to be able to extract value from the consumption of a commodity, our friend, Moneybags, must be so lucky as to find, within the sphere of circulation, in the market, a commodity, whose use-value possesses the peculiar property of being a source of value, whose actual consumption, therefore, is itself an embodiment of labour, and, consequently, a creation of value. The possessor of money does find on the market such a special commodity in capacity for labour or labour-power.

By labour-power or capacity for labour is to be understood the aggregate of those mental and physical capabilities existing in a human being, which he exercises whenever he produces a use-value of any description.

But in order that our owner of money may be able to find labour-power offered for sale as a commodity, various conditions must first be fulfilled. The exchange of commodities of itself implies no other relations of dependence than those which result from its own nature. On this assumption, labour-power can appear upon the market as a commodity, only if, and so far as, its possessor, the individual whose labour-power it is, offers it for sale, or sells it, as a commodity. In order that he may be able to do this, he must have it at his disposal, must be the untrammelled owner of his capacity for labour, i.e. of his person. He and the owner of money meet in the market, and deal with each other as on the basis of equal rights, with this difference alone, that one is buyer, the other seller; both, therefore, equal in the eyes of the law. The continuance of this relation demands that the owner of the labour-power should sell it only for a definite period, for if he were to sell it rump and stump, once for all, he would be selling himself, converting himself from a free man into a slave, from an owner of a commodity into a commodity. He must constantly look upon his labour-power as his own property, his own commodity, and this he can only do by placing it at the disposal of the buyer temporarily, for a definite period of time. By this means alone can he avoid renouncing his rights of ownership over it.

The second essential condition to the owner of money finding labour-power in the market as a commodity is this—that the labourer instead of being in the position to sell commodities in which his labour is incorporated, must be obliged to offer for sale as a commodity that very labour-power, which exists only in his living self.

In order that a man may be able to sell commodities other than labour-power, he must of course have the means of production, as raw material, implements, etc. No boots can be made without leather. He requires also the means of subsistence. Nobody—not even 'a musician of the future'* can live upon future products, or upon use-values in an unfinished state; and ever since the first moment of his appearance on the world's stage, man always has been, and must still be a consumer, both before and while he is producing. In a society where all products assume the form of commodities, these commodities must be sold after they have been produced, it is only after their sale that they can serve in satisfying the requirements of their producer. The time necessary for their sale is superadded to that necessary for their production.

For the conversion of his money into capital, therefore, the owner of money must meet in the market with the free labourer, free in the double sense, that as a free man he can dispose of his labour-power as his own commodity, and that on the other hand he has no other commodity for sale, is short of everything necessary for the realisation of his labour-power.

The question why this free labourer confronts him in the market, has no interest for the owner of money, who regards the labour-market as a branch of the general market for commodities. And for the present it interests us just as little. We cling to the fact theoretically, as he does practically. One thing, however, is clear—Nature does not produce on the one side owners of money or commodities, and on the other men possessing nothing but their own labour-power. This relation has no natural basis, neither is its social basis one that is common to all historical periods. It is clearly the result of a past historical development, the product of many economic revolutions, of the extinction of a whole series of older forms of social production.

So, too, the economic categories, already discussed by us, bear the stamp of history. Definite historical conditions are necessary that a product may become a commodity. It must not be produced as the immediate means of subsistence of the producer himself. Had we gone further, and inquired under what circumstances all, or even the majority of products take the form of commodities, we should have found that this can only happen with production of a very specific kind, capitalist production. Such an inquiry, however, would have been foreign to the analysis of commodities. Production and circulation of commodities can take place, although the great mass of the objects produced are intended for the immediate requirements of their producers, are not turned into commodities, and consequently social production is not yet by a long way dominated in its length and breadth by exchange-value. The appearance of products as commodities pre-supposes such a development of the social division of labour, that the separation of use-value from exchange-value, a separation which first begins with barter, must already have been completed. But such a degree of development is common to many forms of society, which in other respects present the most varying historical features. On the other hand, if we consider money, its existence implies a definite stage in the exchange of commodities. The particular functions of money which it performs, either as the mere equivalent of commodities, or as means of circulation, or means of payment, as hoard or as universal money, point, according to the extent and relative preponderance of the one function or the other, to very different stages in the process of social production. Yet we know by experience that a circulation of commodities relatively primitive, suffices for the production of all these forms. Otherwise with capital. The historical conditions of its existence are by no means given with the mere circulation of money and commodities. It can spring into life, only when the owner of the means of production and subsistence meets in the market with the free labourer selling his labour-power. And this one historical condition comprises a world's history. Capital, therefore, announces from its first appearance a new epoch in the process of social production.

We must now examine more closely this peculiar commodity, labour-power. Like all others it has a value. How is that value determined?

The value of labour-power is determined, as in the case of every other commodity, by the labour-time necessary for the production, and consequently also the reproduction, of this special article. So far as it has value, it represents no more than a definite quantity of the average labour of society incorporated in it. Labour-power exists only as a capacity, or power of the living individual. Its production consequently pre-supposes his existence. Given the individual, the production of labour-power consists in his reproduction of himself or his mainte-nance. For his maintenance he requires a given quantity of the means of subsistence. Therefore the labour-time requisite for the production of labour-power reduces itself to that necessary for the production of those means of subsistence; in other words, the value of labour-power is the value of the means of subsistence necessary for the maintenance of the labourer. Labour-power, however, becomes a reality only by its exercise; it sets itself in action only by working. But thereby a definite quantity of human muscle, nerve, brain, etc., is wasted, and these require to be restored. This increased expenditure demands a larger income. If the owner of labour-power works today, to-morrow he must again be able to repeat the same process in the same conditions as regards health and strength. His means of subsistence must therefore be sufficient to maintain him in his normal state as a labouring indi-vidual. His natural wants, such as food, clothing, fuel, and housing, vary according to the climatic and other physical conditions of his country. On the other hand, the number and extent of his so-called necessary wants, as also the modes of satisfying them, are themselves the product of historical development, and depend therefore to a great extent on the degree of civilisation of a country, more particularly on the conditions under which, and consequently on the habits and de-gree of comfort in which, the class of free labourers has been formed. In contradistinction therefore to the case of other commodities, there enters into the determination of the value of labour-power a historical and moral element. Nevertheless, in a given country, at a given period, the average quantity of the means of subsistence necessary for the labourer is practically known.

The owner of labour-power is mortal. If then his appearance in the market is to be continuous, and the continuous conversion of money into capital assumes this, the seller of labour-power must perpetuate himself, 'in the way that every living individual perpetuates himself, by procreation.' The labour-power withdrawn from the market by wear and tear and death, must be continually replaced by, at the very least, an equal amount of fresh labour-power. Hence the sum of the means of subsistence necessary for the production of labour-power must include the means necessary for the labourer's substitutes, i.e. his children, in order that this race of peculiar commodity-owners may perpetuate its appearance in the market.

In order to modify the human organism, so that it may acquire skill and handiness in a given branch of industry, and become labour-power of a special kind, a special education or training is requisite, and this, on its part, costs an equivalent in commodities of a greater or less amount. This amount varies according to the more or less complicated character of the labour-power. The expenses of this education (excessively small in the case of ordinary labour-power), enter pro tanto into the total value spent in its production.

The minimum limit of the value of labour-power is determined by the value of the commodities, without the daily supply of which the labourer cannot renew his vital energy, consequently by the value of those means of subsistence that are physically indispensable. If the price of labour-power fall to this minimum, it falls below its value, since under such circumstances it can be maintained and developed only in a crippled state. But the value of every commodity is determined by the labour-time requisite to turn it out so as to be of normal quality.

One consequence of the peculiar nature of labour-power as a commodity is, that its use-value does not, on the conclusion of the contract between the buyer and seller, immediately pass into the hands of the former. Its value, like that of every other commodity, is already fixed before it goes into circulation, since a definite quantity of social labour has been spent upon it; but its use-value consists in the subsequent exercise of its force. The alienation of labour-power and its actual appropriation by the buyer, its employment as a use-value, are separated by an interval of time. But in those cases in which the formal alienation by sale of the use-value of a commodity, is not simultaneous with its actual delivery to the buyer, the money of the latter usually functions as means of payment. In every country in which the capitalist mode of production reigns, it is the custom not to pay for labour-power before it has been exercised for the period fixed by the contract, as for example, the end of each week. In all cases, therefore, the use-value of the labour-power is advanced to the capitalist: the labourer allows the buyer to consume it before he receives payment of the price; he everywhere gives credit to the capitalist. That this credit is no mere fiction, is shown not only by the occasional loss of wages on the bankruptcy of the capitalist, but also by a series of more enduring consequences. Nevertheless, whether money serves as a means of purchase or as a means of payment, this makes no alteration in the nature of the exchange of commodities. The price of the labour-power is fixed by the contract, although it is not realised till later, like the rent of a house. The labour-power is sold, although it is only paid for at a later period. It will, therefore, be useful, for a clear comprehension of the relation of the parties, to assume provisionally, that the possessor of labour-power, on the occasion of each sale, immediately receives the price stipulated to be paid for it.

We now know how the value paid by the purchaser to the possessor of this peculiar commodity, labour-power, is determined. The use-value which the former gets in exchange, manifests itself only in the actual usufruct, in the consumption of the labour-power. The money-owner buys everything necessary for this purpose, such as raw material, in the market, and pays for it at its full value. The consumption of labour-power is at one and the same time the production of commodities and of surplus-value. The consumption of labour-power is completed, as in the case of every other commodity, outside the limits of the market or of the sphere of circulation. Accompanied by Mr Moneybags and by the possessor of labour-power, we therefore take leave for a time of this noisy sphere, where everything takes place on the surface and in view of all men, and follow them both into the hidden abode of production, on whose threshold there stares us in the face 'No admittance except on business.' Here we shall see, not only how capital produces, but how capital is produced. We shall at last force the secret of profit making.

This sphere that we are deserting, within whose boundaries the sale and purchase of labour-power goes on, is in fact a very Eden of the innate rights of man. There alone rule Freedom, Equality, Property and Bentham. Freedom, because both buyer and seller of a commodity, say of labour-power, are constrained only by their own free will. They contract as free agents, and the agreement they come to, is but the form in which they give legal expression to their common will. Equality, because each enters into relation with the other, as with a simple owner of commodities, and they exchange equivalent for equivalent. Property, because each disposes only of what is his own. And Bentham because each looks only to himself. The only force that brings them together and puts them in relation with each other, is the selfishness, the gain and the private interests of each. Each looks to himself only, and no one troubles himself about the rest, and just because they do so, do they all, in accordance with the pre-established harmony of things, or under the auspices of an all-shrewd providence, work together to their mutual advantage, for the common weal and in the interest of all.

On leaving this sphere of simple circulation or of exchange of commodities, which furnishes the 'Free-trader Vulgaris' with his views and ideas, and with the standard by which he judges a society based on capital and wages, we think we can perceive a change in the physiognomy of our dramatis personæ. He, who before was the money-owner, now strides in front as capitalist; the possessor of labour-power follows as his labourer. The one with an air of importance, smirking, intent on business; the other, timid and holding back, like one who is bringing his own hide to market and has nothing to expect but—a hiding.

PART III
THE PRODUCTION OF ABSOLUTE SURPLUS-VALUE

CHAPTER 7
THE LABOUR-PROCESS AND THE PROCESS OF PRODUCING SURPLUS-VALUE

Section 1. The Labour-Process or the Production of Use-Values

The capitalist buys labour-power in order to use it; and labour-power in use is labour itself. The purchaser of labour-power consumes it by setting the seller of it to work. By working, the latter becomes actually, what before he only was potentially, labour-power in action, a labourer. In order that his labour may re-appear in a commodity, he must, before all things, expend it on something useful, on something capable of satisfying a want of some sort. Hence, what the capitalist sets the labourer to produce, is a particular use-value, a specified article. The fact that the production of use-values, or goods, is carried on under the control of a capitalist and on his behalf, does not alter the general character of that production. We shall, therefore, in the first place, have to consider the labour-process independently of the particular form it assumes under given social conditions.

Labour is, in the first place, a process in which both man and Nature participate, and in which man of his own accord starts, regulates, and controls the material re-actions between himself and Nature. He opposes himself to Nature as one of her own forces, setting in motion arms and legs, head and hands, the natural forces of his body, in order to appropriate Nature's productions in a form adapted to his own wants. By thus acting on the external world and changing it, he at the same time changes his own nature. He develops his slumbering powers and compels them to act in obedience to his sway. We are not now dealing with those primitive instinctive forms of labour that remind us of the mere animal. An immeasurable interval of time separates the state of things in which a man brings his labour-power to market for sale as a commodity, from that state in which human labour was still in its first instinctive stage. We pre-suppose labour in a form that stamps it as exclusively human. A spider conducts operations that resemble those of a weaver, and a bee puts to shame many an architect in the construction of her cells. But what distinguishes the worst architect from the best of bees is this, that the architect raises his structure in imagination before he erects it in reality. At the end of every labour-process, we get a result that already existed in the imagination of the labourer at its commencement. He not only effects a change of form in the material on which he works, but he also realises a purpose of his own that gives the law to his modus operandi, and to which he must subordinate his will. And this subordination is no mere momentary act. Besides the exertion of the bodily organs, the process demands that, during the whole operation, the workman's will be steadily in consonance with his purpose. This means close attention. The less he is attracted by the nature of the work, and the mode in which it is carried on, and the less, therefore, he enjoys it as something which gives play to his bodily and mental powers, the more close his attention is forced to be.

The elementary factors of the labour-process are 1, the personal activity of man, i.e. work itself, 2, the subject of that work, and 3, its instruments.

The soil (and this, economically speaking, includes water) in the virgin state in which it supplies man with necessaries or the means of subsistence ready to hand, exists independently of him, and is the universal subject of human labour. All those things which labour merely separates from immediate connexion with their environment, are subjects of labour spontaneously provided by Nature. Such are fish which we catch and take from their element, water, timber which we fell in the virgin forest, and ores which we extract from their veins. If, on the other hand, the subject of labour has, so to say, been filtered through previous labour, we call it raw material; such is ore already extracted and ready for washing. All raw material is the subject of labour, but not every subject of labour is raw material: it can only become so, after it has undergone some alteration by means of labour.

An instrument of labour is a thing, or a complex of things, which the labourer interposes between himself and the subject of his labour, and which serves as the conductor of his activity. He makes use of the mechanical, physical, and chemical properties of some substances in order to make other substances subservient to his aims. Leaving out of consideration such ready-made means of subsistence as fruits, in gathering which a man's own limbs serve as the instruments of his labour, the first thing of which the labourer possesses himself is not the subject of labour but its instrument. Thus Nature becomes one of the organs of his activity, one that he annexes to his own bodily organs, adding stature to himself in spite of the Bible. As the earth is his original larder, so too it is his original tool house. It supplies him, for instance, with stones for throwing, grinding, pressing, cutting, etc. The earth itself is an instrument of labour, but when used as such in agriculture implies a whole series of other instruments and a comparatively high development of labour. No sooner does labour undergo the least development, than it requires specially prepared instruments. Thus in the oldest caves we find stone implements and weapons. In the earliest period of human history domesticated animals, i.e. animals which have been bred for the purpose, and have undergone modifications by means of labour, play the chief part as instruments of labour along with specially prepared stones, wood, bones, and shells. The use and fabrication of instruments of labour, although existing in the germ among certain species of animals, is specifically characteristic of the human labour-process, and Franklin therefore defines man as a tool-making animal. Relics of bygone instruments of labour possess the same importance for the investigation of extinct economic forms of society, as do fossil bones for the determination of extinct species of animals. It is not the articles made, but how they are made, and by what instruments, that enables us to distinguish different economic epochs. Instruments of labour not only supply a standard of the degree of development to which human labour has attained, but they are also indicators of the social conditions under which that labour is carried on. Among the instruments of labour, those of a mechanical nature, which, taken as a whole, we may call the bone and muscles of production, offer much more decided characteristics of a given epoch of production, than those which, like pipes, tubs, baskets, jars, etc., serve only to hold the materials for labour, which latter class, we may in a general way, call the vascular system of production. The latter first begins to play an important part in the chemical industries.

In a wider sense we may include among the instruments of labour, in addition to those things that are used for directly transferring labour to its subject, and which therefore, in one way or another, serve as conductors of activity, all such objects as are necessary for carrying on the labour-process. These do not enter directly into the process, but without them it is either impossible for it to take place at all, or possible only to a partial extent. Once more we find the earth to be a universal instrument of this sort, for it furnishes a locus standi to the labourer and a field of employment for his activity. Among instruments that are the result of previous labour and also belong to this class, we find workshops, canals, roads, and so forth.

In the labour-process, therefore, man's activity, with the help of the instruments of labour, effects an alteration, designed from the commencement, in the material worked upon. The process disappears in the product; the latter is a use-value, Nature's material adapted by a change of form to the wants of man. Labour has incorporated itself with its subject: the former is materialised, the latter transformed. That which in the labourer appeared as movement, now appears in the product as a fixed quality without motion. The blacksmith forges and the product is a forging.

If we examine the whole process from the point of view of its result, the product, it is plain that both the instruments and the subject of labour, are means of production, and that the labour itself is productive labour.

Though a use-value, in the form of a product, issues from the labour-process, yet other use-values, products of previous labour, enter into it as means of production. The same use-value is both the product of a previous process, and a means of production in a later process. Products are therefore not only results, but also essential conditions of labour.

With the exception of the extractive industries, in which the material for labour is provided immediately by Nature, such as mining, hunting, fishing, and agriculture (so far as the latter is confined to breaking up virgin soil), all branches of industry manipulate raw material, objects already filtered through labour, already products of labour. Such is seed in agriculture. Animals and plants, which we are accustomed to consider as products of Nature, are in their present form, not only products of, say last year's labour, but the result of a gradual transformation, continued through many generations, under man's superintendence, and by means of his labour. But in the great majority of cases, instruments of labour show even to the most superficial observer, traces of the labour of past ages.

Labour uses up its material factors, its subject and its instruments, consumes them, and is therefore a process of consumption. Such productive consumption is distinguished from individual consumption by this, that the latter uses up products, as means of subsistence for the living individual; the former, as means whereby alone, labour, the labour-power of the living individual, is enabled to act. The product, therefore, of individual consumption, is the consumer himself; the result of productive consumption, is a product distinct from the consumer.

In so far then, as its instruments and subjects are themselves products, labour consumes products in order to create products, or in other words, consumes one set of products by turning them into means of production for another set. But, just as in the beginning, the only participators in the labour-process were man and the earth, which latter exists independently of man, so even now we still employ in the process many means of production, provided directly by Nature, that do not represent any combination of natural substances with human labour.

The labour-process, resolved as above into its simple elementary factors, is human action with a view to the production of use-values, appropriation of natural substances to human requirements; it is the necessary condition for effecting exchange of matter between man and Nature; it is the everlasting Nature-imposed condition of human existence, and therefore is independent of every social phase of that existence, or rather, is common to every such phase. It was, therefore, not necessary to represent our labourer in connexion with other labourers; man and his labour on one side, Nature and its materials on the other, sufficed. As the taste of the porridge does not tell you who grew the oats, no more does this simple process tell you of itself what are the social conditions under which it is taking place, whether under the slave-owner's brutal lash, or the anxious eye of the capitalist, whether Cincinnatus* carries it on in tilling his modest farm or a savage in killing wild animals with stones.

Let us now return to our would-be capitalist. We left him just after he had purchased, in the open market, all the necessary factors of the labour-process; its objective factors, the means of production, as well as its subjective factor, labour-power. With the keen eye of an expert, he has selected the means of production and the kind of labour-power best adapted to his particular trade, be it spinning, bootmaking, or any other kind. He then proceeds to consume the commodity, the labour-power that he has just bought, by causing the labourer, the impersonation of that labour-power, to consume the means of production by his labour. The general character of the labour-process is evidently not changed by the fact, that the labourer works for the capitalist instead of for himself; moreover, the particular methods and operations employed in bootmaking or spinning are not immediately changed by the intervention of the capitalist. He must begin by taking the labour-power as he finds it in the market, and consequently be satisfied with labour of such a kind as would be found in the period immediately preceding the rise of capitalists. Changes in the methods of production by the subordination of labour to capital, can take place only at a later period, and therefore will have to be treated of in a later chapter.

The labour-process, turned into the process by which the capitalist consumes labour-power, exhibits two characteristic phenomena. First, the labourer works under the control of the capitalist to whom his labour belongs; the capitalist taking good care that the work is done in a proper manner, and that the means of production are used with intelligence, so that there is no unnecessary waste of raw material, and no wear and tear of the implements beyond what is necessarily caused by the work.

Secondly, the product is the property of the capitalist and not that of the labourer, its immediate producer. Suppose that a capitalist pays for a day's labour-power at its value; then the right to use that power for a day belongs to him, just as much as the right to use any other commodity, such as a horse that he has hired for the day. To the purchaser of a commodity belongs its use, and the seller of labour-power, by giving his labour, does no more, in reality, than part with the use-value that he has sold. From the instant he steps into the workshop, the use-value of his labour-power, and therefore also its use, which is labour, belongs to the capitalist. By the purchase of labour-power, the capitalist incorporates labour, as a living ferment, with the lifeless constituents of the product. From his point of view, the labour-process is nothing more than the consumption of the commodity purchased, i.e. of labour-power; but this consumption cannot be effected except by supplying the labour-power with the means of production. The labour-process is a process between things that the capitalist has purchased, things that have become his property. The product of this process belongs, therefore, to him, just as much as does the wine which is the product of a process of fermentation completed in his cellar.

Section 2. The Production of Surplus-Value

The product appropriated by the capitalist is a use-value, as yarn, for example, or boots. But, although boots are, in one sense, the basis of all social progress, and our capitalist is a decided 'progressist,' yet he does not manufacture boots for their own sake. Use-value is, by no means, the thing 'qu'on aime pour lui-même'* in the production of commodities. Use-values are only produced by capitalists, because, and in so far as, they are the material substratum, the depositories of exchange-value. Our capitalist has two objects in view: in the first place, he wants to produce a use-value that has a value in exchange, that is to say, an article destined to be sold, a commodity; and secondly, he desires to produce a commodity whose value shall be greater than the sum of the values of the commodities used in its production, that is, of the means of production and the labour-power, that he purchased with his good money in the open market. His aim is to produce not only a use-value, but a commodity also; not only use-value, but value; not only value, but at the same time surplus-value.

It must be borne in mind, that we are now dealing with the production of commodities, and that, up to this point, we have only considered one aspect of the process. Just as commodities are, at the same time, use-values and values, so the process of producing them must be a labour-process, and at the same time, a process of creating value.

Let us now examine production as a creation of value.

We know that the value of each commodity is determined by the quantity of labour expended on and materialised in it, by the working-time necessary, under given social conditions, for its production. This rule also holds good in the case of the product that accrued to our capitalist, as the result of the labour-process carried on for him. Assuming this product to be 10 lbs. of yarn, our first step is to calculate the quantity of labour realised in it.

For spinning the yarn, raw material is required; suppose in this case 10 lbs. of cotton. We have no need at present to investigate the value of this cotton, for our capitalist has, we will assume, bought it at its full value, say of ten shillings. In this price the labour required for the production of the cotton is already expressed in terms of the average labour of society. We will further assume that the wear and tear of the spindle, which, for our present purpose, may represent all other instruments of labour employed, amounts to the value of 2s. If, then, twenty-four hours' labour, or two working-days, are required to produce the quantity of gold represented by twelve shillings, we have here, to begin with, two days' labour already incorporated in the yarn.

We must not let ourselves be misled by the circumstance that the cotton has taken a new shape while the substance of the spindle has to a certain extent been used up. By the general law of value, if the value of 40 lbs. of yarn = the value of 40 lbs. of cotton + the value of a whole spindle, i.e. if the same working-time is required to produce the commodities on either side of this equation, then 10 lbs. of yarn are an equivalent for 10 lbs. of cotton, together with one-fourth of a spindle.

In the case we are considering the same working-time is materialised in the 10 lbs. of yarn on the one hand, and in the 10 lbs. of cotton and the fraction of a spindle on the other. Therefore, whether value appears in cotton, in a spindle, or in yarn, makes no difference in the amount of that value. The spindle and cotton, instead of resting quietly side by side, join together in the process, their forms are altered, and they are turned into yarn; but their value is no more affected by this fact than it would be if they had been simply exchanged for their equivalent in yarn.

The labour required for the production of the cotton, the raw material of the yarn, is part of the labour necessary to produce the yarn, and is therefore contained in the yarn. The same applies to the labour embodied in the spindle, without whose wear and tear the cotton could not be spun.

Hence, in determining the value of the yarn, or the labour-time required for its production, all the special processes carried on at various times and in different places, which were necessary, first to produce the cotton and the wasted portion of the spindle, and then with the cotton and spindle to spin the yarn, may together be looked on as different and successive phases of one and the same process. The whole of the labour in the yarn is past labour; and it is a matter of no importance that the operations necessary for the production of its constituent elements were carried on at times which, referred to the present, are more remote than the final operation of spinning. If a definite quantity of labour, say thirty days, is requisite to build a house, the total amount of labour incorporated in it is not altered by the fact that the work of the last day is done twenty-nine days later than that of the first. Therefore the labour contained in the raw material and the instruments of labour can be treated just as if it were labour expended in an earlier stage of the spinning process, before the labour of actual spinning commenced.

The values of the means of production, i.e. the cotton and the spindle, which values are expressed in the price of twelve shillings, are therefore constituent parts of the value of the yarn, or, in other words, of the value of the product.

Two conditions must nevertheless be fulfilled. First, the cotton and spindle must concur in the production of a use-value; they must in the present case become yarn. Value is independent of the particular use-value by which it is borne, but it must be embodied in a use-value of some kind. Secondly, the time occupied in the labour of production must not exceed the time really necessary under the given social conditions of the case. Therefore, if no more than 1 lb. of cotton be requisite to spin 1 lb. of yarn, care must be taken that no more than this weight of cotton is consumed in the production of 1 lb. of yarn; and similarly with regard to the spindle. Though the capitalist have a hobby, and use a gold instead of a steel spindle, yet the only labour that counts for anything in the value of the yarn is that which would be required to produce a steel spindle, because no more is necessary under the given social conditions.

We now know what portion of the value of the yarn is owing to the cotton and the spindle. It amounts to twelve shillings or the value of two days' work. The next point for our consideration is, what portion of the value of the yarn is added to the cotton by the labour of the spinner.

We have now to consider this labour under a very different aspect from that which it had during the labour-process; there, we viewed it solely as that particular kind of human activity which changes cotton into yarn; there, the more the labour was suited to the work, the better the yarn, other circumstances remaining the same. The labour of the spinner was then viewed as specifically different from other kinds of productive labour, different on the one hand in its special aim, viz., spinning, different, on the other hand, in the special character of its operations, in the special nature of its means of production and in the special use-value of its product. For the operation of spinning, cotton and spindles are a necessity, but for making rifled cannon they would be of no use whatever. Here, on the contrary, where we consider the labour of the spinner only so far as it is value-creating, i.e. a source of value, his labour differs in no respect from the labour of the man who bores cannon, or (what here more nearly concerns us), from the labour of the cotton-planter and spindle-maker incorporated in the means of production. It is solely by reason of this identity, that cotton planting, spindle making and spinning, are capable of forming the component parts, differing only quantitatively from each other, of one whole, namely, the value of the yarn. Here, we have nothing more to do with the quality, the nature and the specific character of the labour, but merely with its quantity. And this simply requires to be calculated. We proceed upon the assumption that spinning is simple, unskilled labour, the average labour of a given state of society. Hereafter we shall see that the contrary assumption would make no difference.

While the labourer is at work, his labour constantly undergoes a transformation: from being motion, it becomes an object without motion; from being the labourer working, it becomes the thing produced.

At the end of one hour's spinning, that act is represented by a definite quantity of yarn; in other words, a definite quantity of labour, namely that of one hour, has become embodied in the cotton. We say labour, i.e. the expenditure of his vital force by the spinner, and not spinning labour, because the special work of spinning counts here, only so far as it is the expenditure of labour-power in general, and not in so far as it is the specific work of the spinner.

In the process we are now considering it is of extreme importance, that no more time be consumed in the work of transforming the cotton into yarn than is necessary under the given social conditions. If under normal, i.e. average social conditions of production, *a* pounds of cotton ought to be made into *b* pounds of yarn by one hour's labour, then a day's labour does not count as 12 hours' labour unless 12 *a* pounds of cotton have been made into 12 *b* pounds of yarn; for in the creation of value, the time that is socially necessary alone counts.

Not only the labour, but also the raw material and the product now appear in quite a new light, very different from that in which we viewed them in the labour-process pure and simple. The raw material serves now merely as an absorbent of a definite quantity of labour. By this absorption it is in fact changed into yarn, because it is spun, because labour-power in the form of spinning is added to it; but the product, the yarn, is now nothing more than a measure of the labour absorbed by the cotton. If in one hour $1\frac{2}{3}$ lbs. of cotton can be spun into $1\frac{2}{3}$ lbs. of yarn, then 10 lbs. of yarn indicate the absorption of 6 hours' labour. Definite quantities of product, these quantities being determined by experience, now represent nothing but definite quantities of labour, definite masses of crystallised labour-time. They are nothing more than the materialisation of so many hours or so many days of social labour.

We are here no more concerned about the facts, that the labour is the specific work of spinning, that its subject is cotton and its product yarn, than we are about the fact that the subject itself is already a product and therefore raw material. If the spinner, instead of spinning, were working in a coal mine, the subject of his labour, the coal, would be supplied by Nature; nevertheless, a definite quantity of extracted coal, a hundredweight for example, would represent a definite quantity of absorbed labour.

We assumed, on the occasion of its sale, that the value of a day's labour-power is three shillings, and that six hours' labour is incorporated in that sum; and consequently that this amount of labour is requisite to produce the necessaries of life daily required on an average by the labourer. If now our spinner by working for one hour, can convert 1⅔ lbs. of cotton into 1⅔ lbs. of yarn, it follows that in six hours he will convert 10 lbs. of cotton into 10 lbs. of yarn. Hence, during the spinning process, the cotton absorbs six hours' labour. The same quantity of labour is also embodied in a piece of gold of the value of three shillings. Consequently by the mere labour of spinning, a value of three shillings is added to the cotton.

Let us now consider the total value of the product, the 10 lbs. of yarn. Two and a half days' labour has been embodied in it, of which two days were contained in the cotton and in the substance of the spindle worn away, and half a day was absorbed during the process of spinning. This two and a half days' labour is also represented by a piece of gold of the value of fifteen shillings. Hence, fifteen shillings is an adequate price for the 10 lbs. of yarn, or the price of one pound is eighteenpence.

Our capitalist stares in astonishment. The value of the product is exactly equal to the value of the capital advanced. The value so advanced has not expanded, no surplus-value has been created, and consequently money has not been converted into capital. The price of the yarn is fifteen shillings, and fifteen shillings were spent in the open market upon the constituent elements of the product, or, what amounts to the same thing, upon the factors of the labour-process; ten shillings were paid for the cotton, two shillings for the substance of the spindle worn away, and three shillings for the labour-power. The swollen value of the yarn is of no avail, for it is merely the sum of the values formerly existing in the cotton, the spindle, and the labour-power: out of such a simple addition of existing values, no surplus-value can possibly arise. These separate values are now all concentrated in one thing; but so they were also in the sum of fifteen shillings, before it was split up into three parts, by the purchase of the commodities.

There is in reality nothing very strange in this result. The value of one pound of yarn being eighteenpence, if our capitalist buys 10 lbs. of yarn in the market, he must pay fifteen shillings for them. It is clear that, whether a man buys his house ready built, or gets it built for him, in neither case will the mode of acquisition increase the amount of money laid out on the house.

Our capitalist, who is at home in his vulgar economy, exclaims: 'Oh! but I advanced my money for the express purpose of making more money.' The way to Hell is paved with good intentions, and he might just as easily have intended to make money, without producing at all. He threatens all sorts of things. He won't be caught napping again. In future he will buy the commodities in the market, instead of manufacturing them himself. But if all his brother capitalists were to do the same, where would he find his commodities in the market? And his money he cannot eat. He tries persuasion. 'Consider my abstinence; I might have played ducks and drakes with the 15 shillings; but instead of that I consumed it productively, and made yarn with it.' Very well, and by way of reward he is now in possession of good yarn instead of a bad conscience; and as for playing the part of a miser, it would never do for him to relapse into such bad ways as that; we have seen before to what results such asceticism leads. Besides, where nothing is, the king has lost his rights; whatever may be the merit of his abstinence, there is nothing wherewith specially to remunerate it, because the value of the product is merely the sum of the values of the commodities that were thrown into the process of production. Let him therefore console himself with the reflection that virtue is its own reward. But no, he becomes importunate. He says: 'The yarn is of no use to me: I produced it for sale.' In that case let him sell it, or, still better, let him for the future produce only things for satisfying his personal wants, a remedy that his physician MacCulloch has already prescribed as infallible against an epidemic of over-production. He now gets obstinate. 'Can the labourer', he asks, 'merely with his arms and legs, produce commodities out of nothing? Did I not supply him with the materials, by means of which, and in which alone, his labour could be embodied? And as the greater part of society consists of such ne'er-do-wells, have I not rendered society incalculable service by my instruments of production, my cotton and my spindle, and not only society, but the labourer also, whom in addition I have provided with the necessaries of life? And am I to be allowed nothing in return for all this service?' Well, but has not the labourer rendered him the equivalent service of changing his cotton and spindle into yarn? Moreover, there is here no question of service. A service is nothing more than the useful effect of a use-value, be it of a commodity, or be it of labour. But here we are dealing with exchange-value. The capitalist paid to the labourer a value of 3 shillings, and the labourer gave him back an exact equivalent in the value of 3 shillings, added by him to the cotton: he gave him value for value. Our friend, up to this time so purse-proud, suddenly assumes the modest demeanour of his own workman, and exclaims: 'Have I myself not worked? Have I not performed the labour of superintendence and of overlooking the spinner? And does not this labour, too, create value?' His overlooker and his manager try to hide their smiles. Meanwhile, after a hearty laugh, he re-assumes his usual mien. Though he chanted to us the whole creed of the economists, in reality, he says, he would not give a brass farthing for it. He leaves this and all such like subterfuges and juggling tricks to the professors of Political Economy, who are paid for it. He himself is a practical man; and though he does not always consider what he says outside his business, yet in his business he knows what he is about.

Let us examine the matter more closely. The value of a day's labour-power amounts to 3 shillings, because on our assumption half a day's labour is embodied in that quantity of labour-power, i.e. because the means of subsistence that are daily required for the production of labour-power, cost half a day's labour. But the past labour that is embodied in the labour-power, and the living labour that it can call into action; the daily cost of maintaining it, and its daily expenditure in work, are two totally different things. The former determines the exchange-value of the labour-power, the latter is its use-value. The fact that half a day's labour is necessary to keep the labourer alive during 24 hours, does not in any way prevent him from working a whole day. Therefore, the value of labour-power, and the value which that labour-power creates in the labour-process, are two entirely different magnitudes; and this difference of the two values was what the capitalist had in view, when he was purchasing the labour-power. The useful qualities that labour-power possesses, and by virtue of which it makes yarn or boots, were to him nothing more than a conditio sine qua non; for in order to create value, labour must be expended in a useful manner. What really influenced him was the specific use-value which this commodity possesses of being *a source not only of value, but of more value than it has itself*. This is the special service that the capitalist expects from labour-power, and in this transaction he acts in accordance with the 'eternal laws' of the exchange of commodities. The seller of labour-power, like the seller of any other commodity, realises its exchange-value, and parts with its use-value. He cannot take the one without giving the other. The use-value of labour-power, or in other words, labour, belongs just as little to its seller, as the use-value of oil after it has been sold belongs to the dealer who has sold it. The owner of the money has paid the value of a day's labour-power; his, therefore, is the use of it for a day; a day's labour belongs to him. The circumstance, that on the one hand the daily sustenance of labour-power costs only half a day's labour, while on the other hand the very same labour-power can work during a whole day, that consequently the value which its use during one day creates, is double what he pays for that use, this circumstance is, without doubt, a piece of good luck for the buyer, but by no means an injury to the seller.

Our capitalist foresaw this state of things, and that was the cause of his laughter. The labourer therefore finds, in the workshop, the means of production necessary for working, not only during six, but during twelve hours. Just as during the six hours' process our 10 lbs. of cotton absorbed six hours' labour, and became 10 lbs. of yarn, so now, 20 lbs. of cotton will absorb 12 hours' labour and be changed into 20 lbs. of yarn. Let us now examine the product of this prolonged process. There is now materialised in this 20 lbs. of yarn the labour of five days, of which four days are due to the cotton and the lost steel of the spindle, the remaining day having been absorbed by the cotton during the spinning process. Expressed in gold, the labour of five days is thirty shillings. This is therefore the price of the 20 lbs. of yarn, giving, as before, eighteenpence as the price of a pound. But the sum of the values of the commodities that entered into the process amounts to 27 shillings. The value of the yarn is 30 shillings. Therefore the value of the product is ⅑ greater than the value advanced for its production; 27 shillings have been transformed into 30 shillings; a surplus-value of 3 shillings has been created. The trick has at last succeeded; money has been converted into capital.

Every condition of the problem is satisfied, while the laws that regulate the exchange of commodities, have been in no way violated. Equivalent has been exchanged for equivalent. For the capitalist as buyer paid for each commodity, for the cotton, the spindle and the labour-power, its full value. He then did what is done by every purchaser of commodities; he consumed their use-value. The consumption of the labour-power, which was also the process of producing commodities, resulted in 20 lbs. of yarn, having a value of 30 shillings. The capitalist, formerly a buyer, now returns to market as a seller, of commodities. He sells his yarn at eighteenpence a pound, which is its exact value. Yet for all that he withdraws 3 shillings more from circulation than he originally threw into it. This metamorphosis, this conversion of money into capital, takes place both within the sphere of circulation and also outside it; within the circulation, because conditioned by the purchase of the labour-power in the market; outside the circulation, because what is done within it is only a stepping-stone to the production of surplus-value, a process which is entirely confined to the sphere of production. Thus 'tout est pour le mieux dans le meilleur des mondes possibles'.*

By turning his money into commodities that serve as the material elements of a new product, and as factors in the labour-process, by incorporating living labour with their dead substance, the capitalist at the same time converts value, i.e. past, materialised, and dead labour into capital, into value big with value, a live monster that is fruitful and multiplies.

If we now compare the two processes of producing value and of creating surplus-value, we see that the latter is nothing but the continuation of the former beyond a definite point. If on the one hand the process be not carried beyond the point, where the value paid by the capitalist for the labour-power is replaced by an exact equivalent, it is simply a process of producing value; if, on the other hand, it be continued beyond that point, it becomes a process of creating surplus-value.

If we proceed further, and compare the process of producing value with the labour-process, pure and simple, we find that the latter consists of the useful labour, the work, that produces use-values. Here we contemplate the labour as producing a particular article; we view it under its qualitative aspect alone, with regard to its end and aim. But viewed as a value-creating process, the same labour-process presents itself under its quantitative aspect alone. Here it is a question merely of the time occupied by the labourer in doing the work; of the period during which the labour-power is usefully expended. Here, the commodities that take part in the process, do not count any longer as necessary adjuncts of labour-power in the production of a definite, useful object. They count merely as depositories of so much absorbed or materialised labour; that labour, whether previously embodied in the means of production, or incorporated in them for the first time during the process by the action of labour-power, counts in either case only according to its duration; it amounts to so many hours or days as the case may be.

Moreover, only so much of the time spent in the production of any article is counted, as, under the given social conditions, is necessary. The consequences of this are various. In the first place, it becomes necessary that the labour should be carried on under normal conditions. If a self-acting mule is the implement in general use for spinning, it would be absurd to supply the spinner with a distaff and spinning wheel. The cotton too must not be such rubbish as to cause extra waste in being worked, but must be of suitable quality. Otherwise the spinner would be found to spend more time in producing a pound of yarn than is socially necessary, in which case the excess of time would create neither value nor money. But whether the material factors of the process are of normal quality or not, depends not upon the labourer, but entirely upon the capitalist. Then again, the labour-power itself must be of average efficacy. In the trade in which it is being employed, it must possess the average skill, handiness and quickness prevalent in that trade, and our capitalist took good care to buy labour-power of such normal goodness. This power must be applied with the average amount of exertion and with the usual degree of intensity; and the capitalist is as careful to see that this is done, as that his workmen are not idle for a single moment. He has bought the use of the labour-power for a definite period, and he insists upon his rights. He has no intention of being robbed. Lastly, and for this purpose our friend has a penal code of his own, all wasteful consumption of raw material or instruments of labour is strictly forbidden, because what is so wasted, represents labour superfluously expended, labour that does not count in the product or enter into its value.[6]

We now see, that the difference between labour, considered on the one hand as producing utilities, and on the other hand, as creating value, a difference which we discovered by our analysis of a commodity, resolves itself into a distinction between two aspects of the process of production.

The process of production, considered on the one hand as the unity of the labour-process and the process of creating value, is production of commodities; considered on the other hand as the unity of the labour-process and the process of producing surplus-value, it is the capitalist process of production, or capitalist production of commodities.

We stated, on a previous page, that in the creation of surplus-value it does not in the least matter, whether the labour appropriated by the capitalist be simple unskilled labour of average quality or more complicated skilled labour. All labour of a higher or more complicated character than average labour is expenditure of labour-power of a more costly kind, labour-power whose production has cost more time and labour, and which therefore has a higher value, than unskilled or simple labour-power. This power being of higher value, its consumption is labour of a higher class, labour that creates in equal times proportionally higher values than unskilled labour does. Whatever difference in skill there may be between the labour of a spinner and that of a jeweller, the portion of his labour by which the jeweller merely replaces the value of his own labour-power, does not in any way differ in quality from the additional portion by which he creates surplus-value. In the making of jewellery, just as in spinning, the surplus-value results only from a quantitative excess of labour, from a lengthening-out of one and the same labour-process, in the one case, of the process of making jewels, in the other of the process of making yarn.[7]

But on the other hand, in every process of creating value, the reduction of skilled labour to average social labour, e.g. one day of skilled to six days of unskilled labour, is unavoidable. We therefore save ourselves a superfluous operation, and simplify our analysis, by the assumption, that the labour of the workman employed by the capitalist is unskilled average labour.

CHAPTER 8

CONSTANT CAPITAL AND VARIABLE CAPITAL

THE various factors of the labour-process play different parts in forming the value of the product.

The labourer adds fresh value to the subject of his labour by expending upon it a given amount of additional labour, no matter what the specific character and utility of that labour may be. On the other hand, the values of the means of production used up in the process are preserved, and present themselves afresh as constituent parts of the value of the product; the values of the cotton and the spindle, for instance, re-appear again in the value of the yarn. The value of the means of production is therefore preserved, by being transferred to the product. This transfer takes place during the conversion of those means into a product, or in other words, during the labour-process. It is brought about by labour; but how?

The labourer does not perform two operations at once, one in order to add value to the cotton, the other in order to preserve the value of the means of production, or, what amounts to the same thing, to transfer to the yarn, to the product, the value of the cotton on which he works, and part of the value of the spindle with which he works. But, by the very act of adding new value, he preserves their former values. Since, however, the addition of new value to the subject of his labour, and the preservation of its former value, are two entirely distinct results, produced simultaneously by the labourer, during one operation, it is plain that this two-fold nature of the result can be explained only by the two-fold nature of his labour; at one and the same time, it must in one character create value, and in another character preserve or transfer value.

Now, in what manner does every labourer add new labour and consequently new value? Evidently, only by labouring productively in a particular way; the spinner by spinning, the weaver by weaving, the smith by forging. But, while thus incorporating labour generally, that is value, it is by the particular form alone of the labour, by the spinning, the weaving and the forging respectively, that the means of production, the cotton and spindle, the yarn and loom, and the iron and anvil become constituent elements of the product, of a new use-value. Each use-value disappears, but only to re-appear under a new form in a new use-value. Now, we saw, when we were considering the process of creating value, that, if a use-value be effectively consumed in the production of a new use-value, the quantity of labour expended in the production of the consumed article, forms a portion of the quantity of labour necessary to produce the new use-value; this portion is therefore labour transferred from the means of production to the new product. Hence, the labourer preserves the values of the consumed means of production, or transfers them as portions of its value to the product, not by virtue of his additional labour, abstractedly considered, but by virtue of the particular useful character of that labour, by virtue of its special productive form. In so far then as labour is such specific productive activity, in so far as it is spinning, weaving, or forging, it raises, by mere contact, the means of production from the dead, makes them living factors of the labour-process, and combines with them to form the new products.

If the special productive labour of the workman were not spinning, he could not convert the cotton into yarn, and therefore could not transfer the values of the cotton and spindle to the yarn. Suppose the same workman were to change his occupation to that of a joiner, he would still by a day's labour add value to the material he works upon. Consequently, we see, first, that the addition of new value takes place not by virtue of his labour being spinning in particular, or joinering in particular, but because it is labour in the abstract, a portion of the total labour of society; and we see next, that the value added is of a given definite amount, not because his labour has a special utility, but because it is exerted for a definite time. On the one hand, then, it is by virtue of its general character, as being expenditure of human labour-power in the abstract, that spinning adds new value to the values of the cotton and the spindle; and on the other hand, it is by virtue of its special character, as being a concrete, useful process, that the same labour of spinning both transfers the values of the means of production to the product, and preserves them in the product. Hence at one and the same time there is produced a two-fold result.

By the simple addition of a certain quantity of labour, new value is added, and by the quality of this added labour, the original values of the means of production are preserved in the product. This two-fold effect, resulting from the two-fold character of labour, may be traced in various phenomena.

Let us assume, that some invention enables the spinner to spin as much cotton in 6 hours as he was able to spin before in 36 hours. His labour is now six times as effective as it was, for the purposes of useful production. The product of 6 hours' work has increased six-fold, from

6 lbs. to 36 lbs. But now the 36 lbs. of cotton absorb only the same amount of labour as formerly did the 6 lbs. One-sixth as much new labour is absorbed by each pound of cotton, and consequently, the value added by the labour to each pound is only one-sixth of what it formerly was. On the other hand, in the product, in the 36 lbs. of yarn, the value transferred from the cotton is six times as great as before. By the 6 hours' spinning, the value of the raw material preserved and transferred to the product is six times as great as before, although the new value added by the labour of the spinner to each pound of the very same raw material is one-sixth what it was formerly. This shows that the two properties of labour, by virtue of which it is enabled in one case to preserve value, and in the other to create value, are essentially different. On the one hand, the longer the time necessary to spin a given weight of cotton into yarn, the greater is the new value added to the material; on the other hand, the greater the weight of the cotton spun in a given time, the greater is the value preserved, by being transferred from it to the product.

Let us now assume, that the productiveness of the spinner's labour, instead of varying, remains constant, that he therefore requires the same time as he formerly did, to convert one pound of cotton into yarn, but that the exchange-value of the cotton varies, either by rising to six times its former value or falling to one-sixth of that value. In both these cases, the spinner puts the same quantity of labour into a pound of cotton, and therefore adds as much value, as he did before the change in the value: he also produces a given weight of yarn in the same time as he did before. Nevertheless, the value that he transfers from the cotton to the yarn is either one-sixth of what it was before the variation, or, as the case may be, six times as much as before. The same result occurs, when the value of the instruments of labour rises or falls, while their useful efficacy in the process remains unaltered.

Again, if the technical conditions of the spinning process remain unchanged, and no change of value takes place in the means of production, the spinner continues to consume in equal working-times equal quantities of raw material, and equal quantities of machinery of unvarying value. The value that he preserves in the product is directly proportional to the new value that he adds to the product. In two weeks he incorporates twice as much labour, and therefore twice as much value, as in one week, and during the same time he consumes twice as much material, and wears out twice as much machinery, of double the value in each case; he therefore preserves, in the product of two weeks, twice as much value as in the product of one week. So long as the conditions of production remain the same, the more value the labourer adds by fresh labour, the more value he transfers and preserves; but he does so merely because this addition of new value takes place under conditions that have not varied and are independent of his own labour. Of course, it may be said in one sense, that the labourer preserves old value always in proportion to the quantity of new value that he adds. Whether the value of cotton rise from one shilling to two shillings, or fall to sixpence, the workman invariably preserves in the product of one hour only one half as much value as he preserves in two hours. In like manner, if the productiveness of his own labour varies by rising or falling, he will in one hour spin either more or less cotton, as the case may be, than he did before, and will consequently preserve in the product of one hour, more or less value of cotton; but, all the same, he will preserve by two hours' labour twice as much value as he will by one.

Value exists only in articles of utility, in objects: we leave out of consideration its purely symbolical representation by tokens. (Man himself, viewed as the impersonation of labour-power, is a natural object, a thing, although a living conscious thing, and labour is the manifestation of this power residing in him.) If therefore an article loses its utility, it also loses its value. The reason why means of production do not lose their value, at the same time that they lose their use-value, is this: they lose in the labour-process the original form of their use-value, only to assume in the product the form of a new use-value. But, however important it may be to value, that it should have some object of utility to embody itself in, yet it is a matter of complete indifference what particular object serves this purpose; this we saw when treating of the metamorphosis of commodities. Hence it follows that in the labour-process the means of production transfer their value to the product only so far as along with their use-value they lose also their exchange-value. They give up to the product that value alone which they themselves lose as means of production. But in this respect the material factors of the labour-process do not all behave alike.

The coal burnt under the boiler vanishes without leaving a trace; so, too, the tallow with which the axles of wheels are greased. Dye stuffs and other auxiliary substances also vanish but re-appear as properties of the product. Raw material forms the substance of the product, but only after it has changed its form. Hence raw material and auxiliary substances lose the characteristic form with which they are clothed on entering the labour-process. It is otherwise with the instruments of labour. Tools, machines, workshops, and vessels, are of use in the labour-process, only so long as they retain their original shape, and are ready each morning to renew the process with their shape unchanged. And just as during their lifetime, that is to say, during the continued labour-process in which they serve, they retain their shape independent of the product, so, too, they do after their death. The corpses of machines, tools, workshops, etc., are always separate and distinct from the product they helped to turn out. If we now consider the case of any instrument of labour during the whole period of its service, from the day of its entry into the workshop, till the day of its banishment into the lumber room, we find that during this period its use-value has been completely consumed, and therefore its exchange-value completely transferred to the product. For instance, if a spinning machine lasts for 10 years, it is plain that during that working period its total value is gradually transferred to the product of the 10 years. The lifetime of an instrument of labour, therefore, is spent in the repetition of a greater or less number of similar operations. Its life may be compared with that of a human being. Every day brings a man 24 hours nearer to his grave: but how many days he has still to travel on that road, no man can tell accurately by merely looking at him. This difficulty, however, does not prevent life insurance offices from drawing, by means of the theory of averages, very accurate, and at the same time very profitable conclusions. So it is with the instruments of labour. It is known by experience how long on the average a machine of a particular kind will last. Suppose its use-value in the labour-process to last only six days. Then, on the average, it loses each day one-sixth of its use-value, and therefore parts with one-sixth of its value to the daily product. The wear and tear of all instruments, their daily loss of use-value, and the corresponding quantity of value they part with to the product, are accordingly calculated upon this basis.

It is thus strikingly clear, that means of production never transfer more value to the product than they themselves lose during the labour-process by the destruction of their own use-value. If such an instrument has no value to lose, if, in other words, it is not the product of human labour, it transfers no value to the product. It helps to create use-value without contributing to the formation of exchange-value. In this class are included all means of production supplied by Nature without human assistance, such as land, wind, water, metals in situ, and timber in virgin forests.

Yet another interesting phenomenon here presents itself. Suppose a machine to be worth £1,000, and to wear out in 1,000 days. Then one thousandth part of the value of the machine is daily transferred to the day's product. At the same time, though with diminishing vitality, the machine as a whole continues to take part in the labour-process. Thus it appears, that one factor of the labour-process, a means of production, continually enters as a whole into that process, while it enters into the process of the formation of value by fractions only. The difference between the two processes is here reflected in their material factors, by the same instrument of production taking part as a whole in the labour-process, while at the same time as an element in the formation of value, it enters only by fractions.

On the other hand, a means of production may take part as a whole in the formation of value, while into the labour-process it enters only bit by bit. Suppose that in spinning cotton, the waste for every 115 lbs. used amounts to 15 lbs., which is converted, not into yarn, but into 'devil's dust'. * Now, although this 15 lbs. of cotton never becomes a constituent element of the yarn, yet assuming this amount of waste to be normal and inevitable under average conditions of spinning, its value is just as surely transferred to the value of the yarn, as is the value of the 100 lbs. that form the substance of the yarn. The use-value of 15 lbs. of cotton must vanish into dust, before 100 lbs. of yarn can be made. The destruction of this cotton is therefore a necessary condition in the production of the yarn. And because it is a necessary condition, and for no other reason, the value of that cotton is transferred to the product. The same holds good for every kind of refuse resulting from a labour-process, so far at least as such refuse cannot be further employed as a means in the production of new and independent use-values. Such an employment of refuse may be seen in the large machine works at Manchester, where mountains of iron turnings are carted away to the foundry in the evening, in order the next morning to reappear in the workshops as solid masses of iron.

We have seen that the means of production transfer value to the new product, so far only as during the labour-process they lose value in the shape of their old use-value. The maximum loss of value that they can suffer in the process, is plainly limited by the amount of the original value with which they came into the process, or in other words, by the labour-time necessary for their production. Therefore, the means of production can never add more value to the product than they themselves possess independently of the process in which they assist. However useful a given kind of raw material, or a machine, or other means of production may be, though it may cost £150, or, say, 500 days' labour, yet it cannot, under any circumstances, add to the value of the product more than £150. Its value is determined not by the labour-process into which it enters as a means of production, but by that out of which it has issued as a product. In the labour-process it only serves as a mere use-value, a thing with useful properties, and could not, therefore, transfer any value to the product, unless it possessed such value previously.

While productive labour is changing the means of production into constituent elements of a new product, their value undergoes a metempsychosis. It deserts the consumed body, to occupy the newly created one. But this transmigration takes place, as it were, behind the back of the labourer. He is unable to add new labour, to create new value, without at the same time preserving old values, and this, because the labour he adds must be of a specific useful kind; and he cannot do work of a useful kind, without employing products as the means of production of a new product, and thereby transferring their value to the new product. The property therefore which labour-power in action, living labour, possesses of preserving value, at the same time that it adds it, is a gift of Nature which costs the labourer nothing, but which is very advantageous to the capitalist inasmuch as it preserves the existing value of his capital. So long as trade is good, the capitalist is too much absorbed in money-grubbing to take notice of this gratuitous gift of labour. A violent interruption of the labour-process by a crisis, makes him sensitively aware of it.

As regards the means of production, what is really consumed is their use-value, and the consumption of this use-value by labour results in the product. There is no consumption of their value, and it would therefore be inaccurate to say that it is reproduced. It is rather preserved; not by reason of any operation it undergoes itself in the process; but because the article in which it originally exists, vanishes, it is true, but vanishes into some other article. Hence, in the value of the product, there is a reappearance of the value of the means of production, but there is, strictly speaking, no reproduction of that value. That which is produced is a new use-value in which the old exchange-value reappears.

It is otherwise with the subjective factor of the labour-process, with labour-power in action. While the labourer, by virtue of his labour being of a specialised kind that has a special object, preserves and transfers to the product the value of the means of production, he at the same time, by the mere act of working, creates each instant an additional or new value. Suppose the process of production to be stopped just when the workman has produced an equivalent for the value of his own labour-power, when, for example, by six hours' labour, he has added a value of three shillings. This value is the surplus, of the total value of the product, over the portion of its value that is due to the means of production. It is the only original bit of value formed during this process, the only portion of the value of the product created by this process. Of course, we do not forget that this new value only replaces the money advanced by the capitalist in the purchase of the labour-power, and spent by the labourer on the necessaries of life. With regard to the money spent, the new value is merely a reproduction; but, nevertheless, it is an actual, and not, as in the case of the value of the means of production, only an apparent, reproduction. The substitution of one value for another, is here effected by the creation of new value.

We know, however, from what has gone before, that the labour-process may continue beyond the time necessary to reproduce and incorporate in the product a mere equivalent for the value of the labour-power. Instead of the six hours that are sufficient for the latter purpose, the process may continue for twelve hours. The action of labour-power, therefore, not only reproduces its own value, but produces value over and above it. This surplus-value is the difference between the value of the product and the value of the elements consumed in the formation of that product, in other words, of the means of production and the labour-power.

By our explanation of the different parts played by the various factors of the labour-process in the formation of the product's value, we have, in fact, disclosed the characters of the different functions allotted to the different elements of capital in the process of expanding its own value. The surplus of the total value of the product, over the sum of the values of its constituent factors, is the surplus of the expanded capital over the capital originally advanced. The means of production on the one hand, labour-power on the other, are merely the different modes of existence which the value of the original capital assumed when from being money it was transformed into the various factors of the labour-process. That part of capital then, which is represented by the means of production, by the raw material, auxiliary material and the instruments of labour, does not, in the process of production, undergo any quantitative alteration of value. I therefore call it the constant part of capital, or, more shortly, *constant capital*.

On the other hand, that part of capital, represented by labour-power, does, in the process of production, undergo an alteration of value. It both reproduces the equivalent of its own value, and also produces an excess, a surplus-value, which may itself vary, may be more or less according to circumstances. This part of capital is continually being transformed from a constant into a variable magnitude. I therefore call it the variable part of capital, or, shortly, *variable capital*. The same elements of capital which, from the point of view of the labour-process, present themselves respectively as the objective and subjective factors, as means of production and labour-power, present themselves, from the point of view of the process of creating surplus-value, as constant and variable capital.

The definition of constant capital given above by no means excludes the possibility of a change of value in its elements. Suppose the price of cotton to be one day sixpence a pound, and the next day, in consequence of a failure of the cotton crop, a shilling a pound. Each pound of the cotton bought at sixpence, and worked up after the rise in value, transfers to the product a value of one shilling; and the cotton already spun before the rise, and perhaps circulating in the market as yarn, likewise transfers to the product twice its original value. It is plain, however, that these changes of value are independent of the increment or surplus-value added to the value of the cotton by the spinning itself. If the old cotton had never been spun, it could, after the rise, be resold at a shilling a pound instead of at sixpence. Further, the fewer the processes the cotton has gone through, the more certain is this result. We therefore find that speculators make it a rule when such sudden changes in value occur, to speculate in that material on which the least possible quantity of labour has been spent: to speculate, therefore, in yarn rather than in cloth, in cotton itself, rather than in yarn. The change of value in the case we have been considering, originates, not in the process in which the cotton plays the part of a means of production, and in which it therefore functions as constant capital, but in the process in which the cotton itself is produced. The value of a commodity, it is true, is determined by the quantity of labour contained in it, but this quantity is itself limited by social conditions. If the time socially necessary for the production of any commodity alters—and a given weight of cotton represents, after a bad harvest, more labour than after a good one—all previously existing commodities of the same class are affected, because they are, as it were, only individuals of the species, and their value at any given time is measured by the labour socially necessary, i.e. by the labour necessary for their production under the then existing social conditions.

As the value of the raw material may change, so, too, may that of the instruments of labour, of the machinery, etc., employed in the process; and consequently that portion of the value of the product transferred to it from them, may also change. If in consequence of a new invention, machinery of a particular kind can be produced by a diminished expenditure of labour, the old machinery becomes depreciated more or less, and consequently transfers so much less value to the product. But here again, the change in value originates outside the process in which the machine is acting as a means of production. Once engaged in this process, the machine cannot transfer more value than it possesses apart from the process.

Just as a change in the value of the means of production, even after they have commenced to take a part in the labour-process, does not alter their character as constant capital, so, too, a change in the proportion of constant to variable capital does not affect the respective functions of these two kinds of capital. The technical conditions of the labour-process may be revolutionised to such an extent, that where formerly ten men using ten implements of small value worked up a relatively small quantity of raw material, one man may now, with the aid of one expensive machine, work up one hundred times as much raw material. In the latter case we have an enormous increase in the constant capital, that is represented by the total value of the means of production used, and at the same time a great reduction in the variable capital, invested in labour-power. Such a revolution, however, alters only the quantitative relation between the constant and the variable capital, or the proportions in which the total capital is split up into its constant and variable constituents; it has not in the least degree affected the essential difference between the two.

CHAPTER 9

THE RATE OF SURPLUS-VALUE

Section 1. The Degree of Exploitation of Labour-Power

The surplus-value generated in the process of production by C, the capital advanced, or in other words, the self-expansion of the value of the capital C, presents itself for our consideration, in the first place, as a surplus, as the amount by which the value of the product exceeds the value of its consituent elements.

The capital C is made up of two components, one, the sum of money c laid out upon the means of production, and the other, the sum of money v expended upon the labour-power; c represents the portion that has become constant capital, and v the portion that has become variable capital. At first then, C = c + v: for example, if £500 is the capital advanced, its components may be such that the £500 = £410 const. + £90 var. When the process of production is finished, we get a commodity whose value = (c + v) + s, where s is the surplus-value; or taking our former figures, the value of this commodity may be (£410 const. + £90 var.) + £90 surpl. The original capital has now changed from C to C´, from £500 to £590. The difference is s or a surplus-value of £90. Since the value of the constituent elements of the product is equal to the value of the advanced capital, it is mere tautology to say, that the excess of the value of the product over the value of its constituent elements, is equal to the expansion of the capital advanced or to the surplus-value produced.

Nevertheless, we must examine this tautology a little more closely. The two things compared are, the value of the product and the value of its constituents consumed in the process of production. Now we have seen how that portion of the constant capital which consists of the instruments of labour, transfers to the production only a fraction of its value, while the remainder of that value continues to reside in those instruments. Since this remainder plays no part in the formation of value, we may at present leave it on one side. To introduce it into the calculation would make no difference. For instance, taking our former example, c = £410: suppose this sum to consist of £312 value of raw material, £44 value of auxiliary material, and £54 value of the machinery worn away in the process; and suppose that the total value of the machinery employed is £1,054. Out of this latter sum, then, we reckon as advanced for the purpose of turning out the product, the sum of £54 alone, which the machinery loses by wear and tear in the process; for this is all it parts with to the product. Now if we also reckon the remaining £1,000, which still continues in the machinery, as transferred to the product, we ought also to reckon it as part of the value advanced, and thus make it appear on both sides of our calculation. We should, in this way, get £1,500 on one side and £1,590 on the other. The difference of these two sums, or the surplus-value, would still be £90. Throughout this Book therefore, by constant capital advanced for the production of value, we always mean, unless the context is repugnant thereto, the value of the means of production actually consumed in the process, and that value alone.

This being so, let us return to the formula $C = c + v$, which we saw was transformed into $C' = (c + v) + s$, C becoming C'. We know that the value of the constant capital is transferred to, and merely reappears in the product. The new value actually created in the process, the value produced, or value-product, is therefore not the same as the value of the product; it is not, as it would at first sight appear $(c + v) + s$ or £410 const. + £90 var. + £90 surpl.; but $v + s$ or £90 var. + £90 surpl., not £590 but £180. If $c = 0$, or in other words, if there were branches of industry in which the capitalist could dispense with all means of production made by previous labour, whether they be raw material, auxiliary material, or instruments of labour, employing only labour-power and materials supplied by Nature, in that case, there would be no constant capital to transfer to the product. This component of the value of the product, i.e. the £410 in our example, would be eliminated, but the sum of £180, the amount of new value created, or the value produced, which contains £90 of surplus-value, would remain just as great as if c represented the highest value imaginable. We should have $C = (0 + v) = v$ or C' the expanded capital $= v + s$ and therefore $C' - C = s$ as before. On the other hand, if $s = 0$, or in other words, if the labour-power, whose value is advanced in the form of variable capital, were to produce only its equivalent, we should have $C = c + v$ or C' the value of the product $= (c + v) + 0$ or $C = C'$. The capital advanced would, in this case, not have expanded its value.

From what has gone before, we know that surplus-value is purely the result of a variation in the value of v, of that portion of the capital which is transformed into labour-power; consequently, $v + s = v + v'$ or v plus an increment of v. But the fact that it is v alone that varies, and the conditions of that variation, are obscured by the circumstance that in consequence of the increase in the variable component of the capital, there is also an increase in the sum total of the advanced capital. It was originally £500 and becomes £590. Therefore in order that our investigation may lead to accurate results, we must make abstraction from that portion of the value of the product, in which constant capital alone appears, and consequently must equate the constant capital to zero or make $c = 0$. This is merely an application of a mathematical rule, employed whenever we operate with constant and variable magnitudes, related to each other by the symbols of addition and subtraction only.

A further difficulty is caused by the original form of the variable capital. In our example, C′ = £410 const. + £90 var. + £90 surpl.; but £90 is a given and therefore a constant quantity; hence it appears absurd to treat it as variable. But in fact, the term £90 var. is here merely a symbol to show that this value undergoes a process. The portion of the capital invested in the purchase of labour-power is a definite quantity of materialised labour, a constant value like the value of the labour-power purchased. But in the process of production the place of the £90 is taken by the labour-power in action, dead labour is replaced by living labour, something stagnant by something flowing, a constant by a variable. The result is the reproduction of v plus an increment of v. From the point of view then of capitalist production, the whole process appears as the spontaneous variation of the originally constant value, which is transformed into labour-power. Both the process and its result, appear to be owing to this value. If, therefore, such expressions as '£90 variable capital', or 'so much self-expanding value', appear contradictory, this is only because they bring to the surface a contradiction immanent in capitalist production.

At first sight it appears a strange proceeding, to equate the constant capital to zero. Yet it is what we do every day. If, for example, we wish to calculate the amount of England's profits from the cotton industry, we first of all deduct the sums paid for cotton to the United States, India, Egypt and other countries; in other words, the value of the capital that merely re-appears in the value of the product, is put $= 0$.

Of course the ratio of surplus-value not only to that portion of the capital from which it immediately springs, and whose change of value it represents, but also to the sum total of the capital advanced is economically of very great importance. We shall, therefore, in the third book,* treat of this ratio exhaustively. In order to enable one portion of a capital to expand its value by being converted into labour-power, it is necessary that another portion be converted into means of production. In order that variable capital may perform its function, constant capital must be advanced in proper proportion, a proportion given by the special technical conditions of each labour-process. The circumstance, however, that retorts and other vessels, are necessary to a chemical process, does not compel the chemist to notice them in the result of his analysis. If we look at the means of production, in their relation to the creation of value, and to the variation in the quantity of value, apart from anything else, they appear simply as the material in which labour-power, the value-creator, incorporates itself. Neither the nature, nor the value of this material is of any importance. The only requisite is that there be a sufficient supply to absorb the labour expended in the process of production. That supply once given, the material may rise or fall in value, or even be, as land and the sea, without any value in itself; but this will have no influence on the creation of value or on the variation in the quantity of value.

In the first place then we equate the constant capital to zero. The capital advanced is consequently reduced from c + v to v, and instead of the value of the product (c + v) + s we have now the value produced (v + s). Given the new value produced = £180, which sum consequently represents the whole labour expended during the process, then subtracting from it £90 the value of the variable captial, we have remaining £90, the amount of the surplus-value. This sum of £90 or s expresses the absolute quantity of surplus-value produced. The relative quantity produced, or the increase per cent of the variable capital, is determined, it is plain, by the ratio of the surplus-value to the variable capital, or is expressed by s/v. In our example this ratio is ⁹⁰⁄₉₀, which gives an increase of 100%. This relative increase in the value of the variable capital, or the relative magnitude of the surplus-value, I call, 'The rate of surplus-value'.

We have seen that the labourer, during one portion of the labour-process, produces only the value of his labour-power, that is, the value of his means of subsistence. Now since his work forms part of a system, based on the social division of labour, he does not directly produce the actual necessaries which he himself consumes; he produces instead a particular commodity, yarn for example, whose value is equal to the value of those necessaries or of the money with which they can be bought. The portion of his day's labour devoted to this purpose, will be greater or less, in proportion to the value of the necessaries that he daily requires on an average, or, what amounts to the same thing, in proportion to the labour-time required on an average to produce them. If the value of those necessaries represent on an average the expenditure of six hours' labour, the workman must on an average work for six hours to produce that value. If instead of working for the capitalist, he worked independently on his own account, he would, other things being equal, still be obliged to labour for the same number of hours, in order to produce the value of his labour-power, and thereby to gain the means of subsistence necessary for his conservation or continued re-production. But as we have seen, during that portion of his day's labour in which he produces the value of his labour-power, say three shilings, he produces only an equivalent for the value of his labour-power already advanced by the capitalist; the new value created only replaces the variable capital advanced. It is owing to this fact, that the pro-duction of the new value of three shillings takes the semblance of a mere reproduction. That portion of the working-day, then, during which this reproduction takes place, I call '*necessary*' labour-time, and the labour expended during that time I cell '*necessary*' labour. Neces-sary, as regards the labourer, because independent of the particular social form of his labour; necessary, as regards capital, and the world of capitalists, because on the continued existence of the labourer depends their existence also.

During the second period of the labour-process, that in which his labour is no longer necessary labour, the workman, it is true, labours, expends labour-power; but, his labour, being no longer necessary labour, he creates no value for himself. He creates surplus-value which, for the capitalists, has all the charms of a creation out of nothing. This portion of the working-day, I name surplus labour-time, and to the labour expended during that time, I give the name of surplus-labour. It is every bit as important, for a correct understanding of surplus-value, to conceive it as a mere congelation of surplus labour-time, as nothing but materialised surplus-labour, as it is, for a proper comprehension of value, to conceive it as a mere congelation of so many hours of labour, as nothing but materialised labour. The essential difference between the various economic forms of society, between, for instance, a society based on slave-labour, and one based on wage-labour, lies only in the mode in which this surplus-labour is in each case extracted from the actual producer, the labourer.

Since, on the one hand, the values of the variable capital and of the labour-power purchased by that capital are equal, and the value of this labour-power determines the necessary portion of the working-day; and since, on the other hand, the surplus-value is determined by the surplus portion of the working-day, it follows that surplus-value bears the same ratio to variable capital, that surplus-labour does to necessary labour, or in other words, the rate of surplus-value $s/v = \text{surplus-labour/necessary labour}$. Both ratios, s/v and surplus-labour/necessary labour, express the same thing in different ways; in the one case by reference to materialised, incorporated labour, in the other by reference to living, fluent labour.

The rate of surplus-value is therefore an exact expression for the degree of exploitation of labour-power by capital, or of the labourer by the capitalist.

CHAPTER 10

THE WORKING-DAY

Section 1. The Limits of the Working-Day

We started with the supposition that labour-power is bought and sold at its value. Its value, like that of all other commodities, is determined by the working-time necessary to its production. If the production of the average daily means of subsistence of the labourer takes up 6 hours, he must work, on the average, 6 hours every day, to produce his daily labour-power, or to reproduce the value received as the result of its sale. The necessary part of his working-day amounts to 6 hours, and is, therefore, *caeteris paribus*, a given quantity. But with this, the extent of the working-day itself is not yet given.

Let us assume that the line A B represents the length of the necessary working-time, say 6 hours. If the labour be prolonged 1, 3, or 6 hours beyond A B, we have 3 other lines:

Working-day I.	Working-day II.	Working-day III.
A—B–C.	A—B–C.	A—B—C.

representing 3 different working-days of 7, 9, and 12 hours. The extension B C of the line A B represents the length of the surplus-labour. As the working-day is A B + B C or A C, it varies with the variable quantity B C. Since A B is constant, the ratio of B C to A B can always be calculated. In working-day I, it is $\frac{1}{6}$, in working-day II, $\frac{3}{6}$, in working-day III, $\frac{6}{6}$ of A B. Since, further, the ratio surplus working-time,/necessary working-time, determines the rate of the surplus-value, the latter is given by the ratio of B C to A B. It amounts in the 3 different working-days respectively to $16\frac{2}{3}$, 50 and 100 per cent. On the other hand, the rate of surplus-value alone would not give us the extent of the working-day. If this rate, e.g. were 100 per cent., the working-day might be of 8, 10, 12, or more hours. It would indicate that the 2 constituent parts of the working-day, necessary-labour and surplus-labour time, were equal in extent, but not how long each of these two constituent parts was.

The working-day is thus not a constant, but a variable quantity. One of its parts, certainly, is determined by the working-time required for the reproduction of the labour-power of the labourer himself. But its total amount varies with the duration of the surplus-labour. The working-day is, therefore, determinable, but is, *per se*, indeterminate.

Although the working-day is not a fixed, but a fluent quantity, it can, on the other hand, only vary within certain limits. The minimum limit is, however, not determinable; of course, if we make the extension line B C or the surplus-labour = 0, we have a minimum limit, i.e. the part of the day which the labourer must necessarily work for his own maintenance. On the basis of capitalist production, however, this necessary labour can form a part only of the working-day; the working-day itself can never be reduced to this minimum. On the other hand, the working-day has a maximum limit. It cannot be prolonged beyond a certain point. This maximum limit is conditioned by two things. First, by the physical bounds of labour-power. Within the 24 hours of the natural day a man can expend only a definite quantity of his vital force. A horse, in like manner, can only work from day to day, 8 hours. During part of the day this force must rest, sleep; during another part the man has to satisfy other physical needs, to feed, wash, and clothe himself. Besides these purely physical limitations, the extension of the working-day encounters moral ones. The labourer needs time for satisfying his intellectual and social wants, the extent and number of which are conditioned by the general state of social advancement. The variation of the working-day fluctuates, therefore, within physical and social bounds. But both these limiting conditions are of a very elastic nature, and allow the greatest latitude. So we find working-days of 8, 10, 12, 14, 16, 18 hours, i.e. of the most different lengths.

The capitalist has bought the labour-power at its day-rate. To him its use-value belongs during one working-day. He has thus acquired the right to make the labourer work for him during one day. But, what is a working-day?

At all events, less than a natural day. By how much? The capitalist has his own views of this *ultima Thule*,* the necessary limit of the working-day. As capitalist, he is only capital personified. His soul is the soul of capital. But capital has one single life impulse, the tendency to create value and surplus-value, to make its constant factor, the means of production, absorb the greatest possible amount of surplus-labour.

Capital is dead labour, that, vampire-like, only lives by sucking living labour, and lives the more, the more labour it sucks. The time during which the labourer works, is the time during which the capitalist consumes the labour-power he has purchased of him.

If the labourer consumes his disposable time for himself, he robs the capitalist.

The capitalist then takes his stand on the law of the exchange of commodities. He, like all other buyers, seeks to get the greatest possible benefit out of the use-value of his commodity. Suddenly the voice of the labourer, which had been stifled in the storm and stress of the process of production, rises:

The commodity that I have sold to you differs from the crowd of other commodities, in that its use creates value, and a value greater than its own. That is why you bought it. That which on your side appears a spontaneous expansion of capital, is on mine extra expenditure of labour-power. You and I know on the market only one law, that of the exchange of commodities. And the consumption of the commodity belongs not to the seller who parts with it, but to the buyer, who acquires it. To you, therefore, belongs the use of my daily labour-power. But by means of the price that you pay for it each day, I must be able to reproduce it daily, and to sell it again. Apart from natural exhaustion through age, etc., I must be able on the morrow to work with the same normal amount of force, health and freshness as today. You preach to me constantly the gospel of 'saving' and 'abstinence'. Good! I will, like a sensible saving owner, husband my sole wealth, labour-power, and abstain from all foolish waste of it. I will each day spend, set in motion, put into action only as much of it as is compatible with its normal duration, and healthy development. By an unlimited extension of the working-day, you may in one day use up a quantity of labour-power greater than I can restore in three. What you gain in labour I lose in substance. The use of my labour-power and the spoliation of it are quite different things. If the average time that (doing a reasonable amount of work) an average labourer can live, is 30 years, the value of my labour-power, which you pay me from day to day is $1/(365 \times 30)$ or $1/10950$ of its total value. But if you consume it in 10 years, you pay me daily $1/10950$ instead of $1/3650$ of its total value, i.e. only $\frac{1}{3}$ of its daily value, and you rob me, therefore, every day of $\frac{2}{3}$ of the value of my commodity. You pay me for one day's labour-power, whilst you use that of 3 days. That is against our contract and the law of exchanges. I demand, therefore, a working-day of normal length, and I demand it without any appeal to your heart, for in money matters sentiment is out of place. You may be a model citizen, perhaps a member of the Society for the Prevention of Cruelty to Animals, and in the odour of sanctity to boot; but the thing that you represent face to face with me has no heart in its breast. That which seems to throb there is my own heart-beating. I demand the normal working-day because I, like every other seller, demand the value of my commodity.

We see then, that, apart from extremely elastic bounds, the nature of the exchange of commodities itself imposes no limit to the working-day, no limit to surplus-labour. The capitalist maintains his rights as a purchaser when he tries to make the working-day as long as possible, and to make, whenever possible, two working-days out of one. On the other hand, the peculiar nature of the commodity sold implies a limit to its consumption by the purchaser, and the labourer maintains his right as seller when he wishes to reduce the working-day to one of definite normal duration. There is here, therefore, an antinomy, right against right, both equally bearing the seal of the law of exchanges. Between equal rights force decides. Hence is it that in the history of capitalist production, the determination of what is a working-day, presents itself as the result of a struggle, a struggle between collective capital, i.e. the class of capitalists, and collective labour, i.e. the working-class.

Section 2. The Greed for Surplus-Labour. Manufacturer and Boyard

Capital has not invented surplus-labour. Wherever a part of society possesses the monopoly of the means of production, the labourer, free or not free, must add to the working-time necessary for his own maintenance an extra working-time in order to produce the means of subsistence for the owners of the means of production, whether this proprietor be the Athenian καλὸς κἀγαθός,* Etruscan theocrat, civis Romanus, Norman baron, American slave-owner, Wallachian Boyard, modern landlord or capitalist. It is, however, clear that in any given economic formation of society, where not the exchange-value but the use-value of the product predominates, surplus-labour will be limited by a given set of wants which may be greater or less, and that here no boundless thirst for surplus-labour arises from the nature of the production itself. Hence in antiquity over-work becomes horrible only when the object is to obtain exchange-value in its specific independent money-form; in the production of gold and silver. Compulsory working to death is here the recognised form of over-work. Only read Diodorus Siculus. Still these are exceptions in antiquity. But as soon as people, whose production still moves within the lower forms of slave-labour, corvée-labour, etc., are drawn into the whirlpool of an international market dominated by the capitalistic mode of production, the sale of their products for export becoming their principal interest, the civilised horrors of over-work are grafted on the barbaric horrors of slavery, serfdom, etc. Hence the negro labour in the Southern States of the American Union preserved something of a patriarchal character, so long as production was chiefly directed to immediate local consumption. But in proportion, as the export of cotton became of vital interest to these states, the over-working of the negro and sometimes the using up of his life in 7 years of labour became a factor in a calculated and calculating system. It was no longer a question of obtaining from him a certain quantity of useful products. It was now a question of production of surplus-labour itself.

These acts curb the passion of capital for a limitless draining of labour-power, by forcibly limiting the working-day by state regulations, made by a state that is ruled by capitalist and landlord. Apart from the working-class movement that daily grew more threatening, the limiting of factory labour was dictated by the same necessity which spread guano over the English fields. The same blind eagerness for plunder that in the one case exhausted the soil, had, in the other, torn up by the roots the living force of the nation. Periodical epidemics speak on this point as clearly as the diminishing military standard in Germany and France.

The Factory Act of 1850 now in force (1867) allows for the average working-day 10 hours, i.e. for the first 5 days 12 hours from 6 a. m. to 6 p. m., including ½ an hour for breakfast, and an hour for dinner, and thus leaving 10½ working-hours, and 8 hours for Saturday, from 6 a. m. to 2 p. m. of which ½ an hour is subtracted for breakfast. 60 working-hours are left, 10½ for each of the first 5 days, 7½ for the last. Certain guardians of these laws are appointed Factory Inspectors directly under the Home Secretary, whose reports are published half-yearly, by order of Parliament. They give regular and official statistics of the capitalistic greed for surplus-labour.

Let us listen, for a moment, to the Factory Inspector. 'The fraudulent mill-owner begins work a quarter of an hour (sometimes more, sometimes less) before 6 a. m., and leaves off a quarter of an hour (sometimes more, sometimes less) after 6 p. m. He takes 5 minutes from the beginning and from the end of the half hour nominally allowed for breakfast, and 10 minutes at the beginning and end of the hour nominally allowed for dinner. He works for a quarter of an hour (sometimes more, sometimes less) after 2 p. m. on Saturday. Thus his gain is—

Before 6 a. m.	15 minutes.
After 6 p. m.	15 "
At breakfast time	10 "
At dinner time	20 "
	60 "

	Five days	300 minutes.
On Saturday before 6 a. m.	15	"
At breakfast time	10	"
After 2 p. m.	15	"
		40 minutes.
Total weekly		340 minutes.

Or 5 hours and 40 minutes weekly, which 'multiplied by 50 working weeks in the year (allowing two for holidays and occasional stoppages) is equal to 27 working-days.'

'Five minutes a day's increased work, multiplied by weeks, are equal to two and a half days of produce in the year.'

'An additional hour a day gained by small instalments before 6 a. m., after 6 p. m., and at the beginning and end of the times nominally fixed for meals, is nearly equivalent to working 13 months in the year.'

'The profit to be gained by it (over-working in violation of the Act) appears to be, to many, a greater temptation than they can resist; they calculate upon the chance of not being found out; and when they see the small amount of penalty and costs, which those who have been convicted have had to pay, they find that if they should be detected there will still be a considerable balance of gain. . . . . . In cases where the additional time is gained by a multiplication of small thefts in the course of the day, there are insuperable difficulties to the inspectors making out a case.'

These 'small thefts' of capital from the labourer's meal and recreation time, the factory inspectors also designate as 'petty pilferings of minutes', 'snatching a few minutes', or, as the labourers technically called them, 'nibbling and cribbling at meal-times'.

It is evident that in this atmosphere the formation of surplus-value by surplus-labour, is no secret. 'If you allow me', said a highly respectable master to me, 'to work only ten minutes in the day over-time, you put one thousand a year in my pocket.' 'Moments are the elements of profit.'

Nothing is from this point of view more characteristic than the designation of the workers who work full time as 'full-timers', and the children under 13 who are only allowed to work 6 hours as 'half-timers'. The worker is here nothing more than personified labour-time. All individual distinctions are merged in those of 'full-timers' and 'half-timers'.

Section 3. Branches of English Industry without Legal Limits to Exploitation

We have hitherto considered the tendency to the extension of the working-day, the were-wolf's hunger for surplus-labour in a department where the monstrous exactions, not surpassed, says an English bourgeois economist, by the cruelties of the Spaniards to the American red-skins, caused capital at last to be bound by the chains of legal regulations. Now, let us cast a glance at certain branches of production in which the exploitation of labour is either free from fetters to this day, or was so yesterday.

Mr Broughton Charlton, county magistrate, declared, as chairman of a meeting held at the Assembly Rooms, Nottingham, on the 14th January, 1860, 'that there was an amount of privation and suffering among that portion of the population connected with the lace trade, unknown in other parts of the kingdom, indeed, in the civilised world. ...Children of nine or ten years are dragged from their squalid beds at two, three, or four o'clock in the morning and compelled to work for a bare subsistence until ten, eleven, or twelve at night, their limbs wearing away, their frames dwindling, their faces whitening, and their humanity absolutely sinking into a stone-like torpor, utterly horrible to contemplate. . . . We are not surprised that Mr Mallett, or any other manufacturer, should stand forward and protest against discussion. . . . The system, as the Rev. Montagu Valpy describes it, is one of unmitigated slavery, socially, physically, morally, and spiritually. . . . What can be thought of a town which holds a public meeting to petition that the period of labour for men shall be diminished to eighteen hours a day? . . . We declaim against the Virginian and Carolinian cotton-planters. Is their black-market, their lash, and their barter of human flesh more detestable than this slow sacrifice of humanity which takes place in order that veils and collars may be fabricated for the benefit of capitalists?'

The potteries of Staffordshire have, during the last 22 years, been the subject of three parliamentary inquiries. The result is embodied in Mr Scriven's Report of 1841 to the 'Children's Employment Commissioners', in the report of Dr Greenhow of 1860 published by order of the medical officer of the Privy Council (Public Health, 3rd Report, 112–113), lastly, in the report of Mr Longe of 1862 in the 'First Report of the Children's Employment Commission, of the 13th June, 1863'. For my purpose it is enough to take, from the reports of 1860 and 1863, some depositions of the exploited children themselves. From the children we may form an opinion as to the adults, especially the girls and women, and that in a branch of industry by the side of which cotton-spinning appears an agreeable and healthful occupation.

William Wood, 9 years old, was 7 years and 10 months when he began to work. He 'ran moulds' (carried ready-moulded articles into the drying-room, afterwards bringing back the empty mould) from the beginning. He came to work every day in the week at 6 a. m., and left off about 9 p. m. 'I work till 9 o'clock at night six days in the week. I have done so seven or eight weeks.' Fifteen hours of labour for a child 7 years old! J. Murray, 12 years of age, says: 'I turn jigger, and run moulds. I come at 6. Sometimes I come at 4. I worked all night last night, till 6 o'clock this morning. I have not been in bed since the night before last. There were eight or nine other boys working last night. All but one have come this morning. I get 3 shillings and sixpence. I do not get any more for working at night. I worked two nights last week.' Fernyhough, a boy of ten: 'I have not always an hour (for dinner). I have only half an hour sometimes; on Thursday, Friday, and Saturday.'

Dr Greenhow states that the average duration of life in the pottery districts of Stoke-on-Trent, and Wolstanton is extraordinarily short. Although in the district of Stoke, only 36.6% and in Wolstanton only 30.4% of the adult male population above 20 are employed in the potteries, among the men of that age in the first district more than half, in the second, nearly ⅖ of the whole deaths are the result of pulmonary diseases among the potters. Dr Boothroyd, a medical practitioner at Hanley, says: 'Each successive generation of potters is more dwarfed and less robust than the preceding one.' In like manner another doctor, Mr M'Bean: 'Since he began to practise among the potters 25 years ago, he had observed a marked degeneration especially shown in diminution of stature and breadth.' These statements are taken from the report of Dr Greenhow in 1860.

From the report of the Commissioners in 1863, the following: Dr J. T. Arledge, senior physician of the North Staffordshire Infirmary, says: 'The potters as a class, both men and women, represent a degenerated population, both physically and morally. They are, as a rule, stunted in growth, ill-shaped, and frequently ill-formed in the chest; they become prematurely old, and are certainly short-lived; they are phlegmatic and bloodless, and exhibit their debility of constitution by obstinate attacks of dyspepsia, and disorders of the liver and kidneys, and by rheumatism. But of all diseases they are especially prone to chest-disease, to pneumonia, phthisis, bronchitis, and asthma. One form would appear peculiar to them, and is known as potter's asthma, or potter's consumption. Scrofula attacking the glands, or bones, or other parts of the body, is a disease of two-thirds or more of the potters. . . . That the 'degenerescence' of the population of this district is not even greater than it is, is due to the constant recruiting from the adjacent country, and intermarriages with more healthy races.'

Mr Charles Parsons, late house surgeon of the same institution, writes in a letter to Commissioner Longe, amongst other things: 'I can only speak from personal observation and not from statistical data, but I do not hesitate to assert that my indignation has been aroused again and again at the sight of poor children whose health has been sacrificed to gratify the avarice of either parents or employers.' He enumerates the causes of the diseases of the potters, and sums them up in the phrase, 'long hours'. The report of the Commission trusts that 'a manufacture which has assumed so prominent a place in the whole world, will not long be subject to the remark that its great success is accompanied with the physical deterioration, widespread bodily suffering, and early death of the workpeople . . . by whose labour and skill such great results have been achieved.' And all that holds of the potteries in England is true of those in Scotland.

The manufacture of lucifer matches dates from 1833, from the discovery of the method of applying phosphorus to the match itself. Since 1845 this manufacture has rapidly developed in England, and has extended especially amongst the thickly populated parts of London as well as in Manchester, Birmingham, Liverpool, Bristol, Norwich, Newcastle and Glasgow. With it has spread the form of lockjaw, which a Vienna physician in 1845 discovered to be a disease peculiar to lucifer-matchmakers. Half the workers are children under thirteen, and young persons under eighteen. The manufacture is on account of its unhealthiness and unpleasantness in such bad odour that only the most miserable part of the labouring class, half-starved widows and so forth, deliver up their children to it, 'the ragged, half-starved, untaught children'.

Of the witnesses that Commissioner White examined (1863), 270 were under 18, 50 under 10, 10 only 8, and 5 only 6 years old. A range of the working-day from 12 to 14 or 15 hours, night-labour, irregular meal-times, meals for the most part taken in the very workrooms that are pestilent with phosphorus. Dante would have found the worst horrors of his Inferno surpassed in this manufacture.

In the manufacture of paper-hangings the coarser sorts are printed by machine; the finer by hand (block-printing). The most active business months are from the beginning of October to the end of April. During this time the work goes on fast and furious without intermission from 6 a. m. to 10 p. m. or further into the night.

J. Leach deposes: 'Last winter six out of nineteen girls were away from ill-health at one time from over-work. I have to bawl at them to keep them awake.' W. Duffy: 'I have seen when the children could none of them keep their eyes open for the work; indeed, none of us could.' J. Lightbourne: 'Am 13 . . . We worked last winter till 9 (evening), and the winter before till 10. I used to cry with sore feet every night last winter.' G. Apsden: 'That boy of mine . . . when he was 7 years old I used to carry him on my back to and fro through the snow, and he used to have 16 hours a day . . . I have often knelt down to feed him as he stood by the machine, for he could not leave it or stop.' Smith, the managing partner of a Manchester factory: 'We (he means his "hands" who work for "us") work on, with no stoppage for meals, so that day's work of 10½ hours is finished by 4.30 p. m., and all after that is overtime.' (Does this Mr Smith take no meals himself during 10½ hours?) 'We (this same Smith) seldom leave off working before 6 p. m. (he means leave off the consumption of "our" labour-power machines), so that we (iterum Crispinus) are really working over-time the whole year round. . . . For all these, children and adults alike (152 children and young persons and 140 adults), the average work for the last 18 months has been at the very least 7 days, 5 hours, or 78½ hours a week. For the six weeks ending May 2nd this year (1862), the average was higher—8 days or 84 hours a week.' Still this same Mr Smith, who is so extremely devoted to the *pluralis majestatis*, adds with a smile, 'Machine-work is not great.' So the employers in the block-printing say: 'Hand labour is more healthy than machine-work.' On the whole, manufacturers declare with indignation against the proposal 'to stop the machines at least during meal-times'. A clause, says Mr Otley, manager of a wall-paper factory in the Borough, 'which allowed work between, say 6 a. m. and 9 p. m. . . . would suit us (!) very well, but the factory hours, 6 a. m. to 6 p. m., are not suitable. Our machine is always stopped for dinner. (What generosity!) There is no waste of paper and colour to speak of. But,' he adds sympathetically, 'I can understand the loss of time not being liked.' The report of the Commission opines with naïveté that the fear of some 'leading firms' of losing time, i.e. the time for appropriating the labour of others, and thence losing profit is not a sufficient reason for allowing children under 13, and young persons under 18, working 12 to 16 hours per day, to lose their dinner, nor for giving it to them as coal and water are supplied to the steam-engine, soap to wool, oil to the wheel—as merely auxiliary material to the instruments of labour, during the process of production itself.

From the motley crowd of labourers of all callings, ages, sexes, that press on us more busily than the souls of the slain on Ulysses, on whom—without referring to the Blue books under their arms—we see at a glance the mark of over-work, let us take two more figures whose striking contrast proves that before capital all men are alike—a milliner and a blacksmith.

In the last week of June, 1863, all the London daily papers published a paragraph with the 'sensational' heading, 'Death from simple over-work'. It dealt with the death of the milliner, Mary Anne Walkley, 20 years of age, employed in a highly-respectable dressmaking establishment, exploited by a lady with the pleasant name of Elise. The old, often-told story, was once more recounted. This girl worked, on an average, 16½ hours, during the season often 30 hours, without a break, whilst her failing labour-power was revived by occasional supplies of sherry, port, or coffee. It was just now the height of the season. It was necessary to conjure up in the twinkling of an eye the gorgeous dresses for the noble ladies bidden to the ball in honour of the newly-imported Princess of Wales. Mary Anne Walkley had worked without intermission for 26½ hours, with 60 other girls, 30 in one room, that only afforded ⅓ of the cubic feet of air required for them. At night, they slept in pairs in one of the stifling holes into which the bedroom was divided by partitions of board. And this was one of the best millinery establishments in London. Mary Anne Walkley fell ill on the Friday, died on Sunday, without, to the astonishment of Madame Elise, having previously completed the work in hand. The doctor, Mr Keys, called too late to the death-bed, duly bore witness before the coroner's jury that 'Mary Anne Walkley had died from long hours of work in an over-crowded work-room, and a too small and badly-ventilated bedroom.' In order to give the doctor a lesson in good manners, the coroner's jury thereupon brought in a verdict that 'the deceased had died of apoplexy, but there was reason to fear that her death had been accelerated by over-work in an over-crowded work-room, etc.' 'Our white slaves,' cried the *Morning Star*, the organ of the Free-traders, Cobden and Bright, 'our white slaves, who are toiled into the grave, for the most part silently pine and die.'

It is not in dressmakers' rooms that working to death is the order of the day, but in a thousand other places; in every place I had almost said, where 'a thriving business' has to be done. . . . We will take the blacksmith as a type. If the poets were true, there is no man so hearty, so merry, as the blacksmith; he rises early and strikes his sparks before the sun; he eats and drinks and sleeps as no other man. Working in moderation, he is, in fact, in one of the best of human positions, physically speaking. But we follow him into the city or town, and we see the stress of work on that strong man, and what then is his position in the death-rate of his country. In Marylebone, blacksmiths die at the rate of 31 per thousand per annum, or 11 above the mean of the male adults of the country in its entirety. The occupation, instinctive almost as a portion of human art, unobjectionable as a branch of human industry, is made by mere excess of work, the destroyer of the man. He can strike so many blows per day, walk so many steps, breathe so many breaths, produce so much work, and live an average, say of fifty years; he is made to strike so many more blows, to walk so many more steps, to breathe so many more breaths per day, and to increase altogether a fourth of his life. He meets the effort; the result is, that producing for a limited time a fourth more work, he dies at 37 for 50.

Section 4. Day and Night Work. The Relay System

Constant capital, the means of production, considered from the stand-point of the creation of surplus-value, only exist to absorb labour, and with every drop of labour a proportional quantity of surplus-labour. While they fail to do this, their mere existence causes a relative loss to the capitalist, for they represent during the time they lie fallow, a useless advance of capital. And this loss becomes positive and absolute as soon as the intermission of their employment necessitates additional outlay at the recommencement of work. The prolongation of the work-ing-day beyond the limits of the natural day, into the night, only acts as a palliative. It quenches only in a slight degree the vampire thirst for the living blood of labour. To appropriate labour during all the 24 hours of the day is, therefore, the inherent tendency of capitalist pro-duction. But as it is physically impossible to exploit the same individual labour-power constantly during the night as well as the day, to over-come this physical hindrance, an alternation becomes necessary be-tween the workpeople whose powers are exhausted by day, and those who are used up by night. This alternation may be effected in various ways; e.g. it may be so arranged that part of the workers are one week employed on day-work, the next week on night-work. It is well known that this relay system, this alternation of two sets of workers, held full sway in the full-blooded youth-time of the English cotton manufac-ture, and that at the present time it still flourishes, among others, in the cotton spinning of the Moscow district. This 24 hours' process of production exists today as a system in many of the branches of industry of Great Britain that are still 'free,' in the blast-furnaces, forges, plate-rolling mills, and other metallurgical establishments in England, Wales, and Scotland. The working-time here includes, besides the 24 hours of the 6 working-days, a great part also of the 24 hours of Sunday. The workers consist of men and women, adults and children of both sexes. The ages of the children and young persons run through all intermediate grades, from 8 (in some cases from 6) to 18.

Mr J. Ellis, one of the firm of Messrs. John Brown & Co., steel and iron works, employing about 3,000 men and boys, part of whose operations, namely iron and heavier steel work, goes on night and day by relays, states 'that in the heavier steel work one or two boys are employed to a score or two men.' Their concern employs upwards of 500 boys under 18, of whom about ⅓ or 170 are under the age of 13. With reference to the proposed alteration of the law, Mr Ellis says: 'I do not think it would be very objectionable to require that no person under the age of 18 should work more than 12 hours in the 24. But we do not think that any line could be drawn over the age of 12, at which boys could be dispensed with for night-work. But we would sooner be prevented from employing boys under the age of 13, or even so high as 14, at all, than not be allowed to employ boys that we do have at night. Those boys who work in the day sets must take their turn in the night sets also, because the men could not work in the night sets only; it would ruin their health. . . . We think, however, that night-work in alternate weeks is no harm. (Messrs. Naylor & Vickers, on the other hand, in conformity with the interest of their business, considered that periodically changed night-labour might possibly do more harm than continual night-labour.) We find the men who do it, as well as the others who do other work only by day. . . . Our objections to not allowing boys under 18 to work at night, would be on account of the increase of expense, but this is the only reason. (What cynical naïveté!) We think that the increase would be more than the trade, with due regard to its being successfully carried out, could fairly bear. (What mealy-mouthed phraseology!) Labour is scarce here, and might fall short if there were such a regulation.' (i.e. Ellis Brown & Co. might fall into the fatal perplexity of being obliged to pay labour-power its full value.)

The 'Cyclops Steel and Iron Works', of Messrs. Cammell & Co., are conducted on the same large scale as those of the above-mentioned John Brown & Co. The managing director had handed in his evidence to the Government Commissioner, Mr White, in writing. Later he found it convenient to suppress the MS. when it had been returned to him for revision. Mr White, however, has a good memory. He remembered quite clearly that for the Messrs. Cyclops the forbidding of the night-labour of children and young persons 'would be impossible, it would be tantamount to stopping their works', and yet their business employs little more than 6% of boys under 18, and less than 1% under 13.

On the same subject Mr E. F. Sanderson, of the firm of Sanderson, Bros., & Co., steel rolling-mills and forges, Attercliffe, says: 'Great difficulty would be caused by preventing boys under 18 from working at night. The chief would be the increase of cost from employing men instead of boys. I cannot say what this would be, but probably it would not be enough to enable the manufacturers to raise the price of steel, and consequently it would fall on them, as of course the men (what queer-headed folk!) would refuse to pay it.' Mr Sanderson does not know how much he pays the children, but 'perhaps the younger boys get from 4s. to 5s. a week. . . . The boys' work is of a kind for which the strength of the boys is generally ('generally', of course not always) quite sufficient, and consequently there would be no gain in the greater strength of the men to counterbalance the loss, or it would be only in the few cases in which the metal is heavy. The men would not like so well not to have boys under them, as men would be less obedient. Besides, boys must begin young to learn the trade. Leaving day-work alone open to boys would not answer this purpose.' And why not? Why could not boys learn their handicraft in the day-time? Your reason? 'Owing to the men working days and nights in alternate weeks, the men would be separated half the time from their boys, and would lose half the profit which they make from them. The training which they give to an apprentice is considered as part of the return for the boys' labour, and thus enables the man to get it at a cheaper rate. Each man would want half of this profit.' In other words, Messrs. Sanderson would have to pay part of the wages of the adult men out of their own pockets instead of by the night-work of the boys. Messrs. Sanderson's profit would thus fall to some extent, and this is the good Sandersonian reason why boys cannot learn their handicraft in the day. In addition to this, it would throw night-labour on those who worked instead of the boys, which they would not be able to stand. The difficulties in fact would be so great that they would very likely lead to the giving up of night-work altogether, and 'as far as the work itself is concerned,' says E. F. Sanderson, 'this would suit as well, but—' But Messrs. Sanderson have something else to make besides steel. Steel-making is simply a pretext for surplus-value making. The smelting furnaces, rolling-mills, etc., the buildings, machinery, iron, coal, etc., have something more to do than transform themselves into steel. They are there to absorb surplus-labour, and naturally absorb more in 24 hours than in 12. In fact they give, by grace of God and law, the Sandersons a cheque on the working-time of a certain number of hands for all the 24 hours of the day, and they lose their character as capital, are therefore a pure loss for the Sandersons, as soon as their function of absorbing labour is interrupted. 'But then there would be the loss from so much expensive machinery, lying idle half the time, and to get through the amount of work which we are able to do on the present system, we should have to double our premises and plant, which would double the outlay.' But why should these Sandersons pretend to a privilege not enjoyed by the other capitalists who only work during the day, and whose buildings, machinery, raw material, therefore lie 'idle' during the night? E. F. Sanderson answers in the name of all the Sandersons: 'It is true that there is this loss from machinery lying idle in those manufactories in which work only goes on by day. But the use of furnaces would involve a further loss in our case. If they were kept up there would be a waste of fuel (instead of, as now, a waste of the living substance of the workers), and if they were not, there would be loss of time in laying the fires and getting the heat up (whilst the loss of sleeping time, even to children of 8 is a gain of working-time for the Sanderson tribe), and the furnaces themselves would suffer from the changes of temperature.' (Whilst those same furnaces suffer nothing from the day and night change of labour.)

Section 5. The Struggle for a Normal Working-Day. Compulsory Laws for the Extension of the Working-Day from the Middle of the 14th to the End of the 17th Century

'What is a working-day? What is the length of time during which capital may consume the labour-power whose daily value it buys? How far may the working-day be extended beyond the working-time necessary for the reproduction of labour-power itself?' It has been seen that to these questions capital replies: the working-day contains the full 24 hours, with the deduction of the few hours of repose without which labour-power absolutely refuses its services again. Hence it is self-evident that the labourer is nothing else, his whole life through, than labour-power, that therefore all his disposable time is by nature and law labour-time, to be devoted to the self-expansion of capital. Time for education, for intellectual development, for the fulfilling of social functions and for social intercourse, for the free-play of his bodily and mental activity, even the rest time of Sunday (and that in a country of Sabbatarians!)[8]—moonshine! But in its blind unrestrainable passion, its were-wolf hunger for surplus-labour, capital oversteps not only the moral, but even the merely physical maximum bounds of the working-day. It usurps the time for growth, development, and healthy mainten-ance of the body. It steals the time required for the consumption of fresh air and sunlight. It higgles over a meal-time, incorporating it where possible with the process of production itself, so that food is given to the labourer as to a mere means of production, as coal is supplied to the boiler, grease and oil to the machinery. It reduces the sound sleep needed for the restoration, reparation, refreshment of the bodily powers to just so many hours of torpor as the revival of an organism, absolutely exhausted, renders essential. It is not the normal maintenance of the labour-power which is to determine the limits of the working-day; it is the greatest possible daily expenditure of labour-power, no matter how diseased, compulsory, and painful it may be, which is to determine the limits of the labourer's period of repose. Capital cares nothing for the length of life of labour-power. All that concerns it is simply and solely the maximum of labour-power, that can be rendered fluent in a working-day. It attains this end by shortening the extent of the labourer's life, as a greedy farmer snatches increased produce from the soil by robbing it of its fertility.

The capitalistic mode of production (essentially the production of surplus-value, the absorption of surplus-labour), produces thus, with the extension of the working-day, not only the deterioration of human labour-power by robbing it of its normal, moral and physical, con-ditions of development and function. It produces also the prema-ture exhaustion and death of this labour-power itself. It extends the labourer's time of production during a given period by shortening his actual lifetime.

But the value of the labour-power includes the value of the com-modities necessary for the reproduction of the worker, or for the keep-ing up of the working-class. If then the unnatural extension of the working-day, that capital necessarily strives after in its unmeasured passion for self-expansion, shortens the length of life of the individual labourer, and therefore the duration of his labour-power, the forces used up have to be replaced at a more rapid rate and the sum of the expenses for the reproduction of labour-power will be greater; just as in a machine the part of its value to be reproduced every day is greater the more rapidly the machine is worn out. It would seem therefore that the interest of capital itself points in the direction of a normal working-day.

The slave-owner buys his labourer as he buys his horse. If he loses his slave, he loses capital that can only be restored by new outlay in the slave-mart. But 'the rice-grounds of Georgia, or the swamps of the Mississippi may be fatally injurious to the human constitution; but the waste of human life which the cultivation of these districts necessitates, is not so great that it cannot be repaired from the teeming preserves of Virginia and Kentucky. Considerations of economy, moreover, which, under a natural system, afford some security for humane treatment by identifying the master's interest with the slave's preservation, when once trading in slaves is practised, become reasons for racking to the uttermost the toil of the slave; for, when his place can at once be supplied from foreign preserves, the duration of his life becomes a matter of less moment than its productiveness while it lasts. It is accordingly a maxim of slave management, in slave-importing countries, that the most effective economy is that which takes out of the human chattel in the shortest space of time the utmost amount of exertion it is capable of putting forth. It is in tropical culture, where annual profits often equal the whole capital of plantations, that negro life is most recklessly sacrificed. It is the agriculture of the West Indies, which has been for centuries prolific of fabulous wealth, that has engulfed millions of the African race. It is in Cuba, at this day, whose revenues are reckoned by millions, and whose planters are princes, that we see in the servile class, the coarsest fare, the most exhausting and unremitting toil, and even the absolute destruction of a portion of its numbers every year.'

*Mutato nomine de te fabula narratur.** For slave-trade read labour-market, for Kentucky and Virginia, Ireland and the agricultural districts of England, Scotland, and Wales, for Africa, Germany. We heard how over-work thinned the ranks of the bakers in London. Nevertheless, the London labour-market is always over-stocked with German and other candidates for death in the bakeries. Pottery, as we saw, is one of the shortest-lived industries. Is there any want therefore of potters? Josiah Wedgwood, the inventor of modern pottery, himself originally a common workman, said in 1785 before the House of Commons that the whole trade employed from 15,000 to 20,000 people. In the year 1861 the population alone of the town centres of this industry in Great Britain numbered 101,302. 'The cotton trade has existed for ninety years. . . . It has existed for three generations of the English race, and

I believe I may safely say that during that period it has destroyed nine generations of factory operatives.'

No doubt in certain epochs of feverish activity the labour-market shows significant gaps. In 1834, e.g. But then the manufacturers proposed to the Poor Law Commissioners that they should send the 'surplus-population' of the agricultural districts to the north, with the explanation 'that the manufacturers would absorb and use it up.' 'Agents were appointed with the consent of the Poor Law Commissioners. . . . An office was set up in Manchester, to which lists were sent of those workpeople in the agricultural districts wanting employment, and their names were registered in books. The manufacturers attended at these offices, and selected such persons as they chose; when they had selected such persons as their "wants required", they gave instructions to have them forwarded to Manchester, and they were sent, ticketed like bales of goods, by canals, or with carriers, others tramping on the road, any many of them were found on the way lost and half-starved. This system had grown up unto a regular trade. This House will hardly believe it, but I tell them, that this traffic in human flesh was as well kept up, they were in effect as regularly sold to these [Manchester] manufacturers as slaves are sold to the cotton-grower in the United States. . . . In 1860, "the cotton trade was at its zenith". . . . The manufacturers again found that they were short of hands. . . . They applied to the "flesh agents", as they are called. Those agents sent to the southern downs of England, to the pastures of Dorsetshire, to the glades of Devonshire, to the people tending kine in Wiltshire, but they sought in vain. The surplus-population was "absorbed".' The *Bury Guardian* said, on the completion of the French treaty,* that '10,000 additional hands could be absorbed by Lancashire, and that 30,000 or 40,000 will be needed'. After the 'flesh agents and sub-agents' had in vain sought through the agricultural districts, 'a deputation came up to London, and waited on the right hon. gentleman [Mr Villiers, President of the Poor Law Board] with a view of obtaining poor children from certain union houses for the mills of Lancashire'.

What experience shows to the capitalist generally is a constant excess of population, i.e. an excess in relation to the momentary requirements of surplus-labour-absorbing capital, although this excess is made up of generations of human beings stunted, short-lived, swiftly replacing each other, plucked, so to say, before maturity. And, indeed, experience shows to the intelligent observer with what swiftness and grip the capitalist mode of production, dating, historically speaking, only from yesterday, has seized the vital power of the people by the very root—shows how the degeneration of the industrial population is only retarded by the constant absorption of primitive and physically uncorrupted elements from the country—shows how even the country labourers, in spite of fresh air and the principle of natural selection, that works so powerfully amongst them, and only permits the survival of the strongest, are already beginning to die off. Capital that has such good reasons for denying the sufferings of the legions of workers that surround it, is in practice moved as much and as little by the sight of the coming degradation and final depopulation of the human race, as by the probable fall of the earth into the sun. In every stock-jobbing swindle every one knows that some time or other the crash must come, but every one hopes that it may fall on the head of his neighbour, after he himself has caught the shower of gold and placed it in safety. *Après moi le déluge!** Is the watchword of every capitalist and of every capitalist nation. Hence Capital is reckless of the health or length of life of the labourer, unless under compulsion from society. To the out-cry as to the physical and mental degradation, the premature death, the torture of over-work, it answers: Ought these to trouble us since they increase our profits?* But looking at things as a whole, all this does not, indeed, depend on the good or ill will of the individual capitalist. Free competition brings out the inherent laws of capitalist production, in the shape of external coercive laws having power over every individual capitalist.[9]

Section 6 The Struggle for the Normal Working-Day. Compulsory Limitation by Law of the Working-Time. The English Factory Acts, 1833 to 1864

After capital had taken centuries in extending the working-day to its normal maximum limit, and then beyond this to the limit of the natural day of 12 hours, there followed on the birth of machinism and modern industry in the last third of the 18th century, a violent encroachment like that of an avalanche in its intensity and extent. All bounds of morals and nature, age and sex, day and night, were broken down. Even the ideas of day and night, of rustic simplicity in the old statutes, became so confused that an English judge, as late as 1860, needed a quite Talmudic sagacity to explain 'judicially' what was day and what was night. Capital celebrated its orgies.

As soon as the working-class, stunned at first by the noise and turmoil of the new system of production, recovered, in some measure, its senses, its resistance began, and first in the native land of machinism, in England. For 30 years, however, the concessions conquered by the workpeople were purely nominal. Parliament passed 5 Labour Laws between 1802 and 1833, but was shrewd enough not to vote a penny for their carrying out, for the requisite officials, etc.

They remained a dead letter. 'The fact is, that prior to the Act of 1833, young persons and children were worked all night, all day, or both *ad libitum*.'

A normal working-day for modern industry only dates from the Factory Act of 1833, which included cotton, wool, flax, and silk factories. Nothing is more characteristic of the spirit of capital than the history of the English Factory Acts from 1833 to 1864.

The Act of 1833 declares the ordinary factory working-day to be from half-past five in the morning to half-past eight in the evening, and within these limits, a period of 15 hours, it is lawful to employ young persons (i.e. persons between 13 and 18 years of age), at any time of the day, provided no one individual young person should work more than 12 hours in any one day, except in certain cases especially provided for. The 6th section of the Act provided: 'That there shall be allowed in the course of every day not less than one and a half hours for meals to every such person restricted as hereinbefore provided.' The employment of children under 9, with exceptions mentioned later, was forbidden; the work of children between 9 and 13 was limited to 8 hours a day, nightwork, i.e. according to this Act, work between 8.30 p. m. and 5.30 a. m., was forbidden for all persons between 9 and 18.

The law-makers were so far from wishing to trench on the freedom of capital to exploit adult labour-power, or, as they called it, 'the freedom of labour', that they created a special system in order to prevent the Factory Acts from having a consequence so outrageous.

'The great evil of the factory system as at present conducted', says the first report of the Central Board of the Commission of June 28th, 1833, 'has appeared to us to be that it entails the necessity of continuing the labour of children to the utmost length of that of the adults. The only remedy for this evil, short of the limitation of the labour of adults, which would, in our opinion, create an evil greater than that which is sought to be remedied, appears to be the plan of working double sets of children.' . . . Under the name of System of Relays, this 'plan' was therefore carried out, so that, e.g. form 5.30 a. m. until 1.30 in the afternoon, one set of children between 9 and 13, and from 1.30 p. m. to 8.30 in the evening another set were 'put to', etc.

In order to reward the manufacturers for having, in the most barefaced way, ignored all the Acts as to children's labour passed during the last twenty-two years, the pill was yet further gilded for them. Parliament decreed that after March 1st, 1834, no child under 11, after March 1st, 1835, no child under 12, and after March 1st, 1836, no child under 13, was to work more than eight hours in a factory. This 'liberalism', so full of consideration for 'capital', was the more noteworthy as, Dr Farre, Sir A. Carlisle, Sir B. Brodie, Sir C. Bell, Mr Guthrie, etc., in a word, the most distinguished physicians and surgeons in London, had declared in their evidence before the House of Commons, that there was danger in delay. Dr Farre expressed himself still more coarsely. 'Legislation is necessary for the prevention of death, in any form in which it can be prematurely inflicted, and certainly this (i.e. the factory method) must be viewed as a most cruel mode of inflicting it.'

That same 'reformed' Parliament, which in its delicate consideration for the manufacturers condemned children under 13, for years to come, to 72 hours of work per week in the Factory Hell, on the other hand, in the Emancipation Act, which also administered freedom drop by drop, forbade the planters, from the outset, to work any negro slave more than 45 hours a week.

But in no wise conciliated, capital now began a noisy agitation that went on for several years. It turned chiefly on the age of those who, under the name of children, were limited to 8 hours' work, and were subject to a certain amount of compulsory education. According to capitalistic anthropology, the age of childhood ended at 10, or at the outside, at 11. The more nearly the time approached for the coming into full force of the Factory Act, the fatal year 1836, the more wildly raged the mob of manufacturers. They managed, in fact, to intimidate the government to such an extent that in 1835 it proposed to lower the limit of the age of childhood from 13 to 12. In the meantime the pressure from without grew more threatening. Courage failed the House of Commons. It refused to throw children of 13 under the Juggernaut Car of capital for more than 8 hours a day, and the Act of 1833 came into full operation. It remained unaltered until June, 1844.

In the ten years during which it regulated factory work, first in part, and then entirely, the official reports of the factory inspectors teem with complaints as to the impossibility of putting the Act into force. As the law of 1833 left it optional with the lords of capital during the 15 hours, from 5.30 a. m. to 8.30 p. m., to make every 'young person,' and 'every child' begin, break off, resume, or end his 12 or 8 hours at any moment they liked, and also permitted them to assign to different persons, different times for meals, there gentlemen soon discovered a new 'system of relays,' by which the labour-horses were not changed at fixed stations, but were constantly re-harnessed at changing stations. We do not pause longer on the beauty of this system, as we shall have to return to it later. But this much is clear at the first glance: that this system annulled the whole Factory Act, not only in the spirit, but in the letter. How could factory inspectors, with this complex book-keeping in respect to each individual child or young person, enforce the legally determined work-time and the granting of the legal meal-times? In a great many of the factories, the old brutalities soon blossomed out again unpunished. In an interview with the Home Secretary (1844), the factory inspectors demonstrated the impossibility of any control under the newly invented relay system. In the meantime, however, circumstances had greatly changed. The factory hands, especially since 1838, had made the Ten Hours' Bill their economic, as they had made the Charter* their political, election-cry. Some of the manufacturers, even, who had managed their factories in conformity with the Act of 1833, overwhelmed Parliament with memorials on the immoral competition of their false brethren whom greater impudence, or more fortunate local circumstances, enabled to break the law. Moreover, however much the individual manufacturer might give the rein to his old lust for gain, the spokesmen and political leaders of the manufacturing class ordered a change of front and of speech towards the workpeople. They had entered upon the contest for the repeal of the Corn Laws, and needed the workers to help them to victory. They promised, therefore, not only a double-sized loaf of bread, but the enactment of the Ten Hours' Bill in the Free-trade millennium. Thus they still less dared to oppose a measure intended only to make the law of 1833 a reality. Threatened in their holiest interest, the rent of land, the Tories thundered with philanthropic indignation against the 'nefarious practices' of their foes.

This was the origin of the additional Factory Act of June 7th, 1844. It came into effect on September 10th, 1844. It places under protection a new category of workers, viz., the women over 18. They were placed in every respect on the same footing as the young persons, their work-time limited to twelve hours, their night-labour forbidden, etc. For the first time, legislation saw itself compelled to control directly and officially the labour of adults. In the Factory Report of 1844–1845, it is said with irony: 'No instances have come to my knowledge of adult women having expressed any regret at their *rights* being thus far interfered with.' The working-time of children under 13 was reduced to 6½, and in certain circumstances to 7 hours a-day.

To get rid of the abuses of the 'spurious relay system', the law established besides others the following important regulation:—'That the hours of work of children and young persons shall be reckoned from the time when any child or young person shall begin to work in the morning.' So that if A, e.g. begins work at 8 in the morning, and B at 10, B's work-day must nevertheless end at the same hour as A's. 'The time shall be regulated by a public clock', for example, the nearest railway clock, by which the factory clock is to be set. The occupier is to hang up a 'legible' printed notice stating the hours for the beginning and ending of work and the times allowed for the several meals. Children beginning work before 12 noon may not be again employed after 1 p. m. The afternoon shift must therefore consist of other children than those employed in the morning. Of the hour and a half for meal-times, 'one hour thereof at the least shall be given before three of the clock in the afternoon . . . and at the same period of the day. No child or young person shall be employed more than five hours before 1 p. m. without an interval for meal-time of at least 30 minutes. No child or young person [or female] shall be employed or allowed to remain in any room in which any manufacturing process is then [i.e. at meal-times] carried on,' etc.

It has been seen that these minutiæ, which, with military uniformity, regulate by stroke of the clock the times, limits, pauses of the work, were not at all the products of Parliamentary fancy. They developed gradually out of circumstances as natural laws of the modern mode of production. Their formulation, official recognition, and proclamation by the State, were the result of a long struggle of classes. One of their first consequences was that in practice the working-day of the adult males in factories became subject to the same limitations, since in most processes of production the co-operation of the children, young persons, and women is indispensable. On the whole, therefore, during the period from 1844 to 1847, the 12 hours' working-day became general and uniform in all branches of industry under the Factory Act.

The manufacturers, however, did not allow this 'progress' without a compensating 'retrogression'. At their instigation the House of Commons reduced the minimum age for exploitable children from 9 to 8, in order to assure that additional supply of factory children which is due to capitalists, according to divine and human law.

The years 1846–47 are epoch-making in the economic history of England. The Repeal of the Corn Laws, and of the duties on cotton and other raw material; Free-trade proclaimed as the guiding star of legislation; in a word, the arrival of the millennium. On the other hand, in the same years, the Chartist movement and the 10 hours' agitation reached their highest point. They found allies in the Tories panting for revenge. Despite the fanatical opposition of the army of perjured Free-traders, with Bright and Cobden at their head, the Ten Hours' Bill, struggled for so long, went through Parliament.

The new Factory Act of June 8th, 1847, enacted that on July 1st, 1847, there should be a preliminary shortening of the working-day for 'young persons' (from 13 to 18), and all females to 11 hours, but that on May 1st, 1848, there should be a definite limitation of the working-day to 10 hours. In other respects, the Act only amended and completed the Acts of 1833 and 1844.

Capital now entered upon a preliminary campaign in order to hinder the Act from coming into full force on May 1st, 1848. And the workers themselves, under the pretence that they had been taught by experience, were to help in the destruction of their own work. The moment was cleverly chosen. 'It must be remembered, too, that there has been more than two years of great suffering (in consequence of the terrible crisis of 1846–47) among the factory operatives, from many mills having worked short time, and many being altogether closed. A considerable number of the operatives must therefore be in very narrow circumstances; many, it is to be feared, in debt; so that it might fairly have been presumed that at the present time they would prefer working the longer time, in order to make up for past losses, perhaps to pay off debts, or get their furniture out of pawn, or replace that sold, or to get a new supply of clothes for themselves and their families.'

The manufacturers tried to aggravate the natural effect of these circumstances by a general reduction of wages by 10%. This was done, so to say, to celebrate the inauguration of the new Free-trade era. Then followed a further reduction of 8⅓% as soon as the working-day was shortened to 11, and a reduction of double that amount as soon as it was finally shortened to 10 hours. Wherever, therefore, circumstances allowed it, a reduction of wages of at least 25% took place. Under such favourably prepared conditions the agitation among the factory workers for the repeal of the Act of 1847 was begun. Neither lies, bribery, nor threats were spared in this attempt. But all was in vain. Concerning the half-dozen petitions in which workpeople were made to complain of 'their oppression by the Act,' the petitioners themselves declared under oral examination, that their signatures had been extorted from them. 'They felt themselves oppressed, but not exactly by the Factory Act.' But if the manufacturers did not succeed in making the work-people speak as they wished, they themselves shrieked all the louder in press and Parliament in the name of the workpeople. They denounced the Factory Inspectors as a kind of revolutionary commissioners like those of the French National Convention* ruthlessly sacrificing the unhappy factory workers to their humanitarian crotchet. This manœuvre also failed. Factory Inspector Leonard Horner conducted in his own person, and through his sub-inspectors, many examinations of witnesses in the factories of Lancashire. About 70% of the workpeople examined declared in favour of 10 hours, a much smaller percentage in favour of 11, and an altogether insignificant minority for the old 12 hours.

Another 'friendly' dodge was to make the adult males work 12 to 15 hours, and then to blazon abroad this fact as the best proof of what the proletariat desired in its heart of hearts. But the 'ruthless' Factory Inspector Leonard Horner was again to the fore. The majority of the 'over-times' declared: 'They would much prefer working ten hours for less wages, but that they had no choice; that so many were out of employment (so many spinners getting very low wages by having to work as piecers, being unable to do better), that if they refused to work the longer time, others would immediately get their places, so that it was a question with them of agreeing to work the longer time, or of being thrown out of employment altogether.'

The preliminary campaign of capital thus came to grief, and the Ten Hours' Act came into force May 1st, 1848. But meanwhile the fiasco of the Chartist party whose leaders were imprisoned, and whose organisation was dismembered, had shaken the confidence of the English working-class in its own strength. Soon after this the June insurrection in Paris and its bloody suppression united, in England as on the Continent, all fractions of the ruling classes, landlords and capitalists, stock-exchange wolves and shop-keepers, Protectionists and Free-traders, government and opposition, priests and freethinkers, young whores and old nuns, under the common cry for the salvation of Property, Religion, the Family and Society. The working-class was everywhere proclaimed, placed under a ban, under a virtual law of suspects.* The manufacturers had no need any longer to restrain themselves. They broke out in open revolt not only against the Ten Hours' Act, but against the whole of the legislation that since 1833 had aimed at restricting in some measure the 'free' exploitation of labour-power. It was a pro-slavery rebellion* in miniature, carried on for over two years with a cynical recklessness, a terrorist energy all the cheaper because the rebel capitalist risked nothing except the skin of his 'hands'.

To understand that which follows we must remember that the Factory Acts of 1833, 1844, and 1847 were all three in force so far as the one did not amend the other: that not one of these limited the working-day of the male worker over 18, and that since 1833 the 15 hours from 5.30 a. m. to 8.30 p. m. had remained the legal 'day', within the limits of which at first the 12, and later the 10 hours' labour of young persons and women had to be performed under the prescribed conditions.

The manufacturers began by here and there discharging a part of, in many cases half of, the young persons and women employed by them, and then, for the adult males, restoring the almost obsolete night-work. The Ten Hours' Act, they cried, leaves no other alternative.

Their second step dealt with the legal pauses for meals. Let us hear the Factory Inspectors. 'Since the restriction of the hours of work to ten, the factory occupiers maintain, although they have not yet practically gone the whole length, that supposing the hours of work to be from 9 a. m. to 7 p. m. they fulfil the provisions of the statutes by allowing an hour before 9 a. m. and half an hour after 7 p. m. [for meals]. In some cases they now allow an hour, or half an hour for dinner, insisting at the same time, that they are not bound to allow any part of the hour and a half in the course of the factory working-day.' The manufacturers maintained therefore that the scrupulously strict provisions of the Act of 1844 with regard to meal-times only gave the operatives permission to eat and drink before coming into, and after leaving the factory—i.e. at home. And why should not the workpeople eat their dinner before 9 in the morning? The crown lawyers, however, decided that the prescribed meal-times 'must be in the interval during the working-hours, and that it will not be lawful to work for 10 hours continuously, from 9 a. m. to 7 p. m., without any interval'.

After these pleasant demonstrations, Capital preluded its revolt by a step which agreed with the letter of the law of 1844, and was therefore legal.

The Act of 1844 certainly prohibited the employment after 1 p. m. of such children, from 8 to 13, as had been employed before noon. But it did not regulate in any way the 6½ hours' work of the children whose work-time began at 12 midday or later. Children of 8 might, if they began work at noon, be employed from 12 to 1, 1 hour; from 2 to 4 in the afternoon, 2 hours; from 5 to 8.30 in the evening, 3½ hours; in all, the legal 6½ hours. Or better still. In order to make their work coincide with that of the adult male labourers up to 8.30 p. m., the manufacturers only had to give them no work till 2 in the afternoon; they could then keep them in the factory without intermission till 8.30 in the evening. 'And it is now expressly admitted that the practice exists in England from the desire of mill-owners to have their machinery at work for more than 10 hours a-day, to keep the children at work with male adults after all the young persons and women have left, and until 8.30 p. m. if the factory-owners choose.' Workmen and factory inspectors protested on hygienic and moral grounds, but Capital answered:

> "My deeds upon my head! I crave the law,
> The penalty and forfeit of my bond."*

In fact, according to statistics laid before the House of Commons on July 26th, 1850, in spite of all protests, on July 15th, 1850, 3,742 children were subjected to this 'practice' in 257 factories. Still, this was not enough. The lynx eye of Capital discovered that the Act of 1844 did not allow 5 hours' work before mid-day without a pause of at least 30 minutes for refreshment, but prescribed nothing of the kind for work after mid-day. Therefore, it claimed and obtained the enjoyment not only of making children of 8 drudge without intermission from 2 to 8.30 p. m., but also of making them hunger during that time.

> "Ay, his heart,
> So says the bond."

This Shylock-clinging to the letter of the law of 1844, so far as it regulated children's labour, was but to lead up to an open revolt against the same law, so far as it regulated the labour of 'young persons and women'. It will be remembered that the abolition of the 'false relay system' was the chief aim and object of that law. The masters began their revolt with the simple declaration that the sections of the Act of 1844 which prohibited the *ad libitum* use of young persons and women in such short fractions of the day of 15 hours as the employer chose, were 'comparatively harmless' so long as the work-time was fixed at 12 hours. But under the Ten Hours' Act they were a 'grievous hardship'. They informed the inspectors in the coolest manner that they should place themselves above the letter of the law, and re-introduce the old system on their own account. They were acting in the interests of the ill-advised operatives themselves, 'in order to be able to pay them higher wages'. 'This was the only possible plan by which to maintain, under the Ten Hours' Act, the industrial supremacy of Great Britain.' 'Perhaps it may be a little difficult to detect irregularities under the relay system; but what of that? Is the great manufacturing interest of this country to be treated as a secondary matter in order to save some little trouble to Inspectors and Sub-Inspectors of Factories?'

All these shifts naturally were of no avail. The Factory Inspectors appealed to the Law Courts. But soon such a cloud of dust in the way of petitions from the masters overwhelmed the Home Secretary, Sir George Grey, that in a circular of August 5th, 1848, he recommends the inspectors not 'to lay informations against mill-owners for a breach of the letter of the Act, or for employment of young persons by relays in cases in which there is no reason to believe that such young persons have been actually employed for a longer period than that sanctioned by law'. Hereupon, Factory Inspector J. Stuart allowed the so-called relay system during the 15 hours of the factory day throughout Scotland, where it soon flourished again as of old. The English Factory Inspectors, on the other hand, declared that the Home Secretary had no power dictatorially to suspend the law, and continued their legal proceedings against the pro-slavery rebellion.

But what was the good of summoning the capitalists when the Courts, in this case the country magistrates—Cobbett's 'Great Unpaid'—acquitted them? In these tribunals, the masters sat in judgment on themselves. An example. One Eskrigge, cotton-spinner, of the firm of Kershaw, Leese, & Co., had laid before the Factory Inspector of his district the scheme of a relay system intended for his mill. Receiving a refusal, he at first kept quiet. A few months later, an individual named Robinson, also a cotton-spinner, and if not his Man Friday, at all events related to Eskrigge, appeared before the borough magistrates of Stockport on a charge of introducing the identical plan of relays invented by Eskrigge. Four Justices sat, among them three cotton-spinners, at their head this same inevitable Eskrigge. Eskrigge acquitted Robinson, and now was of opinion that what was right for Robinson was fair for Eskrigge. Supported by his own legal decision, he introduced the system at once into his own factory. Of course, the composition of this tribunal was in itself a violation of the law. These judicial farces, exclaims Inspector Howell, 'urgently call for a remedy—either that the law should be so altered as to be made to conform to these decisions, or that it should be administered by a less fallible tribunal, whose decisions would conform to the law... when these cases are brought forward. I long for a stipendiary magistrate'.

The crown lawyers declared the masters' interpretation of the Act of 1848 absurd. But the Saviours of Society would not allow themselves to be turned from their purpose. Leonard Horner reports, 'Having endeavoured to enforce the Act... by ten prosecutions in seven magisterial divisions, and having been supported by the magistrates in one case only... I considered it useless to prosecute more for this evasion of the law. That part of the Act of 1848 which was framed for securing uniformity in the hours of work, . . . is thus no longer in force in my district (Lancashire). Neither have the sub-inspectors or myself any means of satisfying ourselves, when we inspect a mill working by shifts, that the young persons and women are not working more than 10 hours a-day. . . . In a return of the 30th April, . . . of mill-owners working by shifts, the number amounts to 114, and has been for some time rapidly increasing. In general, the time of working the mill is extended to 13½ hours, from 6 a. m. to 7½ p. m., . . . in some instances it amounts to 15 hours, from 5½ a. m. to 8½ p. m.' Already, in December, 1848, Leonard Horner had a list of 65 manufacturers and 29 overlookers who unanimously declared that no system of supervision could, under this relay system, prevent enormous over-work. Now, the same children and young persons were shifted from the spinning-room to the weaving-room, now, during 15 hours, from one factory to another. How was it possible to control a system which, 'under the guise of relays, is some one of the many plans for shuffling "the hands" about in endless variety, and shifting the hours of work and of rest for different individuals throughout the day, so that you may never have one complete set of hands working together in the same room at the same time'.

But altogether independently of actual over-work, this so-called relay system was an offspring of capitalistic fantasy, such as Fourier, in his humorous sketches of 'Courtes Séances,'* has never surpassed, except that the 'attraction of labour' was changed into the attraction of capital. Look, for example, at those schemes of the masters which the 'respectable' press praised as models of 'what a reasonable degree of care and method can accomplish.' The *personnel* of the workpeople was sometimes divided into from 12 to 14 categories, which themselves constantly changed and rechanged their constituent parts. During the 15 hours of the factory day, capital dragged in the labourer now for 30 minutes, now for an hour, and then pushed him out again, to drag him into the factory and to thrust him out afresh, hounding him hither and thither, in scattered shreds of time, without ever losing hold of him until the full 10 hours' work was done. As on the stage, the same persons had to appear in turns in the different scenes of the different acts. But as an actor during the whole course of the play belongs to the stage, so the operatives, during 15 hours, belonged to the factory, without reckoning the time for going and coming. Thus the hours of rest were turned into hours of enforced idleness, which drove the youths to the pot-house, and the girls to the brothel. At every new trick that the capitalist, from day to day, hit upon for keeping his machinery going 12 or 15 hours without increasing the number of his hands, the worker had to swallow his meals now in this fragment of time, now in that. At the time of the 10 hours' agitation, the masters cried out that the working mob petitioned in the hope of obtaining 12 hours' wages for 10 hours' work. Now they reversed the medal. They paid 10 hours' wages for 12 or 15 hours' lordship over labour-power. This was the gist of the matter, this the masters' interpretation of the 10 hours' law! These were the same unctuous Free-traders, perspiring with the love of humanity, who for full 10 years, during the Anti-Corn Law agitation, had preached to the operatives, by a reckoning of pounds, shillings, and pence, that with free importation of corn, and with the means possessed by English industry, 10 hours' labour would be quite enough to enrich the capitalists. This revolt of capital, after two years was at last crowned with victory by a decision of one of the four highest Courts of Justice in England, the Court of Exchequer, which in a case brought before it on February 8th, 1850, decided that the manufacturers were certainly acting against the sense of the Act of 1844, but that this Act itself contained certain words that rendered it meaningless. 'By this decision, the Ten Hours' Act was abolished.' A crowd of masters, who until then had been afraid of using the relay system for young persons and women, now took it up heart and soul.

But on this apparently decisive victory of capital, followed at once a revulsion. The workpeople had hitherto offered a passive, although inflexible and unremitting resistance. They now protested in Lancashire and Yorkshire in threatening meetings. The pretended Ten Hours' Act was thus simple humbug, parliamentary cheating, had never existed! The Factory Inspectors urgently warned th Government that the antagonism of classes had arrived at an incredible tension. Some of the masters themselves murmured: 'On account of the contradictory decisions of the magistrates, a condition of things altogether abnormal and anarchical obtains. One law holds in Yorkshire, another in Lancashire; one law in one parish of Lancashire, another in its immediate neighbourhood. The manufacturer in large towns could evade the law, the manufacturer in country districts could not find the people necessary for the relay system, still less for the shifting of hands from one factory to another,' etc. And the first birthright of capital is equal exploitation of labour-power by all capitalists.

Under these circumstances a compromise between masters and men was effected that received the seal of Parliament in the additional Factory Act of August 5th, 1850. The working-day for 'young persons and women', was raised from 10 to 10½ hours for the first five days of the week, and shortened to 7½ on the Saturday. The work was to go on between 6 a. m. and 6 p. m., with pauses of not less than 1½ hours for meal-times, these meal-times to be allowed at one and the same time for all, and conformably to the conditions of 1844. By this an end was put to the relay system once for all. For children's labour, the Act of 1844 remained in force.

One set of masters, this time as before, secured to itself special seigneurial rights over the children of the proletariat. These were the silk manufacturers. In 1833 they had howled out in threatening fashion, 'if the liberty of working children of any age for 10 hours a day were taken away, it would stop their works'. It would be impossible for them to buy a sufficient number of children over 13. They extorted the privilege they desired. The pretext was shown on subsequent investigation to be a deliberate lie. It did not, however, prevent them, during 10 years, from spinning silk 10 hours a day out of the blood of little children who had to be placed upon stools for the performance of their work. The Act of 1844 certainly 'robbed' them of the 'liberty' of employing children under 11 longer than 6½ hours a day. But it secured to them, on the other hand, the privilege of working children between 11 and 13, 10 hours a day, and of annulling in their case the education made compulsory for all other factory children. This time the pretext was 'the delicate texture of the fabric in which they were employed, requiring a lightness of touch, only to be acquired by their early introduction to these factories'. The children were slaughtered out-and-out for the sake of their delicate fingers, as in Southern Russia the horned cattle for the sake of their hide and tallow. At length, in 1850, the privilege granted in 1844, was limited to the departments of silk-twisting and silk-winding. But here, to make amends to capital bereft of its 'freedom', the work-time for children from 11 to 13 was raised from 10 to 10½ hours. Pretext: 'Labour in silk mills was lighter than in mills for other fabrics, and less likely in other respects also to be prejudicial to health.' Official medical inquiries proved afterwards that, on the contrary, 'the average death-rate is exceedingly high in the silk districts and amongst the female part of the population is higher even than it is in the cotton districts of Lancashire'. Despite the protests of the Factory Inspector, renewed every 6 months, the mischief continues to this hour.

The Act of 1850 changed the 15 hours' time from 6 a. m. to 8.30 p. m., into the 12 hours from 6 a. m. to 6 p. m. for 'young persons and women' only. It did not, therefore, affect children who could always be employed for half an hour before and 2½ hours after this period, provided the whole of their labour did not exceed 6½ hours. Whilst the bill was under discussion, the Factory Inspectors laid before Parliament statistics of the infamous abuses due to this anomaly. To no purpose. In the background lurked the intention of screwing up, during prosperous years, the working-day of adult males to 15 hours by the aid of the children. The experience of the three following years showed that such an attempt must come to grief against the resistance of the adult male operatives. The Act of 1850 was therefore finally completed in 1853 by forbidding the 'employment of children in the morning before and in the evening after young persons and women.' Henceforth with a few exceptions the Factory Act of 1850 regulated the working-day of all workers in the branches of industry that come under it. Since the passing of the first Factory Act half a century had elapsed.

Factory legislation for the first time went beyond its original sphere in the 'Printworks' Act of 1845'. The displeasure with which capital received this new 'extravagance' speaks through every line of the Act. It limits the working-day for children from 8 to 13, and for women to 16 hours, between 6 a. m. and 10 p. m., without any legal pause for meal-times. It allows males over 13 to be worked at will day and night. It is a Parliamentary abortion.

However, the principle had triumphed with its victory in those great branches of industry which form the most characteristic creation of the modern mode of production. Their wonderful development from 1853 to 1860, hand-in-hand with the physical and moral regeneration of the factory workers, struck the most purblind. The masters from whom the legal limitation and regulation had been wrung step by step after a civil war of half a century, themselves referred ostentatiously to the contrast with the branches of exploitation still 'free.' The Pharisees of 'Political Economy' now proclaimed the discernment of the necessity of a legally fixed working-day as a characteristic new discovery of their 'science'. It will be easily understood that after the factory magnates had resigned themselves and become reconciled to the inevitable, the power of resistance of capital gradually weakened, whilst at the same time the power of attack of the working-class grew with the number of its allies in the classes of society not immediately interested in the question. Hence the comparatively rapid advance since 1860.

Section 7. The Struggle for the Normal Working-Day. Reaction of the English Factory Acts on Other Countries

The reader will bear in mind that the production of surplus-value, or the extraction of surplus-labour, is the specific end and aim, the sum and substance, of capitalist production, quite apart from any changes in the mode of production, which may arise from the subordination of labour to capital. He will remember that as far as we have at present gone, only the independent labourer, and therefore only the labourer legally qualified to act for himself, enters as a vendor of a commodity into a contract with the capitalist. If, therefore, in our historical sketch, on the one hand, modern industry; on the other, the labour of those who are physically and legally minors, play important parts, the former was to us only a special department, and the latter only a specially striking example of labour exploitation. Without, however, anticipating the subsequent development of our inquiry, from the mere connexion of the historic facts before us, it follows:

First. The passion of capital for an unlimited and reckless extension of the working-day, is first gratified in the industries earliest revolutionised by water-power, steam, and machinery, in those first creations of the modern mode of production, cotton, wool, flax, and silk spinning, and weaving. The changes in the material mode of production, and the corresponding changes in the social relations of the producers gave rise first to an extravagance beyond all bounds, and then in opposition to this, called forth a control on the part of Society which legally limits, regulates, and makes uniform the working-day and its pauses. This control appears, therefore, during the first half of the nineteenth century simply as exceptional legislation. As soon as this primitive dominion of the new mode of production was conquered, it was found that, in the meantime, not only had many other branches of production been made to adopt the same factory system, but that manufactures with more or less obsolete methods, such as potteries, glass-making, etc., that old-fashioned handicrafts, like baking, and, finally, even that the so-called domestic industries, such as nail-making, had long since fallen as completely under capitalist exploitation as the factories themsleves. Legislation was, therefore, compelled to gradually get rid of its exceptional character, or where, as in England, it proceeds after the manner of the Roman Casuists, to declare any house in which work was done to be a factory.

Second. The history of the regulation of the working-day in certain branches of production, and the struggle still going on in others in regard to this regulation, prove conclusively that the isolated labourer, the labourer as 'free' vendor of his labour-power, when capitalist production has once attained a certain stage, succumbs without any power of resistance. The creation of a normal working-day is, therefore, the product of a protracted civil war, more or less dissembled, between the capitalist class and the working-class. As the contest take place in the arena of modern industry, it first breaks out in the home of that industry—England. The English factory workers were the champions, not only of the English, but of the modern working-class generally, as their theorists were the first to throw down the gauntlet to the theory of capital.[10] Hence, the philosopher of the Factory, Ure, denounces as an ineffable disgrace to the English working-class that they inscribed 'the slavery of the Factory Acts' on the banner which they bore against capital, manfully striving for 'perfect freedom of labour'.

France limps slowly behind England. The February revolution was necessary to bring into the world the 12 hours' law, which is much more deficient than its English original. For all that, the French revolutionary method has its special advantages. It once for all commands the same limit to the working-day in all shops and factories without distinction, whilst English legislation reluctantly yields to the pressure of circumstances, now on this point, now on that, and is getting lost in a hopelessly bewildering tangle of contradictory enactments. On the other hand, the French law proclaims as a principle that which in England was only won in the name of children, minors, and women, and has been only recently for the first time claimed as a general right.

Working Men's Association at Geneva, on the proposition of the London General Council, resolved that 'the limitation of the working-day is a preliminary condition without which all further attempts at improvement and emancipation must prove abortive . . . the Congress proposes eight hours as the legal limit of the working-day.'

Thus the movement of the working-class on both sides of the Atlantic, that had grown instinctively out of the conditions of production themselves, endorsed the words of the English Factory Inspector, R. J. Saunders: 'Further steps towards a reformation of society can never be carried out with any hope of success, unless the hours of labour be limited, and the prescribed limit strictly enforced.'

It must be acknowledged that our labourer comes out of the process of production other than he entered. In the market he stood as owner of the commodity 'labour-power' face to face with other owners of commodities, dealer against dealer. The contract by which he sold to the capitalist his labour-power proved, so to say, in black and white that he disposed of himself freely. The bargain concluded, it is discovered that he was no 'free agent', that the time for which he is free to sell his labour-power is the time for which he is forced to sell it, that in fact the vampire will not lose its hold on him 'so long as there is a muscle, a nerve, a drop of blood to be exploited'. For 'protection' against 'the serpent of their agonies', the labourers must put their heads together, and, as a class, compel the passing of a law, an all-powerful social barrier that shall prevent the very workers from selling, by voluntary contract with capital, themselves and their families into slavery and death. In place of the pompous catalogue of the 'inalienable rights of man' comes the modest Magna Charta of a legally limited working-day, which shall make clear 'when the time which the worker sells is ended, and when his own begins'. Quantum mutatus ab illo!*

CHAPTER 11

RATE AND MASS OF SURPLUS-VALUE

IN this chapter, as hitherto, the value of labour-power, and therefore the part of the working-day necessary for the reproduction or maintenance of that labour-power, are supposed to be given, constant magnitudes.

This premised, with the rate, the mass is at the same time given of the surplus-value that the individual labourer furnishes to the capitalist in a definite period of time. If, e.g. the necessary labour amounts to 6 hours daily, expressed in a quantum of gold = 3 shillings, then 3s. is the daily value of one labour-power or the value of the capital advanced in the buying of one labour-power. If, further, the rate of surplus-value be = 100%, this variable capital of 3s. produces a mass of surplus-value of 3s., or the labourer supplies daily a mass of surplus-labour equal to 6 hours.

But the variable capital of a capitalist is the expression in money of the total value of all the labour-powers that he employs simultaneously. Its value is, therefore, equal to the average value of one labour-power, multiplied by the number of labour-powers employed. With a given value of labour-power, therefore, the magnitude of the variable capital varies directly as the number of labourers employed simultaneously. If the daily value of one labour-power = 3s., then a capital of 300s. must be advanced in order to exploit daily 100 labour-powers, of n times 3s., in order to exploit daily n labour-powers.

In the same way, if a variable capital of 3s., being the daily value of one labour-power, produce a daily surplus-value of 3s., a variable capital of 300s. will produce a daily surplus-value of 300s., and one of n times 3s. a daily surplus-value of n × 3s. The mass of the surplus-value produced is therefore equal to the surplus-value which the working-day of one labourer supplies multiplied by the number of labourers employed. But as further the mass of surplus-value which a single labourer produces, the value of labour-power being given, is determined by the rate of the surplus-value, this law follows: the mass of the surplus-value produced is equal to the amount of the variable capital advanced, multiplied by the rate of surplus-value; in other words: it is determined by the compound ratio between the number of labour-powers exploited simultaneously by the same capitalist and the degree of exploitation of each individual labour-power. Diminution of the variable capital may therefore be compensated by a proportionate rise in the degree of exploitation of labour-power, or the decrease in the number of the labourers employed by a proportionate extension of the working-day. Within certain limits therefore the supply of labour exploitable by capital is independent of the supply of labourers. On the contrary, a fall in the rate of surplus-value leaves unaltered the mass of the surplus-value produced, if the amount of the variable capital, or number of the labourers employed, increases in the same proportion.

The absolute limit of the average working-day—this being by nature always less than 24 hours—sets an absolute limit to the compensation of a reduction of variable capital by a higher rate of surplus-value, or of the decrease of the number of labourers exploited by a higher degree of exploitation of labour-power. This palpable law is of importance for the clearing up of many phenomena, arising from a tendency (to be worked out later on)* of capital to reduce as much as possible the number of labourers employed by it, or its variable constituent transformed into labour-power, in contradiction to its other tendency to produce the greatest possible mass of surplus-value. On the other hand, if the mass of labour-power employed, or the amount of variable capital, increases, but not in proportion to the fall in the rate of surplus-value, the mass of the surplus-value produced, falls.

The rate of surplus-value, or the degree of exploitation of labour-power, and the value of labour-power, or the amount of necessary working-time being given, it is self-evident that the greater the variable capital, the greater would be the mass of the value produced and of the surplus-value. If the limit of the working-day is given, and also the limit of its necessary constituent, the mass of value and surplus-value that an individual capitalist produces, is clearly exclusively dependent on the mass of labour that he sets in motion. But this, under the conditions supposed above, depends on the mass of labour-power, or the number of labourers whom he exploits, and this number in its turn is determined by the amount of the variable capital advanced. With a given rate of surplus-value, and a given value of labour-power, therefore, the masses of surplus-value produced vary directly as the amounts of the variable capitals advanced. Now we know that the capitalist divides his capital into two parts. One part he lays out in means of production. This is the constant part of his capital. The other part he lays out in living labour-power. This part forms his variable capital. On the basis of the same mode of social production, the division of capital into constant and variable differs in different branches of production, and within the same branch of production, too, this relation changes with changes in the technical conditions and in the social combinations of the processes of production.

The law demonstrated above now, therefore, takes this form: the masses of value and of surplus-value produced by different capitals—the value of labour-power being given and its degree of exploitation being equal—vary directly as the amounts of the variable constituents of these capitals, i.e. as their constituents transformed into living labour-power.

This law clearly contradicts all experience based on appearance. Everyone knows that a cotton spinner, who, reckoning the percentage on the whole of his applied capital, employs much constant and little variable capital, does not, on account of this, pocket less profit or surplus-value than a baker, who relatively sets in motion much variable and little constant capital. For the solution of this apparent contradiction, many intermediate terms are as yet wanted, as from the standpoint of elementary algebra many intermediate terms are wanted to understand that % may represent an actual magnitude. Classical economy, although not formulating the law, holds instinctively to it, because it is a necessary consequence of the general law of value. It tries to rescue the law from collision with contradictory phenomena by a violent abstraction. It will be seen later how the school of Ricardo has come to grief over this stumbling-block. Vulgar economy which, indeed, 'has really learnt nothing,' here as everywhere sticks to appearances in opposition to the law which regulates and explains them. In opposition to Spinoza, it believes that 'ignorance is a sufficient reason.'*

The labour which is set in motion by the total capital of a society, day in, day out, may be regarded as a single collective working-day. If, e.g. the number of labourers is a million, and the average working-day of a labourer is 10 hours, the social working-day consists of ten million hours. With a given length of this working-day, whether its limits are fixed physically or socially, the mass of surplus-value can only be increased by increasing the number of labourers, i.e. of the labouring population. The growth of population here forms the mathematical limit to the production of surplus-value by the total social capital. On the contrary, with a given amount of population, this limit is formed by the possible lengthening of the working-day. It will, however, be seen in the following chapter that this law only holds for the form of surplus-value dealt with up to the present.

From the treatment of the production of surplus-value, so far, it follows that not every sum of money, or of value, is at pleasure transformable into capital. To effect this transformation, in fact, a certain minimum of money or of exchange-value must be pre-supposed in the hands of the individual possessor of money or commodities. The minimum of variable capital is the cost price of a single labour-power, employed the whole year through, day in, day out, for the production of surplus-value. If this labourer were in possession of his own means of production, and were satisfied to live as a labourer, he need not work beyond the time necessary for the reproduction of his means of subsistence, say 8 hours a day. He would, besides, only require the means of production sufficient for 8 working-hours. The capitalist, on the other hand, who makes him do, besides these 8 hours, say 4 hours' surplus-labour, requires an additional sum of money for furnishing the additional means of production. On our supposition, however, he would have to employ two labourers in order to live, on the surplus-value appropriated daily, as well as, and no better than a labourer, i.e. to be able to satisfy his necessary wants. In this case the mere maintenance of life would be the end of his production, not the increase of wealth; but this latter is implied in capitalist production. That he may live only twice as well as an ordinary labourer, and besides turn half of the surplus-value produced into capital, he would have to raise, with the number of labourers, the minimum of the capital advanced 8 times. Of course he can, like his labourer, take to work himself, participate directly in the process of production, but he is then only a hybrid between capitalist and labourer, a 'small master'. A certain stage of capitalist production necessitates that the capitalist be able to devote the whole of the time during which he functions as a capitalist, i.e. as personified capital, to the appropriation and therefore control of the labour of others, and to the selling of the products of this labour. The guilds of the middle ages therefore tried to prevent by force the transformation of the master of a trade into a capitalist, by limiting the number of labourers that could be employed by one master within a very small maximum. The possessor of money or commodities actually turns into a capitalist in such cases only where the minimum sum advanced for production greatly exceeds the maximum of the middle ages. Here, as in natural science, is shown the correctness of the law discovered by Hegel (in his 'Logic'), that merely quantitative differences beyond a certain point pass into qualitative changes.

The minimum of the sum of value that the individual possessor of money or commodities must command, in order to metamorphose himself into a capitalist, changes with the different stages of development of capitalist production, and is at given stages different in different spheres of production, according to their special and technical conditions. Certain spheres of production demand, even at the very outset of capitalist production, a minimum of capital that is not as yet found in the hands of single individuals. This gives rise partly to state subsidies to private persons, as in France in the time of Colbert, and as in many German states up to our own epoch; partly to the formation of societies with legal monopoly for the exploitation of certain branches of industry and commerce, the fore-runners of our modern joint-stock companies.

Within the process of production, as we have seen, capital acquired the command over labour, i.e. over functioning labour-power or the labourer himself. Personified capital, the capitalist takes care that the labourer does his work regularly and with the proper degree of intensity.

Capital further developed into a coercive relation, which compels the working-class to do more work than the narrow round of its own life-wants prescribes. As a producer of the activity of others, as a pumper-out of surplus-labour and exploiter of labour-power, it surpasses in energy, disregard of bounds, recklessness and efficiency, all earlier systems of production based on directly compulsory labour.

At first, capital subordinates labour on the basis of the technical conditions in which it historically finds it. It does not, therefore, change immediately the mode of production. The production of surplus-value—in the form hitherto considered by us—by means of simple extension of the working-day, proved, therefore, to be independent of any change in the mode of production itself. It was not less active in the old-fashioned bakeries than in the modern cotton factories.

If we consider the process of production from the point of view of the simple labour-process, the labourer stands in relation to the means of production, not in their quality as capital, but as the mere means and material of his own intelligent productive activity. In tanning, e.g. he deals with the skins as his simple object of labour. It is not the capitalist whose skin he tans. But it is different as soon as we deal with the process of production from the point of view of the process of creation of surplus-value. The means of production are at once changed into means for the absorption of the labour of others. It is now no longer the labourer that employs the means of production, but the means of production that employ the labourer. Instead of being consumed by him as material elements of his productive activity, they consume him as the ferment necessary to their own life-process, and the life-process of capital consists only in its movement as value constantly expanding, constantly multiplying itself. Furnaces and workshops that stand idle by night, and absorb no living labour, are 'a mere loss' to the capitalist. Hence, furnaces and workshops constitute lawful claims upon the night-labour of the workpeople. The simple transformation of money into the material factors of the process of production, into means of production, transforms the latter into a title and a right to the labour and surplus-labour of others.

PART IV
THE PRODUCTION OF RELATIVE
SURPLUS-VALUE

CHAPTER 12
THE CONCEPT OF RELATIVE SURPLUS-VALUE

THAT portion of the working-day which merely produces an equivalent for the value paid by the capitalist for his labour-power, has, up to
this point, been treated by us as a constant magnitude, and such in fact
it is, under given conditions of production and at a given stage in the
economic development of society. Beyond this, his necessary labour-
time, the labourer, we saw, could continue to work for 2, 3, 4, 6, etc.,
hours. The rate of surplus-value and the length of the working-day
depended on the magnitude of this prolongation. Though the necessary labour-time was constant, we saw, on the other hand, that the total
working-day was variable. Now suppose we have a working-day whose
length, and whose apportionment between necessary labour and surplus-labour, are given. Let the whole line a c, a———b——c represent, for
example, a working-day of 12 hours; the portion of a b 10 hours of
necessary labour, and the portion b c 2 hours of surplus-labour. How
now can the production of surplus-value be increased, i.e. how can the
surplus-labour be prolonged, without, or independently of, any prolongation of a c?

Although the length of a c is given, b c appears to be capable of
prolongation, if not by extension beyond its end c, which is also the end
of the working-day a c, yet, at all events, by pushing back its starting-
point b in the direction of a. Assume that b′——b in the line a b′ b c is
equal to half of b c

$$a———b′——b———c$$

or to one hour's labour-time. If now, in a c, the working-day of 12
hours, we move the point b to b′, b c becomes b′ c; the surplus-labour
increases by one half, from 2 hours to 3 hours, although the working-
day remains as before at 12 hours. This extension of the surplus
labour-time from b c to b′ c, from 2 hours to 3 hours, is, however,
evidently impossible, without a simultaneous contraction of the necessary labour-time from a b into a b′, from 10 hours to 9 hours. The

prolongation of the surplus-labour would correspond to a shortening of the necessary labour; or a portion of the labour-time previously consumed, in reality, for the labourer's own benefit, would be converted into labour-time for the benefit of the capitalist. There would be an alteration, not in the length of the working-day, but in its division into necessary labour-time and surplus labour-time.

On the other hand, it is evident that the duration of the surplus-labour is given, when the length of the working-day, and the value of labour-power, are given. The value of labour-power, i.e. the labour-time requisite to produce labour-power, determines the labour-time necessary for the reproduction of that value. If one working-hour be embodied in sixpence, and the value of a day's labour-power be five shillings, the labourer must work 10 hours a day, in order to replace the value paid by capital for his labour-power, or to produce an equivalent for the value of his daily necessary means of subsistence. Given the value of these means of subsistence, the value of his labour-power is given; and given the value of his labour-power, the duration of his necessary labour-time is given. The duration of the surplus-labour, however, is arrived at, by subtracting the necessary labour-time from the total working-day. Ten hours subtracted from twelve, leave two, and it is not easy to see, how, under the given conditions, the surplus-labour can possibly be prolonged beyond two hours. No doubt, the capitalist can, instead of five shillings, pay the labourer four shillings and sixpence or even less. For the reproduction of this value of four shillings and sixpence, nine hours' labour-time would suffice; and consequently three hours of surplus-labour, instead of two, would accrue to the capitalist, and the surplus-value would rise from one shilling to eighteen-pence. This result, however, would be obtained only by lowering the wages of the labourer below the value of his labour-power. With the four shillings and sixpence which he produces in nine hours, he commands one-tenth less of the necessaries of life than before, and consequently the proper reproduction of his labour-power is crippled. The surplus-labour would in this case be prolonged only by an over-stepping of its normal limits; its domain would be extended only by a usurpation of part of the domain of necessary labour-time. Despite the important part which this method plays in actual practice, we are excluded from considering it in this place, by our assumption, that all commodities, including labour-power, are bought and sold at their full value. Granted this, it follows that the labour-time necessary for the production of labour-power, or for the reproduction of its value, cannot be lessened by a fall in the labourer's wages below the value of his labour-power, but only by a fall in this value itself. Given the length of the working-day, the prolongation of the surplus-labour must of necessity originate in the curtailment of the necessary labour-time; the latter cannot arise from the former. In the example we have taken, it is necessary that the value of labour-power should actually fall by one-tenth, in order that the necessary labour-time may be diminished by one-tenth, i.e. from ten hours to nine, and in order that the surplus-labour may consequently be prolonged from two hours to three.

Such a fall in the value of labour-power implies, however, that the same necessaries of life which were formerly produced in ten hours, can now be produced in nine hours. But this is impossible without an increase in the productiveness of labour. For example, suppose a shoe-maker, with given tools, makes in one working-day of twelve hours, one pair of boots. If he must make two pairs in the same time, the productiveness of his labour must be doubled; and this cannot be done, except by an alteration in his tools or in his mode of working, or in both. Hence, the conditions of production, i.e. his mode of production, and the labour-process itself, must be revolutionised. By increase in the productiveness of labour, we mean, generally, an alteration in the labour-process, of such a kind as to shorten the labour-time socially necessary for the production of a commodity, and to endow a given quantity of labour with the power of producing a greater quantity of use-value. Hitherto in treating of surplus-value, arising from a simple prolongation of the working-day, we have assumed the mode of production to be given and invariable. But when surplus-value has to be produced by the conversion of necessary labour into surplus-labour, it by no means suffices for capital to take over the labour-process in the form under which it has been historically handed down, and then simply to prolong the duration of that process. The technical and social conditions of the process, and consequently the very mode of production must be revolutionised, before the productiveness of labour can be increased. By that means alone can the value of labour-power be made to sink, and the portion of the working-day necessary for the reproduction of that value, be shortened.

The surplus-value produced by prolongation of the working-day, I call *absolute surplus-value*. On the other hand, the surplus-value arising from the curtailment of the necessary labour-time, and from the corresponding alteration in the respective lengths of the two components of the working-day, I call *relative surplus-value*.

In order to effect a fall in the value of labour-power, the increase in the productiveness of labour must seize upon those branches of industry, whose products determine the value of labour-power, and consequently either belong to the class of customary means of subsistence, or are capable of supplying the place of those means. But the value of a commodity is determined, not only by the quantity of labour which the labourer directly bestows upon that commodity, but also by the labour contained in the means of production. For instance, the value of a pair of boots depends, not only on the cobbler's labour, but also on the value of the leather, wax, thread, etc. Hence, a fall in the value of labour-power is also brought about by an increase in the productiveness of labour, and by a corresponding cheapening of commodities in those industries which supply the instruments of labour and the raw material, that form the material elements of the constant capital required for producing the necessaries of life. But an increase in the productiveness of labour in those branches of industry which supply neither the necessaries of life, nor the means of production for such necessaries, leaves the value of labour-power undisturbed.

The cheapened commodity, of course, causes only a pro tanto fall in the value of labour-power, a fall proportional to the extent of that commodity's employment in the reproduction of labour-power. Shirts, for instance, are a necessary means of subsistence, but are only one out of many. The totality of the necessaries of life consists, however, of various commodities, each the product of a distinct industry; and the value of each of those commodities enters as a component part into the value of labour-power. This latter value decreases with the decrease of the labour-time necessary for its reproduction; the total decrease being the sum of all the different curtailments of labour-time effected in those various and distinct industries. This general result is treated, here, as if it were the immediate result directly aimed at in each individual case. Whenever an individual capitalist cheapens shirts, for instance, by increasing the productiveness of labour, he by no means necessarily aims at reducing the value of labour-power and shortening, pro tanto, the necessary labour-time. But it is only in so far as he ultimately contributes to this result, that he assists in raising the general rate of surplus-value. The general and necessary tendencies of capital must be distinguished from their forms of manifestation.

It is not our intention to consider, here, the way in which the laws, immanent in capitalist production, manifest themselves in the movements of individual masses of capital, where they assert themselves as coercive laws of competition, and are brought home to the mind and consciousness of the individual capitalist as the directing motives of his operations. But this much is clear; a scientific analysis of competition is not possible, before we have a conception of the inner nature of capital, just as the apparent motions of the heavenly bodies are not intelligible to any but him, who is acquainted with their real motions, motions which are not directly perceptible by the senses. Nevertheless, for the better comprehension of the production of relative surplus-value, we may add the following remarks, in which we assume nothing more than the results we have already obtained.

If one hour's labour is embodied in sixpence, a value of six shillings will be produced in a working-day of 12 hours. Suppose, that with the prevailing productiveness of labour, 12 articles are produced in these 12 hours. Let the value of the means of production used up in each article be sixpence. Under these circumstances, each article costs one shilling: sixpence for the value of the means of production, and six-pence for the value newly added in working with those means. Now let some one capitalist contrive to double the productiveness of labour, and to produce in the working-day of 12 hours, 24 instead of 12 such articles. The value of the means of production remaining the same, the value of each article will fall to ninepence, made up of sixpence for the value of the means of production and threepence for the value newly added by the labour. Despite the doubled productiveness of labour, the day's labour creates, as before, a new value of six shillings and no more, which, however, is now spread over twice as many articles. Of this value each article now has embodied in it 1/24th, instead of 1/12th, threepence instead of sixpence; or, what amounts to the same thing, only half an hour's instead of a whole hour's labour-time, is now added to the means of production while they are being transformed into each article. The individual value of these articles is now below their social value; in other words, they have cost less labour-time than the great bulk of the same article produced under the average social conditions. Each article costs, on an average, one shilling, and represents 2 hours of social labour; but under the altered mode of production it costs only ninepence, or contains only 1½ hours' labour. The real value of a commodity is, however, not its individual value, but its social value; that is to say, the real value is not measured by the labour-time that the article in each individual case costs the producer, but by the labour-time socially required for its production. If therefore, the capitalist who applies the new method, sells his commodity at its social value of one shilling, he sells it for threepence above its individual value, and thus realises an extra surplus-value of threepence. On the other hand, the working-day of 12 hours is, as regards him, now represented by 24 articles instead of 12. Hence, in order to get rid of the product of one working-day, the demand must be double what it was, i.e. the market

must become twice as extensive. Other things being equal, his commodities can command a more extended market only by a diminution
of their prices. He will therefore sell them above their individual but
under their social value, say at tenpence each. By this means he still
squeezes an extra surplus-value of one penny out of each. This augmentation of surplus-value is pocketed by him, whether his commodities belong or not to the class of necessary means of subsistence that
participate in determining the general value of labour-power. Hence,
independently of this latter circumstance, there is a motive for each
individual capitalist to cheapen his commodities, by increasing the
productiveness of labour.

Nevertheless, even in this case, the increased production of surplus-
value arises from the curtailment of the necessary labour-time, and
from the corresponding prolongation of the surplus-labour.

Hence, the capitalist who applies the improved method of production, appropriates to surplus-labour a greater portion of the
working-day, than the other capitalists in the same trade. He does
individually, what the whole body of capitalists engaged in producing
relative surplus-value, do collectively. On the other hand, however, this
extra surplus-value vanishes, so soon as the new method of production
has become general, and has consequently caused the difference between the individual value of the cheapened commodity and its social
value to vanish. The law of the determination of value by labour-time,
a law which brings under its sway the individual capitalist who applies
the new method of production, by compelling him to sell his goods
under their social value, this same law, acting as a coercive law of
competition, forces his competitors to adopt the new method. The
general rate of surplus-value is, therefore, ultimately affected by the
whole process, only when the increase in the productiveness of labour,
has seized upon those branches of production that are connected
with, and has cheapened those commodities that form part of, the
necessary means of subsistence, and are therefore elements of the value
of labour-power.

The value of commodities is in inverse ratio to the productiveness of
labour. And so, too, is the value of labour-power, because it depends on
the values of commodities. Relative surplus-value is, on the contrary,
directly proportional to that productiveness. It rises with rising and
falls with falling productiveness. The value of money being assumed to
be constant, an average social working-day of 12 hours always produces
the same new value, six shillings, no matter how this sum may be
apportioned between surplus-value and wages. But if, in consequence

of increased productiveness, the value of the necessaries of life fall, and the value of a day's labour-power be thereby reduced from five shillings to three, the surplus-value increases from one shilling to three. Ten hours were necessary for the reproduction of the value of the labour-power; now only six are required. Four hours have been set free, and can be annexed to the domain of surplus-labour. Hence there is imma-nent in capital an inclination and constant tendency, to heighten the productiveness of labour, in order to cheapen commodities, and by such cheapening to cheapen the labourer himself.

The value of a commodity is, in itself, of no interest to the capitalist. What alone interests him, is the surplus-value that dwells in it, and is realisable by sale. Realisation of the surplus-value necessarily carries with it the refunding of the value that was advanced. Now, since relative surplus-value increases in direct proportion to the develop-ment of the productiveness of labour, while, on the other hand, the value of commodities diminishes in the same proportion; since one and the same process cheapens commodities, and augments the surplus-value contained in them; we have here the solution of the riddle: why does the capitalist, whose sole concern is the production of exchange-value, continually strive to depress the exchange-value of commodi-ties? A riddle with which Quesnay, one of the founders of Political Economy, tormented his opponents, and to which they could give him no answer. 'You acknowledge', he says, 'that the more expenses and the cost of labour can, in the manufacture of industrial products, be re-duced without injury to production, the more advantageous is such reduction, because it diminishes the price of the finished article. And yet, you believe that the production of wealth, which arises from the labour of the workpeople, consists in the augmentation of the ex-change-value of their products.'

The shortening of the working-day is, therefore, by no means what is aimed at, in capitalist production, when labour is economised by increasing its productiveness. It is only the shortening of the labour-time, necessary for the production of a definite quantity of com-modities, that is aimed at. The fact that the workman, when the productiveness of his labour has been increased, produces, say 10 times as many commodities as before, and thus spends one-tenth as much labour-time on each, by no means prevents him from continuing to work 12 hours as before, nor from producing in those 12 hours 1,200 articles instead of 120. Nay, more, his working-day may be prolonged at the same time, so as to make him produce, say 1,400 articles in 14 hours. In the treatises, therefore, of economists of the stamp of

MacCulloch, Ure, Senior, and tutti quanti, we may read upon one page, that the labourer owes a debt of gratitude to capital for developing his productiveness, because the necessary labour-time is thereby shortened, and on the next page, that he must prove his gratitude by working in future for 15 hours instead of 10. The object of all development of the productiveness of labour, within the limits of capitalist production, is to shorten that part of the working-day, during which the workman must labour for his own benefit, and by that very shortening, to lengthen the other part of the day, during which he is at liberty to work gratis for the capitalist. How far this result is also attainable, without cheapening commodities, will appear from an examination of the particular modes of producing relative surplus-value, to which examination we now proceed.

CHAPTER 13

CO-OPERATION

CAPITALIST production only then really begins, as we have already seen, when each individual capital employs simultaneously a comparatively large number of labourers; when consequently the labour-process is carried on on an extensive scale and yields, relatively, large quantities of products. A greater number of labourers working together, at the same time, in one place (or, if you will, in the same field of labour), in order to produce the same sort of commodity under the mastership of one capitalist, constitutes, both historically and logically, the starting-point of capitalist production. With regard to the mode of production itself, manufacture, in its strict meaning, is hardly to be distinguished, in its earliest stages, from the handicraft trades of the guilds, otherwise than by the greater number of workmen simultaneously employed by one and the same individual capital. The workshop of the mediæval master handicraftsman is simply enlarged.

Nevertheless, within certain limits, a modification takes place. The labour realised in value, is labour of an average social quality; is consequently the expenditure of average labour-power. Any average magnitude, however, is merely the average of a number of separate magnitudes all of one kind, but differing as to quantity. In every industry, each individual labourer, be he Peter or Paul, differs from the average labourer. These individual differences, or 'errors' as they are called in mathematics, compensate one another, and vanish, whenever a certain minimum number of workmen are employed together. The celebrated sophist and sycophant, Edmund Burke, goes so far as to make the following assertion, based on his practical observations as a farmer; viz., that 'in so small a platoon' as that of five farm labourers, all individual differences in the labour vanish, and that consequently any given five adult farm labourers taken together, will in the same time do as much work as any other five. But, however that may be, it is clear, that the collective working-day of a large number of workmen simultaneously employed, divided by the number of these workmen, gives one day of average social labour.

Thus the laws of the production of value are only fully realised for the individual producer, when he produces as a capitalist, and employs a number of workmen together, whose labour, by its collective nature, is at once stamped as average social labour.

Even without an alteration in the system of working, the simultaneous employment of a large number of labourers effects a revolution in the material conditions of the labour-process. The buildings in which they work, the store-houses for the raw material, the implements and utensils used simultaneously or in turns by the workmen; in short, a portion of the means of production, are now consumed in common. On the one hand, the exchange-value of these means of production is not increased; for the exchange-value of a commodity is not raised by its use-value being consumed more thoroughly and to greater advantage. On the other hand, they are used in common, and therefore on a larger scale than before. A room where twenty weavers work at twenty looms must be larger than the room of a single weaver with two assistants. But it costs less labour to build one workshop for twenty persons than to build ten to accommodate two weavers each; thus the value of the means of production that are concentrated for use in common on a large scale does not increase in direct proportion to the expansion and to the increased useful effect of those means. When consumed in common, they give up a smaller part of their value to each single product; partly because the total value they part with is spread over a greater quantity of products, and partly because their value, though absolutely greater, is, having regard to their sphere of action in the process, relatively less than the value of isolated means of production. Owing to this, the value of a part of the constant capital falls, and in proportion to the magnitude of the fall, the total value of the commodity also falls. The effect is the same as if the means of production had cost less. The economy in their application is entirely owing to their being consumed in common by a large number of workmen. Moreover, this character of being necessary conditions of social labour, a character that distinguishes them from the dispersed and relatively more costly means of production of isolated, independent labourers, or small masters, is acquired even when the numerous workmen assembled together do not assist one another, but merely work side by side. A portion of the instruments of labour acquires this social character before the labour-process itself does so.

When numerous labourers work together side by side, whether in one and the same process, or in different but connected processes, they are said to co-operate, or to work in co-operation.

Just as the offensive power of a squadron of cavalry, or the defensive power of a regiment of infantry, is essentially different from the sum of the offensive or defensive powers of the individual cavalry or infantry soldiers taken separately, so the sum total of the mechanical forces exerted by isolated workmen differs from the social force that is developed, when many hands take part simultaneously in one and the same undivided operation, such as raising a heavy weight, turning a winch, or removing an obstacle. In such cases the effect of the combined labour could either not be produced at all by isolated individual labour, or it could only be produced by a great expenditure of time, or on a very dwarfed scale. Not only have we here an increase in the productive power of the individual, by means of co-operation, but the creation of a new power, namely, the collective power of masses.

Apart from the new power that arises from the fusion of many forces into one single force, mere social contact begets in most industries an emulation and a stimulation of the animal spirits that heightens the efficiency of each individual workman. Hence it is that a dozen persons working together will, in their collective working-day of 144 hours, produce far more than twelve isolated men each working 12 hours, or than one man who works twelve days in succession. The reason of this is that man is, if not as Aristotle contends, a political, at all events a social animal.

Although a number of men may be occupied together at the same time on the same, or the same kind of work, yet the labour of each, as a part of the collective labour, may correspond to a distinct phase of the labour-process, through all whose phases, in consequence of co-operation, the subject of their labour passes with greater speed. For instance, if a dozen masons place themselves in a row, so as to pass stones from the foot of a ladder to its summit, each of them does the same thing; nevertheless, their separate acts form connected parts of one total operation; they are particular phases, which must be gone through by each stone; and the stones are thus carried up quicker by the 24 hands of the row of men than they could be if each man went separately up and down the ladder with his burden. The object is carried over the same distance in a shorter time. Again, a combination of labour occurs whenever a building, for instance, is taken in hand on different sides simultaneously; although here also the co-operating masons are doing the same, or the same kind of work. The 12 masons, in their collective working-day of 144 hours, make much more progress with the building than one mason could make working for 12 days, or 144 hours. The reason is, that a body of men working in concert has hands and eyes both before and behind, and is, to a certain degree, omnipresent. The various parts of the work progress simultaneously.

In the above instances we have laid stress upon the point that the men do the same, or the same kind of work, because this, the most simple form of labour in common, plays a great part in co-operation, even in its most fully developed stage. If the work be complicated, then the mere number of the men who co-operate allows of the various operations being apportioned to different hands, and, consequently, of being carried on simultaneously. The time necessary for the completion of the whole work is thereby shortened.

In many industries, there are critical periods, determined by the nature of the process, during which certain definite results must be obtained. For instance, if a flock of sheep has to be shorn, or a field of wheat to be cut and harvested, the quantity and quality of the product depends on the work being begun and ended within a certain time. In these cases, the time that ought to be taken by the process is prescribed, just as it is in herring fishing. A single person cannot carve a working-day of more than, say 12 hours, out of the natural day, but 100 men co-operating extend the working-day to 1,200 hours. The shortness of the time allowed for the work is compensated for by the large mass of labour thrown upon the field of production at the decisive moment. The completion of the task within the proper time depends on the simultaneous application of numerous combined working-days; the amount of useful effect depends on the number of labourers; this number, however, is always smaller than the number of isolated labourers required to do the same amount of work in the same period. It is owing to the absence of this kind of co-operation that, in the western part of the United States, quantities of corn, and in those parts of East India where English rule has destroyed the old communities, quantities of cotton, are yearly wasted.

On the one hand, co-operation allows of the work being carried on over an extended space; it is consequently imperatively called for in certain undertakings, such as draining, constructing dykes, irrigation works, and the making of canals, roads and railways. On the other hand, while extending the scale of production, it renders possible a relative contraction of the arena. This contraction of arena simultaneous with, and arising from, extension of scale, whereby a number of useless expenses are cut down, is owing to the conglomeration of labourers, to the aggregation of various processes, and to the concentration of the means of production.

The combined working-day produces, relatively to an equal sum of isolated working-days, a greater quantity of use-values, and, consequently, diminishes the labour-time necessary for the production of a given useful effect. Whether the combined working-day, in a given case, acquires this increased productive power, because it heightens the mechanical force of labour, or extends its sphere of action over a greater space, or contracts the field of production relatively to the scale of production, or at the critical moment sets large masses of labour to work, or excites emulation between individuals and raises their animal spirits, or impresses on the similar operations carried on by a number of men the stamp of continuity and many-sidedness, or performs simultaneously different operations, or economises the means of production by use in common, or lends to individual labour the character of average social labour—whichever of these be the cause of the increase, the special productive power of the combined working-day is, under all circumstances, the social productive power of labour, or the productive power of social labour. This power is due to co-operation itself. When the labourer co-operates systematically with others, he strips off the fetters of his individuality, and develops the capabilities of his species.

As a general rule, labourers cannot co-operate without being brought together: their assemblage in one place is a necessary condition of their co-operation. Hence wage-labourers cannot co-operate, unless they are employed simultaneously by the same capital, the same capitalist, and unless therefore their labour-powers are bought simultaneously by him. The total value of these labour-powers, or the amount of the wages of these labourers for a day, or a week, as the case may be, must be ready in the pocket of the capitalist, before the workmen are assembled for the process of production. The payment of 300 workmen at once, though only for one day, requires a greater outlay of capital, than does the payment of a smaller number of men, week by week, during a whole year. Hence the number of the labourers that co-operate, or the scale of co-operation, depends, in the first instance, on the amount of capital that the individual capitalist can spare for the purchase of labour-power; in other words, on the extent to which a single capitalist has command over the means of subsistence of a number of labourers.

And as with the variable, so it is with the constant capital. For example, the outlay on raw material is 30 times as great, for the capitalist who employs 300 men, as it is for each of the 30 capitalists who employ 10 men. The value and quantity of the instruments of labour used in common do not, it is true, increase at the same rate as the number of workmen, but they do increase very considerably. Hence, concentration of large masses of the means of production in the hands of individual capitalists, is a material condition for the co-operation of wage-labourers, and the extent of the co-operation or the scale of production, depends on the extent of this concentration.

We saw in a former chapter, that a certain minimum amount of capital was necessary, in order that the number of labourers simultaneously employed, and, consequently, the amount of surplus-value produced, might suffice to liberate the employer himself from manual labour, to convert him from a small master into a capitalist, and thus formally to establish capitalist production. We now see that a certain minimum amount is a necessary condition for the conversion of numerous isolated and independent processes into one combined social process.

We also saw that at first, the subjection of labour to capital was only a formal result of the fact, that the labourer, instead of working for himself, works for and consequently under the capitalist. By the co-operation of numerous wage-labourers, the sway of capital develops into a requisite for carrying on the labour-process itself, into a real requisite of production. That a capitalist should command on the field of production, is now as indispensable as that a general should command on the field of battle.

All combined labour on a large scale requires, more or less, a directing authority, in order to secure the harmonious working of the individual activities, and to perform the general functions that have their origin in the action of the combined organism, as distinguished from the action of its separate organs. A single violin player is his own conductor; an orchestra requires a separate one. The work of directing, superintending, and adjusting, becomes one of the functions of capital, from the moment that the labour under the control of capital, becomes co-operative. Once a function of capital, it acquires special characteristics.

The directing motive, the end and aim of capitalist production, is to extract the greatest possible amount of surplus-value, and consequently to exploit labour-power to the greatest possible extent. As the number of the co-operating labourers increases, so too does their resistance to the domination of capital, and with it, the necessity for capital to overcome this resistance by counterpressure. The control exercised by the capitalist is not only a special function, due to the nature of the social labour-process, and peculiar to that process, but it is, at the same time, a function of the exploitation of a social labour-process, and is consequently rooted in the unavoidable antagonism between the exploiter and the living and labouring raw material he exploits.

Again, in proportion to the increasing mass of the means of production, now no longer the property of the labourer, but of the capitalist, the necessity increases for some effective control over the proper application of those means. Moreover, the co-operation of wage-labourers is entirely brought about by the capital that employs them. Their union into one single productive body and the establishment of a connexion between their individual functions, are matters foreign and external to them, are not their own act, but the act of the capital that brings and keeps them together. Hence the connexion existing between their various labours appears to them, ideally, in the shape of a preconceived plan of the capitalist, and practically in the shape of the authority of the same capitalist, in the shape of the powerful will of another, who subjects their activity to his aims. If, then, the control of the capitalist is in substance two-fold by reason of the two-fold nature of the process of production itself,—which, on the one hand, is a social process for producing use-values, on the other, a process for creating surplus-value—in form that control is despotic. As co-operation extends its scale, this despotism takes forms peculiar to itself. Just as at first the capitalist is relieved from actual labour so soon as his capital has reached that minimum amount with which capitalist production, as such, begins, so now, he hands over the work of direct and constant supervision of the individual workmen, and groups of workmen, to a special kind of wage-labourer. An industrial army of workmen, under the command of a capitalist, requires, like a real army, officers (managers), and sergeants (foremen, overlookers), who, while the work is being done, command in the name of the capitalist. The work of supervision becomes their established and exclusive function. When comparing the mode of production of isolated peasants and artisans with production by slave-labour, the political economist counts this labour of superintendence among the *faux frais* of production. But, when considering the capitalist mode of production, he, on the contrary, treats the work of control made necessary by the co-operative character of the labour-process as identical with the different work of control, necessitated by the capitalist character of that process and the antagonism of interests between capitalist and labourer. It is not because he is a leader of industry that a man is a capitalist; on the contrary, he is a leader of industry because he is a capitalist. The leadership of industry is an attribute of capital, just as in feudal times the functions of general and judge, were attributes of landed property.

The labourer is the owner of his labour-power until he has done bargaining for its sale with the capitalist; and he can sell no more than what he has—i.e. his individual, isolated labour-power. This state of things is in no way altered by the fact that the capitalist, instead of buying the labour-power of one man, buys that of 100, and enters into separate contracts with 100 unconnected men instead of with one. He is at liberty to set the 100 men to work, without letting them co-operate. He pays them the value of 100 independent labour-powers, but he does not pay for the combined labour-power of the hundred. Being independent of each other, the labourers are isolated persons, who enter into relations with the capitalist, but not with one another. This co-operation begins only with the labour-process, but they have then ceased to belong to themselves. On entering that process, they become incorporated with capital. As co-operators, as members of a working organism they are but special modes of existence of capital. Hence, the productive power developed by the labourer when working in co-operation, is the productive power of capital. This power is developed gratuitously, whenever the workmen are placed under given conditions, and it is capital that places them under such conditions. Because this power costs capital nothing, and because, on the other hand, the labourer himself does not develop it before his labour belongs to capital, it appears as a power with which capital is endowed by Nature—a productive power that is immanent in capital.

CHAPTER 14

DIVISION OF LABOUR AND MANUFACTURE

Section 1. Two-Fold Origin of Manufacture

That co-operation which is based on division of labour, assumes its typical form in manufacture, and is the prevalent characteristic form of the capitalist process of production throughout the manufacturing period properly so called. That period, roughly speaking, extends from the middle of the 16th to the last third of the 18th century.

Manufacture takes its rise in two ways:—

(1) By the assemblage, in one workshop under the control of a single capitalist, of labourers belonging to various independent handicrafts, but through whose hands a given article must pass on its way to completion. A carriage, for example, was formerly the product of the labour of a great number of independent artificers, such as wheel-wrights, harness-makers, tailors, locksmiths, upholsterers, turners, fringe-makers, glaziers, painters, polishers, gilders, etc. In the manufacture of carriages, however, all these different artificers are assembled in one building where they work into one another's hands. It is true that a carriage cannot be gilt before it has been made. But if a number of carriages are being made simultaneously, some may be in the hands of the gilders while others are going through an earlier process. So far, we are still in the domain of simple co-operation, which finds its materials ready to hand in the shape of men and things But very soon an important change takes place. The tailor, the locksmith, and the other artificers, being now exclusively occupied in carriage-making, each gradually loses, through want of practice, the ability to carry on, to its full extent, his old handicraft. But, on the other hand, his activity now confined in one groove, assumes the form best adapted to the narrowed sphere of action. At first, carriage manufacture is a combination of various independent handicrafts. By degrees, it becomes the splitting up of carriage-making into its various detail processes, each of which crystallises into the exclusive function of a particular workman, the manufacture, as a whole, being carried on by the men in conjunction. In the same way, cloth manufacture, as also a whole series of other manufactures, arose by combining different handicrafts together under the control of a single capitalist.

(2) Manufacture also arises in a way exactly the reverse of this—namely, by one capitalist employing simultaneously in one workshop a number of artificers, who all do the same, or the same kind of work, such as making paper, type, or needles. This is co-operation in its most elementary form. Each of these artificers (with the help, perhaps, of one or two apprentices), makes the entire commodity, and he consequently performs in succession all the operations necessary for its production. He still works in his old handicraft-like way. But very soon external circumstances cause a different use to be made of the concentration of the workmen on one spot, and of the simultaneousness of their work. An increased quantity of the article has perhaps to be delivered within a given time. The work is therefore re-distributed. Instead of each man being allowed to perform all the various operations in succession, these operations are changed into disconnected, isolated ones, carried on side by side; each is assigned to a different artificer, and the whole of them together are performed simultaneously by the co-operating workmen. This accidental repartition gets repeated, develops advantages of its own, and gradually ossifies into a systematic division of labour. The commodity, from being the individual product of an independent artificer, becomes the social product of a union of artificers, each of whom performs one, and only one, of the constituent partial operations. The same operations which, in the case of a papermaker belonging to a German Guild, merged one into the other as the successive acts of one artificer, became in the Dutch paper manufacture so many partial operations carried on side by side by numerous co-operating labourers. The needlemaker of the Nuremberg Guild was the cornerstone on which the English needle manufacture was raised. But while in Nuremberg that single artificer performed a series of perhaps 20 operations one after another, in England it was not long before there were 20 needle-makers side by side, each performing one alone of those 20 operations, and in consequence of further experience, each of those 20 operations was again split up, isolated, and made the exclusive function of a separate workman.

The mode in which manufacture arises, its growth out of handicrafts, is therefore two-fold. On the one hand, it arises from the union of various independent handicrafts, which become stripped of their independence and specialised to such an extent as to be reduced to mere supplementary partial processes in the production of one particular commodity. On the other hand, it arises from the co-operation of artificers of one handicraft; it splits up that particular handicraft into its various detail operations, isolating, and making these operations independent of one another up to the point where each becomes the exclusive function of a particular labourer. On the one hand, therefore, manufacture either introduces division of labour into a process of production, or further develops that division; on the other hand, it unites together handicrafts that were formerly separate. But whatever may have been its particular starting-point, its final form is invariably the same—a productive mechanism whose parts are human beings.

For a proper understanding of the division of labour in manufacture, it is essential that the following points be firmly grasped. First, the decomposition of a process of production into its various successive steps coincides, here, strictly with the resolution of a handicraft into its successive manual operations. Whether complex or simple, each operation has to be done by hand, retains the character of a handicraft, and is therefore dependent on the strength, skill, quickness, and sureness, of the individual workman in handling his tools. The handicraft continues to be the basis. This narrow technical basis excludes a really scientific analysis of any definite process of industrial production, since it is still a condition that each detail process gone through by the product must be capable of being done by hand and of forming, in its way, a separate handicraft. It is just because handicraft skill continues, in this way, to be the foundation of the process of production, that each workman becomes exclusively assigned to a partial function, and that for the rest of his life, his labour-power is turned into the organ of this detail function.

Secondly, this division of labour is a particular sort of co-operation, and many of its disadvantages spring from the general character of co-operation, and not from this particular form of it.

Section 2. The Detail Labourer and his Implements

If we now go more into detail, it is, in the first place, clear that a labourer who all his life performs one and the same simple operation, converts his whole body into the automatic, specialised implement of that operation. Consequently, he takes less time in doing it, than the artificer who performs a whole series of operations in succession. But the collective labourer, who constitutes the living mechanism of manufacture, is made up solely of such specialised detail labourers. Hence, in comparison with the independent handicraft, more is produced in a given time, or the productive power of labour is increased. Moreover, when once this fractional work is established as the exclusive function of one person, the methods it employs become perfected. The work-man's continued repetition of the same simple act, and the concen-tration of his attention on it, teach him by experience how to attain the desired effect with the minimum of exertion. But since there are always several generations of labourers living at one time, and working together at the manufacture of a given article, the technical skill, the tricks of the trade thus acquired, become established, and are accumu-lated and handed down. Manufacture, in fact, produces the skill of the detail labourer, by reproducing, and systematically driving to an ex-treme within the workshop, the naturally developed differentiation of trades which it found ready to hand in society at large. On the other hand, the conversion of fractional work into the life-calling of one man, corresponds to the tendency shown by earlier societies, to make trades hereditary; either to petrify them into castes, or whenever definite historical conditions beget in the individual a tendency to vary in a manner incompatible with the nature of castes, to ossify them into guilds. Castes and guilds arise from the action of the same natural law, that regulates the differentiation of plants and animals into species and varieties, except that, when a certain degree of development has been reached, the heredity of castes and the exclusiveness of guilds are ordained as a law of society. 'The muslins of Dakka in fineness, the calicoes and other piece goods of Coromandel in brilliant and durable colours, have never been surpassed. Yet they are produced without capital, machinery, division of labour, or any of those means which give such facilities to the manufacturing interest of Europe. The weaver is merely a detached individual, working a web when ordered of a cus-tomer, and with a loom of the rudest construction, consisting some-times of a few branches or bars of wood, put roughly together. There is even no expedient for rolling up the warp; the loom must therefore be kept stretched to its full length, and becomes so inconveniently large, that it cannot be contained within the hut of the manufacturer, who is therefore compelled to ply his trade in the open air, where it is interrupted by every vicissitude of the weather.' It is only the special skill accumulated from generation to generation, and transmitted from father to son, that gives to the Hindu, as it does to the spider, this proficiency. And yet the work of such a Hindu weaver is very compli-cated, compared with that of a manufacturing labourer.

An artificer, who performs one after another the various fractional operations in the production of a finished article, must at one time change his place, at another his tools. The transition from one oper-ation to another interrupts the flow of his labour, and creates, so to say, gaps in his working-day. These gaps close up so soon as he is tied to one and the same operation all day long; they vanish in proportion as the changes in his work diminish. The resulting increased productive power is owing either to an increased expenditure of labour-power in a given time—i.e. to increased intensity of labour—or to a decrease in the amount of labour-power unproductively consumed. The extra expenditure of power, demanded by every transition from rest to motion, is made up for by prolonging the duration of the normal velocity when once acquired. On the other hand, constant labour of one uniform kind disturbs the intensity and flow of a man's animal spirits, which find recreation and delight in mere change of activity.

The productiveness of labour depends not only on the proficiency of the workman, but on the perfection of his tools. Tools of the same kind, such as knives, drills, gimlets, hammers, etc., may be employed in different processes; and the same tool may serve various purposes in a single process. But so soon as the different operations of a labour-process are disconnected the one from the other, and each fractional operation acquires in the hands of the detail labourer a suitable and peculiar form, alterations become necessary in the implements that previously served more than one purpose. The direction taken by this change is determined by the difficulties experienced in consequence of the unchanged form of the implement. Manufacture is characterised by the differentiation of the instruments of labour—a differentiation whereby implements of a given sort acquire fixed shapes, adapted to each particular application, and by the specialisation of those instruments, giving to each special implement its full play only in the hands of a specific detail labourer. In Birmingham alone 500 varieties of hammers are produced, and not only is each adapted to one particular process, but several varieties often serve exclusively for the different operations in one and the same process. The manufacturing period simplifies, improves, and multiplies the implements of labour, by adapting them to the exclusively special functions of each detail labourer. It thus creates at the same time one of the material conditions for the existence of machinery, which consists of a combination of simple instruments.

The detail labourer and his implements are the simplest elements of manufacture. Let us now turn to its aspect as a whole.

Section 3. The Two Fundamental Forms of Manufacture: Heterogeneous Manufacture, Serial Manufacture

The organisation of manufacture has two fundamental forms which, in spite of occasional blending, are essentially different in kind, and, moreover, play very distinct parts in the subsequent transformation of manufacture into modern industry carried on by machinery. This double character arises from the nature of the article produced. This article either results from the mere mechanical fitting together of partial products made independently, or owes its completed shape to a series of connected processes and manipulations.

A locomotive, for instance, consists of more than 5,000 independent parts. It cannot, however, serve as an example of the first kind of genuine manufacture, for it is a structure produced by modern mechanical industry. But a watch can; and William Petty used it to illustrate the division of labour in manufacture. Formerly the individual work of a Nuremberg artificer, the watch has been transformed into the social product of an immense number of detail labourers, such as mainspring makers, dial makers, spiral spring makers, jewelled hole makers, ruby lever makers, hand makers, case makers, screw makers, gilders, with numerous subdivisions, such as wheel makers (brass and steel separate), pin makers, movement makers, acheveur de pignon (fixes the wheels on the axles, polishes the facets, etc.), pivot makers, planteur de finissage (puts the wheels and springs in the works), finisseur de barillet (cuts teeth in the wheels, makes the holes of the right size, etc.), escapement makers, cylinder makers for cylinder escapements, escapement wheel makers, balance wheel makers, raquette makers (apparatus for regulating the watch), the planteur d'échappement (escapement maker proper); then the repasseur de barillet (finishes the box for the spring, etc.), steel polishers, wheel polishers, screw polishers, figure painters, dial enamellers (melt the enamel on the copper), fabricant de pendants (makes the ring by which the case is hung), finisseur de charnière (puts the brass hinge in the cover, etc.), faiseur de secret (puts in the springs that open the case), graveur, ciseleur, polisseur de boîte, etc., etc., and last of all the repasseur, who fits together the whole watch and hands it over in a going state. Only a few parts of the watch pass through several hands; and all these membra disjecta come together for the first time in the hand that binds them into one mechanical whole. This external relation between the finished product, and its various and diverse elements makes it, as well in this case as in the case of all similar finished articles, a matter of chance whether the detail labourers are brought together in one workshop or not. The detail operations may further be carried on like so many independent handicrafts, as they are in the Cantons of Vaud and Neufchâtel; while in Geneva there exist large watch manufactories where the detail labourers directly co-operate under the control of a single capitalist. And even in the latter case the dial, the springs, and the case, are seldom made in the factory itself. To carry on the trade as a manufacture, with concentration of workmen, is, in the watch trade, profitable only under exceptional conditions, because competition is greater between the labourers who desire to work at home, and because the splitting up of the work into a number of heterogeneous processes, permits but little use of the instruments of labour in common, and the capitalist, by scattering the work, saves the outlay on workshops, etc. Nevertheless the position of this detail labourer who, though he works at home, does so for a capitalist (manufacturer, établisseur), is very different from that of the independent artificer, who works for his own customers.

The second kind of manufacture, its perfected form, produces articles that go through connected phases of development, through a series of processes step by step, like the wire in the manufacture of needles, which passes through the hands of 72 and sometimes even 92 different detail workmen.

In so far as such a manufacture, when first started, combines scattered handicrafts, it lessens the space by which the various phases of production are separated from each other. The time taken in passing from one stage to another is shortened, so is the labour that effectuates this passage. In comparison with a handicraft, productive power is gained, and this gain is owing to the general co-operative character of manufacture. On the other hand, division of labour, which is the distinguishing principle of manufacture, requires the isolation of the various stages of production and their independence of each other. The establishment and maintenance of a connexion between the isolated functions necessitates the incessant transport of the article from one hand to another, and from one process to another. From the standpoint of modern mechanical industry, this necessity stands forth as a characteristic and costly disadvantage, and one that is immanent in the principle of manufacture.

If we confine our attention to some particular lot of raw materials, of rags, for instance, in paper manufacture, or of wire in needle manufacture, we perceive that it passes in succession through a series of stages in the hands of the various detail workmen until completion. On the other hand, if we look at the workshop as a whole, we see the raw material in all the stages of its production at the same time. The collective labourer, with one set of his many hands armed with one kind of tools, draws the wire, with another set, armed with different tools, he, at the same time, straightens it, with another, he cuts it, with another, points it, and so on. The different detail processes, which were successive in time, have become simultaneous, go on side by side in space. Hence, production of a greater quantum of finished commodities in a given time. This simultaneity, it is true, is due to the general co-operative form of the process as a whole; but Manufacture not only finds the conditions for co-operation ready to hand, it also, to some extent, creates them by the sub-division of handicraft labour. On the other hand, it accomplishes this social organisation of the labour-process only by riveting each labourer to a single fractional detail.

Since the fractional product of each detail labourer is, at the same time, only a particular stage in the development of one and the same finished article, each labourer, or each group of labourers, prepares the raw material for another labourer or group. The result of the labour of the one is the starting-point for the labour of the other. The one workman therefore gives occupation directly to the other. The labour-time necessary in each partial process, for attaining the desired effect, is learnt by experience; and the mechanism of Manufacture, as a whole, is based on the assumption that a given result will be obtained in a given time. It is only on this assumption that the various supplementary labour-processes can proceed uninterruptedly, simultaneously, and side by side. It is clear that this direct dependence of the operations, and therefore of the labourers, on each other, compels each one of them to spend on his work no more than the necessary time, and thus a continuity, uniformity, regularity, order, and even intensity of labour, of quite a different kind, is begotten than is to be found in an independent handicraft or even in simple co-operation. The rule, that the labour-time expended on a commodity should not exceed that which is socially necessary for its production, appears, in the production of commodities generally, to be established by the mere effect of competition; since, to express ourselves superficially, each single producer is obliged to sell his commodity at its market-price. In Manufacture, on the contrary, the turning out of a given quantum of product in a given time is a technical law of the process of production itself.

Different operations take, however, unequal periods, and yield therefore, in equal times unequal quantities of fractional products. If, therefore, the same labourer has, day after day, to perform the same operation, there must be a different number of labourers for each operation; for instance, in type manufacture, there are four founders and two breakers to one rubber: the founder casts 2,000 type an hour, the breaker breaks up 4,000, and the rubber polishes 8,000. Here we have again the principle of co-operation in its simplest form, the simultaneous employment of many doing the same thing; only now, this principle is the expression of an organic relation. The division of labour, as carried out in Manufacture, not only simplifies and multiplies the qualitatively different parts of the social collective labourer, but also creates a fixed mathematical relation or ratio which regulates the quantitative extent of those parts—i.e. the relative number of labourers, or the relative size of the group of labourers, for each detail operation. It developss, along with the qualitative sub-division of the social labour-process, a quantitative rule and proportionality for that process.

When once the most fitting proportion has been experimentally established for the numbers of the detail labourers in the various groups when producing on a given scale, that scale can be extended only by employing a multiple of each particular group. There is this to boot, that the same individual can do certain kinds of work just as well on a large as on a small scale; for instance, the labour of superintendence, the carriage of the fractional product from one stage to the next, etc. The isolation of such functions, their allotment to a particular labourer, does not become advantageous till after an increase in the number of labourers employed; but this increase must affect every group proportionally.

The isolated group of labourers to whom any particular detail function is assigned, is made up of homogeneous elements, and is one of the constituent parts of the total mechanism. In many manufactures, however, the group itself is an organised body of labour, the total mechanism being a repetition or multiplication of these elementary organisms. Take, for instance, the manufacture of glass bottles. It may be resolved into three essentially different stages. First, the preliminary stage, consisting of the preparation of the components of the glass, mixing the sand and lime, etc., and melting them into a fluid mass of glass. Various detail labourers are employed in this first stage, as also in the final one of removing the bottles from the drying furnace, sorting and packing them, etc. In the middle, between these two stages, comes the glass melting proper, the manipulation of the fluid mass. At each mouth of the furnace, there works a group, called 'the hole,' consisting of one bottlemaker or finisher, one blower, one gatherer, one putter-up or whetter-off, and one taker-in. These five detail workers are so many special organs of a single working organism that acts only as a whole, and therefore can operate only by the direct co-operation of the whole five. The whole body is paralysed if but one of its members be wanting. But a glass furnace has several openings (in England from

4 to 6), each of which contains an earthenware melting-pot full of molten glass, and employs a similar five-membered group of workers. The organisation of each group is based on division of labour, but the bond between the different groups is simple co-operation, which, by using in common one of the means of production, the furnace, causes it to be more economically consumed. Such a furnace, with its 4–6 groups, constitutes a glass house; and a glass manufactory comprises a number of such glass houses, together with the apparatus and workmen requisite for the preparatory and final stages.

Finally, just as Manufacture arises in part from the combination of various handicrafts, so, too, it develops into a combination of various manufactures. The larger English glass manufacturers, for instance, make their own earthenware melting-pots, because, on the quality of these depends, to a great extent, the success or failure of the process. The manufacture of one of the means of production is here united with that of the product. On the other hand, the manufacture of the product may be united with other manufactures, of which that product is the raw material, or with the products of which it is itself subsequently mixed. Thus, we find the manufacture of flint glass combined with that of glass cutting and brass founding; the latter for the metal settings of various articles of glass. The various manufactures so combined form more or less separate departments of a larger manufacture, but are at the same time independent processes, each with its own divison of labour. In spite of the many advantages offered by this combination of manufactures, it never grows into a complete technical system on its own foundation. That happens only on its transformation into an industry carried on by machinery.

The collective labourer, formed by the combination of a number of detail labourers, is the machinery specially characteristic of the manufacturing period. The various operations that are performed in turns by the producer of a commodity, and coalesce one with another during the progress of production, lay claim to him in various ways. In one operation he must exert more strength, in another more skill, in another more attention; and the same individual does not possess all these qualities in an equal degree. After Manufacture has once separated, made independent, and isolated the various operations, the labourers are divided, classified, and grouped according to their predominating qualities. If their natural endowments are, on the one hand, the foundation on which the division of labour is built up, on the other hand, Manufacture, once introduced, develops in them new powers that are by nature fitted only for limited and special functions. The collective labourer now possesses, in an equal degree of excellence, all the qualities requisite for production, and expends them in the most economical manner, by exclusively employing all his organs, consisting of particular labourers, or groups of labourers, in performing their special functions. The one-sidedness and the deficiencies of the detail labourer become perfections when he is a part of the collective labourer. The habit of doing only one thing converts him into a never failing instrument, while his connexion with the whole mechanism compels him to work with the regularity of the parts of a machine.

Since the collective labourer has functions, both simple and complex, both high and low, his members, the individual labour-powers, require different degrees of training, and must therefore have different values. Manufacture, therefore, develops a hierarchy of labour-powers, to which there corresponds a scale of wages. If, on the one hand, the individual labourers are appropriated and annexed for life by a limited function; on the other hand, the various operations of the hierarchy are parcelled out among the labourers according to both their natural and their acquired capabilities. Every process of production, however, requires certain simple manipulations, which every man is capable of doing. They too are now severed from their connexion with the more pregnant moments of activity, and ossified into exclusive functions of specially appointed labourers. Hence, Manufacture begets, in every handicraft that it seizes upon, a class of so-called unskilled labourers, a class which handicraft industry strictly excluded. If it develops a one-sided speciality into a perfection, at the expense of the whole of a man's working capacity, it also begins to make a speciality of the absence of all development. Alongside of the hierarchic gradation there steps the simple separation of the labourers into skilled and unskilled. For the latter, the cost of apprenticeship vanishes; for the former, it diminishes, compared with that of artificers, in consequence of the functions being simplified. In both cases the value of labour-power falls. An exception to this law holds good whenever the decomposition of the labour-process begets new and comprehensive functions, that either had no place at all, or only a very modest one, in handicrafts. The fall in the value of labour-power, caused by the disappearance or diminution of the expenses of apprenticeship, implies a direct increase of surplus-value for the benefit of capital; for everything that shortens the necessary labour-time required for the reproduction of labour-power, extends the domain of surplus-labour.

Section 4. Division of Labour in Manufacture, and Division of Labour in Society

We first considered the origin of Manufacture, then its simple elements, then the detail labourer and his implements, and finally, the totality of the mechanism. We shall now lightly touch upon the relation between the division of labour in manufacture, and the social division of labour, which forms the foundation of all production of commodities.

If we keep labour alone in view, we may designate the separation of social production into its main divisions or *genera*—viz., agriculture, industries, etc., as division of labour in general, and the splitting up of these families into species and sub-species, as division of labour in particular, and the division of labour within the workshop as division of labour in singular or in detail.

Division of labour in a society, and the corresponding tying down of individuals to a particular calling, develops itself, just as does the division of labour in manufacture, from opposite starting-points. Within a family, and after further development within a tribe, there springs up naturally a division of labour, caused by differences of sex and age, a division that is consequently based on a purely physiological foundation, which division enlarges its materials by the expansion of the community, by the increase of population, and more especially, by the conflicts between different tribes, and the subjugation of one tribe by another. On the other hand, as I have already remarked,* the exchange of products springs up at the points where different families, tribes, communities, come in contact; for, in the beginning of civilisation, it is not private individuals but families, tribes, etc., that meet on an independent footing. Different communities find different means of production, and different means of subsistence in their natural environment. Hence, their modes of production, and of living, and their products are different. It is this spontaneously developed difference which, when different communities come in contact, calls forth the mutual exchange of products, and the consequent gradual conversion of those products into commodities. Exchange does not create the differences between the spheres of production, but brings what are already different into relation, and thus converts them into more or less inter-dependent branches of the collective production of an enlarged society. In the latter case, the social division of labour arises from the exchange between spheres of production, that are originally distinct and independent of one another. In the former, where the physiological division of labour is the starting-point, the particular organs of a compact whole grow loose, and break off, principally owing to the exchange of commodities with foreign communities, and then isolate themselves so far, that the sole bond, still connecting the various kinds of work, is the exchange of the products as commodities. In the one case, it is the making dependent what was before independent; in the other case, the making independent what was before dependent.

The foundation of every division of labour that is well developed, and brought about by the exchange of commodities, is the separation between town and country. It may be said, that the whole economic history of society is summed up in the movement of this antithesis. We pass it over, however, for the present.

Just as a certain number of simultaneously employed labourers are the material pre-requisites for division of labour in manufacture, so are the number and density of the population, which here correspond to the agglomeration in one workshop, a necessary condition for the division of labour in society. Nevertheless, this density is more or less relative. A relatively thinly populated country, with well-developed means of communication, has a denser population than a more numerously populated country, with badly-developed means of communication; and in this sense the Northern States of the American Union, for instance, are more thickly populated than India.

Since the production and the circulation of commodities are the general pre-requisites of the capitalist mode of production, division of labour in manufacture demands, that division of labour in society at large should previously have attained a certain degree of development. Inversely, the former division reacts upon and develops and multiplies the latter. Simultaneously, with the differentiation of the instruments of labour, the industries that produce these instruments, become more and more differentiated. If the manufacturing system seize upon an industry, which, previously, was carried on in connexion with others, either as a chief or as a subordinate industry, and by one producer, these industries immediately separate their connexion, and become independent. If it seize upon a particular stage in the production of a commodity, the other stages of its production become converted into so many independent industries. It has already been stated, that where the finished article consists merely of a number of parts fitted together, the detail operations may re-establish themselves as genuine and separate handicrafts. In order to carry out more perfectly the division of labour in manufacture, a single branch of production is, according to the varieties of its raw material, or the various forms that one and the same raw material may assume, split up into numerous, and to some extent, entirely new manufactures. Accordingly, in France alone, in the first half of the 18th century, over 100 different kinds of silk stuffs were woven, and, in Avignon, it was law, that 'every apprentice should devote himself to only one sort of fabrication, and should not learn the preparation of several kinds of stuff at once'. The territorial division of labour, which confines special branches of production to special districts of a country, acquires fresh stimulus from the manufacturing system, which exploits every special advantage. The Colonial system and the opening out of the markets of the world, both of which are included in the general conditions of existence of the manufacturing period, furnish rich material for developing the division of labour in society. It is not the place, here, to go on to show how division of labour seizes upon, not only the economic, but every other sphere of society, and everywhere lays the foundation of that all engrossing system of specialising and sorting men, that development in a man of one single faculty at the expense of all other faculties, which caused A. Ferguson, the master of Adam Smith, to exclaim: 'We make a nation of Helots, and have no free citizens.'

But, in spite of the numerous analogies and links connecting them, division of labour in the interior of a society, and that in the interior of a workshop, differ not only in degree, but also in kind. The analogy appears most indisputable where there is an invisible bond uniting the various branches of trade. For instance the cattle-breeder produces hides, the tanner makes the hides into leather, and the shoemaker, the leather into boots. Here the thing produced by each of them is but a step towards the final form, which is the product of all their labours combined. There are, besides, all the various industries that supply the cattle-breeder, the tanner, and the shoemaker with the means of production. Now it is quite possible to imagine, with Adam Smith, that the difference between the above social division of labour, and the division in manufacture, is merely subjective, exists merely for the observer, who, in a manufacture, can see with one glance, all the numerous operations being performed on one spot, while in the instance given above, the spreading out of the work over great areas, and the great number of people employed in each branch of labour, obscure the connexion. But what is it that forms the bond between the independent labours of the cattle-breeder, the tanner, and the shoemaker? It is the fact that their respective products are commodities. What, on the other hand, characterises division of labour in manufactures? The fact that the detail labourer produces no commodities. It is only the common product of all the detail labourers that becomes a commodity. Division of labour in society is brought about by the purchase and sale of the products of different branches of industry, while the connexion between the detail operations in a workshop, is due to the sale of the labour-power of several workmen to one capitalist, who applies it as combined labour-power. The division of labour in the workshop implies concentration of the means of production in the hands of one capitalist; the division of labour in society implies their dispersion among many independent producers of commodities. While within the workshop, the iron law of proportionality subjects definite numbers of workmen to definite functions, in the society outside the workshop, chance and caprice have full play in distributing the producers and their means of production among the various branches of industry. The different spheres of production, it is true, constantly tend to an equilibrium: for, on the one hand, while each producer of a commodity is bound to produce a use-value, to satisfy a particular social want, and while the extent of these wants differs quantitatively, still there exists an inner relation which settles their proportions into a regular system, and that system one of spontaneous growth; and, on the other hand, the law of the value of commodities ultimately determines how much of its disposable working-time society can expend on each particular class of commodities. But this constant tendency to equilibrium, of the various spheres of production, is exercised, only in the shape of a reaction against the constant upsetting of this equilibrium. The *a priori* system on which the division of labour, within the workshop, is regularly carried out, becomes in the division of labour within the society, an *a posteriori*, nature-imposed necessity, controlling the lawless caprice of the producers, and perceptible in the barometrical fluctuations of the market-prices. Division of labour within the workshop implies the undisputed authority of the capitalist over men, that are but parts of a mechanism that belongs to him. The division of labour within the society brings into contact independent commodity-producers, who acknowledge no other authority but that of competition, of the coercion exerted by the pressure of their mutual interests; just as in the animal kingdom, the *bellum omnium contra omnes* more or less preserves the conditions of existence of every species. The same bourgeois mind which praises division of labour in the workshop, life-long annexation of the labourer to a partial operation, and his complete subjection to capital, as being an organisation of labour that increases its productiveness—that same bourgeois mind denounces with equal vigour every conscious attempt to socially control and regulate the process of production, as an inroad upon such sacred things as the rights of property, freedom and unrestricted play for the bent of the individual capitalist. It is very characteristic that the enthusiastic apologists of the factory system have nothing more damning to urge against a general organisation of the labour of society, than that it would turn all society into one immense factory.

If, in a society with capitalist production, anarchy in the social division of labour and despotism in that of the workshop are mutual conditions the one of the other, we find, on the contrary, in those earlier forms of society in which the separation of trades has been spontaneously developed, then crystallised, and finally made permanent by law, on the one hand, a specimen of the organisation of the labour of society, in accordance with an approved and authoritative plan, and on the other, the entire exclusion of division of labour in the workshop, or at all events a mere dwarflike or sporadic and accidental development of the same.

Those small and extremely ancient Indian communities, some of which have continued down to this day, are based on possession in common of the land, on the blending of agriculture and handicrafts, and on an unalterable division of labour, which serves, whenever a new community is started, as a plan and scheme ready cut and dried. Occupying areas of from 100 up to several thousand acres, each forms a compact whole producing all it requires. The chief part of the products is destined for direct use by the community itself, and does not take the form of a commodity. Hence, production here is independent of that division of labour brought about, in Indian society as a whole, by means of the exchange of commodities. It is the surplus alone that becomes a commodity, and a portion of even that, not until it has reached the hands of the State, into whose hands from time immemorial a certain quantity of these products has found its way in the shape of rent in kind. The constitution of these communities varies in different parts of India. In those of the simplest form, the land is tilled in common, and the produce divided among the members. At the same time, spinning and weaving are carried on in each family as subsidiary industries. Side by side with the masses thus occupied with one and the same work, we find the 'chief inhabitant', who is judge, police, and tax-gatherer in one; the book-keeper, who keeps the accounts of the tillage and registers everything relating thereto; another official, who prosecutes criminals, protects strangers travelling through and escorts them to the next village; the boundary man, who guards the boundaries against neighbouring communities; the water-overseer, who distributes the water from the common tanks for irrigation; the Brahmin, who conducts the religious services; the schoolmaster, who on the sand teaches the children reading and writing; the calendar-Brahmin, or astrologer, who makes known the lucky or unlucky days for seed-time and harvest, and for every other kind of agricultural work; a smith and a carpenter, who make and repair all the agricultural implements; the potter, who makes all the pottery of the village; the barber, the washerman, who washes clothes, the silversmith, here and there the poet, who in some communities replaces the silversmith, in others the schoolmaster. This dozen of individuals is maintained at the expense of the whole community. If the population increases, a new community is founded, on the pattern of the old one, on unoccupied land. The whole mechanism discloses a systematic division of labour; but a division like that in manufactures is impossible, since the smith and the carpenter, etc., find an unchanging market, and at the most there occur, according to the sizes of the villages, two or three of each, instead of one. The law that regulates the division of labour in the community acts with the irresistible authority of a law of Nature, at the same time that each individual artificer, the smith, the carpenter, and so on, conducts in his workshop all the operations of his handicraft in the traditional way, but independently, and without recognising any authority over him. The simplicity of the organisation for production in these self-sufficing communities that constantly reproduce themselves in the same form, and when accidentally destroyed, spring up again on the spot and with the same name—this simplicity supplies the key to the secret of the unchangeableness of Asiatic societies, an unchangeableness in such striking contrast with the constant dissolution and refounding of Asiatic States, and the never-ceasing changes of dynasty. The structure of the economic elements of society remains untouched by the storm-clouds of the political sky.

The rules of the guilds, as I have said before, by limiting most strictly the number of apprentices and journeymen that a single master could employ, prevented him from becoming a capitalist. Moreover, he could not employ his journeymen in many other handicrafts than the one in which he was a master. The guilds zealously repelled every encroachment by the capital of merchants, the only form of free capital with which they came in contact. A merchant could buy every kind of commodity, but labour as a commodity he could not buy. He existed only on sufferance, as a dealer in the products of the handicrafts. If circumstances called for a further division of labour, the existing guilds split themselves up into varieties, or founded new guilds by the side of the old ones; all this, however, without concentrating various handicrafts in a single workshop. Hence, the guild organisation, however much it may have contributed by separating, isolating, and perfecting the handicrafts, to create the material conditions for the existence of manufacture, excluded division of labour in the workshop. On the whole, the labourer and his means of production remained closely united, like the snail with its shell, and thus there was wanting the principal basis of manufacture, the separation of the labourer from his means of production, and the conversion of these means into capital.

While division of labour in society at large, whether such division be brought about or not by exchange of commodities, is common to economic formations of society the most diverse, division of labour in the workshop, as practised by manufacture, is a special creation of the capitalist mode of production alone.

Section 5. The Capitalistic Character of Manufacture

An increased number of labourers under the control of one capitalist is the natural starting-point, as well of co-operation generally, as of manufacture in particular. But the division of labour in manufacture makes this increase in the number of workmen a technical necessity. The minimum number that any given capitalist is bound to employ is here prescribed by the previously established division of labour. On the other hand, the advantages of further division are obtainable only by adding to the number of workmen, and this can be done only by adding multiples of the various detail groups. But an increase in the variable component of the capital employed necessitates an increase in its constant component, too, in the workshops, implements, etc., and, in particular, in the raw material, the call for which grows quicker than the number of workmen. The quantity of it consumed in a given time, by a given amount of labour, increases in the same ratio as does the productive power of that labour in consequence of its division. Hence, it is a law, based on the very nature of manufacture, that the minimum amount of capital, which is bound to be in the hands of each capitalist, must keep increasing; in other words, that the transformation into capital of the social means of production and subsistence must keep extending.

In manufacture, as well as in simple co-operation, the collective working organism is a form of existence of capital. The mechanism that is made up of numerous individual detail labourers belongs to the capitalist. Hence, the productive power resulting from a combination of labours appears to be the productive power of capital. Manufacture proper not only subjects the previously independent workman to the discipline and command of capital, but, in addition, creates a hierarchic gradation of the workmen themselves. While simple co-operation leaves the mode of working by the individual for the most part unchanged, manufacture thoroughly revolutionises it, and seizes labour-power by its very roots. It converts the labourer into a crippled monstrosity, by forcing his detail dexterity at the expense of a world of productive capabilities and instincts; just as in the States of La Plata* they butcher a whole beast for the sake of his hide or his tallow. Not only is the detail work distributed to the different individuals, but the individual himself is made the automatic motor of a fractional operation, and the absurd fable of Menenius Agrippa,* which makes man a mere fragment of his own body, becomes realised. If, at first, the workman sells his labour-power to capital, because the material means of producing a commodity fail him, now his very labour-power refuses its services unless it has been sold to capital. Its functions can be exercised only in an environment that exists in the workshop of the capitalist after the sale. By nature unfitted to make anything independently, the manufacturing labourer develops productive activity as a mere appendage of the capitalist's workshop. As the chosen people bore in their features the sign manual of Jehovah, so division of labour brands the manufacturing workman as the property of capital.

The knowledge, the judgment, and the will, which, though in ever so small a degree, are practised by the independent peasant or handicraftsman, in the same way as the savage makes the whole art of war consist in the exercise of his personal cunning—these faculties are now required only for the workshop as a whole. Intelligence in production expands in one direction, because it vanishes in many others. What is lost by the detail labourers, is concentrated in the capital that employs them. It is a result of the division of labour in manufactures, that the labourer is brought face to face with the intellectual potencies of the material process of production, as the property of another, and as a ruling power. This separation begins in simple co-operation, where the capitalist represents to the single workman, the oneness and the will of the associated labour. It is developed in manufacture which cuts down the labourer into a detail labourer. It is completed in modern industry, which makes science a productive force distinct from labour and presses it into the service of capital.

In manufacture, in order to make the collective labourer, and through him capital, rich in social productive power, each labourer must be made poor in individual productive powers. 'Ignorance is the mother of industry as well as of superstition. Reflection and fancy are subject to err; but a habit of moving the hand or the foot is independent of either. Manufactures, accordingly, prosper most where the mind is least consulted, and where the workshop may . . . be considered as an engine, the parts of which are men.' As a matter of fact, some few manufacturers in the middle of the 18th century preferred, for certain operations that were trade secrets, to employ half-idiotic persons.

'The understandings of the greater part of men', says Adam Smith, 'are necessarily formed by their ordinary employments. The man whose whole life is spent in performing a few simple operations . . . has no occasion to exert his understanding. . . . He generally becomes as stupid and ignorant as it is possible for a human creature to become.' After describing the stupidity of the detail labourer he goes on: 'The uniformity of his stationary life naturally corrupts the courage of his mind. . . . It corrupts even the activity of his body and renders him incapable of exerting his strength with vigour and perseverance in any other employments than that to which he has been bred. His dexterity at his own particular trade seems in this manner to be acquired at the expense of his intellectual, social, and martial virtues. But in every improved and civilised society, this is the state into which the labouring poor, that is, the great body of the people, must necessarily fall.' For preventing the complete deterioration of the great mass of the people by division of labour, A. Smith recommends education of the people by the State, but prudently, and in homœopathic doses. G. Garnier, his French translator and commentator, who, under the first French Empire, quite naturally developed into a senator, quite as naturally opposes him on this point. Education of the masses, he urges, violates the first law of the division of labour, and with it 'our whole social system would be proscribed'. 'Like all other divisions of labour,' he says, 'that between hand labour and head labour is more pronounced and decided in proportion as society (he rightly uses this word, for capital, landed property and their State) becomes richer. This division of labour, like every other, is an effect of past, and a cause of future progress . . . ought the government then to work in opposition to this division of labour, and to hinder its natural course? Ought it to expend a part of the public money in the attempt to confound and blend together two classes of labour, which are striving after division and separation?'

Some crippling of body and mind is inseparable even from division of labour in society as a whole. Since, however, manufacture carries this social separation of branches of labour much further, and also, by its peculiar division, attacks the individual at the very roots of his life, it is the first to afford the materials for, and to give a start to, industrial pathology.

'To subdivide a man is to execute him, if he deserves the sentence, to assassinate him if he does not. . . . The subdivision of labour is the assassination of a people.'

Co-operation based on division of labour, in other words, manufacture, commences as a spontaneous formation. So soon as it attains some consistence and extension, it becomes the recognised methodical and systematic form of capitalist production. History shows how the division of labour peculiar to manufacture, strictly so called, acquires the best adapted form at first by experience, as it were behind the backs of the actors, and then, like the guild handicrafts, strives to hold fast that form when once found, and here and there succeeds in keeping it for centuries. Any alteration in this form, except in trivial matters, is solely owing to a revolution in the instruments of labour. Modern manufacture wherever it arises—I do not here allude to modern industry based on machinery—either finds the disjecta membra poetæ* ready to hand, and only waiting to be collected together, as is the case in the manufacture of clothes in large towns, or it can easily apply the principle of division, simply by exclusively assigning the various operations of a handicraft (such as book-binding) to particular men. In such cases, a week's experience is enough to determine the proportion between the numbers of the hands necessary for the various functions.

By decomposition of handicrafts, by specialisation of the instruments of labour, by the formation of detail labourers, and by grouping and combining the latter into a single mechanism, division of labour in manufacture creates a qualitative gradation, and a quantitative proportion in the social process of production; it consequently creates a definite organisation of the labour of society, and thereby develops at the same time new productive forces in the society. In its specific capitalist form—and under the given conditions, it could take no other form than a capitalistic one—manufacture is but a particular method of begetting relative surplus-value, or of augmenting at the expense of the labourer the self-expansion of capital—usually called social wealth, 'Wealth of Nations', etc. It increases the social productive power of labour, not only for the benefit of the capitalist instead of for that of the labourer, but it does this by crippling the individual labourers. It creates new conditions for the lordship of capital over labour. If, therefore, on the one hand, it presents itself historically as a progress and as a necessary phase in the economic development of society, on the other hand, it is a refined and civilised method of exploitation.

Political Economy, which as an independent science, first sprang into being during the period of manufacture, views the social division of labour only from the standpoint of manufacture, and sees in it only the means of producing more commodities with a given quantity of labour, and, consequently, of cheapening commodities and hurrying on the accumulation of capital. In most striking contrast with this accentuation of quantity and exchange-value, is the attitude of the writers of classical antiquity, who hold exclusively by quality and use-value. In consequence of the separation of the social branches of production, commodities are better made, the various bents and talents of men select a suitable field, and without some restraint no important results can be obtained anywhere. Hence both product and producer are improved by division of labour. If the growth of the quantity produced is occasionally mentioned, this is only done with reference to the greater abundance of use-values. There is not a word alluding to exchange-value or to the cheapening of commodities. This aspect, from the standpoint of use-value alone, is taken as well by Plato, who treats division of labour as the foundation on which the division of society into classes is based, as by Xenophon, who with characteristic bourgeois instinct, approaches more nearly to division of labour within the workshop. Plato's Republic, in so far as division of labour is treated in it, as the formative principle of the State, is merely the Athenian idealisation of the Egyptian system of castes, Egypt having served as the model of an industrial country to many of his contemporaries also, amongst others to Isocrates, and it continued to have this importance to the Greeks of the Roman Empire.

During the manufacturing period proper, i.e. the period during which manufacture is the predominant form taken by capitalist production, many obstacles are opposed to the full development of the peculiar tendencies of manufacture. Although manufacture creates, as we have already seen, a simple separation of the labourers into skilled and unskilled, simultaneously with their hierarchic arrangement in classes, yet the number of the unskilled labourers, owing to the preponderating influence of the skilled, remains very limited. Although it adapts the detail operations to the various degrees of maturity, strength, and development of the living instruments of labour, thus conducing to exploitation of women and children, yet this tendency as a whole is wrecked on the habits and the resistance of the male labourers. Although the splitting up of handicrafts lowers the cost of forming the workman, and thereby lowers his value, yet for the more difficult detail work, a longer apprenticeship is necessary, and, even where it would be superfluous, is jealously insisted upon by the workmen. In England, for instance, we find the laws of apprenticeship, with their seven years' probation, in full force down to the end of the manufacturing period, and they are not thrown on one side till the advent of Modern Industry. Since handicraft skill is the foundation of manufacture, and since the mechanism of manufacture as a whole possesses no framework, apart from the labourers themselves, capital is constantly compelled to wrestle with the insubordination of the workmen. 'By the infirmity of human nature,' says friend Ure, 'it happens that the more skilful the workman, the more self-willed and intractable he is apt to become, and of course the less fit a component of a mechanical system in which . . . he may do great damage to the whole.' Hence throughout the whole manufacturing period there runs the complaint of want of discipline among the workmen. And had we not the testimony of contemporary writers, the simple facts, that during the period between the 16th century and the epoch of Modern Industry, capital failed to become the master of the whole disposable working-time of the manufacturing labourers, that manufactures are short-lived, and change their locality from one country to another with the emigrating or immigrating workmen, these facts would speak volumes. 'Order must in one way or another be established', exclaims in 1770 the oft-cited author of the 'Essay on Trade and Commerce'. 'Order,' re-echoes Dr Andrew Ure 66 years later, 'Order' was wanting in manufacture based on 'the scholastic dogma of division of labour,' and 'Arkwright created order.'

At the same time manufacture was unable, either to seize upon the production of society to its full extent, or to revolutionise that production to its very core. It towered up as an economic work of art, on the broad foundation of the town handicrafts, and of the rural domestic industries. At a given stage in its development, the narrow technical basis on which manufacture rested, came into conflict with requirements of production that were created by manufacture itself.

One of its most finished creations was the workshop for the production of the instruments of labour themselves, including especially the complicated mechanical apparatus then already employed. A machine-factory, says Ure, 'displayed the division of labour in manifold gradations—the file, the drill, the lathe, having each its different workman in the order of skill'. This workshop, the product of the division of labour in manufacture, produced in its turn—machines. It is they that sweep away the handicraftsman's work as the regulating principle of social production. Thus, on the one hand, the technical reason for the life-long annexation of the workman to a detail function is removed. On the other hand, the fetters that this same principle laid on the dominion of capital, fall away.

CHAPTER 15

MACHINERY AND MODERN INDUSTRY

Section 1. The Development of Machinery

John Stuart Mill says in his 'Principles of Political Economy': 'It is questionable if all the mechanical inventions yet made have lightened the day's toil of any human being.' That is, however, by no means the aim of the capitalistic application of machinery. Like every other increase in the productiveness of labour, machinery is intended to cheapen commodities, and, by shortening that portion of the working-day, in which the labourer works for himself, to lengthen the other portion that he gives, without an equivalent, to the capitalist. In short, it is a means for producing surplus-value.

In manufacture, the revolution in the mode of production begins with the labour-power, in modern industry it begins with the instruments of labour. Our first inquiry then is, how the instruments of labour are converted from tools into machines, or what is the difference between a machine and the implements of a handicraft? We are only concerned here with striking and general characteristics; for epochs in the history of society are no more separated from each other by hard and fast lines of demarcation, than are geological epochs.

Mathematicians and mechanicians, and in this they are followed by a few English economists, call a tool a simple machine, and a machine a complex tool. They see no essential difference between them, and even give the name of machine to the simple mechanical powers, the lever, the inclined plane, the screw, the wedge, etc. As a matter of fact, every machine is a combination of those simple powers no matter how they may be disguised. From the economic standpoint this explanation is worth nothing, because the historical element is wanting. Another explanation of the difference between tool and machine is that in the case of a tool, man is the motive power, while the motive power of a machine is something different from man, as, for instance, an animal, water, wind, and so on. According to this, a plough drawn by oxen, which is a contrivance common to the most different epochs, would be a machine, while Claussen's circular loom, which, worked by a single labourer, weaves 96,000 picks per minute, would be a mere tool. Nay, this very loom, though a tool when worked by hand, would, if worked by steam, be a machine. And since the application of animal power is one of man's earliest inventions, production by machinery would have preceded production by handicrafts. When in 1735, John Wyatt brought out his spinning machine, and began the industrial revolution of the 18th century, not a word did he say about an ass driving it instead of a man, and yet this part fell to the ass. He described it as a machine 'to spin without fingers'.[11]

All fully developed machinery consists of three essentially different parts, the motor mechanism, the transmitting mechanism, and finally the tool or working machine. The motor mechanism is that which puts the whole in motion. It either generates its own motive power, like the steam-engine, the caloric engine, the electromagnetic machine, etc., or it receives its impulse from some already existing natural force, like the water-wheel from a head of water, the wind-mill from wind, etc. The transmitting mechanism, composed of fly-wheels, shafting, toothed wheels, pullies, straps, ropes, bands, pinions, and gearing of the most varied kinds, regulates the motion, changes its form where necessary, as for instance, from linear to circular, and divides and distributes it among the working machines. These two first parts of the whole mechanism are there, solely for putting the working machines in motion, by means of which motion the subject of labour is seized upon and modified as desired. The tool or working machine is that part of the machinery with which the industrial revolution of the 18th century started. And to this day it constantly serves as such a starting-point, whenever a handicraft, or a manufacture, is turned into an industry carried on by machinery.

As soon as man, instead of working with an implement on the subject of his labour, becomes merely the motive power of an implement-machine, it is a mere accident that motive power takes the disguise of human muscle; and it may equally well take the form of wind, water or steam. Of course, this does not prevent such a change of form from producing great technical alterations in the mechanism that was originally constructed to be driven by man alone. Now-a-days, all machines that have their way to make, such as sewing-machines, bread-making machines, etc., are, unless from their very nature their use on a small scale is excluded, constructed to be driven both by human and by purely mechanical motive power.

The machine, which is the starting-point of the industrial revolution, supersedes the workman, who handles a single tool, by a mechanism operating with a number of similar tools, and set in motion by a single motive power, whatever the form of that power may be. Here we have the machine, but only as an elementary factor of production by machinery.

Increase in the size of the machine, and in the number of its working tools, calls for a more massive mechanism to drive it; and this mechanism requires, in order to overcome its resistance, a mightier moving power than that of man, apart from the fact that man is a very imperfect instrument for producing uniform continued motion. But assuming that he is acting simply as a motor, that a machine has taken the place of his tool, it is evident that he can be replaced by natural forces. Of all the great motors handed down from the manufacturing period, horse-power is the worst, partly because a horse has a head of his own, partly because he is costly, and the extent to which he is applicable in factories is very restricted. Nevertheless the horse was extensively used during the infancy of Modern Industry. This is proved, as well by the complaints of contemporary agriculturists, as by the term 'horse-power', which has survived to this day as an expression for mechanical force.

Wind was too inconstant and uncontrollable, and besides, in England, the birthplace of Modern Industry, the use of water-power preponderated even during the manufacturing period. In the 17th century attempts had already been made to turn two pairs of millstones with a single water-wheel. But the increased size of the gearing was too much for the water-power, which had now become insufficient, and this was one of the circumstances that led to a more accurate investigation of the laws of friction. In the same way the irregularity caused by the motive power in mills that were put in motion by pushing and pulling a lever, led to the theory, and the application, of the fly-wheel, which afterwards plays so important a part in Modern Industry. In this way, during the manufacturing period, were developed the first scientific and technical elements of Modern Mechanical Industry. Arkwright's throstle-spinning mill was from the very first turned by water. But for all that, the use of water, as the predominant motive power, was beset with difficulties. It could not be increased at will, it failed at certain seasons of the year, and, above all, it was essentially local. Not till the invention of Watt's second and so-called double-acting steam-engine, was a prime mover found, that begot its own force by the consumption of coal and water, whose power was entirely under man's control, that was mobile and a means of locomotion, that was urban and not, like the water-wheel, rural, that permitted production to be concentrated in towns instead of, like the water-wheels, being scattered up and down the country, that was of universal technical application, and, relatively speaking, little affected in its choice of residence by local circumstances. The greatness of Watt's genius showed itself in the specification of the patent that he took out in April, 1784. In that specification his steam-engine is described, not as an invention for a specific purpose, but as an agent universally applicable in Mechanical Industry. In it he points out applications, many of which, as for instance, the steam-hammer, were not introduced till half a century later. Nevertheless he doubted the use of steam-engines in navigation. His successors, Boulton and Watt, sent to the exhibition of 1851 steam-engines of colossal size for ocean steamers.

As soon as tools had been converted from being manual implements of man into implements of a mechanical apparatus, of a machine, the motive mechanism also acquired an independent form, entirely emancipated from the restraints of human strength. Thereupon the individual machine, that we have hitherto been considering, sinks into a mere factor in production by machinery. One motive mechanism was now able to drive many machines at once. The motive mechanism grows with the number of the machines that are turned simultaneously, and the transmitting mechanism becomes a wide-spreading apparatus.

We now proceed to distinguish the co-operation of a number of machines of one kind from a complex system of machinery.

In the one case, the product is entirely made by a single machine, which performs all the various operations previously done by one handicraftsman with his tool; as, for instance, by a weaver with his loom; or by several handicraftsmen successively, either separately or as members of a system of Manufacture. For example, in the manufacture of envelopes, one man folded the paper with the folder, another laid on the gum, a third turned the flap over, on which the device is impressed, a fourth embossed the device, and so on; and for each of these operations the envelope had to change hands. One single envelope machine now performs all these operations at once, and makes more than 3,000 envelopes in an hour. In the London exhibition of 1862, there was an American machine for making paper cornets. It cut the paper, pasted, folded, and finished 300 in a minute. Here, the whole process, which, when carried on as Manufacture, was split up into, and carried out by, a series of operations, is completed by a single machine, working a combination of various tools. Now, whether such a machine be merely a reproduction of a complicated manual implement, or a combination of various simple implements specialised by Manufacture, in either case, in the factory, i.e. in the workshop in which machinery alone is used, we meet again with simple co-operation; and, leaving the workman out of consideration for the moment, this co-operation presents itself to us, in the first instance, as the conglomeration in one place of similar and simultaneously acting machines. Thus, a weaving factory is constituted of a number of power-looms, working side by side, and a sewing factory of a number of sewing-machines all in the same building. But there is here a technical oneness in the whole system, owing to all the machines receiving their impulse simultaneously, and in an equal degree, from the pulsations of the common prime mover, by the intermediary of the transmitting mechanism; and this mechanism, to a certain extent, is also common to them all, since only particular ramifications of it branch off to each machine. Just as a number of tools, then, form the organs of a machine, so a number of machines of one kind constitute the organs of the motive mechanism.

A real machinery system, however, does not take the place of these independent machines, until the subject of labour goes through a connected series of detail processes, that are carried out by a chain of machines of various kinds, the one supplementing the other. Here we have again the co-operation by division of labour that characterises Manufacture; only now, it is a combination of detail machines. The special tools of the various detail workmen, such as those of the beaters, combers, spinners, etc., in the woollen manufacture, are now transformed into the tools of specialised machines, each machine constituting a special organ, with a special function, in the system. In those branches of industry in which the machinery system is first introduced, Manufacture itself furnishes, in a general way, the natural basis for the division, and consequent organisation, of the process of production. Nevertheless an essential difference at once manifests itself. In Manufacture it is the workmen who, with their manual implements, must, either singly or in groups, carry on each particular detail process. If, on the one hand, the workman becomes adapted to the process, on the other, the process was previously made suitable to the workman. This subjective principle of the division of labour no longer exists in production by machinery. Here, the process as a whole is examined objectively, in itself, that is to say, without regard to the question of its execution by human hands, it is analysed into its constituent phases; and the problem, how to execute each detail process, and bind them all into a whole, is solved by the aid of machines, chemistry, etc. But, of course, in this case also, theory must be perfected by accumulated experience on a large scale. Each detail machine supplies raw material to the machine next in order; and since they are all working at the same time, the product is always going through the various stages of its fabrication, and is also constantly in a state of transition, from one phase to another. Just as in Manufacture, the direct co-operation of the detail labourers establishes a numerical proportion between the special groups, so in an organised system of machinery, where one detail machine is constantly kept employed by another, a fixed relation is established between their numbers, their size, and their speed. The collective machine, now an organised system of various kinds of single machines, and of groups of single machines, becomes more and more perfect, the more the process as a whole becomes a continuous one, i.e. the less the raw material is interrupted in its passage from its first phase to its last; in other words, the more its passage from one phase to another is effected, not by the hand of man, but by the machinery itself. In Manufacture the isolation of each detail process is a condition imposed by the nature of division of labour, but in the fully developed factory the continuity of those processes is, on the contrary, imperative.

A system of machinery, whether it reposes on the mere co-operation of similar machines, as in weaving, or on a combination of different machines, as in spinning, constitutes in itself a huge automaton, when-ever it is driven by a self-acting prime mover. But although the factory as a whole be driven by its steam-engine, yet either some of the indi-vidual machines may require the aid of the workman for some of their movements (such aid was necessary for the running in of the mule carriage, before the invention of the self-acting mule, and is still necess-ary in fine-spinning mills); or, to enable a machine to do its work, certain parts of it may require to be handled by the workman like a manual tool; this was the case in machine-makers' workshops, before the conversion of the slide rest into a self-actor. As soon as a machine executes, without man's help, all the movements requisite to elaborate the raw material, needing only attendance from him, we have an auto-matic system of machinery, and one that is susceptible of constant improvement in its details. Such improvements as the apparatus that stops a drawing frame, whenever a sliver breaks, and the self-acting stop, that stops the power-loom so soon as the shuttle bobbin is emp-tied of weft, are quite modern inventions. As an example, both of continuity of production, and of the carrying out of the automatic principle, we may take a modern paper mill. In the paper industry generally, we may advantageously study in detail not only the dis-tinctions between modes of production based on different means of production, but also the connexion of the social conditions of pro-duction with those modes: for the old German paper-making furnishes us with a sample of handicraft production; that of Holland in the 17th and of France in the 18th century with a sample of manufacturing in the strict sense; and that of modern England with a sample of automatic fabrication of this article. Besides these, there still exist, in India and China, two distinct antique Asiatic forms of the same industry.

An organised system of machines, to which motion is communicated by the transmitting mechanism from a central automaton, is the most developed form of production by machinery. Here we have, in the place of the isolated machine, a mechanical monster whose body fills whole factories, and whose demon power, at first veiled under the slow and measured motions of his giant limbs, at length breaks out into the fast and furious whirl of his countless working organs.

There were mules and steam-engines before there were any labourers, whose exclusive occupation it was to make mules and steam-engines; just as men wore clothes before there were such people as tailors. The inventions of Vaucanson, Arkwright, Watt, and others, were, however, practicable, only because those inventors found, ready to hand, a considerable number of skilled mechanical workmen, placed at their disposal by the manufacturing period. Some of these workmen were independent handicraftsmen of various trades, others were grouped together in manufactures, in which, as before-mentioned, division of labour was strictly carried out. As inventions increased in number, and the demand for the newly discovered machines grew larger, the machine-making industry split up, more and more, into numerous independent branches, and division of labour in these manufactures was more and more developed. Here, then, we see in Manufacture the immediate technical foundation of Modern Industry. Manufacture produced the machinery, by means of which Modern Industry abolished the handicraft and manufacturing systems in those spheres of production that it first seized upon. The factory system was therefore raised, in the natural course of things, on an inadequate foundation. When the system attained to a certain degree of development, it had to root up this ready-made foundation, which in the meantime had been elaborated on the old lines, and to build up for itself a basis that should correspond to its methods of production. Just as the individual machine retains a dwarfish character, so long as it is worked by the power of man alone, and just as no system of machinery could be properly developed before the steam-engine took the place of the earlier motive powers, animals, wind, and even water; so, too, Modern Industry was crippled in its complete development, so long as its characteristic instrument of production, the machine, owed its existence to personal strength and personal skill, and depended on the muscular development, the keenness of sight, and the cunning of hand, with which the detail workmen in manufactures, and the manual labourers in handicrafts, wielded their dwarfish implements. Thus, apart from the dearness of the machines made in this way, a circumstance that is ever present to the mind of the capitalist, the expansion of industries carried on by means of machinery, and the invasion by machinery of fresh branches of production, were dependent on the growth of a class of workmen, who, owing to the almost artistic nature of their employment, could increase their numbers only gradually, and not by leaps and bounds. But besides this, at a certain stage of its development, Modern Industry became technologically incompatible with the basis furnished for it by handicraft and Manufacture. The increasing size of the prime movers, of the transmitting mechanism, and of the machines proper, the greater complication, multiformity and regularity of the details of these machines, as they more and more departed from the model of those originally made by manual labour, and acquired a form, untrammelled except by the conditions under which they worked, the perfecting of the automatic system, and the use, every day more unavoidable, of a more refractory material, such as iron instead of wood—the solution of all these problems, which sprang up by the force of circumstances, everywhere met with a stumbling-block in the personal restrictions, which even the collective labourer of Manufacture could not break through, except to a limited extent. Such machines as the modern hydraulic press, the modern power-loom, and the modern carding engine, could never have been furnished by Manufacture.

A radical change in the mode of production in one sphere of industry involves a similar change in other spheres. This happens at first in such branches of industry as are connected together by being separate phases of a process, and yet are isolated by the social division of labour, in such a way, that each of them produces an independent commodity. Thus spinning by machinery made weaving by machinery a necessity, and both together made the mechanical and chemical revolution that took place in bleaching, printing, and dyeing, imperative. So too, on the other hand, the revolution in cotton-spinning called forth the invention of the gin, for separating the seeds from the cotton fibre; it was only by means of this invention, that the production of cotton became possible on the enormous scale at present required. But more especially, the revolution in the modes of production of industry and agriculture made necessary a revolution in the general conditions of the social process of production, i.e. in the means of communication and of transport. In a society whose pivot, to use an expression of Fourier, was agriculture on a small scale, with its subsidiary domestic industries, and the urban handicrafts, the means of communication and transport were so utterly inadequate to the productive requirements of the manufacturing period, with its extended division of social labour, its concentration of the instruments of labour, and of the workmen, and its colonial markets, that they became in fact revolutionised. In the same way the means of communication and transport handed down from the manufacturing period soon became unbearable trammels on Modern Industry, with its feverish haste of production, its enormous extent, its constant flinging of capital and labour from one sphere of production into another, and its newly-created connexions with the markets of the whole world. Hence, apart from the radical changes introduced in the construction of sailing vessels, the means of communication and transport became gradually adapted to the modes of production of mechanical industry, by the creation of a system of river steamers, railways, ocean steamers, and telegraphs. But the huge masses of iron that had now to be forged, to be welded, to be cut, to be bored, and to be shaped, demanded, on their part, cyclopean machines, for the construction of which the methods of the manufacturing period were utterly inadequate.

Modern Industry had therefore itself to take in hand the machine, its characteristic instrument of production, and to construct machines by machines. It was not till it did this, that it built up for itself a fitting technical foundation, and stood on its own feet. Machinery, simultaneously with the increasing use of it, in the first decades of this century, appropriated, by degrees, the fabrication of machines proper. But it was only during the decade preceding 1866, that the construction of railways and ocean steamers on a stupendous scale called into existence the cyclopean machines now employed in the construction of prime movers.

The most essential condition to the production of machines by machines was a prime mover capable of exerting any amount of force, and yet under perfect control. Such a condition was already supplied by the steam-engine. But at the same time it was necessary to produce the geometrically accurate straight lines, planes, circles, cylinders, cones, and spheres, required in the detail parts of the machines. This problem Henry Maudsley solved in the first decade of this century by the invention of the slide rest, a tool that was soon made automatic, and in a modified form was applied to other constructive machines besides the lathe, for which it was originally intended. This mechanical appliance replaces, not some particular tool, but the hand itself, which produces a given form by holding and guiding the cutting tool along the iron or other material operated upon. Thus it became possible to produce the forms of the individual parts of machinery 'with a degree of ease, accuracy, and speed, that no accumulated experience of the hand of the most skilled workman could give'.

If we now fix our attention on that portion of the machinery employed in the construction of machines, which constitutes the operating tool, we find the manual implements re-appearing, but on a cyclopean scale. The operating part of the boring machine is an immense drill driven by a steam-engine; without this machine, on the other hand, the cylinders of large steam-engines and of hydraulic presses could not be made. The mechanical lathe is only a cyclopean reproduction of the ordinary foot-lathe; the planing machine, an iron carpenter, that works on iron with the same tools that the human carpenter employs on wood; the instrument that, on the London wharves, cuts the veneers, is a gigantic razor; the tool of the shearing machine, which shears iron as easily as a tailor's scissors cut cloth, is a monster pair of scissors; and the steam-hammer works with an ordinary hammer head, but of such a weight that not Thor himself could wield it. These steam-hammers are an invention of Nasmyth, and there is one that weighs over 6 tons and strikes with a vertical fall of 7 feet, on an anvil weighing 36 tons. It is mere child's-play for it to crush a block of granite into powder, yet it is no less capable of driving, with a succession of light taps, a nail into a piece of soft wood.

The implements of labour, in the form of machinery, necessitate the substitution of natural forces for human force, and the conscious application of science, instead of rule of thumb. In Manufacture, the organisation of the social labour-process is purely subjective; it is a combination of detail labourers; in its machinery system, Modern Industry has a productive organism that is purely objective, in which the labourer becomes a mere appendage to an already existing material condition of production. In simple co-operation, and even in that founded on division of labour, the suppression of the isolated, by the collective, workman still appears to be more or less accidental. Machinery, with a few exceptions to be mentioned later, operates only by means of associated labour, or labour in common. Hence the co-operative character of the labour-process is, in the latter case, a technical necessity dictated by the instrument of labour itself.

Section 2. The Value Transferred by Machinery to the Product

We saw that the productive forces resulting from co–operation and division of labour cost capital nothing. They are natural forces of social labour. So also physical forces, like steam, water, etc., when appropriated to productive processes, cost nothing. But just as a man requires lungs to breathe with, so he requires something that is work of man's hand, in order to consume physical forces productively. A water-wheel is necessary to exploit the force of water, and a steam–engine to exploit the elasticity of steam. Once discovered, the law of the deviation of the magnetic needle in the field of an electric current, or the law of the magnetisation of iron, around which an electric current circulates, cost never a penny. But the exploitation of these laws for the purposes of telegraphy, etc., necessitates a costly and extensive apparatus. The tool, as we have seen, is not exterminated by the machine. From being a dwarf implement of the human organism, it expands and multiplies into the implement of a mechanism created by man. Capital now sets the labourer to work, not with a manual tool, but with a machine which itself handles the tools. Although, therefore, it is clear at the first glance that, by incorporating both stupendous physical forces, and the natural sciences, with the process of production, Modern Industry raises the productiveness of labour to an extraordinary degree, it is by no means equally clear, that this increased productive force is not, on the other hand, purchased by an increased expenditure of labour. Machinery, like every other component of constant capital, creates no new value, but yields up its own value to the product that it serves to beget. In so far as the machine has value, and, in consequence, parts with value to the product, it forms an element in the value of that product. Instead of being cheapened, the product is made dearer in proportion to the value of the machine. And it is clear as noon-day, that machines and systems of machinery, the characteristic instruments of labour of Modern Industry, are incomparably more loaded with value than the implements used in handicrafts and manufactures.

In the first place, it must be observed that the machinery, while always entering as a whole into the labour-process, enters into the value-begetting process only by bits.It never adds more value than it loses, on an average, by wear and tear. Hence there is a great difference between the value of a machine, and the value transferred in a given time by that machine to the product. The longer the life of the machine in the labour-process, the greater is that difference. It is true, no doubt, as we have already seen, that every instrument of labour enters as a whole into the labour-process, and only piece-meal, proportionally to its average daily loss by wear and tear, into the value-begetting process. But this difference between the instrument as a whole and its daily wear and tear, is much greater in a machine than in a tool, because the machine, being made from more durable material, has a longer life; because its employment, being regulated by strictly scientific laws, allows of greater economy in the wear and tear of its parts, and in the materials it consumes; and lastly, because its field of production is incomparably larger than that of a tool. After making allowance, both in the case of the machine and of the tool, for their average daily cost, that is for the value they transmit to the product by their average daily wear and tear, and for their consumption of auxiliary substance, such as oil, coal, and so on, they each do their work gratuitously, just like the forces furnished by Nature without the help of man. The greater the productive power of the machinery compared with that of the tool, the greater is the extent of its gratuitous service compared with that of the tool. In Modern Industry man succeeded for the first time in making the product of his past labour work on a large scale gratuitously, like the forces of Nature.

In treating of Co-operation and Manufacture, it was shown that certain general factors of production, such as buildings, are, in comparison with the scattered means of production of the isolated workman, economised by being consumed in common, and that they therefore make the product cheaper. In a system of machinery, not only is the framework of the machine consumed in common by its numerous operating implements, but the prime mover, together with a part of the transmitting mechanism, is consumed in common by the numerous operative machines.

Given the difference between the value of the machinery, and the value transferred by it in a day to the product, the extent to which this latter value makes the product dearer, depends in the first instance, upon the size of the product; so to say, upon its area. Mr Baynes, of Blackburn, in a lecture published in 1858, estimates that 'each real mechanical horse-power will drive 450 self-acting mule spindles, with preparation, or 200 throstle spindles, or 15 looms for 40 inch cloth with the appliances for warping, sizing, etc.'. In the first case, it is the day's produce of 450 mule spindles, in the second, of 200 throstle spindles, in the third, of 15 power-looms, over which the daily cost of one horse-power, and the wear and tear of the machinery set in motion by that power, are spread; so that only a very minute value is transferred by such wear and tear to a pound of yarn or a yard of cloth. The same is the case with the steam-hammer mentioned above. Since its daily wear and tear, its coal-consumption, etc., are spread over the stupendous masses of iron hammered by it in a day, only a small value is added to a hundred weight of iron; but that value would be very great, if the cyclopean instrument were employed in driving in nails.

Given a machine's capacity for work, that is, the number of its operating tools, or, where it is a question of force, their mass, the amount of its product will depend on the velocity of its working parts, on the speed, for instance, of the spindles, or on the number of blows given by the hammer in a minute. Many of these colossal hammers strike seventy times in a minute, and Ryder's patent machine for forging spindles with small hammers gives as many as 700 strokes per minute.

Given the rate at which machinery transfers its value to the product, the amount of value so transferred depends on the total value of the machinery. The less labour it contains, the less value it imparts to the product. The less value it gives up, so much the more productive it is, and so much the more its services approximate to those of natural forces. But the production of machinery by machinery lessens its value relatively to its extension and efficacy.

An analysis and comparison of the prices of commodities produced by handicrafts or manufactures, and of the prices of the same commodities produced by machinery, shows generally, that, in the product of machinery, the value due to the instruments of labour increases relatively, but decreases absolutely. In other words, its absolute amount decreases, but its amount, relatively to the total value of the product, of a pound of yarn, for instance, increases.

It is evident that whenever it costs as much labour to produce a machine as is saved by the employment of that machine, there is nothing but a transposition of labour; consequently the total labour required to produce a commodity is not lessened or the productiveness of labour is not increased. It is clear, however, that the difference between the labour a machine costs, and the labour it saves, in other words, that the degree of its productiveness does not depend on the difference between its own value and the value of the implement it replaces. As long as the labour spent on a machine, and consequently the portion of its value added to the product, remains smaller than the value added by the workman to the product with his tool, there is always a difference of labour saved in favour of the machine. The productiveness of a machine is therefore measured by the human labour-power it replaces. According to Mr Baynes, 2½ operatives are required for the 450 mule spindles, inclusive of preparation machinery, that are driven by one-horse power; each self-acting mule spindle, working ten hours, produces 13 ounces of yarn (average number of thickness); consequently 2½ operatives spin weekly 365⅝ lbs. of yarn. Hence, leaving waste on one side, 366 lbs. of cotton absorb, during their conversion into yarn, only 150 hours' labour, or fifteen days' labour of ten hours each. But with a spinning-wheel, supposing the hand-spinner to produce thirteen ounces of yarn in sixty hours, the same weight of cotton would absorb 2,700 days' labour of ten hours each, or 27,000 hours' labour. Where blockprinting, the old method of printing calico by hand, has been superseded by machine printing, a single machine prints, with the aid of one man or boy, as much calico of four colours in one hour, as it formerly took 200 men to do. Before Eli Whitney invented the cotton gin in 1793, the separation of the seed from a pound of cotton cost an average day's labour. By means of his invention one negress was enabled to clean 100 lbs. daily; and since then, the efficacy of the gin has been considerably increased. A pound of cotton wool, previously costing 50 cents to produce, included after that invention more unpaid labour, and was consequently sold with greater profit, at 10 cents. In India they employ for separating the wool from the seed, an instrument, half machine, half tool, called a churka; with this one man and a woman can clean 28 lbs. daily. With the churka invented some years ago by Dr Forbes, one man and a boy produce 250 lbs. daily. If oxen, steam, or water, be used for driving it, only a few boys and girls as feeders are required. Sixteen of these machines driven by oxen do as much work in a day as formerly 750 people did on an average.

As already stated, a steam-plough does as much work in one hour at a cost of threepence, as 66 men at a cost of 15 shillings. I return to this example in order to clear up an erroneous notion. The 15 shillings are by no means the expression in money of all the labour expended in one hour by the 66 men. If the ratio of surplus-labour to necessary labour were 100%, these 66 men would produce in one hour a value of 30 shillings, although their wages, 15 shillings, represent only their labour for half an hour. Suppose, then, a machine cost as much as the wages for a year of the 150 men it displaces, say £3,000; this £3,000 is by no means the expression in money of the labour added to the object produced by these 150 men before the introduction of the machine, but only of that portion of their year's labour which was expended for themselves and represented by their wages. On the other hand, the

£3,000, the money-value of the machine, expresses all the labour expended on its production, no matter in what proportion this labour constitutes wages for the workman, and surplus-value for the capitalist. Therefore, though a machine cost as much as the labour-power displaced by it costs, yet the labour materialised in it is even then much less than the living labour it replaces.

The use of machinery for the exclusive purpose of cheapening the product, is limited in this way, that less labour must be expended in producing the machinery than is displaced by the employment of that machinery. For the capitalist, however, this use is still more limited. Instead of paying for the labour, he only pays the value of the labour-power employed; therefore, the limit to his using a machine is fixed by the difference between the value of the machine and the value of the labour-power replaced by it. Since the division of the day's work into necessary and surplus-labour differs in different countries, and even in the same country at different periods, or in different branches of industry; and further, since the actual wage of the labourer at one time sinks below the value of his labour-power, at another rises above it, it is possible for the difference between the price of the machinery and the price of the labour-power replaced by that machinery to vary very much, although the difference between the quantity of labour requisite to produce the machine and the total quantity replaced by it, remain constant. But it is the former difference alone that determines the cost, to the capitalist, of producing a commodity, and, through the pressure of competition, influences his action. Hence the invention now-a-days of machines in England that are employed only in North America; just as in the sixteenth and seventeenth centuries, machines were invented in Germany to be used only in Holland, and just as many a French invention of the eighteenth century was exploited in England alone. In the older countries, machinery, when employed in some branches of industry, creates such a redundancy of labour in other branches that in these latter the fall of wages below the value of labour-power impedes the use of machinery, and, from the standpoint of the capitalist, whose profit comes, not from a diminution of the labour employed, but of the labour paid for, renders that use superfluous and often impossible. In some branches of the woollen manufacture in England the employment of children has during recent years been considerably diminished, and in some cases has been entirely abolished. Why? Because the Factory Acts made two sets of children necessary, one working six hours, the other four, or each working five hours. But the parents refused to sell the 'half-timers' cheaper than the 'full-timers'. Hence the substitution of machinery for the 'half-timers'. Before the labour of women and of children under 10 years of age was forbidden in mines, capitalists considered the employment of naked women and girls, often in company with men, so far sanctioned by their moral code, and especially by their ledgers, that it was only after the passing of the Act that they had recourse to machinery. The Yankees have invented a stone-breaking machine. The English do not make use of it, because the 'wretch' who does this work gets paid for such a small portion of his labour, that machinery would increase the cost of production to the capitalist. In England women are still occasionally used instead of horses for hauling canal boats, because the labour required to produce horses and machines is an accurately known quantity, while that required to maintain the women of the surplus-population is below all calculation. Hence nowhere do we find a more shameful squandering of human labour-power for the most despicable purposes than in England, the land of machinery.

Section 3. The Proximate Effects of Machinery on the Workman

The starting-point of Modern Industry is, as we have shown, the revolution in the instruments of labour, and this revolution attains its most highly developed form in the organised system of machinery in a factory. Before we inquire how human material is incorporated with this objective organism, let us consider some general effects of this revolution on the labourer himself.

(a) *Appropriation of Supplementary Labour-Power by Capital. The Employment of Women and Children*

In so far as machinery dispenses with muscular power, it becomes a means of employing labourers of slight muscular strength, and those whose bodily development is incomplete, but whose limbs are all the more supple. The labour of women and children was, therefore, the first thing sought for by capitalists who used machinery. That mighty substitute for labour and labourers was forthwith changed into a means for increasing the number of wage-labourers by enrolling, under the direct sway of capital, every member of the workman's family, without distinction of age or sex. Compulsory work for the capitalist usurped the place, not only of the children's play, but also of free labour at home within moderate limits for the support of the family.

The value of labour-power was determined, not only by the labour-time necessary to maintain the individual adult labourer, but also by that necessary to maintain his family. Machinery, by throwing every member of that family on to the labour-market, spreads the value of the man's labour-power over his whole family. It thus depreciates his labour-power. To purchase the labour-power of a family of four workers may, perhaps, cost more than it formerly did to purchase the labour-power of the head of the family, but, in return, four day's labour takes the place of one, and their price falls in proportion to the excess of the surplus-labour of four over the surplus-labour of one. In order that the family may live, four people must now, not only labour, but expend surplus-labour for the capitalist. Thus we see, that machinery, while augmenting the human material that forms the principal object of capital's exploiting power, at the same time raises the degree of exploitation.

Machinery also revolutionises out and out the contract between the labourer and the capitalist, which formally fixes their mutual relations. Taking the exchange of commodities as our basis, our first assumption was that capitalist and labourer met as free persons, as independent owners of commodities; the one possessing money and means of production, the other labour-power. But now the capitalist buys children and young persons under age. Previously, the workman sold his own labour-power, which he disposed of nominally as a free agent. Now he sells wife and child. He has become a slave-dealer. The demand for children's labour often resembles in form the inquiries for negro slaves, such as were formerly to be read among the advertisements in American journals. 'My attention', says an English factory inspector, 'was drawn to an advertisement in the local paper of one of the most important manufacturing towns of my district, of which the following is a copy: Wanted, 12 to 20 young persons, not younger than what can pass for 13 years. Wages, 4 shillings a week. Apply etc.' The phrase 'what can pass for 13 years', has reference to the fact, that by the Factory Act, children under 13 years may work only 6 hours. A surgeon officially appointed must certify their age. The manufacturer, therefore, asks for children who look as if they were already 13 years old. The decrease, often by leaps and bounds in the number of children under 13 years employed in factories, a decrease that is shown in an astonishing manner by the English statistics of the last 20 years, was for the most part, according to the evidence of the factory inspectors themselves, the work of the certifying surgeons, who overstated the age of the children, agreeably to the capitalist's greed for exploitation, and the sordid trafficking needs of the parents. In the notorious district of Bethnal Green, a public market is held every Monday and Tuesday morning, where children of both sexes from 9 years of age upwards, hire themselves out to the silk manufacturers. 'The usual terms are 1s. 8d. a week (this belongs to the parents) and "2d. for myself and tea." The contract is binding only for the week. The scene and language while this market is going on are quite disgraceful.' It has also occurred in England, that women have taken 'children from the workhouse and let any one have them out for 2s. 6d. a week'. In spite of legislation, the number of boys sold in Great Britain by their parents to act as live chimney-sweeping machines (although there exist plenty of machines to replace them) exceeds 2,000. The revolution effected by machinery in the juridical relations between the buyer and the seller of labour-power, causing the transaction as a whole to lose the appearance of a contract between free persons, afforded the English Parliament an excuse, founded on juridical principles, for the interference of the state with factories. Whenever the law limits the labour of children to 6 hours in industries not before interfered with, the complaints of the manufacturers are always renewed. They allege that numbers of the parents withdraw their children from the industry brought under the Act, in order to sell them where 'freedom of labour' still rules, i.e. where children under 13 years are compelled to work like grown-up people, and therefore can be got rid of at a higher price. But since capital is by nature a leveller, since it exacts in every sphere of production equality in the conditions of the exploitation of labour, the limitation by law of children's labour, in one branch of industry, becomes the cause of its limitation in others.

We have already alluded to the physical deterioration as well of the children and young persons as of the women, whom machinery, first directly in the factories that shoot up on its basis, and then indirectly in all the remaining branches of industry, subjects to the exploitation of capital. In this place, therefore, we dwell only on one point, the enormous mortality, during the first few years of their life, of the children of the operatives. Married women, who work in gangs along with boys and girls, are, for a stipulated sum of money, placed at the disposal of the farmer, by a man called the 'undertaker', who contracts for the whole gang. 'These gangs will sometimes travel many miles from their own village; they are to be met morning and evening on the roads, dressed in short petticoats, with suitable coats and boots, and some-times trousers, looking wonderfully strong and healthy, but tainted with a customary immorality and heedless of the fatal results which their love of this busy and independent life is bringing on their unfortunate offspring who are pining at home.' Every phenomenon of the factory districts is here reproduced, including, but to a greater extent, ill-disguised infanticide, and dosing children with opiates. 'My knowledge of such evils,' says Dr Simon, the medical officer of the Privy Council and editor in chief of the Reports on Public Health, 'may excuse the profound misgiving with which I regard any large industrial employment of adult women.' 'Happy indeed,' exclaims Mr Baker, the factory inspector, in his official report, 'happy indeed will it be for the manufacturing districts of England, when every married woman having a family is prohibited from working in any textile works at all.'

(b) *Prolongation of the Working-Day*

If machinery be the most powerful means for increasing the productiveness of labour—i.e. for shortening the working-time required in the production of a commodity, it becomes in the hands of capital the most powerful means, in those industries first invaded by it, for lengthening the working-day beyond all bounds set by human nature. It creates, on the one hand, new conditions by which capital is enabled to give free scope to this its constant tendency, and on the other hand, new motives with which to whet capital's appetite for the labour of others.

In the first place, in the form of machinery, the implements of labour become automatic, things moving and working independent of the workman. They are thenceforth an industrial *perpetuum mobile*, that would go on producing forever, did it not meet with certain natural obstructions in the weak bodies and the strong wills of its human attendants. The automaton, as capital, and because it is capital, is endowed, in the person of the capitalist, with intelligence and will; it is therefore animated by the longing to reduce to a minimum the resistance offered by that repellent yet elastic natural barrier, man. This resistance is moreover lessened by the apparent lightness of machine work, and by the more pliant and docile character of the women and children employed on it.

The productiveness of machinery is, as we saw, inversely proportional to the value transferred by it to the product. The longer the life of the machine, the greater is the mass of the products over which the value transmitted by the machine is spread, and the less is the portion of that value added to each single commodity. The active lifetime of a machine is, however, clearly dependent on the length of the working-day, or on the duration of the daily labour-process multiplied by the number of days for which the process is carried on.

The wear and tear of a machine is not exactly proportional to its working-time. And even if it were so, a machine working 16 hours daily for 7½ years, covers as long a working period as, and transmits to the total product no more value than, the same machine would if it worked only 8 hours daily for 15 years. But in the first case the value of the machine would be reproduced twice as quickly as in the latter, and the capitalist would, by this use of the machine, absorb in 7½ years as much surplus-value as in the second case he would in 15.

The material wear and tear of a machine is of two kinds. The one arises from use, as coins wear away by circulating, the other from non-use, as a sword rusts when left in its scabbard. The latter kind is due to the elements. The former is more or less directly proportional, the latter to a certain extent inversely proportional, to the use of the machine.

But in addition to the material wear and tear, a machine also undergoes, what we may call a moral depreciation. It loses exchange-value, either by machines of the same sort being produced cheaper than it, or by better machines entering into competition with it. In both cases, be the machine ever so young and full of life, its value is no longer determined by the labour actually materialised in it, but by the labour-time requisite to reproduce either it or the better machine. It has, therefore, lost value more or less. The shorter the period taken to reproduce its total value, the less is the danger of moral depreciation; and the longer the working-day, the shorter is that period. When machinery is first introduced into an industry, new methods of reproducing it more cheaply follow blow upon blow, and so do improvements, that not only affect individual parts and details of the machine, but its entire build. It is, therefore, in the early days of the life of machinery that this special incentive to the prolongation of the working-day makes itself felt most acutely.

Given the length of the working-day, all other circumstances remaining the same, the exploitation of double the number of workmen demands, not only a doubling of that part of constant capital which is invested in machinery and buildings, but also of that part which is laid out in raw material and auxiliary substances. The lengthening of the working-day, on the other hand, allows of production on an extended scale without any alteration in the amount of capital laid out on machinery and buildings. Not only is there, therefore, an increase of surplus-value, but the outlay necessary to obtain it diminishes. It is true that this takes place, more or less, with every lengthening of the working-day; but in the case under consideration, the change is more marked, because the capital converted into the instruments of labour preponderates to a greater degree. The development of the factory system fixes a constantly increasing portion of the capital in a form, in which, on the one hand, its value is capable of continual self-expansion, and in which, on the other hand, it loses both use-value and exchange-value whenever it loses contact with living labour. 'When a labourer', said Mr Ashworth, a cotton magnate, to Professor Nassau W. Senior, 'lays down his spade, he renders useless, for that period, a capital worth eighteen-pence. When one of our people leaves the mill, he renders useless a capital that has cost £100,000.' Only fancy! making 'useless' for a single moment, a capital that has cost £100,000! It is, in truth, monstrous, that a single one of our people should ever leave the factory! The increased use of machinery, as Senior after the instruction he received from Ashworth clearly perceives, makes a constantly increasing lengthening of the working-day 'desirable'.

Machinery produces relative surplus-value; not only by directly depreciating the value of labour-power, and by indirectly cheapening the same through cheapening the commodities that enter into its re-production, but also, when it is first introduced sporadically into an industry, by converting the labour employed by the owner of that machinery, into labour of a higher degree and greater efficacy, by raising the social value of the article produced above its individual value, and thus enabling the capitalist to replace the value of a day's labour-power by a smaller portion of the value of a day's product. During this transition period, when the use of machinery is a sort of monopoly, the profits are therefore exceptional, and the capitalist endeavours to exploit thoroughly 'the sunny time of this his first love', by prolonging the working-day as much as possible. The magnitude of the profit whets his appetite for more profit.

As the use of machinery becomes more general in a particular industry, the social value of the product sinks down to its individual value, and the law that surplus-value does not arise from the labour-power that has been replaced by the machinery, but from the labour-power actually employed in working with the machinery, asserts itself. Surplus-value arises from variable capital alone, and we saw that the amount of surplus-value depends on two factors, viz., the rate of surplus-value and the number of the workmen simultaneously employed. Given the length of the working-day, the rate of surplus-value is determined by the relative duration of the necessary labour and of the surplus-labour in a day. The number of the labourers simultaneously employed depends, on its side, on the ratio of the variable to the constant capital. Now, however much the use of machinery may increase the surplus-labour at the expense of the necessary labour by heightening the productiveness of labour, it is clear that it attains this result, only by diminishing the number of workmen employed by a given amount of capital. It converts what was formerly variable capital, invested in labour-power, into machinery which, being constant capital, does not produce surplus-value. It is impossible, for instance, to squeeze as much surplus-value out of 2 as out of 24 labourers. If each of these 24 men gives only one hour of surplus-labour in 12, the 24 men give together 24 hours of surplus-labour, while 24 hours is the total labour of the two men. Hence, the application of machinery to the production of surplus-value implies a contradiction which is immanent in it, since of the two factors of the surplus-value created by a given amount of capital, one, the rate of surplus-value , cannot be increased, except by diminishing the other, the number of workmen. This contradiction comes to light, as soon as by the general employment of machinery in a given industry, the value of the machine-produced commodity regulates the value of all commodities of the same sort; and it is this contradiction, that in its turn, drives the capitalist, without his being conscious of the fact, to excessive lengthening of the working-day, in order that he may compensate the decrease in the relative number of labourers exploited, by an increase not only of the relative, but of the absolute surplus-labour.

If, then, the capitalistic employment of machinery, on the one hand, supplies new and powerful motives to an excessive lengthening of the working-day, and radically changes, as well the methods of labour, as also the character of the social working organism, in such a manner as to break down all opposition to this tendency, on the other hand it produces, partly by opening out to the capitalist new strata of the working-class, previously inaccessible to him, partly by setting free the labourers it supplants, a surplus working population, which is compelled to submit to the dictation of capital. Hence that remarkable phenomenon in the history of Modern Industry, that machinery sweeps away every moral and natural restriction on the length of the working-day. Hence, too, the economic paradox, that the most powerful instrument for shortening labour-time, becomes the most unfailing means for placing every moment of the labourer's time and that of his family, at the disposal of the capitalist for the purpose of expanding the value of his capital. 'If,' dreamed Aristotle, the greatest thinker of antiquity, 'if every tool, when summoned, or even of its own accord, could do the work that befits it, just as the creations of Dædalus moved of themselves, or the tripods of Hephæstos went of their own accord to their sacred work, if the weavers' shuttles were to weave of themselves, then there would be no need either of apprentices for the master workers, or of slaves for the lords.' And Antipatros, a Greek poet of the time of Cicero, hailed the invention of the water-wheel for grinding corn, an invention that is the elementary form of all machinery, as the giver of freedom to female slaves, and the bringer back of the golden age. Oh! those heathens! They understood, as the learned Bastiat, and before him the still wiser MacCulloch have discovered, nothing of Political Economy and Christianity. They did not, for example, comprehend that machinery is the surest means of lengthening the working-day. They perhaps excused the slavery of one on the ground that it was a means to the full development of another. But to preach slavery of the masses, in order that a few crude and half-educated parvenus, might become 'eminent spinners', 'extensive sausage-makers', and 'influential shoe-black dealers', to do this, they lacked the bump of Christianity.

(c) *Intensification of Labour*

The immoderate lengthening of the working-day, produced by machinery in the hands of capital, leads to a reaction on the part of society, the very sources of whose life are menaced; and, thence, to a normal working-day whose length is fixed by law. Thenceforth a phenomenon that we have already met with, namely, the intensification of labour, develops into great importance. Our analysis of absolute surplus-value had reference primarily to the extension or duration of the labour, its intensity being assumed as given. We now proceed to consider the substitution of a more intensified labour for labour of more extensive duration, and the degree of the former.

It is self-evident, that in proportion as the use of machinery spreads, and the experience of a special class of workmen habituated to machinery accumulates, the rapidity and intensity of labour increase as a natural consequence. Thus in England, during half a century, lengthening of the working-day went hand in hand with increasing intensity of factory labour. Nevertheless the reader will clearly see, that where we have labour, not carried on by fits and starts, but repeated day after day with unvarying uniformity, a point must inevitably be reached, where extension of the working-day and intensity of the labour mutually exclude one another, in such a way that lengthening of the working-day becomes compatible only with a lower degree of intensity, and a higher degree of intensity, only with a shortening of the working-day. So soon as the gradually surging revolt of the working-class compelled Parliament to shorten compulsorily the hours of labour, and to begin by imposing a normal working-day on factories proper, so soon consequently as an increased production of surplus-value by the prolongation of the working-day was once for all put a stop to, from that moment capital threw itself with all its might into the production of relative surplus-value, by hastening on the further improvement of machinery. At the same time a change took place in the nature of relative surplus-value. Generally speaking, the mode of producing relative surplus-value consists in raising the productive power of the workman, so as to enable him to produce more in a given time with the same expenditure of labour. Labour-time continues to transmit as before the same value to the total product, but this unchanged amount of exchange-value is spread over more use-value; hence the value of each single commodity sinks. Otherwise, however, so soon as the compulsory shortening of the hours of labour takes place, the immense impetus it gives the development of productive power, and to economy in the means of production, imposes on the workman increased expenditure of labour in a given time, heightened tension of labour-power, and closer filling up of the pores of the working-day, or condensation of labour to a degree that is attainable only within the limits of the shortened working-day. This condensation of a greater mass of labour into a given period thenceforward counts for what it really is, a greater quantity of labour. In addition to a measure of its extension, i.e. duration, labour now acquires a measure of its intensity or of the degree of its condensation or density. The denser hour of the ten hours' working-day contains more labour, i.e. expended labour-power, than the more porous hour of the twelve hours' working-day. The product therefore of one of the former hours has as much or more value than has the product of $1\frac{1}{5}$ of the latter hours. Apart from the increased yield of relative surplus-value through the heightened productiveness of labour, the same mass of value is now produced for the capitalist say by $3\frac{1}{3}$ hours of surplus-labour, and $6\frac{2}{3}$ hours of necessary labour, as was previously produced by four hours of surplus-labour and eight hours of necessary labour.

We now come to the question: How is the labour intensified?

The first effect of shortening the working-day results from the self-evident law, that the efficiency of labour-power is in an inverse ratio to the duration of its expenditure. Hence, within certain limits what is lost by shortening the duration is gained by the increasing tension of labour-power. That the workman moreover really does expend more labour-power, is ensured by the mode in which the capitalist pays him. In those industries, such as potteries, where machinery plays little or no part, the introduction of the Factory Acts has strikingly shown that the mere shortening of the working-day increases to a wonderful degree the regularity, uniformity, order, continuity, and energy of the labour. It seemed, however, doubtful whether this effect was produced in the factory proper, where the dependence of the workman on the continuous and uniform motion of the machinery had already created the strictest discipline. Hence, when in 1844 the reduction of the working-day to less than twelve hours was being debated, the masters almost unanimously declared 'that their overlookers in the different rooms took good care that the hands lost no time', that 'the extent of vigilance and attention on the part of the workmen was hardly capable of being increased', and, therefore, that the speed of the machinery and other conditions remaining unaltered, 'to expect in a well-managed factory any important result from increased attention of the workmen was an absurdity'. This assertion was contradicted by experiments. Mr Robert Gardner reduced the hours of labour in his two large factories at Preston, on and after the 20th April, 1844, from twelve to eleven hours a day. The result of about a year's working was that 'the same amount of product for the same cost was received, and the workpeople as a whole earned in eleven hours as much wages as they did before in twelve'. I pass over the experiments made in the spinning and carding rooms, because they were accompanied by an increase of 2% in the speed of the machines. But in the weaving department, where, moreover, many sorts of figured fancy articles were woven, there was not the slightest alteration in the conditions of the work. The result was: 'From 6th January to 20th April, 1844, with a twelve hours' day, average weekly wages of each hand 10s. 1½d., from 20th April to 29th June, 1844, with day of eleven hours, average weekly wages 10s. 3½d.' Here we have more produced in eleven hours than previously in twelve, and entirely in consequence of more steady application and economy of time by the workpeople. While they got the same wages and gained one hour of spare time, the capitalist got the same amount produced and saved the cost of coal, gas, and other such items, for one hour. Similar experiments, and with the like success, were carried out in the mills of Messrs. Horrocks and Jacson.

The shortening of the hours of labour creates, to begin with, the subjective conditions for the condensation of labour, by enabling the workman to exert more strength in a given time. So soon as that shortening becomes compulsory, machinery becomes in the hands of capital the objective means, systematically employed for squeezing out more labour in a given time. This is effected in two ways: by increasing the speed of the machinery, and by giving the workman more machinery to tent. Improved construction of the machinery is necessary, partly because without it greater pressure cannot be put on the workman, and partly because the shortened hours of labour force the capitalist to exercise the strictest watch over the cost of production. The improvements in the steam-engine have increased the piston speed, and at the same time have made it possible, by means of a greater economy of power, to drive with the same or even a smaller consumption of coal more machinery with the same engine. The improvements in the transmitting mechanism have lessened friction, and, what so strikingly distinguishes modern from the older machinery, have reduced the diameter and weight of the shafting to a constantly decreasing minimum. Finally, the improvements in the operative machines have, while reducing their size, increased their speed and efficiency, as in the modern power-loom; or, while increasing the size of their framework, have also increased the extent and number of their working parts, as in spinning-mules, or have added to the speed of these working parts by imperceptible alterations of detail, such as those which ten years ago increased the speed of the spindles in self-acting mules by one-fifth.

The reduction of the working-day to 12 hours dates in England from 1832. In 1836 a manufacturer stated: 'The labour now undergone in the factories is much greater than it used to be . . . compared with thirty or forty years ago . . . owing to the greater attention and activity required by the greatly increased speed which is given to the machinery.' In the year 1844, Lord Ashley now Lord Shaftesbury, made in the House of Commons the following statements, supported by documentary evidence:

The labour performed by those engaged in the processes of manufacture, is three times as great as in the beginning of such operations. Machinery has executed, no doubt, the work that would demand the sinews of millions of men; but it has also prodigiously multiplied the labour of those who are governed by its fearful movements. . . . In 1815, the labour of following a pair of mules spinning cotton of No. 40—reckoning 12 hours to the working-day—involved a necessity of walking 8 miles. In 1832, the distance travelled in following a pair of mules, spinning cotton yarn of the same number, was 20 miles, and frequently more. In 1835 [query—1815 or 1825?] the spinner put up daily, on each of these mules, 820 stretches, making a total of 1,640 stretches in the course of the day. In 1832, the spinner put up on each mule 2,200 stretches, making a total of 4,400. In 1844, 2,400 stretches, making a total of 4,800; and in some cases the amount of labour required is even still greater. . . . I have another document sent to me in 1842, stating that the labour is progressively increasing—increasing not only because the distance to be travelled is greater, but because the quantity of goods produced is multiplied, while the hands are fewer in proportion than before; and, moreover, because an inferior species of cotton is now often spun, which it is more difficult to work. . . . In the carding-room there has also been a great increase of labour. One person there does the work formerly divided between two. In the weaving-room, where a vast number of persons are employed, and principally females . . . the labour has increased within the last few years fully 10 per cent, owing to the increased speed of the machinery in spinning. In 1838, the number of hanks spun per week was 18,000, in 1843 it amounted to 21,000. In 1819, the number of picks in power-loom-weaving per minute was 60—in 1842 it was 140, showing a vast increase of labour.

In the face of this remarkable intensity of labour which had already been reached in 1844 under the Twelve Hours' Act, there appeared to be a justification for the assertion made at that time by the English manufacturers, that any further progress in that direction was impossible, and therefore that every further reduction of the hours of labour meant a lessened production. The apparent correctness of their reasons will be best shown by the following contemporary statement by Leonard Horner, the factory inspector, their ever watchful censor.

Now, as the quantity produced must, in the main, be regulated by the speed of the machinery, it must be the interest of the mill-owner to drive it at the utmost rate of speed consistent with these following conditions, viz., the preservation of the machinery from too rapid deterioration; the preservation of the quality of the article manufactured; and the capability of the workman to follow the motion without a greater exertion than he can sustain for a constancy. One of the most important problems, therefore, which the owner of a factory has to solve is to find out the maximum speed at which he can run, with a due regard to the above conditions. It frequently happens that he finds he has gone too fast, that breakages and bad work more than counterbalance the increased speed, and that he is obliged to slacken his pace. I therefore concluded, that as an active and intelligent mill-owner would find out the safe maximum, it would not be possible to produce as much in eleven hours as in twelve. I further assumed that the operative paid by piece-work, would exert himself to the utmost consistent with the power of continuing at the same rate.

Horner, therefore, came to the conclusion that a reduction of the working-hours below twelve would necessarily diminish production. He himself, ten years later, cites his opinion of 1845 in proof of how much he under-estimated in that year the elasticity of machinery, and of man's labour-power, both of which are simultaneously stretched to an extreme by the compulsory shortening of the working-day.

We now come to the period that follows the introduction of the Ten Hours' Act in 1847 into the English cotton, woollen, silk, and flax mills.

'The speed of the spindles has increased upon throstles 500, and upon mules 1,000 revolutions a minute, i.e. the speed of the throstle spindle, which in 1839 was 4,500 times a minute, is now (1862) 5,000; and of the mule spindle, that was 5,000, is now 6,000 times a minute, amounting in the former case to one-tenth, and in the second case to one-fifth additional increase.' James Nasmyth, the eminent civil engineer of Patricroft, near Manchester, explained in a letter to Leonard Horner, written in 1852, the nature of the improvements in the steam-engine that had been made between the years 1848 and 1852. After remarking that the horse-power of steam-engines, being always estimated in the official returns according to the power of similar engines in 1828, is only nominal, and can serve only as an index of their real power, he goes on to say:

I am confident that from the same weight of steam-engine machinery, we are now obtaining at least 50 per cent. more duty or work performed on the average, and that in many cases the identical steam-engines which in the days of the restricted speed of 220 feet per minute, yielded 50 horse-power, are now yielding upwards of 100. . . . The modern steam-engine of 100 horse-power is capable of being driven at a much greater force than formerly, arising from improvements in its construction, the capacity and construction of the boilers, etc. . . . Although the same number of hands are employed in proportion to the horse-power as at former periods, there are fewer hands employed in proportion to the machinery. In the year 1850, the factories of the United Kingdom employed 134,217 nominal horse-power to give motion to 25,638,716 spindles and 301,445 looms. The number of spindles and looms in 1856 was respectively 33,503,580 of the former, and 369,205 of the latter, which, reckoning the force of the nominal horse-power required to be the same as in 1850, would require a force equal to 175,000 horses, but the actual power given in the return for 1856 is 161,435, less by above 10,000 horses than, calculating upon the basis of the return of 1850, the factories ought to have required in 1856. The facts thus brought out by the Return (of 1856) appear to be that the factory system is increasing rapidly; that although the same number of hands are employed in proportion to the horse-power as at former periods, there are fewer hands employed in proportion to the machinery; that the steam-engine is enabled to drive an increased weight of machinery by economy of force and other methods, and that an increased quantity of work can be turned off by improvements in machinery, and in methods of manufacture, by increase of speed of the machinery, and by a variety of other causes.

The great improvements made in machines of every kind have raised their productive power very much. Without any doubt, the shortening of the hours of labour . . . gave the impulse to these improvements. The latter, combined with the more intense strain on the workman, have had the effect, that at least as much is produced in the shortened (by two hours or one-sixth) working-day as was previously produced during the longer one.

One fact is sufficient to show how greatly the wealth of the manufacturers increased along with the more intense exploitation of labour-power. From 1838 to 1850, the average proportional increase in English cotton and other factories was 32%, while from 1850 to 1856 it amounted to 86%.

But however great the progress of English industry had been during the 8 years from 1848 to 1856 under the influence of a working-day of 10 hours, it was far surpassed during the next period of 6 years from 1856 to 1862. In silk factories, for instance, there were in 1856, spindles 1,093,799; in 1862, 1,388,544; in 1856, looms 9,260; in 1862, 10,709. But the number of operatives was, in 1856, 56,131; in 1862, 52,429. The increase in the spindles was therefore 26.9% and in the looms 15.6%, while the number of the operatives decreased 7%. In the year 1850 there were employed in worsted mills 875,830 spindles; in 1856, 1,324,549 (increase 51.2%), and in 1862, 1,289,172 (decrease 2.7%). But if we deduct the doubling spindles that figure in the numbers for 1856, but not in those for 1862, it will be found that after 1856, the number of spindles remained nearly stationary. On the other hand, after 1850, the speed of the spindles and looms was in many cases doubled. The number of power-looms in worsted mills was, in 1850, 32,617; in 1856, 38,956; in 1862, 43,048. The number of the operatives was, in 1850, 79,737; in 1856, 87,794; in 1862, 86,063; included in these, however, the children under 14 years of age were, in 1850, 9,956; in 1856, 11,228; in 1862, 13,178. In spite, therefore, of the greatly increased number of looms in 1862, compared with 1856, the total number of the workpeople employed decreased, and that of the children exploited increased.

On the 27th April, 1863, Mr Ferrand said in the House of Commons:

I have been informed by delegates from 16 districts of Lancashire and Cheshire, in whose behalf I speak, that the work in the factories is, in consequence of the improvements in machinery, constantly on the increase. Instead of as formerly one person with two helps tenting two looms, one person now tents three looms without helps, and it is no uncommon thing for one person to tent four. Twelve hours' work, as is evident from the facts adduced, is now compressed into less than 10 hours. It is therefore self-evident, to what an enormous extent the toil of the factory operative has increased during the last 10 years.

Although, therefore, the Factory Inspectors unceasingly and with justice, commend the results of the Acts of 1844 and 1850, yet they admit that the shortening of the hours of labour has already called forth such an intensification of the labour as is injurious to the health of the workman and to his capacity for work. 'In most of the cotton, worsted, and silk mills, an exhausting state of excitement necessary to enable the workers satisfactorily to mind the machinery, the motion of which has been greatly accelerated within the last few years, seems to me not unlikely to be one of the causes of that excess of mortality from lung disease, which Dr Greenhow has pointed out in his recent report on this subject.' There cannot be the slightest doubt that the tendency that urges capital, so soon as a prolongation of the hours of labour is once for all forbidden, to compensate itself, by a systematic heightening of the intensity of labour, and to convert every improvement in machinery into a more perfect means of exhausting the workman, must soon lead to a state of things in which a reduction of the hours of labour will again be inevitable. On the other hand, the rapid advance of English industry between 1848 and the present time, under the influence of a day of 10 hours, surpasses the advance made between 1833 and 1847, when the day was 12 hours long, by far more than the latter surpasses the advance made during the half century after the first introduction of the factory system, when the working-day was without limits.

Section 4. The Factory

At the commencement of this chapter we considered that which we may call the body of the factory, i.e. machinery organised into a system. We there saw how machinery, by annexing the labour of women and children, augments the number of human beings who form the material for capitalistic exploitation, how it confiscates the whole of the workman's disposable time, by immoderate extension of the hours of labour; and how finally its progress, which allows of enormous increase of production in shorter and shorter periods, serves as a means of systematically getting more work done in a shorter time, or of exploiting labour-power more intensely. We now turn to the factory as a whole, and that in its most perfect form.

Dr Ure, the Pindar of the automatic factory, describes it, on the one hand, as 'Combined co-operation of many orders of workpeople, adult and young, in tending with assiduous skill, a system of productive machines, continuously impelled by a central power' (the prime mover); on the other hand, as 'a vast automaton, composed of various mechanical and intellectual organs, acting in uninterrupted concert for the production of a common object, all of them being subordinate to a self-regulated moving force'. These two descriptions are far from being identical. In one, the collective labourer, or social body of labour, appears as the dominant subject, and the mechanical automaton as the object; in the other, the automaton itself is the subject, and the workmen are merely conscious organs, co-ordinate with the unconscious organs of the automaton, and together with them, subordinated to the central moving-power. The first description is applicable to every possible employment of machinery on a large scale, the second is characteristic of its use by capital, and therefore of the modern factory system. Ure prefers therefore, to describe the central machine, from which the motion comes, not only as an automaton, but as an autocrat. 'In these spacious halls the benignant power of steam summons around him his myriads of willing menials.'

Along with the tool, the skill of the workman in handing it passes over to the machine. The capabilities of the tool are emancipated from the restraints that are inseparable from human labour-power. Thereby the technical foundation on which is based the division of labour in Manufacture, is swept away. Hence, in the place of the hierarchy of specialised workmen that characterises manufacture, there steps, in the automatic factory, a tendency to equalise and reduce to one and the same level every kind of work that has to be done by the minders of the machines; in the place of the artificially produced differentiations of the detail workmen, step the natural differences of age and sex.

So far as division of labour re-appears in the factory, it is primarily a distribution of the workmen among the specialised machines; and of masses of workmen, not however organised into groups, among the various departments of the factory, in each of which they work at a number of similar machines placed together; their co-operation, therefore, is only simple. The organised group, peculiar to manufacture, is replaced by the connexion between the head workman and his few assistants. The essential division is, into workmen who are actually employed on the machines (among whom are included a few who look after the engine), and into mere attendants (almost exclusively children) of these workmen. Among the attendants are reckoned more or less all 'Feeders' who supply the machines with the material to be worked. In addition to these two principal classes, there is a numerically unimportant class of persons, whose occupation it is to look after the whole of the machinery and repair it from time to time; such as engineers, mechanics, joiners, etc. This is a superior class of workmen, some of them scientifically educated, others brought up to a trade; it is distinct from the factory operative class, and merely aggregated to it. This division of labour is purely technical.

To work at a machine, the workman should be taught from child-hood, in order that he may learn to adapt his own movements to the uniform and unceasing motion of an automaton. When the machinery, as a whole, forms a system of manifold machines, working simultane-ously and in concert, the co-operation based upon it, requires the distribution of various groups of workmen among the different kinds of machines. But the employment of machinery does away with the necessity of crystallising this distribution after the manner of Manufac-ture, by the constant annexation of a particular man to a particular function. Since the motion of the whole system does not proceed from the workman, but from the machinery, a change of persons can take place at any time without an interruption of the work. The most striking proof of this is afforded by the *relays system*, put into operation by the manufacturers during their revolt from 1848–1850.* Lastly, the quickness with which machine work is learnt by young people, does away with the necessity of bringing up for exclusive employment by machinery, a special class of operatives. With regard to the work of the mere attendants, it can, to some extent, be replaced in the mill by machines, and owing to its extreme simplicity, it allows of a rapid and constant change of the individuals burdened with this drudgery.

Although then, technically speaking, the old system of division of labour is thrown overboard by machinery, it hangs on in the factory, as a traditional habit handed down from Manufacture, and is afterwards systematically re-moulded and established in a more hideous form by capital, as a means of exploiting labour-power. The life-long speciality of handling one and the same tool, now becomes the life-long speciality of serving one and the same machine. Machinery is put to a wrong use, with the object of transforming the workman, from his very childhood, into a part of a detail-machine. In this way, not only are the expenses of his reproduction considerably lessened, but at the same time his help-less dependence upon the factory as a whole, and therefore upon the capitalist, is rendered complete. Here as everywhere else, we must distinguish between the increased productiveness due to the develop-ment of the social process of production, and that due to the capitalist exploitation of that process. In handicrafts and manufacture, the workman makes use of a tool, in the factory, the machine makes use of him. There the movements of the instrument of labour proceed from him, here it is the movements of the machine that he must follow. In manufacture the workmen are parts of a living mechanism. In the factory we have a lifeless mechanism independent of the workman, who becomes its mere living appendage. 'The miserable routine of endless drudgery and toil in which the same mechanical process is gone through over and over again, is like the labour of Sisyphus. The burden of labour, like the rock, keeps ever falling back on the worn-out labourer.' At the same time that factory work exhausts the nervous system to the uttermost, it does away with the many-sided play of the muscles, and confiscates every atom of freedom, both in bodily and intellectual activity. The lightening of the labour, even, becomes a sort of torture, since the machine does not free the labourer from work, but deprives the work of all interest. Every kind of capitalist production, in so far as it is not only a labour-process, but also a process of creating surplus-value, has this in common, that it is not the workman that employs the instruments of labour, but the instruments of labour that employ the workman. But it is only in the factory system that this inversion for the first time acquires technical and palpable reality. By means of its conversion into an automaton, the instrument of labour confronts the labourer, during the labour-process, in the shape of capital, of dead labour, that dominates, and pumps dry, living labour-power. The separation of the intellectual powers of production from the manual labour, and the conversion of those powers into the might of capital over labour, is, as we have already shown, finally completed by modern industry erected on the foundation of machinery. The special skill of each individual insignificant factory operative vanishes as an infinitesimal quantity before the science, the gigantic physical forces, and the mass of labour that are embodied in the factory mechanism and, together with that mechanism, constitute the power of the 'master'. This 'master', therefore, in whose brain the machinery and his monopoly of it are inseparably united, whenever he falls out with his 'hands', contemptuously tells them: 'The factory operatives should keep in wholesome remembrance the fact that theirs is really a low species of skilled labour; and that there is none which is more easily acquired, or of its quality more amply remunerated, or which by a short training of the least expert can be more quickly, as well as abundantly, acquired. . . . The master's machinery really plays a far more important part in the business of production than the labour and the skill of the operative, which six months' education can teach, and a common labourer can learn.' The technical subordination of the workman to the uniform motion of the instruments of labour, and the peculiar composition of the body of workpeople, consisting as it does of individuals of both sexes and of all ages, give rise to a barrack discipline, which is elaborated into a complete system in the factory, and which fully develops the before mentioned labour of overlooking, thereby dividing the workpeople into operatives and overlookers, into private soldiers and sergeants of an industrial army.

The main difficulty [in the automatic factory] . . . lay . . . above all in training human beings to renounce their desultory habits of work, and to identify themselves with the unvarying regularity of the complex automaton. To devise and administer a successful code of factory discipline, suited to the necessities of factory diligence, was the Herculean enterprise, the noble achievement of Arkwright! Even at the present day, when the system is perfectly organised and its labour lightened to the utmost, it is found nearly impossible to convert persons past the age of puberty, into useful factory hands.

The factory code in which capital formulates, like a private legislator, and at his own good will, his autocracy over his workpeople, unaccompanied by that division of responsibility, in other matters so much approved of by the bourgeoisie, and unaccompanied by the still more approved representative system, this code is but the capitalistic caricature of that social regulation of the labour-process which becomes requisite in co-operation on a great scale, and in the employment in common, of instruments of labour and especially of machinery. The place of the slave-driver's lash in taken by the overlooker's book of penalties. All punishments naturally resolve themselves into fines and deductions from wages, and the law-giving talent of the factory Lycurgus so arranges matters, that a violation of his laws is, if possible, more profitable to him than the keeping of them.

We shall here merely allude to the material conditions under which factory labour is carried on. Every organ of sense is injured in an equal degree by artificial elevation of the temperature, by the dust-laden atmosphere, by the deafening noise, not to mention danger to life and limb among the thickly crowded machinery, which, with the regularity of the seasons, issues its list of the killed and wounded in the industrial battle. Economy of the social means of production, matured and forced as in a hothouse by the factory system, is turned, in the hands of capital, into systematic robbery of what is necessary for the life of the workman while he is at work, robbery of space, light, air, and of protection to his person against the dangerous and unwholesome accompaniments of the productive process, not to mention the robbery of appliances for the comfort of the workman. Is Fourier wrong when he calls factories 'tempered jails'?

Section 5. The Strife between Workman and Machine

The contest between the capitalist and the wage-labourer dates back to the very origin of capital. It raged on throughout the whole manufacturing period. But only since the introduction of machinery has the workman fought against the instrument of labour itself, the material embodiment of capital. He revolts against this particular form of the means of production, as being the material basis of the capitalist mode of production.

The contests about wages in Manufacture, pre-suppose manufacture, and are in no sense directed against its existence. The opposition against the establishment of new manufactures, proceeds from the guilds and privileged towns, not from the workpeople. Hence the writers of the manufacturing period treat the division of labour chiefly as a means of virtually supplying a deficiency of labourers, and not as a means of actually displacing those in work. This distinction is self-evident. If it be said that 100 millions of people would be required in England to spin with the old spinning-wheel the cotton that is now spun with mules by 500,000 people, this does not mean that the mules took the place of those millions who never existed. It means only this, that many millions of workpeople would be required to replace the spinning machinery. If, on the other hand, we say, that in England the power-loom threw 800,000 weavers on the streets, we do not refer to existing machinery, that would have to be replaced by a definite number of workpeople, but to a number of weavers in existence who were actually replaced or displaced by the looms. During the manufacturing period, handicraft labour, altered though it was by division of labour, was yet the basis. The demands of the new colonial markets could not be satisfied owing to the relatively small number of town operatives handed down from the middle ages, and the manufactures proper opened out new fields of production to the rural population, driven from the land by the dissolution of the feudal system. At that time, therefore, division of labour and co-operation in the workshops, were viewed more from the positive aspect, that they made the workpeople more productive. Long before the period of Modern Industry, co-operation and the concentration of the instruments of labour in the hands of a few, gave rise, in numerous countries where these methods were applied in agriculture, to great, sudden and forcible revolutions in the modes of production, and consequentially, in the conditions of existence, and the means of employment of the rural populations. But this contest at first takes place more between the large and the small landed proprietors, than between capital and wage-labour; on the other hand, when the labourers are displaced by the instruments of labour, by sheep, horses, etc., in this case force is directly resorted to in the first instance as the prelude to the industrial revolution. The labourers are first driven from the land, and then come the sheep. Land grabbing on a great scale, such as was perpetrated in England, is the first step in creating a field for the establishment of agriculture on a great scale. Hence this subversion of agriculture puts on, at first, more the appearance of a political revolution.

The instrument of labour, when it takes the form of a machine, immediately becomes a competitor of the workman himself. The self-expansion of capital by means of machinery is thenceforward directly proportional to the number of the workpeople, whose means of livelihood have been destroyed by that machinery. The whole system of capitalist production is based on the fact that the workman sells his labour-power as a commodity. Division of labour specialises this labour-power, by reducing it to skill in handing a particular tool. So soon as the handing of this tool becomes the work of a machine, then, with the use-value, the exchange-value too, of the workman's labour-power vanishes; the workman becomes unsaleable, like paper money thrown out of currency by legal enactment. That portion of the working-class, thus by machinery rendered superfluous, i.e. no longer immediately necessary for the self-expansion of capital, either goes to the wall in the unequal contest of the old handicrafts and manufactures with machinery, or else floods all the more easily accessible branches of industry, swamps the labour-market, and sinks the price of labour-power below its value. It is impressed upon the workpeople, as a great consolation, first, that their sufferings are only temporary ('a temporary inconvenience'), secondly, that machinery acquires the mastery over the whole of a given field of production, only by degrees, so that the extent and intensity of its destructive effect is diminished. The first consolation neutralises the second. When machinery seizes on an industry by degrees, it produces chronic misery among the operatives who compete with it. Where the transition is rapid, the effect is acute and felt by great masses. History discloses no tragedy more horrible than the gradual extinction of the English hand-loom weavers, an extinction that was spread over several decades, and finally sealed in 1838. Many of them died of starvation, many with families vegetated for a long time on 2½*d*. a day. On the other hand, the English cotton machinery produced an acute effect in India. The Governor General reported 1834–35: 'The misery hardly finds a parallel in the history of commerce. The bones of the cotton-weavers are bleaching the plains of India.' No doubt, in turning them out of this 'temporal' world, the machinery caused them no more than 'a temporary inconvenience'. For the rest, since machinery is continually seizing upon new fields of production, its temporary effect is really permanent. Hence, the character of independence and estrangement which the capitalist mode of production as a whole gives to the instruments of labour and to the product, as against the workman, is developed by means of machinery into a thorough antagonism. Therefore, it is with the advent of machinery, that the workman for the first time brutally revolts against the instruments of labour.

The instrument of labour strikes down the labourer. This direct antagonism between the two comes out most strongly, whenever newly introduced machinery competes with handicrafts or manufactures, handed down from former times. But even in Modern Industry the continual improvement of machinery, and the development of the automatic system, has an analogous effect. 'The object of improved machinery is to diminish manual labour, to provide for the performance of a process or the completion of a link in a manufacture by the aid of an iron instead of the human apparatus.' 'The adaptation of power to machinery heretofore moved by hand, is almost of daily occurrence ...the minor improvements in machinery having for their object economy of power, the production of better work, the turning off more work in the same time, or in supplying the place of a child, a female, or a man, are constant, and although sometimes apparently of no great moment, have somewhat important results.' 'Whenever a process requires peculiar dexterity and steadiness of hand, it is withdrawn, as soon as possible, from the cunning workman, who is prone to irregularities of many kinds, and it is placed in charge of a peculiar mechanism, so self-regulating that a child can superintend it.' 'On the automatic plan skilled labour gets progressively superseded.' 'The effect of improvements in machinery, not merely in superseding the necessity for the employment of the same quantity of adult labour as before, in order to produce a given result, but in substituting one description of human labour for another, the less skilled for the more skilled, juvenile for adult, female for male, causes a fresh disturbance in the rate of wages.' 'The effect of substituting the self-acting mule for the common mule, is to discharge the greater part of the men spinners, and to retain adolescents and children.' The extraordinary power of expansion of the factory system owing to accumulated practical experience, to the mechanical means at hand, and to constant technical progress, was proved to us by the giant strides of that system under the pressure of a shortened working-day. But who, in 1860, the Zenith year of the English cotton industry, would have dreamt of the galloping improvements in machinery, and the corresponding displacement of working people, called into being during the following 3 years, under the stimulus of the American Civil War? A couple of examples from the Reports of the Inspectors of Factories will suffice on this point. A Manchester manufacturer states: 'We formerly had 75 carding engines, now we have 12, doing the same quantity of work. . . . We are doing with fewer hands by 14, at a saving in wages of £10 a-week. Our estimated saving in waste is about 10% in the quantity of cotton consumed.' 'In another fine-spinning mill in Manchester, I was informed that through increased speed and the adoption of some self-acting processes, a reduction had been made, in number, of a fourth in one department, and of above half in another, and that the introduction of the combing machine in place of the second carding, had considerably reduced the number of hands formerly employed in the carding-room.' Another spinning-mill is estimated to effect a saving of labour of 10%. The Messrs Gilmour, spinners at Manchester, state: 'In our blowing-room department we consider our expense with new machinery is fully one-third less in wages and hands . . . in the jack-frame and drawing-frame room, about one-third less in expense, and likewise one-third less in hands; in the spinning-room about one-third less in expenses. But this is not all; when our yarn goes to the manufacturers, it is so much better by the application of our new machinery, that they will produce a greater quantity of cloth, and cheaper than from the yarn produced by old machinery.' Mr Redgrave further remarks in the same Report: 'The reduction of hands against increased production is, in fact, constantly taking place, in woollen mills the reduction commenced some time since, and is continuing; a few days since, the master of a school in the neighbourhood of Rochdale said to me, that the great falling off in the girls' school is not only caused by the distress, but by the changes of machinery in the woollen mills, in consequence of which a reduction of 70 short-timers had taken place.'

Hence, between 1861 and 1868, 338 cotton factories disappeared, in other words more productive machinery on a larger scale was concentrated in the hands of a smaller number of capitalists. The number of power-looms decreased by 20,663; but since their product increased in the same period, an improved loom must have yielded more than an old one. Lastly the number of spindles increased by 1,612,541, while the number of operatives decreased by 50,505. The 'temporary' misery inflicted on the workpeople by the cotton-crisis, was heightened, and from being temporary made permanent, by the rapid and persistent progress of machinery.

But machinery not only acts as a competitor who gets the better of the workman, and is constantly on the point of making him superfluous. It is also a power inimical to him, and as such capital proclaims it from the roof tops and as such makes use of it. It is the most powerful weapon for repressing strikes, those periodical revolts of the working-class against the autocracy of capital. According to Gaskell, the steam-engine was from the very first an antagonist of human power, an antagonist that enabled the capitalist to tread under foot the growing claims of the workmen, who threatened the newly born factory system with a crisis. It would be possible to write quite a history of the inventions, made since 1830, for the sole purpose of supplying capital with weapons against the revolts of the working-class. At the head of these in importance, stands the self-acting mule, because it opened up a new epoch in the automatic system.

Nasmyth, the inventor of the steam-hammer, gives the following evidence before the Trades' Union Commission, with regard to the improvements made by him in machinery and introduced in consequence of the wide-spread and long strikes of the engineers in 1851. 'The characteristic feature of our modern mechanical improvements, is the introduction of self-acting tool machinery. What every mechanical workman has now to do, and what every boy can do, is not to work himself but to superintend the beautiful labour of the machine. The whole class of workmen that depend exclusively on their skill, is now done away with. Formerly, I employed four boys to every mechanic. Thanks to these new mechanical combinations, I have reduced the number of grown-up men from 1,500 to 750. The result was a considerable increase in my profits.'

Ure says of a machine used in calico printing: 'At length capitalists sought deliverance from this intolerable bondage [namely the, in their eyes, burdensome terms of their contracts with the workmen] in the resources of science, and were speedily re-instated in their legitimate rule, that of the head over the inferior members.' Speaking of an invention for dressing warps: 'Then the combined malcontents, who fancied themselves impregnably intrenched behind the old lines of division of labour, found their flanks turned and their defences rendered useless by the new mechanical tactics, and were obliged to sur-render at discretion.' With regard to the invention of the self-acting mule, he says: 'A creation destined to restore order among the industri-ous classes. . . . This invention confirms the great doctrine already propounded, that when capital enlists science into her service, the refractory hand of labour will always be taught docility.' Although Ure's work appeared 30 years ago, at a time when the factory system was comparatively but little developed, it still perfectly expresses the spirit of the factory, not only by its undisguised cynicism, but also by the naïveté with which it blurts out the stupid contradictions of the capitalist brain. For instance, after propounding the 'doctrine' stated above, that capital, with the aid of science taken into its pay, always reduces the refractory hand of labour to docility, he grows indignant because 'it [physico-mechanical science] has been accused of lending itself to the rich capitalist as an instrument for harassing the poor'. After preaching a long sermon to show how advantageous the rapid development of machinery is to the working-classes, he warns them, that by their obstinacy and their strikes they hasten that development. 'Violent revulsions of this nature', he says, 'display short-sighted man in the contemptible character of a self-tormentor.' A few pages before he states the contrary. 'Had it not been for the violent collisions and interruptions resulting from erroneous views among the factory oper-atives, the factory system would have been developed still more rapidly and beneficially for all concerned.' Then he exclaims again: 'Fortu-nately for the state of society in the cotton districts of Great Britain, the improvements in machinery are gradual.' 'It' [improvement in ma-chinery] 'is said to lower the rate of earnings of adults by displacing a portion of them, and thus rendering their number superabundant as compared with the demand for their labour. It certainly augments the demand for the labour of children and increases the rate of *their* wages. On the other hand, this same dispenser of consolation defends the lowness of the children's wages on the ground that it prevents parents from sending their children at too early an age into the factory. The whole of his book is a vindication of a working-day of unrestricted length; that Parliament should forbid children of 13 years to be exhausted by working 12 hours a day, reminds his liberal soul of the darkest days of the middle ages. This does not prevent him from calling upon the factory operatives to thank Providence, who by means of machinery has given them the leisure to think of their 'immortal interests'.

Section 6. The Theory of Compensation as Regards the Workpeople Displaced by Machinery

James Mill, MacCulloch, Torrens, Senior, John Stuart Mill, and a whole series besides, of bourgeois political economists, insist that all machinery that displaces workmen, simultaneously and necessarily sets free an amount of capital adequate to employ the same identical workmen.

The real facts, which are travestied by the optimism of economists, are as follows: The labourers, when driven out of the workshop by the machinery, are thrown upon the labour-market, and there add to the number of workmen at the disposal of the capitalists. In Part VII of this book it will be seen that this effect of machinery, which, as we have seen, is represented to be a compensation to the working-class, is on the contrary a most frightful scourge. For the present I will only say this: The labourers that are thrown out of work in any branch of industry, can no doubt seek for employment in some other branch. If they find it, and thus renew the bond between them and the means of subsistence, this takes place only by the intermediary of a new and additional capital that is seeking investment; not at all by the intermediary of the capital that formerly employed them and was afterwards converted into machinery. And even should they find employment, what a poor look-out is theirs! Crippled as they are by division of labour, these poor devils are worth so little outside their old trade, that they cannot find admission into any industries, except a few of inferior kind, that are over-supplied with underpaid workmen. Further, every branch of industry attracts each year a new stream of men, who furnish a contingent from which to fill up vacancies, and to draw a supply for expansion. So soon as machinery sets free a part of the workmen employed in a given branch of industry, the reserve men are also diverted into new channels of employment, and become absorbed in other branches; meanwhile the original victims, during the period of transition, for the most part starve and perish.

Although machinery necessarily throws men out of work in those industries into which it is introduced, yet it may, notwithstanding this, bring about an increase of employment in other industries. This effect, however, has nothing in common with the so-called theory of compensation. Since every article produced by a machine is cheaper than a similar article produced by hand, we deduce the following infallible law: If the total quantity of the article produced by machinery, be equal to the total quantity of the article previously produced by a handicraft or by manufacture, and now made by machinery, then the total labour expended is diminished. The new labour spent on the instruments of labour, on the machinery, on the coal, and so on, must necessarily be less than the labour displaced by the use of the machinery; otherwise the product of the machine would be as dear, or dearer, than the product of the manual labour. But, as a matter of fact, the total quantity of the article produced by machinery with a diminished number of workmen, instead of remaining equal to, by far exceeds the total quantity of the hand-made article that has been displaced. Suppose that 400,000 yards of cloth have been produced on power-looms by fewer weavers than could weave 100,000 yards by hand. In the quadrupled product there lies four times as much raw material. Hence the production of raw material must be quadrupled. But as regards the instruments of labour, such as buildings, coal, machinery, and so on, it is different; the limit up to which the additional labour required for their production can increase, varies with the difference between the quantity of the machine-made article, and the quantity of the same article that the same number of workmen could make by hand.

Hence, as the use of machinery extends in a given industry, the immediate effect is to increase production in the other industries that furnish the first with means of production. How far employment is thereby found for an increased number of men, depends, given the length of the working-day and the intensity of labour, on the composition of the capital employed, i.e. on the ratio of its constant to its variable component. This ratio, in its turn, varies considerably with the extent to which machinery has already seized on, or is then seizing on, those trades. The number of the men condemned to work in coal and metal mines increased enormously owing to the progress of the English factory system; but during the last few decades this increase of number has been less rapid, owing to the use of new machinery in mining. A new type of workman springs into life along with the machine, namely, its maker. We have already learnt that machinery has possessed itself even of this branch of production on a scale that grows greater every day. As to raw material, there is not the least doubt that the rapid strides of cotton spinning, not only pushed on with tropical luxuriance the growth of cotton in the United States, and with it the African slave trade, but also made the breeding of slaves the chief business of the border slave-states.* When, in 1790, the first census of slaves was taken in the United States, their number was 697,000; in 1861 it had nearly reached four millions. On the other hand, it is no less certain that the rise of the English woollen factories, together with the gradual conversion of arable land into sheep pasture, brought about the superfluity of agricultural labourers that led to their being driven in masses into the towns. Ireland, having during the last twenty years reduced its population by nearly one half, is at this moment undergoing the process of still further reducing the number of its inhabitants, so as exactly to suit the requirements of its landlords and of the English woollen manufacturers.

When machinery is applied to any of the preliminary or intermediate stages through which the subject of labour has to pass on its way to completion, there is an increased yield of material in those stages, and simultaneously an increased demand for labour in the handicrafts or manufactures supplied by the produce of the machines. Spinning by machinery, for example, supplied yarn so cheaply and so abundantly that the hand-loom weavers were, at first, able to work full time without increased outlay. Their earnings accordingly rose. Hence a flow of people into the cotton-weaving trade, till at length the 800,000 weavers, called into existence by the Jenny, the throstle and the mule, were overwhelmed by the power-loom. So also, owing to the abundance of clothing materials produced by machinery, the number of tailors, seamstresses and needlewomen, went on increasing until the appearance of the sewing-machine.

In proportion as machinery, with the aid of a relatively small number of workpeople, increases the mass of raw materials, intermediate products, instruments of labour, etc., the working-up of these raw materials and intermediate products becomes split up into numberless branches; social production increases in diversity. The factory system carries the social division of labour immeasurably further than does manufacture, for it increases the productiveness of the industries it seizes upon, in a far higher degree.

The immediate result of machinery is to augment surplus-value and the mass of products in which surplus-value is embodied. And, as the substances consumed by the capitalists and their dependants become more plentiful, so too do these orders of society. Their growing wealth, and the relatively diminished number of workmen required to produce the necessaries of life beget, simultaneously with the rise of new and luxurious wants, the means of satisfying those wants. A larger portion of the produce of society is changed into surplus-produce, and a larger part of the surplus-produce is supplied for consumption in a multiplicity of refined shapes. In other words, the production of luxuries increases. The refined and varied forms of the products are also due to new relations with the markets of the world, relations that are created by Modern Industry. Not only are greater quantities of foreign articles of luxury exchanged for home products, but a greater mass of foreign raw materials, ingredients, and intermediate products, are used as means of production in the home industries. Owing to these relations with the markets of the world, the demand for labour increases in the carrying trades, which split up into numerous varieties.

The increase of the means of production and subsistence, accompanied by a relative diminution in the number of labourers, causes an increased demand for labour in making canals, docks, tunnels, bridges, and so on, works that can only bear fruit in the far future. Entirely new branches of production, creating new fields of labour, are also formed, as the direct result either of machinery or of the general industrial changes brought about by it. But the place occupied by these branches in the general production is, even in the most developed countries, far from important. The number of labourers that find employment in them is directly proportional to the demand, created by those industries, for the crudest form of manual labour. The chief industries of this kind are, at present, gas-works, telegraphs, photography, steam navigation, and railways. According to the census of 1861 for England and Wales, we find in the gas industry (gas-works, production of mechanical apparatus, servants of the gas companies, etc.), 15,211 persons; in telegraphy, 2,399; in photography, 2,366; steam navigation, 3,570; and in railways, 70,599, of whom the unskilled 'navvies', more or less permanently employed, and the whole administrative and commercial staff, make up about 28,000. The total number of persons, therefore, employed in these five new industries amounts to 94,145.

Lastly, the extraordinary productiveness of modern industry, accompanied as it is by both a more extensive and a more intense exploitation of labour-power in all other spheres of production, allows of the unproductive employment of a larger and larger part of the working-class, and the consequent reproduction, on a constantly extending scale, of the ancient domestic slaves under the name of a servant class, including men-servants, women-servants, lackeys, etc. According to the census of 1861, the population of England and Wales was 20,066,244; of these, 9,766,259 males, and 10,289,965 females. If we deduct from this population all who are too old or too young for work, all unproductive women, young persons and children, the 'ideological' classes, such as government officials, priests, lawyers, soldiers, etc.; further, all who have no occupation but to consume the labour of others in the form of rent, interest, etc.; and, lastly, paupers, vagabonds, and criminals, there remain in round numbers eight millions of the two sexes of every age, including in that number every capitalist who is in any way engaged in industry, commerce, or finance. Among these 8 millions are:

	Persons
Agricultural labourers (including shepherds, farm servants, and maidservants living in the houses of farmers)	1,098,261
All who are employed in cotton, woollen, worsted, flax, hemp, silk, and jute factories, in stocking making and lace making by machinery	642,607
All who are employed in coal mines and metal mines	565,835
All who are employed in metal works (blast-furnaces, rolling mills, etc.), and metal manufactures of every kind	396,998
The servant class	1,208,648

All the persons employed in textile factories and in mines, taken together, number 1,208,442; those employed in textile factories and metal industries, taken together, number 1,039,605; in both cases less than the number of modern domestic slaves. What a splendid result of the capitalist exploitation of machinery!

Section 7. Repulsion and Attraction of Workpeople by the Factory System. Crises in the Cotton Trade

All political economists of any standing admit that the introduction of new machinery has a baneful effect on the workmen in the old handicrafts and manufactures with which this machinery at first competes. Almost all of them bemoan the slavery of the factory operative. And what is the great trump-card that they play? That machinery, after the horrors of the period of introduction and development have subsided, instead of diminishing, in the long run increases the number of the slaves of labour! Yes, Political Economy revels in the hideous theory, hideous to every 'philanthropist' who believes in the eternal Nature-ordained necessity for capitalist production, that after a period of growth and transition, even its crowning success, the factory system based on machinery, grinds down more workpeople than on its first introduction it throws on the streets.

So long as, in a given branch of industry, the factory system extends itself at the expense of the old handicrafts or of manufacture, the result is as sure as is the result of an encounter between an army furnished with breach-loaders, and one armed with bows and arrows. This first period, during which machinery conquers its field of action, is of decisive importance owing to the extraordinary profits that it helps to produce. These profits not only form a source of accelerated accumulation, but also attract into the favoured sphere of production a large part of the additional social capital that is being constantly created, and is ever on the look-out for new investments. The special advantages of this first period of fast and furious activity are felt in every branch of production that machinery invades. So soon, however, as the factory system has gained a certain breadth of footing and a definite degree of maturity, and, especially, so soon as its technical basis, machinery, is itself produced by machinery; so soon as coal mining and iron mining, the metal industries, and the means of transport have been revolutionised; so soon, in short, as the general conditions requisite for production by the modern industrial system have been established, this mode of production acquires an elasticity, a capacity for sudden extension by leaps and bounds that finds no hindrance except in the supply of raw material and in the disposal of the produce. On the one hand, the immediate effect of machinery is to increase the supply of raw material in the same way, for example, as the cotton gin augmented the production of cotton. On the other hand, the cheapness of the articles produced by machinery, and the improved means of transport and communication furnish the weapons for conquering foreign markets. By ruining handicraft production in other countries, machinery forcibly converts them into fields for the supply of its raw material. In this way East India was compelled to produce cotton, wool, hemp, jute, and indigo for Great Britain. By constantly making a part of the hands 'supernumerary', modern industry, in all countries where it has taken root, gives a spur to emigration and to the colonisation of foreign lands, which are thereby converted into settlements for growing the raw material of the mother country; just as Australia, for example, was converted into a colony for growing wool. A new and international division of labour, a division suited to the requirements of the chief centres of modern industry springs up, and converts one part of the globe into a chiefly agricultural field of production, for supplying the other part which remains a chiefly industrial field. This revolution hangs together with radical changes in agriculture which we need not here further inquire into.

The enormous power, inherent in the factory system, of expanding by jumps, and the dependence of that system on the markets of the world, necessarily beget feverish production, followed by over-filling of the markets, whereupon contraction of the markets brings on crippling of production. The life of modern industry becomes a series of periods of moderate activity, prosperity, over-production, crisis and stagnation. The uncertainty and instability to which machinery subjects the employment, and consequently the conditions of existence, of the operatives become normal, owing to these periodic changes of the industrial cycle. Except in the periods of prosperity, there rages between the capitalists the most furious combat for the share of each in the markets. This share is directly proportional to the cheapness of the product. Besides the rivalry that this struggle begets in the application of improved machinery for replacing labour-power, and of new methods of production, there also comes a time in every industrial cycle, when a forcible reduction of wages beneath the value of labour-power, is attempted for the purpose of cheapening commodities.

A necessary condition, therefore, to the growth of the number of factory hands, is a proportionally much more rapid growth of the amount of capital invested in mills. This growth, however, is conditioned by the ebb and flow of the industrial cycle. It is, besides, constantly interrupted by the technical progress that at one time virtually supplies the place of new workmen, at another, actually displaces old ones. This qualitative change in mechanical industry continually discharges hands from the factory, or shuts its doors against the fresh stream of recruits, while the purely quantitative extension of the factories absorbs not only the men thrown out of work, but also fresh contingents. The workpeople are thus continually both repelled and attracted, hustled from pillar to post, while, at the same time, constant changes take place in the sex, age, and skill of the levies.

The lot of the factory operatives will be best depicted by taking a rapid survey of the course of the English cotton industry.

From 1770 to 1815 this trade was depressed or stagnant for 5 years only. During this period of 45 years the English manufacturers had a monopoly of machinery and of the markets of the world. From 1815 to 1821 depression; 1822 and 1823 prosperity; 1824 abolition of the laws against Trades' Unions, great extension of factories everywhere; 1825 crisis; 1826 great misery and riots among the factory operatives; 1827 slight improvement; 1828 great increase in power-looms, and in exports; 1829 exports, especially to India, surpass all former years; 1830 glutted markets, great distress; 1831 to 1833 continued depression, the monopoly of the trade with India and China withdrawn from the East

India Company; 1834 great increase of factories and machinery, shortness of hands. The new poor law furthers the migration of agricultural labourers into the factory districts. The country districts swept of children. White slave trade; 1835 great prosperity, contemporaneous starvation of the hand-loom weavers; 1836 great prosperity; 1837 and 1838 depression and crisis; 1839 revival; 1840 great depression, riots, calling out of the military; 1841 and 1842 frightful suffering among the factory operatives; 1842 the manufacturers lock the hands out of the factories in order to enforce the repeal of the Corn Laws. The operatives stream in thousands into the towns of Lancashire and Yorkshire, are driven back by the military, and their leaders brought to trial at Lancaster; 1843 great misery; 1844 revival; 1845 great prosperity; 1846 continued improvement at first, then reaction. Repeal of the Corn Laws; 1847 crisis, general reduction of wages by 10 and more per cent. in honour of the 'big loaf';* 1848 continued depression; Manchester under military protection; 1849 revival; 1850 prosperity; 1851 falling prices, low wages, frequent strikes; 1852 improvement begins, strikes continue, the manufacturers threaten to import foreign hands; 1853 increasing exports. Strike for 8 months, and great misery at Preston; 1854 prosperity, glutted markets; 1855 news of failures stream in from the United States, Canada, and the Eastern markets; 1856 great prosperity; 1857 crisis; 1858 improvement; 1859 great prosperity, increase in factories; 1860 Zenith of the English cotton trade, the Indian, Australian, and other markets so glutted with goods that even in 1863 they had not absorbed the whole lot; the French Treaty of Commerce, enormous growth of factories and machinery; 1861 prosperity continues for a time, reaction, the American Civil War, cotton famine: 1862 to 1863 complete collapse.

Section 8. Revolution Effected in Manufacture, Handicrafts, and Domestic Industry by Modern Industry

(a) *Overthrow of Co-operation Based on Handicraft and on the Division of Labour*

We have seen how machinery does away with co-operation based on handicrafts, and with manufacture based on the division of handicraft labour. An example of the first sort is the mowing-machine; it replaces co-operation between mowers. A striking example of the second kind, is the needle-making machine. According to Adam Smith, 10 men, in his day, made in co-operation, over 48,000 needles a-day. On the other hand, a single needle-machine makes 145,000 in a working-day of 11 hours. One woman or one girl superintends four such machines, and so produces near upon 600,000 needles in a day, and upwards of 3,000,000 in a week. A single machine, when it takes the place of co-operation or of manufacture, may itself serve as the basis of an industry of a handicraft character. Still, such a return to handicrafts is but a transition to the factory system, which, as a rule, makes its appearance so soon as the human muscles are replaced, for the purpose of driving the machines, by a mechanical motive power, such as steam or water. Here and there, but in any case only for a time, an industry may be carried on, on a small scale, by means of mechanical power. This is effected by hiring steam-power, as is done in some of the Birmingham trades, or by the use of small caloric-engines, as in some branches of weaving. In the Coventry silk weaving industry the experiment of 'cottage factories' was tried. In the centre of a square surrounded by rows of cottages, an engine-house was built and the engine connected by shafts with the looms in the cottages. In all cases the power was hired at so much per loom. The rent was payable weekly, whether the looms worked or not. Each cottage held from 2 to 6 looms; some belonged to the weaver, some were bought on credit, some were hired. The struggle between these cottage factories and the factory proper, lasted over 12 years. It ended with the complete ruin of the 300 cottage factories. Wherever the nature of the process did not involve production on a large scale, the new industries that have sprung up in the last few decades, such as envelope making, steel-pen making, etc., have, as a general rule, first passed through the handicraft stage, and then the manufacturing stage, as short phases of transition to the factory stage. The transition is very difficult in those cases where the production of the article by manufacture consists, not of a series of graduated processes, but of a great number of disconnected ones. This circumstance formed a great hindrance to the establishment of steel-pen factories. Nevertheless, about 15 years ago, a machine was invented that automatically performed 6 separate operations at once. The first steel-pens were supplied by the handicraft system, in the year 1820, at £7 4 *s.* the gross; in 1830 they were supplied by manufacture at 8*s.*, and today the factory system supplies them to the trade at from 2*s.* to 6*d.* the gross.

(b) *Reaction of the Factory System on Manufacture and Domestic Industries*

Along with the development of the factory system and of the revolution in agriculture that accompanies it, production in all the other branches of industry not only extends, but alters its character. The principle, carried out in the factory system, of analysing the process of production into its constituent phases, and of solving the problems thus proposed by the application of mechanics, of chemistry, and of the whole range of the natural sciences, becomes the determining principle everywhere. Hence, machinery squeezes itself into the manufacturing industries first for one detail process, then for another. Thus the solid crystal of their organisation, based on the old division of labour, becomes dissolved, and makes way for constant changes. Independently of this, a radical change takes place in the composition of the collective labourer, a change of the persons working in combination. In contrast with the manufacturing period, the division of labour is thenceforth based, wherever possible, on the employment of women, of children of all ages, and of unskilled labourers, in one word, on cheap labour, as it is characteristically called in England. This is the case not only with all production on a large scale, whether employing machinery or not, but also with the so-called domestic industry, whether carried on in the houses of the workpeople or in small workshops. This modern so-called domestic industry has nothing, except the name, in common with the old-fashioned domestic industry, the existence of which pre-supposes independent urban handicrafts, independent peasant farming, and above all, a dwelling-house for the labourer and his family. That old-fashioned industry has now been converted into an outside department of the factory, the manufactory, or the warehouse. Besides the factory operatives, the manufacturing workmen and the handicraftsmen, whom it concentrates in large masses at one spot, and directly commands, capital also sets in motion, by means of invisible threads, another army; that of the workers in the domestic industries, who dwell in the large towns and are also scattered over the face of the country. An example: The shirt factory of Messrs. Tillie at Londonderry, which employs 1,000 operatives in the factory itself, and 9,000 people spread up and down the country and working in their own houses.

The exploitation of cheap and immature labour-power is carried out in a more shameless manner in modern Manufacture than in the factory proper. This is because the technical foundation of the factory system, namely, the substitution of machines for muscular power, and the light character of the labour, is almost entirely absent in Manufacture, and at the same time women and over-young children are subjected, in a most unconscionable way, to the influence of poisonous or injurious substances. This exploitation is more shameless in the so-called domestic industry than in manufactures, and that because the power of resistance in the labourers decreases with their dissemination;

because a whole series of plundering parasites insinuate themselves between the employer and the workman; because a domestic industry has always to compete either with the factory system, or with manufacturing in the same branch of production; because poverty robs the workman of the conditions most essential to his labour, of space, light and ventilation; because employment becomes more and more irregular; and, finally, because in these the last resorts of the masses made 'redundant' by Modern Industry and Agriculture, competition for work attains its maximum. Economy in the means of production, first systematically carried out in the factory system, and there, from the very beginning, coincident with the most reckless squandering of labour-power, and robbery of the conditions normally requisite for labour—this economy now shows its antagonistic and murderous side more and more in a given branch of industry, the less the social productive power of labour and the technical basis for a combination of processes are developed in that branch.

(c) *Modern Manufacture*

I now proceed, by a few examples, to illustrate the principles laid down above. As a matter of fact, the reader is already familiar with numerous instances given in the chapter on the working-day. In the hardware manufactures of Birmingham and the neighbourhood, there are employed, mostly in very heavy work, 30,000 children and young persons, besides 10,000 women. There they are to be seen in the unwholesome brass-foundries, button factories, enamelling, galvanising, and lackering works. Owing to the excessive labour of their workpeople, both adult and non-adult, certain London houses where newspapers and books are printed, have got the ill-omened name of 'slaughter-houses'. Similar excesses are practised in book-binding, where the victims are chiefly women, girls, and children; young persons have to do heavy work in rope-walks and night-work in salt mines, candle manufactories, and chemical works; young people are worked to death at turning the looms in silk weaving, when it is not carried on by machinery. One of the most shameful, the most dirty, and the worst paid kinds of labour, and one on which women and young girls are by preference employed, is the sorting of rags. It is well known that Great Britain, apart from its own immense store of rags, is the emporium for the rag trade of the whole world. They flow in from Japan, from the most remote States of South America, and from the Canary Islands. But the chief sources of their supply are Germany, France, Russia,

Italy, Egypt, Turkey, Belgium, and Holland. They are used for manure, for making bedflocks, for shoddy, and they serve as the raw material of paper. The rag-sorters are the medium for the spread of small-pox and other infectious diseases, and they themselves are the first victims. A classical example of over-work, of hard and inappropriate labour, and of its brutalising effects on the workman from his childhood upwards, is afforded not only by coal-mining and miners generally, but also by tile and brick making, in which industry the recently invented machinery is, in England, used only here and there. Between May and September the work lasts from 5 in the morning till 8 in the evening, and where the drying is done in the open air, it often lasts from 4 in the morning till 9 in the evening. Work from 5 in the morning till 7 in the evening is considered 'reduced' and 'moderate'. Both boys and girls of 6 and even of 4 years of age are employed. They work for the same number of hours, often longer, than the adults. The work is hard and the summer heat increases the exhaustion. In a certain tile-field at Mosley, e.g. a young woman, 24 years of age, was in the habit of making 2,000 tiles a day, with the assistance of 2 little girls, who carried the clay for her, and stacked the tiles. These girls carried daily 10 tons up the slippery sides of the clay pits, from a depth of 30 feet, and then for a distance of 210 feet.

It is impossible for a child to pass through the purgatory of a tile-field without great moral degradation . . . the low language, which they are accustomed to hear from their tenderest years, the filthy, indecent, and shameless habits, amidst which, unknowing, and half wild, they grow up, make them in after-life lawless, abandoned, dissolute. . . . A frightful source of demoralisation is the mode of living. Each moulder, who is always a skilled labourer, and the chief of a group, supplies his 7 subordinates with board and lodging in his cottage. Whether members of his family or not, the men, boys, and girls all sleep in the cottage, which contains generally two, exceptionally 3 rooms, all on the ground floor, and badly ventilated. These people are so exhausted after the day's hard work, that neither the rules of health, of cleanliness, nor of decency are in the least observed. Many of these cottages are models of untidiness, dirt, and dust. . . . The greatest evil of the system that employs young girls on this sort of work, consists in this, that, as a rule, it chains them fast from childhood for the whole of their after-life to the most abandoned rabble. They become rough, foul-mouthed boys, before Nature has taught them that they are women. Clothed in a few dirty rags, the legs naked far above the knees, hair and face besmeared with dirt, they learn to treat all feelings of decency and of shame with contempt. During meal-times they lie at full length in the fields, or watch the boys bathing in a neighbouring canal. Their heavy day's work at length completed, they put on better clothes, and accompany the men to the public houses.

That excessive insobriety is prevalent from childhood upwards among the whole of this class, is only natural. 'The worst is that the brickmakers despair of themselves. You might as well, said one of the better kind to a chaplain of Southall-field, try to raise and improve the devil as a brickie, sir!'

As to the manner, in which capital effects an economy in the requisites of labour, in modern Manufacture (in which I include all workshops of larger size, except factories proper), official and most ample material bearing on it is to be found in the Public Health Reports IV (1863) and VI (1864). The description of the workshops, more especially those of the London printers and tailors, surpasses the most loathsome phantasies of our romance writers. The effect on the health of the workpeople is self-evident. Dr Simon, the chief medical officer of the Privy Council and the official editor of the 'Public Health Reports', says:

In my fourth Report (1863) I showed, how it is practically impossible for the workpeople to insist upon that which is their first sanitary right, viz., the right that, no matter what the work for which their employer brings them together, the labour, so far as it depends upon him, should be freed from all avoidably unwholesome conditions. I pointed out, that while the workpeople are practically incapable of doing themselves this sanitary justice, they are unable to obtain any effective support from the paid administrations of the sanitary police. . . . The life of myriads of workmen and workwomen is now uselessly tortured and shortened by the never-ending physical suffering that their mere occupation begets.

In illustration of the way in which the workrooms influence the state of health Dr Simon gives the following table of mortality.

Number of persons of all ages employed in the respective industries	Industries compared as regards health	Death-rate per 100,000 men in the respective industries between the stated ages		
		Age 25–35	Age 35–45	Age 45–55
958,265	Agriculture in England and Wales	743	805	1,145
22,301 men 12,379 women }	London tailors	958	1,262	2,093
13,803	London printers	894	1,747	2,367

(e) *Passage of Modern Manufacture, and Domestic Industry into Modern Mechanical Industry. The Hastening of This Revolution by the Application of the Factory Acts to Those Industries*

The cheapening of labour-power, by sheer abuse of the labour of women and children, by sheer robbery of every normal condition requisite for working and living, and by the sheer brutality of overwork and night-work, meets at last with natural obstacles that cannot be overstepped. So also, when based on these methods, do the cheapening of commodities and capitalist exploitation in general. So soon as this point is at last reached—and it takes many years—the hour has struck for the introduction of machinery, and for the thenceforth rapid conversion of the scattered domestic industries and also of manufactures into factory industries.

The production of wearing apparel is carried on partly in manufactories in whose workrooms there is but a reproduction of that division of labour, the membra disjecta* of which were found ready to hand; partly by small master-handicraftsmen; these, however, do not, as formerly, work for individual consumers, but for manufactories and warehouses, and to such an extent that often whole towns and stretches of country carry on certain branches, such as shoemaking, as a speciality; finally, on a very great scale by the so-called domestic workers, who form an external department of the manufactories, warehouses, and even of the workshops of the smaller masters.

The raw material, etc., is supplied by mechanical industry, the mass of cheap human material (taillable à merci et miséricorde)* is composed of the individuals 'liberated' by mechanical industry and improved agriculture. The manufactures of this class owed their origin chiefly to the capitalist's need of having at hand an army ready equipped to meet any increase of demand. These manufactures, nevertheless, allowed the scattered handicrafts and domestic industries to continue to exist as a broad foundation. The great production of surplus-value in these branches of labour, and the progressive cheapening of their articles, were and are chiefly due to the minimum wages paid, no more than requisite for a miserable vegetation, and to the extension of working-time up to the maximum endurable by the human organism. It was in fact by the cheapness of the human sweat and the human blood, which were converted into commodities, that the markets were constantly being extended, and continue daily to be extended; more especially was this the case with England's colonial markets, where, besides, English tastes and habits prevail. At last the critical point was reached. The basis of the old method, sheer brutality in the exploitation of the workpeople, accompanied more or less by a systematic division of labour, no longer sufficed for the extending markets and for the still more rapidly extending competition of the capitalists. The hour struck for the advent of machinery. The decisively revolutionary machine, the machine which attacks in an equal degree the whole of the numberless branches of this sphere of production, dressmaking, tailoring, shoemaking, sewing, hat-making, and many others, is the sewing-machine.

Its immediate effect on the workpeople is like that of all machinery, which, since the rise of modern industry, has seized upon new branches of trade. Children of too tender an age are sent adrift. The wage of the machine hands rises compared with that of the house-workers, many of whom belong to the poorest of the poor. That of the better situated handicraftsmen, with whom the machine competes, sinks. The new machine hands are exclusively girls and young women. With the help of mechanical force, they destroy the monopoly that male labour had of the heavier work, and they drive off from the lighter work numbers of old women and very young children. The over-powering competition crushes the weakest of the manual labourers. The fearful increase in death from starvation during the last 10 years in London runs parallel with the extension of machine sewing. The new workwomen turn the machines by hand and foot, or by hand alone, sometimes sitting, sometimes standing, according to the weight, size, and special make of the machine, and expend a great deal of labour-power. Their occupation is unwholesome, owing to the long hours, although in most cases they are not so long as under the old system. Wherever the sewing-machine locates itself in narrow and already over-crowded workrooms, it adds to the unwholesome influences. 'The effect', says Mr Lord, 'on entering low-ceiled workrooms in which 30 to 40 machine hands are working is unbearable. . . . The heat, partly due to the gas stoves used for warming the irons, is horrible. . . . Even when moderate hours of work, i.e. from 8 in the morning till 6 in the evening, prevail in such places, yet 3 or 4 persons fall into a swoon regularly every day.'

The revolution in the industrial methods which is the necessary result of the revolution in the instruments of production, is effected by a medley of transition forms. These forms vary according to the extent to which the sewing-machine has become prevalent in one branch of industry or the other, to the time during which it has been in operation, to the previous condition of the workpeople, to the preponderance of manufacture, of handicrafts or of domestic industry, to the rent of the workrooms, etc. In dressmaking, for instance, where the labour for the most part was already organised, chiefly by simple co-operation, the sewing-machine at first formed merely a new factor in that manufacturing industry. In tailoring, shirtmaking, shoemaking, etc., all the forms are intermingled. Here the factory system proper. There middlemen receive the raw material from the capitalist *en chef*, and group around their sewing-machines, in 'chambers' and 'garrets', from 10 to 50 or more workwomen. Finally, as is always the case with machinery when not organised into a system, and when it can also be used in dwarfish proportions, handicraftsmen and domestic workers, along with their families, or with a little extra labour from without, make use of their own sewing-machines. The system actually prevalent in England is, that the capitalist concentrates a large number of machines on his premises, and then distributes the produce of those machines for further manipulation amongst the domestic workers. The variety of the transition forms, however, does not conceal the tendency to conversion into the factory system proper. This tendency is nurtured by the very nature of the sewing-machine, the manifold uses of which push on the concentration, under one roof, and one management, of previously separated branches of a trade. It is also favoured by the circumstance that preparatory needlework, and certain other operations, are most conveniently done on the premises where the machine is at work; as well as by the inevitable expropriation of the hand sewers, and of the domestic workers who work with their own machines. This fate has already in part overtaken them. The constantly increasing amount of capital invested in sewing-machines, gives the spur to the production of, and gluts the markets with, machine-made articles, thereby giving the signal to the domestic workers for the sale of their machines. The overproduction of sewing-machines themselves, causes their producers, in bad want of a sale, to let them out for so much a week, thus crushing by their deadly competition the small owners of machines. Constant changes in the construction of the machines, and their ever-increasing cheapness, depreciate day by day the older makes, and allow of their being sold in great numbers, at absurd prices, to large capitalists, who alone can thus employ them at a profit. Finally, the substitution of the steam-engine for man gives in this, as in all similar revolutions, the finishing blow. At first, the use of steam power meets with mere technical difficulties, such as unsteadiness in the machines, difficulty in controlling their speed, rapid wear and tear of the lighter machines, etc., all of which are soon overcome by experience. If, on the one had, the concentration of many machines in large manufactories leads to the use of steam power, on the other hand, the competition of steam with human muscles hastens on the concentration of workpeople and machines in large factories. Thus England is at present experiencing, not only in the colossal industry of making wearing apparel, but in most of the other trades mentioned above, the conversion of manufacture, of handicrafts, and of domestic work into the factory system, after each of those forms of production, totally changed and disorganised under the influence of modern industry, has long ago reproduced, and even overdone, all the horrors of the factory system, without participating in any of the elements of social progress it contains.

This industrial revolution which takes place spontaneously, is artificially helped on by the extension of the Factory Acts to all industries in which women, young persons and children are employed. The compulsory regulation of the working-day as regards its length, pauses, beginning and end, the system of relays of children, the exclusion of all children under a certain age, etc., necessitate on the one hand more machinery and the substitution of steam as a motive power in the place of muscles. On the other hand, in order to make up for the loss of time, an expansion occurs of the means of production used in common, of the furnaces, buildings, etc., in one word, greater concentration of the means of production and a correspondingly greater concourse of workpeople. The chief objection, repeatedly and passionately urged on behalf of each manufacture threatened with the Factory Act, is in fact this, that in order to continue the business on the old scale a greater outlay of capital will be necessary. But as regards labour in the so-called domestic industries and the intermediate forms between them and Manufacture, so soon as limits are put to the working-day and to the employment of children, those industries go to the wall. Unlimited exploitation of cheap labour-power is the sole foundation of their power to compete.

One of the essential conditions for the existence of the factory system, especially when the length of the working-day is fixed, is certainty in the result, i.e. the production in a given time of a given quantity of commodities, or of a given useful effect. The statutory pauses in the working-day, moreover, imply the assumption that periodical and sudden cessation of the work does no harm to the article undergoing the process of production. This certainty in the result, and this possibility of interrupting the work are, of course, easier to be attained in the purely mechanical industries than in those in which chemical and physical processes play a part; as, for instance, in the earthenware trade, in bleaching, dyeing, baking, and in most of the metal industries. Wherever there is a working-day without restriction as to length, wherever there is night-work and unrestricted waste of human life, there the slightest obstacle presented by the nature of the work to a change for the better is soon looked upon as an everlasting barrier erected by Nature. No poison kills vermin with more certainty than the Factory Act removes such everlasting barriers. No one made a greater outcry over 'impossibilities' than our friends the earthenware manufacturers. In 1864, however, they were brought under the Act, and within sixteen months every 'impossibility' had vanished. 'The improved method', called forth by the Act, 'of making slip by pressure instead of by evaporation, the newly-constructed stoves for drying the ware in its green state, etc., are each events of great importance in the pottery art, and mark an advance which the preceding century could not rival. . . . It has even considerably reduced the temperature of the stoves themselves with a considerable saving of fuel, and with readier effect on the ware.' In spite of every prophecy, the cost-price of earthenware did not rise, but the quantity produced did, and to such an extent that the export for the twelve months, ending December, 1865, exceeded in value by £138,628 the average of the preceding three years. In the manufacture of matches it was thought to be an indispensable requirement, that boys, even while bolting their dinner, should go on dipping the matches in melted phosphorus, the poisonous vapour from which rose into their faces. The Factory Act (1864) made the saving of time a necessity, and so forced into existence a dipping machine, the vapour from which could not come in contact with the workers. So, at the present time, in those branches of the lace manufacture not yet subject to the Factory Act, it is maintained that the meal-times cannot be regular owing to the different periods required by the various kinds of lace for drying, which periods vary from three minutes up to an hour and more. To this the Children's Employment Commissioners answer:

The circumstances of this case are precisely analogous to that of the paper-stainers, dealt with in our first report. Some of the principal manufacturers in the trade urged that in consequence of the nature of the materials used, and their various processes, they would be unable, without serious loss, to stop for meal-times at any given moment. But it was seen from the evidence that, by due care and previous arrangement, the apprehended difficulty would be got over; and accordingly, by clause 6 of section 6 of the Factory Acts Extension Act, passed during this Session of Parliament, an interval of eighteen months is given to them from the passing of the Act before they are required to conform to the meal hours, specified by the Factory Acts.

Hardly had the Act been passed when our friends the manufacturers found out: 'The inconveniences we expected to arise from the introduction of the Factory Acts into our branch of manufacture, I am happy to say, have not arisen. We do not find the production at all interfered with; in short, we produce more in the same time.' It is evident that the English legislature, which certainly no one will venture to reproach with being overdosed with genius, has been led by experience to the conclusion that a simple compulsory law is sufficient to enact away all the so-called impediments, opposed by the nature of the process, to the restriction and regulation of the working-day. Hence, on the introduction of the Factory Act into a given industry, a period varying from six to eighteen months is fixed within which it is incumbent on the manufacturers to remove all technical impediments to the working of the Act. Mirabeau's 'Impossible! ne me dites jamais ce bête de mot!'* is particularly applicable to modern technology. But though the Factory Acts thus artificially ripen the material elements necessary for the conversion of the manufacturing system into the factory system, yet at the same time, owing to the necessity they impose for greater outlay of capital, they hasten on the decline of the small masters, and the concentration of capital.

Besides the purely technical impediments that are removable by technical means, the irregular habits of the workpeople themselves obstruct the regulation of the hours of labour. This is especially the case where piece-wage predominates, and where loss of time in one part of the day or week can be made good by subsequent over-time, or by night-work, a process which brutalises the adult workman, and ruins his wife and children. Although this absence of regularity in the expenditure of labour-power is a natural and rude reaction against the tedium of monotonous drudgery, it originates, also, to a much greater degree from anarchy in production, anarchy that in its turn presupposes unbridled exploitation of labour-power by the capitalist. Besides the general periodic changes of the industrial cycle, and the special fluctuations in the markets to which each industry is subject, we may also reckon what is called 'the season', dependent either on the periodicity of favourable seasons of the year for navigation; or on fashion, and the sudden placing of large orders that have to be executed in the shortest possible time. The habit of giving such orders becomes more frequent with the extension of railways and telegraphs.

The extension of the railway system throughout the country has tended very much to encourage giving short notice. Purchasers now come up from Glasgow, Manchester, and Edinburgh once every fortnight or so to the wholesale city warehouses which we supply, and give small orders requiring immediate execution, instead of buying from stock as they used to do. Years ago we were always able to work in the slack times, so as to meet demand of the next season, but now no one can say beforehand what will be the demand then.

In those factories and manufactories that are not yet subject to the Factory Acts, the most fearful over-work prevails periodically during what is called the season, in consequence of sudden orders. In the outside department of the factory, of the manufactory, and of the warehouse, the so-called domestic workers, whose employment is at the best irregular, are entirely dependent for their raw material and their orders on the caprice of the capitalist, who, in this industry, is not hampered by any regard for depreciation of his buildings and machinery, and risks nothing by a stoppage of work, but the skin of the worker himself. Here then he sets himself systematically to work to form an industrial reserve force that shall be ready at a moment's notice; during one part of the year he decimates this force by the most inhuman toil, during the other part, he lets it starve for want of work. 'The employers avail themselves of the habitual irregularity in the homework, when any extra work is wanted at a push, so that the work goes on till 11, and 12 p. m. or 2 a. m., or as the usual phrase is, 'all hours', and that in localities where 'the stench is enough to knock you down, you go to the door, perhaps, and open it, but shudder to go further'. 'They are curious men,' said one of the witnesses, a shoemaker, speaking of the masters, 'they think it does a boy no harm to work too hard for half the year, if he is nearly idle for the other half.'

In the same way as technical impediments, so, too, those 'usages which have grown with the growth of trade' were and still are proclaimed by interested capitalists as obstacles due to the nature of the work. This was a favourite cry of the cotton lords at the time they were first threatened with the Factory Acts. Although their industry more than any other depends on navigation, yet experience has given them the lie. Since then, every pretended obstruction to business has been treated by the Factory inspectors as a mere sham. The thoroughly conscientious investigations of the Children's Employment Commission prove that the effect of the regulation of the hours of work, in some industries, was to spread the mass of labour previously employed more evenly over the whole year; that this regulation was the first rational bridle on the murderous, meaningless caprices of fashion, caprices that consort so badly with the system of modern industry; that the development of ocean navigation and of the means of communication generally, has swept away the technical basis on which season-work was really supported, and that all other so-called unconquerable difficulties vanish before larger buildings, additional machinery, increase in the number of workpeople employed, and the alterations caused by all these in the mode of conducting the wholesale trade. But for all that, capital never becomes reconciled to such changes—and this is admitted over and over again by its own representatives—except 'under the pressure of a General Act of Parliament' for the compulsory regulation of the hours of labour.

Section 9. The Factory Acts. Sanitary and Educational Clauses of the Same. Their General Extension in England

Factory legislation, that first conscious and methodical reaction of society against the spontaneously developed form of the process of production, is, as we have seen, just as much the necessary product of modern industry as cotton yarn, self-actors, and the electric telegraph. Before passing to the consideration of the extension of that legislation in England, we shall shortly notice certain clauses contained in the Factory Acts, and not relating to the hours of work.

Paltry as the education clauses of the Act appear on the whole, yet they proclaim elementary education to be an indispensable condition to the employment of children. The success of those clauses proved for the first time the possibility of combining education and gymnastics with manual labour, and, consequently, of combining manual labour with education and gymnastics. The factory inspectors soon found out by questioning the schoolmasters, that the factory children, although receiving only one half the education of the regular day scholars, yet learnt quite as much and often more. 'This can be accounted for by the simple fact that, with only being at school for one half of the day, they are always fresh, and nearly always ready and willing to receive instruction. The system on which they work, half manual labour, and half school, renders each employment a rest and a relief to the other; consequently, both are far more congenial to the child, than would be the case were he kept constantly at one. It is quite clear that a boy who has been at school all the morning, cannot (in hot weather particularly) cope with one who comes fresh and bright from his work.' Further information on this point will be found in Senior's speech at the Social Science Congress at Edinburgh in 1863. He there shows, amongst other things, how the monotonous and uselessly long school hours of the children of the upper and middle classes, uselessly add to the labour of the teacher, 'while he not only fruitlessly but absolutely injuriously, wastes the time, health, and energy of the children'. From the Factory system budded, as Robert Owen has shown us in detail, the germ of the education of the future, an education that will, in the case of every child over a given age, combine productive labour with instruction and gymnastics, not only as one of the methods of adding to the efficiency of production, but as the only method of producing fully developed human beings.

Modern Industry, as we have seen, sweeps away by technical means the manufacturing division of labour, under which each man is bound hand and foot for life to a single detail-operation. At the same time, the capitalistic form of that industry reproduces this same division of labour in a still more monstrous shape; in the factory proper, by converting the workman into a living appendage of the machine; and everywhere outside the Factory, partly by the sporadic use of machinery and machine workers, partly by re-establishing the division of labour on a fresh basis by the general introduction of the labour of women and children, and of cheap unskilled labour.

The antagonism between the manufacturing division of labour and the methods of Modern Industry makes itself forcibly felt. It manifests itself, amongst other ways, in the frightful fact that a great part of the children employed in modern factories and manufactures, are from their earliest years riveted to the most simple manipulations, and exploited for years, without being taught a single sort of work that would afterwards make them of use, even in the same manufactory or factory. In the English letter-press printing trade, for example, there existed formerly a system, corresponding to that in the old manufactures and handicrafts, of advancing the apprentices from easy to more and more difficult work. They went through a course of teaching till they were finished printers. To be able to read and write was for every one of them a requirement of their trade. All this was changed by the printing machine. It employs two sorts of labourers, one grown up, tenters, the other, boys mostly from 11 to 17 years of age whose sole business in either to spread the sheets of paper under the machine, or to take from it the printed sheets. They perform this weary task, in London especially, for 14, 15, and 16 hours at a stretch, during several days in the week, and frequently for 36 hours, with only 2 hours' rest for meals and sleep. A great part of them cannot read, and they are, as a rule, utter savages and very extraordinary creatures. 'To qualify them for the work which they have to do, they require no intellectual training; there is little room in it for skill, and less for judgment; their wages, though rather high for boys, do not increase proportionately as they grow up, and the majority of them cannot look for advancement to the better paid and more responsible post of machine minder, because while each machine has but one minder, it has at least two, and often four boys attached to it.' As soon as they get too old for such child's work, that is about 17 at the latest, they are discharged from the printing establishments. They become recruits of crime. Several attempts to procure them employment elsewhere, were rendered of no avail by their ignorance and brutality, and by their mental and bodily degradation.

As with the division of labour in the interior of the manufacturing workshops, so it is with the division of labour in the interior of society. So long as handicraft and manufacture form the general groundwork of social production, the subjection of the producer to one branch exclusively, the breaking up of the multifariousness of his employment, is a necessary step in the development. On that groundwork each separate branch of production acquires empirically the form that is technically suited to it, slowly perfects it, and, so soon as a given degree of maturity has been reached, rapidly crystallises that form. The only thing, that here and there causes a change, besides new raw material supplied by commerce, is the gradual alteration of the instruments of labour. But their form, too, once definitely settled by experience, petrifies, as is proved by their being in many cases handed down in the same form by one generation to another during thousands of years. A characteristic feature is, that, even down into the eighteenth century, the different trades were called 'mysteries' (mystères); into their secrets none but those duly initiated could penetrate. Modern Industry rent the veil that concealed from men their own social process of production, and that turned the various, spontaneously divided branches of production into so many riddles, not only to outsiders, but even to the initiated. The principle which it pursued, of resolving each process into its constituent movements, without any regard to their possible execution by the hand of man, created the new modern science of technology. The varied apparently unconnected, and petrified forms of the industrial processes now resolved themselves into so many conscious and systematic applications of natural science to the attainment of given useful effects. Technology also discovered the few main fundamental forms of motion, which, despite the diversity of the instruments used, are necessarily taken by every productive action of the human body; just as the science of mechanics sees in the most complicated machinery nothing but the continual repetition of the simple mechanical powers.

Modern Industry never looks upon and treats the existing form of a process as final. The technical basis of that industry is therefore revolutionary, while all earlier modes of production were essentially conservative. By means of machinery, chemical processes and other methods, it is continually causing changes not only in the technical basis of production, but also in the functions of the labourer, and in the social combinations of the labour-process. At the same time, it thereby also revolutionises the division of labour within the society, and incessantly launches masses of capital and of workpeople from one branch of production to another. But if Modern Industry, by its very nature, therefore necessitates variation of labour, fluency of function, universal mobility of the labourer, on the other hand, in its capitalistic form, it reproduces the old division of labour with its ossified particularisations. We have seen how this absolute contradiction between the technical necessities of Modern Industry, and the social character inherent in its capitalistic form, dispels all fixity and security in the situation of the labourer; how it constantly threatens, by taking away the instruments of labour, to snatch from his hands his means of subsistence, and, by suppressing his detail-function, to make him superfluous. We have seen, too, how this antagonism vents its rage in the creation of that monstrosity, an industrial reserve army, kept in misery in order to be always at the disposal of capital; in the incessant human sacrifices from among the working-class, in the most reckless squandering of labour-power, and in the devastation caused by a social anarchy which turns every economic progress into a social calamity. This is the negative side. But if, on the one hand, variation of work at present imposes itself after the manner of an overpowering natural law, and with the blindly destructive action of a natural law that meets with resistance at all points, Modern Industry, on the other hand, through its catastrophes imposes the necessity of recognising, as a fundamental law of production, variation of work, consequently fitness of the labourer for varied work, consequently the greatest possible development of his varied aptitudes. It becomes a question of life and death for society to adapt the mode of production to the normal functioning of this law. Modern Industry, indeed, compels society, under penalty of death, to replace the detail-worker of today, crippled by life-long repetition of one and the same trivial operation, and thus reduced to the mere fragment of a man, by the fully developed individual, fit for a variety of labours, ready to face any change of production, and to whom the different social functions he performs, are but so many modes of giving free scope to his own natural and acquired powers.

One step already spontaneously taken towards effecting this revolution is the establishment of technical and agricultural schools, and of 'écoles d'enseignement professionnel',* in which the children of the working-men receive some little instruction in technology and in the practical handling of the various implements of labour. Though the Factory Act, that first and meagre concession wrung from capital, is limited to combining elementary education with work in the factory, there can be no doubt that when the working-class comes into power, as inevitably it must, technical instruction, both theoretical and practical, will take its proper place in the working-class schools. There is also no doubt that such revolutionary ferments, the final result of which is the abolition of the old division of labour, are diametrically opposed to the capitalistic form of production, and to the economic status of the labourer corresponding to that form. But the historical development of the antagonisms, immanent in a given form of production, is the only way in which that form of production can be dissolved and a new form established. 'Ne sutor ultra crepidam'*—this nec plus ultra of handicraft wisdom became sheer nonsense, from the moment the watchmaker Watt invented the steam-engine, the barber Arkwright, the throstle, and the working-jeweller, Fulton, the steamship.

So long as Factory legislation is confined to regulating the labour in factories, manufactories, etc., it is regarded as a mere interference with the exploiting rights of capital. But when it comes to regulating the so-called 'home-labour', it is immediately viewed as a direct attack on the patria potestas, on parental authority. The tender-hearted English Parliament long affected to shrink from taking this step. The force of facts, however, compelled it at last to acknowledge that modern industry, in overturning the economic foundation on which was based the traditional family, and the family labour corresponding to it, had also unloosened all traditional family ties. The rights of the children had to be proclaimed. The final report of the Ch. Empl. Comm. of 1866, states: 'It is unhappily, to a painful degree, apparent throughout the whole of the evidence, that against no persons do the children of both sexes so much require protection as against their parents.' The system of unlimited exploitation of children's labour in general and the so-called home-labour in particular is 'maintained only because the parents are able, without check or control, to exercise this arbitrary and mischievous power over their young and tender offspring. . . . Parents must not possess the absolute power of making their children mere 'machines to earn so much weekly wage. . . .' The children and young persons, therefore, in all such cases may justifiably claim from the legislature, as a natural right, that an exemption should be secured to them, from what destroys prematurely their physical strength, and lowers them in the scale of intellectual and moral beings.' It was not, however, the misuse of parental authority that created the capitalistic exploitation, whether direct or indirect, of children's labour; but, on the contrary, it was the capitalistic mode of exploitation which, by sweeping away the economic basis of parental authority, made its exercise degenerate into a mischievous misuse of power. However terrible and disgusting the dissolution, under the capitalist system, of the old family ties may appear, nevertheless, modern industry, by assigning as it does an important part in the process of production, outside the domestic sphere, to women, to young persons, and to children of both sexes, creates a new economic foundation for a higher form of the family and of the relations between the sexes. It is, of course, just as absurd to hold the Teutonic-Christian form of the family to be absolute and final as it would be to apply that character to the ancient Roman, the ancient Greek, or the Eastern forms which, moreover, taken together form a series in historical development. Moreover, it is obvious that the fact of the collective working group being composed of individuals of both sexes and all ages, must necessarily, under suitable conditions, become a source of humane development; although in its spontaneously developed, brutal, capitalistic form, where the labourer exists for the process of production, and not the process of production for the labourer, that fact is a pestiferous source of corruption and slavery.

The necessity for a generalisation of the Factory Acts, for transforming them from an exceptional law relating to mechanical spinning and weaving—those first creations of machinery—into a law affecting social production as a whole, arose, as we have seen, from the mode in which Modern Industry was historically developed. In the rear of that industry, the traditional form of manufacture, of handicraft, and of domestic industry, is entirely revolutionised; manufactures are constantly passing into the factory system, and handicrafts into manufactures; and lastly, the spheres of handicraft and of the domestic industries become, in a, comparatively speaking, wonderfully short time, dens of misery in which capitalistic exploitation obtains free play for the wildest excesses. There are two circumstances that finally turn the scale: first, the constantly recurring experience that capital, so soon as it finds itself subject to legal control at one point, compensates itself all the more recklessly at other points; secondly, the cry of the capitalists for equality in the conditions of competition, i.e. for equal restraint on all exploitation of labour. On this point let us listen to two heartbroken cries. Messrs. Cooksley of Bristol, nail and chain, etc., manufacturers, spontaneously introduced the regulations of the Factory Act into their business. 'As the old irregular system prevails in neighbouring works, the Messrs. Cooksley are subject to the disadvantage of having their boys enticed to continue their labour elsewhere after 6 p. m. 'This', they naturally say, 'is an unjustice and loss to us, as it exhausts a portion of the boy's strength, of which we ought to have the full benefit'. Mr J. Simpson (paper box and bagmaker, London) states before the commissioners of the Ch. Empl. Comm.: 'He would sign any petition for it' (legislative interference). . . . 'As it was, he always felt restless at night, when he had closed his place, lest others should be working later than him and getting away his orders.' Summarising, the Ch. Empl. Comm. says:

It would be unjust to the larger employers that their factories should be placed under regulation, while the hours of labour in the smaller places in their own branch of business were under no legislative restriction. And to the injustice arising from the unfair conditions of competition, in regard to hours, that would be created if the smaller places of work were exempt, would be added the disadvantage to the larger manufacturers, of finding their supply of juvenile and female labour drawn off to the places of work exempt from legislation. Further, a stimulus would be given to the multiplication of the smaller places of work, which are almost invariably the least favourable to the health, comfort, education, and general improvement of the people.

In its final report the Commission proposes to subject to the Factory Act more than 1,400,000 children, young persons, and women, of which number about one half are exploited in small industries and by the so-called home-work. It says,

But if it should seem fit to Parliament to place the whole of that large number of children, young persons and females under the protective legislation above adverted to . . . it cannot be doubted that such legislation would have a most beneficent effect, not only upon the young and the feeble, who are its more immediate objects, but upon the still larger body of adult workers, who would in all these employments, both directly and indirectly, come immediately under its influence. It would enforce upon them regular and moderate hours; it would lead to their places of work being kept in a healthy and cleanly state; it would therefore husband and improve that store of physical strength on which their own well-being and that of the country so much depends; it would save the rising generation from that over-exertion at an early age which undermines their constitutions and leads to premature decay; finally, it would ensure them—at least up to the age of 13—the opportunity of receiving the elements of education, and would put an end to that utter ignorance . . . so faithfully exhibited in the Reports of our Assistant Commissioners, and which cannot be regarded without the deepest pain, and a profound sense of national degradation.

The Workshops' Regulation Act, wretched in all its details, remained a dead letter in the hands of the municipal and local authorities who were charged with its execution. When, in 1871, Parliament withdrew from them this power, in order to confer it on the Factory Inspectors, to whose province it thus added by a single stroke more than one hundred thousand workshops, and three hundred brickworks, care was taken at the same time not to add more than eight assistants to their already undermanned staff.

If the general extension of factory legislation to all trades for the purpose of protecting the working-class both in mind and body has become inevitable, on the other hand, as we have already pointed out, that extension hastens on the general conversion of numerous isolated small industries into a few combined industries carried on upon a large scale; it therefore accelerates the concentration of capital and the exclusive predominance of the factory system. It destroys both the ancient and the transitional forms, behind which the dominion of capital is still in part concealed, and replaces them by the direct and open sway of capital; but thereby it also generalises the direct opposition to this sway. While in each individual workshop it enforces uniformity, regularity, order, and economy, it increases by the immense spur which the limitation and regulation of the working-day give to technical improvement, the anarchy and the catastrophes of capitalist production as a whole, the intensity of labour, and the competition of machinery with the labourer. By the destruction of petty and domestic industries it destroys the last resort of the 'redundant population', and with it the sole remaining safety-valve of the whole social mechanism. By maturing the material conditions, and the combination on a social scale of the processes of production, it matures the contradictions and antagonisms of the capitalist form of production, and thereby provides, along with the elements for the formation of a new society, the forces for exploding the old one.

Section 10. Modern Industry and Agriculture

The revolution called forth by modern industry in agriculture, and in the social relations of agricultural producers, will be investigated later on. In this place we shall merely indicate a few results by way of anticipation. If the use of machinery in agriculture is for the most part free from the injurious physical effect it has on the factory operative, its action in superseding the labourers is more intense, and finds less resistance, as well shall see later in detail. In the counties of Cambridge and Suffolk, for example, the area of cultivated land has extended very much within the last 20 years (up to 1868), while in the same period the rural population has diminished, not only relatively, but absolutely. In the United States it is as yet only virtually that agricultural machines replace labourers; in other words, they allow of the cultivation by the farmer of a larger surface, but do not actually expel the labourers employed. In 1861 the number of persons occupied in England and Wales in the manufacture of agricultural machines was, 1,034, whilst the number of agricultural labourers employed in the use of agricultural machines and steam-engines did not exceed 1,205.

In the sphere of agriculture, modern industry has a more revolutionary effect than elsewhere, for this reason, that it annihilates the peasant, that bulwark of the old society, and replaces him by the wage-labourer. Thus the desire for social changes, and the class antagonisms are brought to the same level in the country as in the towns. The irrational, old-fashioned methods of agriculture are replaced by scientific ones. Capitalist production completely tears asunder the old bond of union which held together agriculture and manufacture in their infancy. But at the same time it creates the material conditions for a higher synthesis in the future, viz., the union of agriculture and industry on the basis of the more perfected forms they have each acquired during their temporary separation. Capitalist production, by collecting the population in great centres, and causing an ever-increasing preponderance of town population, on the one hand concentrates the historical motive power of society; on the other hand, it disturbs the circulation of matter between man and the soil, i.e. prevents the return to the soil of its elements consumed by man in the form of food and clothing; it therefore violates the conditions necessary to lasting fertility of the soil. By this action it destroys at the same time the health of the town labourer and the intellectual life of the rural labourer. But while upsetting the naturally grown conditions for the maintenance of that circulation of matter, it imperiously calls for its restoration as a system, as a regulating law of social production, and under a form appropriate to the full development of the human race. In agriculture as in manufacture, the transformation of production under the sway of capital, means, at the same time, the martyrdom of the producer; the instrument of labour becomes the means of enslaving, exploiting, and impoverishing the labourer; the social combination and organisation of labour-processes is turned into an organised mode of crushing out the workman's individual vitality, freedom, and independence. The dispersion of the rural labourers over larger areas breaks their power of resistance while concentration increases that of the town operatives. In modern agriculture, as in the urban industries, the increased productiveness and quantity of the labour set in motion are bought at the cost of laying waste and consuming by disease labour-power itself. Moreover, all progress in capitalistic agriculture is a progress in the art, not only of robbing the labourer, but of robbing the soil; all progress in increasing the fertility of the soil for a given time, is a progress towards ruining the lasting sources of that fertility. The more a country starts its development on the foundation of modern industry, like the United States, for example, the more rapid is this process of destruction. Capitalist production, therefore, develops technology, and the combining together of various processes into a social whole, only by sapping the original sources of all wealth—the soil and the labourer.

PART V

THE PRODUCTION OF ABSOLUTE AND OF RELATIVE SURPLUS-VALUE

CHAPTER 16

ABSOLUTE AND RELATIVE SURPLUS-VALUE

IN considering the labour-process, we began (see Chapter 7) by treating it in the abstract, apart from its historical forms, as a process between man and Nature. We there stated, p. 118: 'If we examine the whole process from the point of view of its result, the product, it is plain that both the instruments and the subject of labour, are means of production, and that the labour itself is productive labour.' And in Note 2, same page, we further added: 'This method of determining, from the standpoint of the labour-process alone, what is productive labour, is by no means directly applicable to the case of the capitalist process of production.' We now proceed to the further development of this subject.

So far as the labour-process is purely individual, one and the same labourer unites in himself all the functions, that later on become separated. When an individual appropriates natural objects for his livelihood, no one controls him but himself. Afterwards he is controlled by others. A single man cannot operate upon Nature without calling his own muscles into play under the control of his own brain. As in the natural body head and hand wait upon each other, so the labour-process unites the labour of the hand with that of the head. Later on they part company and even become deadly foes. The product ceases to be the direct product of the individual, and becomes a social product, produced in common by a collective labourer, i.e. by a combination of workmen, each of whom takes only a part, greater or less, in the manipulation of the subject of their labour. As the co-operative character of the labour-process becomes more and more marked, so, as a necessary consequence, does our notion of productive labour, and of its agent the productive labourer, become extended. In order to labour productively, it is no longer necessary for you to do manual work yourself; enough, if you are an organ of the collective labourer, and perform one of its subordinate functions. The first definition given above of productive labour, a definition deduced from the very nature of the production of material objects, still remains correct for the collective labourer, considered as a whole. But it no longer holds good for each member taken individually.

On the other hand, however, our notion of productive labour becomes narrowed. Capitalist production is not merely the production of commodities, it is essentially the production of surplus-value. The labourer produces, not for himself, but for capital. It no longer suffices, therefore, that he should simply produce. He must produce surplus-value. That labourer alone is productive, who produces surplus-value for the capitalist, and thus works for the self-expansion of capital. If we may take an example from outside the sphere of production of material objects, a schoolmaster is a productive labourer, when, in addition to belabouring the heads of his scholars, he works like a horse to enrich the school proprietor. That the latter has laid out his capital in a teaching factory, instead of in a sausage factory, does not alter the relation. Hence the notion of a productive labourer implies not merely a relation between work and useful effect, between labourer and product of labour, but also a specific, social relation of production, a relation that has sprung up historically and stamps the labourer as the direct means of creating surplus-value. To be a productive labourer is, therefore, not a piece of luck, but a misfortune. In Book IV, which treats of the history of the theory,* it will be more clearly seen, that the production of surplus-value has at all times been made, by classical political economists, the distinguishing characteristic of the productive labourer. Hence their definition of a productive labourer changes with their comprehension of the nature of surplus-value. Thus the Physiocrats insist that only agricultural labour is productive, since that alone, they say, yields a surplus-value. And they say so because, with them, surplus-value has no existence except in the form of rent.

The prolongation of the working-day beyond the point at which the labourer would have produced just an equivalent for the value of his labour-power, and the appropriation of that surplus-labour by capital, this is production of absolute surplus-value. It forms the general groundwork of the capitalist system, and the starting-point for the production of relative surplus-value. The latter pre-supposes that the working-day is already divided into two parts, necessary labour, and surplus-labour. In order to prolong the surplus-labour, the necessary labour is shortened by methods whereby the equivalent for the wages is produced in less time. The production of absolute surplus-value turns exclusively upon the length of the working-day; the production of relative surplus-value, revolutionises out and out the technical processes of labour, and the composition of society. It therefore pre-supposes a specific mode, the capitalist mode of production, a mode which, along with its methods, means, and conditions, arises and develops itself spontaneously on the foundation afforded by the formal subjection of labour to capital. In the course of this development, the formal subjection is replaced by the real subjection of labour to capital.

Once the capitalist mode of production is established and become general, the difference between absolute and relative surplus-value makes itself felt, whenever there is a question of raising the rate of surplus-value. Assuming that labour-power is paid for at its value, we are confronted by this alternative: given the productiveness of labour and its normal intensity, the rate of surplus-value can be raised only by the actual prolongation of the working-day; on the other hand, given the length of the working-day, that rise can be effected only by a change in the relative magnitudes of the components of the working-day, viz., necessary labour and surplus-labour; a change which, if the wages are not to fall below the value of labour-power, pre-supposes a change either in the productiveness or in the intensity of the labour.

If the labourer wants all his time to produce the necessary means of subsistence for himself and his race, he has no time left in which to work gratis for others. Without a certain degree of productiveness in his labour, he has no such superfluous time at his disposal; without such superfluous time, no surplus-labour and therefore no capitalists, no slave-owners, no feudal lords, in one word, no class of large proprietors.

Thus we may say that surplus-value rests on a natural basis; but this is permissible only in the very general sense, that there is no natural obstacle absolutely preventing one man from disburdening himself of the labour requisite for his own existence, and burdening another with it, any more, for instance, than unconquerable natural obstacles prevent one man from eating the flesh of another. No mystical ideas must in any way be connected, as sometimes happens, with this historically developed productiveness of labour. It is only after men have raised themselves above the rank of animals, when therefore their labour has been to some extent socialised, that a state of things arises in which the surplus-labour of the one becomes a condition of existence for the other. At the dawn of civilisation the productiveness acquired by labour is small, but so too are the wants which develop with and by the means of satisfying them. Further, at that early period, the portion of society that lives on the labour of others is infinitely small compared with the mass of direct producers. Along with the progress in the productiveness of labour, that small portion of society increases both absolutely and relatively. Besides, capital with its accompanying relations springs up from an economic soil that is the product of a long process of development. The productiveness of labour that serves as its foundation and starting-point, is a gift, not of Nature, but of a history embracing thousands of centuries.

Favourable natural conditions alone, give us only the possibility, never the reality, of surplus-labour, nor, consequently, of surplus-value and a surplus-product. The result of difference in the natural conditions of labour is this, that the same quantity of labour satisfies, in different countries, a different mass of requirements, consequently, that under circumstances in other respects analogous, the necessary labour-time is different. These conditions affect surplus-labour only as natural limits, i.e. by fixing the points at which labour for others can begin. In proportion as industry advances, these natural limits recede.

CHAPTER 17

CHANGES OF MAGNITUDE
IN THE PRICE OF LABOUR-POWER
AND IN SURPLUS-VALUE

THE value of labour-power is determined by the value of the necessaries of life habitually required by the average labourer. The quantity of these necessaries is known at any given epoch of a given society, and can therefore be treated as a constant magnitude. What changes, is the value of this quantity. There are, besides, two other factors that enter into the determination of the value of labour-power. One, the expenses of developing that power, which expenses vary with the mode of production; the other, its natural diversity, the difference between the labour-power of men and women, of children and adults. The employment of these different sorts of labour-power, an employment which is, in its turn, made necessary by the mode of production, makes a great difference in the cost of maintaining the family of the labourer, and in the value of the labour-power of the adult male. Both these factors, however, are excluded in the following investigation.

I assume (1) that commodities are sold at their value; (2) that the price of labour-power rises occasionally above its value, but never sinks below it.

On this assumption we have seen that the relative magnitudes of surplus-value and of price of labour-power are determined by three circumstances; (1) the length of the working-day, or the extensive magnitude of labour; (2) the normal intensity of labour, its intensive magnitude, whereby a given quantity of labour is expended in a given time; (3) the productiveness of labour, whereby the same quantum of labour yields, in a given time, a greater or less quantum of product, dependent on the degree of development in the conditions of production. Very different combinations are clearly possible, according as one of the three factors is constant and two variable, or two constant and one variable, or lastly, all three simultaneously variable. And the number of these combinations is augmented by the fact that, when these factors simultaneously vary, the amount and direction of their respective variations may differ. In what follows the chief combinations alone are considered.

I. Length of the Working-Day and Intensity of Labour Constant. Productiveness of Labour Variable

On these assumptions the value of labour-power, and the magnitude of surplus-value, are determined by three laws.

(1) A working-day of given length always creates the same amount of value, no matter how the productiveness of labour, and, with it, the mass of the product, and the price of each single commodity produced, may vary.

If the value created by a working-day of 12 hours be, say, six shillings, then, although the mass of the articles produced varies with the productiveness of labour, the only result is that the value represented by six shillings is spread over a greater or less number of articles.

(2) Surplus-value and the value of labour-power vary in opposite directions. A variation in the productiveness of labour, its increase or diminution, causes a variation in the opposite direction in the value of labour-power, and in the same direction in surplus-value.

The value created by a working-day of 12 hours is a constant quantity, say, six shillings. This constant quantity is the sum of the surplus-value plus the value of the labour-power, which latter value the labourer replaces by an equivalent. It is self-evident, that if a constant quantity consists of two parts, neither of them can increase without the other diminishing. Let the two parts at starting be equal; 3 shillings value of labour-power, 3 shillings surplus-value. Then the value of the labour-power cannot rise from three shillings to four, without the surplus-value falling from three shillings to two; and the surplus-value cannot rise from three shillings to four, without the value of labour-power falling from three shillings to two. Under these circumstances, therefore, no change can take place in the absolute magnitude, either of the surplus-value, or of the value of labour-power, without a simultaneous change in their relative magnitudes, i.e. relatively to each other. It is impossible for them to rise or fall simultaneously.

Futher, the value of labour-power cannot fall, and consequently surplus-value cannot rise, without a rise in the productiveness of labour. For instance, in the above case, the value of the labour-power cannot sink from three shillings to two, unless an increase in the productiveness of labour makes it possible to produce in 4 hours the same quantity of necessaries as previously required 6 hours to produce.

(3) Increase or diminution in surplus-value is always consequent on, and never the cause of, the corresponding diminution or increase in the value of labour-power.

According to the third law, a change in the magnitude of surplus-value, pre-supposes a movement in the value of labour-power, which movement is brought about by a variation in the productiveness of labour. The limit of this change is given by the altered value of labour-power.

The value of labour-power is determined by the value of a given quantity of necessaries. It is the value and not the mass of these necessaries that varies with the productiveness of labour. It is, however, possible that, owing to an increase of productiveness, both the labourer and the capitalist may simultaneously be able to appropriate a greater quantity of these necessaries, without any change in the price of labour-power or in surplus-value. If the value of labour-power be 3 shillings, and the necessary labour-time amount to 6 hours, if the surplus-value, likewise be 3 shillings, and the surplus-labour 6 hours, then if the productiveness of labour were doubled without altering the ratio of necessary labour to surplus-labour, there would be no change of magnitude in surplus-value and price of labour-power. The only result would be that each of them would represent twice as many use-values as before; these use-values being twice as cheap as before. Although labour-power would be unchanged in price, it would be above its value. If, however, the price of labour-power had fallen, not to 1s. 6d., the lowest possible point consistent with its new value, but to 2s. 10d. or 2s. 6d., still this lower price would represent an increased mass of necessaries. In this way it is possible with an increasing productiveness of labour, for the price of labour-power to keep on falling, and yet this fall to be accompanied by a constant growth in the mass of the labourer's means of subsistence. But even in such case, the fall in the value of labour-power would cause a corresponding rise of surplus-value, and thus the abyss between the labourer's position and that of the capitalist would keep widening.

II. Working-Day Constant.
Productiveness of Labour Constant.
Intensity of Labour Variable

Increased intensity of labour means increased expenditure of labour in a given time. Hence a working-day of more intense labour is embodied in more products than is one of less intense labour, the length of each day being the same. Increased productiveness of labour also, it is true, will supply more products in a given working-day. But in this latter case, the value of each single product falls, for it costs less labour than before; in the former case, that value remains unchanged, for each article costs the same labour as before. Here we have an increase in the number of products, unaccompanied by a fall in their individual prices: as their number increases, so does the sum of their prices. But in the case of increased productiveness, a given value is spread over a greater mass of products. Hence the length of the working-day being constant, a day's labour of increased intensity will be incorporated in an increased value, and, the value of money remaining unchanged, in more money. The value created varies with the extent to which the intensity of labour deviates from its normal intensity in the society.

(2) *Increasing Intensity and Productiveness of Labour with Simultaneous Shortening of the Working-Day*

Increased productiveness and greater intensity of labour, both have a like effect. They both augment the mass of articles produced in a given time. Both, therefore, shorten that portion of the working-day which the labourer needs to produce his means of subsistence or their equivalent. The minimum length of the working-day is fixed by this necessary but contractile portion of it. If the whole working-day were to shrink to the length of this portion, surplus-labour would vanish, a consummation utterly impossible under the régime of capital. Only by suppressing the capitalist form of production could the length of the working-day be reduced to the necessary labour-time. But, even in that case, the latter would extend its limits. On the one hand, because the notion of 'means of subsistence' would considerably expand, and the labourer would lay claim to an altogether different standard of life. On the other hand, because a part of what is now surplus-labour, would then count as necessary labour; I mean the labour of forming a fund for reserve and accumulation.

The more the productiveness of labour increases, the more can the working-day be shortened; and the more the working-day is shortened, the more can the intensity of labour increase. From a social point of view, the productiveness increases in the same ratio as the economy of labour, which, in its turn, includes not only economy of the means of production, but also the avoidance of all useless labour. The capitalist mode of production, while on the one hand, enforcing economy in each individual business, on the other hand, begets, by its anarchical system of competition, the most outrageous squandering of labour-power and of the social means of production, not to mention the creation of a vast number of employments, at present indispensable, but in themselves superfluous.

The intensity and productiveness of labour being given, the time which society is bound to devote to material production is shorter, and as a consequence, the time at its disposal for the free development, intellectual and social, of the individual is greater, in proportion as the work is more and more evenly divided among all the able-bodied members of socity, and as a particular class is more and more deprived of the power to shift the natural burden of labour from its own shoulders to those of another layer of society. In this direction, the shortening of the working-day finds at last a limit in the generalisation of labour. In capitalist society spare time is acquired for one class by converting the whole life-time of the masses into labour-time.

PART VI

WAGES

CHAPTER 19

THE TRANSFORMATION OF THE VALUE (AND RESPECTIVELY THE PRICE) OF LABOUR-POWER INTO WAGES

On the surface of bourgeois society the wage of the labourer appears as the price of labour, a certain quantity of money that is paid for a certain quantity of labour. Thus people speak of the value of labour and call its expression in money its necessary or natural price. On the other hand they speak of the market-prices of labour, i.e. prices oscillating above or below its natural price.

But what is the value of a commodity? The objective form of the social labour expended in its production. And how do we measure the quantity of this value? By the quantity of the labour contained in it. How then is the value, e.g. of a 12 hours' working-day to be determined? By the 12 working-hours contained in a working-day of 12 hours, which is an absurd tautology.

In order to be sold as a commodity in the market, labour must at all events exist before it is sold. But could the labourer give it an independent objective existence, he would sell a commodity and not labour.

Apart from these contradictions, a direct exchange of money, i.e. of realised labour, with living labour would either do away with the law of value which only begins to develop itself freely on the basis of capitalist production, or do away with capitalist production itself, which rests directly on wage-labour. The working-day of 12 hours embodies itself, e.g. in a money-value of 6s. Either equivalents are exchanged, and then the labourer receives 6s. for 12 hours' labour; the price of his labour would be equal to the price of his product. In this case he produces no surplus-value for the buyer of his labour, the 6s. are not transformed into capital, the basis of capitalist production vanishes. But it is on this very basis that he sells his labour and that his labour is wage-labour. Or else he receives for 12 hours' labour less than 6s., i.e. less than 12 hours' labour. Twelve hours' labour are exchanged against 10, 6, etc., hours' labour. This equalisation of unequal quantities not merely does away with the determination of value. Such a self-destructive contradiction cannot be in any way even enunciated or formulated as a law.

It is of no avail to deduce the exchange of more labour against less, from their difference of form, the one being realised, the other living. This is the more absurd as the value of a commodity is determined not by the quantity of labour actually realised in it, but by the quantity of living labour necessary for its production. A commodity represents, say 6 working-hours. If an invention is made by which it can be produced in 3 hours, the value, even of the commodity already produced, falls by half. It represents now 3 hours of social labour instead of the 6 formerly necessary. It is the quantity of labour required for its production, not the realised form of that labour, by which the amount of the value of a commodity is determined.

That which comes directly face to face with the possessor of money on the market, is in fact not labour, but the labourer. What the latter sells is his labour-power. As soon as his labour actually begins, it has already ceased to belong to him; it can therefore no longer be sold by him. Labour is the substance, and the immanent measure of value, but *has itself no value*.

In the expression 'value of labour', the idea of value is not only completely obliterated, but actually reversed. It is an expression as imaginary as the value of the earth. These imaginary expressions, arise, however, from the relations of production themselves. They are categories for the phenomenal forms of essential relations. That in their appearance things often represent themselves in inverted form is pretty well known in every science except Political Economy.

Classical Political Economy borrowed from every-day life the category 'price of labour' without further criticism, and then simply asked the question, how is this price determined? It soon recognised that the change in the relations of demand and supply explained in regard to the price of labour, as of all other commodities, nothing except its changes, i.e. the oscillations of the market-price above or below a certain mean. If demand and supply balance, the oscillation of prices ceases, all other conditions remaining the same. But then demand and supply also cease to explain anything. The price of labour, at the moment when demand and supply are in equilibrium, is its natural price, determined independently of the relation of demand and supply. And how this price is determined, is just the question. Or a larger period of oscillations in the market-price is taken, e.g. a year, and they are found to cancel one the other, leaving a mean average quantity, a relatively constant magnitude. This had naturally to be determined otherwise than by its own compensating variations. This price which always finally predominates over the accidental market-prices of labour and regulates them, this 'necessary price' (physiocrats) or 'natural price' of labour (Adam Smith) can, as with all other commodities, be nothing else than its value expressed in money. In this way Political Economy expected to penetrate athwart the accidental prices of labour, to the value of labour. As with other commodities, this value was determined by the cost of production. But what is the cost of production—of the labourer, i.e. the cost of producing or reproducing the labourer himself? This question unconsciously substituted itself in Political Economy for the original one; for the search after the cost of production of labour as such turned in a circle and never left the spot. What economists therefore call value of labour, is in fact the value of labour-power, as it exists in the personality of the labourer, which is as different from its function, labour, as a machine is from the work it performs. Occupied with the difference between the market-price of labour and its so-called value, with the relation of this value to the rate of profit, and to the values of the commodities produced by means of labour, etc., they never discovered that the course of the analysis had led not only from the market-prices of labour to its presumed value, but had led to the resolution of this value of labour itself into the value of labour-power. Classical economy never arrived at a consciousness of the results of its own analysis; it accepted uncritically the categories 'value of labour', 'natural price of labour', etc., as final and as adequate expressions for the value-relation under consideration, and was thus led, as will be seen later,* into inextricable confusion and contradiction, while it offered to the vulgar economists a secure basis of operations for their shallowness, which on principle worships appearances only.

Let us next see how value (and price) of labour-power, present themselves in this transformed condition as wages.

We know that the daily value of labour-power is calculated upon a certain length of the labourer's life, to which, again, corresponds a certain length of working-day. Assume the habitual working-day as 12 hours, the daily value of labour-power as 3*s.*, the expression in money of a value that embodies 6 hours of labour. If the labourer receives 3*s.*, then he receives the value of his labour-power functioning through 12 hours. If, now, this value of a day's labour-power is expressed as the value of a day's labour itself, we have the formula: Twelve hours' labour has a value of 3*s.* The value of labour-power thus determines the value of labour, or, expressed in money, its necessary price. If, on the other hand, the price of labour-power differs from its value, in like manner the price of labour differs from its so-called value.

As the value of labour is only an irrational expression for the value of labour-power, it follows, of course, that the value of labour must always be less than the value it produces, for the capitalist always makes labour-power work longer than is necessary for the reproduction of its own value. In the above example, the value of the labour-power that functions through 12 hours is 3*s*., a value for the reproduction of which 6 hours are required. The value which the labour-power produces is, on the other hand, 6*s*., because it, in fact, functions during 12 hours, and the value it produces depends, not on its own value, but on the length of time it is in action. Thus, we have a result absurd at first sight—that labour which creates a value of 6*s*. possesses a value of 3*s*.

We see, further: The value of 3*s*. by which a part only of the working-day—i.e. 6 hours' labour—is paid for, appears as the value or price of the whole working-day of 12 hours, which thus includes 6 hours unpaid for. The wage-form thus extinguishes every trace of the division of the working-day into necessary labour and surplus-labour, into paid and unpaid labour. All labour appears as paid labour. In the corvée, the labour of the worker for himself, and his compulsory labour for his lord, differ in space and time in the clearest possible way. In slave-labour, even that part of the working-day in which the slave is only replacing the value of his own means of existence, in which, therefore, in fact, he works for himself alone, appears as labour for his master. All the slave's labour appears as unpaid labour. In wage-labour, on the contrary, even surplus-labour, or unpaid labour, appears as paid. There the property-relation conceals the labour of the slave for himself; here the money-relation conceals the unrequited labour of the wage-labourer.

Hence, we may understand the decisive importance of the transformation of value and price of labour-power into the form of wages, or into the value and price of labour itself. This phenomenal form, which makes the actual relation invisible, and, indeed, shows the direct opposite of that relation, forms the basis of all the juridical notions of both labourer and capitalist, of all the mystifications of the capitalistic mode of production, of all its illusions as to liberty, of all the apologetic shifts of the vulgar economists.

If history took a long time to get at the bottom of the mystery of wages, nothing, on the other hand, is more easy to understand than the necessity, the *raison d'être*, of this phenomenon.

The exchange between capital and labour at first presents itself to the mind in the same guise as the buying and selling of all other commodities. The buyer gives a certain sum of money, the seller an article of a nature different from money. The jurist's consciousness recognises in this, at most, a material difference, expressed in the juridically equivalent formulæ: 'Do ut des, do ut facias, facio ut des, facio ut facias.'

Further. Exchange-value and use-value, being intrinsically incommensurable magnitudes, the expressions 'value of labour', 'price of labour', do not seem more irrational than the expressions 'value of cotton', 'price of cotton', Moreover, the labourer is paid after he has given his labour. In its function of means of payment, money realises subsequently the value or price of the article supplied—i.e. in this particular case, the value or price of the labour supplied. Finally, the use-value supplied by the labourer to the capitalist is not, in fact, his labour-power, but its function, some definite useful labour, the work of tailoring, shoemaking, spinning, etc. That this same labour is, on the other hand, the universal value-creating element, and thus possesses a property by which it differs from all other commodities, is beyond the cognisance of the ordinary mind.

Let us put ourselves in the place of the labourer who receives for 12 hours' labour, say the value produced by 6 hours' labour, say 3s. For him, in fact, his 12 hours' labour is the means of buying the 3s. The value of his labour-power may vary, with the value of his usual means of subsistence, from 3 to 4 shillings, or from 3 to 2 shillings; or, if the value of his labour-power remains constant, its price may, in consequence of changing relations of demand and supply, rise to 4s. or fall to 2s. He always gives 12 hours of labour. Every change in the amount of the equivalent that he receives appears to him, therefore, necessarily as a change in the value or price of his 12 hours' work. This circumstance misled Adam Smith, who treated the working-day as a constant quantity, to the assertion that the value of labour is constant, although the value of the means of subsistence may vary, and the same working-day, therefore, may represent itself in more or less money for the labourer.

Let us consider, on the other hand, the capitalist. He wishes to receive as much labour as possible for as little money as possible. Practically, therefore, the only thing that interests him is the difference between the price of labour-power and the value which its function creates. But, then, he tries to buy all commodities as cheaply as possible, and always accounts for his profit by simple cheating, by buying under, and selling over the value. Hence, he never comes to see that, if such a thing as the value of labour really existed, and he really paid this value, no capital would exist, his money would not be turned into capital.

Moreover, the actual movement of wages presents phenomena which seem to prove that not the value of labour-power is paid, but the value of its function, of labour itself. We may reduce these phenomena to two great classes: (1) Change of wages with the changing length of the working-day. One might as well conclude that not the value of a machine is paid, but that of its working, because it costs more to hire a machine for a week than for a day. (2) The individual difference in the wages of different labourers who do the same kind of work. We find this individual difference, but are not deceived by it, in the system of slavery, where, frankly and openly, without any circumlocution, labour-power itself is sold. Only, in the slave system, the advantage of a labour-power above the average, and the disadvantage of a labour-power below the average, affects the slave-owner; in the wage-labour system it affects the labourer himself, because his labour-power is, in the one case, sold by himself, in the other, by a third person.

For the rest, in respect to the phenomenal form, 'value and price of labour', or 'wages', as contrasted with the essential relation manifested therein, viz., the value and price of labour-power, the same difference holds that holds in respect to all phenomena and their hidden substratum. The former appear directly and spontaneously as current modes of thought; the latter must first be discovered by science. Classical Political Economy nearly touches the true relation of things, without, however, consciously formulating it. This it cannot so long as it sticks in its bourgeois skin.

PART VII
THE ACCUMULATION OF CAPITAL

THE conversion of a sum of money into means of production and labour-power, is the first step taken by the quantum of value that is going to function as capital. This conversion takes place in the market, within the sphere of circulation. The second step, the process of production, is complete so soon as the means of production have been converted into commodities whose value exceeds that of their component parts, and, therefore, contains the capital originally advanced, plus a surplus-value. These commodities must then be thrown into circulation. They must be sold, their value realised in money, this money afresh converted into capital, and so over and over again. This circular movement, in which the same phases are continually gone through in succession, forms the circulation of capital.

The first condition of accumulation is that the capitalist must have contrived to sell his commodities, and to reconvert into capital the greater part of the money so received. In the following pages we shall assume that capital circulates in its normal way. The detailed analysis of the process will be found in Book II.

The capitalist who produces surplus-value—i.e. who extracts unpaid labour directly from the labourers, and fixes it in commodities, is, indeed, the first appropriator, but by no means the ultimate owner, of this surplus-value. He has to share it with capitalists, with landowners, etc., who fulfil other functions in the complex of social production. Surplus-value, therefore, splits up into various parts. Its fragments fall to various categories of persons, and take various forms, independent the one of the other, such as profit, interest, merchants' profit, rent, etc. It is only in Book III that we can take in hand these modified forms of surplus-value.

On the one hand, then, we assume that the capitalist sells at their value the commodities he has produced, without concerning ourselves either about the new forms that capital assumes while in the sphere of circulation, or about the concrete conditions of reproduction hidden under these forms. On the other hand, we treat the capitalist producer as owner of the entire surplus-value, or, better perhaps, as the representative of all the sharers with him in the booty. We, therefore, first of all consider accumulation from an abstract point of view—i.e. as a mere phase in the actual process of production.

So far as accumulation takes place, the capitalist must have succeeded in selling his commodities, and in reconverting the sale-money
into capital. Moreover, the breaking-up of surplus-value into fragments neither alters its nature nor the conditions under which it
becomes an element of accumulation. Whatever be the proportion of
surplus-value which the industrial capitalist retains for himself, or
yields up to others, he is the one who, in the first instance, appropriates
it. We, therefore, assume no more than what actually takes place. On
the other hand, the simple fundamental form of the process of accumulation is obscured by the incident of the circulation which brings it
about, and by the splitting up of surplus-value. An exact analysis of the
process, therefore, demands that we should, for a time, disregard all
phenomena that hide the play of its inner mechanism.

CHAPTER 23

SIMPLE REPRODUCTION

WHATEVER the form of the process of production in a society, it must be a continuous process, must continue to go periodically through the same phases. A society can no more cease to produce than it can cease to consume. When viewed, therefore, as a connected whole, and as flowing on with incessant renewal, every social process of production is, at the same time, a process of reproduction.

The conditions of production are also those of reproduction. No society can go on producing, in other words, no society can reproduce, unless it constantly reconverts a part of its products into means of production, or elements of fresh products. All other circumstances remaining the same, the only mode by which it can reproduce its wealth, and maintain it at one level, is by replacing the means of production—i.e. the instruments of labour, the raw material, and the auxiliary substances consumed in the course of the year—by an equal quantity of the same kind of articles; these must be separated from the mass of the yearly products, and thrown afresh into the process of production. Hence, a definite portion of each year's product belongs to the domain of production. Destined for productive consumption from the very first, this portion exists, for the most part, in the shape of articles totally unfitted for individual consumption.

If production be capitalistic in form, so, too, will be reproduction. Just as in the former the labour-process figures but as a means towards the self-expansion of capital, so in the latter it figures but as a means of reproducing as capital—i.e. as self-expanding value,—the value advanced. It is only because his money constantly functions as capital that the economic guise of a capitalist attaches to a man. If, for instance, a sum of £100 has this year been converted into capital, and produced a surplus-value of £20, it must continue during next year, and subsequent years, to repeat the same operation. As a periodic increment of the capital advanced, or periodic fruit of capital in process, surplus-value acquires the form of a revenue flowing out of capital.

If this revenue serve the capitalist only as a fund to provide for his consumption, and be spent as periodically as it is gained, then, *cæteris paribus*, simple reproduction will take place. And although this reproduction is a mere repetition of the process of production on the old scale, yet this mere repetition, or continuity, gives a new character to the process, or, rather, causes the disappearance of some apparent characteristics which it possessed as an isolated discontinuous process.

The purchase of labour-power for a fixed period is the prelude to the process of production; and this prelude is constantly repeated when the stipulated term comes to an end, when a definite period of production, such as a week or a month, has elapsed. But the labourer is not paid until after he has expended his labour-power, and realised in commodities not only its value, but surplus-value. He has, therefore, produced not only surplus-value, which we for the present regard as a fund to meet the private consumption of the capitalist, but he has also produced, before it flows back to him in the shape of wages, the fund out of which he himself is paid, the variable capital; and his employment lasts only so long as he continues to reproduce this fund. Hence, that formula of the economists, referred to in Chapter 18, which represents wages as a share in the product itself. What flows back to the labourer in the shape of wages is a portion of the product that is continuously reproduced by him. The capitalist, it is true, pays him in money, but this money is merely the transmuted form of the product of his labour. While he is converting a portion of the means of production into products, a portion of his former product is being turned into money. It is his labour of last week, or of last year, that pays for his labour-power this week or this year. The illusion begotten by the intervention of money vanishes immediately, if, instead of taking a single capitalist and a single labourer, we take the class of capitalists and the class of labourers as a whole. The capitalist class is constantly giving to the labouring class order-notes, in the form of money, on a portion of the commodities produced by the latter and appropriated by the former. The labourers give these order-notes back just as constantly to the capitalist class, and in this way get their share of their own product. The transaction is veiled by the commodity-form of the product and the money-form of the commodity.

Variable capital is therefore only a particular historical form of appearance of the fund for providing the necessaries of life, or the labour-fund which the labourer requires for the maintenance of himself and family, and which, whatever be the system of social production, he must himself produce and reproduce. If the labour-fund constantly flows to him in the form of money that pays for his labour, it is because the product he has created moves constantly away from him in the form of capital. But all this does not alter the fact, that it is the labourer's own labour, realised in a product, which is advanced to him by the capitalist. Let us take a peasant liable to do compulsory service for his lord. He works on his own land, with his own means of production, for, say, 3 days a week. The 3 other days he does forced work on the lord's domain. He constantly reproduces his own labour-fund, which never, in his case, takes the form of a money payment for his labour, advanced by another person. But in return, his unpaid forced labour for the lord, on its side, never acquires the character of voluntary paid labour. If one fine morning the lord appropriates to himself the land, the cattle, the seed, in a word, the means of production of this peasant, the latter will thenceforth be obliged to sell his labour-power to the lord. He will, *cæteris paribus*, labour 6 days a week as before, 3 for himself, 3 for his lord, who thenceforth becomes a wages-paying capitalist. As before, he will use up the means of production as means of production, and transfer their value to the product. As before, a definite portion of the product will be devoted to reproduction. But from the moment that the forced labour is changed into wage-labour, from that moment the labour-fund, which the peasant himself continues as before to produce and reproduce, takes the form of a capital advanced in the form of wages by the lord. The bourgeois economist whose narrow mind is unable to separate the form of appearance from the thing that appears, shuts his eyes to the fact, that it is but here and there on the face of the earth, that even now-a-days the labour-fund crops up in the form of capital.

Variable capital, it is true, only then loses its character of a value advanced out of the capitalist's funds, when we view the process of capitalist production in the flow of its constant renewal. But that process must have had a beginning of some kind. From our present standpoint it therefore seems likely that the capitalist, once upon a time, became possessed of money, by some accumulation that took place independently of the unpaid labour of others, and that this was, therefore, how he was enabled to frequent the market as a buyer of labour-power. However this may be, the mere continuity of the process, the simple reproduction, brings about some other wonderful changes, which affect not only the variable, but the total capital.

If a capital of £1,000 beget yearly a surplus-value of £200, and if this surplus-value be consumed every year, it is clear that at the end of 5 years the surplus-value consumed will amount to 5 × £200 or the £1,000 originally advanced. If only a part, say one half, were consumed, the same result would follow at the end of 10 years, since 10 × £100 = £1,000. General Rule: The value of the capital advanced divided by the surplus-value annually consumed, gives the number of years, or reproduction periods, at the expiration of which the capital originally advanced has been consumed by the capitalist and has disappeared. The capitalist thinks, that he is consuming the produce of the unpaid labour of others, i.e. the surplus-value, and is keeping intact his original capital; but what he thinks cannot alter facts. After the lapse of a certain number of years, the capital value he then possesses is equal to the sum total of the surplus-value appropriated by him during those years, and the total value he has consumed is equal to that of his original capital. It is true, he has in hand a capital whose amount has not changed, and of which a part, viz., the buildings, machinery, etc., were already there when the work of his business began. But what we have to do with here, is not the material elements, but the value, of that capital. When a person gets through all his property, by taking upon himself debts equal to the value of that property, it is clear that his property represents nothing but the sum total of his debts. And so it is with the capitalist; when he has consumed the equivalent of his original capital, the value of his present capital represents nothing but the total amount of the surplus-value appropriated by him without payment. Not a single atom of the value of his old capital continues to exist.

Apart then from all accumulation, the mere continuity of the process of production, in other words simple reproduction, sooner or later, and of necessity, converts every capital into accumulated capital, or capitalised surplus-value. Even if that capital was originally acquired by the personal labour of its employer, it sooner or later becomes value appropriated without an equivalent, the unpaid labour of others materialised either in money or in some other object. We saw in Chapters 4–6 that in order to convert money into capital something more is required than the production and circulation of commodities. We saw that on the one side the possessor of value or money, on the other, the possessor of the value-creating substance; on the one side, the possessor of the means of production and subsistence, on the other, the possessor of nothing but labour-power, must confront one another as buyer and seller. The separation of labour from its product, of subjective labour-power from the objective conditions of labour, was therefore the real foundation in fact, and the starting-point of capitalist production.

But that which at first was but a starting-point, becomes, by the mere continuity of the process, by simple reproduction, the peculiar result, constantly renewed and perpetuated, of capitalist production. On the one hand, the process of production incessantly converts material wealth into capital, into means of creating more wealth and means of enjoyment for the capitalist. On the other hand, the labourer, on quitting the process, is what he was on entering it, a source of wealth, but devoid of all means of making that wealth his own. Since, before entering on the process, his own labour has already been alienated from himself by the sale of his labour-power, has been appropriated by the capitalist and incorporated with capital, it must, during the process, be realised in a product that does not belong to him. Since the process of production is also the process by which the capitalist consumes labour-power, the product of the labourer is incessantly converted, not only into commodities, but into capital, into value that sucks up the value-creating power, into means of subsistence that buy the person of the labourer, into means of production that command the producers. The labourer therefore constantly produces material, objective wealth, but in the form of capital, of an alien power that dominates and exploits him: and the capitalist as constantly produces labour-power, but in the form of a subjective source of wealth, separated from the objects in and by which it can alone be realised; in short he produces the labourer, but as a wage-labourer. This incessant reproduction, this perpetuation of the labourer, is the sine qua non of capitalist production.

The labourer consumes in a two-fold way. While producing he consumes by his labour the means of production, and converts them into products with a higher value than that of the capital advanced. This is his productive consumption. It is at the same time consumption of his labour-power by the capitalist who bought it. On the other hand, the labourer turns the money paid to him for his labour-power, into means of subsistence: this is his individual consumption. The labourer's productive consumption, and his individual consumption, are therefore totally distinct. In the former, he acts as the motive power of capital, and belongs to the capitalist. In the latter, he belongs to himself, and performs his necessary vital functions outside the process of production. The result of the one is, that the capitalist lives; of the other, that the labourer lives.

When treating of the working-day, we saw that the labourer is often compelled to make his individual consumption a mere incident of production. In such a case, he supplies himself with necessaries in order to maintain his labour-power, just as coal and water are supplied to the steam-engine and oil to the wheel. His means of consumption, in that case, are the mere means of consumption required by a means of production; his individual consumption is directly productive consumption. This, however, appears to be an abuse not essentially appertaining to capitalist production.

The matter takes quite another aspect, when we contemplate, not the single capitalist, and the single labourer, but the capitalist class and the labouring class, not an isolated process of production, but capitalist production in full swing, and on its actual social scale. By converting part of his capital into labour-power, the capitalist augments the value of his entire capital. He kills two birds with one stone. He profits, not only by what he receives from but by what he gives to, the labourer. The capital given in exchange for labour-power is converted into necessaries, by the consumption of which the muscles, nerves, bones, and brains of existing labourers are reproduced, and new labourers are begotten. Within the limits of what is strictly necessary, the individual consumption of the working-class is, therefore, the reconversion of the means of subsistence given by capital in exchange for labour-power, into fresh labour-power at the disposal of capital for exploitation. It is the production and reproduction of that means of production so indispensable to the capitalist: the labourer himself. The individual consumption of the labourer, whether it proceed within the workshop or outside it, whether it be part of the process of production or not, forms therefore a factor of the production and reproduction of capital; just as cleaning machinery does, whether it be done while the machinery is working or while it is standing. The fact that the labourer consumes his means of subsistence for his own purposes, and not to please the capitalist, has no bearing on the matter. The consumption of food by a beast of burden is none the less a necessary factor in the process of production, because the beast enjoys what it eats. The maintenance and reproduction of the working-class is, and must ever be, a necessary condition to the reproduction of capital. But the capitalist may safely leave its fulfilment to the labourer's instincts of self-preservation and of propagation. All the capitalist cares for, is to reduce the labourer's individual consumption as far as possible to what is strictly necessary, and he is far away from imitating those brutal South Americans, who force their labourers to take the more substantial, rather than the less substantial, kind of food.

Hence both the capitalist and his ideological representative, the political economist, consider that part alone of the labourer's individual consumption to be productive, which is requisite for the perpetuation of the class, and which therefore must take place in order that the capitalist may have labour-power to consume; what the labourer consumes for his own pleasure beyond that part, is unproductive consumption. If the accumulation of capital were to cause a rise of wages and an increase in the labourer's consumption, unaccompanied by increase in the consumption of labour-power by capital, the additional capital would be consumed unproductively. In reality, the individual consumption of the labourer is unproductive as regards himself, for it reproduces nothing but the needy individual; it is productive to the capitalist and to the State, since it is the production of the power that creates their wealth.

From a social point of view, therefore, the working-class, even when not directly engaged in the labour-process, is just as much an append-age of capital as the ordinary instruments of labour. Even its individual consumption is, within certain limits, a mere factor in the process of production. That process, however, takes good care to prevent these self-conscious instruments from leaving it in the lurch, for it removes their product, as fast as it is made, from their pole to the opposite pole of capital. Individual consumption provides, on the one hand, the means for their maintenance and reproduction: on the other hand, it secures by the annihilation of the necessaries of life, the continued re-appearance of the workman in the labour-market. The Roman slave was held by fetters: the wage-labourer is bound to his owner by invis-ible threads. The appearance of independence is kept up by means of a constant change of employers, and by the *fictio juris* of a contract.

Capitalist production, therefore, of itself reproduces the separation between labour-power and the means of labour. It thereby reproduces and perpetuates the condition for exploiting the labourer. It incessantly forces him to sell his labour-power in order to live, and enables the capitalist to purchase labour-power in order that he may enrich him-self. It is no longer a mere accident, that capitalist and labourer con-front each other in the market as buyer and seller. It is the process itself that incessantly hurls back the labourer on to the market as a vendor of his labour-power, and that incessantly converts his own product into a means by which another man can purchase him. In reality, the labourer belongs to capital before he has sold himself to capital. His economic bondage is both brought about and concealed by the periodic sale of himself, by his change of masters, and by the oscillations in the market-price of labour-power.

Capitalist production, therefore, under its aspect of a continuous connected process, of a process of reproduction, produces not only commodities, not only surplus-value, but it also produces and repro-duces the capitalist relation; on the one side the capitalist, on the other the wage-labourer.

CHAPTER 24

CONVERSION OF SURPLUS-VALUE INTO CAPITAL

Section 1. Capitalist Production on a Progressively Increasing Scale. Transition of the Laws of Property that Characterise Production of Commodities into Laws of Capitalist Appropriation

HITHERTO we have investigated how surplus-value emanates from capital; we have now to see how capital arises from surplus-value. Employing surplus-value as capital, reconverting it into capital, is called accumulation of capital.

First let us consider this transaction from the standpoint of the individual capitalist. Suppose a spinner to have advanced a capital of £10,000, of which four-fifths (£8,000) are laid out in cotton, machinery, etc., and one-fifth (£2,000) in wages. Let him produce 240,000 lbs. of yarn annually, having a value of £12,000. The rate of surplus-value being 100%, the surplus-value lies in the surplus or net product of 40,000 lbs. of yarn, one-sixth of the gross product, with a value of £2,000 which will be realised by a sale. £2,000 is £2,000. We can neither see nor smell in this sum of money a trace of surplus-value. When we know that a given value is surplus-value, we know how its owner came by it; but that does not alter the nature either of value or of money.

In order to convert this additional sum of £2,000 into capital, the master-spinner will, all circumstances remaining as before, advance four-fifths of it (£1,600) in the purchase of cotton, etc., and one-fifth (£400) in the purchase of additional spinners, who will find in the market the necessaries of life whose value the master has advanced to them. Then the new capital of £2,000 functions in the spinning-mill, and brings in, in its turn, a surplus-value of £400.

The capital-value was originally advanced in the money-form. The surplus-value on the contrary is, originally, the value of a definite portion of the gross product. If this gross product be sold, converted into money, the capital-value regains its original form. From this moment the capital-value and the surplus-value are both of them sums of money, and their reconversion into capital takes place in precisely the same way. The one, as well as the other, is laid out by the capitalist in the purchase of commodities that place him in a position to begin afresh the fabrication of his goods, and this time, on an extended scale. But in order to be able to buy those commodities, he must find them ready in the market.

His own yarns circulate, only because he brings his annual product to market, as all other capitalists likewise do with their commodities. But these commodities, before coming to market, were part of the general annual product, part of the total mass of objects of every kind, into which the sum of the individual capitals, i.e. the total capital of society, had been converted in the course of the year, and of which each capitalist had in hand only an aliquot part. The transactions in the market effectuate only the interchange of the individual components of this annual product, transfer them from one hand to another, but can neither augment the total annual production, nor alter the nature of the objects produced. Hence the use that can be made of the total annual product, depends entirely upon its own composition, but in no way upon circulation.

The annual production must in the first place furnish all those objects (use-values) from which the material components of capital, used up in the course of the year, have to be replaced. Deducting these there remains the net or surplus-product, in which the surplus-value lies. And of what does this surplus-product consist? Only of things destined to satisfy the wants and desires of the capitalist class, things which, consequently, enter into the consumption-fund of the capital-ists? Were that the case, the cup of surplus-value would be drained to the very dregs, and nothing but simple reproduction would ever take place.

To accumulate it is necessary to convert a portion of the surplus-product into capital. But we cannot, except by a miracle, convert into capital anything but such articles as can be employed in the labour-process (i.e. means of production), and such further articles as are suitable for the sustenance of the labourer (i.e. means of subsistence). Consequently, a part of the annual surplus-labour must have been applied to the production of additional means of production and sub-sistence, over and above the quantity of these things required to replace the capital advanced. In one word, surplus-value is convertible into capital solely because the surplus-product, whose value it is, already comprises the material elements of new capital.

Now in order to allow of these elements actually functioning as capital, the capitalist class requires additional labour. If the exploi-

tation of the labourers already employed do not increase, either extensively or intensively, then additional labour-power must be found. For
this the mechanism of capitalist production provides beforehand, by
converting the working-calss into a class dependent on wages, a class
whose ordinary wages suffice, not only for its maintenance, but for its
increase. It is only necessary for capital to incorporate this additional
labour-power, annually supplied by the working-class in the shape of
labourers of all ages, with the surplus means of production comprised
in the annual produce, and the conversion of surplus-value into capital
is complete. From a concrete point of view, accumulation resolves itself
into the reproduction of capital on a progressively increasing scale.
The circle in which simple reproduction moves, alters its form, and, to
use Sismondi's expression, changes into a spiral.

Let us now return to our illustration. It is the old story: Abraham
begat Isaac, Isaac begat Jacob, and so on. The original capital of
£10,000 brings in a surplus-value of £2,000, which is capitalised. The
new capital of £2,000 brings in a surplus-value of £400, and this, too,
is capitalised, converted into a second additional capital, which, in its
turn, produces a further surplus-value of £80. And so the ball rolls on.

We here leave out of consideration the portion of the surplus-value
consumed by the capitalist. Just as little does it concern us, for the
moment, whether the additional capital is joined on to the original
capital, or is separated from it to function independently; whether the
same capitalist, who accumulated it, employs it, or whether he hands it
over to another. This only we must not forget, that by the side of the
newly-formed capital, the original capital continues to reproduce itself,
and to produce surplus-value, and that this is also true of all accumulated capital, and the additional capital engendered by it.

The original capital was formed by the advance of £10,000. How did
the owner become possessed of it? 'By his own labour and that of his
forefather', answer unanimously the spokesmen of Political Economy.
And, in fact, their supposition appears the only one consonant with the
laws of the production of commodities.

But it is quite otherwise with regard to the additional capital of
£2,000. How that originated we know perfectly well. There is not one
single atom of its value that does not owe its existence to unpaid labour.
The means of production, with which the additional labour-power is
incorporated, as well as the necessaries with which the labourers are
sustained, are nothing but component parts of the surplus-product, of
the tribute annually exacted from the working-class by the capitalist
class. Though the latter with a portion of that tribute purchases the

additional labour-power even at its full price, so that equivalent is exchanged for equivalent, yet the transaction is for all that only the old dodge of every conqueror who buys commodities from the conquered with the money he has robbed them of.

If the additional capital employs the person who produced it, this producer must not only continue to augment the value of the original capital, but must buy back the fruits of his previous labour with more labour than they cost. When viewed as a transaction between the capitalist class and the working-class, it makes no difference that additional labourers are employed by means of the unpaid labour of the previously employed labourers. The capitalist may even convert the additional capital into a machine that throws the producers of that capital out of work, and that replaces them by a few children. In every case the working-class creates by the surplus-labour of one year the capital destined to employ additional labour in the following year. And this is what is called: creating capital out of capital.

The accumulation of the first additional capital of £2,000 pre-supposes a value of £10,000 belonging to the capitalist by virtue of his 'primitive labour', and advanced by him. The second additional capital of £400 pre-supposes, on the contrary, only the previous accumulation of the £2,000, of which the £400 is the surplus-value capitalised. The ownership of past unpaid labour is thenceforth the sole condition for the appropriation of living unpaid labour on a constantly increasing scale. The more the capitalist has accumulated, the more is he able to accumulate.

In so far as the surplus-value, of which the additional capital, No. 1, consists, is the result of the purchase of labour-power with part of the original capital, a purchase that conformed to the laws of the exchange of commodities, and that, from a legal standpoint, pre-supposes nothing beyond the free disposal, on the part of the labourer, of his own capacities, and on the part of the owner of money or commodities, of the values that belong to him; in so far as the additional capital, No. 2, etc., is the mere result of No. 1, and, therefore, a consequence of the above conditions; in so far as each single transaction invariably conforms to the laws of the exchange of commodities, the capitalist buying labour-power, the labourer selling it, and we will assume at its real value; in so far as all this is true, it is evident that the laws of appropriation or of private property, laws that are based on the production and circulation of commodities, become by their own inner and inexorable dialectic changed into their very opposite. The exchange of equivalents, the original operation with which we started, has now become turned round in such a way that there is only an apparent exchange. This is owing to the fact, first, that the capital which is exchanged for labour-power is itself but a portion of the product of others' labour appropriated without an equivalent; and, secondly, that this capital must not only be replaced by its producer, but replaced together with an added surplus. The relation of exchange subsisting between capitalist and labourer becomes a mere semblance appertaining to the process of circulation, a mere form, foreign to the real nature of the transaction, and only mystifying it. The ever repeated purchase and sale of labour-power is now the mere form; what really takes place is this—the capitalist again and again appropriates, without equivalent, a portion of the previously materialised labour of others, and exchanges it for a greater quantity of living labour. At first the rights of property seemed to us to be based on a man's own labour. At least, some such assumption was necessary since only commodity-owners with equal rights confronted each other, and the sole means by which a man could become possessed of the commodities of others, was by alienating his own commodities; and these could be replaced by labour alone. Now, however, property turns out to be the right, on the part of the capitalist, to appropriate the unpaid labour of others or its product, and to be the impossibility, on the part of the labourer, of appropriating his own product. The separation of property from labour has become the necessary consequence of a law that apparently originated in their identity.

Therefore, however much the capitalist mode of appropriation may seem to fly in the face of the original laws of commodity production, it nevertheless arises, not from a violation, but, on the contrary, from the application of these laws. Let us make this clear once more by briefly reviewing the consecutive phases of motion whose culminating point is capitalist accumulation.

We saw, in the first place, that the original conversion of a sum of values into capital was achieved in complete accordance with the laws of exchange. One party to the contract sells his labour-power, the other buys it. The former receives the value of his commodity, whose use-value—labour—is thereby alienated to the buyer. Means of production which already belong to the latter are then transformed by him, with the aid of labour equally belonging to him, into a new product which is likewise lawfully his.

The value of this product includes: first, the value of the used-up means of production. Useful labour cannot consume these means of production without transferring their value to the new product, but, to be saleable, labour-power must be capable of supplying useful labour in the branch of industry in which it is to be employed.

The value of the new product further includes: the equivalent of the value of the labour-power together with a surplus-value. This is so because the value of the labour-power—sold for a definite length of time, say a day, a week, etc.—is less than the value created by its use during that time. But the worker has received payment for the exchange-value of his labour-power and by so doing has alienated its use-value—this being the case in every sale and purchase.

The fact that this particular commodity, labour-power, possesses the peculiar use-value of supplying labour, and therefore of creating value, cannot affect the general law of commodity production. If, therefore, the magnitude of value advanced in wages is not merely found again in the product, but is found there augmented by a surplus-value, this is not because the seller has been defrauded, for he has really received the value of his commodity; it is due solely to the fact that this commodity has been used up by the buyer.

The law of exchange requires equality only between the exchange-values of the commodities given in exchange for one another. From the very outset it pre-supposes even a difference between their use-values and it has nothing whatever to do with their consumption, which only begins after the deal is closed and executed.

Thus the original conversion of money into capital is achieved in the most exact accordance with the economic laws of commodity production and with the right of property derived from them. Nevertheless, its result is:

(1) that the product belongs to the capitalist and not to the worker;
(2) that the value of this product includes, besides the value of the capital advanced, a surplus-value which costs the worker labour but the capitalist nothing, and which none the less becomes the legitimate property of the capitalist;
(3) that the worker has retained his labour-power and can sell it anew if he can find a buyer.

Simple reproduction is only the periodical repetition of this first operation; each time money is converted afresh into capital. Thus the law is not broken; on the contrary, it is merely enabled to operate continuously.

Nor does it matter if simple reproduction is replaced by reproduction on an extended scale, by accumulation. In the former case the capitalist squanders the whole surplus-value in dissipation, in the latter he demonstrates his bourgeois virtue by consuming only a portion of it and converting the rest into money.

The surplus-value is his property; it has never belonged to anyone else. If he advances it for the purposes of production, the advances made come from his own funds, exactly as on the day when he first entered the market. The fact that on this occasion the funds are derived from the unpaid labour of his workers makes absolutely no difference. If worker B is paid out of the surplus-value which worker A produced, then, in the first place, A furnished that surplus-value without having the just price of his commodity cut by a halfpenny, and, in the second place, the transaction is no concern of B's whatever. What B claims, and has a right to claim, is that the capitalist should pay him the value of his labour-power. 'Both were still gainers: the worker because he was advanced the fruits of his labour' (should read: of the unpaid labour of other workers); 'before the work was done' (should read: before his own labour had borne fruit); 'the employer (*le maître*), because the labour of this worker was worth more than his wages' (should read: produced more value than the value of his wages).

To be sure, the matter looks quite different if we consider capitalist production in the uninterrupted flow of its renewal, and if, in place of the individual capitalist and the individual worker, we view in their totality, the capitalist class and the working-class confronting each other. But in so doing we should be applying standards entirely foreign to commodity production.

Only buyer and seller, mutually independent, face each other in commodity production. The relations between them cease on the day when the term stipulated in the contract they concluded expires. If the transaction is repeated, it is repeated as the result of a new agreement which has nothing to do with the previous one and which only by chance brings the same seller together again with the same buyer.

If, therefore, commodity production, or one of its associated processes, is to be judged according to its own economic laws, we must consider each act of exchange by itself, apart from any connexion with the act of exchange preceding it and that following it. And since sales and purchases are negotiated solely between particular individuals, it is not admissible to seek here for relations between whole social classes.

However long a series of periodical reproductions and preceding accumulations the capital functioning to-day may have passed through, it always preserves its original virginity. So long as the laws of exchange are observed in every single act of exchange the mode of appropriation can be completely revolutionised without in any way affecting the property rights which correspond to commodity production. These same rights remain in force both at the outset, when the product belongs to its producer, who, exchanging equivalent for equivalent, can enrich himself only by his own labour, and also in the period of capitalism, when social wealth becomes to an ever-increasing degree the property of those who are in a position to appropriate continually and ever afresh the unpaid labour of others.

This result becomes inevitable from the moment there is a free sale, by the labourer himself, of labour-power as a commodity. But it is also only from then onwards that commodity production is generalised and becomes the typical form of production; it is only from then onwards that, from the first, every product is produced for sale and all wealth produced goes through the sphere of circulation. Only when and where wage-labour is its basis does commodity production impose itself upon society as a whole; but only then and there also does it unfold all its hidden potentialities. To say that the supervention of wage-labour adulterates commodity production is to say that commodity production must not develop if it is to remain unadulterated. To the extent that commodity production, in accordance with its own inherent laws, develops further, into capitalist production, the property laws of commodity production change into the laws of capitalist appropriation.

We have seen that even in the case of simple reproduction, all capital, whatever its original source, becomes converted into accumulated capital, capitalised surplus-value. But in the flood of production all the capital originally advanced becomes a vanishing quantity (*magnitudo evanescens*, in the mathematical sense), compared with the directly accumulated capital, i.e. with the surplus-value or surplus-product that is reconverted into capital, whether it functions in the hands of its accumulator, or in those of others. Hence, Political Economy describes capital in general as 'accumulated wealth' (converted surplus-value or revenue), 'that is employed over again in the production of surplus-value,' and the capitalist as 'the owner of surplus-value'. It is merely another way of expressing the same thing to say that all existing capital is accumulated or capitalised interest, for interest is a mere fragment of surplus-value.

Section 3. Separation of Surplus-Value into Capital and Revenue. The Abstinence Theory

In the last preceding chapter, we treated surplus-value (or the surplus-product) solely as a fund for supplying the individual consumption of the capitalist. In this chapter we have, so far, treated it solely as a fund for accumulation. It is, however, neither the one nor the other, but is both together. One portion is consumed by the capitalist as revenue, the other is employed as capital, is accumulated.

Given the mass of surplus-value, then, the larger the one of these parts, the smaller is the other. *Cæteris paribus*, the ratio of these parts determines the magnitude of the accumulation. But it is by the owner of the surplus-value, by the capitalist alone, that the division is made. It is his deliberate act. That part of the tribute exacted by him which he accumulates, is said to be saved by him, because he does not eat it, i.e. because he performs the function of a capitalist, and enriches himself.

Except as personified capital, the capitalist has no historical value, and no right to that historical existence, which, to use an expression of the witty Lichnowsky, 'hasn't got no date'.* And so far only is the necessity for his own transitory existence implied in the transitory necessity for the capitalist mode of production. But, so far as he is personified capital, it is not values in use and the enjoyment of them, but exchange-value and its augmentation, that spur him into action. Fanatically bent on making value expand itself, he ruthlessly forces the human race to produce for production's sake; he thus forces the development of the productive powers of society, and creates those material conditions, which alone can form the real basis of a higher form of society, a society in which the full and free development of every individual forms the ruling principle. Only as personified capital is the capitalist respectable. As such, he shares with the miser the passion for wealth as wealth. But that which in the miser is a mere idiosyncrasy, is, in the capitalist, the effect of the social mechanism, of which he is but one of the wheels. Moreover, the development of capitalist production makes it constantly necessary to keep increasing the amount of the capital laid out in a given industrial undertaking, and competition makes the immanent laws of capitalist production to be felt by each individual capitalist, as external coercive laws. It compels him to keep constantly extending his capital, in order to preserve it, but extend it he cannot, except by means of progressive accumulation.

So far, therefore, as his actions are a mere function of capital—endowed as capital is, in his person, with consciousness and a will—his own private consumption is a robbery perpetrated on accumulation, just as in book-keeping by double entry, the private expenditure of the capitalist is placed on the debtor side of his account against his capital. To accumulate, is to conquer the world of social wealth, to increase the mass of human beings exploited by him, and thus to extend both the direct and the indirect sway of the capitalist.

But original sin is at work everywhere. As capitalist production, accumulation, and wealth, become developed, the capitalist ceases to be the mere incarnation of capital. He has a fellow-feeling for his own Adam, and his education gradually enables him to smile at the rage for asceticism, as a mere prejudice of the old-fashioned miser. While the capitalist of the classical type brands individual consumption as a sin against his function, and as 'abstinence' from accumulating, the modernised capitalist is capable of looking upon accumulation as 'abstinence' from pleasure.

> 'Two souls, alas, do dwell with in his breast;
> The one is ever parting from the other.'*

At the historical dawn of capitalist production,—and every capitalist upstart has personally to go through this historical stage—avarice, and desire to get rich, are the ruling passions. But the progress of capitalist production not only creates a world of delights; it lays open, in speculation and the credit system, a thousand sources of sudden enrichment. When a certain stage of development has been reached, a conventional degree of prodigality, which is also an exhibition of wealth, and consequently a source of credit, becomes a business necessity to the 'unfortunate' capitalist. Luxury enters into capital's expenses of representation. Moreover, the capitalist gets rich, not like the miser, in proportion to his personal labour and restricted consumption, but at the same rate as he squeezes out the labour-power of others, and enforces on the labourer abstinence from all life's enjoyments. Although, therefore, the prodigality of the capitalist never possesses the bona-fide character of the open-handed feudal lord's prodigality, but, on the contrary, has always lurking behind it the most sordid avarice and the most anxious calculation, yet his expenditure grows with his accumulation, without the one necessarily restricting the other. But along with this growth, there is at the same time developed in his breast, a Faustian conflict between the passion for accumulation, and the desire for enjoyment.

Dr Aikin says in a work published in 1795: 'The trade of Manchester may be divided into four periods. First, when manufacturers were obliged to work hard for their livelihood.' They enriched themselves chiefly by robbing the parents, whose children were bound as apprentices to them; the parents paid a high premium, while the apprentices were starved. On the other hand, the average profits were low, and to accumulate, extreme parsimony was requisite. They lived like misers, and were far from consuming even the interest on their capital. 'The second period, when they had begun to acquire little fortunes, but worked as hard as before,'—for direct exploitation of labour costs labour, as every slave-driver knows—'and lived in as plain a manner as before. . . . The third, when luxury began, and the trade was pushed by sending out riders for orders into every market town in the Kingdom. . . . It is probable that few or no capitals of £3,000 to £4,000 acquired by trade existed here before 1690. However, about that time, or a little later, the traders had got money beforehand, and began to build modern brick houses, instead of those of wood and plaster.' Even in the early part of the 18th century, a Manchester manufacturer, who placed a pint of foreign wine before his guests, exposed himself to the remarks and headshakings of all his neighbours. Before the rise of machinery, a manufacturer's evening expenditure at the public house where they all met, never exceeded sixpence for a glass of punch, and a penny for a screw of tobacco. It was not till 1758, and this marks an epoch, that a person actually engaged in business was seen with an equipage of his own. 'The fourth period,' the last 30 years of the 18th century, 'is that in which expense and luxury have made great progress, and was supported by a trade extended by means of riders and factors through every part of Europe'. What would the good Dr Aikin say if he could rise from his grave and see the Manchester of to-day?

Accumulate, accumulate! That is Moses and the prophets! 'Industry furnishes the material which saving accumulates.' Therefore, save, save, i.e. reconvert the greatest possible portion of surplus-value, or surplus-product into capital! Accumulation for accumulation's sake, production for production's sake: by this formula classical economy expressed the historical mission of the bourgeoisie, and did not for a single instant deceive itself over the birth-throes of wealth. But what avails lamentation in the face of historical necessity? If to classical economy, the proletarian is but a machine for the production of surplus-value; on the other hand, the capitalist is in its eyes only a machine for the conversion of this surplus-value into additional capital.

Section 5. The So-Called Labour-Fund

It has been shown in the course of this inquiry that capital is not a fixed magnitude, but is a part of social wealth, elastic and constantly fluctuating with the division of fresh surplus-value into revenue and additional capital. It has been seen further that, even with a given magnitude of functioning capital, the labour-power, the science, and the land (by which are to be understood, economically, all conditions of labour furnished by Nature independently of man), embodied in it, form elastic powers of capital, allowing it, within certain limits, a field of action independent of its own magnitude. In this inquiry we have neglected all effects of the process of circulation, effects which may produce very different degrees of efficiency in the same mass of capital. And as we pre-supposed the limits set by capitalist production, that is to say, pre-supposed the process of social production in a form developed by purely spontaneous growth, we neglected any more rational combination, directly and systematically practicable with the means of production, and the mass of labour-power at present disposable. Classical economy always loved to conceive social capital as a fixed magnitude of a fixed degree of efficiency. But this prejudice was first established as a dogma by the arch-Philistine, Jeremy Bentham, that insipid, pedantic, leather-tongued oracle of the ordinary bourgeois intelligence of the 19th century. Bentham is among philosophers what Martin Tupper is among poets. Both could only have been manufactured in England.[12] In the light of his dogma the commonest phenomena of the process of production, as, e.g. its sudden expansions and contractions, nay, even accumulation itself, become perfectly inconceivable. The dogma was used by Bentham himself, as well as by Malthus, James Mill, MacCulloch, etc., for an apologetic purpose, and especially in order to represent one part of capital, namely, variable capital, or that part convertible into labour-power, as a fixed magnitude. The material of variable capital, i.e. the mass of the means of subsistence it represents for the labourer, or the so-called labour-fund, was fabled as a separate part of social wealth, fixed by natural laws and unchangeable. To set in motion the part of social wealth which is to function as constant capital, or, to express it in a material form, as means of production, a definite mass of living labour is required. This mass is given technologically. But neither is the number of labourers required to render fluid this mass of labour-power given (it changes with the degree of exploitation of the individual labour-power), nor is the price of this labour-power given, but only its minimum limit, which is moreover very variable. The facts that lie at the botton of this dogma are these: on the one hand, the labourer has no right to interfere in the division of social wealth into means of enjoyment for the non-labourer and means of production. On the other hand, only in favourable and exceptional cases, has he the power to enlarge the so-called labour-fund at the expense of the 'revenue' of the wealthy.

What silly tautology results from the attempt to represent the capitalistic limits of the labour-fund as its natural and social limits may be seen, e.g. in Professor Fawcett. 'The circulating capital of a country', he says, 'is its wage-fund. Hence, if we desire to calculate the average money wages received by each labourer, we have simply to divide the amount of this capital by the number of the labouring population.' That is to say, we first add together the individual wages actually paid, and then we affirm that the sum thus obtained, forms the total value of the 'labour-fund' determined and vouchsafed to us by God and Nature. Lastly, we divide the sum thus obtained by the number of labourers to find out again how much may come to each on the average. An uncommonly knowing dodge this. It did not prevent Mr Fawcett saying in the same breath: 'The aggregate wealth which is annually saved in England, is divided into two portions; one portion is employed as capital to maintain our industry, and the other portion is exported to foreign countries . . . Only a portion, and perhaps, not a large portion of the wealth which is annually saved in this country, is invested in our own industry.'

The greater part of the yearly accruing surplus-product, embezzled, because abstracted without return of an equivalent, from the English labourer, is thus used as capital, not in England, but in foreign countries. But with the additional capital thus exported, a part of the 'labour-fund' invented by God and Bentham is also exported.

CHAPTER 25

THE GENERAL LAW OF CAPITALIST ACCUMULATION

Section 1. The Increased Demand for Labour-Power that Accompanies Accumulation, the Composition of Capital Remaining the Same

IN this chapter we consider the influence of the growth of capital on the lot of the labouring class. The most important factor in this inquiry is the composition of capital and the changes it undergoes in the course of the process of accumulation.

The composition of capital is to be understood in a two-fold sense. On the side of value, it is determined by the proportion in which it is divided into constant capital or value of the means of production, and variable capital or value of labour-power, the sum total of wages. On the side of material, as it functions in the process of production, all capital is divided into means of production and living labour-power. This latter composition is determined by the relation between the mass of the means of production employed, on the one hand, and the mass of labour necessary for their employment on the other. I call the former the *value-composition*, the latter the *technical composition* of capital. Between the two there is a strict correlation. To express this, I call the value-composition of capital, in so far as it is determined by its technical composition and mirrors the changes of the latter, the *organic composition* of capital. Wherever I refer to the composition of capital, without further qualification, its organic composition is always understood.

The many individual capitals invested in a particular branch of production have, one with another, more or less different compositions. The average of their individual compositions gives us the composition of the total capital in this branch of production. Lastly, the average of these averages, in all branches of production, gives us the composition of the total social capital of a country, and with this alone are we, in the last resort, concerned in the following investigation.

Growth of capital involves growth of its variable constituent or of the part invested in labour-power. A part of the surplus-value turned into additional capital must always be re-transformed into variable capital, or additional labour-fund. If we suppose that, all other circumstances remaining the same, the composition of capital also remains constant (i.e. that a definite mass of means of production constantly needs the same mass of labour-power to set it in motion), then the demand for labour and the subsistence-fund of the labourers clearly increase in the same proportion as the capital, and the more rapidly, the more rapidly the capital increases. Since the capital produces yearly a surplus-value, of which one part is yearly added to the original capital; since this increment itself grows yearly along with the augmentation of the capital already functioning; since lastly, under special stimulus to enrichment, such as the opening of new markets, or of new spheres for the outlay of capital in consequence of newly developed social wants, etc., the scale of accumulation may be suddenly extended, merely by a change in the division of the surplus-value or surplus-product into capital and revenue, the requirements of accumulating capital may exceed the increase of labour-power or of the number of labourers; the demand for labourers may exceed the supply, and, therefore, wages may rise. This must, indeed, ultimately be the case if the conditions supposed above continue. For since in each year more labourers are employed than in its predecessor, sooner or later a point must be reached, at which the requirements of accumulation begin to surpass the customary supply of labour, and, therefore, a rise of wages takes place. A lamentation on this score was heard in England during the whole of the fifteenth, and the first half of the eighteenth centuries. The more or less favourable circumstances in which the wage-working class supports and multiplies itself, in no way alter the fundamental character of capitalist production. As simple reproduction constantly reproduces the capital-relation itself, i.e. the relation of capitalists on the one hand, and wage-workers on the other, so reproduction on a progressive scale, i.e. accumulation, reproduces the capital-relation on a progressive scale, more capitalists or larger capitalists at this pole, more wage-workers at that. The reproduction of a mass of labour-power, which must incessantly re-incorporate itself with capital for that capital's self-expansion; which cannot get free from capital, and whose enslavement to capital is only concealed by the variety of individual capitalists to whom it sells itself, this reproduction of labour-power forms, in fact, an essential of the reproduction of capital itself. Accumulation of capital is, therefore, increase of the proletariat.

Classical economy grasped this fact so thoroughly that Adam Smith, Ricardo, etc., as mentioned earlier, inaccurately identified accumulation with the consumption, by the productive labourers, of all the capitalised part of the surplus-product, or with its transformation into additional wage-labourers. As early as 1696 John Bellers says: 'For if one had a hundred thousand acres of land and as many pounds in money, and as many cattle, without a labourer, what would the rich man be, but a labourer? And as the labourers make men rich, so the more labourers there will be, the more rich men . . . the labour of the poor being the mines of the rich.' So also Bernard de Mandeville at the beginning of the eighteenth century:

It would be easier, where property is well secured, to live without money than without poor; for who would do the work? . . . As they [the poor] ought to be kept from starving, so they should receive nothing worth saving. If here and there one of the lowest class by uncommon industry, and pinching his belly, lifts himself above the condition he was brought up in, nobody ought to hinder him; nay, it is undeniably the wisest course for every person in the society, and for every private family to be frugal; but it is the interest of all rich nations, that the greatest part of the poor should almost never be idle, and yet continually spend what they get. . . . Those that get their living by their daily labour . . . have nothing to stir them up to be serviceable but their wants which it is prudence to relieve, but folly to cure. The only thing then that can render the labouring man industrious, is a moderate quantity of money, for as too little will, according as his temper is, either dispirit or make him desperate, so too much will make him insolent and lazy. . . . From what has been said, it is manifest, that, in a free nation, where slaves are not allowed of, the surest wealth consists in a multitude of laborious poor; for besides, that they are the never-failing nursery of fleets and armies, without them there could be no enjoyment, and no product of any country could be valuable. To make the society [which of course consists of non-workers] happy and people easier under the meanest circumstances, it is requisite that great numbers of them should be ignorant as well as poor; knowledge both enlarges and multiplies our desires, and the fewer things a man wishes for, the more easily his necessities may be supplied.

What Mandeville, an honest, clear-headed man, had not yet seen, is that the mechanism of the process of accumulation itself increases, along with the capital, the mass of 'labouring poor', i.e. the wage-labourers, who turn their labour-power into an increasing power of self-expansion of the growing capital, and even by doing so must eternise their dependent relation on their own product, as personified in the capitalists. In reference to this relation of dependence, Sir F. M. Eden in his 'The State of the Poor, an History of the Labouring Classes in England', says,

the natural produce of our soil is certainly not fully adequate to our subsistence; we can neither be clothed, lodged nor fed but in consequence of some previous labour. A portion at least of the society must be indefatigably employed. . . . There are others who, though they 'neither toil nor spin', can yet command the produce of industry, but who owe their exemption from labour solely to civilisation and order. . . . They are peculiarly the creatures of civil institutions, which have recognised that individuals may acquire property by various other means besides the exertion of labour. . . . Persons of independent fortune . . . owe their superior advantages by no means to any superior abilities of their own, but almost entirely . . . to the industry of others. It is not the possession of land, or of money, but the command of labour which distinguishes the opulent from the labouring part of the community. . . . This [scheme approved by Eden] would give the people of property sufficient (but by no means too much) influence and authority over those who . . . work for them; and it would place such labourers, not in an abject or servile condition, but in such a state of easy and liberal dependence as all who know human nature, and its history, will allow to be necessary for their own comfort.

Sir F. M. Eden, it may be remarked in passing, is the only disciple of Adam Smith during the eighteenth century that produced any work of importance.[13]

Under the conditions of accumulation supposed thus far, which conditions are those most favourable to the labourers, their relation of dependence upon capital takes on a form endurable or, as Eden says: 'easy and liberal'. Instead of becoming more intensive with the growth of capital, this relation of dependence only becomes more extensive, i.e. the sphere of capital's exploitation and rule merely extends with its own dimensions and the number of its subjects. A larger part of their own surplus-product, always increasing and continually transformed into additional capital, comes back to them in the shape of means of payment, so that they can extend the circle of their enjoyments; can make some additions to their consumption-fund of clothes, furniture, etc., and can lay by small reserve-funds of money. But just as little as better clothing, food, and treatment, and a larger peculium, do away with the exploitation of the slave, so little do they set aside that of the wage-worker. A rise in the price of labour, as a consequence of accumulation of capital, only means, in fact, that the length and weight of the golden chain the wage-worker has already forged for himself, allow of a relaxation of the tension of it. In the controversies on this subject the chief fact has generally been overlooked, viz., the *differentia specifica* of capitalistic production. Labour-power is sold today, not with a view of satisfying, by its service or by its product, the personal needs of the buyer. His aim is augmentation of his capital, production of commodities containing more labour than he pays for, containing therefore a portion of value that costs him nothing, and that is nevertheless realised when the commodities are sold. Production of surplus-value is the absolute law of this mode of production. Labour-power is only saleable so far as it preserves the means of production in their capacity of capital, reproduces its own value as capital, and yields in unpaid labour a source of additional capital. The conditions of its sale, whether more or less favourable to the labourer, include therefore the necessity of its constant re-selling, and the constantly extended reproduction of all wealth in the shape of capital. Wages, as we have seen, by their very nature, always imply the performance of a certain quantity of unpaid labour on the part of the labourer. Altogether, irrespective of the case of a rise of wages with a falling price of labour, etc., such an increase only means at best a quantitative diminution of the unpaid labour that the worker has to supply. This diminution can never reach the point at which it would threaten the system itself. Apart from violent conflicts as to the rate of wages (and Adam Smith has already shown that in such a conflict, taken on the whole, the master is always master), a rise in the price of labour resulting from accumulation of capital implies the following alternative:

Either the price of labour keeps on rising, because its rise does not interfere with the progress of accumulation. In this there is nothing wonderful, for, says Adam Smith, 'after these (profits) are diminished, stock may not only continue to increase, but to increase much faster than before. . . . A great stock, though with small profits, generally increases faster than a small stock with great profits.' In this case it is evident that a diminution in the unpaid labour in no way interferes with the extension of the domain of capital.—Or, on the other hand, accumulation slackens in consequence of the rise in the price of labour, because the stimulus of gain is blunted. The rate of accumulation lessens; but with its lessening, the primary cause of that lessening vanishes, i.e. the disproportion between capital and exploitable labour-power. The mechanism of the process of capitalist production removes the very obstacles that it temporarily creates. The price of labour falls again to a level corresponding with the needs of the self-expansion of capital, whether the level be below, the same as, or above the one which was normal before the rise of wages took place. We see thus: In the first case, it is not the diminished rate either of the absolute, or of the proportional, increase in labour-power, or labouring population, which causes capital to be in excess, but conversely the excess of capital that makes exploitable labour-power insufficient. In the second case, it is not the increased rate either of the absolute, or of the proportional, increase in labour-power, or labouring population, that makes capital insufficient; but, conversely, the relative diminution of capital that causes the exploitable labour-power, or rather its price, to be in excess. It is these absolute movements of the accumulation of capital which are reflected as relative movements of the mass of exploitable labour-power, and therefore seem produced by the latter's own independent movement. To put it mathematically: the rate of accumulation is the independent, not the dependent, variable; the rate of wages, the dependent, not the independent, variable. Thus, when the industrial cycle is in the phase of crisis, a general fall in the price of commodities is expressed as a rise in the value of money, and, in the phase of prosperity, a general rise in the price of commodities, as a fall in the value of money. The so-called currency school* concludes from this that with high prices too much, with low prices too little money is in circulation. Their ignorance and complete misunderstanding of facts are worthily paralleled by the economists, who interpret the above phenomena of accumulation by saying that there are now too few, now too many wage-labourers.

The law of capitalist production, that is at the bottom of the pretended 'natural law of population', reduces itself simply to this: The correlation between accumulation of capital and rate of wages is nothing else than the correlation between the unpaid labour transformed into capital, and the additional paid labour necessary for the setting in motion of this additional capital. It is therefore in no way a relation between two magnitudes, independent one of the other: on the one hand, the magnitude of the capital; on the other, the number of the labouring population; it is rather, at bottom, only the relation between the unpaid and the paid labour of the same labouring population. If the quantity of unpaid labour supplied by the working-class, and accumulated by the capitalist class, increases so rapidly that its conversion into capital requires an extraordinary addition of paid labour, then wages rise, and, all other circumstances remaining equal, the unpaid labour diminishes in proportion. But as soon as this diminution touches the point at which the surplus-labour that nourishes capital is no longer supplied in normal quantity, a reaction sets in: a smaller part of revenue is capitalised, accumulation lags, and the movement of rise in wages receives a check. The rise of wages therefore is confined within limits that not only leave intact the foundations of the capitalistic system, but also secure its reproduction on a progressive scale. The law of capitalistic accumulation, metamorphosed by economists into pretended law of Nature, in reality merely states that the very nature of accumulation excludes every diminution in the degree of exploitation of labour, and every rise in the price of labour, which could seriously imperil the continual reproduction, on an ever-enlarging scale, of the capitalistic relation. It cannot be otherwise in a mode of production in which the labourer exists to satisfy the needs of self-expansion of existing values, instead of, on the contrary, material wealth existing to satisfy the needs of development on the part of the labourer. As, in religion, man is governed by the products of his own brain, so in capitalistic production, he is governed by the products of his own hand.

Section 2. Relative Diminution of the Variable Part of Capital Simultaneously with the Progress of Accumulation and of the Concentration that Accompanies it

According to the economists themselves, it is neither the actual extent of social wealth, nor the magnitude of the capital already functioning, that lead to a rise of wages, but only the constant growth of accumulation and the degree of rapidity of that growth. So far, we have only considered one special phase of this process, that in which the increase of capital occurs along with a constant technical composition of capital. But the process goes beyond this phase.

Once given the general basis of the capitalistic system, then, in the course of accumulation, a point is reached at which the development of the productivity of social labour becomes the most powerful lever of accumulation. 'The same cause', says Adam Smith, 'which raises the wages of labour, the increase of stock, tends to increase its productive powers, and to make a smaller quantity of labour produce a greater quantity of work.'

Apart from natural conditions, such as fertility of the soil, etc., and from the skill of independent and isolated producers (shown rather qualitatively in the goodness than quantitatively in the mass of their products), the degree of productivity of labour, in a given society, is expressed in the relative extent of the means of production that one labourer, during a given time, with the same tension of labour-power, turns into products. The mass of the means of production which he thus transforms, increases with the productiveness of his labour. But those means of production play a double part. The increase of some is a consequence, that of the others a condition of the increasing productivity of labour. E.g. with the division of labour in manufacture, and with the use of machinery, more raw material is worked up in the same time, and, therefore, a greater mass of raw material and auxiliary substances enter into the labour-process. That is the consequence of the increasing productivity of labour. On the other hand, the mass of machinery, beasts of burden, mineral manures, drain-pipes, etc., is a condition of the increasing productivity of labour. So also is it with the means of production concentrated in buildings, furnaces, means of transport, etc. But whether condition or consequence, the growing extent of the means of production, as compared with the labour-power incorporated with them, is an expression of the growing productiveness of labour. The increase of the latter appears, therefore, in the diminution of the mass of labour in proportion to the mass of means of production moved by it, or in the diminution of the subjective factor of the labour-process as compared with the objective factor.

This change in the technical composition of capital, this growth in the mass of means of production, as compared with the mass of the labour-power that vivifies them, is reflected again in its value-composition, by the increase of the constant constituent of capital at the expense of its variable constituent. There may be, e.g. originally 50 per cent. of a capital laid out in means of production, and 50 per cent. in labour-power; later on, with the development of the productivity of labour, 80 per cent. in means of production, 20 per cent. in labour-power, and so on. This law of the progressive increase in constant capital, in proportion to the variable, is confirmed at every step (as already shown) by the comparative analysis of the prices of commodities, whether we compare different economic epochs or different nations in the same epoch. The relative magnitude of the element of price, which represents the value of the means of production only, or the constant part of capital consumed, is in direct, the relative magnitude of the other element of price that pays labour (the variable part of capital) is in inverse proportion to the advance of accumulation.

This diminution in the variable part of capital as compared with the constant, or the altered value-composition of the capital, however, only shows approximately the change in the composition of its material constituents. If, e.g. the capital-value employed today in spinning is $7/8$ constant and $1/8$ variable, whilst at the beginning of the 18th century it was $1/2$ constant and $1/2$ variable, on the other hand, the mass of raw material, instruments of labour, etc., that a certain quantity of spinning labour consumes productively today, is many hundred times greater than at the beginning of the 18th century. The reason is simply that, with the increasing productivity of labour, not only does the mass of the means of production consumed by it increase, but their value compared with their mass diminishes. Their value therefore rises absolutely, but not in proportion to their mass. The increase of the difference between constant and variable capital, is, therefore, much less than that of the difference between the mass of the means of production into which the constant, and the mass of the labour-power into which the variable, capital is converted. The former difference increases with the latter, but in a smaller degree.

But, if the progress of accumulation lessens the relative magnitude of the variable part of capital, it by no means, in doing this, excludes the possibility of a rise in its absolute magnitude. Suppose that a capital-value at first is divided into 50 per cent of constant and 50 per cent. of variable capital; later into 80 per cent of constant and 20 per cent. of variable. If in the meantime the original capital, say £6,000, has increased to £18,000, its variable constituent has also increased. It was £3,000, it is now £3,600. But whereas formerly an increase of capital by 20 per cent would have sufficed to raise the demand for labour 20 per cent, now this latter rise requires a tripling of the original capital.

In Part IV it was shown, how the development of the productiveness of social labour pre-supposes co-operation on a large scale; how it is only upon this supposition that division and combination of labour can be organised, and the means of production economised by concentration on a vast scale; how instruments of labour which, from their very nature, are only fit for use in common, such as a system of machinery, can be called into being; how huge natural forces can be pressed into the service of production; and how the transformation can be effected of the process of production into a technological application of science. On the basis of the production of commodities, where the means of production are the property of private persons, and where the artisan therefore either produces commodities, isolated from and independent of others, or sells his labour-power as a commodity, because he lacks the means for independent industry, co-operation on a large scale can realise itself only in the increase of individual capitals, only in proportion as the means of social production and the means of subsistence are transformed into the private property of capitalists. The basis of the production of commodities can admit of production on a large scale in the capitalistic form alone. A certain accumulation of capital, in the hands of individual producers of commodities, forms therefore the necessary preliminary of the specifically capitalistic mode of production. We had, therefore, to assume that this occurs during the transition from handicraft to capitalistic industry. It may be called primitive accumulation, because it is the historic basis, instead of the historic result of specifically capitalist production. How it itself originates, we need not here inquire as yet. It is enough that it forms the starting-point. But all methods for raising the social productive power of labour that are developed on this basis, are at the same time methods for the increased production of surplus-value or surplus-product, which in its turn is the formative element of accumulation. They are, therefore, at the same time methods of the production of capital by capital, or methods of its accelerated accumulation. The continual re-transformation of surplus-value into capital now appears in the shape of the increasing magnitude of the capital that enters into the process of production. This in turn is the basis of an extended scale of production, of the methods for raising the productive power of labour that accompany it, and of accelerated production of surplus-value. If, therefore, a certain degree of accumulation of capital appears as a condition of the specifically capitalist mode of production, the latter causes conversely an accelerated accumulation of capital. With the accumulation of capital, therefore, the specifically capitalistic mode of production develops, and with the capitalist mode of production the accumulation of capital. Both these economic factors bring about, in the compound ratio of the impulses they reciprocally give one another, that change in the technical composition of capital by which the variable constituent becomes always smaller and smaller as compared with the constant.

Every individual capital is a larger or smaller concentration of means of production, with a corresponding command over a larger or smaller labour-army. Every accumulation becomes the means of new accumulation. With the increasing mass of wealth which functions as capital, accumulation increases the concentration of that wealth in the hands of individual capitalists, and thereby widens the basis of production on a large scale and of the specific methods of capitalist production. The growth of social capital is effected by the growth of many individual capitals. All other circumstances remaining the same, individual capitals, and with them the concentration of the means of production, increase in such proportion as they form aliquot parts of the total social capital. At the same time portions of the original capitals disengage themselves and function as new independent capitals. Besides other causes, the division of property, within capitalist families, plays a great part in this. With the accumulation of capital, therefore, the number of capitalists grows to a greater or less extent. Two points characterise this kind of concentration which grows directly out of, or rather is identical with, accumulation. First: The increasing concentration of the social means of production in the hands of individual capitalists is, other things remaining equal, limited by the degree of increase of social wealth. Second: The part of social capital domiciled in each particular sphere of production is divided among many capitalists who face one another as independent commodity-producers competing with each other. Accumulation and the concentration accompanying it are, therefore, not only scattered over many points, but the increase of each functioning capital is thwarted by the formation of new and the subdivision of old capitals. Accumulation, therefore, presents itself on the one hand as increasing concentration of the means of production, and of the command over labour; on the other, as repulsion of many individual capitals one from another.

This splitting-up of the total social capital into many individual capitals or the repulsion of its fractions one from another, is counteracted by their attraction. This last does not mean that simple concentration of the means of production and of the command over labour, which is identical with accumulation. It is concentration of capitals already formed, destruction of their individual independence, expropriation of capitalist by capitalist, transformation of many small into few large capitals. This process differs from the former in this, that it only pre-supposes a change in the distribution of capital already to hand, and functioning; its field of action is therefore not limited by the absolute growth of social wealth, by the absolute limits of accumulation. Capital grows in one place to a huge mass in a single hand, because it has in another place been lost by many. This is centralisation proper, as distinct from accumulation and concentration.

The laws of this centralisation of capitals, or of the attraction of capital by capital, cannot be developed here. A brief hint at a few facts must suffice. The battle of competition is fought by cheapening of commodities. The cheapness of commodities depends, *cæteris paribus*, on the productiveness of labour, and this again on the scale of production. Therefore, the larger capitals beat the smaller. It will further be remembered that, with the development of the capitalist mode of production, there is an increase in the minimum amount of individual capital necessary to carry on a business under its normal conditions. The smaller capitals, therefore, crowd into spheres of production which Modern Industry has only sporadically or incompletely got hold of. Here competition rages in direct proportion to the number, and in inverse proportion to the magnitudes, of the antagonistic capitals. It always ends in the ruin of many small capitalists, whose capitals partly pass into the hands of their conquerors, partly vanish. Apart from this, with capitalist production an altogether new force comes into play— the credit system, which in its first stages furtively creeps in as the humble assistant of accumulation, drawing into the hands of individual or associated capitalists, by invisible threads, the money resources which lie scattered, over the surface of society, in larger or smaller amounts; but it soon becomes a new and terrible weapon in the battle of competition and is finally transformed into an enormous social mechanism for the centralisation of capitals.

Commensurately with the development of capitalist production and accumulation there develop the two most powerful levers of centralisation—competition and credit. At the same time the progress of accumulation increases the material amenable to centralisation, i.e. the individual capitals, whilst the expansion of capitalist production creates, on the one hand, the social want, and, on the other, the technical means necessary for those immense industrial undertakings which require a previous centralisation of capital for their accomplishment. Today, therefore, the force of attraction, drawing together individual capitals, and the tendency to centralisation are stronger than ever before. But if the relative extension and energy of the movement towards centralisation is determined, in a certain degree, by the magnitude of capitalist wealth and superiority of economic mechanism already attained, progress in centralisation does not in any way depend upon a positive growth in the magnitude of social capital. And this is the specific difference between centralisation and concentration, the latter being only another name for reproduction on an extended scale. Centralisation may result from a mere change in the distribution of capitals already existing, from a simple alteration in the quantitative grouping of the component parts of social capital. Here capital can grow into powerful masses in a single hand because there it has been withdrawn from many individual hands. In any given branch of industry centralisation wiould reach its extreme limit if all the individual capitals invested in it were fused into a single capital. In a given society the limit would be reached only when the entire social capital was united in the hands of either a single capitalist or a single capitalist company.

Centralisation completes the work of accumulation by enabling industrial capitalists to extend the scale of their operations. Whether this latter result is the consequence of accumulation or centralisation, whether centralisation is accomplished by the violent method of annexation—when certain capitals become such preponderant centres of attraction for others that they shatter the individual cohesion of the latter and then draw the separate fragments to themselves—or whether the fusion of a number of capitals already formed or in process of formation takes place by the smoother process of organising joint-stock companies—the economic effect remains the same. Everywhere the increased scale of industrial establishments is the starting-point for a more comprehensive organisation of the collective work of many, for a wider development of their material motive forces—in other words, for the progressive transformation of isolated processes of production, carried on by customary methods, into processes of production socially combined and scientifically arranged.

But accumulation, the gradual increase of capital by reproduction as it passes from the circular to the spiral form, is clearly a very slow procedure compared with centralisation, which has only to change the quantitative groupings of the constituent parts of social capital. The world would still be without railways if it had had to wait until accumulation had got a few individual capitals far enough to be adequate for the construction of a railway. Centralisation, on the contrary, accomplished this in the twinkling of an eye, by means of joint-stock companies. And whilst centralisation thus intensifies and accelerates the effects of accumulation, it simultaneously extends and speeds those revolutions in the technical composition of capital which raise its constant portion at the expense of its variable portion, thus diminishing the relative demand for labour.

The masses of capital fused together overnight by centralisation reproduce and multiply as the others do, only more rapidly, thereby becoming new and powerful levers in social accumulation. Therefore, when we speak of the progress of social accumulation we tacitly include—today—the effects of centralisation.

The additional capitals formed in the normal course of accumulation (see Chapter 24, Section 1) serve particularly as vehicles for the exploitation of new inventions and discoveries, and industrial improvements in general. But in time the old capital also reaches the moment of renewal from top to toe, when it sheds its skin and is reborn like the others in perfected technical form, in which a smaller quantity of labour will suffice to set in motion a larger quantity of machinery and raw materials. The absolute reduction in the demand for labour which necessarily follows from this is obviously so much the greater the higher the degree in which the capitals undergoing this process of renewal are already massed together by virtue of the centralisation movement.

On the one hand, therefore, the additional capital formed in the course of accumulation attracts fewer and fewer labourers in proportion to its magnitude. On the other hand, the old capital periodically reproduced with change of composition, repels more and more of the labourers formerly employed by it.

Section 3. Progressive Production of a Relative Surplus-Population or Industrial Reserve Army

The accumulation of capital, though originally appearing as its quantitative extension only, is effected, as we have seen, under a progressive qualitative change in its composition, under a constant increase of its constant, at the expense of its variable constituent.

The specifically capitalist mode of production, the development of the productive power of labour corresponding to it, and the change thence resulting in the organic composition of capital, do not merely keep pace with the advance of accumulation, or with the growth of social wealth. They develop at a much quicker rate, because mere accumulation, the absolute increase of the total social capital, is accompanied by the centralisation of the individual capitals of which that total is made up; and because the change in the technological composition of the additional capital goes hand in hand with a similar change in the technological composition of the original capital. With the advance of accumulation, therefore, the proportion of constant to variable capital changes. If it was originally say 1:1, it now becomes successively 2:1, 3:1, 4:1, 5:1, 7:1, etc., so that, as the capital increases, instead of ½ of its total value, only ⅓, ¼, ⅕, ⅙, ⅛, etc., is transformed into labour-power, and, on the other hand, ⅔, ¾, ⅘, ⅚, ⅞, into means of production. Since the demand for labour is determined not by the amount of capital as a whole, but by its variable constituent alone, that demand falls progressively with the increase of the total capital, instead of, as previously assumed, rising in proportion to it. It falls relatively to the magnitude of the total capital, and at an accelerated rate, as this magnitude increases. With the growth of the total capital, its variable constituent or the labour incorporated in it, also does increase, but in a constantly diminishing proportion. The intermediate pauses are shortened, in which accumulation works as simple extension of production, on a given technical basis. It is not merely that an accelerated accumulation of total capital, accelerated in a constantly growing progression, is needed to absorb an additional number of labourers, or even, on account of the constant metamorphosis of old capital, to keep employed those already functioning. In its turn, this increasing accumulation and centralisation becomes a source of new changes in the composition of capital, of a more accelerated diminution of its variable, as compared with its constant constituent. This accelerated relative diminution of the variable constituent, that goes along with the accelerated increase of the total capital, and moves more rapidly than this increase, takes the inverse form, at the other pole, of an apparently absolute increase of the labouring population, an increase always moving more rapidly than that of the variable capital or the means of employment. But in fact, it is capitalistic accumulation itself that constantly produces, and produces in the direct ratio of its own energy and extent, a relatively redundant population of labourers, i.e. a population of greater extent than suffices for the average needs of the self-expansion of capital, and therefore a surplus-population.

Considering the social capital in its totality, the movement of its accumulation now causes periodical changes, affecting it more or less as a whole, now distributes its various phases simultaneously over the different spheres of production. In some spheres a change in the composition of capital occurs without increase of its absolute magnitude, as a consequence of simple centralisation; in others the absolute growth of capital is connected with absolute diminution of its variable constituent, or of the labour-power absorbed by it; in others again, capital continues growing for a time on its given technical basis, and attracts additional labour-power in proportion to its increase, while at other times it undergoes organic change, and lessens its variable constituent; in all spheres, the increase of the variable part of capital, and therefore of the number of labourers employed by it, is always connected with violent fluctuations and transitory production of surplus-population, whether this takes the more striking form of the repulsion of labourers already employed, or the less evident but not less real form of the more difficult absorption of the additional labouring population through the usual channels. With the magnitude of social capital already functioning, and the degree of its increase, with the extension of the scale of production, and the mass of the labourers set in motion, with the development of the productiveness of their labour, with the greater breadth and fulness of all sources of wealth, there is also an extension of the scale on which greater attraction of labourers by capital is accompanied by their greater repulsion; the rapidity of the change in the organic composition of capital, and in its technical form increases, and an increasing number of spheres of production becomes involved in this change, now simultaneously, now alternately. The labouring population therefore produces, along with the accumulation of capital produced by it, the means by which it itself is made relatively superfluous, is turned into a relative surplus-population; and it does this to an always increasing extent. This is a law of population peculiar to the capitalist mode of production; and in fact every special historic mode of production has its own special laws of population, historically valid within its limits alone. An abstract law of population exists for plants and animals only, and only in so far as man has not interfered with them.

But if a surplus labouring population is a necessary product of accumulation or of the development of wealth on a capitalist basis, this surplus-population becomes, conversely, the lever of capitalistic accumulation, nay, a condition of existence of the capitalist mode of production. It forms a disposable industrial reserve army, that belongs to capital quite as absolutely as if the latter had bred it at its own cost. Independently of the limits of the actual increase of population, it creates, for the changing needs of the self-expansion of capital, a mass of human material always ready for exploitation. With accumulation, and the development of the productiveness of labour that accompanies it, the power of sudden expansion of capital grows also; it grows, not merely because the elasticity of the capital already functioning increases, not merely because the absolute wealth of society expands, of which capital only forms an elastic part, not merely because credit, under every special stimulus, at once places an unusual part of this wealth at the disposal of production in the form of additional capital; it grows, also, because the technical conditions of the process of production themselves—machinery, means of transport, etc.—now admit of the rapidest transformation of masses of surplus-product into additional means of production. The mass of social wealth, overflowing with the advance of accumulation, and transformable into additional capital, thrusts itself frantically into old branches of production, whose market suddenly expands, or into newly formed branches, such as railways, etc., the need for which grows out of the development of the old ones. In all such cases, there must be the possibility of throwing great masses of men suddenly on the decisive points without injury to the scale of production in other spheres. Overpopulation supplies these masses. The course characteristic of modern industry, viz., a decennial cycle (interrupted by smaller oscillations), of periods of average activity, production at high pressure, crisis and stagnation, depends on the constant formation, the greater or less absorption, and the reformation of the industrial reserve army or surplus-population. In their turn, the varying phases of the industrial cycle recruit the surplus-population, and become one of the most energetic agents of its reproduction. This peculiar course of modern industry, which occurs in no earlier period of human history, was also impossible in the childhood of capitalist production. The composition of capital changed but very slowly. With its accumulation, therefore, there kept pace, on the whole, a corresponding growth in the demand for labour. Slow as was the advance of accumulation compared with that of more modern times, it found a check in the natural limits of the exploitable labouring population, limits which could only be got rid of by forcible means to be mentioned later. The expansion by fits and starts of the scale of production is the preliminary to its equally sudden contraction; the latter again evokes the former, but the former is impossible without disposable human material, without an increase in the number of labourers independently of the absolute growth of the population. This increase is effected by the simple process that constantly 'sets free' a part of the labourers; by methods which lessen the number of labourers employed in proportion to the increased production. The whole form of the movement of modern industry depends, therefore, upon the constant transformation of a part of the labouring population into unemployed or half-employed hands. The superficiality of Political Economy shows itself in the fact that it looks upon the expansion and contraction of credit, which is a mere symptom of the periodic changes of the industrial cycle, as their cause. As the heavenly bodies, once thrown into a certain definite motion, always repeat this, so is it with social production as soon as it is once thrown into this movement of alternate expansion and contraction. Effects, in their turn, become causes, and the varying accidents of the whole process, which always reproduces its own conditions, take on the form of periodicity. When this periodicity is once consolidated, even Political Economy then sees that the production of a relative surplus-population—i.e. surplus with regard to the average needs of the self-expansion of capital—is a necessary condition of modern industry.

Capitalist production can by no means content itself with the quantity of disposable labour-power which the natural increase of population yields. It requires for its free play an industrial reserve army independent of these natural limits.

Up to this point it has been assumed that the increase or diminution of the variable capital corresponds rigidly with the increase or diminution of the number of labourers employed.

The number of labourers commanded by capital may remain the same, or even fall, while the variable capital increases. This is the case if the individual labourer yields more labour, and therefore his wages increase, and this although the price of labour remains the same or even falls, only more slowly than the mass of labour rises. Increase of variable capital, in this case, becomes an index of more labour, but not of more labourers employed. It is the absolute interest of every capitalist to press a given quantity of labour out of a smaller, rather than a greater number of labourers, if the cost is about the same. In the latter case, the outlay of constant capital increases in proportion to the mass of labour set in action; in the former that increase is much smaller. The more extended the scale of production, the stronger this motive. Its force increases with the accumulation of capital.

We have seen that the development of the capitalist mode of production and of the productive power of labour—at once the cause and effect of accumulation—enables the capitalist, with the same outlay of variable capital, to set in action more labour by greater exploitation (extensive or intensive) of each individual labour-power. We have further seen that the capitalist buys with the same capital a greater mass of labour-power, as he progressively replaces skilled labourers by less skilled, mature labour-power by immature, male by female, that of adults by that of young persons or children.

On the one hand, therefore, with the progress of accumulation, a larger variable capital sets more labour in action without enlisting more labourers; on the other, a variable capital of the same magnitude sets in action more labour with the same mass of labour-power; and, finally, a greater number of inferior labour-powers by displacement of higher.

The production of a relative surplus-population, or the setting free of labourers, goes on therefore yet more rapidly than the technical revolution of the process of production that accompanies, and is accelerated by, the advance of accumulation; and more rapidly than the corresponding diminution of the variable part of capital as compared with the constant. If the means of production, as they increase in extent and effective power, become to a less extent means of employment of labourers, this state of things is again modified by the fact that in proportion as the productiveness of labour increases, capital increases its supply of labour more quickly than its demand for labourers. The over-work of the employed part of the working-class swells the ranks of the reserve, whilst conversely the greater pressure that the latter by its competition exerts on the former, forces these to submit to over-work and to subjugation under the dictates of capital. The condemnation of one part of the working-class to enforced idleness by the over-work of the other part, and the converse, becomes a means of enriching the individual capitalists, and accelerates at the same time the production of the industrial reserve army on a scale corresponding with the advance of social accumulation. How important is this element in the formation of the relative surplus-population, is shown by the example of England. Her technical means for saving labour are colossal. Nevertheless, if to-morrow morning labour generally were reduced to a rational amount, and proportioned to the different sections of the working-class according to age and sex, the working population to hand would be absolutely insufficient for the carrying on of national production on its present scale. The great majority of the labourers now 'unproductive' would have to be turned into 'productive' ones.

Taking them as a whole, the general movements of wages are exclusively regulated by the expansion and contraction of the industrial reserve army, and these again correspond to the periodic changes of the industrial cycle. They are, therefore, not determined by the variations of the absolute number of the working population, but by the varying proportions in which the working-class is divided into active and reserve army, by the increase or diminution in the relative amount of the surplus-population, by the extent to which it is now absorbed, now set free. For Modern Industry with its decennial cycles and periodic phases, which, moreover, as accumulation advances, are complicated by irregular oscillations following each other more and more quickly, that would indeed be a beautiful law, which pretends to make the action of capital dependent on the absolute variation of the population, instead of regulating the demand and supply of labour by the alternate expansion and contraction of capital, the labour-market now appearing relatively under-full, because capital is expanding, now again over-full, because it is contracting. Yet this is the dogma of the economists. According to them, wages rise in consequence of accumulation of capital. The higher wages stimulate the working population to more rapid multiplication, and this goes on until the labour-market becomes too full, and therefore capital, relatively to the supply of labour, becomes insufficient. Wages fall, and now we have the reverse of the medal. The working population is little by little decimated as the result of the fall in wages, so that capital is again in excess relatively to them, or, as others explain it, falling wages and the corresponding increase in the exploitation of the labourer again accelerates accumulation, whilst, at the same time, the lower wages hold the increase of the working-class in check. Then comes again the time, when the supply of labour is less than the demand, wages rise, and so on. A beautiful mode of motion this for developed capitalist production! Before, in consequence of the rise of wages, any positive increase of the population really fit for work could occur, the time would have been passed again and again, during which the industrial campaign must have been carried through, the battle fought and won.

Between 1849 and 1859, a rise of wages practically insignificant, though accompanied by falling prices of corn, took place in the English agricultural districts. In Wiltshire, e.g. the weekly wages rose from 7s. to 8s.; in Dorsetshire from 7s. or 8s., to 9s., etc. This was the result of an unusual exodus of the agricultural surplus-population caused by the demands of war,* the vast extension of railroads, factories, mines, etc. The lower the wages, the higher is the proportion in which ever so insignificant a rise of them expresses itself. If the weekly wage, e.g. is 20s. and it rises to 22s., that is a rise of 10 per cent; but if it is only 7s. and it rises to 9s., that is a rise of 28½ per cent, which sounds very fine. Everywhere the farmers were howling, and the London *Economist*, with reference to these starvation-wages, prattled quite seriously of 'a general and substantial advance'. What did the farmers do now? Did they wait until, in consequence of this brilliant remuneration, the agricultural labourers had so increased and multiplied that their wages must fall again, as prescribed by the dogmatic economic brain? They introduced more machinery, and in a moment the labourers were redundant again in a proportion satisfactory even to the farmers. There was now 'more capital' laid out in agriculture than before, and in a more productive form. With this the demand for labour fell, not only relatively, but absolutely.

The above economic fiction confuses the laws that regulate the general movement of wages, or the ratio between the working-class—i.e. the total labour-power—and the total social capital, with the laws that distribute the working population over the different spheres of production. If, e.g. in consequence of favourable circumstances, accumulation in a particular sphere of production becomes especially active, and profits in it, being greater than the average profits, attract additional capital, of course the demand for labour rises and wages also rise. The higher wages draw a larger part of the working population into the more favoured sphere, until it is glutted with labour-power, and wages at length fall again to their average level or below it, if the pressure is too great. Then, not only does the immigration of labourers into the branch of industry in question cease; it gives place to their emigration. Here the political economist thinks he sees the why and wherefore of an absolute increase of workers accompanying an increase of wages, and of a diminution of wages accompanying an absolute increase of labourers. But he sees really only the local oscillation of the labour-market in a particular sphere of production—he sees only the phenomena accompanying the distribution of the working population into the different spheres of outlay of capital, according to its varying needs.

The industrial reserve army, during the periods of stagnation and average prosperity, weighs down the active labour-army; during the periods of over-production and paroxysm, it holds its pretensions in check. Relative surplus-population is therefore the pivot upon which the law of demand and supply of labour works. It confines the field of action of this law within the limits absolutely convenient to the activity of exploitation and to the domination of capital.

Capital works on both sides at the same time. If its accumulation, on the one hand, increases the demand for labour, it increases on the other the supply of labourers by the 'setting free' of them, whilst at the same time the pressure of the unemployed compels those that are employed to furnish more labour, and therefore makes the supply of labour, to a certain extent, independent of the supply of labourers. The action of the law of supply and demand of labour on this basis completes the despotism of capital. As soon, therefore, as the labourers learn the secret, how it comes to pass that in the same measure as they work more, as they produce more wealth for others, and as the productive power of their labour increases, so in the same measure even their function as a means of the self-expansion of capital becomes more and more precarious for them; as soon as they discover that the degree of intensity of the competition among themselves depends wholly on the pressure of the relative surplus-population; as soon as, by Trades' Unions, etc., they try to organise a regular co-operation between employed and unemployed in order to destroy or to weaken the ruinous effects of this natural law of capitalistic production on their class, so soon capital and its sycophant, Political Economy, cry out at the infringement of the 'eternal' and so to say 'sacred' law of supply and demand. Every combination of employed and unemployed disturbs the 'harmonious' action of this law. But, on the other hand, as soon as (in the colonies, e.g.) adverse circumstances prevent the creation of an industrial reserve army and, with it, the absolute dependence of the working-class upon the capitalist class, capital, along with its commonplace Sancho Panza, rebels against the 'sacred' law of supply and demand, and tries to check its inconvenient action by forcible means and State interference.

Section 4. Different Forms of the Relative Surplus-Population. The General Law of Capitalistic Accumulation

The relative surplus-population exists in every possible form. Every labourer belongs to it during the time when he is only partially employed or wholly unemployed. Not taking into account the great periodically recurring forms that the changing phases of the industrial cycle impress on it, now an acute form during the crisis, then again a chronic form during dull times—it has always three forms, the floating, the latent, the stagnant.

In the centres of modern industry—factories, manufactures, iron-works, mines, etc.—the labourers are sometimes repelled, sometimes attracted again in greater masses, the number of those employed increasing on the whole, although in a constantly decreasing proportion to the scale of production. Here the surplus-population exists in the floating form.

In the automatic factories, as in all the great workshops, where machinery enters as a factor, or where only the modern division of labour is carried out, large numbers of boys are employed up to the age of maturity. When this term is once reached, only a very small number continue to find employment in the same branches of industry, whilst the majority are regularly discharged. This majority forms an element of the floating surplus-population, growing with the extension of those branches of industry. Part of them emigrates, following in fact capital that has emigrated. One consequence is that the female population grows more rapidly than the male, *teste* England. That the natural increase of the number of labourers does not satisfy the requirements of the accumulation of capital, and yet all the time is in excess of them, is a contradiction inherent to the movement of capital itself. It wants larger numbers of youthful labourers, a smaller number of adults. The contradiction is not more glaring than that other one that there is a complaint of the want of hands, while at the same time many thousands are out of work, because the division of labour chains them to a particular branch of industry.

The consumption of labour-power by capital is, besides, so rapid that the labourer, half-way through his life, has already more or less completely lived himself out. He falls into the ranks of the super-numeraries, or is thrust down from a higher to a lower step in the scale. It is precisely among the workpeople of modern industry that we meet with the shortest duration of life. Dr Lee, Medical Officer of Health for

Manchester, stated 'that the average age at death of the Manchester . . . upper middle class was 38 years, while the average age at death of the labouring class was 17; while at Liverpool those figures were represented as 35 against 15. It thus appeared that the well-to-do classes had a lease of life which was more than double the value of that which fell to the lot of the less favoured citizens.' In order to conform to these circumstances, the absolute increase of this section of the proletariat must take place under conditions that shall swell their numbers, although the individual elements are used up rapidly. Hence, rapid renewal of the generations of labourers (this law does not hold for the other classes of the population). This social need is met by early marriages, a necessary consequence of the conditions in which the labourers of modern industry live, and by the premium that the exploitation of children sets on their production.

As soon as capitalist production takes possession of agriculture, and in proportion to the extent to which it does so, the demand for an agricultural labouring population falls absolutely, while the accumulation of the capital employed in agriculture advances, without this repulsion being, as in non-agricultural industries, compensated by a greater attraction. Part of the agricultural population is therefore constantly on the point of passing over into an urban or manufacturing proletariat, and on the look-out for circumstances favourable to this transformation. (Manufacture is used here in the sense of all non-agricultural industries.) This source of relative surplus-population is thus constantly flowing. But the constant flow towards the towns presupposes, in the country itself, a constant latent surplus-population, the extent of which becomes evident only when its channels of outlet open to exceptional width. The agricultural labourer is therefore reduced to the minimum of wages, and always stands with one foot already in the swamp of pauperism.

The third category of the relative surplus-population, the stagnant, forms a part of the active labour army, but with extremely irregular employment. Hence it furnishes to capital an inexhaustible reservoir of disposable labour-power. Its conditions of life sink below the average normal level of the working-class; this makes it at once the broad basis of special branches of capitalist exploitation. It is characterised by maximum of working-time, and minimum of wages. We have learnt to know its chief form under the rubric of 'domestic industry'. It recruits itself constantly from the supernumerary forces of modern industry and agriculture, and specially from those decaying branches of industry where handicraft is yielding to manufacture, manufacture to machinery. Its extent grows, as with the extent and energy of accumulation, the creation of a surplus-population advances. But it forms at the same time a self-reproducing and self-perpetuating element of the working-class, taking a proportionally greater part in the general increase of that class than the other elements. In fact, not only the number of births and deaths, but the absolute size of the families stand in inverse proportion to the height of wages, and therefore to the amount of means of subsistence of which the different categories of labourers dispose. This law of capitalistic society would sound absurd to savages, or even civilised colonists. It calls to mind the boundless reproduction of animals individually weak and constantly hunted down.

The lowest sediment of the relative surplus-population finally dwells in the sphere of pauperism. Exclusive of vagabonds, criminals, prostitutes, in a word, the 'dangerous' classes, this layer of society consists of three categories. First, those able to work. One need only glance superficially at the statistics of English pauperism to find that the quantity of paupers increases with every crisis, and diminishes with every revival of trade. Second, orphans and pauper children. These are candidates for the industrial reserve army, and are, in times of great prosperity, as 1860, e.g. speedily and in large numbers enrolled in the active army of labourers. Third, the demoralised and ragged, and those unable to work, chiefly people who succumb to their incapacity for adaptation, due to the division of labour; people who have passed the normal age of the labourer; the victims of industry, whose number increases with the increase of dangerous machinery, of mines, chemical works, etc., the mutilated, the sickly, the widows, etc. Pauperism is the hospital of the active labour-army and the dead weight of the industrial reserve army. Its production is included in that of the relative surplus-population, its necessity in theirs; along with the surplus-population, pauperism forms a condition of capitalist production, and of the capitalist development of wealth. It enters into the *faux frais** of capitalist production; but capital knows how to throw these, for the most part, from its own shoulders on to those of the working-class and the lower middle class.

The greater the social wealth, the functioning capital, the extent and energy of its growth, and, therefore, also the absolute mass of the proletariat and the productiveness of its labour, the greater is the industrial reserve army. The same causes which develop the expansive power of capital, develop also the labour-power at its disposal. The relative mass of the industrial reserve army increases therefore with the potential energy of wealth. But the greater this reserve army in proportion to the active labour-army, the greater is the mass of a consolidated surplus-population, whose misery is in inverse ratio to its torment of labour. The more extensive, finally, the lazarus-layers of the working-class, and the industrial reserve army, the greater is official pauperism. *This is the absolute general law of capitalist accumulation.* Like all other laws it is modified in its working by many circumstances, the analysis of which does not concern us here.

The folly is now patent of the economic wisdom that preaches to the labourers the accommodation of their number to the requirements of capital. The mechanism of capitalist production and accumulation constantly effects this adjustment. The first word of this adaptation is the creation of a relative surplus-population, or industrial reserve army. Its last word is the misery of constantly extending strata of the active army of labour, and the dead weight of pauperism.

The law by which a constantly increasing quantity of means of production, thanks to the advance in the productiveness of social labour, may be set in movement by a progressively diminishing expenditure of human power, this law, in a capitalist society—where the labourer does not employ the means of production, but the means of production employ the labourer—undergoes a complete inversion and is expressed thus: the higher the productiveness of labour, the greater is the pressure of the labourers on the means of employment, the more precarious, therefore, becomes their condition of existence, viz., the sale of their own labour-power for the increasing of another's wealth, or for the self-expansion of capital. The fact that the means of production, and the productiveness of labour, increase more rapidly than the productive population, expresses itself, therefore, capitalistically in the inverse form that the labouring population always increases more rapidly than the conditions under which capital can employ this increase for its own self-expansion.

We saw in Part IV, when analysing the production of relative surplus-value: within the capitalist system all methods for raising the social productiveness of labour are brought about at the cost of the individual labourer; all means for the development of production transform themselves into means of domination over, and exploitation of, the producers; they mutilate the labourer into a fragment of a man, degrade him to the level of an appendage of a machine, destroy every remnant of charm in his work and turn it into a hated toil; they estrange from him the intellectual potentialities of the labour-process in the same proportion as science is incorporated in it as an independent power; they distort the conditions under which he works, subject him during the labour-process to a despotism the more hateful for its meanness; they transform his life-time into working-time, and drag his wife and child beneath the wheels of the Juggernaut of capital. But all methods for the production of surplus-value are at the same time methods of accumulation; and every extension of accumulation becomes again a means for the development of those methods. It follows therefore that in proportion as capital accumulates, the lot of the labourer, be his payment high or low, must grow worse. The law, finally, that always equilibrates the relative surplus-population, or industrial reserve army, to the extent and energy of accumulation, this law rivets the labourer to capital more firmly than the wedges of Vulcan did Prometheus to the rock. It establishes an accumulation of misery, corresponding with accumulation of capital. Accumulation of wealth at one pole is, therefore, at the same time accumulation of misery, agony of toil slavery, ignorance, brutality, mental degradation, at the opposite pole, i.e. on the side of the class that produces its own product in the form of capital.

PART VIII
THE SO-CALLED PRIMITIVE
ACCUMULATION

CHAPTER 26
THE SECRET OF PRIMITIVE ACCUMULATION

WE have seen how money is changed into capital; how through capital surplus-value is made, and from surplus-value more capital. But the accumulation of capital pre-supposes surplus-value; surplus-value pre-supposes capitalistic production; capitalistic production pre-supposes the pre-existence of considerable masses of capital and of labour-power in the hands of producers of commodities. The whole movement, therefore, seems to turn in a vicious circle, out of which we can only get by supposing a primitive accumulation (previous accumulation of Adam Smith) preceding capitalistic accumulation; an accumulation not the result of the capitalist mode of production, but its starting-point.

This primitive accumulation plays in Political Economy about the same part as original sin in theology. Adam bit the apple, and thereupon sin fell on the human race. Its origin is supposed to be explained when it is told as an anecdote of the past. In times long gone by there were two sorts of people; one, the diligent, intelligent, and, above all, frugal élite; the other, lazy rascals, spending their substance, and more, in riotous living. The legend of theological original sin tells us certainly how man came to be condemned to eat his bread in the sweat of his brow; but the history of economic original sin reveals to us that there are people to whom this is by no means essential. Never mind! Thus it came to pass that the former sort accumulated wealth, and the latter sort had at last nothing to sell except their own skins. And from this original sin dates the poverty of the great majority that, despite all its labour, has up to now nothing to sell but itself, and the wealth of the few that increases constantly although they have long ceased to work. Such insipid childishness is every day preached to us in the defence of property. M. Thiers, e.g. had the assurance to repeat it with all the solemnity of a statesman, to the French people, once so *spirituel*. But as soon as the question of property crops up, it becomes a sacred duty to proclaim the intellectual food of the infant as the one thing fit for all ages and for all stages of development. In actual history it is notorious that conquest. enslavement, robbery, murder, briefly force, play the great part. In the tender annals of Political Economy, the idyllic reigns from time immemorial. Right and 'labour' were from all time the sole means of enrichment, the present year of course always excepted. As a matter of fact, the methods of primitive accumulation are anything but idyllic.

In themselves money and commodities are no more capital than are the means of production and of subsistence. They want transforming into capital. But this transformation itself can only take place under certain circumstances that centre in this, viz., that two very different kinds of commodity-possessors must come face to face and into contact; on the one hand, the owners of money, means of production, means of subsistence, who are eager to increase the sum of values they possess, by buying other people's labour-power; on the other hand, free labourers, the sellers of their own labour-power, and therefore the sellers of labour. Free labourers, in the double sense that neither they themselves form part and parcel of the means of production, as in the case of slaves, bondsmen, etc., nor do the means of production belong to them, as in the case of peasant-proprietors; they are, therefore, free from, unencumbered by, any means of production of their own. With this polarisation of the market for commodities, the fundamental conditions of capitalist production are given. The capitalist system presupposes the complete separation of the labourers from all property in the means by which they can realise their labour. As soon as capitalist production is once on its own legs, it not only maintains this separation, but reproduces it on a continually extending scale. The process, therefore, that clears the way for the capitalist system, can be none other than the process which takes away from the labourer the possession of his means of production; a process that transforms, on the one hand, the social means of subsistence and of production into capital, on the other, the immediate producers into wage-labourers. The so-called primitive accumulation, therefore, is nothing else than the historical process of divorcing the producer from the means of production. It appears as primitive, because it forms the pre-historic stage of capital and of the mode of production corresponding with it.

The economic structure of capitalistic society has grown out of the economic structure of feudal society. The dissolution of the latter set free the elements of the former.

The immediate producer, the labourer, could only dispose of his own person after he had ceased to be attached to the soil and ceased to be the slave, serf, or bondman of another. To become a free seller of labour-power, who carries his commodity wherever he finds a market, he must further have escaped from the regime of the guilds, their rules for apprentices and journeymen, and the impediments of their labour regulations. Hence, the historical movement which changes the producers into wage-workers, appears, on the one hand, as their emancipation from serfdom and from the fetters of the guilds, and this side alone exists for our bourgeois historians. But, on the other hand, these new freedmen became sellers of themselves only after they had been robbed of all their own means of production, and of all the guarantees of existence afforded by the old feudal arrangements. And the history of this, their expropriation, is written in the annals of mankind in letters of blood and fire.

In the history of primitive accumulation, all revolutions are epoch-making that act as levers for the capitalist class in course of formation; but, above all, those moments when great masses of men are suddenly and forcibly torn from their means of subsistence, and hurled as free and 'unattached' proletarians on the labour-market. The expropriation of the agricultural producer, of the peasant, from the soil, is the basis of the whole process. The history of this expropriation, in different countries, assumes different aspects, and runs through its various phases in different orders of succession, and at different periods. In England alone, which we take as our example, has it the classic form.

CHAPTER 27

EXPROPRIATION OF THE AGRICULTURAL POPULATION FROM THE LAND

In England, serfdom had practically disappeared in the last part of the 14th century. The immense majority of the population consisted then, and to a still larger extent, in the 15th century, of free peasant proprietors, whatever was the feudal title under which their right of property was hidden. In the larger seignorial domains, the old bailiff, himself a serf, was displaced by the free farmer. The wage-labourers of agriculture consisted partly of peasants, who utilised their leisure time by working on the large estates, partly of an independent special class of wage-labourers, relatively and absolutely few in numbers. The latter also were practically at the same time peasant farmers, since, besides their wages, they had allotted to them arable land to the extent of 4 or more acres, together with their cottages. Besides they, with the rest of the peasants, enjoyed the usufruct of the common land, which gave pasture to their cattle, furnished them with timber, fire-wood, turf, etc. In all countries of Europe, feudal production is characterised by division of the soil amongst the greatest possible number of subfeudatories. The might of the feudal lord, like that of the sovereign, depended not on the length of his rent-roll, but on the number of his subjects, and the latter depended on the number of peasant proprietors. Although, therefore, the English land, after the Norman conquest, was distributed in gigantic baronies, one of which often included some 900 of the old Anglo-Saxon lordships, it was bestrewn with small peasant properties, only here and there interspersed with great seignorial domains. Such conditions, together with the prosperity of the towns so characteristic of the 15th century, allowed of that wealth of the people which Chancellor Fortescue so eloquently paints in his 'Laudes legum Angliæ'; but it excluded the possibility of capitalistic wealth.

The prelude of the revolution that laid the foundation of the capitalist mode of production, was played in the last third of the 15th, and the first decade of the 16th century. A mass of free proletarians was hurled on the labour-market by the breaking-up of the bands of feudal retainers, who, as Sir James Steuart well says, 'everywhere uselessly filled house and castle'. Although the royal power, itself a product of bourgeois development, in its strife after absolute sovereignty forcibly hastened on the dissolution of these bands of retainers, it was by no means the sole cause of it. In insolent conflict with king and parliament, the great feudal lords created an incomparably larger proletariat by the forcible driving of the peasantry from the land, to which the latter had the same feudal right as the lord himself, and by the usurpation of the common lands. The rapid rise of the Flemish wool manufactures, and the corresponding rise in the price of wool in England, gave the direct impulse to these evictions. The old nobility had been devoured by the great feudal wars. The new nobility was the child of its time, for which money was the power of all powers. Transformation of arable land into sheep-walks was, therefore, its cry.

The process of forcible expropriation of the people received in the 16th century a new and frightful impulse from the Reformation, and from the consequent colossal spoliation of the church property. The Catholic church was, at the time of the Reformation, feudal proprietor of a great part of the English land. The suppression of the monasteries, etc., hurled their inmates into the proletariat. The estates of the church were to a large extent given away to rapacious royal favourites, or sold at a nominal price to speculating farmers and citizens, who drove out, *en masse*, the hereditary sub-tenants and threw their holdings into one. The legally guaranteed property of the poorer folk in a part of the church's tithes was tacitly confiscated. 'Pauper ubique jacet',* cried Queen Elizabeth, after a journey through England. In the 43rd year of her reign the nation was obliged to recognise pauperism officially by the introduction of a poor-rate. 'The authors of this law seem to have been ashamed to state the grounds of it, for [contrary to traditional usage] it has no preamble whatever.' By the 16th of Charles I, ch. 4, it was declared perpetual, and in fact only in 1834 did it take a new and harsher form. These immediate results of the Reformation were not its most lasting ones. The property of the church formed the religious bulwark of the traditional conditions of landed property. With its fall these were no longer tenable.

Even in the last decade of the 17th century, the yeomanry, the class of independent peasants, were more numerous than the class of farmers. They had formed the backbone of Cromwell's strength, and, even according to the confession of Macaulay, stood in favourable contrast to the drunken squires and to their servants, the country clergy, who had to marry their masters' cast-off mistresses. About 1750, the yeomanry had disappeared, and so had, in the last decade of the 18th century, the last trace of the common land of the agricultural labourer. We leave on one side here the purely economic causes of the agricultural revolution. We deal only with the forcible means employed.

After the restoration of the Stuarts, the landed proprietors carried, by legal means, an act of usurpation, effected everywhere on the Continent without any legal formality. They abolished the feudal tenure of land, i.e. they got rid of all its obligations to the State, 'indemnified' the State by taxes on the peasantry and the rest of the mass of the people, vindicated for themselves the rights of modern private property in estates to which they had only a feudal title, and, finally, passed those laws of settlement, which, *mutatis mutandis*, had the same effect on the English agricultural labourer, as the edict of the Tartar Boris Godunof* on the Russian peasantry.

The 'glorious Revolution' brought into power, along with William of Orange, the landlord and capitalist appropriators of surplus-value. They inaugurated the new era by practising on a colossal scale thefts of state lands, thefts that had been hitherto managed more modestly. These estates were given away, sold at a ridiculous figure, or even annexed to private estates by direct seizure. All this happened without the slightest observation of legal etiquette. The Crown lands thus fraudulently appropriated, together with the robbery of the Church estates, as far as these had not been lost again during the republican revolution, form the basis of the today princely domains of the English oligarchy. The bourgeois capitalists favoured the operation with the view, among others, to promoting free trade in land, to extending the domain of modern agriculture on the large farm-system, and to increasing their supply of the free agricultural proletarians ready to hand. Besides, the new landed aristocracy was the natural ally of the new bankocracy, of the newly-hatched *haute finance*, and of the large manufacturers, then depending on protective duties. The English bourgeoisie acted for its own interest quite as wisely as did the Swedish bourgeoisie who, reversing the process, hand in hand with their economic allies, the peasantry, helped the kings in the forcible resumption of the Crown lands from the oligarchy. This happened since 1604 under Charles X and Charles XI.

Communal property—always distinct from the State property just dealt with—was an old Teutonic institution which lived on under cover of feudalism. We have seen how the forcible usurpation of this, generally accompanied by the turning of arable into pasture land, begins at the end of the 15th and extends into the 16th century. But, at that time, the process was carried on by means of individual acts of violence against which legislation, for a hundred and fifty years, fought in vain. The advance made by the 18th century shows itself in this, that the law itself becomes now the instrument of the theft of the people's land, although the large farmers make use of their little independent methods as well. The parliamentary form of the robbery is that of Acts for enclosures of Commons, in other words, decrees by which the landlords grant themselves the people's land as private property, decrees of expropriation of the people. Sir F. M. Eden refutes his own crafty special pleading, in which he tries to represent communal property as the private property of the great landlords who have taken the place of the feudal lords, when he, himself, demands a 'general Act of Parliament for the enclosure of Commons' (admitting thereby that a parliamentary *coup d'état* is necessary for its transformation into private property), and moreover calls on the legislature for the indemnification for the expropriated poor.

Whilst the place of the independent yeoman was taken by tenants at will, small farmers on yearly leases, a servile rabble dependent on the pleasure of the landlords, the systematic robbery of the Communal lands helped especially, next to the theft of the State domains, to swell those large farms, that were called in the 18th century capital farms or merchant farms, and to 'set free' the agricultural population as proletarians for manufacturing industry.

In the 19th century, the very memory of the connexion between the agricultural labourer and the communal property had, of course, vanished. To say nothing of more recent times, have the agricultural population received a farthing of compensation for the 3,511,770 acres of common land which between 1801 and 1831 were stolen from them and by parliamentary devices presented to the landlords by the landlords?

The last process of wholesale expropriation of the agricultural population from the soil is, finally, the so-called clearing of estates, i.e. the sweeping men off them. All the English methods hitherto considered culminated in 'clearing'. As we saw in the picture of modern conditions given in a former chapter, where there are no more independent peasants to get rid of, the 'clearing' of cottages begins; so that the agricultural labourers do not find on the soil cultivated by them even the spot necessary for their own housing. But what 'clearing of estates' really and properly signifies, we learn only in the promised land of modern romance, the Highlands of Scotland. There the process is distinguished by its systematic character, by the magnitude of the scale on which it is carried out at one blow (in Ireland landlords have gone to the length of sweeping away several villages at once; in

Scotland areas as large as German principalities are dealt with), finally by the peculiar form of property, under which the embezzled lands were held.

The Highland Celts were organised in clans, each of which was the owner of the land on which it was settled. The representative of the clan, its chief or 'great man', was only the titular owner of this property, just as the Queen of England is the titular owner of all the national soil. When the English government succeeded in suppressing the intestine wars of these 'great men', and their constant incursions into the Lowland plains, the chiefs of the clans by no means gave up their time-honoured trade as robbers; they only changed its form. On their own authority they transformed their nominal right into a right of private property, and as this brought them into collision with their clansmen, resolved to drive them out by open force. 'A king of England might as well claim to drive his subjects into the sea', says Professor Newman. This revolution, which began in Scotland after the last rising* of the followers of the Pretender, can be followed through its first phases in the writings of Sir James Steuart and James Anderson. In the 18th century the hunted-out Gaels were forbidden to emigrate from the country, with a view to driving them by force to Glasgow and other manufacturing towns. As an example of the method obtaining in the 19th century, the 'clearing' made by the Duchess of Sutherland will suffice here. This person, well instructed in economy, resolved, on entering upon her government, to effect a radical cure, and to turn the whole country, whose population had already been, by earlier processes of the like kind, reduced to 15,000, into a sheep-walk. From 1814 to 1820 these 15,000 inhabitants, about 3,000 families, were systematically hunted and rooted out. All their villages were destroyed and burnt, all their fields turned into pasturage. British soldiers enforced this eviction, and came to blows with the inhabitants. One old woman was burnt to death in the flames of the hut, which she refused to leave. Thus this fine lady appropriated 794,000 acres of land that had from time immemorial belonged to the clan. She assigned to the expelled inhabitants about 6,000 acres on the sea-shore—2 acres per family. The 6,000 acres had until this time lain waste, and brought in no income to their owners. The Duchess, in the nobility of her heart, actually went so far as to let these at an average rent of 2*s.* 6*d.* per acre to the clansmen, who for centuries had shed their blood for her family. The whole of the stolen clanland she divided into 29 great sheep farms, each inhabited by a single family, for the most part imported English farm-servants. In the year 1835 the 15,000 Gaels were already replaced by

131,000 sheep. The remnant of the aborigines flung on the sea-shore, tried to live by catching fish. They became amphibious and lived, as an English author says, half on land and half on water, and withal only half on both.

But the brave Gaels must expiate yet more bitterly their idolatry, romantic and of the mountains, for the 'great men' of the clan. The smell of their fish rose to the noses of the great men. They scented some profit in it, and let the sea-shore to the great fishmongers of London. For the second time the Gaels were hunted out.

The spoliation of the church's property, the fraudulent alienation of the State domains, the robbery of the common lands, the usurpation of feudal and clan property, and its transformation into modern private property under circumstances of reckless terrorism, were just so many idyllic methods of primitive accumulation. They conquered the field for capitalistic agriculture, made the soil part and parcel of capital, and created for the town industries the necessary supply of a 'free' and outlawed proletariat.

CHAPTER 28

BLOODY LEGISLATION AGAINST THE EXPROPRIATED, FROM THE END OF THE 15TH CENTURY. FORCING DOWN OF WAGES BY ACTS OF PARLIAMENT

THE proletariat created by the breaking up of the bands of feudal retainers and by the forcible expropriation of the people from the soil, this 'free' proletariat could not possibly be absorbed by the nascent manufactures as fast as it was thrown upon the world. On the other hand, these men, suddenly dragged from their wonted mode of life, could not as suddenly adapt themselves to the discipline of their new condition. They were turned *en masse* into beggars, robbers, vagabonds, partly from inclination, in most cases from stress of circumstances. Hence at the end of the 15th and during the whole of the 16th century, throughout Western Europe a bloody legislation against vagabondage. The fathers of the present working-class were chastised for their enforced transformation into vagabonds and paupers. Legislation treated them as 'voluntary' criminals, and assumed that it depended on their own good will to go on working under the old conditions that no longer existed.

Thus were the agricultural people, first forcibly expropriated from the soil, driven from their homes, turned into vagabonds, and then whipped, branded, tortured by laws grotesquely terrible, into the discipline necessary for the wage system.

It is not enough that the conditions of labour are concentrated in a mass, in the shape of capital, at the one pole of society, while at the other are grouped masses of men, who have nothing to sell but their labour-power. Neither is it enough that they are compelled to sell it voluntarily. The advance of capitalist production develops a working-class, which by education, tradition, habit, looks upon the conditions of that mode of production as self-evident laws of Nature. The organisation of the capitalist process of production, once fully developed, breaks down all resistance. The constant generation of a relative surplus-population keeps the law of supply and demand of labour, and therefore keeps wages, in a rut that corresponds with the wants of capital. The dull compulsion of economic relations completes the subjection of the labourer to the capitalist. Direct force, outside economic conditions, is of course still used, but only exceptionally. In the ordinary run of things, the labourer can be left to the 'natural laws of production', i.e. to his dependence on capital, a dependence springing from, and guaranteed in perpetuity by, the conditions of production themselves. It is otherwise during the historic genesis of capitalist production. The bourgeoisie, at its rise, wants and uses the power of the state to 'regulate' wages, i.e. to force. them within the limits suitable for surplus-value making, to lengthen the working-day and to keep the labourer himself in the normal degree of dependence. This is an essential element of the so-called primitive accumulation.

The provisions of the labour statutes as to contracts between master and workman, as to giving notice and the like, which only allow of a civil action against the contract-breaking master, but on the contrary permit a criminal action against the contract-breaking workman, are to this hour (1873) in full force. The barbarous laws against Trades' Unions fell in 1825 before the threatening bearing of the proletariat. Despite this, they fell only in part. Certain beautiful fragments of the old statute vanished only in 1859. Finally, the act of Parliament of June 29, 1871, made a pretence of removing the last traces of this class of legislation by legal recognition of Trades' Unions. But an act of Parliament of the same date (an act to amend the criminal law relating to violence, threats, and molestation), re-established, in point of fact, the former state of things in a new shape. By this Parliamentary escamotage the means which the labourers could use in a strike or lock-out were withdrawn from the laws common to all citizens, and placed under exceptional penal legislation, the interpretation of which fell to the masters themselves in their capacity as justices of the peace. Two years earlier, the same House of Commons and the same Mr Gladstone in the well-known straightforward fashion brought in a bill for the abolition of all exceptional penal legislation against the working-class. But this was never allowed to go beyond the second reading, and the matter was thus protracted until at last the 'great Liberal party,' by an alliance with the Tories, found courage to turn against the very proletariat that had carried it into power. Not content with this treachery, the 'great Liberal party' allowed the English judges, ever complaisant in the service of the ruling classes, to dig up again the earlier laws against 'conspiracy', and to apply them to coalitions of labourers. We see that only against its will and under the pressure of the masses did the English Parliament give up the laws against Strikes and Trades' Unions, after it had itself, for 500 years, held, with shameless egoism, the position of a permanent Trades' Union of the capitalists against the labourers.

During the very first storms of the revolution, the French bourgeoisie dared to take away from the workers the right of association but just acquired. By a decree of June 14, 1791, they declared all coalition of the workers as 'an attempt against liberty and the declaration of the rights of man,' punishable by a fine of 500 livres, together with deprivation of the rights of an active citizen for one year. This law which, by means of State compulsion, confined the struggle between capital and labour within limits comfortable for capital, has outlived revolutions and changes of dynasties. Even the Reign of Terror left it untouched. It was but quite recently struck out of the Penal Code. Nothing is more characteristic than the pretext for this bourgeois *coup d'état*. 'Granting', says Chapelier, the reporter of the Select Committee on this law, 'that wages ought to be a little higher than they are, . . . that they ought to be high enough for him that receives them, to be free from that state of absolute dependence due to the want of the necessaries of life, and which is almost that of slavery,' yet the workers must not be allowed to come to any understanding about their own interests, nor to act in common and thereby lessen their 'absolute dependence, which is almost that of slavery', because, forsooth, in doing this they injure 'the freedom of their cidevant masters, the present entrepreneurs', and because a coalition against the despotism of the quondam masters of the corporations is—guess what!—is a restoration of the corporations abolished by the French constitution.

CHAPTER 31

GENESIS OF THE INDUSTRIAL CAPITALIST

THE genesis of the industrial capitalist did not proceed in such a gradual way as that of the farmer. Doubtless many small guild-masters, and yet more independent small artisans, or even wage-labourers, transformed themselves into small capitalists, and (by gradually extending exploitation of wage-labour and corresponding accumulation) into full-blown capitalists. In the infancy of capitalist production, things often happened as in the infancy of mediæval towns, where the question, which of the escaped serfs should be master and which servant, was in great part decided by the earlier or later date of their flight. The snail's pace of this method corresponded in no wise with the commercial requirements of the new world-market that the great discoveries of the end of the 15th century created. But the middle ages had handed down two distinct forms of capital, which mature in the most different economic social formations, and which, before the era of the capitalist mode of production, are considered as capital quand même—usurer's capital and merchant's capital.

At present, all the wealth of society goes first into the possession of the capitalist . . . he pays the landowner his rent, the labourer his wages, the tax and tithe gatherer their claims, and keeps a large, indeed the largest, and a continually augmenting share, of the annual produce of labour for himself. The capitalist may now be said to be the first owner of all the wealth of the community, though no law has conferred on him the right to this property . . . this change has been effected by the taking of interest on capital . . . and it is not a little curious that all the law-givers of Europe endeavoured to prevent this by statutes, viz., statutes against usury. . . . The power of the capitalist over all the wealth of the country is a complete change in the right of property, and by what law, or series of laws, was it effected?

The author should have remembered that revolutions are not made by laws.

The money capital formed by means of usury and commerce was prevented from turning into industrial capital, in the country by the feudal constitution, in the towns by the guild organisation. These fetters vanished with the dissolution of feudal society, with the expropriation and partial eviction of the country population. The new manufactures were established at sea-ports, or at inland points beyond the control of the old municipalities and their guilds. Hence in England an embittered struggle of the corporate towns against these new industrial nurseries.

The discovery of gold and silver in America, the extirpation, enslavement and entombment in mines of the aboriginal population, the beginning of the conquest and looting of the East Indies, the turning of Africa into a warren for the commercial hunting of black-skins, signalised the rosy dawn of the era of capitalist production. These idyllic proceedings are the chief momenta of primitive accumulation. On their heels treads the commercial war of the European nations, with the globe for a theatre. It begins with the revolt of the Netherlands from Spain, assumes giant dimensions in England's Anti-Jacobin War, and is still going on in the opium wars against Chian, etc.

The different momenta of primitive accumulation distribute themselves now, more or less in chronological order, particularly over Spain, Portugal, Holland, France, and England. In England at the end of the 17th century, they arrive at a systematical combination, embracing the colonies, the national debt, the modern mode of taxation, and the protectionist system. These methods depend in part on brute force, e.g. the colonial system. But they all employ the power of the State, the concentrated and organised force of society, to hasten, hot-house fashion, the process of transformation of the feudal mode of production into the capitalist mode, and to shorten the transition. Force is the midwife of every old society pregnant with a new one. It is itself an economic power.

With the development of capitalist production during the manufacturing period, the public opinion of Europe had lost the last remnant of shame and conscience. The nations bragged cynically of every infamy that served them as a means to capitalistic accumulation. Read, e.g. the naïve Annals of Commerce of the worthy A. Anderson. Here it is trumpeted forth as a triumph of English statecraft that at the Peace of Utrecht, England extorted from the Spaniards by the Asiento Treaty the privilege of being allowed to ply the negro-trade, until then only carried on between Africa and the English West Indies, between Africa and Spanish America as well. England thereby acquired the right of supplying Spanish America until 1743 with 4,800 negroes yearly. This threw, at the same time, an official cloak over British smuggling. Liverpool waxed fat on the slave-trade. This was its method of primitive accumulation. And, even to the present day, Liverpool 'respectability' is the Pindar of the slave-trade* which—compare the work of Aikin [1795] already quoted—'has coincided with that spirit of bold adventure which has characterised the trade of Liverpool and rapidly carried it to its present state of prosperity; has occasioned vast employ-ment for shipping and sailors, and greatly augmented the demand for the manufactures of the country' (p. 339). Liverpool employed in the slave-trade, in 1730, 15 ships; in 1751, 53; in 1760, 74; in 1770, 96; and in 1792, 132.

Whilst the cotton industry introduced child-slavery in England, it gave in the United States a stimulus to the transformation of the earlier, more or less patriarchal slavery, into a system of commercial exploitation. It fact, the veiled slavery of the wage-workers in Europe needed, for its pedestal, slavery pure and simple in the new world.

Tantæ molis erat,* to establish the 'eternal laws of Nature' of the capitalist mode of production, to complete the process of separation between labourers and conditions of labour, to transform, at one pole, the social means of production and subsistence into capital, at the opposite pole, the mass of the population into wage-labourers, into 'free labouring poor', that artificial product of modern society. If money, according to Augier, 'comes into the world with a congenital blood-stain on one cheek', capital comes dripping from head to foot, from every pore, with blood and dirt.

CHAPTER 32

HISTORICAL TENDENCY OF CAPITALIST ACCUMULATION

WHAT does the primitive accumulation of capital, i.e. its historical genesis, resolve itself into? In so far as it is not immediate transformation of slaves and serfs into wage-labourers, and therefore a mere change of form, it only means the expropriation of the immediate producers, i.e. the dissolution of private property based on the labour of its owner. Private property, as the antithesis to social, collective property, exists only where the means of labour and the external conditions of labour belong to private individuals. But according as these private individuals are labourers or not labourers, private property has a different character. The numberless shades, that it at first sight presents, correspond to the intermediate stages lying between these two extremes. The private property of the labourer in his means of production is the foundation of petty industry, whether agricultural, manufacturing, or both; petty industry, again, is an essential condition for the development of social production and of the free individuality of the labourer himself. Of course, this petty mode of production exists also under slavery, serfdom, and other states of dependence. But it flourishes, it lets loose its whole energy, it attains its adequate classical form, only where the labourer is the private owner of his own means of labour set in action by himself: the peasant of the land which he cultivates, the artisan of the tool which he handles as a virtuoso. This mode of production pre-supposes parcelling of the soil, and scattering of the other means of production. As it excludes the concentration of these means of production, so also it excludes co-operation, division of labour within each separate process of production, the control over, and the productive application of the forces of Nature by society, and the free development of the social productive powers. It is compatible only with a system of production, and a society, moving within narrow and more or less primitive bounds. To perpetuate it would be, as Pecqueur rightly says, 'to decree universal mediocrity'. At a certain stage of development it brings forth the material agencies for its own dissolution. From that moment new forces and new passions spring up in the bosom of society; but the old social organisation fetters them and keeps them down. It must be annihilated; it is annihilated. Its annihilation, the transformation of the individualised and scattered means of production into socially concentrated ones, of the pigmy property of the many into the huge property of the few, the expropriation of the great mass of the people from the soil, from the means of subsistence, and from the means of labour, this fearful and painful expropriation of the mass of the people forms the prelude to the history of capital. It comprises a series of forcible methods, of which we have passed in review only those that have been epoch-making as methods of the primitive accumulation of capital. The expropriation of the immediate producers was accomplished with merciless Vandalism, and under the stimulus of passions the most infamous, the most sordid, the pettiest, the most meanly odious. Self-earned private property, that is based, so to say, on the fusing together of the isolated, independent labouring-individual with the conditions of his labour, is supplanted by capitalistic private property, which rests on exploitation of the nominally free labour of others, i.e. on wage-labour.

As soon as this process of transformation has sufficiently decomposed the old society from top to bottom, as soon as the labourers are turned into proletarians, their means of labour into capital, as soon as the capitalist mode of production stands on its own feet, then the further socialisation of labour and further transformation of the land and other means of production into socially exploited and, therefore, common means of production, as well as the further expropriation of private proprietors, takes a new form. That which is now to be expropriated is no longer the labourer working for himself, but the capitalist exploiting many labourers. This expropriation is accomplished by the action of the immanent laws of capitalistic production itself, by the centralisation of capital. One capitalist always kills many. Hand in hand with this centralisation, or this expropriation of many capitalists by few, develop, on an ever-extending scale, the co-operative form of the labour-process, the conscious technical application of science, the methodical cultivation of the soil, the transformation of the instruments of labour into instruments of labour only usable in common, the economising of all means of production by their use as the means of production of combined, socialised labour, the entanglement of all peoples in the net of the world-market, and with this, the international character of the capitalistic regime. Along with the constantly diminishing number of the magnates of capital, who usurp and monopolise all advantages of this process of transformation, grows the mass of misery, oppression, slavery, degradation, exploitation; but with this too grows the revolt of the working-class, a class always increasing in numbers, and disciplined, united, organised by the very mechanism of the process of capitalist production itself. The monopoly of capital becomes a fetter upon the mode of production, which has sprung up and flourished along with, and under it. Centralisation of the means of production and socialisation of labour at last reach a point where they become incompatible with their capitalist integument. Thus integument is burst asunder. The knell of capitalist private property sounds. The expropriators are expropriated.

The capitalist mode of appropriation, the result of the capitalist mode of production, produces capitalist private property. This is the first negation of individual private property, as founded on the labour of the proprietor. But capitalist production begets, with the inexorability of a law of Nature, its own negation. It is the negation of negation. This does not re-establish private property for the producer, but gives him individual property based on the acquisitions of the capitalist era: i.e. on co-operation and the possession in common of the land and of the means of production.

The transformation of scattered private property, arising from individual labour, into capitalist private property is, naturally, a process, incomparably more protracted, violent, and difficult, than the transformation of capitalistic private property, already practically resting on socialised production, into socialised property. In the former case, we had the expropriation of the mass of the people by a few usurpers; in the latter, we have the expropriation of a few usurpers by the mass of the people.

From RESULTS OF THE
IMMEDIATE PROCESS OF
PRODUCTION

From RESULTS OF THE IMMEDIATE PROCESS OF PRODUCTION

Alienation in the Productive Process

. . . But everything is changed when we examine the process of valorization. Here it is not the worker who uses the means of production, but the means of production which use the worker. It is not living labour which realizes itself in material labour as its objective organ, but it is material labour which conserves itself and grows by absorbing living labour to such an extent that it becomes value creating value, capital in movement. . . .

In circulation, the capitalist and the worker only face each other as sellers of commodities. But, owing to the specifically bipolar nature of the commodities that they sell each other, the worker necessarily enters into the productive process as an integral part of the use-value or real mode of existence or value-existence of capital: thus their relationship is only realized *inside* the productive process and the capitalist potential (which has bought labour) only really becomes capitalist when the labourer (potential wage-earner through the sale of his labour-power) really passes under the direction of capital in the productive process.

The functions exercised by the capitalist are no more than the consciously and wilfully executed functions of capital-value which valorizes itself by absorbing living labour. The capitalist only functions as the personification of capital, capital in person, just as the worker is only labour personified, labour which belongs to the worker as far as its hardship and effort goes and to the capitalist as far as it is a substance creating ever greater riches; in short, the worker appears as an element incorporated into capital within the productive process, as its living and variable factor.

The domination of the capitalist over the worker is thus the domination of the thing over man, of dead labour over living labour, of the product over the producer; for the commodities which become the means of domination (in fact only over the worker) are themselves merely the results of the productive process, *its* products.

At the level of material production, the true process of social life—which is nothing but the productive process—we find the same relationship as obtains at the level of ideology, in religion: the subject is transformed into object and vice versa.

From the historical point of view, this inversion represents a transitional phase which is necessary in order to force the majority of humanity to produce wealth for itself by inexorably developing the productive forces of social labour which alone can constitute the material basis for a free human society. It is necessary to go through this antagonistic form, just as it is necessary at first to give man's spiritual forces a religious form by erecting them into autonomous power over against him.

This is the 'process of alienation' of man's own labour. From the start, the worker is superior to the capitalist in that the capitalist is rooted in his 'process of alienation' and is completely content therein, whereas the worker who is its victim finds himself from the beginning in a state of rebellion against it and experiences the process as one of enslavement. . . . The self-valorization of capital—the creation of surplus value—is the determining, supreme, and dominant aim of the capitalist, the complete motive and content of his actions, the rationalized instinct and aim of the miser—a poor content which demonstrates that the capitalist is in the same slavish relation to capital as the worker, although at the opposite pole.

Man can only live if he produces means of subsistence, but he can only produce these means if he holds the means of production, the material conditions for labour. It is easy to understand that, if the worker is deprived of the means of production, he is also deprived of the means of subsistence, just as, inversely, if he is deprived of the means of subsistence, he cannot create his means of production.

What first of all—even before the real transformation of money or the commodity into capital—gives the character of *capital* to the conditions of labour is not the nature of money, commodities, or material use-values as means of subsistence and means of production; it is the fact that this money and these commodities, these means of subsistence, arise as autonomous powers, personified by their owners, over against labour power which is deprived of all material wealth; it is the fact that the material conditions, indispensable to the realization of labour, are alienated from the worker and, what is more, appear as fetishes endowed with their own will and soul; it is finally the fact that commodities figure as buyers of people. . . .

Money cannot become capital without first of all being exchanged for the labour power that the worker sells as a commodity; on the other hand, labour can only earn wages from the moment when the worker's own objective conditions arise over against him as autonomous forces, the property of someone else, value existing for itself and bringing everything back to itself—in short, capital. Therefore, if from the point of view of its matter—that is, its use-value—capital is reduced to the objective conditions of labour, from the formal point of view these conditions must oppose labour as autonomous and alien powers, as value (objectified labour) which treats living labour simply as a means of conserving and increasing itself. Wage-labour is thus a form of labour that is socially necessary for capitalist production, just as capital—value concentrated into a power—in the socially necessary form that the objective conditions of labour must assume in order for it to be wage-labour.

It follows that wage-labour is the necessary condition for the formation of capital and always remains the necessary premiss of capitalist production. This is why, even if the first process—that of the exchange of money for labour power or purchase of labour power—does not as such form part of the immediate process of production, it does on the other hand form part of the general production of the relationship.

In the eyes of the capitalist, the worker, and the economist (who cannot conceive of the work process outside the process of capitalist appropriation) the material elements of the labour process appear, in virtue of their material properties, as capital. This is why the economist is incapable of distinguishing between these simple factors in the labour process and the social property that is amalgamated with them—that of capital. He is incapable because, in reality, it is one and the same labour process (in which the means of production, by their material properties, simply serve as aids to labour) which transforms these means of production into simple means for the absorption of labour.

In the labour process considered in itself, the worker was the means of production; in the labour process which is at the same time the capitalist process of production, the means of production employ the worker in such a way that the labour is no more than a means by which a given sum of values, or a determinate mass of objectified labour, absorbs living labour in order to conserve and increase itself. The labour process is thus the process of the self-valorization of objectified labour thanks to living labour.

Thus capital uses the worker, the worker does not use capital: and capital is only composed of the objects which employ the worker and thus have an existence, a will, and a consciousness personified in the capitalist. . . .

Classical political economy had the great merit of conceiving the whole process of production as taking place between objectified labour and living labour, living labour being opposed to capital, simple objectified labour, that is, value which valorizes itself thanks to living labour.

Its only faults are: (1) It has not been able to show how this exchange of a greater quantity of living labour against a lesser quantity of objectified labour does not contradict the law of the exchange of commodities, in other words, the determination of the value of commodities by labour time. (2) As a result, it identifies the exchange of a determinate quantity of objectified labour for labour power in the circulation process purely and simply with the assumption of living labour in the production process by objectified labour under the form of the means of production; whence the confusion between the exchange process of variable capital for labour power and the assumption process of living labour by constant capital in the production process.

These errors are explicable in terms of the hold that capital exercises on the economists. In fact, the exchange of a lesser quantity of objectified labour against a larger quantity of living labour appears as a single and unique process without, in the capitalist's eyes, any intermediary: does he not pay for the labour only after it has been valorized? . . .

The axiom of classical economics is the mobility of the labour force and the fluidity of capital. This is accurate in as much as the capitalist mode of production tends in that direction remorselessly, despite all the obstacles that it creates—for the most part of its own accord. In any case, in order to lay bare the laws of economics in their purity, we must make an abstraction of these obstacles, just as in pure mechanics we ignore secondary frictions which, in each particular case, must be removed so that the law can be applied. . . .

Capitalism as a Stage towards Socialism

In the course of their development, society's forces of production or productive forces of labour are socialized, and become directly social (collective) thanks to co-operation, the division of labour on the shopfloor, the use of mechanization and, in general, the changes which the process of production undergoes thanks to the conscious use of the natural sciences, mechanics, chemistry, etc. applied to definite technological ends, and thanks to all that is related to labour performed on a large scale, etc. It is only this socialized labour that is able to apply the general products of human development—for example mathematics—to the process of immediate production, as the development of these sciences is in its turn determined by the level reached by the material process of production.

All this development of the productive force of socialized labour—just like the application of science, that general product of social development—is opposed to the more or less remote and scattered labour of the particular individual. This is all the more true inasmuch as everything is presented directly as a productive force of capital, and not as a productive force of labour, whether it is the force of the isolated worker, or of workers associated in the process of production, or even of a productive force of labour which could be identified with capital.

This mystification, proper to the capitalist relationship in general, will develop from now on much more than could be the case in the simple formal submission of labour to capital. Furthermore, it is only at this level that the historical significance of capitalist production appears in a striking (specific) way, precisely through the changes undergone by the immediate process of production and through the development of the productive social forces of labour.

Factory Worker and Artisan

It is evident that the worker works with more continuity for the capitalist than does the artisan for his chance customers; his labour is not limited by the fortuitous needs of particular buyers but only by the exploitation needs of the capital which employs him. Compared to the labour of the slave, that of the free worker is more productive, because it is more intense. The slave only works swayed by fear, and it is not his existence itself which is at stake, since it is guaranteed to him even if it does not belong to him. The free worker, on the other hand, is impelled by his needs. The consciousness (or rather the idea) of being solely determined by himself, of being free, as well as the feeling (sense) of the responsibility which is connected with this, make him a much better worker, because like every seller of goods, he is responsible for the goods which he supplies and obliged to supply them at a certain quality, at the risk of being ousted by the other sellers of the same goods.

The continuity of the relationship between the slave and the supporter of slavery was assured by the constraint experienced directly by the slave. On the other hand, the free worker himself is obliged to assure the continuity of his relationship, for his existence and that of his family depend on the continued renewal of the sale of his labour force to the capitalist.

Productive and Unproductive Labour

In capitalist production, the absolute rule becomes, on the one hand, the production of articles in the form of commodities and, on the other hand, wage-earning labour. A great number of functions and activities which, now adorned with a halo and considered as ends in themselves, were formerly carried on gratuitously or remunerated in an indirect way (in Britain, for example, the learned professions, doctors, barristers, etc., could not and still cannot bring an action in law to be paid), change directly into wage-earning labour (however diverse their content) or fall within the scope of laws regulating wage value, as far as concerns the estimation of their value and the cost of the different services, from that of the whore to that of the king. . . .

With the development of capitalist production, all services change into wage-earning labour and all those who carry them on into wage-earning workers, so that they acquire this character in common with the productive workers. This is what leads some people to confuse these two categories, inasmuch as wages are a phenomenon and a creation characterizing capitalist production. Moreover, this gives capital's apologists the opportunity to change the productive worker, under the pretence that he is a wage-earner, with a worker who simply exchanges his services (that is his labour as use-value) for money. This is to overlook a little conveniently what characterize in a fundamental way the productive worker and capitalist production: the production of surplus value and the self-valorization process of capital which incorporates living labour as simple money. The soldier is a wage-earner, if he is a mercenary, but he is not for all that a productive worker.

The process of capitalist production does not simply create commodities, it absorbs unpaid labour and changes the means of production into means of absorbing unpaid labour.

From the above it follows that productive labour in no way implies that it has an exact content, a particular usefulness, a definite use-value in which it is materialized. This is what explains why labour of the same content can be either productive or unproductive.

For example, Milton, the author of *Paradise Lost*, is an unproductive worker, whereas a writer who supplies his publisher with a manufactured work is a productive worker. Milton has produced his poem as a silkworm produces silk, by expressing his nature through his activity. By later selling his product for the sum of £5, he was, to this extent, a merchant. On the other hand, the proletarian man of letters in Leipzig who, at his publisher's command, produces books—for example, economics texts—is similar to the productive worker to the extent that his production is subject to capital and only exists with a view to its valorization.

A singer who sings like a bird is an unproductive worker, to the extent that she sells her song for money she is a wage-earner and a merchant. But this very singer becomes a productive worker, when she is engaged by a contractor to sing and make money, since she directly produces capital. The teacher in the class-room is not a productive worker; but he becomes productive if he is engaged with others as a wage-earner in order to valorize, with his labour, the money of the contractor of an establishment which exploits learning. Indeed, most of these labours are scarcely subject formally to capital: they are transitory forms.

On the whole, labour which can only be utilized as service, because its products are inseparable from their author so that they cannot become autonomous commodities (which does not prevent them, nevertheless, from being exploited in a directly capitalist way), represents a derisory amount in relation to that of capitalist production.

The same labour (for example, that of a gardener, a tailor) can be performed by the same worker on behalf of a capitalist or on immediate uses. In the two cases, he is wage-earning or hired by the day, but, if he works for the capitalist, he is a productive worker, since he produces capital, whereas if he works for a direct user he is unproductive. Indeed, in the first case, his labour represents an element of the process of self-valorization of capital, but not in the second.

A great part of the annual product which is consumed as income and no longer returns to production as means of production consists of the most nefarious products (use-values), satisfying the most unhealthy envies and caprices. However that may be, their content is completely indifferent as regards determining productive labour. (It is obvious, however, that if a disproportionate part was consumed in this way, at the expense of the means of production and subsistence which enter into the reproduction whether of goods or of the labour force, the development of wealth would suffer a stoppage.) This sort of productive labour creates use-values, and is crystallized in products destined solely for unproductive consumption and themselves deprived of any use-value for the process of reproduction.

They would only be able to acquire usefulness by exchanging themselves for use-values destined for reproduction. However, that would be a simple displacement, as they must necessarily be consumed somewhere in a non-reproductive way.

Here are some comments in advance about this subject: current economics is incapable of saying anything sensible whatever—even from the capitalist point of view—on the limits of the production of luxury products. None the less, the question becomes very simple, if we analyse the elements of the process of reproduction correctly. From the capitalist point of view, luxury becomes condemnable from the time when the process of reproduction—or its progress accomplished by the simple natural progression of population—meets a check in the disproportionate application of productive labour to the creation of articles which are not used for reproduction, so that there is insufficient reproduction of the necessary means of subsistence and means of production. Furthermore, luxury is an absolute necessity for a mode of production which, creating wealth for non-producers, must give it forms which only permit its appropriation by those who are sybarites.

For the worker, this productive labour is, like any other, the sole means of which he disposes to reproduce his necessary means of subsistence. For his capitalist, who is indifferent to the nature of use-value and to the character of utilized concrete labour, it is only a means of coining money and of producing surplus value.

The supreme ideal of capitalist production is—at the same time as it increases net produce in a relative way—to reduce as much as possible the number of those who live on wages, and to increase as much as possible the number of those who live on net produce.

Alienated Labour

Even in the purely formal relationship—valid in general for any capitalist production, since the latter conserves, even in its full development, the characteristics of its underdeveloped mode—the means of production, the material conditions of labour, are not subject to the worker, but it is he who is subject to them: it is capital which employs labour. In this simple manner, this relationship enhances the personification of objects and the reification of people.

But the relationship becomes more complex and apparently more mysterious when, with the development of the specifically capitalist mode of production, it is no longer only the objects—those products of labour, use-values and exchange-values—which rear themselves as capital over against the worker, but also the social forms of labour which present themselves as forms of development of capital, so that the productive forces, thus developed, of social labour appear as productive forces of capital: as such, they are 'capitalized', over against labour. Indeed, collective unity is found in co-operation, the association and division of labour, the utilization of natural forces, sciences and products of labour in the form of machines. All that is opposed to the individual worker as something which is alien to him and exists at the outset in a material form; what is more, it seems to him that he has not contributed anything, or even that all this exists despite what he does.

In short, all the things become independent of him, simple modes of existence of the means of labour which dominate him as objects. The intelligence and will of the collective workshop seem embodied in its representatives—the capitalist or his lieutenants—to the extent that the workers are associated in the workshop and the functions of capital embodied in the capitalist are opposed to them.

The social forms of labour of the individual workers—subjectively as well as objectively—or, in other words, the form of their own social labour, are relationships established according to a mode quite independent of them: by being subject to capital, the workers become elements of these social formations, which rear up over against them like forms of capital itself, as if they belonged to it—unlike the labour power of the workers—and as if they were derived from capital and were immediately incorporated in it.

All this adopts forms that are all the more real in that, on the one hand, the labour power itself is modified by these forms to the point where it becomes powerless when it is separated from them. In other words, its autonomous productive force is shattered when it is no longer in the capitalist relationship. On the other hand, machinery develops so that the conditions of labour manage, even from the technological point of view, to dominate labour at the same time as they replace it, suppress it, and make it superfluous in the forms where it is autonomous.

In this process, the social characteristics of labour appear to the workers as if they were capitalized over against them: in machinery, for example, the visible products of labour appear to dominate labour. The same of course goes for the forces of nature and science (that product of general historical development in its abstract quintessence), which oppose the worker as powers of capital, by actually being separate from the art and knowledge of the individual worker. Although they are, in their origin, the product of labour, they appear as if they are incorporated in capital, and the worker scarcely enters into the process of labour. The capitalist who uses a machine does not need to understand it (cf. Ure); yet science realized in the machine appears as capital over against the workers. In fact, all these applications—based on associated labour—of science, of the forces of nature, and of the products of labour in bulk appear solely as means of exploiting labour and appropriating surplus labour, and therefore as forces themselves belonging to capital. Of course, capital utilizes all these means with the sole aim of exploiting labour, but, to do this, it has to apply them to production. It is in this way that the development of productive social forces of labour and the conditions of this development appear as the work of capital, and the worker finds himself, confronted with all this, in a relationship which is not only passive but also antagonistic.

Capital thus becomes a quite mysterious being.

The conditions of labour are gathered as social forces over against the worker, and it is in this form that they are capitalized.

Capital appears therefore as productive:

(1) Because it compels the worker to perform surplus labour. Now if labour is productive, it is precisely due to the fact that it performs surplus labour and that a difference is effected between the value of labour power and that of its valorization;

(2) Because it personified and represents, in an objectified form, the 'forces of the social production of labour' or productive forces of social labour.

We have already seen that the law of capitalist production—the creation of surplus value, etc.—imposes itself as a compulsion which the capitalists exert on one another as well as on the workers; in short it is a law of capital which works against both.

The force, of a social nature, of labour does not develop in the process of valorization as such, but in the process of real labour. This is why it appears as a characteristic quality inherent in capital as a thing, like its use-value. Productive (of value) labour continues to oppose capital as the labour of individual workers, whatever the social combination in which these workers enter the process of production. While capital is opposed to workers as a social force of labour, productive labour itself always appears over against capital as the labour of individual workers.

By analysing the process of accumulation, we have seen that it is as the immanent force of capital that there appears the element thanks to which past labour—in the form of productive forces and of conditions of production already produced—increases reproduction. This happens from the point of view of use-value as well as of exchange-value, whose value aggregate is conserved by a definite quantity of living labour, just as the aggregate of use-values is produced afresh. In fact, objectified labour always operates by capitalizing itself over against the worker.

The Reproduction of the Capitalist Relationship

The product of capitalist production is not only surplus value—it is capital.

Even after its change into factors of the labour process—into means of production, constant capital, and into the labour power into which variable capital changes—the sum of money or of value advanced is only capital in itself and potentially, but it was this still more before this transformation. It is only in the heat of the production process, when in reality living labour is incorporated into the material elements of capital and when the additional labour is in fact absorbed, that not only this labour, but also the sum of value advanced, becomes real and active capital. Instead of just possible capital, capital by destination.

What is happening during the total process? The worker sells the disposal of his capacity to labour in exchange for a certain value, determined by the value of his labour power, so as to make sure of the necessary means of subsistence. What is the result of it for him? Simply and purely, the reproduction of his labour power. What does he give in exchange? The activity which conserves, creates, and increases value: his labour. Setting aside the wastage of his labour power, it comes out of the process as it went in, a simple subjective labour power which has to run through the same cycle to conserve itself.

Capital, on the other hand, does not come out of the process as it went into it: it is only in this process that it changes into true capital, into value which valorizes itself. The global product which is born of it is now the form of existence of realized capital: as such, it again meets the worker as the property of the capitalist, as an autonomous power, although it has been created by labour.

Thus this process not only reproduces capital but also produces it. In the beginning, the production conditions oppose the worker as capital to the extent that he finds them objectified beforehand over against him; now it is the very product of his labour that he finds before him, as production conditions changed into capital. What was a premiss has now become the result of the production process.

To say that the production process creates capital is only another way of saying that it creates surplus value. But that is not all.

Surplus value is reconverted into additional capital and therefore appears as the creation of new capital or of enlarged capital. Capital not only realizes itself but also creates more capital. Thus the accumulation process is immanent to the capitalist production process: it implies the creation of new wage-earning workers and new means of realizing and increasing the existing capital, whether capital subjects to itself strata of the population which up till then still escaped it, for example women and children, or whether it acquires an increased number of workers by the natural rise in population.

On closer inspection we notice that capital regulates, according to the demands of its exploitation, the production of the labour forces and of the exploited human masses. Thus capital produces not only capital but also a growing mass of workers, thanks to which alone it can operate as additional capital. Labour therefore does not only produce—in opposition to itself and on a continually increased scale—labour conditions in the form of capital; capital produces, on an always enlarged scale, the productive wage-earning workers whom it needs. Labour produces its own production conditions like capital, and capital produces labour in a wage-earning form as a means of realizing it as capital.

Capitalist production is not only reproduction of the relationship, it is its reproduction on an ever wider scale. To the very extent that the force of the social production of labour develops, with the capitalist mode of production, the wealth accumulated over against the worker increases and dominates him as capital: the world of wealth swells before the worker like a world which is alien to him and which dominates him, in proportion as poverty, want, and dependence increase for him. His destitution accompanies this plethora, while there increases yet further the mass of this living means of production of capital which is the working proletariat.

The growth of capital there goes hand in hand with the increase in the proletariat: they are two products burgeoning at opposite poles of one and the same process.

The relationship is not only reproduced, but continues to produce on a still more immense scale, by always creating more workers, by continually subjecting to itself new branches of production. While it is reproduced—as we have emphasized, when describing the specifically capitalist mode of production—in conditions ever more favourable to one of these poles, that of the capitalists, it is reproduced in conditions ever more unfavourable to the other, that of the wage-earning workers.

From the point of view of the continuity of the production process, wages are only the part of the product which, after being created by the worker, changes into means of subsistence, in other words into means of conserving and increasing the labour power necessary to capital for its self-valorization and its vital process. This conservation and this increase in labour force—the result of the process—therefore appear simply as the reproduction and enlargement of the conditions of reproduction and accumulation which belong to capital.

Thus there disappears even the appearance which still continued to exist on the surface, namely that capitalist and worker free each other as owners of commodities, equal in law, in circulation, and in the market and that like all the other owners of commodities the only thing that distinguishes them is the material content of their goods, the particular use-value of the goods which they sell to each other. In other words, this original form of relationship only continues to exist as the pure reflection of the underlying capitalist relationship.

Here we must distinguish two stages: the reproduction of the relationship itself on an ever wider scale, such as it results from the capitalist production process, and the form that it assumes historically at the time of its birth and that it assumes again continually on the surface of developed capitalist society.

1. The introductory process, which develops inside the sphere of circulation, is the sale and purchase of labour power. The capitalist process of production is not only transformation into capital of the value of the goods which the capitalist throws on to the market or puts back into the labour process: these changed products are not his products, but those of the worker. The capitalist constantly sells, for labour, a part of this product—the means of subsistence necessary for the conservation and growth of labour power, and he constantly lends to it another of them—the objective conditions of labour—as means of self-valorization of capital, as capital. In this way, whereas the worker reproduces his products as capital, the capitalist reproduces the worker as wage-earner, that is as a seller of his own labour. The relationship between simple sellers of goods would imply that they exchanged their own labour incorporated in different use-values. The purchase/sale of labour force, as a constant result of capitalist production implies, on the contrary, that the worker is constantly buying again a fraction of his own product, in exchange for his living labour.

It is in this way that there disappears the appearance of the simple relationship between owners of goods: the constant act of purchase/sale of labour power and the ceaseless confrontation of the goods produced by the worker himself as purchaser of his labour power and as variable capital are only forms which mediate his subjection to capital, living labour being only a simple means of conservation and increase of objectified labour, become autonomous over against it.

The form of mediation inherent in the capitalist mode of production is therefore used to perpetuate the relationship between the capital which purchases the labour, and the worker who sells it; however, it is only different in form from the other more or less direct modes of subjection and appropriation of labour by the owners of the conditions of production. It conceals under the simple monetary relationship the true transaction and the dependence perpetuated thanks to the mediation of the sale/purchase act which is renewed constantly. This relationship continually reproduces not only the conditions of this trade but also its results, namely what one purchases and what the other sells. The perpetual renewal of this relationship of purchase/sale only serves to mediate the continuity of the specific relationship of dependence, by giving it the mystifying appearance of a transaction, a contract between owners of good endowed with equal rights and similarly equally free one in front of the other. Thus, the initial relationship becomes itself an immanent stage in the domination of living labour by objectified labour which has established itself with capitalist production.

Both the following groups are therefore mistaken:

Those who consider wage-earning labour, the sale of labour to capital, in short the status of the wage-earner, as external to capitalist production. In fact, wage-earning labour is a form of mediation that is essential and continually reproduced by the relationship of capitalist production.

Those who see the substance itself in the superficial relationship of purchase/sale, in this essential formality and in this reflection of the capitalist relationship, and who as a result claim to subordinate the relationship between workers and capitalists to the general relationship between owners of goods, in order to vindicate it and efface its specific differences.

2. The premisses of the formation of the capitalist relationship in general arise at a definite historical level of social production. It is necessary that in the womb of the previous mode of production, the means of production and circulation, and even needs must be developed to the point when they tend to surpass the former relations of production and change them into capitalist relationships. In the long term, it is sufficient for them to permit a formal surrender of labour to

capital. On the basis of this new relationship, there develops a specifically different mode of production which, on the one hand, creates new material productive forces and, on the other hand, develops on this basis to create new actual conditions. It is a question of a complete economic revolution: on the one hand capital begins by producing the actual conditions of the domination of capital over labour—then it perfects them and gives them an adequate form; on the other hand, as regards the productive forces of labour, the conditions of production are relationships of circulation developed by it in opposition to the workers, it creates the actual conditions of a new mode of production which, by abolishing the antagonistic form of capitalism, lays the material foundations of a new social life and of a new form of society.

Our conception differs fundamentally from that of the economists who, imprisoned in the capitalist system, see clearly how one produces in the capitalist relationship, but not how this relationship itself is produced and at the same time creates the material conditions of its dissolution, doing away at the same stroke with its historical justification as a necessary form of the economic development and the production of social wealth.

On the contrary, we have seen not only how capital produces but also how it is itself produced, and how it comes out of the production process essentially different from what it was on going in to it. In fact, on the one hand, it changes the former mode of production; on the other hand, this change, together with a given level of the development of the material productive forces, form the basis and the preliminary condition of its own revolution.

Man is distinct from all other animal species in that his needs have no limits and are completely elastic; no other animal can repress his needs in as extraordinary a way, and limit his conditions of life to such a minimum. In short, there is no animal with more tendency to *irelandization*. In the value of labour power, there is no room for the consideration of this psychological minimum of existence.

The price of labour power—like that of any other commodity—can rise above or fall below it value, in other words deviate, in one direction or the other, from the price which is the monetary expression of value. The level of vital needs, whose sum total represents the value of labour power, can increase or diminish. . . .

Later on in our study, we shall see that, for the analysis of capital, it is quite immaterial whether we presuppose a low or high level of the needs of the workers. Moreover, in theory as in practice, we start from the value of labour power as a given quantity. For example, if a fortunate individual wishes to convert his money into capital—into, let us say, capital to exploit a cotton factory—he will first of all inquire about the average level of wages in the area where he intends to establish himself. He knows that wages—like the price of cotton—continually deviate from the average, but that these fluctuations in the end counterbalance each other. In the settlement of his accounts, he therefore takes wages as a given quantity of value.

Moreover, the value of labour power constitutes the rational and declared basis of the Trades Unions, whose importance for the working class it is vital not to underestimate. The aim of the Trade Unions is to prevent the level of wages from falling below the amount traditionally paid in the various branches of industry, and to prevent the price of the labour power from falling below its value. Of course they know that if the relationship between offer and demand changes, the market price also changes. However, on the one hand, such a change is far from being the simple unilateral act of the purchaser, in our case of the capitalist; on the other hand, there is a great difference between on the one hand, the amount of wages as it is determined by supply and demand (that is the amount resulting from the 'honest' operation of the exchange of goods, when purchaser and seller deal on an equal footing) and, on the other hand, the amount of wages which the seller—the worker—is forced to accept, when the capitalist deals with each worker taken in isolation and imposes a low wage on him, exploiting the exceptional adversity of the solitary worker, independently of the general relationship of supply and demand.

From VOLUME THREE

CHAPTER 9

FORMATION OF A GENERAL
RATE OF PROFIT (AVERAGE RATE OF PROFIT)
AND TRANSFORMATION OF THE
VALUES OF COMMODITIES INTO
PRICES OF PRODUCTION

THE organic composition of capital depends at any given time on two circumstances: first, on the technical relation of labour-power employed to the mass of the means of production employed; secondly, on the price of these means of production. This composition, as we have seen, must be examined on the basis of percentage ratios. We express the organic composition of a certain capital consisting $\frac{4}{5}$ of constant and $\frac{1}{5}$ of variable capital, by the formula $80_c + 20_v$. It is furthermore assumed in this comparison that the rate of surplus-value is unchangeable. Let it be any rate picked at random; say, 100%. The capital of $80_c + 20_v$ then produces a surplus-value of 20_s, and this yields a rate of profit of 20% on the total capital. The magnitude of the actual value of its product depends on the magnitude of the fixed part of the constant capital, and on the portion which passes from it through wear and tear into the product. But since this circumstance has absolutely no bearing on the rate of profit, and hence, in the present analysis, we shall assume, for the sake of simplicity, that the constant capital is everywhere uniformly and entirely transferred to the annual product of the capitals. It is further assumed that the capitals in the different spheres of production annually realise the same quantities of surplus-value proportionate to the magnitude of their variable parts. For the present, therefore, we disregard the difference which may be produced in this respect by variations in the duration of turnovers. This point will be discussed later.

Let us take five different spheres of production and let the capital in each have a different organic composition as follows:

Capitals	Rate of surplus-value %	Surplus-value	Value of product	Rate of profit %
I. $80_c + 20_v$	100	20	120	20
II. $70_c + 30_v$	100	30	130	30
III. $60_c + 40_v$	100	40	140	40
IV. $85_c + 15_v$	100	15	115	15
V. $95_c + 5_v$	100	5	105	5

Here, in different spheres of production with the same degree of exploitation, we find considerably different rates of profit corresponding to the different organic composition of these capitals.

The sum total of the capitals invested in these five spheres of production = 500; the sum total of the surplus-value produced by them = 110; the aggregate value of the commodities produced by them = 610. If we consider the 500 as a single capital, and capitals I to V merely as its component parts (as, say, different departments of a cotton mill, which has different ratios of constant to variable capital in its carding, preparatory spinning, spinning, and weaving shops, and in which the average ratio for the factory as a whole has still to be calculated), the mean composition of this capital of 500 would $= 390_c + 110_v$, or, in per cent, $= 78_c + 22_v$. Should each of the capitals of 100 be regarded as one-fifth of the total capital, its composition would equal this average of $78_c + 22_v$; for every 100 there would be an average surplus-value of 22; thus, the average rate of profit would = 22%, and, finally, the price of every fifth of the total product produced by the 500 would = 122. The product of each fifth of the advanced total capital would then have to be sold at 122.

But to avoid entirely erroneous conclusions it must not be assumed that all cost-prices = 100.

With $80_c + 20_v$ and a rate of surplus-value = 100%, the total value of commodities produced by capital I = 100 would be $80_c + 20_v + 20_s = 120$, provided the entire constant capital went into the annual product. Now, this may under certain circumstances be the case in some spheres of production. But hardly in cases where the proportion of c:v = 4:1. We must, therefore, remember in comparing the values produced by each 100 of the different capitals, that they will differ in accordance with the different composition of c as to its fixed and circulating parts, and that, in turn, the fixed portions of each of the different capitals depreciate slowly or rapidly as the case may be, thus transferring unequal quantities of their value to the product in equal periods of time. But this is immaterial to the rate of profit. No matter whether the 80_c give up a value of 80, or 50, or 5, to the annual product, and the annual product consequently $= 80_c + 20_v + 20_s = 120$, or $50_c + 20_v + 20_s = 90$, or $5_c + 20_v + 20_s = 45$; in all these cases the redundance of the product's value over its cost-price $= 20$, and in calculating the rate of profit these 20 are related to the capital of 100 in all of them. The rate of profit of capital I, therefore, is 20% in every case. To make this still plainer, we let different portions of constant capital go into the value of the product of the same five capitals in the following table:

Capitals	Rate of surplus-value %	Surplus-value	Rate of profit %	Used up c	Value of commodities	Cost-price	
I. $80_c + 20_v$	100	20	20	50	90	70	
II. $70_c + 30_v$	100	30	30	51	111	81	
III. $60_c + 40_v$	100	40	40	51	131	91	
IV. $85_c + 15_v$	100	15	15	40	70	55	
V. $95_c + 5_v$	100	5	5	10	20	15	
$390_c + 110_v$	—	110	110	—	—	—	Total
$78_c + 22_v$	—	22	22	—	—	—	Average

If we now again consider capitals I to V as a single total capital, we shall see that, in this case as well, the composition of the sums of these five capitals $= 500 = 390_c + 110_v$, so that we get the same average composition $= 78_c + 22_v$, and, similarly, the average surplus-value remains 22. If we divide this surplus-value uniformly among capitals I to V, we get the following commodity-prices:

Capitals	Surplus-value	Value of commodities	Cost-Price of commodities	Price of commodities	Rate of profit %	Deviation of price from value
I. $80_c + 20_v$	20	90	70	92	22	+ 2
II. $70_c + 30_v$	30	111	81	103	22	− 8
III. $60_c + 40_v$	40	131	91	113	22	− 18
IV. $85_c + 15_v$	15	70	55	77	22	+ 7
V. $95_c + 5_v$	5	20	15	37	22	+ 17

Taken together, the commodities are sold at $2 + 7 + 17 = 26$ above, and $8 + 18 = 26$ below their value, so that the deviations of price from value balance out one another through the uniform distribution of surplus-value, or through addition of the average profit of 22 per 100 units of advanced capital to the respective cost-prices of the commodities I to V. One portion of the commodities is sold above its value in the same proportion in which the other is sold below it. And it is only the sale of the commodities at such prices that enables the rate of profit for capitals I to V to be uniformly 22%, regardless of their different organic composition. The prices which obtain as the average of the various rates of profit in the different spheres of production added to the cost-prices of the different spheres of production, constitute the *prices of production*. They have as their prerequisite the existence of a general rate of profit, and this, again, presupposes that the rates of profit in every individual sphere of production taken by itself have previously been reduced to just as many average rates. These particular rates of profit $= s/C$ in every sphere of production, and must, as occurs in Part I of this book, be deduced out of the values of the commodities. Without such deduction the general rate of profit (and consequently the price of production of commodities) remains a vague and senseless conception. Hence, the price of production of a commodity is equal to its cost-price plus the profit, allotted to it in per cent, in accordance with the general rate of profit, or, in other words, to its cost-price plus the average profit.

Owing to the different organic compositions of capitals invested in different lines of production, and, hence, owing to the circumstance that—depending on the different percentage which the variable part makes up in a total capital of a given magnitude—capitals of equal magnitude put into motion very different quantities of labour, they also appropriate very different quantities of surplus-labour or produce very different quantities of surplus-value. Accordingly, the rates of profit prevailing in the various branches of production are originally very different. These different rates of profit are equalised by competition to a single general rate of profit, which is the average of all these different rates of profit. The profit accruing in accordance with this general rate of profit to any capital of a given magnitude, whatever its organic composition, is called the average profit. The price of a commodity, which is equal to its cost-price plus the share of the annual average profit on the total capital invested (not merely consumed) in its production that falls to it in accordance with the conditions of turnover, is called its price of production. Take, for example, a capital of 500, of which 100 is fixed capital, and let 10% of this wear out during one turnover of the circulating capital of 400. Let the average profit for the period of turnover be 10%. In that case the cost-price of the product created during this turnover will be 10_c for wear plus 400 $(c + v)$ circulating capital = 410, and its price of production will be 410 cost-price plus (10% profit on 500) 50 = 460.

Thus, although in selling their commodities the capitalists of the various spheres of production recover the value of the capital consumed in their production, they do not secure the surplus-value, and consequently the profit, created in their own sphere by the production of these commodities. What they secure is only as much surplus-value, and hence profit, as falls, when uniformly distributed, to the share of every aliquot part of the total social capital from the total social surplus-value, or profit, produced in a given time by the social capital in all spheres of production. Every 100 of an invested capital, whatever its composition, draws as much profit in a year, or any other period of time, as falls to the share of every 100, the n'th part of the total capital, during the same period. So far as profits are concerned, the various capitalists are just so many stockholders in a stock company in which the shares of profit are uniformly divided per 100, so that profits differ in the case of the individual capitalists only in accordance with the amount of capital invested by each in the aggregate enterprise, i.e. according to his investment in social production as a whole, according to the number of his shares. Therefore, the portion of the price of commodities which replaces the elements of capital consumed in the production of these commodities, the portion, therefore, which will have to be used to buy back these consumed capital-values, i.e. their cost-price, depends entirely on the outlay of capital within the respective spheres of production. But the other element of the price of commodities, the profit added to this cost-price, does not depend on the amount of profit produced in a given sphere of production by a given capital in a given period of time. It depends on the mass of profit which falls as an average for any given period to each individual capital as an aliquot part of the total social capital invested in social production.

When a capitalist sells his commodities at their price of production, therefore, he recovers money in proportion to the value of the capital consumed in their production and secures profit in proportion to his advanced capital as the aliquot part in the total social capital. His cost-prices are specific. But the profit added to them is independent of his particular sphere of production, being a simple average per 100 units of invested capital.

Let us assume that the five different investments I to V of the foregoing illustration belong to one man. The quantity of variable and constant capital consumed per 100 of the invested capital in each of the departments I to V in the production of commodities would be known, and this portion of the value of the commodities I to V would, needless to say, make up a part of their price, since at least this price is required to recover the advanced and consumed portions of the capital. These cost-prices would therefore be different for each class of the commodities I to V, and would as such be set differently by the owner. But as regards the different quantities of surplus-value, or profit, produced by I to V, they might easily be regarded by the capitalist as profit on his advanced aggregate capital, so that each 100 units would get their definite aliquot part. Hence, the cost-prices of the commodities produced in the various departments I to V would be different; but that portion of their selling price derived from the profit added per 100 capital would be the same for all these commodities. The aggregate price of the commodities I to V would therefore equal their aggregate value, i.e. the sum of the cost-prices I to V plus the sum of the surplus-values, or profits, produced in I to V. It would hence actually be the money-expression of the total quantity of past and newly applied labour incorporate in commodities I to V. And in the same way the sum of the prices of production of all commodities produced in society—the totality of all branches of production—is equal to the sum of their values.

This statement seems to conflict with the fact that under capitalist production the elements of productive capital are, as a rule, bought on the market, and that for this reason their prices include profit which has already been realised, hence, include the price of production of the respective branch of industry together with the profit contained in it, so that the profit of one branch of industry goes into the cost-price of another. But if we place the sum of the cost-prices of the commodities of an entire country on one side, and the sum of its surplus-values, or profits, on the other, the calculation must evidently be right. For instance, take a certain commodity A. Its cost-price may contain the profits of B, C, D, etc., just as the cost-prices of B, C, D, etc., may contain the profits of A. Now, as we make our calculation the profit of A will not be included in its cost-price, nor will the profits of B, C, D, etc., be included in theirs. Nobody ever includes his own profit in his cost-price. If there are, therefore, n spheres of production, and if each makes a profit amounting to p, then their aggregate cost-price = k—np. Considering the calculation as a whole we see that since the profits of one sphere of production pass into the cost-price of another, they are therefore included in the calculation as constituents of the total price of the end-product, and so cannot appear a second time on the profit side. If any do appear on this side, however, then only because the commodity in question is itself an ultimate product, whose price of production does not pass into the cost-price of some other commodity.

If the cost-price of a commodity includes a sum = p, which stands for the profits of the producers of the means of production, and if a profit = p_1 is added to this cost-price, the aggregate profit $P = p + p_1$. The aggregate cost-price of the commodity, considered without the profit portions, is then its own cost-price minus P. Let this cost-price be k. Then, obviously, $k + p = k + p + p_1$. In dealing with surplus-values, we have seen in Book I (Ch. 7, sect. 2) that the product of every capital may be so treated, as though a part of it replaces only capital, while the other part represents only surplus-value. In applying this approach to the aggregate product of society, we must make some rectifications. Looking upon society as a whole, the profit contained in, say, the price of flax cannot appear twice—not both as a portion of the linen price and as the profit of the flax.

There is no difference between surplus-value and profit, as long as, e.g. A's surplus-value passes into B's constant capital. It is, after all, quite immaterial to the value of the commodities, whether the labour contained in them is paid or unpaid. This merely shows that B pays for A's surplus-value. A's surplus-value cannot be entered twice in the total calculation.

But the difference is this: Aside from the fact that the price of a particular product, let us say that of capital B, differs from its value because the surplus–value realised in B may be greater or smaller than the profit added to the price of the products of B, the same circumstance applies also to those commodities which form the constant part of capital B, and indirectly also its variable part, as the labourers' necessities of life. So far as the constant portion is concerned, it is itself equal to the cost-price plus the surplus–value, here therefore equal to cost-price plus profit, and this profit may again be greater or smaller than the surplus–value for which it stands. As for the variable capital, the average daily wage is indeed always equal to the value produced in the number of hours the labourer must work to produce the necessities of life. But this number of hours is in its turn obscured by the deviation of the prices of production of the necessities of life from their values. However, this always resolves itself to one commodity receiving too little of the surplus–value while another receives too much, so that the deviations from the value which are embodied in the prices of production compensate one another. Under capitalist production, the general law acts as the prevailing tendency only in a very complicated and approximate manner, as a never ascertainable average of ceaseless fluctuations.

Since the general rate of profit is formed by taking the average of the various rates of profit for each 100 of capital invested in a definite period, e.g. a year, it follows that in it the difference brought about by different periods of turnover of different capitals is also effaced. But these differences have a decisive bearing on the different rates of profit in the various spheres of production whose average forms the general rate of profit.

In the preceding illustration concerning the formation of the average rate of profit we assumed each capital in each sphere of production = 100, and we did so to show the difference in the rates of profit in per cent, and thus also the difference in the values of commodities produced by equal amounts of capital. But it goes without saying that the actual amounts of surplus–value produced in each sphere of production depend on the magnitude of the invested capitals, since the composition of capital is given in each sphere of production. Yet the actual *rate* of profit in any particular sphere of production is not affected by the fact that the capital invested is 100, or m times 100, or xm times 100. The rate of profit remains 10%, whether the total profit is 10:100, or 1,000:10,000.

However, since the rates of profit differ in the various spheres of production, with very much different quantities of surplus–value, or profit, being produced in them, depending on the proportion of the variable to the total capital, it is evident that the average profit per 100 of the social capital, and hence the average, or general, rate of profit, will differ considerably in accordance with the respective magnitudes of the capitals invested in the various spheres. Let us take four capitals A, B, C, D. Let the rate of surplus-value for all = 100%. Let the variable capital for each 100 of the total be 25 in A, 40 in B, 15 in C, and 10 in D. Then each 100 of the total capital would yield a surplus-value, or profit, of 25 in A, 40 in B, 15 in C, and 10 in D. This would total 90, and if these four capitals are of the same magnitude, the average rate of profit would then be 90/4 or 22½%.

Suppose, however, the total capitals are as follows: A = 200, B = 300, C = 1,000, D = 4,000. The profits produced would then respectively = 50, 120, 150, and 400. This makes a profit of 720, and an average rate of profit of 13 1/11% for 5,500, the sum of the four capitals.

The masses of the total value produced differ in accordance with the magnitudes of the total capitals invested in A, B, C, D, respectively. The formation of the average rate of profit is, therefore, not merely a matter of obtaining the simple average of the different *rates* of profit in the various spheres of production, but rather one of the relative weight which these different rates of profit have in forming this average. This, however, depends on the relative magnitude of the capital invested in each particular sphere, or on the aliquot part which the capital invested in each particular sphere forms in the aggregate social capital. There will naturally be a very great difference, depending on whether a greater or smaller part of the total capital produces a higher or lower rate of profit. And this, again, depends on how much capital is invested in spheres, in which the variable capital is relatively small or large compared to the total capital. It is just like the average interest obtained by a usurer who lends various quantities of capital at different interest rates; for instance, at 4, 5, 6, 7%, etc. The average rate will depend entirely on how much of his capital he has loaned out at each of the different rates of interest.

The general rate of profit is, therefore, determined by two factors:

(1) The organic composition of the capitals in the different spheres of production, and thus, the different rates of profit in the individual spheres.

(2) The distribution of the total social capital in these different spheres, and thus, the relative magnitude of the capital invested in each particular sphere at the specific rate of profit prevailing in it; i.e. the relative share of the total social capital absorbed by each individual sphere of production.

In Books I and II we dealt only with the *value* of commodities. On the one hand, the *cost-price* has now been singled out as a part of this value, and, on the other, the *price of production* of commodities has been developed as its converted form.

Suppose the composition of the average social capital is $80_c + 20_v$, and the annual rate of surplus-value, s', is 100%. In that case the average annual profit for a capital of $100 = 20$, and the general annual rate of profit $= 20$%. Whatever the cost-price, k, of the commodities annually produced by a capital of 100, their price of production would then be $k + 20$. In those spheres of production in which the composition of capital would $= (80 - x)_c + (20 + x)_v$, the actually produced surplus-value, or the annual profit produced in that particular sphere, would be $20 + x$, that is, greater than 20, and the value of the produced commodities $= k + 20 + x$, that is, greater than $k + 20$, or greater than their price of production. In those spheres, in which the composition of the capital $= (80 + x)_c + (20 - x)_v$, the annually produced surplus-value, or profit, would $= 20 - x$, or less than 20, and consequently the value of the commodities $k + 20 - x$ less than the price of production, which $= k + 20$. Aside from possible differences in the periods of turnover, the price of production of the commodities would then equal their value only in spheres, in which the composition would happen to be $80_c + 20_v$.

The specific development of the social productivity of labour in each particular sphere of production varies in degree, higher or lower, depending on how large a quantity of means of production are set in motion by a definite quantity of labour, hence in a given working-day by a definite number of labourers, and, consequently, on how small a quantity of labour is required for a given quantity of means of production. Such capitals as contain a larger percentage of constant and a smaller percentage of variable capital than the average social capital are, therefore, called capitals of *higher* composition, and, conversely, those capitals in which the constant is relatively smaller, and the variable relatively greater than in the average social capital, are called capitals of *lower* composition. Finally, we call those capitals whose composition coincides with the average, capitals of average composition. Should the average social capital be composed in per cent of $80_c + 20_v$, then a capital of $90_c + 10_v$ is *higher*, and a capital of $70_c + 30_v$ *lower* than the social average. Generally speaking, if the composition of the average social capital $= m_c + n_v$, in which m and n are constant magnitudes and $m + n = 100$, the formula $(m + x)_c + (n - x)_v$ represents the higher composition, and $(m - x)_c + (n + x)_v$ the lower composition of an individual capital or group of capitals. The way in which these capitals perform their functions after establishment of an average rate of profit and assuming one turnover per year, is shown in the following tabulation, in which I represents the average composition with an average rate of profit of 20%.

I. $80_c + 20_v + 20_s$.   Rate of profit $= 20\%$.
                               Price of product $= 120$. Value $= 120$.
II. $90_c + 10_v + 10_s$.   Rate of profit $= 20\%$.
                               Price of product $= 120$. Value $= 110$.
III. $70_c + 30_v + 30_s$.   Rate of profit $= 20\%$.
                               Price of product $= 120$. Value $= 130$.

The value of the commodities produced by capital II would, therefore, be smaller than their price of production, the price of production of the commodities of III smaller than their value, and only in the case of capital I in branches of production in which the composition happens to coincide with the social average, would value and price of production be equal. In applying these terms to any particular cases note must, however, be taken whether a deviation of the ratio between c and v is simply due to a change in the value of the elements of constant capital, rather than to a difference in the technical composition.

The foregoing statements have at any rate modified the original assumption concerning the determination of the cost-price of commodities. We had originally assumed that the cost-price of a commodity equalled the *value* of the commodities consumed in its production. But for the buyer the price of production of a specific commodity is its cost-price, and may thus pass as cost-price into the prices of other commodities. Since the price production may differ from the value of a commodity, it follows that the cost-price of a commodity containing this price of production of another commodity may also stand above or below that portion of its total value derived from the value of the means of production consumed by it. It is necessary to remember this modified significance of the cost-price, and to bear in mind that there is always the possibility of an error if the cost-price of a commodity in any particular sphere is identified with the value of the means of production consumed by it. Our present analysis does not necessitate a closer examination of this point. It remains true, nevertheless, that the cost-price of a commodity is always smaller than its value. For no matter how much the cost-price of a commodity may differ from the value of the means of production consumed by it, this past mistake is immaterial to the capitalist. The cost-price of a particular commodity is a definite condition which is given, and independent of the production of our capitalist, while the result of his production is a commodity containing surplus-value, therefore an excess of value over and above its cost-price. For all other purposes, the statement that the cost-price is smaller than the value of a commodity has now changed practically into the statement that the cost-price is smaller than the price of production. As concerns the total social capital, in which the price of production is equal to the value, this statement is identical with the former, namely that the cost-price is smaller than the value. And while it is modified in the individual spheres of production, the fundamental fact always remains that in the case of the total social capital the cost-price of the commodities produced by it is smaller than their value, or, in the case of the total mass of social commodities, smaller than their price of production, which is identical with their value. The cost-price of a commodity refers only to the quantity of paid labour contained in it, while its value refers to all the paid and unpaid labour contained in it. The price of production refers to the sum of the paid labour plus a certain quantity of unpaid labour determined for any particular sphere of production by conditions over which it has no control.

The formula that the price of production of a commodity $= k + p$, i.e. equals its cost-price plus profit, is now more precisely defined with $p = kp'$ (p' being the general rate of profit). Hence the price of production $= k + kp'$. If $k = 300$ and $p' = 15\%$, then the price of production is $k + kp' = 300 + 300 \times 15/100$, or 345.

The price of production of the commodities in any particular sphere may change in magnitude:

(1) If the general rate of profit changes independently of this particular sphere, while the value of the commodities remains the same (the same quantities of congealed and living labour being consumed in their production as before).

(2) If there is a change of value, either in this particular sphere in consequence of technical changes, or in consequence of a change in the value of those commodities which form the elements of its constant capital, while the general rate of profit remains unchanged.

(3) Finally, if a combination of the two aforementioned circumstances takes place.

In spite of the great changes occurring continually, as we shall see, in the actual rates of profit within the individual spheres of production, any real change in the general rate of profit, unless brought about by way of an exception by extraordinary economic events, is the belated effect of a series of fluctuations extending over very long periods, fluctuations which require much time before consolidating and equal-ising one another to bring about a change in the general rate of profit. In all shorter periods (quite aside from fluctuations of market-prices), a change in the prices of production is, therefore, always traceable *prima facie* to actual changes in the value of commodities, i.e. to changes in the total amount of labour-time required for their produc-tion. Mere changes in the money-expression of the same values are, naturally, not at all considered here.

On the other hand, it is evident that from the point of view of the total social capital the value of the commodities produced by it (or, expressed in money, their price) = value of constant capital + value of variable capital + surplus-value. Assuming the degree of labour exploi-tation to be constant, the rate of profit cannot change so long as the mass of surplus-value remains the same, unless there is a change in either the value of the constant capital, the value of the variable capital, or the value of both, so that C changes, and thereby s/C, which represents the general rate of profit. In each case, therefore, a change in the general rate of profit implies a change in the value of commodities which form the elements of the constant or variable capital, or of both.

Or, the general rate of profit may change, while the value of the commodities remains the same, when the degree of labour exploitation changes.

Or, if the degree of labour exploitation remains the same, the general rate of profit may change through a change in the amount of labour employed relative to the constant capital as a result of technical changes in the labour-process. But such technical changes must always show themselves in, and be attended by, a change in the value of the commodities, whose production would then require more or less la-bour than before.

We saw in Part I that surplus-value and profit are identical from the standpoint of their mass. But the rate of profit is from the very outset distinct from the rate of surplus-value, which appears at first sight as merely a different form of calculating. But at the same time this serves, also from the outset, to obscure and mystify the actual origin of sur-plus-value, since the rate of profit can rise or fall while the rate of surplus-value remains the same, and vice versa, and since the capitalist is in practice solely interested in the rate of profit. Yet there was difference of magnitude only between the rate of surplus-value and the rate of profit and not between the surplus-value itself and profit. Since in the rate of profit the surplus-value is calculated in relation to the total capital and the latter is taken as its standard of measurement, the surplus-value itself appears to originate from the total capital, uniformly derived from all its parts, so that the organic difference between constant and variable capital is obliterated in the conception of profit. Disguised as profit, surplus-value actually denies its origin, loses its character, and becomes unrecognisable. However, hitherto the distinction between profit and surplus-value applied solely to a qualitative change, or change of form, while there was no real difference of magnitude in this first stage of the change between surplus-value and profit, but only between the rate of profit and the rate of surplus-value.

But it is different, as soon as a general rate of profit, and thereby an average profit corresponding to the magnitude of invested capital given in the various spheres of production, have been established.

It is then only an accident if the surplus-value, and thus the profit, actually produced in any particular sphere of production, coincides with the profit contained in the selling price of a commodity. As a rule, surplus-value and profit and not their rates alone, are then different magnitudes. At a given degree of exploitation, the mass of surplus-value produced in a particular sphere of production is then more important for the aggregate average profit of social capital, and thus for the capitalist class in general, than for the individual capitalist in any specific branch of production. It is of importance to the latter only in so far as the quantity of surplus-value produced in his branch helps to regulate the average profit. But this is a process which occurs behind his back, one he does not see, nor understand, and which indeed does not interest him. The actual difference of magnitude between profit and surplus-value—not merely between the rate of profit and the rate of surplus-value—in the various spheres of production now completely conceals the true nature and origin of profit not only from the capitalist, who has a special interest in deceiving himself on this score, but also from the labourer. The transformation of values into prices of production serves to obscure the basis for determining value itself. Finally, since the mere transformation of surplus-value into profit distinguishes the portion of the value of a commodity forming the profit from the portion forming its cost-price, it is natural that the conception of value should elude the capitalist at this juncture, for he does not see the total labour put into the commodity, but only that portion of the total labour for which he has paid in the shape of means of production, be they living or not, so that his profit appears to him as something outside the immanent value of the commodity. Now this idea is fully confirmed, fortified, and ossified in that, from the standpoint of his particular sphere of production, the profit added to the cost-price is not actually determined by the limits of the formation of value within his own sphere, but through completely outside influences.

The fact that this intrinsic connection is here revealed for the first time; that up to the present time political economy, as we shall see in the following and in Book IV,* either forcibly abstracted itself from the distinctions between surplus-value and profit, and their rates, so it could retain value determination as a basis, or else abandoned this value determination and with it all vestiges of a scientific approach, in order to cling to the differences that strike the eye in this phenomenon—this confusion of the theorists best illustrates the utter incapacity of the practical capitalist, blinded by competition as he is, and incapable of penetrating its phenomena, to recognise the inner essence and inner structure of this process behind its outer appearance.

In fact, all the laws evolved in Part I concerning the rise and fall of the rate of profit have the following two-fold meaning:

(1) On the one hand, they are the laws of the general rate of profit. In view of the many different causes which make the rate of profit rise or fall one would think, after everything that has been said and done, that the general rate of profit must change every day. But a trend in one sphere of production compensates for that in another, their effects cross and paralyse one another. We shall later examine to which side these fluctuations ultimately gravitate. But they are slow. The suddenness, multiplicity, and different duration of the fluctuations in the individual spheres of production make them compensate for one another in the order of their succession in time, a fall in prices following a rise, and vice versa, so that they remain limited to local, i.e. individual, spheres. Finally, the various local fluctuations neutralise one another. Within each individual sphere of production, there take place changes, i.e. deviations from the general rate of profit, which counterbalance one another in a definite time on the one hand, and thus have no influence upon the general rate of profit, and which, on the other, do not react upon it, because they are balanced by other simultaneous local fluctuations. Since the general rate of profit is not only determined by the average rate of profit in each sphere, but also by the distribution of the total social capital among the different individual spheres, and since this distribution is continually changing, it becomes another constant cause of change in the general rate of profit. But it is a cause of change which mostly paralyses itself, owing to the uninterrupted and many-sided nature of this movement.

(2) Within each sphere, there is some room for play for a longer or shorter space of time, in which the rate of profit of this sphere may fluctuate, before this fluctuation consolidates sufficiently after rising or falling to gain time for influencing the general rate of profit and therefore assuming more than local importance. The laws of the rate of profit, as developed in Part I of this book, likewise remain applicable within these limits of space and time.

The theoretical conception concerning the first transformation of surplus-value into profit, that every part of a capital yields a uniform profit, expresses a practical fact. Whatever the composition of an industrial capital, whether it sets in motion one-quarter of congealed labour and three-quarters of living labour, or three-quarters of congealed labour and one-quarter of living labour, whether in one case it absorbs three times as much surplus-labour, or produces three times as much surplus-value than in another—in either case it yields the same profit, given the same degree of labour exploitation and leaving aside individual differences, which, incidentally, disappear because we are dealing in both cases with the average composition of the entire sphere of production. The individual capitalist (or all the capitalists in each individual sphere of production), whose outlook is limited, rightly believes that his profit is not derived solely from the labour employed by him, or in his line of production. This is quite true, as far as his average profit is concerned. To what extent this profit is due to the aggregate exploitation of labour on the part of the total social capital, i.e. by all his capitalist colleagues—this interrelation is a complete mystery to the individual capitalist; all the more so, since no bourgeois theorists, the political economists, have so far revealed it. A saving of labour—not only labour necessary to produce a certain product, but also the number of employed labourers—and the employment of more congealed labour (constant capital), appear to be very sound operations from the economic standpoint and do not seem to exert the least influence on the general rate of profit and the average profit. How could living labour be the sole source of profit, in view of the fact that a reduction in the quantity of labour required for production appears not to exert any influence on profit? Moreover, it even seems in certain circumstances to be the nearest source of an increase of profits, at least for the individual capitalist.

If in any particular sphere of production there is a rise or fall of the portion of the cost-price which represents the value of constant capital, this portion comes from the circulation and, either enlarged or reduced, passes from the very outset into the process of production of the

commodity. If, on the other hand, the same number of labourers produces more or less in the same time, so that the quantity of labour
required for the production of a definite quantity of commodities
varies while the number of labourers remains the same, that portion of
the cost-price which represents the value of the variable capital may
remain the same, i.e. contribute the same amount to the cost-price of
the total product. But every one of the individual commodities whose
sum makes up the total product, shares in more or less labour (paid and
therefore also unpaid), and shares consequently in the greater or
smaller outlay for this labour, i.e. a larger or smaller portion of the
wage. The total wages paid by the capitalist remain the same, but wages
differ if calculated per piece of the commodity. Thus, there is a change
in this portion of the cost-price of the commodity. But no matter
whether the cost-price of the individual commodity (or, perhaps, the
cost-price of the sum of commodities produced by a capital of a given
magnitude) rises or falls, be it due to such changes in its own value, or
in that of its elements, the average profit of, e.g. 10% remains 10%.
Still, 10% of an individual commodity may represent very different
amounts, depending on the change of magnitude caused in the cost-
price of the individual commodity by such changes of value as we have
assumed.

So far as the variable capital is concerned—and this is most important, because it is the source of surplus-value, and because anything
which conceals its relation to the accumulation of wealth by the capitalist serves to mystify the entire system—matters get cruder or appear
to the capitalist in the following light: A variable capital of £100
represents the weekly wage of, say, 100 labourers. If these 100 labourers
weekly produce 200 pieces of a commodity = 200C, in a given working-
time, then 1C—abstracted from that portion of its cost-price which is
added by the constant capital, costs £100/200 = 10 shillings, since
£100 = 200C. Now suppose that a change occurs in the productiveness
of labour. Suppose it doubles, so that the same number of labourers
now produces twice 200C in the time which it previously took to
produce 200C. In that case (considering only that part of the cost-price
which consists of wages) 1C = £100/400 = 5 shillings, since now
£100 = 400C. Should the productiveness decrease one-half, the same
labour would produce only 200C/2 and since £100 = 200C/2,
1C = £200/200 = £1. The changes in the labour-time required for the
production of the commodities, and hence the changes in their value,
thus appear in regard to the cost-price, and hence to the price of
production, as a different distribution of the same wage for more or

fewer commodities, depending on the greater or smaller quantity of commodities produced in the same working-time for the same wage. What the capitalist, and consequently also the political economist, see is that the part of the paid labour per piece of commodity changes with the productivity of labour, and that the value of each piece also changes accordingly. What they do not see is that the same applies to unpaid labour contained in every piece of the commodity, and this is perceived so much less since the average profit actually is only accidentally determined by the unpaid labour absorbed in the sphere of the individual capitalist. It is only in such crude and meaningless form that we can glimpse that the value of commodities is determined by the labour contained in them.

CHAPTER 13

THE LAW AS SUCH

ASSUMING a given wage and working-day, a variable capital, for instance of 100, represents a certain number of employed labourers. It is the index of this number. Suppose £100 are the wages of 100 labourers for, say, one week. If these labourers perform equal amounts of necessary and surplus-labour, if they work daily as many hours for themselves, i.e. for the reproduction of their wage, as they do for the capitalist, i.e. for the production of surplus-value, then the value of their total product = £200, and the surplus-value they produce would amount to £100. The rate of surplus-value, s/v, would = 100%. But, as we have seen, this rate of surplus-value would nonetheless express itself in very different rates of profit, depending on the different volumes of constant capital c and consequently of the total capital C, because the rate of profit = s/C. The rate of surplus-value is 100%:

If $c = 50$, and $v = 100$, then $p' = 100/150 = 66\frac{2}{3}\%$;
" $c = 100$, and $v = 100$, then $p' = 100/200 = 50\%$;
" $c = 200$, and $v = 100$, then $p' = 100/300 = 33\frac{1}{3}\%$;
" $c = 300$, and $v = 100$, then $p' = 100/400 = 25\%$;
" $c = 400$, and $v = 100$, then $p' = 100/500 = 20\%$.

This is how the same rate of surplus-value would express itself under the same degree of labour exploitation in a falling rate of profit, because the material growth of the constant capital implies also a growth—albeit not in the same proportion—in its value, and consequently in that of the total capital.

If it is further assumed that this gradual change in the composition of capital is not confined only to individual spheres of production, but that it occurs more or less in all, or at least in the key spheres of production, so that it involves changes in the average organic composition of the total capital of a certain society, then the gradual growth of constant capital in relation to variable capital must necessarily lead to a *gradual fall of the general rate of profit*, so long as the rate of surplus-value, or the intensity of exploitation of labour by capital, remain the same. Now we have seen that it is a law of capitalist production that its development is attended by a relative decrease of variable in relation to constant capital, and consequently to the total capital set in motion. This is just another way of saying that owing to the distinctive methods of production developing in the capitalist system the same number of labourers, i.e. the same quantity of labour-power set in motion by a variable capital of a given value, operate, work up and productively consume in the same time span an ever-increasing quantity of means of labour, machinery and fixed capital of all sorts, raw and auxiliary materials—and consequently a constant capital of an ever-increasing value. This continual relative decrease of the variable capital vis-à-vis the constant, and consequently the total capital, is identical with the progressively higher organic composition of the social capital in its average. It is likewise just another expression for the progressive development of the social productivity of labour, which is demonstrated precisely by the fact that the same number of labourers, in the same time, i.e. with less labour, convert an ever-increasing quantity of raw and auxiliary materials into products, thanks to the growing application of machinery and fixed capital in general. To this growing quantity of value of the constant capital—although indicating the growth of the real mass of use-values of which the constant capital materially consists only approximately—corresponds a progressive cheapening of products. Every individual product, considered by itself, contains a smaller quantity of labour than it did on a lower level of production, where the capital invested in wages occupies a far greater place compared to the capital invested in means of production. The hypothetical series drawn up at the beginning of this chapter expresses, therefore, the actual tendency of capitalist production. This mode of production produces a progressive relative decrease of the variable capital as compared to the constant capital, and consequently a continuously rising organic composition of the total capital. The immediate result of this is that the rate of surplus-value, at the same, or even a rising, degree of labour exploitation, is represented by a continually falling general rate of profit. (We shall see later why this fall does not manifest itself in an absolute form, but rather as a tendency toward a progressive fall.) The progressive tendency of the general rate of profit to fall is, therefore, just *an expression peculiar to the capitalist mode of production* of the progressive development of the social productivity of labour. This does not mean to say that the rate of profit may not fall temporarily for other reasons. But proceeding from the nature of the capitalist mode of production, it is thereby proved a logical necessity that in its development the general average rate of surplus-value must express itself in a falling general rate of profit. Since the mass of the employed living labour is continually on the decline as compared to the mass of materialised labour set in motion by it, i.e. to the productively consumed means of production, it follows that the portion of living labour, unpaid and congealed in surplus-value, must also be continually on the decrease compared to the amount of value represented by the invested total capital. Since the ratio of the mass of surplus-value to the value of the invested total capital forms the rate of profit, this rate must constantly fall.

Simple as this law appears from the foregoing statements, all of political economy has so far had little success in discovering it, as we shall see in a later part. The economists perceived the phenomenon and cudgelled their brains in tortuous attempts to interpret it. Since this law is of great importance to capitalist production, it may be said to be a mystery whose solution has been the goal of all political economy since Adam Smith, the difference between the various schools since Adam Smith having been in the divergent approaches to a solution. When we consider, on the other hand, that up to the present political economy has been running in circles round the distinction between constant and variable capital, but has never known how to define it accurately; that it has never separated surplus-value from profit, and never even considered profit in its pure form as distinct from its different, independent components, such as industrial profit, commercial profit, interest, and ground-rent; that it has never thoroughly analysed the differences in the organic composition of capital, and, for this reason, has never thought of analysing the formation of the general rate of profit—if we consider all this, the failure to solve this riddle is no longer surprising.

We intentionally present this law before going on to the division of profit into different independent categories. The fact that this analysis is made independently of the division of profit into different parts, which fall to the share of different categories of people, shows from the outset that this law is, in its entirety, independent of this division, and just as independent of the mutual relations of the resultant categories of profit. The profit to which we are here referring is but another name for surplus-value itself, which is presented only in its relation to total capital rather than to variable capital, from which it arises. The drop in the rate of profit, therefore, expresses the falling relation of surplus-value to advanced total capital, and is for this reason independent of any division whatsoever of this surplus-value among the various categories.

We have seen that at a certain stage of capitalist development, where the organic composition of capital c:v was 50:100, a rate of surplus-value of 100% was expressed in a rate of profit of 66⅔%, and that at a higher stage, where c:v was 400:100, the same rate of surplus-value was expressed in a rate of profit of only 20%. What is true of different successive stages of development in one country, is also true of different coexisting stages of development in different countries. In an undeveloped country, in which the former composition of capital is the average, the general rate of profit would $= 66\frac{2}{3}\%$, while in a country with the latter composition and a much higher stage of development it would $= 20\%$.

The difference between the two national rates of profit might disappear, or even be reversed, if labour were less productive in the less developed country, so that a larger quantity of labour were to be represented in a smaller quantity of the same commodities, and a larger exchange-value were represented in less use-value. The labourer would then spend more of his time in reproducing his own means of subsistence, or their value, and less time in producing surplus-value; consequently, he would perform less surplus-labour, with the result that the rate of surplus-value would be lower. Suppose, the labourer of the less developed country were to work $\frac{2}{3}$ of the working-day for himself and $\frac{1}{3}$ for the capitalist; in accordance with the above illustration, the same labour-power would then be paid with $133\frac{1}{3}$ and would furnish a surplus of only $66\frac{2}{3}$. A constant capital of 50 would correspond to a variable capital of $133\frac{1}{3}$. The rate of surplus-value would amount to $66\frac{2}{3}:133\frac{1}{3} = 50\%$, and the rate of profit to $66\frac{2}{3}:183\frac{1}{3}$, or approximately $36\frac{1}{2}\%$.

Since we have not so far analysed the different component parts of profit, i.e. they do not for the present exist for us, we make the following remarks beforehand merely to avoid misunderstanding: In comparing countries in different stages of development it would be a big mistake to measure the level of the national rate of profit by, say, the level of the national rate of interest, namely when comparing countries with a developed capitalist production with countries in which labour has not yet been formally subjected to capital, although in reality the labourer is exploited by the capitalist (as, for instance, in India, where the ryot manages his farm as an independent producer whose production as such is not, therefore, as yet subordinated to capital, although the usurer may not only rob him of his entire surplus-labour by means of interest, but may also, to use a capitalist term, hack off a part of his wage). This interest comprises all the profit, and more than the profit, instead of merely expressing an aliquot part of the produced surplus-value, or profit, as it does in countries with a developed capitalist production. On the other hand, the rate of interest is, in this case, mostly determined by relations (loans granted by usurers to owners of larger estates who draw ground-rent) which have nothing to do with profit, and rather indicate to what extent usury appropriates ground-rent.

As regards countries possessing different stages of development of capitalist production, and consequently capitals of different organic composition, a country where the normal working-day is shorter than another's may have a higher rate of surplus-value (one of the factors which determines the rate of profit). *First*, if the English ten-hour working-day is, on account of its higher intensity, equal to an Austrian working-day of 14 hours, then, dividing the working-day equally in both instances, 5 hours of English surplus-labour may represent a greater value on the world-market than 7 hours of Austrian surplus-labour. *Second*, a larger portion of the English working-day than of the Austrian may represent surplus-labour.

The law of the falling rate of profit, which expresses the same, or even a higher, rate of surplus-value, states, in other words, that any quantity of the average social capital, say, a capital of 100, comprises an ever larger portion of means of labour, and an ever smaller portion of living labour. Therefore, since the aggregate mass of living labour operating the means of production decreases in relation to the value of these means of production, it follows that the unpaid labour and the portion of value in which it is expressed must decline as compared to the value of the advanced total capital. Or: An ever smaller aliquot part of invested total capital is converted into living labour, and this total capital, therefore, absorbs in proportion to its magnitude less and less surplus-labour, although the unpaid part of the labour applied may at the same time grow in relation to the paid part. The relative decrease of the variable and increase of the constant capital, however much both parts may grow in absolute magnitude, is, as we have said, but another expression for greater productivity of labour.

Let a capital of 100 consist of $80_c + 20_v$, and the latter $= 20$ labourers. Let the rate of surplus-value be 100%, i.e. the labourers work half the day for themselves and the other half for the capitalist. Now let the capital of 100 in a less developed country $= 20_c + 80_v$, and let the latter $= 80$ labourers. But these labourers require ⅔ of the day for themselves, and work only ⅓ for the capitalist. Everything else being equal, the labourers in the first case produce a value of 40, and in the second of 120. The first capital produces $80_c + 20_v + 20_s = 120$; rate of profit $= 20\%$. The second capital, $20_c + 80_v + 40_s = 140$; rate of profit 40%. In the second case the rate of profit is, therefore, double the first, although the rate of surplus-value in the first = 100%, which is double that of the second, where it is only 50%. But then, a capital of the same magnitude appropriates the surplus-labour of only 20 labourers in the first case, and of 80 labourers in the second case.

The law of the progressive falling of the rate of profit, or the relative decline of appropriated surplus-labour compared to the mass of materialised labour set in motion by living labour, does not rule out in any way that the absolute mass of exploited labour set in motion by the social capital, and consequently the absolute mass of the surplus-labour it appropriates, may grow; nor, that the capitals controlled by individual capitalists may dispose of a growing mass of labour and, hence, of surplus-labour, the latter even though the number of labourers they employ does not increase.

Take a certain working population of, say, two million. Assume, furthermore, that the length and intensity of the average working-day, and the level of wages, and thereby the proportion between necessary and surplus-labour, are given. In that case the aggregate labour of these two million, and their surplus-labour expressed in surplus-value, always produces the same magnitude of value. But with the growth of the mass of the constant (fixed and circulating) capital set in motion by this labour, this produced quantity of value declines in relation to the value of this capital, which value grows with its mass, even if not in quite the same proportion. This ratio, and consequently the rate of profit, shrinks in spite of the fact that the mass of commanded living labour is the same as before, and the same amount of surplus-labour is sucked out of it by the capital. It changes because the mass of materialised labour set in motion by living labour increases, and not because the mass of living labour has shrunk. It is a relative decrease, not an absolute one, and has, in fact, nothing to do with the absolute magnitude of the labour and surplus-labour set in motion. The drop in the rate of profit is not due to an absolute, but only to a relative decrease of the variable part of the total capital, i.e. to its decrease in relation to the constant part.

What applies to any given mass of labour and surplus-labour, also applies to a growing number of labourers, and, thus, under the above assumption, to any growing mass of commanded labour in general, and to its unpaid part, the surplus-labour, in particular. If the working population increases from two million to three, and if the variable capital invested in wages also rises to three million from its former two million, while the constant capital rises from four million to fifteen million, then, under the above assumption of a constant working-day and a constant rate of surplus-value, the mass of surplus-labour, and of surplus-value, rises by one-half, i.e. 50%, from two million to three. Nevertheless, in spite of this growth of the absolute mass of surplus-labour, and hence of surplus-value, by 50%, the ratio of variable to constant capital would fall from 2:4 to 3:15, and the ratio of surplus-value to total capital would be (in millions)

$$\text{I.} \quad 4_c + 2_v + 2_s; \ C = 6, \quad p' = 33\tfrac{1}{3}\%.$$
$$\text{II.} \quad 15_c + 3_v + 3_s; \ C = 18, \ p' = 16\tfrac{2}{3}\%.$$

While the mass of surplus-value has increased by one-half, the rate of profit has fallen by one-half. However, the profit is only the surplus-value calculated in relation to the total social capital, and the mass of profit, its absolute magnitude, is socially equal to the absolute magnitude of the surplus-value. The absolute magnitude of the profit, its total amount, would, therefore, have grown by 50%, in spite of its enormous relative decrease compared to the advanced total capital, or in spite of the enormous decrease in the general rate of profit. The number of labourers employed by capital, hence the absolute mass of the labour set in motion by it, and therefore the absolute mass of surplus-labour absorbed by it, the mass of the surplus-value produced by it, and therefore the absolute mass of the profit produced by it, *can*, consequently, increase, and increase progressively, in spite of the progressive drop in the rate of profit. And this not only *can* be so. Aside from temporary fluctuations it *must* be so, on the basis of capitalist production.

Essentially, the capitalist process of production is simultaneously a process of accumulation. We have shown that with the development of capitalist production the mass of values to be simply reproduced, or maintained, increases as the productivity of labour grows, even if the labour-power employed should remain constant. But with the development of social productivity of labour the mass of produced use-values, of which the means of production form a part, grows still more. And the additional labour, through whose appropriation this additional wealth can be reconverted into capital, does not depend on the value, but on the mass of these means of production (including means of subsistence), because in the production process the labourers have nothing to do with the value, but with the use-value, of the means of production. Accumulation itself, however, and the concentration of capital that goes with it, is a material means of increasing productiveness. Now, this growth of the means of production includes the growth of the working population, the creation of a working population, which corresponds to the surplus-capital, or even exceeds its general requirements, thus leading to an over-population of workers. A momentary excess of surplus-capital over the working population it has commandeered, would have a two-fold effect. It would, on the one hand, by raising wages, mitigate the adverse conditions which decimate the offspring of the labourers and would make marriages easier among them, so as gradually to increase the population. On the other hand, by applying methods which yield relative surplus-value (introduction and improvement of machinery) it would produce a far more rapid, artificial, relative over-population, which in its turn, would be a breeding-ground for a really swift propagation of the population, since under capitalist production misery produces population. It therefore follows of itself from the nature of the capitalist process of accumulation, which is but one facet of the capitalist production process, that the increased mass of means of production that is to be converted into capital always finds a correspondingly increased, even excessive, exploitable worker population. As the process of production and accumulation advances therefore, the mass of available and appropriated surplus-labour, and hence the absolute mass of profit appropriated by the social capital, *must* grow. Along with the volume, however, the same laws of production and accumulation increase also the value of the constant capital in a mounting progression more rapidly than that of the variable part of capital, invested as it is in living labour. Hence, the same laws produce for the social capital a growing absolute mass of profit, and a falling rate of profit.

We shall entirely ignore here that with the advance of capitalist production and the attendant development of the productiveness of social labour and multiplication of production branches, hence products, the same amount of value represents a progressively increasing mass of use-values and enjoyments.

The development of capitalist production and accumulation lifts labour-processes to an increasingly enlarged scale and thus imparts to them ever greater dimensions, and involves accordingly larger investments of capital for each individual establishment. A mounting concentration of capitals (accompanied, though on a smaller scale, by an increase in the number of capitalists) is, therefore, one of its material requirements as well as one of its results. Hand in hand with it, mutually interacting, there occurs a progressive expropriation of the more or less direct producers. It is, then, natural for the individual capitalists to command increasingly large armies of labourers (no matter how much the variable capital may decrease in relation to the constant), and natural, too, that the mass of surplus-value, and hence profit, appropriated by them, should grow simultaneously with, and in spite of, the fall in the rate of profit. The causes which concentrate masses of labourers under the command of individual capitalists, are the very same that swell the mass of the invested fixed capital, and auxiliary and raw materials, in mounting proportion as compared to the mass of employed living labour.

It requires no more than a passing remark at this point to indicate that, given a certain labouring population, the mass of surplus-value, hence the absolute mass of profit, must grow if the rate of surplus-value increases, be it through a lengthening or intensification of the working-day, or through a drop in the value of wages due to an increase in the productiveness of labour, and that it must do so in spite of the relative decrease of variable capital in respect to constant.

The same development of the productiveness of social labour, the same laws which express themselves in a relative decrease of variable as compared to total capital, and in the thereby facilitated accumulation, while this accumulation in its turn becomes a starting-point for the further development of the productiveness and for a further relative decrease of variable capital—this same development manifests itself, aside from temporary fluctuations, in a progressive increase of the total employed labour-power and a progressive increase of the absolute mass of surplus-value, and hence of profit.

Now, what must be the form of this double-edged law of a decrease in the *rate* of profit and a simultaneous increase in the absolute *mass* of profit arising from the same causes? As a law based on the fact that under given conditions the appropriated mass of surplus-labour, hence of surplus-value, increases, and that, so far as the total capital is concerned, or the individual capital as an aliquot part of the total capital, profit and surplus-value are identical magnitudes?

Let us take an aliquot part of capital upon which we calculate the rate of profit, e.g. 100. These 100 represent the average composition of the total capital, say, $80_c + 20_v$. We have seen in the second part of this book that the average rate of profit in the various branches of production is determined not by the particular composition of each individual capital, but by the average social composition. As the variable capital decreases relative to the constant, hence the total capital of 100, the rate of profit, or the relative magnitude of surplus-value, i.e. its ratio to the advanced total capital of 100, falls even though the intensity of exploitation were to remain the same, or even to increase. But it is not this relative magnitude alone which falls. The magnitude of the surplus-value or profit absorbed by the total capital of 100 also falls absolutely. At a rate of surplus-value of 100%, a capital of $60_c + 40_v$ produces a mass of surplus-value, and hence of profit, amounting to 40; a capital of $70_c + 30_v$ a mass of profit of 30; and for a capital of $80_c + 20_v$ the profit falls to 20. This falling applies to the mass of surplus-value, and hence of profit, and is due to the fact that the total capital of 100 employs less living labour, and, the intensity of labour exploitation remaining the same, sets in motion less surplus-labour, and therefore produces less surplus-value. Taking any aliquot part of the social capital, i.e. a capital of average composition, as a standard by which to measure surplus-value—and this is done in all profit calculations—a relative fall of surplus-value is generally identical with its absolute fall. In the cases given above, the rate of profit sinks from 40% to 30% and to 20%, because, in fact, the mass of surplus-value, and hence of profit, produced by the same capital falls absolutely from 40 to 30 and to 20. Since the magnitude of the value of the capital, by which the surplus-value is measured, is given as 100, a fall in the proportion of surplus-value to this given magnitude can be only another expression for the decrease of the absolute magnitude of surplus-value and profit. This is, indeed, a tautology. But, as shown, the fact that this decrease occurs at all, arises from the nature of the development of the capitalist process of production.

On the other hand, however, the same causes which bring about an absolute decrease of surplus-value, and hence profit, on a given capital, and consequently of the rate of profit calculated in per cent, produce an increase in the absolute mass of surplus-value, and hence of profit, appropriated by the social capital (i.e. by all capitalists taken as a whole). How does this occur, what is the only way in which this can occur, or what are the conditions obtaining in this seeming contradiction?

If any aliquot part = 100 of the social capital, and hence any 100 of average social composition, is a given magnitude, for which therefore a fall in the rate of profit coincides with a fall in the absolute magnitude of the profit because the capital which here serves as a standard of measurement is a constant magnitude, then the magnitude of the social capital like that of the capital in the hands of individual capitalists, is variable, and in keeping with our assumptions it must vary inversely with the decrease of its variable portion.

In our former illustration, when the percentage of composition was $60_c + 40_v$, the corresponding surplus-value, or profit, was 40, and hence the rate of profit 40%. Suppose, the total capital in this stage of composition was one million. Then the total surplus-value, and hence the total profit, amounted to 400,000. Now, if the composition later $= 80_c + 20_v$, while the degree of labour exploitation remained the same, then the surplus-value or profit for each $100 = 20$. But since the absolute mass of surplus-value or profit increases, as demonstrated, in spite of the decreasing rate of profit or the decreasing production of surplus-value by every 100 of capital—increase, say, from 400,000 to 440,000, then this occurs solely because the total capital which formed at the time of this new composition has risen to 2,200,000. The mass of the total capital set in motion has risen to 220%, while the rate of profit has fallen by 50%. Had the total capital no more than doubled, it would have to produce as much surplus-value and profit to obtain a rate of profit of 20% as the old capital of 1,000,000 produced at 40%. Had it grown to less than double, it would have produced less surplus-value, or profit, than the old capital of 1,000,000, which, in its former composition, would have had to grow from 1,000,000 to no more than 1,100,000 to raise its surplus-value from 400,000 to 440,000.

We again meet here the previously defined law that the relative decrease of the variable capital, hence the development of the social productiveness of labour, involves an increasingly large mass of total capital to set in motion* the same quantity of labour-power and squeeze out the same quantity of surplus-labour. Consequently, the possibility of a relative surplus of labouring people develops proportionately to the advances made by capitalist production not because the productiveness of social labour *decreases*, but because it *increases*. It does not therefore arise out of an absolute disproportion between labour and the means of subsistence, or the means for the production of these means of subsistence, but out of a disproportion occasioned by capitalist exploitation of labour, a disproportion between the progressive growth of capital and its relatively shrinking need for an increasing population.

Should the rate of profit fall by 50%, it would shrink one-half. If the mass of profit is to remain the same, the capital must be doubled. For the mass of profit made at a declining rate of profit to remain the same, the multiplier indicating the growth of the total capital must be equal to the divisor indicating the fall of the rate of profit. If the rate of profit falls from 40 to 20, the total capital must rise inversely at the rate of 20:40 to obtain the same result. If the rate of profit falls from 40 to 8, the capital would have to increase at the rate of 8:40, or five-fold. A capital of 1,000,000 at 40% produces 400,000, and a capital of 5,000,000 at 8% likewise produces 400,000. This applies if we want the result to remain the same. But if the result is to be higher, then the capital must grow at a greater rate than the rate of profit falls. In other words, for the variable portion of the total capital not to remain the same in absolute terms, but to increase absolutely, in spite of its falling in percentage of the total capital, the total capital must grow at a faster rate than the percentage of the variable capital falls. It must grow so considerably that in its new composition it should require more than the old portion of variable capital to purchase labour-power. If the variable portion of a capital = 100 should fall from 40 to 20, the total capital must rise higher than 200 to be able to employ a larger variable capital than 40.

Even if the exploited mass of the working population were to remain constant, and only the length and intensity of the working-day were to increase, the mass of the invested capital would have to increase, since it would have to be greater in order to employ the same mass of labour under the old conditions of exploitation after the composition of capital changes.

Thus, the same development of the social productiveness of labour expresses itself with the progress of capitalist production on the one hand in a tendency of the rate of profit to fall progressively and, on the other, in a progressive growth of the absolute mass of the appropriated surplus-value, or profit; so that on the whole a relative decrease of variable capital and profit is accompanied by an absolute increase of both. This two-fold effect, as we have seen, can express itself only in a growth of the total capital at a pace more rapid than that at which the rate of profit falls. For an absolutely increased variable capital to be employed in a capital of higher composition, or one in which the constant capital has increased relatively more, the total capital must not only grow proportionately to its higher composition, but still more rapidly. It follows, then, that as the capitalist mode of production develops, an ever larger quantity of capital is required to employ the same, let alone an increased, amount of labour-power. Thus, on a capitalist foundation, the increasing productiveness of labour necessarily and permanently creates a seeming over-population of labouring people. If the variable capital forms just ⅙ of the total capital instead of the former ½, the total capital must be trebled to employ the same amount of labour-power. And if twice as much labour-power is to be employed, the total capital must increase six-fold.

Political economy, which has until now been unable to explain the law of the tendency of the rate of profit to fall, pointed self-consolingly to the increasing mass of profit, i.e. to the growth of the absolute magnitude of profit, be it for the individual capitalist or for the social capital, but this was also based on mere platitude and speculation.

To say that the mass of profit is determined by two factors—first, the rate of profit, and, secondly, the mass of capital invested at this rate, is mere tautology. It is therefore but a corollary of this tautology to say that there is a possibility for the mass of profit to grow even though the rate of profit may fall at the same time. It does not help us one step farther, since it is just as possible for the capital to increase without the mass of profit growing, and for it to increase even while the mass of profit falls. For 100 at 25% yields 25, and 400 at 5% yields only 20. But if the same causes which make the rate of profit fall, entail the accumulation, i.e. the formation, of additional capital, and if each additional capital employs additional labour and produces additional surplus-value; if, on the other hand, the mere fall in the rate of profit implies that the constant capital, and with it the total old capital, have increased, then this process ceases to be mysterious. We shall see later* to what deliberate falsifications some people resort in their calculations to spirit away the possibility of an increase in the mass of profit simultaneous with a decrease in the rate of profit.

We have shown how the same causes that bring about a tendency for the general rate of profit to fall necessitate an accelerated accumulation of capital and, consequently, an increase in the absolute magnitude, or total mass, of the surplus-labour (surplus-value, profit) appropriated by it. Just as everything appears reversed in competition, and thus in the consciousness of the agents of competition, so also this law, this inner and necessary connection between two seeming contradictions. It is evident that within the proportions indicated above a capitalist disposing of a large capital will receive a larger mass of profit than a small capitalist making seemingly high profits. Even a cursory examination of competition shows, furthermore, that under certain circumstances, when the greater capitalist wishes to make room for himself on the market, and to crowd out the smaller ones, as happens in times of crises, he makes practical use of this, i.e. he deliberately lowers his rate of profit in order to drive the smaller ones to the wall. Merchant's capital, which we shall describe in detail later, also notably exhibits phenomena which appear to attribute a fall in profit to an expansion of business, and thus of capital. The scientific expression for this false conception will be given later. Similar superficial observations result from a comparison of rates of profit in individual lines of business, distinguished either as subject to free competition, or to monopoly. The utterly shallow conception existing in the minds of the agents of competition is found in Roscher, namely, that a reduction in the rate of profit is 'more prudent and humane'. The fall in the rate of profit appears in this case as an *effect* of an increase in capital and of the concomitant calculation of the capitalist that the mass of profits pocketed by him will be greater at a smaller rate of profit. This entire conception (with the exception of Adam Smith's, which we shall mention later) rests on an utter misapprehension of what the general rate of profit is, and on the crude notion that prices are actually determined by adding a more or less arbitrary quota of profit to the true value of commodities. Crude as these ideas are, they arise necessarily out of the inverted aspect which the immanent laws of capitalist production represent in competition.

The law that a fall in the rate of profit due to the development of productiveness is accompanied by an increase in the mass of profit, also expresses itself in the fact that a fall in the price of commodities produced by a capital is accompanied by a relative increase of the masses of profit contained in them and realised by their sale.

Since the development of the productiveness and the correspondingly higher composition of capital sets in motion an ever-increasing quantity of means of production through a constantly decreasing quantity of labour, every aliquot part of the total product, i.e. every single commodity, or each particular lot of commodities in the total mass of products, absorbs less living labour, and also contains less materialised labour, both in the depreciation of the fixed capital applied and in the raw and auxiliary materials consumed. Hence every single commodity contains a smaller sum of labour materialised in means of production and of labour newly added during production. This causes the price of the individual commodity to fall. But the mass of profits contained in the individual commodities may nevertheless increase if the rate of the absolute or relative surplus-value grows. The commodity contains less newly added labour, but its unpaid portion grows in relation to its paid portion. However, this is the case only within certain limits. With the absolute amount of living labour newly incorporated in individual commodities decreasing enormously as production develops, the absolute mass of unpaid labour contained in them will likewise decrease, however much it may have grown as compared to the paid portion. The mass of profit on each individual commodity will shrink considerably with the development of the productiveness of labour, in spite of a growth in the rate of surplus-value. And this reduction, just as the fall in the rate of profit, is only delayed by the cheapening of the elements of constant capital and by the other circumstances set forth in the first part of this book, which increase the rate of profit at a given, or even falling, rate of surplus-value.

That the price of individual commodities whose sum makes up the total product of capital falls, means simply that a certain quantity of labour is realised in a larger quantity of commodities, so that each individual commodity contains less labour than before. This is the case even if the price of one part of constant capital, such as raw material, etc., should rise. Outside of a few cases (for instance, if the productiveness of labour uniformly cheapens all elements of the constant, and the variable, capital), the rate of profit will fall, in spite of the higher rate of surplus-value, (1) because even a larger unpaid portion of the smaller total amount of newly added labour is smaller than a smaller aliquot unpaid portion of the former larger amount, and (2) because the higher composition of capital is expressed in the individual commodity by the fact that the portion of its value in which newly added labour is materialised decreases in relation to the portion of its value which represents raw and auxiliary material, and the wear and tear of fixed capital. This change in the proportion of the various component parts in the price of individual commodities, i.e. the decrease of that portion of the price in which newly added living labour is materialised, and the increase of that portion of it in which formerly materialised labour is represented, is the form which expresses the decrease of the variable in relation to the constant capital through the price of the individual commodities. Just as this decrease is absolute for a certain amount of capital, say of 100, it is also absolute for every individual commodity as an aliquot part of the reproduced capital. However, the rate of profit, if calculated merely on the elements of the price of an individual commodity, would be different from what it actually is. And for the following reason:

[The rate of profit is calculated on the total capital invested, but for a definite time, actually a year. The rate of profit is the ratio of the surplus-value, or profit, produced and realised in a year, to the total capital calculated in per cent. It is, therefore, not necessarily equal to a rate of profit calculated for the period of turnover of the invested capital rather than for a year. It is only if the capital is turned over exactly in one year that the two coincide.

On the other hand, the profit made in the course of a year is merely the sum of profits on commodities produced and sold during that same year. Now, if we calculate the profit on the cost-price of commodities, we obtain a rate of profit $= p/k$ in which p stands for the profit realised during one year, and k for the sum of the cost-prices of commodities produced and sold within the same period. It is evident that this rate of profit p/k will not coincide with the actual rate of profit p/C, mass of profit divided by total capital, unless k = C, that is, unless the capital is turned over in exactly one year.

Let us take three different conditions of an industrial capital.

I. A capital of £8,000 produces and sells annually 5,000 pieces of a commodity at 30*s*. per piece, thus making an annual turnover of £7,500. It makes a profit of 10*s*. on each piece, or £2,500 per year. Every piece, then, contains 20*s*. advanced capital and 10*s*. profit, so that the rate of profit per piece is 10/20 = 50%. The turned-over sum of £7,500 contains £5,000 advanced capital and £2,500 profit. Rate of profit per turnover, p/k, likewise = 50%. But calculated on the total capital the rate of profit p/C = 2,500/8,000 = 31¼%.

II. The capital rises to £10,000. Owing to increased productivity of labour it is able to produce annually 10,000 pieces of the commodity at a cost-price of 20*s*. per piece. Suppose, the commodity is sold at a profit of 4*s*., hence at 24*s*. per piece. In that case the price of the annual product = £12,000, of which £10,000 is advanced capital and £2,000 is profit. The rate of profit p/k = 4/20 per piece, and 2,000/10,000 for the annual turnover, or in both cases = 20%. And since the total capital is equal to the sum of the cost-prices, namely £10,000, it follows that p/C, the actual rate of profit, is in this case also 20%.

III. Let the capital rise to £15,000 owing to a constant growth of the productiveness of labour, and let it annually produce 30,000 pieces of the commodity at a cost-price of 13*s*. per piece, each piece being sold at a profit of 2*s*., or at 15*s*. The annual turnover therefore = 30,000 × 15*s*. = £22,500, of which £19,500 is advanced capital and £3,000 profit. The rate of profit p/k then = 2/13 = 3,000/19,500 = 15⁵⁄₁₃%. But p/C = 3,000/15,000 = 20%.

We see, therefore, that only in case II, where the turned-over capital-value is equal to the total capital, the rate of profit per piece, or per total amount of turnover, is the same as the rate of profit calculated on the total capital. In case I, in which the amount of the turnover is smaller than the total capital, the rate of profit calculated on the cost-price of the commodity is higher; and in case III, in which the total capital is smaller than the amount of the turnover, it is lower than the actual rate calculated on the total capital. This is a general rule.

In commercial practice, the turnover is generally calculated inaccurately. It is assumed that the capital has been turned over once as soon as the sum of the realised commodity-prices equals the sum of the invested total capital. But the *capital* can complete one whole turnover only when the sum of the *cost-prices* of the realised commodities equals the sum of the total capital.—*F. E.*]

This again shows how important it is in capitalist production to regard individual commodities, or the commodity-product of a certain period, as products of advanced capital and in relation to the total capital which produces them, rather than in isolation, by themselves, as mere commodities.

The *rate* of profit must be calculated by measuring the mass of produced and realised surplus-value not only in relation to the consumed portion of capital reappearing in the commodities, but also to this part plus that portion of unconsumed but applied capital which continues to operate in production. However, the *mass* of profit cannot be equal to anything but the mass of profit or surplus-value, contained in the commodities themselves, and to be realised by their sale.

If the productivity of industry increases, the price of individual commodities falls. There is less labour in them, less paid and unpaid labour. Suppose, the same labour produces, say, triple its former product. Then ⅔ less labour yields an individual product. And since profit can make up but a portion of the amount of labour contained in an individual commodity, the mass of profit in the individual commodity must decrease, and this takes place within certain limits, even if the rate of surplus-value should rise. In any case, the mass of profit on the total product does not fall below the original mass of profit so long as the capital employs the same number of labourers at the same degree of exploitation. (This may also occur if fewer labourers are employed at a higher rate of exploitation.) For the mass of profit on the individual product decreases proportionately to the increase in the number of products. The mass of profit remains the same, but it is distributed differently over the total amount of commodities. Nor does this alter the distribution between the labourers and capitalists of the amount of value created by newly added labour. The mass of profit cannot increase so long as the same amount of labour is employed, unless the unpaid surplus-labour increases, or, should intensity of exploitation remain the same, unless the number of labourers grows. Or, both these causes may combine to produce this result. In all these cases—which, however, in accordance with our assumption, presuppose an increase of constant capital as compared to variable, and an increase in the magnitude of total capital—the individual commodity contains a smaller mass of profit and the rate of profit falls even if calculated on the individual commodity. A given quantity of newly added labour materialises in a larger quantity of commodities. The price of the individual commodity falls. Considered abstractly the rate of profit may remain the same, even though the price of the individual commodity may fall as a result of greater productiveness of labour and a simultaneous increase in the number of this cheaper commodity if, for instance, the increase in productiveness of labour acts uniformly and simultaneously on all the elements of the commodity, so that its total price falls in the same proportion in which the productivity of labour increases, while, on the other hand, the mutual relation of the different elements of the price of the commodity remains the same. The rate of profit could even rise if a rise in the rate of surplus-value were accompanied by a substantial reduction in the value of the elements of constant, and particularly of fixed, capital. But in reality, as we have seen, the rate of profit will fall in the long run. In no case does a fall in the price of any individual commodity by itself give a clue to the rate of profit. Everything depends on the magnitude of the total capital invested in its production. For instance, if the price of one yard of fabric falls from 3s. to 1⅔s., if we know that before this price reduction it contained 1⅔s. constant capital, yarn, etc., ⅔s. wages, and ⅔s. profit, while after the reduction it contains 1s. constant capital, ⅓s. wages, and ⅓s. profit, we cannot tell if the rate of profit has remained the same or not. This depends on whether, and by how much, the advanced total capital has increased, and how many yards more it produces in a given time.

The phenomenon, springing from the nature of the capitalist mode of production, that increasing productivity of labour implies a drop in the price of the individual commodity, or of a certain mass of commodities, an increase in the number of commodities, a reduction in the mass of profit on the individual commodity and in the rate of profit on the aggregate of commodities, and an increase in the mass of profit on the total quantity of commodities—this phenomenon appears on the surface only in a reduction of the mass of profit on the individual commodity, a fall in its price, an increase in the mass of profit on the augmented total number of commodities produced by the total social capital or an individual capitalist. It then appears as if the capitalist adds less profit to the price of the individual commodity of his own free will, and makes up for it through the greater number of commodities he produces. This conception rests upon the notion of profit upon alienation, which, in its turn, is deduced from the conception of merchant capital.

We have previously seen in Book I (Parts 4 and 7) that the mass of commodities growing along with the productivity of labour and the cheapening of the individual commodity as such (as long as these commodities do not enter the price of labour-power as determinants)—that this does not affect the proportion between paid and unpaid labour in the individual commodity, in spite of the falling price.

Since all things appear distorted, namely, reversed in competition, the individual capitalist may imagine: 1) that he is reducing his profit on the individual commodity by cutting its price, but still making a greater profit by selling a larger quantity of commodities; 2) that he fixes the price of the individual commodities and that he determines the price of the total product by multiplication, while the original process is really one of division (see Book I, Ch.12, p. 193), and multiplication is only correct secondarily, since it is based on that division. The vulgar economist does practically no more than translate the singular concepts of the capitalists, who are in the thrall of competition, into a seemingly more theoretical and generalised language, and attempt to substantiate the justice of those conceptions.

The fall in commodity-prices and the rise in the mass of profit on the augmented mass of these cheapened commodities is, in fact, but another expression for the law of the falling rate of profit attended by a simultaneously increasing mass of profit.

The analysis of how far a falling rate of profit may coincide with rising prices no more belongs here than that of the point previously discussed in Book I (Ch. 12, pp. 192–4), concerning relative surplus-value. A capitalist working with improved but not as yet generally adopted methods of production sells below the market-price, but above his individual price of production; his rate of profit rises until competition levels it out. During this equalisation period the second requisite, expansion of the invested capital, makes its appearance. According to the degree of this expansion the capitalist will be able to employ a part of his former labourers, actually perhaps all of them, or even more, under the new conditions, and hence to produce the same, or a greater, mass of profit.

CHAPTER 14

COUNTERACTING INFLUENCES

IF we consider the enormous development of the productive forces of social labour in the last 30 years alone as compared with all preceding periods; if we consider, in particular, the enormous mass of fixed capital, aside from the actual machinery, which goes into the process of social production as a whole, then the difficulty which has hitherto troubled the economist, namely to explain the falling rate of profit, gives place to its opposite, namely to explain why this fall is not greater and more rapid. There must be some counteracting influences at work, which cross and annul the effect of the general law, and which give it merely the characteristic of a tendency, for which reason we have referred to the fall of the general rate of profit as a tendency to fall.

The following are the most general counterbalancing forces:

I. Increasing Intensity of Exploitation

The degree of exploitation of labour, the appropriation of surplus-labour and surplus-value, is raised notably by lengthening the working-day and intensifying labour. These two points have been comprehensively treated in Book I as incidental to the production of absolute and relative surplus-value. There are many ways of intensifying labour which imply an increase of constant, as compared to variable, capital, and hence a fall in the rate of profit, such as compelling a labourer to operate a larger number of machines. In such cases—and in most procedures serving the production of relative surplus-values—the same causes which increase the rate of surplus-value, may also, from the standpoint of given quantities of invested total capital, involve a fall in the mass of surplus-value. But there are other aspects of intensification, such as the greater velocities of machinery, which consume more raw material in the same time, but, so far as the fixed capital is concerned, wear out the machinery so much faster, and yet do not in any way affect the relation of its value to the price of the labour which sets it in motion. But notably, it is prolongation of the working-day, this invention of modern industry, which increases the mass of appropriated surplus-labour without essentially altering the proportion of the employed labour-power to the constant capital set in motion by it, and which rather tends to reduce this capital relatively. Moreover, it has already been demonstrated—and this constitutes the real secret of the tendency of the rate of profit to fall—that the manipulations to produce relative surplus-value amount, on the whole, to transforming as much as possible of a certain quantity of labour into surplus-value, on the one hand, and employing as little labour as possible in proportion to the invested capital, on the other, so that the same reasons which permit raising the intensity of exploitation rule out exploiting the same quantity of labour as before by the same capital. These are the counteracting tendencies, which, while effecting a rise in the rate of surplus-value, also tend to decrease the mass of surplus-value, and hence the rate of profit produced by a certain capital. Mention should also be made here of the widespread introduction of female and child labour, in so far as the whole family must now perform more surplus-labour for capital than before, even when the total amount of their wages increases, which is by no means always the case.—Everything that promotes the production of relative surplus-value by mere improvement in methods, as in agriculture, without altering the magnitude of the invested capital, has the same effect. The constant capital, it is true, does not, in such cases, increase in relation to the variable, inasmuch as we regard the variable capital as an index of the amount of labour-power employed, but the mass of the product does increase in proportion to the labour-power employed. The same occurs, if the productiveness of labour (no matter, whether its product goes into the labourer's consumption or into the elements of constant capital) is freed from hindrances in communications, from arbitrary or other restrictions which have become obstacles in the course of time; from fetters of all kinds, without directly affecting the ratio of variable to constant capital.

It might be asked whether the factors that check the fall of the rate of profit, but that always hasten its fall in the last analysis, whether these include the temporary, but always recurring, elevations in surplus-value above the general level, which keep occurring now in this and now in that line of production redounding to the benefit of those individual capitalists, who make use of inventions, etc., before these are introduced elsewhere. This question must be answered in the affirmative.

The mass of surplus-value produced by a capital of a given magnitude is the product of two factors—the rate of surplus-value multiplied by the number of labourers employed at this rate. At a given rate of surplus-value it therefore depends on the number of labourers, and it depends on the rate of surplus-value when the number of labourers is given. Generally, therefore, it depends on the composite ratio of the absolute magnitudes of the variable capital and the rate of surplus-value. Now we have seen that, on the average, the same factors which raise the rate of relative surplus-value lower the mass of the employed labour-power. It is evident, however, that this will occur to a greater or lesser extent, depending on the definite proportion in which this conflicting movement obtains, and that the tendency towards a reduction in the rate of profit is notably weakened by a rise in the rate of absolute surplus-value, which originates with the lengthening of the working-day.

We saw in the case of the rate of profit that a drop in the rate was generally accompanied by an increase in the mass of profit, due to the increasing mass of total capital employed. From the standpoint of the total variable capital of society, the surplus-value it has produced is equal to the profit it has produced. Both the absolute mass and the rate of surplus-value have increased; the one because the quantity of labour-power employed by society has grown, and the other, because the intensity of exploitation of this labour-power has increased. But in the case of a capital of a given magnitude, e.g. 100, the rate of surplus-value may increase, while the average mass may decrease; for the rate is determined by the proportion, in which the variable capital produces value, while the mass is determined by the proportion of variable capital to the total capital.

The rise in the rate of surplus-value is a factor which determines the mass of surplus-value, and hence also the rate of profit, for it takes place especially under conditions, in which, as we have previously seen, the constant capital is either not increased at all, or not proportionately increased, in relation to the variable capital. This factor does not abolish the general law. But it causes that law to act rather as a tendency, i.e. as a law whose absolute action is checked, retarded, and weakened, by counteracting circumstances. But since the same influences which raise the rate of surplus-value (even a lengthening of the working-time is a result of large-scale industry) tend to decrease the labour-power employed by a certain capital, it follows that they also tend to reduce the rate of profit and to retard this reduction. If one labourer is compelled to perform as much labour as would rationally be performed by at least two, and if this is done under circumstances in which this one labourer can replace three, then this one labourer will perform as much surplus-labour as was formerly performed by two, and the rate of surplus-value will have risen accordingly. But he will not perform as much as three had performed, and the mass of surplus-value will have decreased accordingly. But this reduction in mass will be compensated, or limited, by the rise in the rate of surplus-value. If the entire population is employed at a higher rate of surplus-value, the mass of surplus-value will increase, in spite of the population remaining the same. It will increase still more if the population increases. And although this is tied up with a relative reduction of the number of employed labourers in proportion to the magnitude of the total capital, this reduction is moderated, or checked, by the rise in the rate of surplus-value.

Before leaving this point, it is to be emphasised once more that with a capital of a given magnitude the *rate* of surplus-value may rise, while its *mass* is decreasing, and vice versa. The mass of surplus-value is equal to the rate multiplied by the number of labourers; however, the rate is never calculated on the total, but only on the variable capital, actually only for every working-day. On the other hand, with a given magnitude of capital-value, the *rate of profit* can neither rise nor fall without the *mass of surplus-value* also rising or falling.

II. Depression of Wages below the Value of Labour-Power

This is mentioned here only empirically, since, like many other things which might be enumerated, it has nothing to do with the general analysis of capital, but belongs in an analysis of competition, which is not presented in this work. However, it is one of the most important factors checking the tendency of the rate of profit to fall.

III. Cheapening of Elements of Constant Capital

Everything said in Part I of this book about factors which raise the rate of profit while the rate of surplus-value remains the same, or regardless of the rate of surplus-value, belongs here. Hence also, with respect to the total capital, that the value of the constant capital does not increase in the same proportion as its material volume. For instance, the quantity of cotton worked up by a single European spinner in a modern factory has grown tremendously compared to the quantity formerly worked up by a European spinner with a spinning-wheel. Yet the value of the worked-up cotton has not grown in the same proportion as its mass. The same applies to machinery and other fixed capital. In short, the same development which increases the mass of the constant capital in relation to the variable reduces the value of its elements as a result of the increased productivity of labour, and therefore prevents the value of constant capital, although it continually increases, from increasing at the same rate as its material volume, i.e. the material volume of the means of production set in motion by the same amount of labour-power. In isolated cases the mass of the elements of constant capital may even increase, while its value remains the same, or falls.

The foregoing is bound up with the depreciation of existing capital (that is, of its material elements), which occurs with the development of industry. This is another continually operating factor which checks the fall of the rate of profit, although it may under certain circumstances encroach on the mass of profit by reducing the mass of the capital yielding a profit. This again shows that the same influences which tend to make the rate of profit fall, also moderate the effects of this tendency.

IV. Relative Over-Population

Its propagation is inseparable from, and hastened by, the development of the productivity of labour as expressed by a fall in the rate of profit. The relative over-population becomes so much more apparent in a country, the more the capitalist mode of production is developed in it. This, again, is the reason why, on the one hand, the more or less imperfect subordination of labour to capital continues in many branches of production, and continues longer than seems at first glance compatible with the general stage of development. This is due to the cheapness and abundance of disposable or unemployed wage-labourers, and to the greater resistance, which some branches of production, by their very nature, render to the transformation of manual work into machine production. On the other hand, new lines of production are opened up, especially for the production of luxuries, and it is these that take as their basis this relative over-population, often set free in other lines of production through the increase of their constant capital. These new lines start out predominantly with living labour, and by degrees pass through the same evolution as the other lines of production. In either case the variable capital makes up a considerable portion of the total capital and wages are below the average, so that both the rate and mass of surplus-value in these lines of production are unusually high. Since the general rate of profit is formed by levelling the rates of profit in the individual branches of production, however, the same factor which brings about the tendency in the rate of profit to fall, again produces a counterbalance to this tendency and more or less paralyses its effects.

V. Foreign Trade

Since foreign trade partly cheapens the elements of constant capital, and partly the necessities of life for which the variable capital is exchanged, it tends to raise the rate of profit by increasing the rate of surplus-value and lowering the value of constant capital. It generally acts in this direction by permitting an expansion of the scale of production. It thereby hastens the process of accumulation, on the one hand, but causes the variable capital to shrink in relation to the constant capital, on the other, and thus hastens a fall in the rate of profit. In the same way, the expansion of foreign trade, although the basis of the capitalist mode of production in its infancy, has become its own product, however, with the further progress of the capitalist mode of production, through the innate necessity of this mode of production, its need for an ever-expanding market. Here we see once more the dual nature of this effect. (Ricardo has entirely over-looked this side of foreign trade.)

Another question—really beyond the scope of our analysis because of its special nature—is this: Is the general rate of profit raised by the higher rate of profit produced by capital invested in foreign, and particularly colonial, trade?

Capitals invested in foreign trade can yield a higher rate of profit, because, in the first place, there is competition with commodities produced in other countries with inferior production facilities, so that the more advanced country sells its goods above their value even though cheaper than the competing countries. In so far as the labour of the more advanced country is here realised as labour of a higher specific weight, the rate of profit rises, because labour which has not been paid as being of a higher quality is sold as such. The same may obtain in relation to the country, to which commodities are exported and to that from which commodities are imported; namely, the latter may offer more materialised labour *in kind* than it receives, and yet thereby receive commodities cheaper than it could produce them. Just as a manufacturer who employs a new invention before it becomes generally used, undersells his competitors and yet sells his commodity above its individual value, that is, realises the specifically higher productiveness of the labour he employs as surplus-labour. He thus secures a surplus–profit. As concerns capitals invested in colonies, etc., on the other hand, they may yield higher rates of profit for the simple reason that the rate of profit is higher there due to backward development, and likewise the exploitation of labour, because of the use of slaves, coolies, etc. Why should not these higher rates of profit, realised by capitals invested in certain lines and sent home by them, enter into the equalisation of the general rate of profit and thus tend, *pro tanto*, to raise it, unless it is the monopolies that stand in the way. There is so much less reason for it, since these spheres of investment of capital are subject to the laws of free competition. What Ricardo fancies is mainly this: with the higher prices realised abroad commodities are bought there in return and sent home. These commodities are thus sold on the home market, which fact can at best be but a temporary extra disadvantage of these favoured spheres of production over others. This illusion falls away as soon as it is divested of its money-form. The favoured country recovers more labour in exchange for less labour, although this difference, this excess is pocketed, as in any exchange between labour and capital, by a certain class. Since the rate of profit is higher, therefore, because it is generally higher in a colonial country, it may, provided natural conditions are favourable, go hand in hand with low commodity-prices. A levelling takes place but not a levelling to the old level, as Ricardo feels.

This same foreign trade develops the capitalist mode of production in the home country, which implies the decrease of variable capital in relation to constant, and, on the other hand, causes over-production in respect to foreign markets, so that in the long run it again has an opposite effect.

We have thus seen in a general way that the same influences which produce a tendency in the general rate of profit to fall, also call forth counter-effects, which hamper, retard, and partly paralyse this fall. The latter do not do away with the law, but impair its effect. Otherwise, it would not be the fall of the general rate of profit, but rather its relative slowness, that would be incomprehensible. Thus, the law acts only as a tendency. And it is only under certain circumstances and only after long periods that its effects become strikingly pronounced.

Before we go on, in order to avoid misunderstandings, we should recall two, repeatedly treated, points.

First: The same process which brings about a cheapening of commodities in the course of the development of the capitalist mode of production, causes a change in the organic composition of the social capital invested in the production of commodities, and consequently lowers the rate of profit. We must be careful, therefore, not to identify the reduction in the relative cost of an individual commodity, including that portion of it which represents wear and tear of machinery, with the rise in the value of the constant in relation to variable capital, although, conversely, every reduction in the relative cost of the constant capital assuming the volume of its material elements remains the same, or increases, tends to raise the rate of profit, i.e. to reduce *pro tanto* the value of the constant capital in relation to the shrinking proportions of the employed variable capital.

Second: The fact that the newly added living labour contained in the individual commodities, which taken together make up the product of capital, decreases in relation to the materials they contain and the means of labour consumed by them; the fact, therefore, that an ever-decreasing quantity of additional living labour is materialised in them, because their production requires less labour with the development of the social productiveness—this fact does not affect the ratio, in which the living labour contained in the commodities breaks up into paid and unpaid labour. Quite the contrary. Although the total quantity of additional living labour contained in the commodities decreases, the unpaid portion increases in relation to the paid portion, either by an absolute or a relative shrinking of the paid portion; for the same mode of production which reduces the total quantity of additional living labour in a commodity is accompanied by a rise in the absolute and relative surplus-value. The tendency of the rate of profit to fall is bound up with a tendency of the rate of surplus-value to rise, hence with a tendency for the rate of labour exploitation to rise. Nothing is more absurd, for this reason, than to explain the fall in the rate of profit by a rise in the rate of wages, although this may be the case by way of an exception. Statistics is not able to make actual analyses of the rates of wages in different epochs and countries, until the conditions which shape the rate of profit are thoroughly understood. The rate of profit does not fall because labour becomes less productive, but because it becomes more productive. Both the rise in the rate of surplus-value and the fall in the rate of profit are but specific forms through which growing productivity of labour is expressed under capitalism.

VI. The Increase of Stock Capital

The foregoing five points may still be supplemented by the following, which, however, cannot be more fully treated for the present. With the progress of capitalist production, which goes hand in hand with accelerated accumulation, a portion of capital is calculated and applied only as interest-bearing capital. Not in the sense in which every capitalist who lends out capital is satisfied with interest, while the industrial capitalist pockets the investor's profit. This has no bearing on the level of the general rate of profit, because for the latter profit = interest + profit of all kinds + ground-rent, the division into these particular categories being immaterial to it. But in the sense that these capitals, although invested in large productive enterprises, yield only large or small amounts of interest, so-called dividends, after all costs have been deducted. In railways, for instance. These do not therefore go into levelling the general rate of profit, because they yield a lower than average rate of profit. If they did enter into it, the general rate of profit would fall much lower. Theoretically, they may be included in the calculation, and the result would then be a lower rate of profit than the seemingly existing rate, which is decisive for the capitalists; it would be lower, because the constant capital particularly in these enterprises is largest in its relation to the variable capital.

CHAPTER 15

EXPOSITION OF THE INTERNAL CONTRADICTIONS OF THE LAW

I. General

We have seen in the first part of this book that the rate of profit expresses the rate of surplus-value always lower than it actually is. We have just seen that even a rising rate of surplus-value has a tendency to express itself in a falling rate of profit. The rate of profit would equal the rate of surplus-value only if $c = 0$, i.e. if the total capital were paid out in wages. A falling rate of profit does not express a falling rate of surplus-value, unless the proportion of the value of the constant capital to the quantity of labour-power which sets it in motion remains unchanged or the amount of labour-power increases in relation to the value of the constant capital.

On the plea of analysing the rate of profit, Ricardo actually analyses the rate of surplus-value alone, and this only on the assumption that the working-day is intensively and extensively a constant magnitude.

A fall in the rate of profit and accelerated accumulation are different expressions of the same process only in so far as both reflect the development of productiveness. Accumulation, in turn, hastens the fall of the rate of profit, inasmuch as it implies concentration of labour on a large scale, and thus a higher composition of capital. On the other hand, a fall in the rate of profit again hastens the concentration of capital and its centralisation through expropriation of minor capitalists, the few direct producers who still have anything left to be expropriated. This accelerates accumulation with regard to mass, although the rate of accumulation falls with the rate of profit.

On the other hand, the rate of self-expansion of the total capital, or the rate of profit, being the goad of capitalist production (just as self-expansion of capital is its only purpose), its fall checks the formation of new independent capitals and thus appears as a threat to the development of the capitalist production process. It breeds over-production, speculation, crises, and surplus-capital alongside surplus-population. Those economists, therefore, who, like Ricardo, regard the capitalist mode of production as absolute, feel at this point that it creates a barrier itself, and for this reason attribute the barrier to Nature (in the theory of rent), not to production. But the main thing about their horror of the falling rate of profit is the feeling that capitalist production meets in the development of its productive forces a barrier which has nothing to do with the production of wealth as such; and this peculiar barrier testifies to the limitations and to the merely historical, transitory character of the capitalist mode of production; testifies that for the production of wealth, it is not an absolute mode, moreover, that at a certain stage it rather conflicts with its further development.

True, Ricardo and his school considered only industrial profit, which includes interest. But the rate of ground-rent likewise has a tendency to fall, although its absolute mass increases, and may also increase proportionately more than industrial profit. (See Ed. West, who developed the law of ground-rent *before* Ricardo.) If we consider the total social capital C, and use p_1 for the industrial profit that remains after deducting interest and ground-rent, i for interest, and r for ground-rent, then $s/C = p/C = p_1 + i + r/C = p_1/C + i/C + r/C$. We have seen that while s, the total amount of surplus-value, is continually increasing in the course of capitalist development, s/C is just as steadily declining, because C grows still more rapidly than s. Therefore it is by no means a contradiction for p_1, i, and r to be steadily increasing, each individually, while $s/C = p/C$, as well as p_1/C, i/C, and r/C, should each by itself be steadily shrinking, or that p_1 should increase in relation to i, or r in relation to p_1, or to p_1 and i. With a rising total surplus-value or profit s = p, and a simultaneously falling rate of profit $s/C = p/C$, the proportions of the parts p_1, i, and r, which make up s = p, may change at will within the limits set by the total amount of s without thereby affecting the magnitude of s or s/C.

The mutual variation of p_1, i, and r is merely a varying distribution of s among different classes. Consequently, p_1/C, i/C, or r/C, the rate of individual industrial profit, the rate of interest, and the ratio of ground-rent to the total capital, may rise in relation to one another, while s/C, the general rate of profit, falls. The only condition is that the sum of all three = s/C. If the rate of profit falls from 50% to 25%, because the composition of a certain capital with, say, a rate of surplus-value = 100% has changed from $50_c + 50_v$ to $75_c + 25_v$, then a capital of 1,000 will yield a profit of 500 in the first case, and in the second a capital of 4,000 will yield a profit of 1,000. We see that s or p have doubled, while p´ has fallen by one-half. And if that 50% was formerly divided into 20 profit, 10 interest, and 20 rent, then $p_1/C = 20\%$, $i/C = 10\%$, and $r/C = 20\%$. If the proportions had remained the same after the change from 50% to 25%, then $p_1/C = 10\%$, $i/C = 5\%$, and $r/C = 10\%$. If, however, p_1/C should fall to 8% and i/C to 4%, then r/C would rise to 13%. The relative magnitude of r would have risen as against p_1 and i, while p would have remained the same. Under both assumptions, the sum of p_1, i, and r would have increased, because produced by a capital four times as large. Furthermore, Ricardo's assumption that originally industrial profit (plus interest) contains the entire surplus-value is historically and logically false. It is rather the progress of capitalist production which 1) gives the whole profit directly to the industrial and commercial capitalists for further distribution, and 2) reduces rent to the excess over the profit. On this capitalist basis, again, the rent grows, being a portion of profit (i.e. of the surplus-value viewed as the product of the total capital), but not that specific portion of the product, which the capitalist pockets.

Given the necessary means of production, i.e. a sufficient accumulation of capital, the creation of surplus-value is only limited by the labouring population if the rate of surplus-value, i.e. the intensity of exploitation, is given; and no other limit but the intensity of exploitation if the labouring population is given. And the capitalist process of production consists essentially of the production of surplus-value, represented in the surplus-product or that aliquot portion of the produced commodities materialising unpaid labour. It must never be forgotten that the production of this surplus-value—and the reconversion of a portion of it into capital, or the accumulation, forms an integrate part of this production of surplus-value—is the immediate purpose and compelling motive of capitalist production. It will never do, therefore, to represent capitalist production as something which it is not, namely as production whose immediate purpose is enjoyment or the manufacture of the means of enjoyment for the capitalist. This would be overlooking its specific character, which is revealed in all its inner essence.

The creation of this surplus-value makes up the direct process of production, which, as we have said, has no other limits but those mentioned above. As soon as all the surplus-labour it was possible to squeeze out has been embodied in commodities, surplus-value has been produced. But this production of surplus-value completes but the first act of the capitalist process of production—the direct production process. Capital has absorbed so and so much unpaid labour. With the development of the process, which expresses itself in a drop in the rate of profit, the mass of surplus-value thus produced swells to immense dimensions. Now comes the second act of the process. The entire mass of commodities, i.e. the total product, including the portion which replaces the constant and variable capital, and that representing surplus-value, must be sold. If this is not done, or done only in part, or only at prices below the prices of production, the labourer has been indeed exploited, but his exploitation is not realised as such for the capitalist, and this can be bound up with a total or partial failure to realise the surplus-value pressed out of him, indeed even with the partial or total loss of the capital. The conditions of direct exploitation, and those of realising it, are not identical. They diverge not only in place and time, but also logically. The first are only limited by the productive power of society, the latter by the proportional relation of the various branches of production and the consumer power of society. But this last-named is not determined either by the absolute productive power, or by the absolute consumer power, but by the consumer power based on antagonistic conditions of distribution, which reduce the consumption of the bulk of society to a minimum varying within more or less narrow limits. It is furthermore restricted by the tendency to accumulate, the drive to expand capital and produce surplus-value on an extended scale. This is law for capitalist production, imposed by incessant revolutions in the methods of production themselves, by the depreciation of existing capital always bound up with them, by the general competitive struggle and the need to improve production and expand its scale merely as a means of self-preservation and under penalty of ruin. The market must, therefore, be continually extended, so that its interrelations and the conditions regulating them assume more and more the form of a natural law working independently of the producer, and become ever more uncontrollable. This internal contradiction seeks to resolve itself through expansion of the outlying field of production. But the more productiveness develops, the more it finds itself at variance with the narrow basis on which the conditions of consumption rest. It is no contradiction at all on this self-contradictory basis that there should be an excess of capital simultaneously with a growing surplus of population. For while a combination of these two would, indeed, increase the mass of produced surplus-value, it would at the same time intensify the contradiction between the conditions under which this surplus-value is produced and those under which it is realised.

If a certain rate of profit is given, the mass of profit will always depend on the magnitude of the advanced capital. The accumulation, however, is then determined by that portion of this mass which is reconverted into capital. As for this portion, being equal to the profit minus the revenue consumed by the capitalists, it will depend not merely on the value of this mass, but also on the cheapness of the commodities which the capitalist can buy with it, commodities which pass partly into his consumption, his revenue, and partly into his constant capital. (Wages are here assumed to be given.)

The mass of capital set in motion by the labourer, whose value he preserves by his labour and reproduces in his product, is quite different from the value which he adds to it. If the mass of the capital = 1,000 and the added labour = 100, the reproduced capital = 1,100. If the mass = 100 and the added labour = 20, the reproduced capital = 120. In the first case the rate of profit = 10%, in the second = 20%. And yet more can be accumulated out of 100 than out of 20. And thus the river of capital rolls on (aside from its depreciation through increase of the productiveness), or its accumulation does, not in proportion to the rate of profit, but in proportion to the impetus it already possesses. So far as it is based on a high rate of surplus-value, a high rate of profit is possible when the working-day is very long, although labour is not highly productive. It is possible, because the wants of the labourers are very small, hence average wages very low, although the labour itself is unproductive. The low wages will correspond to the labourers' lack of energy. Capital then accumulates slowly, in spite of the high rate of profit. Population is stagnant and the working-time which the product costs, is great, while the wages paid to the labourer are small.

The rate of profit does not sink because the labourer is exploited any less, but because generally less labour is employed in proportion to the employed capital.

If, as shown, a falling rate of profit is bound up with an increase in the mass of profit, a larger portion of the annual product of labour is appropriated by the capitalist under the category of capital (as a replacement for consumed capital) and a relatively smaller portion under the category of profit. Hence the fantastic idea of priest Chalmers, that the less of the annual product is expended by capitalists as capital, the greater the profits they pocket. In which case the state church comes to their assistance, to care for the consumption of the greater part of the surplus-product, rather than having it used as capital. The preacher confounds cause with effect. Furthermore, the mass of profit increases in spite of its slower rate with the growth of the invested capital. However, this requires a simultaneous concentration of capital, since the conditions of production then demand employment of capital on a larger scale. It also requires its centralisation, i.e. the swallowing up of the small capitalists by the big and their deprivation of capital. It is again but an instance of separating—raised to the second power—the conditions of production from the producers to whose number these small capitalists still belong, since their own labour continues to play a role in their case. The labour of a capitalist stands altogether in inverse proportion to the size of his capital, i.e. to the degree in which he is a capitalist. It is this same severance of the conditions of production, on the one hand, from the producers, on the other, that forms the conception of capital. It begins with primitive accumulation (Vol. I, Ch. 24), appears as a permanent process in the accumulation and concentration of capital, and expresses itself finally as centralisation of existing capitals in a few hands and a deprivation of many of their capital (to which expropriation is now changed). This process would soon bring about the collapse of capitalist production if it were not for counteracting tendencies, which have a continuous decentralising effect alongside the centripetal one.

II. Conflict between Expansion of Production and Production of Surplus-Value

The development of the social productiveness of labour is manifested in two ways: first, in the magnitude of the already produced productive forces, the value and mass of the conditions of production under which new production is carried on, and in the absolute magnitude of the already accumulated productive capital; secondly, in the relative smallness of the portion of total capital laid out in wages, i.e. in the relatively small quantity of living labour required for the reproduction and self-expansion of a given capital, for mass production. This also implies concentration of capital.

In relation to employed labour-power the development of the productivity again reveals itself in two ways: First, in the increase of surplus-labour, i.e. the reduction of the necessary labour-time required for the reproduction of labour-power. Secondly, in the decrease of the quantity of labour-power (the number of labourers) generally employed to set in motion a given capital.

The two movements not only go hand in hand, but mutually influence one another and are phenomena in which the same law expresses itself. Yet they affect the rate of profit in opposite ways. The total mass of profit is equal to the total mass of surplus-value, the rate of profit $= s/C =$ surplus-value/advanced total capital. The surplus-value, however, as a total, is determined first by its rate, and second by the mass of labour simultaneously employed at this rate, or, what amounts to the same, by the magnitude of the variable capital. One of these factors, the rate of surplus-value, rises, and the other, the number of labourers, falls (relatively or absolutely). Inasmuch as the development of the productive forces reduces the paid portion of employed labour, it raises the surplus-value, because it raises its rate; but inasmuch as it reduces the total mass of labour employed by a given capital, it reduces the factor of the number by which the rate of surplus-value is multiplied to obtain its mass. Two labourers, each working 12 hours daily, cannot produce the same mass of surplus-value as 24 who work only 2 hours, even if they could live on air and hence did not have to work for themselves at all. In this respect, then, the compensation of the reduced number of labourers by intensifying the degree of exploitation has certain insurmountable limits. It may, for this reason, well check the fall in the rate of profit, but cannot prevent it altogether.

With the development of the capitalist mode of production, therefore, the rate of profit falls, while its mass increases with the growing mass of the capital employed. Given the rate, the absolute increase in the mass of capital depends on its existing magnitude. But, on the other hand, if this magnitude is given, the proportion of its growth, i.e. the rate of its increment, depends on the rate of profit. The increase in the productiveness (which, moreover, we repeat, always goes hand in hand with a depreciation of the available capital) can directly only increase the value of the existing capital if by raising the rate of profit it increases that portion of the value of the annual product which is reconverted into capital. As concerns the productivity of labour, this can only occur (since this productivity has nothing direct to do with the *value* of the existing capital) by raising the relative surplus-value, or reducing the value of the constant capital, so that the commodities which enter either the reproduction of labour-power, or the elements of constant capital, are cheapened. Both imply a depreciation of the existing capital, and both go hand in hand with a reduction of the variable capital in relation to the constant. Both cause a fall in the rate of profit, and both slow it down. Furthermore, inasmuch as an increased rate of profit causes a greater demand for labour, it tends to increase the working population and thus the material, whose exploitation makes real capital out of capital.

Indirectly, however, the development of the productivity of labour contributes to the increase of the value of the existing capital by increasing the mass and variety of use-values in which the same exchange-value is represented and which form the material substance, i.e. the material elements of capital, the material objects making up the constant capital directly, and the variable capital at least indirectly.

More products which may be converted into capital, whatever their exchange-value, are created with the same capital and the same labour. These products may serve to absorb additional labour, hence also additional surplus-labour, and therefore create additional capital. The amount of labour which a capital can command does not depend on its value, but on the mass of raw and auxiliary materials, machinery and elements of fixed capital and necessities of life, all of which it comprises, whatever their value may be. As the mass of the labour employed, and thus of surplus-labour increases, there is also a growth in the value of the reproduced capital and in the surplus-value newly added to it.

These two elements embraced by the process of accumulation, however, are not to be regarded merely as existing side by side in repose, as Ricardo does. They contain a contradiction which manifests itself in contradictory tendencies and phenomena. These antagonistic agencies counteract each other simultaneously.

Alongside the stimulants of an actual increase of the labouring population, which spring from the increase of the portion of the total social product serving as capital, there are agencies which create a merely relative over-population.

Alongside the fall in the rate of profit mass of capitals grows, and hand in hand with this there occurs a depreciation of existing capitals which checks the fall and gives an accelerating motion to the accumulation of capital-values.

Alongside the development of productivity there develops a higher composition of capital, i.e. the relative decrease of the ratio of variable to constant capital.

These different influences may at one time operate predominantly side by side in space, and at another succeed each other in time. From time to time the conflict of antagonistic agencies finds vent in crises. The crises are always but momentary and forcible solutions of the existing contradictions. They are violent eruptions which for a time restore the disturbed equilibrium.

The contradiction, to put it in a very general way, consists in that the capitalist mode of production involves a tendency towards absolute development of the productive forces, regardless of the value and surplus-value it contains, and regardless of the social conditions under which capitalist production takes place; while, on the other hand, its aim is to preserve the value of the existing capital and promote its self-expansion to the highest limit (i.e. to promote an ever more rapid growth of this value). The specific feature about it is that it uses the existing value of capital as a means of increasing this value to the utmost. The methods by which it accomplishes this include the fall of the rate of profit, depreciation of existing capital, and development of the productive forces of labour at the expense of already created productive forces.

The periodical depreciation of existing capital—one of the means immanent in capitalist production to check the fall of the rate of profit and hasten accumulation of capital-value through formation of new capital—disturbs the given conditions, within which the process of circulation and reproduction of capital takes place, and is therefore accompanied by sudden stoppages and crises in the production process.

The decrease of variable in relation to constant capital, which goes hand in hand with the development of the productive forces, stimulates the growth of the labouring population, while continually creating an artificial over-population. The accumulation of capital in terms of value is slowed down by the falling rate of profit, to hasten still more the accumulation of use-values, while this, in its turn, adds new momentum to accumulation in terms of value.

Capitalist production seeks continually to overcome these immanent barriers, but overcomes them only by means which again place these barriers in its way and on a more formidable scale.

The *real barrier* of capitalist production is *capital itself*. It is that capital and its self-expansion appear as the starting and the closing point, the motive and the purpose of production; that production is only production for *capital* and not vice versa, the means of production are not mere means for a constant expansion of the living process of the *society* of producers. The limits within which the preservation and self-expansion of the value of capital resting on the expropriation and pauperisation of the great mass of producers can alone move—these limits come continually into conflict with the methods of production employed by capital for its purposes, which drive towards unlimited extension of production, towards production as an end in itself, towards unconditional development of the social productivity of labour. The means—unconditional development of the productive forces of society—comes continually into conflict with the limited purpose, the self-expansion of the existing capital. The capitalist mode of production is, for this reason, a historical means of developing the material forces of production and creating an appropriate world-market and is, at the same time, a continual conflict between this its historical task and its own corresponding relations of social production.

III. Excess Capital and Excess Population

A drop in the rate of profit is attended by a rise in the minimum capital required by an individual capitalist for the productive employment of labour; required both for its exploitation generally, and for making the consumed labour-time suffice as the labour-time necessary for the production of the commodities, so that it does not exceed the average social labour-time required for the production of the commodities. Concentration increases simultaneously, because beyond certain limits a large capital with a small rate of profit accumulates faster than a small capital with a large rate of profit. At a certain high point this increasing concentration in its turn causes a new fall in the rate of profit. The mass of small dispersed capitals is thereby driven along the adventurous road of speculation, credit frauds, stock swindles, and crises. The so-called plethora of capital always applies essentially to a plethora of the capital for which the fall in the rate of profit is not compensated through the mass of profit—this is always true of newly developing fresh offshoots of capital—or to a plethora which places capitals incapable of action on their own at the disposal of the managers of large enterprises in the form of credit. This plethora of capital arises from the same causes as those which call forth relative over-population, and is, therefore, a phenomenon supplementing the latter, although they stand at opposite poles—unemployed capital at one pole, and unemployed worker population at the other.

Over-production of capital, not of individual commodities—although over-production of capital always includes over-production of commodities—is therefore simply over-accumulation of capital. To appreciate what this over-accumulation is (its closer analysis follows later), one need only assume it to be absolute. When would over-production of capital be absolute? Over-production which would affect not just one or another, or a few important spheres of production, but would be absolute in its full scope, hence would extend to all fields of production?

There would be absolute over-production of capital as soon as additional capital for purposes of capitalist production = 0. The purpose of capitalist production, however, is self-expansion of capital, i.e. appropriation of surplus-labour, production of surplus-value, of profit. As soon as capital would, therefore, have grown in such a ratio to the labouring population that neither the absolute working-time supplied by this population, nor the relative surplus working-time, could be expanded any further (this last would not be feasible at any rate in the case when the demand for labour were so strong that there were a tendency for wages to rise); at a point, therefore, when the increased capital produced just as much, or even less, surplus-value than it did before its increase, there would be absolute over-production of capital; i.e. the increased capital C + ΔC would produce no more, or even less, profit than capital C before its expansion by ΔC. In both cases there would be a steep and sudden fall in the general rate of profit, but this time due to a change in the composition of capital not caused by the development of the productive forces.

CHAPTER 42

GENESIS OF CAPITALIST GROUND-RENT

II. Labour Rent

If we consider ground-rent in its simplest form, that of *labour rent*, where the direct producer, using instruments of labour (plough, cattle, etc.) which actually or legally belong to him, cultivates soil actually owned by him during part of the week, and works during the remaining days upon the estate of the feudal lord without any compensation from the feudal lord, the situation here is still quite clear, for in this case rent and surplus-value are identical. Rent, not profit, is the form here through which unpaid surplus-labour expresses itself. To what extent the labourer (a self-sustaining serf) can secure in this case a surplus above his indispensable necessities of life, i.e. a surplus above that which we would call wages under the capitalist mode of production, depends, other circumstances remaining unchanged, upon the proportion in which his labour-time is divided into labour-time for himself and enforced labour-time for his feudal lord. This surplus above the indispensable requirements of life, the germ of what appears as profit under the capitalist mode of production, is therefore wholly determined by the amount of ground-rent, which in this case is not only directly unpaid surplus-labour, but also appears as such. It is unpaid surplus-labour for the 'owner' of the means of production, which here coincide with the land, and so far as they differ from it, are mere accessories to it. That the product of the serf must here suffice to reproduce his conditions of labour, in addition to his subsistence, is a circumstance which remains the same under all modes of production. For it is not the result of their specific form, but a natural requisite of all continuous and reproductive labour in general, of any continuing production, which is always simultaneously reproduction, i.e. including reproduction of its own operating conditions. It is furthermore evident that in all forms in which the direct labourer remains the 'possessor' of the means of production and labour conditions necessary for the production of his own means of subsistence, the property relationship must simultaneously appear as a direct relation of lordship and servitude, so that the direct producer is not free; a lack of freedom which may be reduced from serfdom with enforced labour to a mere tributary relationship. The direct producer, according to our assumption, is to be found here in possession of his own means of production, the necessary material labour conditions required for the realisation of his labour and the production of his means of subsistence. He conducts his agricultural activity and the rural home industries connected with it independently. This independence is not undermined by the circumstance that the small peasants may form among themselves a more or less natural production community, as they do in India, since it is here merely a question of independence from the nominal lord of the manor. Under such conditions the surplus-labour for the nominal owner of the land can only be extorted from them by other than economic pressure, whatever the form assumed may be. This differs from slave or plantation economy in that the slave works under alien conditions of production and not independently. Thus, conditions of personal dependence are requisite, a lack of personal freedom, no matter to what extent, and being tied to the soil as its accessory, bondage in the true sense of the word. Should the direct producers not be confronted by a private landowner, but rather, as in Asia, under direct subordination to a state which stands over them as their landlord and simultaneously as sovereign, then rent and taxes coincide, or rather, there exists no tax which differs from this form of ground-rent. Under such circumstances, there need exist no stronger political or economic pressure than that common to all subjection to that state. The state is then the supreme lord. Sovereignty here consists in the ownership of land concentrated on a national scale. But, on the other hand, no private ownership of land exists, although there is both private and common possession and use of land.

The specific economic form, in which unpaid surplus-labour is pumped out of direct producers, determines the relationship of rulers and ruled, as it grows directly out of production itself and, in turn, reacts upon it as a determining element. Upon this, however, is founded the entire formation of the economic community which grows up out of the production relations themselves, thereby simultaneously its specific political form. It is always the direct relationship of the owners of the conditions of production to the direct producers—a relation always naturally corresponding to a definite stage in the development of the methods of labour and thereby its social productivity—which reveals the innermost secret, the hidden basis of the entire social structure, and with it the political form of the relation of sovereignty and dependence, in short, the corresponding specific form of the state. This does not prevent the same economic basis—the same from the standpoint of its main conditions—due to innumerable different empirical circumstances, natural environment, racial relations, external historical influences, etc., from showing infinite variations and gradations in appearance, which can be ascertained only by analysis of the empirically given circumstances.

So much is evident with respect to labour rent, the simplest and most primitive form of rent: Rent is here the primeval form of surplus-labour and coincides with it. But this identity of surplus-value with unpaid labour of others need not be analysed here, because it still exists in its visible, palpable form, since the labour of the direct producer for himself is still separated in space and time from his labour for the landlord, and the latter appears directly in the brutal form of enforced labour for a third person. In the same way the 'attribute' possessed by the soil to produce rent is here reduced to a tangibly open secret, for the disposition to furnish rent here also includes human labour-power bound to the soil, and the property relation which compels the owner of labour-power to drive it on and activate it beyond such measure as is required to satisfy his own indispensable needs. Rent consists directly in the appropriation of this surplus expenditure of labour-power by the landlord; for the direct producer pays him no additional rent. Here, where surplus-value and rent are not only identical but where surplus-value has the tangible form of surplus-labour, the natural conditions or limits of rent, being those of surplus-value in general, are plainly clear. The direct producer must (1) possess enough labour-power, and (2) the natural conditions of his labour, above all the soil cultivated by him, must be productive enough, in a word, the natural productivity of his labour must be big enough to give him the possibility of retaining some surplus-labour over and above that required for the satisfaction of his own indispensable needs. It is not this possibility which creates the rent, but rather compulsion which turns this possibility into reality. But the possibility itself is conditioned by subjective and objective natural circumstances. And here too lies nothing at all mysterious. Should labour-power be minute, and the natural conditions of labour scanty, then the surplus-labour is small, but in such a case so are the wants of the producers on the one hand and the relative number of exploiters of surplus-labour on the other, and finally so is the surplus-product, whereby this barely productive surplus-labour is realised for those few exploiting landowners.

Finally, labour rent in itself implies that, all other circumstances remaining equal, it will depend wholly upon the relative amount of surplus-labour, or enforced labour, to what extent the direct producer shall be enabled to improve his own condition, to acquire wealth, to produce an excess over and above his indispensable means of subsistence, or, if we wish to anticipate the capitalist mode of expression, whether he shall be able to produce a profit for himself, and how much of a profit, i.e. an excess over his wages which have been produced by himself. Rent here is the normal, all-absorbing, so to say legitimate form of surplus-labour, and far from being excess over profit, which means in this case being above any other excess over wages, it is rather that the amount of such profit, and even its very existence, depends, other circumstances being equal, upon the amount of rent, i.e. the enforced surplus-labour to be surrendered to the landowners.

Since the direct producer is not the owner, but only a possessor, and since all his surplus-labour *de jure* actually belongs to the landlord, some historians have expressed astonishment that it should be at all possible for those subject to enforced labour, or serfs, to acquire any independent property, or relatively speaking, wealth, under such circumstances. However, it is evident that tradition must play a dominant role in the primitive and undeveloped circumstances on which these social production relations and the corresponding mode of production are based. It is furthermore clear that here as always it is in the interest of the ruling section of society to sanction the existing order as law and to legally establish its limits given through usage and tradition. Apart from all else, this, by the way, comes about of itself as soon as the constant reproduction of the basis of the existing order and its fundamental relations assumes a regulated and orderly form in the course of time. And such regulation and order are themselves indispensable elements of any mode of production, if it is to assume social stability and independence from mere chance and arbitrariness. These are precisely the form of its social stability and therefore its relative freedom from mere arbitrariness and mere chance. Under backward conditions of the production process as well as the corresponding social relations, it achieves this form by mere repetition of their very reproduction. If this has continued on for some time, it entrenches itself as custom and tradition and is finally sanctioned as an explicit law. However, since the form of this surplus-labour, enforced labour, is based upon the imperfect development of all social productive powers and the crudeness of the methods of labour itself, it will naturally absorb a relatively much smaller portion of the direct producer's total labour than under developed modes of production, particularly the capitalist mode of production. Take it, for instance, that the enforced labour for the landlord originally amounted to two days per week. These two days of enforced labour per week are thereby fixed, are a constant magnitude, legally regulated by prescriptive or written law. But the productivity of the remaining days of the week, which are at the disposal of the direct producer himself, is a variable magnitude, which must develop in the course of his experience, just as the new wants he acquires, and just as the expansion of the market for his product and the increasing assurance with which he disposes of this portion of his labour-power will spur him on to a greater exertion of his labour-power, whereby it should not be forgotten that the employment of his labour-power is by no means confined to agriculture, but includes rural home industry. The possibility is here presented for definite economic development taking place, depending, of course, upon favourable circumstances, inborn racial characteristics, etc.

III. Rent in Kind

The transformation of labour rent into rent in kind changes nothing from the economic standpoint in the nature of ground-rent. The latter consists, in the forms considered here, in that rent is the sole prevailing and normal form of surplus-value, or surplus-labour. This is further expressed in the fact that it is the only surplus-labour, or the only surplus-product, which the direct producer, who is in *possession* of the labour conditions needed for his own reproduction, must give up to the *owner* of the land, which in this situation is the all-embracing condition of labour. And, furthermore, that land is the only condition of labour which confronts the direct producer as alien property, independent of him, and personified by the landlord. To whatever extent rent in kind is the prevailing and dominant form of ground-rent, it is furthermore always more or less accompanied by survivals of the earlier form, i.e. of rent paid directly in labour, corvée-labour, no matter whether the landlord be a private person or the state. Rent in kind presupposes a higher stage of civilisation for the direct producer, i.e. a higher level of development of his labour and of society in general. And it is distinct from the preceding form in that surplus-labour needs no longer to be performed in its natural form, thus no longer under the direct supervision and compulsion of the landlord or his representatives; the direct producer is driven rather by force of circumstances than by direct coercion, through legal enactment rather than the whip, to perform it on his own responsibility. Surplus-production, in the sense of production beyond the indispensable needs of the direct producer, and within the field of production actually belonging to him, upon the land exploited by himself instead of, as earlier, upon the nearby lord's estate beyond his own land, has already become a self-understood rule here. In this relation the direct producer more or less disposes of his entire labour-time, although, as previously, a part of this labour-time, at first practically the entire surplus portion of it, belongs to the landlord without compensation; except that the landlord no longer directly receives this surplus-labour in its natural form, but rather in the products' natural form in which it is realised. The burdensome, and according to the way in which enforced labour is regulated, more or less disturbing interruption by work for the landlord (see Vol. I, Ch. 10, section 2) ('Manufacturer and Boyard') stops wherever rent in kind appears in pure form, or at least it is reduced to a few short intervals during the year, when a continuation of some corvée-labour side by side with rent in kind takes place. The labour of the producer for himself and his labour for the landlord are no longer palpably separated by time and space. This rent in kind, in its pure form, while it may drag fragments along into more highly developed modes of production and production relations, still presupposes for its existence a natural economy, i.e. that the conditions of the economy are either wholly or for the overwhelming part produced by the economy itself, directly replaced and reproduced out of its gross product. It furthermore presupposes the combination of rural home industry with agriculture. The surplus-product, which forms the rent, is the product of this combined agricultural and industrial family labour, no matter whether rent in kind contains more or less of the industrial product, as is often the case in the Middle Ages, or whether it is paid only in the form of actual products of the land. In this form of rent it is by no means necessary for rent in kind, which represents the surplus-labour, to fully exhaust the entire surplus-labour of the rural family. Compared with labour rent, the producer rather has more room for action to gain time for surplus-labour whose product shall belong to himself, as well as the product of his labour which satisfies his indispensable needs. Similarly, this form will give rise to greater differences in the economic position of the individual direct producers. At least the possibility for such a differentiation exists, and the possibility for the direct producer to have in turn acquired the means to exploit other labourers directly. This, however, does not concern us here, since we are dealing with rent in kind in its pure form; just as in general we cannot enter into the endless variety of combinations wherein the various forms of rent may be united, adulterated and amalgamated. The form of rent in kind, by being bound to a definite type of product and production itself and through its indispensable combination of agriculture and domestic industry, through its almost complete self-sufficiency whereby the peasant family supports itself through its independence from the market and the movement of production and history of that section of society lying outside of its sphere, in short owing to the character of natural economy in general, this form is quite adapted to furnishing the basis for stationary social conditions as we see, e.g. in Asia. Here, as in the earlier form of labour rent, ground-rent is the normal form of surplus-value, and thus of surplus-labour, i.e. of the entire excess labour which the direct producer must perform gratis, hence actually under compulsion although this compulsion no longer confronts him in the old brutal form—for the benefit of the owner of his essential condition of labour, the land. The profit, if by erroneously anticipating we may thus call that portion of the direct producer's labour excess over his necessary labour, which he retains for himself, has so little to do with determining rent in kind, that this profit, on the contrary, grows up behind the back of rent and finds its natural limit in the size of rent in kind. The latter may assume dimensions which seriously imperil reproduction of the conditions of labour, the means of production themselves, rendering the expansion of production more or less impossible and reducing the direct producers to the physical minimum of means of subsistence. This is particularly the case, when this form is met with and exploited by a conquering commercial nation, e.g. the English in India.

CHAPTER 43

THE TRINITY FORMULA

I

Capital—profit (profit of enterprise plus interest), land—ground-rent, labour—wages, this is the trinity formula which comprises all the secrets of the social production process.

Furthermore, since as previously demonstrated interest appears as the specific characteristic product of capital and profit of enterprise on the contrary appears as wages independent of capital, the above trinity formula reduces itself more specifically to the following:

Capital—interest, land—ground-rent, labour—wages, where profit, the specific characteristic form of surplus-value belonging to the capitalist mode of production, is fortunately eliminated.

On closer examination of this economic trinity, we find the following:

First, the alleged sources of the annually available wealth belong to widely dissimilar spheres and are not at all analogous with one another. They have about the same relation to each other as lawyer's fees, red beets, and music.

Capital, land, labour! However, capital is not a thing, but rather a definite social production relation, belonging to a definite historical formation of society, which is manifested in a thing and lends this thing a specific social character. Capital is not the sum of the material and produced means of production. Capital is rather the means of production transformed into capital, which in themselves are no more capital than gold or silver in itself is money. It is the means of production monopolised by a certain section of society, confronting living labour-power as products and working conditions rendered independent of this very labour-power, which are personified through this antithesis in capital. It is not merely the products of labourers turned into independent powers, products as rulers and buyers of their producers, but rather also the social forces and the future . . . [? illegible] form of this labour, which confront the labourers as properties of their products. Here, then, we have a definite and, at first glance, very mystical, social form, of one of the factors in a historically produced social production process.

And now alongside of this we have the land, inorganic nature as such, *rudis indigestaque moles*;* in all its primeval wildness. Value is labour. Therefore surplus-value cannot be earth. Absolute fertility of the soil effects nothing more than the following: a certain quantity of labour produces a certain product—in accordance with the natural fertility of the soil. The difference in soil fertility causes the same quantities of labour and capital, hence the same value, to be manifested in different quantities of agricultural products; that is, causes these products to have different individual values. The equalisation of these individual values into market-values is responsible for the fact that the 'advantages of fertile over inferior soil . . . are transferred from the cultivator or consumer to the landlord'. (Ricardo, *Principles*, London, 1821, p. 62.)

And finally, as third party in this union, a mere ghost—'the' Labour, which is no more than an abstraction and taken by itself does not exist at all, or, if we take . . . [illegible], the productive activity of human beings in general, by which they promote the interchange with Nature, divested not only of every social form and well-defined character, but even in its bare natural existence, independent of society, removed from all societies, and as an expression and confirmation of life which the still non-social man in general has in common with the one who is in any way social.

II

Capital—interest; landed property, private ownership of the Earth, and, to be sure, modern and corresponding to the capitalist mode of production—rent; wage-labour—wages. The connection between the sources of revenue is supposed to be represented in this form. Wage-labour and landed property, like capital, are historically determined social forms; one of labour, the other of monopolised terrestrial globe, and indeed both forms corresponding to capital and belonging to the same economic formation of society.

The first striking thing about this formula is that side by side with capital, with this form of an element of production belonging to a definite mode of production, to a definite historical form of social process of production, side by side with an element of production amalgamated with and represented by a definite social form are indiscriminately placed: the land on the one hand and labour on the other, two elements of the real labour-process, which in this material form are common to all modes of production, which are the material elements of every process of production and have nothing to do with its social form.

Secondly. In the formula: capital—interest, land—ground-rent, labour—wages, capital, land and labour appear respectively as sources of interest (instead of profit), ground-rent and wages, as their products, or fruits; the former are the basis, the latter the consequence, the former are the cause, the latter the effect; and indeed, in such a manner that each individual source is related to its product as to that which is ejected and produced by it. All the proceeds, interest (instead of profit), rent, and wages, are three components of the value of the products, i.e. generally speaking, components of value or expressed in money, certain money components, price components. The formula: capital—interest is now indeed the most meaningless formula of capital, but still one of its formulas. But how should land create value, i.e. a socially defined quantity of labour, and moreover that particular portion of the value of its own products which forms the rent? Land, e.g. takes part as an agent of production in creating a use-value, a material product, wheat. But it has nothing to do with the production of the *value of wheat*. In so far as value is represented by wheat, the latter is merely considered as a definite quantity of materialised social labour, regardless of the particular substance in which this labour is manifested or of the particular use-value of this substance. This nowise contradicts that (1) other circumstances being equal, the cheapness or dearness of wheat depends upon the productivity of the soil. The productivity of agricultural labour is dependent on natural conditions, and the same quantity of labour is represented by more or fewer products, use-values, in accordance with such productivity. How large the quantity of labour represented in one bushel of wheat depends upon the number of bushels yielded by the same quantity of labour. It depends, in this case, upon the soil productivity in what quantities of product the value shall be manifested. But this value is given, independent of this distribution. Value is represented in use-value; and use-value is a prerequisite for the creation of value; but it is folly to create an antithesis by placing a use-value, like land, on one side and on the other side value, and a particular portion of value at that. (2) . . . [here the manuscript breaks off].

III

Vulgar economy actually does no more than interpret, systematise and defend in doctrinaire fashion the conceptions of the agents of bourgeois production who are entrapped in bourgeois production relations. It should not astonish us, then, that vulgar economy feels particularly at home in the estranged outward appearances of economic relations in which these *prima facie* absurd and perfect contradictions appear and that these relations seem the more self-evident the more their internal relationships are concealed from it, although they are understandable to the popular mind. But all science would be superfluous if the outward appearance and the essence of things directly coincided. Thus, vulgar economy has not the slightest suspicion that the trinity which it takes as its point of departure, namely, land—rent, capital—interest, labour—wages or the price of labour, are *prima facie* three impossible combinations. First we have the use-value *land*, which has no value, and the exchange-value *rent*: so that a social relation conceived as a thing is made proportional to Nature, i.e. two incommensurable magnitudes are supposed to stand in a given ratio to one another. Then *capital—interest*. If capital is conceived as a certain sum of values represented independently by money, then it is *prima facie* nonsense to say that a certain value should be worth more than it is worth. It is precisely in the form: capital—interest that all intermediate links are eliminated, and capital is reduced to its most general formula, which therefore in itself is also inexplicable and absurd. The vulgar economist prefers the formula capital—interest with its occult quality of making a value unequal to itself, to the formula capital—profit, precisely for the reason that this already more nearly approaches actual capitalist relations. Then again, driven by the disturbing thought that 4 is not 5 and that 100 taler cannot possibly be 110 taler, he flees from capital as value to the material substance of capital; to its use-value as a condition of production of labour, to machinery, raw materials, etc. Thus, he is able once more to substitute in place of the first incomprehensible relation, whereby $4 = 5$, a wholly incommensurable one between a use-value, a thing on one side, and a definite social production relation, surplus-value, on the other, as in the case of landed property. As soon as the vulgar economist arrives at this incommensurable relation, everything becomes clear to him, and he no longer feels the need for further thought. For he has arrived precisely at the 'rational' in bourgeois conception. Finally, *labour—wages*, or price of labour, is an expression, as shown in Book I, which *prima facie* contradicts the conception of value as well as of price—the latter generally being but a definite expression of value. And 'price of labour' is just as irrational as a yellow logarithm. But here the vulgar economist is all the more satisfied, because he has gained the profound insight of the bourgeois, namely, that he pays money for labour, and since precisely the contradiction between the formula and the conception of value relieves him from all obligation to understand the latter.

We have seen that the capitalist process of production is a historically determined form of the social process of production in general. The latter is as much a production process of material conditions of human life as a process taking place under specific historical and economic production relations, producing and reproducing these production relations themselves, and thereby also the bearers of this process, their material conditions of existence and their mutual relations, i.e. their particular socio-economic form. For the aggregate of these relations, in which the agents of this production stand with respect to Nature and to one another, and in which they produce, is precisely society, considered from the standpoint of its economic structure. Like all its predecessors, the capitalist process of production proceeds under definite material conditions, which are, however, simultaneously the bearers of definite social relations entered into by individuals in the process of reproducing their life. Those conditions, like these relations, are on the one hand prerequisites, on the other hand results and creations of the capitalist process of production; they are produced and reproduced by it. We saw also that capital—and the capitalist is merely capital personified and functions in the process of production solely as the agent of capital—in its corresponding social process of production, pumps a definite quantity of surplus-labour out of the direct producers, or labourers; capital obtains this surplus-labour without an equivalent, and in essence it always remains forced labour—no matter how much it may seem to result from free contractual agreement. This surplus-labour appears as surplus-value, and this surplus-value exists as a surplus-product. Surplus-labour in general, as labour performed over and above the given requirements, must always remain. In the capitalist as well as in the slave system, etc., it merely assumes an antagonistic form and is supplemented by complete idleness of a stratum of society. A definite quantity of surplus-labour is required as insurance against accidents, and by the necessary and progressive expansion of the process of reproduction in keeping with the development of the needs and the growth of population, which is called accumulation from the viewpoint of the capitalist. It is one of the civilising aspects of capital that it enforces this surplus-labour in a manner and under conditions which are more advantageous to the development of the productive forces, social relations, and the creation of the elements for a new and higher form than under the preceding forms of slavery, serfdom, etc. Thus it gives rise to a stage, on the one hand, in which coercion and monopolisation of social development (including its material and intellectual advantages) by one portion of society at the expense of the other are eliminated; on the other hand, it creates the material means and embryonic conditions, making it possible in a higher form of society to combine this surplus-labour with a greater reduction of time devoted to material labour in general. For, depending on the development of labour productivity, surplus-labour may be large in a small total working-day, and relatively small in a large total working-day. If the necessary labour-time = 3 and the surplus-labour = 3, then the total working-day = 6 and the rate of surplus-labour = 100%. If the necessary labour = 9 and the surplus-labour = 3, then the total working-day = 12 and the rate of surplus-labour only = 33⅓%. In that case, it depends upon the labour productivity how much use-value shall be produced in a definite time, hence also in a definite surplus labour-time. The actual wealth of society, and the possibility of constantly expanding its reproduction process, therefore, do not depend upon the duration of surplus-labour, but upon its productivity and the more or less copious conditions of production under which it is performed. In fact, the realm of freedom actually begins only where labour which is determined by necessity and mundane considerations ceases; thus in the very nature of things it lies beyond the sphere of actual material production. Just as the savage must wrestle with Nature to satisfy his wants, to maintain and reproduce life, so must civilised man, and he must do so in all social formations and under all possible modes of production. With his development this realm of physical necessity expands as a result of his wants; but, at the same time, the forces of production which satisfy these wants also increase. Freedom in this field can only consist in socialised man, the associated producers, rationally regulating their interchange with Nature, bringing it under their common control, instead of being ruled by it as by the blind forces of Nature; and achieving this with the least expenditure of energy and under conditions most favourable to, and worthy of, their human nature. But it nonetheless still remains a realm of necessity. Beyond it begins that development of human energy which is an end in itself, the true realm of freedom, which, however, can blossom forth only with this realm of necessity as its basis. The shortening of the working-day is its basic prerequisite.

In a capitalist society, this surplus-value, or this surplus-product (leaving aside chance fluctuations in its distribution and considering only its regulating law, its standardising limits), is divided among capitalists as dividends proportionate to the share of the social capital each holds. In this form surplus-value appears as average profit which falls to the share of capital, an average profit which in turn divides into profit of enterprise and interest, and which under these two categories may fall into the laps of different kinds of capitalists. This appropriation and distribution of surplus-value, or surplus-product, on the part of capital, however, has its barrier in landed property. Just as the operating capitalist pumps surplus-labour, and thereby surplus-value and surplus-product in the form of profit, out of the labourer, so the landlord in turn pumps a portion of this surplus-value, or surplus-product, out of the capitalist in the form of rent in accordance with the laws already elaborated.

Hence, when speaking here of profit as that portion of surplus-value falling to the share of capital, we mean average profit (equal to profit of enterprise plus interest) which is already limited by the deduction of rent from the aggregate profit (identical in mass with aggregate surplus-value); the deduction of rent is assumed. Profit of capital (profit of enterprise plus interest) and ground-rent are thus no more than particular components of surplus-value, categories by which surplus-value is differentiated depending on whether it falls to the share of capital or landed property, headings which in no whit however alter its nature. Added together, these form the sum of social surplus-value. Capital pumps the surplus-labour, which is represented by surplus-value and surplus-product, directly out of the labourers. Thus, in this sense, it may be regarded as the producer of surplus-value. Landed property has nothing to do with the actual process of production. Its role is confined to transferring a portion of the produced surplus-value from the pockets of capital to its own. However, the landlord plays a role in the capitalist process of production not merely through the pressure he exerts upon capital, nor merely because large landed property is a prerequisite and condition of capitalist production since it is a prerequisite and condition of the expropriation of the labourer from the means of production, but particularly because he appears as the personification of one of the most essential conditions of production.

Finally, the labourer in the capacity of owner and seller of his individual labour-power receives a portion of the product under the label of wages, in which that portion of his labour appears which we call necessary labour, i.e. that required for the maintenance and reproduction of this labour-power, be the conditions of this maintenance and reproduction scanty or bountiful, favourable or unfavourable.

Whatever may be the disparity of these relations in other respects, they all have this in common: Capital yields a profit year after year to the capitalist, land a ground-rent to the landlord, and labour-power, under normal conditions and so long as it remains useful labour-power, a wage to the labourer. These three portions of total value annually produced, and the corresponding portions of the annually created total product (leaving aside for the present any consideration of accumulation), may be annually consumed by their respective owners, without exhausting the source of their reproduction. They are like the annually consumable fruits of a perennial tree, or rather three trees; they form the annual incomes of three classes, capitalist, landowner and labourer, revenues distributed by the functioning capitalist in his capacity as direct extorter of surplus-labour and employer of labour in general. Thus, capital appears to the capitalist, land to the landlord, and labour-power, or rather labour itself, to the labourer (since he actually sells labour-power only as it is manifested, and since the price of labour-power, as previously shown, inevitably appears as the price of labour under the capitalist mode of production), as three different sources of their specific revenues, namely, profit, ground-rent and wages. They are really so in the sense that capital is a perennial pumping-machine of surplus-labour for the capitalist, land a perennial magnet for the land-lord, attracting a portion of the surplus-value pumped out by capital, and finally, labour the constantly self-renewing condition and ever self-renewing means of acquiring under the title of wages a portion of the value created by the labourer and thus a part of the social product measured by this portion of value, i.e. the necessities of life. They are so, furthermore, in the sense that capital fixes a portion of the value and thereby of the product of the annual labour in the form of profit; landed property fixes another portion in the form of rent; and wage-labour fixes a third portion in the form of wages, and precisely by this transformation converts them into revenues of the capitalist, land-owner, and labourer, without, however, creating the substance itself which is transformed into these various categories. The distribution rather presupposes the existence of this substance, namely, the total value of the annual product, which is nothing but materialised social labour. Nevertheless, it is not in this form that the matter appears to the agents of production, the bearers of the various functions in the production process, but rather in a distorted form. Why this takes place will be developed in the further course of our analysis. Capital landed property and labour appear to those agents of production as three different, independent sources, from which as such there arise three different components of the annually produced value—and thereby the product in which it exists; thus, from which there arise not merely the different forms of this value as revenues falling to the share of particular factors in the social process of production, but from which this value itself arises, and thereby the substance of these forms of revenue.

[Here one folio sheet of the manuscript is missing.]

. . . Differential rent is bound up with the relative soil fertility, in other words, with properties arising from the soil as such. But, in the first place, in so far as it is based upon the different individual values of the products of different soil types, it is but the determination just mentioned; secondly, in so far as it is based upon the regulating general market-value, which differs from these individual values, it is a social law carried through by means of competition, which has to do neither with the soil nor the different degrees of its fertility.

It might seem as if a rational relation were expressed at least in 'labour—wages'. But this is no more the case than with 'land—ground-rent'. In so far as labour is value-creating, and is manifested in the value of commodities, it has nothing to do with the distribution of this value among various categories. In so far as it has the specifically social character of wage-labour, it is not value-creating. It has already been shown in general that wages of labour, or price of labour, is but an irrational expression for the value, or price of labour-power; and the specific social conditions, under which this labour-power is sold, have nothing to do with labour as a general agent in production. Labour is also materialised in that value component of a commodity which as wages forms the price of labour-power; it creates this portion just as much as the other portions of the product; but it is materialised in this portion no more and no differently than in the portions forming rent or profit. And, in general, when we establish labour as value-creating, we do not consider it in its concrete form as a condition of production, but in its social delimitation which differs from that of wage-labour.

Even the expression 'capital—profit' is incorrect here. If capital is viewed in the only relation in which it produces surplus-value, namely, its relation to the labourer whereby it extorts surplus-labour by compulsion exerted upon labour-power, i.e. the wage-labourer, then this surplus-value comprises, outside of profit (profit of enterprise plus interest), also rent, in short, the entire undivided surplus-value. Here, on the other hand, as a source of revenue, it is placed only in relation to that portion falling to the share of the capitalist. This is not the surplus-value which it extracts generally but only that portion which it extracts for the capitalist. Still more does all connection vanish no sooner the formula is transformed into 'capital—interest.'

If we at first considered the disparity of the above three sources, we now note that their products, their offshoots, or revenues, on the other hand, all belong to the same sphere, that of value. However, this is compensated for (this relation not only between incommensurable magnitudes, but also between wholly unlike, mutually unrelated, and non-comparable things) in that capital, like land and labour, is simply considered as a material substance, that is, simply as a produced means of production, and thus is abstracted both as a relation to the labourer and as value.

Thirdly, if understood in this way, the formula, capital—interest (profit), land—rent, labour—wages, presents a uniform and symmetrical incongruity. In fact, since wage-labour does not appear as a socially determined form of labour, but rather all labour appears by its nature as wage-labour (thus appearing to those in the grip of capitalist production relations), the definite specific social forms assumed by the material conditions of labour—the produced means of production and the land—with respect to wage-labour (just as they, in turn, conversely presuppose wage-labour), directly coincide with the material existence of these conditions of labour or with the form possessed by them generally in the actual labour-process, independent of its concrete historically determined social form, or indeed independent of *any* social form. The changed form of the conditions of labour, i.e. alienated from labour and confronting it independently, whereby the produced means of production are thus transformed into capital, and the land into monopolised land, or landed property—this form belonging to a definite historical period thereby coincides with the existence and function of the produced means of production and of the land in the process of production in general. These means of production are in themselves capital by nature; capital is merely an 'economic appellation' for these means of production; and so, in itself land is by nature the earth monopolised by a certain number of landowners. Just as products confront the producer as an independent force in capital and capitalists—who actually are but the personification of capital— so land becomes personified in the landlord and likewise gets on its hind legs to demand, as an independent force, its share of the product created with its help. Thus, not the land receives its due portion of the product for the restoration and improvement of its productivity, but instead the landlord takes a share of this product to chaffer away or squander. It is clear that capital presupposes labour as wage-labour.

But it is just as clear that if labour as wage-labour is taken as the point of departure, so that the identity of labour in general with wage-labour appears to be self-evident, then capital and monopolised land must also appear as the natural form of the conditions of labour in relation to labour in general. To be capital, then, appears as the natural form of the means of labour and thereby as the purely real character arising from their function in the labour-process in general. Capital and produced means of production thus become identical terms. Similarly, land and land monopolised through private ownership become identical. The means of labour as such, which are by nature capital, thus become the source of profit, much as the land as such becomes the source of rent.

Labour as such, in its simple capacity as purposive productive activity, relates to the means of production, not in their social determinate form, but rather in their concrete substance, as material and means of labour; the latter likewise are distinguished from one another merely materially, as use-values, i.e. the land as unproduced, the others as produced, means of labour. If, then, labour coincides with wage-labour, so does the particular social form in which the conditions of labour confront labour coincide with their material existence. The means of labour as such are then capital, and the land as such is landed property. The formal independence of these conditions of labour in relation to labour, the unique form of this independence with respect to wage-labour, is then a property inseparable from them as things, as material conditions of production, an inherent, immanent, intrinsic character of them as elements of production. Their definite social character in the process of capitalist production bearing the stamp of a definite historical epoch is a natural, and intrinsic substantive character belonging to them, as it were, from time immemorial, as elements of the production process. Therefore, the respective part played by the earth as the original field of activity of labour, as the realm of forces of Nature, as the pre-existing arsenal of all objects of labour, and the other respective part played by the produced means of production (instruments, raw materials, etc.) in the general process of production, must seem to be expressed in the respective shares claimed by them as capital and landed property, i.e. which fall to the share of their social representatives in the form of profit (interest) and rent, like to the labourer—the part his labour plays in the process of production is expressed in wages. Rent, profit and wages thus seem to grow out of the role played by the land, produced means of production, and labour in the simple labour-process, even when we consider this labour-process as one carried on merely between man and Nature, leaving aside any historical determination. It is merely the same thing again, in another form, when it is argued: the product in which a wage-labourer's labour for himself is manifested, his proceeds or revenue, is simply wages, the portion of value (and thereby the social product measured by this value) which his wages represent. Thus, if wage-labour coincides with labour generally, then so do wages with the produce of labour, and the value portion representing wages with the value created by labour generally. But in this way the other portions of value, profit and rent also appear independent with respect to wages, and must arise from sources of their own, which are specifically different and independent of labour; they must arise from the participating elements of production, to the share of whose owners they fall; i.e. profit arises from the means of production, the material elements of capital, and rent arises from the land, or Nature, as represented by the landlord (Roscher).

Landed property, capital and wage-labour are thus transformed from sources of revenue—in the sense that capital attracts to the capitalist, in the form of profit, a portion of the surplus-value extracted by him from labour, that monopoly in land attracts for the landlord another portion in the form of rent; and that labour grants the labourer the remaining portion of value in the form of wages—from sources by means of which one portion of value is transformed into the form of profit, another into the form of rent, and a third into the form of wages—into actual sources from which these value portions and respective portions of the product in which they exist, or for which they are exchangeable, arise themselves, and from which, therefore, in the final analysis, the value of the product itself arises.

In the case of the simplest categories of the capitalist mode of production, and even of commodity-production, in the case of commodities and money, we have already pointed out the mystifying character that transforms the social relations, for which the material elements of wealth serve as bearers in production, into properties of these things themselves (commodities) and still more pronouncedly transforms the production relation itself into a thing (money). All forms of society, in so far as they reach the stage of commodity-production and money circulation, take part in this perversion. But under the capitalist mode of production and in the case of capital, which forms its dominant category, its determining production relation, this enchanted and perverted world develops still more. If one considers capital, to begin with, in the actual process of production as a means of extracting surplus-labour, then this relationship is still very simple, and the actual connection impresses itself upon the bearers of this process, the capitalists themselves, and remains in their consciousness. The violent struggle over the limits of the working-day demonstrates this strikingly. But even within this non-mediated sphere, the sphere of direct action between labour and capital, matters do not rest in this simplicity. With the development of relative surplus-value in the actual specifically capitalist mode of production, whereby the productive powers of social labour are developed, these productive powers and the social interrelations of labour in the direct labour-process seem transferred from labour to capital. Capital thus becomes a very mystic being since all of labour's social productive forces appear to be due to capital, rather than labour as such, and seem to issue from the womb of capital itself. Then the process of circulation intervenes, with its changes of substance and form, on which all parts of capital, even agricultural capital, devolve to the same degree that the specifically capitalist mode of production develops. This is a sphere where the relations under which value is originally produced are pushed completely into the background. In the direct process of production the capitalist already acts simultaneously as producer of commodities and manager of commodity-production. Hence this process of production appears to him by no means simply as a process of producing surplus-value. But whatever may be the surplus-value extorted by capital in the actual production process and appearing in commodities, the value and surplus-value contained in the commodities must first be realised in the circulation process. And both the restitution of the values advanced in production and, particularly, the surplus-value contained in the commodities seem not merely to be realised in the circulation, but actually to arise from it; an appearance which is especially reinforced by two circumstances: first, the profit made in selling depends on cheating, deceit, inside knowledge, skill and a thousand favourable market opportunities; and then by the circumstance that added here to labour-time is a second determining element—time of circulation. This acts, in fact, only as a negative barrier against the formation of value and surplus-value, but it has the appearance of being as definite a basis as labour itself and of introducing a determining element that is independent of labour and resulting from the nature of capital. In Book II we naturally had to present this sphere of circulation merely with reference to the form determinations which it created and to demonstrate the further development of the structure of capital taking place in this sphere. But in reality this sphere is the sphere of competition, which, considered in each individual case, is dominated by chance; where, then, the inner law, which prevails in these accidents and regulates them, is only visible when these accidents are grouped together in large numbers, where it remains, therefore, invisible and unintelligible to the individual agents in production. But furthermore: the actual process of production, as a unity of the direct production process and the circulation process, gives rise to new formations, in which the vein of internal connections is increasingly lost, the production relations are rendered independent of one another, and the component values become ossified into forms independent of one another.

The conversion of surplus-value into profit, as we have seen, is determined as much by the process of circulation as by the process of production. Surplus-value, in the form of profit, is no longer related back to that portion of capital invested in labour from which it arises, but to the total capital. The rate of profit is regulated by laws of its own, which permit, or even require, it to change while the rate of surplus-value remains unaltered. All this obscures more and more the true nature of surplus-value and thus the actual mechanism of capital. Still more is this achieved through the transformation of profit into average profit and of values into prices of production, into the regulating averages of market-prices. A complicated social process intervenes here, the equalisation process of capitals, which divorces the relative average prices of the commodities from their values, as well as the average profits in the various spheres of production (quite aside from the individual investments of capital in each particular sphere of production) from the actual exploitation of labour by the particular capitals. Not only does it appear so, but it is true in fact that the average price of commodities differs from their value, thus from the labour realised in them, and the average profit of a particular capital differs from the surplus-value which this capital has extracted from the labourers employed by it. The value of commodities appears, directly, solely in the influence of fluctuating productivity of labour upon the rise and fall of the prices of production, upon their movement and not upon their ultimate limits. Profit seems to be determined only secondarily by direct exploitation of labour, in so far as the latter permits the capitalist to realise a profit deviating from the average profit at the regulating market-prices, which apparently prevail independent of such exploitation. Normal average profits themselves seem immanent in capital and independent of exploitation; abnormal exploitation, or even average exploitation under favourable, exceptional conditions, seems to determine only the deviations from average profit, not this profit itself. The division of profit into profit of enterprise and interest (not to mention the intervention of commercial profit and profit from money-dealing, which are founded upon circulation and appear to arise completely from it, and not from the process of production itself) consummates the individualisation of the form of surplus-value, the ossification of its form as opposed to its substance, its essence. One portion of profit, as opposed to the other, separates itself entirely from the relationship of capital as such and appears as arising not out of the function of exploiting wage-labour, but out of the wage-labour of the capitalist himself. In contrast thereto, interest then seems to be independent both of the labourer's wage-labour and the capitalist's own labour, and to arise from capital as its own independent source. If capital originally appeared on the surface of circulation as a fetishism of capital, as a value-creating value, so it now appears again in the form of interest-bearing capital, as in its most estranged and characteristic form. Wherefore also the formula capital—interest, as the third to land—rent and labour—wages, is much more consistent than capital—profit, since in profit there still remains a recollection of its origin, which is not only extinguished in interest, but is also placed in a form thoroughly antithetical to this origin.

Finally, capital as an independent source of surplus-value is joined by landed property, which acts as a barrier to average profit and transfers a portion of surplus-value to a class that neither works itself, nor directly exploits labour, nor can find morally edifying rationalisations, as in the case of interest-bearing capital, e.g. risk and sacrifice of lending capital to others. Since here a part of the surplus-value seems to be bound up directly with a natural element, the land, rather than with social relations, the form of mutual estrangement and ossification of the various parts of surplus-value is completed, the inner connection completely disrupted, and its source entirely buried, precisely because the relations of production, which are bound to the various material elements of the production process, have been rendered mutually independent.

In capital—profit, or still better capital—interest, land—rent, labour—wages, in this economic trinity represented as the connection between the component parts of value and wealth in general and its sources, we have the complete mystification of the capitalist mode of production, the conversion of social relations into things, the direct coalescence of the material production relations with their historical and social determination. It is an enchanted, perverted, topsy-turvy world, in which Monsieur le Capital and Madame la Terre do their ghost-walking as social characters and at the same time directly as mere things. It is the great merit of classical economy to have destroyed this false appearance and illusion, this mutual independence and ossification of the various social elements of wealth, this personification of things and conversion of production relations into entities, this religion of everyday life. It did so by reducing interest to a portion of profit, and rent to the surplus above average profit, so that both of them converge in surplus-value; and by representing the process of circulation as a mere metamorphosis of forms, and finally reducing value and surplus-value of commodities to labour in the direct production process. Nevertheless even the best spokesmen of classical economy remain more or less in the grip of the world of illusion which their criticism had dissolved, as cannot be otherwise from a bourgeois standpoint, and thus they all fall more or less into inconsistencies, half-truths and unsolved contradictions. On the other hand, it is just as natural for the actual agents of production to feel completely at home in these estranged and irrational forms of capital—interest, land—rent, labour—wages, since these are precisely the forms of illusion in which they move about and find their daily occupation. It is therefore just as natural that vulgar economy, which is no more than a didactic, more or less dogmatic, translation of everyday conceptions of the actual agents of production, and which arranges them in a certain rational order, should see precisely in this trinity, which is devoid of all inner connection, the natural and indubitable lofty basis for its shallow pompousness. This formula simultaneously corresponds to the interests of the ruling classes by proclaiming the physical necessity and eternal justification of their sources of revenue and elevating them to a dogma.

In our description of how production relations are converted into entities and rendered independent in relation to the agents of production, we leave aside the manner in which the interrelations, due to the world-market, its conjunctures, movements of market-prices, periods of credit, industrial and commercial cycles, alternations of prosperity and crisis, appear to them as overwhelming natural laws that irresistibly enforce their will over them, and confront them as blind necessity. We leave this aside because the actual movement of competition belongs beyond our scope, and we need present only the inner organisation of the capitalist mode of production, in its ideal average, as it were.

In preceding forms of society this economic mystification arose principally with respect to money and interest-bearing capital. In the nature of things it is excluded, in the first place, where production for the use-value, for immediate personal requirements, predominates; and, secondly, where slavery or serfdom form the broad foundation of social production, as in antiquity and during the Middle Ages. Here, the domination of the producers by the conditions of production is concealed by the relations of dominion and servitude, which appear and are evident as the direct motive power of the process of production. In early communal societies in which primitive communism prevailed, and even in the ancient communal towns, it was this communal society itself with its conditions which appeared as the basis of production, and its reproduction appeared as its ultimate purpose. Even in the medieval guild system neither capital nor labour appear untrammelled, but their relations are rather defined by the corporate rules, and by the same associated relations, and corresponding conceptions of professional duty, craftsmanship, etc. Only when the capitalist mode of production*—

MARX'S SELECTED FOOTNOTES

1. It is one of the chief failings of classical economy that it has never succeeded, by means of its analysis of commodities, and, in particular, of their value, in discovering that form under which value becomes exchange-value. Even Adam Smith and Ricardo, the best representatives of the school, treat the form of value as a thing of no importance, as having no connexion with the inherent nature of commodities. The reason for this is not solely because their attention is entirely absorbed in the analysis of the magnitude of value. It lies deeper. The value-form of the product of labour is not only the most abstract, but is also the most universal form, taken by the product in bourgeois production, and stamps that production as a particular species of social production, and thereby gives it its special historical character. If then we treat this mode of production as one eternally fixed by Nature for every state of society, we necessarily overlook that which is the differentia specifica of the value-form, and consequently of the commodity-form, and of its further developments, money-form, capital-form, etc. We consequently find that economists, who are thoroughly agreed as to labour-time being the measure of the magnitude of value, have the most strange and contradictory ideas of money, the perfected form of the general equivalent. This is seen in a striking manner when they treat of banking, where the commonplace definitions of money will no longer hold water. This led to the rise of a restored mercantile system (Ganilh, etc.), which sees in value nothing but a social form, or rather the unsubstantial ghost of that form. Once for all I may here state, that by classical Political Economy, I understand that economy which, since the time of W. Petty, has investigated the real relations of production in bourgeois society, in contradistinction to vulgar economy, which deals with appearances only, ruminates without ceasing on the materials long since provided by scientific economy, and there seeks plausible explanations of the most obtrusive phenomena, for bourgeois daily use, but for the rest, confines itself to systematising in a pedantic way, and proclaiming for everlasting truths, the trite ideas held by the self-complacent bourgeoisie with regard to their own world, to them the best of all possible worlds.

2. Truly comical is M. Bastiat, who imagines that the ancient Greeks and Romans lived by plunder alone. But when people plunder for centuries, there must always be something at hand for them to seize; the objects of plunder must be continually reproduced. It would thus appear that even Greeks and Romans had some process of production, consequently, an economy, which just as much constituted the material basis of their world, as bourgeois economy constitutes that of our modern world. Or perhaps Bastiat means, that a mode of production based on slavery is based on a system of plunder. In that case he treads on dangerous ground. If a giant

thinker like Aristotle erred in his appreciation of slave labour, why should a dwarf economist like Bastiat be right in his appreciation of wage-labour?—I seize this opportunity of shortly answering an objection taken by a German paper in America, to my work, 'Zur Kritik der Pol. Oekonomie, 1859'. In the estimation of that paper, my view that each special mode of production and the social relations corresponding to it, in short, that the economic structure of society, is the real basis on which the juridical and political superstructure is raised, and to which definite social forms of thought correspond; that the mode of production determines the character of the social, political, and intellectual life generally, all this is very true for our own times, in which material interests preponderate, but not for the middle ages, in which Catholicism, nor for Athens and Rome, where politics, reigned supreme. In the first place it strikes one as an odd thing for any one to suppose that these well-worn phrases about the middle ages and the ancient world are unknown to anyone else. This much, however, is clear, that the middle ages could not live on Catholicism, nor the ancient world on politics. On the contrary, it is the mode in which they gained a livelihood that explains why here politics, and there Catholicism, played the chief part. For the rest, it requires but a slight acquaintance with the history of the Roman republic, for example, to be aware that its secret history is the history of its landed property. On the other hand, Don Quixote long ago paid the penalty for wrongly imagining that knight errantry was compatible with all economic forms of society.

3. From this we may form an estimate of the shrewdness of the petit-bour-geois socialism, which, while perpetuating the production of commodities, aims at abolishing the 'antagonism' between money and commodities, and consequently, since money exists only by virtue of this antagonism, at abolishing money itself. We might just as well try to retain Catholicism without the Pope.

4. The question—Why does not money directly represent labour-time, so that a piece of paper may represent, for instance, x hours' labour, is at bottom the same as the question why, given the production of com-modities, must products take the form of commodities? This is evident, since their taking the form of commodities implies their differentiation into commodities and money. Or, why cannot private labour—labour for the account of private individuals—be treated as its opposite, immediate social labour? I have elsewhere examined thoroughly the Utopian idea of 'labour-money' in a society founded on the production of commodities. On this point I will only say further, that Owen's 'labour-money', for instance, is no more 'money' than a ticket for the theatre. Owen pre-supposes directly associated labour, a form of production that is entirely inconsistent with the production of commodities. The certificate of labour is merely evidence of the part taken by the individual in the common labour, and of his right to a certain portion of the common produce destined for consumption. But it never enters into Owen's head to pre-

suppose the production of commodities, and at the same time, by juggling with money, to try to evade the necessary conditions of that production.

5. Jerome had to wrestle hard, not only in his youth with the bodily flesh, as is shown by his fight in the desert with the handsome women of his imagination, but also in his old age with the spiritual flesh. 'I thought,' he says, 'I was in the spirit before the Judge of the Universe.' 'Who art thou?' asked a voice. 'I am a Christian.' 'Thou liest,' thundered back the great Judge, 'thou art nought but a Ciceronian.'

6. This is one of the circumstances that makes production by slave labour such a costly process. The labourer here is, to use a striking expression of the ancients, distinguishable only as instrumentum vocale, from an animal as instrumentum semi-vocale, and from an implement as instrumentum mutum. But he himself takes care to let both beast and implement feel that he is none of them, but is a man. He convinces himself with immense satisfaction, that he is a different being, by treating the one unmercifully and damaging the other con amore. Hence the principle, universally applied in this method of production, only to employ the rudest and heaviest implements and such as are difficult to damage owing to their sheer clumsiness. In the slave-states bordering on the Gulf of Mexico, down to the date of the civil war, ploughs constructed on old Chinese models, which turned up the soil like a hog or a mole, instead of making furrows, were alone to be found. Conf. J. E. Cairnes. 'The Slave Power', London, 1862, p. 46 sqq. In his 'Sea Board Slave States', Olmsted tells us: 'I am here shown tools that no man in his senses, with us, would allow a labourer, for whom he was paying wages, to be encumbered with; and the excessive weight and clumsiness of which, I would judge, would make work at least ten per cent greater than with those ordinarily used with us. And I am assured that, in the careless and clumsy way they must be used by the slaves, anything lighter or less rude could not be furnished them with good economy, and that such tools as we constantly give our labourers and find our profit in giving them, would not last out a day in a Virginia cornfield— much lighter and more free from stones though it be than ours. So, too, when I ask why mules are so universally substituted for horses on the farm, the first reason given, and confessedly the most conclusive one, is that horses cannot bear the treatment that they always must get from negroes; horses are always soon foundered or crippled by them, while mules will bear cudgelling, or lose a meal or two now and then, and not be materially injured, and they do not take cold or get sick, if neglected or overworked. But I do not need to go further than to the window of the room in which I am writing, to see at almost any time, treatment of cattle that would ensure the immediate discharge of the driver by almost any farmer owning them in the North.'

7. The distinction between skilled and unskilled labour rests in part on pure illusion, or, to say the least, on distinctions that have long since ceased to be real, and that survive only by virtue of a traditional convention; in part

on the helpless condition of some groups of the working-class, a condition that prevents them from exacting equally with the rest the value of their labour-power. Accidental circumstances here play so great a part, that these two forms of labour sometimes change places. Where, for instance, the physique of the working-class has deteriorated, and is, relatively speaking, exhausted, which is the case in all countries with a well developed capitalist production, the lower forms of labour, which demand great expenditure of muscle, are in general considered as skilled, compared with much more delicate forms of labour; the latter sink down to the level of unskilled labour. Take as an example the labour of a bricklayer, which in England occupies a much higher level than that of a damask-weaver. Again, although the labour of a fustian cutter demands great bodily exertion, and is at the same time unhealthy, yet it counts only as unskilled labour. And then, we must not forget, that the so-called skilled labour does not occupy a large space in the field of national labour. Laing estimates that in England (and Wales) the livelihood of 11,300,000 people depends on unskilled labour. If from the total population of 18,000,000 living at the time when he wrote, we deduct 1,000,000 for the 'genteel population', and 1,500,000 for paupers, vagrants, criminals, prostitutes, etc., and 4,650,000 who compose the middle-class, there remain the above mentioned 11,000,000. But in his middle-class he includes people that live on the interest of small investments, officials, men of letters, artists, schoolmasters and the like, and in order to swell the number he also includes in these 4,650,000 the better paid portion of the factory operatives! The bricklayers, too, figure amongst them. (S. Laing: 'National Distress', etc., London, 1844.) 'The great class who have nothing to give for food but ordinary labour, are the great bulk of the people.' (James Mill, in art.: 'Colony', Supplement to the Encyclop. Brit., 1831.)

8. In England even now occasionally in rural districts a labourer is condemned to imprisonment for desecrating the Sabbath, by working in his front garden. The same labourer is punished for breach of contract if he remains away from his metal, paper, or glass works on the Sunday, even if it be from a religious whim. The orthodox Parliament will hear nothing of Sabbath-breaking if it occurs in the process of expanding capital. A memorial (August 1863), in which the London day-labourers in fish and poultry shops asked for the abolition of Sunday labour, states that their work lasts for the first 6 days of the week on an average 15 hours a-day, and on Sunday 8–10 hours. From this same memorial we learn also that the delicate gourmands among the aristocratic hypocrites of Exeter Hall, especially encourage this 'Sunday labour'. These 'holy ones', so zealous *in cute curanda** show their Christianity by the humility with which they bear the overwork, the privations, and the hunger of others. *Obsequium ventris istis (the labourers) perniciosius est.**

9. We, therefore, find, e.g., that in the beginning of 1863, 26 firms owning extensive potteries in Staffordshire, amongst others, Josiah Wedgwood, &

Sons, petition in a memorial for 'some legislative enactment'. Competition with other capitalists permits them no voluntary limitation of working-time for children, etc. 'Much as we deplore the evils before mentioned, it would not be possible to prevent them by any scheme of agreement between the manufacturers. . . . Taking all these points into consideration, we have come to the conviction that some legislative enactment is wanted.' ('Children's Employment Comm.' Rep. 1, 1863, p. 322.) Most recently a much more striking example offers. The rise in the price of cotton during a period of feverish activity, had induced the manufacturers in Blackburn to shorten, by mutual consent, the working-time in their mills during a certain fixed period. This period terminated about the end of November, 1871. Meanwhile, the wealthier manufacturers, who combined spinning with weaving, used the diminution of production resulting from this agreement, to extend their own business and thus to make great profits at the expense of the small employers. The latter thereupon turned in their extremity to the operatives, urged them earnestly to agitate for the 9 hours' system, and promised contributions in money to this end.

10. Robert Owen, soon after 1810, not only maintained the necessity of a limitation of the working-day in theory, but actually introduced the 10 hours' day into his factory at New Lanark. This was laughed at as a communistic Utopia; so were his 'Combination of children's education with productive labour' and the Co-operative Societies of working-men, first called into being by him. Today, the first Utopia is a Factory Act, the second figures as an official phrase in all Factory Acts, the third is already being used as a cloak for reactionary humbug.

11. Before his time, spinning machines, although very imperfect ones, had already been used, and Italy was probably the country of their first appearance. A critical history of technology would show how little any of the inventions of the 18th century are the work of a single individual. Hitherto there is no such book. Darwin has interested us in the history of Nature's Technology, i.e. in the formation of the organs of plants and animals, which organs serve as instruments of production for sustaining life. Does not the history of the productive organs of man, of organs that are the material basis of all social organisation, deserve equal attention? And would not such a history be easier to compile, since, as Vico says, human history differs from natural history in this, that we have made the former, but not the latter? Technology discloses man's mode of dealing with Nature, the process of production by which he sustains his life, and thereby also lays bare the mode of formation of his social relations, and of the mental conceptions that flow from them. Every history of religion, even, that fails to take account of this material basis, is uncritical. It is, in reality, much easier to discover by analysis the earthly core of the misty creations of religion, than, conversely, it is, to develop from the actual relations of life the corresponding celestialised forms of those relations. The latter method is the only materialistic, and therefore the only scien-

tific one. The weak points in the abstract materialism of natural science, a materialism that excludes history and its process, are at once evident from the abstract and ideological conceptions of its spokesmen, whenever they venture beyond the bounds of their own speciality.

12. Bentham is a purely English phenomenon. Not even excepting our philosopher, Christian Wolff, in no time and in no country has the most homespun commonplace ever strutted about in so self-satisfied a way. The principle of utility was no discovery of Bentham. He simply reproduced in his dull way what Helvétius and other Frenchmen had said with esprit in the 18th century. To know what is useful for a dog, one must study dog-nature. This nature itself is not to be deduced from the principle of utility. Applying this to man, he that would criticise all human acts, movements, relations, etc., by the principle of utility, must first deal with human nature in general, and then with human nature as modified in each historical epoch. Bentham makes short work of it. With the dryest naïveté he takes the modern shopkeeper, especially the English shopkeeper, as the normal man. Whatever is useful to this queer normal man, and to his world, is absolutely useful. This yard-measure, then, he applies to past, present, and future. The Christian religion, e.g. is 'useful', because it forbids in the name of religion the same faults that the penal code condemns in the name of the law. Artistic criticism is 'harmful', because it disturbs worthy people in their enjoyment of Martin Tupper, etc. With such rubbish has the brave fellow, with his motto, 'nulla dies sine linea', piled up mountains of books. Had I the courage of my friend, Heinrich Heine, I should call Mr Jeremy a genius in the way of bourgeois stupidity.

13. If the reader reminds me of Malthus, whose 'Essay on Population' appeared in 1798, I remind him that this work in its first form is nothing more than a schoolboyish, superficial plagiary of De Foe, Sir James Steuart, Townsend, Franklin, Wallace, etc., and does not contain a single sentence thought out by himself. The great sensation this pamphlet caused, was due solely to party interest. The French Revolution had found passionate defenders in the United Kingdom; the 'principle of population', slowly worked out in the eighteenth century, and then, in the midst of a great social crisis, proclaimed with drums and trumpets as the infallible antidote to the teachings of Condorcet, etc., was greeted with jubilance by the English oligarchy as the great destroyer of all hankerings after human development. Malthus, hugely astonished at his success, gave himself to stuffing into his book materials superficially compiled, and adding to it new matter, not discovered but annexed by him. Note further: Although Malthus was a parson of the English State Church, he had taken the monastic vow of celibacy—one of the conditions of holding a Fellowship in Protestant Cambridge University: 'Socios collegiorum maritos esse non permittimus, sed statim postquam quis uxorem duxerit socius collegii desinat esse.' ('Reports of Cambridge University Commission', p. 172.) This circumstance favourably distinguishes Malthus from the other Prot-

estant parsons, who have shuffled off the command enjoining celibacy of the priesthood and have taken, 'Be fruitful and multiply', as their special Biblical mission in such a degree that they generally contribute to the increase of population to a really unbecoming extent, whilst they preach at the same time to the labourers the 'principle of population'. It is characteristic that the economic fall of man, the Adam's apple, the urgent appetite, 'the checks which tend to blunt the shafts of Cupid', as Parson Townsend waggishly puts it, that this delicate question was and is monopolised by the Reverends of Protestant Theology, or rather of the Protestant Church. With the exception of the Venetian monk, Ortes, an original and clever writer, most of the population-theory teachers are Protestant parsons. For instance, Bruckner, 'Théorie du Systeme animal', Leyde, 1767, in which the whole subject of the modern population theory is exhausted, and to which the passing quarrel between Quesnay and his pupil, the elder Mirabeau, furnished ideas on the same topic; then Parson Wallace, Parson Townsend, Parson Malthus and his pupil, the arch-Parson Thomas Chalmers, to say nothing of lesser reverend scribblers in this line. Originally, Political Economy was studied by philosophers like Hobbes, Locke, Hume; by businessmen and statesmen, like Thomas More, Temple, Sully, De Witt, North, Law, Vanderlint, Cantillon, Franklin; and especially, and with the greatest success, by medical men like Petty, Barbon, Mandeville, Quesnay. Even in the middle of the eighteenth century, the Rev. Mr Tucker, a notable economist of his time, excused himself for meddling with the things of Mammon. Later on, and in truth with this very 'Principle of population', struck the hour of the Protestant parsons. Petty, who regarded the population as the basis of wealth, and was, like Adam Smith, an outspoken foe to parsons, says, as if he had a presentiment of their bungling interference, 'that Religion best flourishes when the Priests are most mortified, as was before said of the Law, which best flourisheth when lawyers have least to do'. He advises the Protestant priests, therefore, if they, once for all, will not follow the Apostle Paul and 'mortify' themselves by celibacy, 'not to breed more Churchmen than the Benefices, as they now stand shared out, will receive, that is to say, if there be places for about twelve thousand in England and Wales, it will not be safe to breed up 24,000 ministers, for then the twelve thousand which are unprovided for, will seek ways how to get themselves a livelihood, which they cannot do more easily than by persuading the people that the twelve thousand incumbents do poison or starve their souls, and misguide them in their way to Heaven'. (Petty: 'A Treatise of Taxes and Contributions', London, 1667, p. 57.) Adam Smith's position with the Protestant priesthood of his time is shown by the following. In 'A Letter to A. Smith, L.L.D. On the Life, Death, and Philosophy of his Friend, David Hume. By one of the People called Christians', 4th Edition, Oxford, 1784, Dr Horne, Bishop of Norwich, reproves Adam Smith, because in a published letter to Mr Strahan, he 'embalmed his friend David' (sc. Hume); because he told the world how 'Hume amused himself on his deathbed with Lucian and Whist', and because he even had the impudence to write of Hume: 'I have always considered him, both in his life-time and since his death, as approaching as nearly to the idea of a perfectly wise and virtuous man, as, perhaps, the nature of human frailty will permit.' The bishop cries out in a passion: 'Is it right in you, Sir, to hold up to our view as 'perfectly wise and virtuous', the *character* and *conduct* of one, who seems to have been possessed with an incurable antipathy to all that is called *Religion*; and who strained every nerve to explode, suppress and extirpate the spirit of it among men, that its very name, if he could effect it, might no more be had in remembrance?' (l. c., p. 8.) 'But let not the lovers of truth be discouraged. Atheism cannot be of long continuance.' (p. 17.) Adam Smith, 'had the atrocious wickedness to propagate atheism through the land (viz., by his 'Theory of Moral Sentiments'). Upon the whole, Doctor, your meaning is good; but I think you will not succed this time. You would persuade us, by the example of *David Hume. Esq.*, that atheism is the only cordial for low spirits, and the proper antidote against the fear of death. . . . You may smile over *Babylon* in ruins and congratulate the hardened *Pharaoh* on his overthrow in the Red Sea.' (l. c., pp. 21, 22.) One orthodox individual, amongst Adam Smith's college friends, writes after his death: 'Smith's well-placed affection for Hume . . . hindered him from being a Christian. . . . When he met with honest men whom he liked . . . he would believe almost anything they said. Had he been a friend of the worthy ingenious Horrox he would have believed that the moon some times disappeared in a clear sky without the interposition of a cloud. . . . He approached to republicanism in his political principles.' ('The Bee'. By James Anderson, 18 Vols., Vol. 3, pp. 166, 165, Edinburgh, 1791–93.) Parson Thomas Chalmers has his suspicions as to Adam Smith having invented the category of 'unproductive labourers', solely for the Protestant parsons, in spite of their blessed work in the vineyard of the Lord.

EXPLANATORY NOTES

3 *De te fabula narratur*: this story is told about you yourself (Horace, *Satires*, I. i. 69–70).

4 *Le mort saisit le vif*: the dead man clutches the living.

6 *Segui il tuo corso e lascia dir le genti*: follow your own path and let people say what they will (an emended version of Dante, *Divine Comedy: Purgatory*, Canto 5, l. 13).

23 *Dame Quickly . . . 'where to have it'*: cf. *1 Henry IV*, I. iii, Falstaff (of Dame Quickly): 'Why, she's neither fish nor flesh; a man knows not where to have her.'

27 *Paris vaut bien une messe*: Paris is well worth a Mass. The supposed words of Henri IV on his conversion to Catholicism in 1593, in order to become king of France.

46 *post festum*: after the feast, i.e. after what is being reflected upon has already taken place.

49 *Intermundia*: spaces between different worlds, which is where, according to Epicurus, the gods lived, who had no influence on human affairs.

51 *Maritornes herself*: a character in the novel *Don Quixote* by Cervantes.

52 *Im Anfang war die That*: in the beginning was the deed (Goethe, *Faust*, pt. I, sc. iii).

64 *Assai bene . . .* : the alloy and weight of this coin have been well tested; but tell me now whether you have it in your purse (Dante, *Divine Comedy: Paradise*, Canto 24, ll. 84–5).

66 *salto mortale*: deathly leap. Cf. K. Marx, *Critique of Political Economy* (Progress Publishers, Moscow, 1953), p. 88.

70 *Non olet*: money does not smell. A saying attributed to the Roman emperor Vespasian when reproached by his son Titus for taxing public lavatories.

82 *ce n'est que le premier pas qui coûte*: it all depends on the first step. A remark attributed to St Denis who, after being beheaded, walked four miles from the place of his execution to Notre Dame in the centre of Paris.

86 *'Soyons riches ou paraissons riches'*: 'Let us be rich, or let us appear rich'.

107 *Hic Rhodus, hic salta!*: Rhodes is here—jump here! A challenge issued to a boaster who claimed to have jumped an enormous length in Rhodes. Also a reference to the end of the Preface to Hegel's *Philosophy of Right* where Hegel uses this saying to illustrate his view that philosophy should deal with what is and not what ought to be.

109 *musician of the future*: a builder of castles in the air, a utopian dreamer.

119 *Cincinnatus*: ruler of Rome in the middle of the fifth century BC, who was said to live an austere life on his own small farm which he worked himself as an example to his fellow Romans.

120 '[*la chose*] *qu'on aime pour lui-même*' [*sic*]: the thing desired for its own sake.

128 *tout est pour le mieux* . . . : everything is for the best in the best of all possible worlds. The reiterated opinion of Dr Pangloss in Voltaire's *Candide*.

137 '*devil's dust*': flock converted from cotton waste by a machine.

144 *in the third book*: see *Capital*, vol. iii, ch. 2.

149 *ultima Thule*: furthest limit. An expression used by the Romans to indicate the end of the known world.

151 *kalos kagathos*: handsome and good, a Greek expression for those of aristocratic birth.

164 *de te fabula narratur*: the name has been changed but the story is about you. (Horace, *Satires*, I. i. 69–70.)

165 *the French treaty*: the Treaty of Commerce of 1860 between Britain and France which lowered tariff barriers on both sides.

166 *après moi le déluge*: after me comes the downfall. A version of a remark attributed to Madame de Pompadour, mistress of Louis XV.

   ought these to trouble us . . . ?: this question is a quotation from Goethe, 'An Suleika,' *West-östlicher Divan*, in *Werke* (Beck, Munich, 1981), ii. 61.

169 *Charter*: the foundation document of the Chartist movement, a manifesto published in May 1848 demanding fundamental electoral reform, including universal male suffrage.

172 *Convention*: the Assembly during the French Revolution which lasted from 1792 until 1795 and presided over the Terror.

   law of suspects: this refers to a law passed by the Convention in September 1793 against those suspected of counter-revolution. It formed what legal basis there was to the Terror.

   pro-slavery rebellion: the American Civil War of 1861–5.

174 *My deeds upon my head*: this quotation, and the following one, are taken from Shylock's speech in Shakespeare's *The Merchant of Venice*, IV. i.

176 '*Courtes séances*': 'short sessions' or brief periods of work which Fourier proposed in his utopia to satisfy human need for variety.

182 *Quantum mutatus ab illo*: how much changed from the previous one! From Virgil's *Aeneid*, bk. II, l. 274.

184 *to be worked out later on*: see Ch. 25 on the General Law of Capitalist Accumulation, particularly sections 2 and 3.

185 *'ignorance is a sufficient reason'*: Spinoza in his *Ethics* argued that we should not presume God created the world for a particular purpose just because of our ignorance of other possible causes.

216 *already remarked*: see above, p. 53.

223 *states of La Plata*: Argentina, Uruguay, and Paraguay, which border the river Plate.

Menenius Agrippa: a patrician ruler of Rome in the fifth century BC who is said to have dissuaded the plebeians from overthrowing patrician rule by persuading them to see an analogy between the relationship of the plebeians to the patricians and the limbs to the stomach: if the stomach was not fed, the limbs would wither—and so would the plebeians without patrician rule.

225 *disjecta membra poetæ*: the scattered members of the poet (Horace, *Satires*, I. iv. 62).

260 *revolt from 1848 to 1850*: see above, pp. 175–7.

270 *border slave-states*: states such as Virginia, Kentucky, or Missouri on the border between the North and the South which had a mixture of slave and free labour until the Civil War.

276 *'big loaf'*: those who supported the repeal of the Corn Laws claimed that the free trade in corn would result in a bigger loaf than that previously provided for the workers.

282 *membra disjecta*: scattered elements.

taillable à merci et miséricorde: to be shaped at pleasure and mercy. An expression used of serfs in the Middle Ages to indicate their complete subordination to their masters.

287 *. . . ce bête de mot*: impossible? never use that ridiculous word to me!

293 *écoles d'enseignment professionel*: schools of vocational teaching.

Ne sutor ultra crepidam: the cobbler should stick to his last.

300 *the history of the theory*: i.e. the *Theories of Surplus Value* which Kautsky edited and published in three volumes between 1905 and 1910.

311 *as will be seen later*: a reference to the *Theories of Surplus Value*.

332 *hasn't got no date*: this illiterate phrase became a byword for backwardness and stupidity in the Prussian aristocracy. It was used by Prince Felix von Lichnowsky in the Frankfurt Assembly in 1848 to reject Poland's claim to independence.

333 *parting from the other*: from Goethe's *Faust*, pt. I.

342 *currency school*: see above, pp. 92–3.

356 *the demands of war*: i.e. the Crimean War from 1854 to 1856.

360 *faux frais*: incidental expenses.

367 *pauper ubique jacet*: the poor are oppressed everywhere.

368 *edict of the Tartar Boris Godunof*: issued in 1597, this edict allowed
peasants who had fled from their lords to be pursued and recovered for a
period of five years.

370 *the last rising*: the rebellion of 1745–6 led by the Young Pretender Charles
Edward Stuart.

376 *Pindar of the slave-trade*: the Greek lyric poet Pindar (522–442 BC) wrote
triumphal odes celebrating the winners of the Olympic games.

377 *Tantæ molis erat*: so great an effort was required (to found the Roman
nation)—Virgil, *Aeneid*, I. 33.

415 *Book IV*: i.e. the *Theories of Surplus Value*.

429 *set in motion*: see Chapter 25 of Volume One.

431 *We shall see later*: these references are all to pt. II of the *Theories of Surplus
Value*.

466 *Rudis indigestaque moles*: a rude and motley mass (Ovid, *Metamorphoses*,
I. 7).

481 The manuscript breaks off here.

486 *in cute curanda*: in looking after their own bodies. From Horace, *Epistles*,
I. ii. 9.

Obsequium ventris: gluttony is more destructive of their stomachs. A
slightly altered version of Horace, *Satires*, II. vii. 104 where Horace wrote:
'gluttony is more destructive of my stomach'.

SUBJECT INDEX

NAME INDEX

Women's Writing 1778–1838

WILLIAM BECKFORD — **Vathek**

JAMES BOSWELL — **Life of Johnson**

FRANCES BURNEY — **Camilla**
Cecilia
Evelina
The Wanderer

LORD CHESTERFIELD — **Lord Chesterfield's Letters**

JOHN CLELAND — **Memoirs of a Woman of Pleasure**

DANIEL DEFOE — **A Journal of the Plague Year**
Moll Flanders
Robinson Crusoe
Roxana

HENRY FIELDING — **Joseph Andrews** and **Shamela**
A Journey from This World to the Next and
The Journal of a Voyage to Lisbon
Tom Jones

WILLIAM GODWIN — **Caleb Williams**

OLIVER GOLDSMITH — **The Vicar of Wakefield**

MARY HAYS — **Memoirs of Emma Courtney**

ELIZABETH HAYWOOD — **The History of Miss Betsy Thoughtless**

ELIZABETH INCHBALD — **A Simple Story**

SAMUEL JOHNSON — **The History of Rasselas**
The Major Works

CHARLOTTE LENNOX — **The Female Quixote**

MATTHEW LEWIS — **Journal of a West India Proprietor**
The Monk

HENRY MACKENZIE — **The Man of Feeling**

ALEXANDER POPE — **Selected Poetry**

American Literature

British and Irish Literature

Children's Literature

Classics and Ancient Literature

Colonial Literature

Eastern Literature

European Literature

History

Medieval Literature

Oxford English Drama

Poetry

Philosophy

Politics

Religion

The Oxford Shakespeare